iOS Apps
for Masterminds

How to take advantage of Swift
to create insanely great apps
for iPhones and iPads

J.D Gauchat
www.jdgauchat.com

Cover Illustration by **Patrice Garden**
www.smartcreativz.com

HTML5 for Masterminds

How to take advantage of HTML5 to create responsive websites and revolutionary web applications

www.formasterminds.com

Table of Contents

Chapter 14—Table Views

Chapter 15—Collection Views

Chapter 16—Split View Controllers

Introduction

In 2007 Apple introduced the first iPhone to the market. The smartphone was regarded by many as a revolutionary piece of technology, but not for the right reasons. The innovations presented by this device were clearly changing our understanding of telecommunications and challenging the preconceptions we had of what a phone could do, but nobody, not even Apple, was able to predict the impact that it would have in the software industry.

At first, Apple's plan was to follow the trend. They wanted to provide a new communication device with enhanced capabilities but under their strict control. The device would be capable of running its own applications, also called *apps* or *native apps*, but only those created by the company would be available. Each user would have the same apps as everybody else and only access third-party applications from the web and through the browser that was delivered with the system. Apple was trying to focus its strategy on web applications and emerging web technologies, like everybody else, but the incredible possibilities offered by the iPhone inevitably altered its plans.

The new features and mobile capabilities introduced by this powerful device caught developers' attention all around the world, and the interest to create native applications grew fast. Soon, methods to install unauthorized applications were created and popularized. Dozens of third-party applications were developed and shared online through open markets. The success of these first apps and the willingness of users to install them (under the risk of damaging their devices) made clear that not many people agreed with the company's initial intentions. It was evident that users preferred to tap on an icon and work with the app right away rather than open a browser, remember a domain, type it, and wait for the web application to load. These applications were easy to access, focused on a single purpose, and visually more appealing than a website. Developers wanted to create and users wanted to consume native apps.

This external pressure, along with internal demands from executives in Apple's headquarters, motivated a change in Steve Jobs's mind, and the creation of the App Store was announced. The creation of the App Store not only meant that an official place to sell apps was going to be available, but also that a whole set of tools was going to be provided by the company itself to create them. The App Store and the iOS SDK (Software Development Kit) changed everything for good. Developers now had the right tools to build their apps and users had a safe place to buy them. Soon, thousands of native apps were available, generating an excellent alternative to web applications and creating a whole new market. The new apps attracted more customers for Apple devices, which motivated the creation of more apps, in a positive spiral that generated billions of dollars. Several applications created by developers working alone from their bedrooms became an overnight success, triggering a gold rush, the effects of which are still visible nowadays.

The new distribution channels and the production tools provided by Apple have initiated a golden era for developers. The possibility and opportunities are infinite. Native applications are here to stay, the market they have created is growing by the day, and now you can be part of it.

 IMPORTANT: Links with additional information, examples, projects, videos, and resources are available at **www.formasterminds.com**. Apple's official documentation is available at **developer.apple.com**. Frameworks and APIs references are available at **developer.apple.com/reference**.

Chapter 1
App Development

1.1 Overview

The decision to create the App Store and open the platform to developers was not an easy one. Steve Jobs did not like the idea of exposing his highly praised new creation to the same threats of personal computers. He did not want his devices to be affected by viruses or attacked by hackers and get a bad reputation. He insisted on keeping the platform closed until he realized that they could take advantage of the systems already developed by Apple for the iTunes Store to stay in control of quality and sales. This decision did not come without a price for developers. The system is open enough to allow full creativity, but it's still under Apple's strict supervision, which means developers can only work according to the company's rules.

Requirements

Apple requires developers to use the software provided by the company to create apps for its mobile devices. This software only works in Apple computers and requires the developer to have an Apple account. For these reasons, the options are very limited, but the good news is that most of the things we need are provided for free.

Mac Computer—This in theory could be any Intel-based Mac computer, but the development software always requires the latest operative system (macOS), so in practice we need a relatively new computer.

Apple Developer Account—This is a basic account we can get for free; it gives us access to the Member Center where we can watch videos, download programming guides, read the official documentation, get sample codes, and more.

Xcode—This is the software provided by Apple for development. The latest version is number 10. It's free and the package comes with everything we need to create our apps, including an editor, the SDK (Software Development Kit), and a simulator to test the applications.

Apple Developer Program—This is the developer account we need to publish our apps. Membership to this program is not only required to publish our apps in the App Store but also to test services like iCloud. The membership costs $99 US dollars per year.

Mobile Device—This could be any of the devices available in the market, including iPads, iPhones, and iPods Touch, but at the time of picking one for testing we must consider that old models do not support the current versions of Apple's mobile operative system (iOS), and the latest version of this system, iOS 12, only runs on devices with a 64bit processor. Testing our applications on a real device is highly recommended and necessary before publishing.

The setup is relatively simple. We have to get a Mac Computer capable of running the operative system currently required by Xcode (at the time of this writing, it is macOS High Sierra), open an Apple developer account from **developer.apple.com** using our personal Apple ID (the one that is created when we initialized our computer), and install the latest version of Xcode (currently 10).

Mobile Operative System

iOS is the name of the operative system delivered by Apple with every mobile device (except for the Apple Watch that has its own OS called *watchOS*). The system is currently in version number 12. Although we could develop our applications for older systems, this is not recommended unless we have very strong reasons to do so. Statistics show that at any given time, the latest operative system is installed in over 90 % of active devices, and therefore most developers only create applications for the latest version of iOS.

1.2 Xcode

Xcode is a general-purpose IDE (Integrated Development Environment). It includes a very powerful editor with graphic tools to help us write our code, the SDKs (Software Development Kits) for the creation of software for the iOS, macOS, watchOS, and tvOS operative systems, and compilers for the C, C++, Objective-C and Swift languages. From Xcode, we can program software for every Apple platform using any of these programming languages.

Xcode is available as an app on the Mac App Store. To download this application, we must open the App Store from Launchpad (the application organizer that comes with macOS) or double click the App Store icon inside the Applications folder in Finder (macOS file explorer). From the App Store, we have to search for the term "Xcode". The window will show Xcode's icon at the top (Figure 1-1, number 1). Then, we have to click on the *GET* button to download and install the software.

Figure 1-1: Xcode in the Mac App Store

 IMPORTANT: The examples of this book were developed in Xcode 10 and only run in devices with iOS 12 installed. At the moment of this writing, only the Beta versions of Xcode 10 and iOS 12 are available. Beta software is not available in the App Store, you have to download it from Apple's developer website (**https://developer.apple.com/download/**). The procedure required to install this software is different from the one used to install the final versions. For more information, visit our website and follow the links for this chapter.

Running Xcode

Once the downloading process is over, the software is automatically installed. To open Xcode, we have to go to Launchpad and click on the icon or search for the program inside the Applications folder in Finder. Figure 1-2 shows Xcode's welcome screen.

Welcome to Xcode
Version 10.0

No Recent Projects

Get started with a playground
Explore new ideas quickly and easily.

Create a new Xcode project
Create an app for iPhone, iPad, Mac, Apple Watch, or Apple TV.

Clone an existing project
Start working on something from a Git repository.

Figure 1-2: Xcode's welcome screen

The welcome screen offers a list of the recent projects on the right and buttons on the left to initiate a new project or find those already created and stored in a repository. The following are the options currently available.

Get started with a playground—This option creates a single file and provides a simplified interface called *Playground* that we can use to experiment and learn about the Swift language and the basic frameworks included in the SDK.

Create a new Xcode project—This is the option we choose when we want to create a new application. The option generates a new Xcode project from a template that provides basic files and settings to start from.

Clone an existing project—This option allows us to open and work on a project stored on a server. It is used to download a project already initiated by other developers or share a project online.

 IMPORTANT: The first two options are the ones we are going to use in this book. We will open a Playground to learn fundamental programming concepts in the following chapters and work with Xcode projects from **Chapter 5** to learn how to create real applications.

1.3 Development

Even though some simple projects could be developed without programming a single line of code, we always have to write our own code if we want to create a useful application, and for that, we need programming languages.

Programming Languages

Several years ago, Apple adopted and implemented a language called Objective-C to allow developers to create applications for its devices. Due to the technical level required to work with this language, the spectacular success of Apple's mobile devices did not impress developers the same way as consumers. The demand for more and better applications was growing fast, but the complicated nature of the system did not appeal to most developers who were used to working with more traditional tools. To solve this problem, the company introduced some innovations to Xcode and engaged in active work to promote the evolution of Objective-C. But no matter how hard they tried, some complex features of the language, such as the extensive use of pointers and its verbose syntax, were difficult to remove and were still scaring developers away, especially web developers transitioning from simpler languages like HTML, CSS, and JavaScript.

In the middle of 2014, with the purpose of putting an end to this situation, the company introduced a new programming language called *Swift*. Swift presents a simpler syntax that developers find familiar, while at the same time preserves that low-level nature necessary to take advantage of every aspect of Apple's devices. Swift was designed to replace Objective-C and, therefore, is the language recommended to new developers.

 IMPORTANT: Because of the recent introduction of the Swift language, a huge part of the SDK is still programmed in Apple's previous languages (Objective-C and C). Although the company's intention is to focus on its new language, the migration of the APIs, documentation, and examples from one language to another will take some time. If you come across examples or tutorials written in Objective-C, there is a guide provided by Apple that explains how this code may be translated to Swift called "Using Swift with Cocoa and Objective-C". Also, you can always learn the basics of Objective-C from Apple's official guide. For more information, visit our website at **www.formasterminds.com** and follow the links for this chapter.

Cocoa Touch API

Programming languages by themselves cannot do much. They provide all the elements to interact with the system but are basic tools for the manipulation of data. Because of the complexity of the information required to control sophisticated technologies and access every aspect of a system, it could take years to develop an application from scratch working with just the instructions of a programming language. Doing simple things like printing graphics on the screen or storing data in files would become a nightmare if programmers had to depend on the tools provided by programming languages alone. For this reason, the languages are always accompanied by sets of pre-programmed routines grouped in libraries and frameworks that through a simple interface called *API* (Application programming interface) allow programmers to incorporate to their apps amazing functionality with just a few lines of code.

Xcode comes with an SDK that includes all the frameworks and APIs we need to work with every component of an Apple device. In Apple's environment, this large group of development tools is referred to as Cocoa Touch API (named after the Cocoa API created for Mac computers).

 IMPORTANT: Frameworks are critical for app development. Learning the APIs (public interfaces) to interact with these frameworks will become the main subject of study in following chapters.

Compiler

Computers do not understand Swift or any other programming language. These languages were created for us to give machines instructions we can understand. Our code has to be converted to elemental orders that work at an electronic level, turning multiple switches on and off to represent the abstraction humans work with. The translation from the language humans understand to the language computers understand is done by a program called *compiler*.

Compilers have specific routines to translate instructions from programming languages to machine code. They are language and platform specific, which means that we need a specific compiler to program in one language and for one particular device. There are a few compilers available for Apple systems, but the one currently used by Xcode is called *LLVM*. LLVM is capable of compiling code written in Swift, C, C++, and Objective-C.

App Development

With the compiler, the machinery to build an app is complete. Figure 1-3 shows all the elements involved. There are three main sources of code the compiler uses to build the application: our code in Swift, the frameworks our program requires, and a set of basic routines necessary for the app to run (called Application Loop in Figure 1-3). The process starts from Xcode. In this program we write our code, access frameworks through their APIs, and configure the app to be compiled (built). Combining our code, the codes from the frameworks our app requires and the basic routines (Application Loop), the compiler creates an executable program that may be run in a simulator, a device, or submitted to the App Store for distribution.

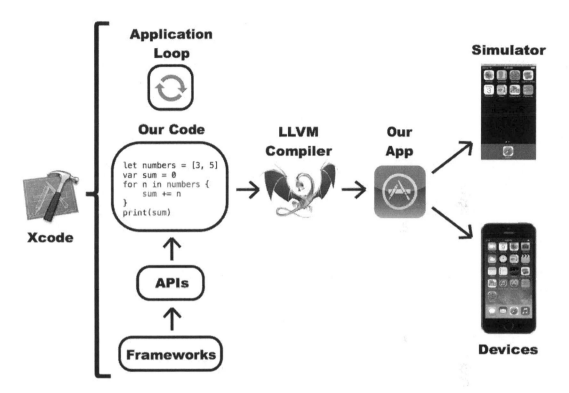

Figure 1-3: Building an App

The Basics: The Application Loop is a group of elemental routines, common to every program, that connects your app to the operative system and provides a loop (a code that executes itself over and over again) to constantly check for events produced by the user or coming from the system. Although you never work directly with these routines, they are connected to your code to inform the state of the program, as we will see in further chapters.

App Development

Chapter 2
Introduction to Swift

2.1 Computer Programs

To get a computer to do what we want, we have to write a program. A program is a succession of instructions that the computer has to follow. We write the program using the instructions provided by a specific programming language, then a compiler translates these instructions into orders the computer can understand, and when we tell the computer to run the program, the orders are executed sequentially one by one.

The instructions are always listed in sequential order, but programming languages offer different ways to group them together and organize the code and the data that is going to be processed. Although the instructions provided by programming languages are limited, the possible combinations are infinite. Developing an app demands a deep understanding of these instructions and the combinations required to achieve the results we want. Since this may be daunting for those who want to create their first app, Xcode includes a tool called *Playground* to learn how to program and test our code.

 IMPORTANT: This chapter introduces basic concepts of computer programming and the Swift language. If you are familiar with this information, feel free to skip the parts you already know. Our approach to Swift is introductory. We work with basic and complex features, but only apply those that we consider essential to understand the examples of the book. To expand your knowledge of the language, we recommend you read the book published by Apple called "*The Swift Programming Language*", which is available for free from the iBook store.

Playground

There are two alternatives to work in Xcode: we can initiate a project to create an application or open a Playground file to experiment with the code before to include it in our app. Although we could use the first option and create our application right away, it's better to work with Playground first to learn how to program with the Swift language and how to take advantage of some the fundamental frameworks included in the SDK.

When we create an app, we have to program the code, build it (turn it into code the computer can understand), and execute it. The results of our work are visible only when we run the final product. Playground, on the other hand, is a real-time interpreter that can show the results of the execution of our code as we type. It is a great tool for learning and that's the reason why we are going to use it in this and following chapters.

To start with Playground, we have to select the option *Get started with a playground* on the Xcode's welcome window (Figure 1-2). The first window we see after we click on this option includes a few icons to select the template we want to use. These are files with pre-programmed code to help us get started with our project. The templates available at the moment are called Blank (with just a few lines of code to start from scratch), Game (with basic code to program a video game), Map (with the code to display a map), and Single View (with the same code required to create a view for an application).

Figure 2-1: *Playground's templates*

After we select the template, Xcode asks for the name of the Playground file and the place on our hard drive where we want to store it. Once the file is created, Xcode shows the Playground's interface on the screen. Figure 2-2 illustrates what we see when we create a Blank template.

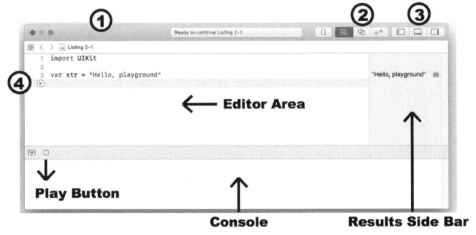

Figure 2-2: *Playground's interface*

 The Basics: The Xcode's menu at the top of the screen also includes the option to create the Playground file. If you cannot see Xcode's welcome window, open the *File* menu from the menu bar, select the option *New* and click on *Playground*.

Playground presents a simple interface with a toolbar at the top that includes a few buttons for configuration (number 1) and two main areas, the *Editor Area* where we write our code, and the *Results Side Bar* where the results produced by our code are printed. This interface can be expanded from the buttons on the toolbar. The first group of buttons on the right (number 2) are called Standard Editor, Assistant Editor, and Version editor. These buttons allow us to split the Editor Area into two panels. The most useful are the Standard Editor, which presents only the panel where the code is displayed (default), and the Assistant Editor, which presents a second panel on the right with a live view where the graphics produced by the application are displayed. The second set of buttons (number 3) is used to open or close the removable panels. The first button opens a panel on the left-hand side of the window called Navigator Area where we can see the resources included in our Playground, the second button opens the Console at the bottom of the window, where we can read the errors produced by the code and print our own messages (as shown in Figure 2-2), and the third button opens a panel on the right-hand side of the window called Utilities Area, which contains information about the selected resource.

Introduction to Swift

As illustrated by Figure 2-2, the Editor Area includes a button at the bottom of the panel to execute and stop the code. Every time we insert a change in the code, we must press this button to execute it, but if the code is already running, we have to stop it first. For this reason, Xcode also includes a play button on the left side of the Editor Area that we can press every time something new is added to the code (number 4).

 The Basics: When a Playground file is opened for the first time, Xcode only shows the Editor Area in the Standard mode and no extra panels. If you want to see the console, click on the middle button on the right-hand side of the toolbar (number 3). We will learn more about Xcode's interface in Chapter 5.

In the Editor Area, we can see the code we have programmed so far. When a new Playground file is created, Xcode offers a template that includes a few basic lines of code to start from. Listing 2-1 shows the code currently generated for the Blank template.

```
import UIKit

var str = "Hello, playground"
```

Listing 2-1: Playground template

A computer program is just text written in a specific format. Each line of text represents an instruction. Sometimes a single line includes several instructions, and this is why each line is usually called *statement*. Every statement is an order for the computer to perform a task. In the code of Listing 2-1, the first statement uses the instruction **import** to include in our code the pre-programmed codes from a framework called *UIKit*, and the second statement uses the instruction **var** to store the text "Hello, playground" in memory.

Inside the Results Side Bar, on the same vertical line of the last statement, there is an indication of what the code does (in this case, it shows the text stored in memory by the **var** instruction). When we move the mouse over this indication, two small buttons show up, as illustrated by Figure 2-3.

Figure 2-3: Quick Look and Show Result buttons

The button on the left is called the *Quick Look*, and it shows a popup window with a visual representation of the final result of the execution of the code, such as formatted text or an image (in this case, no visual effect is associated with the code so only the plain text is shown on that window).

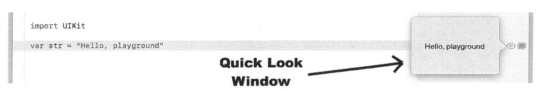

Figure 2-4: Quick Look window

The button on the right is called *Show Result*, and what it does is to open a window within our code with a visual representation of the results of the execution of the code over time (in this case, nothing changes, so only the "Hello, playground" text is shown).

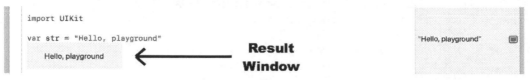

Figure 2-5: *Result window*

 The Basics: If you don't see any values in the Results Side Bar, press the Play button at the bottom of the Editor Area to execute the code (see Figure 2-2).

The code provided by Xcode for the Blank template is useless, but it shows the basic syntax of the Swift language and how to do elemental things in a program such as importing frameworks to add functionality to our programs and storing data in memory. The reason why one of the statements is storing data in memory is because this is the most important task of a program. A program's main functions are storing, retrieving, and processing data. Working with data in the computer's memory is a delicate process that demands meticulous organization. If we are not careful, data may be accidentally deleted, corrupted, or completely overwritten. To make sure this does not happen, programming languages introduce the concept of variables.

2.2 Variables

Variables are names representing values stored in memory. Once a variable is defined, its name remains the same but the value in memory they represent may change. This allows us to store and retrieve a value from memory without the need of remembering where in the memory the value was stored. The system takes care of memory management in the background. With just mentioning the name of the variable created to store a value, we can get that value back or replace it with a new one. Let's see how all of this works.

Memory

The computer's memory is like a huge honeycomb, with consecutive cells that can be in two possible states: activated or deactivated. They are actually electronic switches with on and off positions established by low and high energy levels.

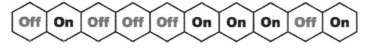

Figure 2-6: *Memory cells*

Because of their two possible states, each cell is a small unit of information. One cell may represent two possible states (switch on or off), but by combining a sequence of cells we can represent more states. For example, if we combine two cells, we have four possible states.

Combination 1   **Combination 2**   **Combination 3**   **Combination 4**

Figure 2-7: *Combining two cells*

With these two cells, we can now represent up to four states (4 possible combinations). If we had used three cells instead, then the possible combinations would have been 8 (eight states). The number of combinations is duplicated every time we add another cell to the group. This can be extended to represent any number of states we want.

Because of its characteristics, this system of switches is used to represent binary numbers, which are numbers expressed by only two digits: 0 and 1. An on switch corresponds to the value 1 and an off switch corresponds to the value 0. For practical purposes, basic units were determined with the purpose of identifying parts of this endless series of digits. One cell was called a *bit* and a group of 8 bits was called a *byte*. Figure 2-8 shows how a byte looks like in memory, with some of its switches on representing the binary number 00011101.

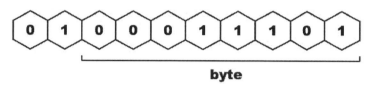

byte

Figure 2-8: Representation of one byte in memory

The possible combinations of 8 bits is 256, therefore, a byte can represent binary numbers of 8 digits, which in turn can be converted to numbers humans can understand, such as decimal numbers. With its 256 possible combinations, a byte can represent decimal numbers from 0 to 255. For instance, when the value of the byte in the example of figure 2-8 is converted to the decimal system, we get the number 29 (00011101 = 29).

 The Basics: Numbers of one numeral system, like binary, can be converted to any other numeral system, like decimal. The binary system is the one computers can understand because it translates directly to the electronic switches they are built off, but humans find this is difficult to read, so we use other systems to express numbers. The decimal system is the one we use every day, but in computer programming you will often see numbers expressed in other systems, like hexadecimal (base-16).

To represent larger numbers, bytes are grouped together. For example, if we take two bytes from memory, we get a binary number composed of a total of 16 bits (16 zeros and ones). A binary number of 16 bits can represent decimal numbers from 0 to 65535 (a total of 65536 possible combinations). For coherence and to establish clearly defined data structures, each programming language declares its own units of data of a predetermined size. These units are language specific, but there are some elemental units that we will find in almost every language because they are the building blocks of more complex types of data. These units are usually called *primitive types*.

Primitive Types

Primitive types are types of units of data defined by the language. They have always the same size, so when we store a value of one of these types the computer knows exactly how much memory to use and how to read it later. Of all these data types, probably the most useful is `Int`.

Int—This type is for integer numbers, which are numbers with no fractional component. In 64 bits systems, the size of this type is 8 bytes and therefore it can store values from -9,223,372,036,854,775,808 to 9,223,372,036,854,775,807.

Although it is recommended to always use the `Int` type to store integer numbers, there are frameworks that require a very specific type of integer. For this reason, Swift also defines the following types.

Int8—This type is for integer numbers of a size of 1 byte (8 bits). Because of its size, it can store values from -128 to 127.

Int16—This type is for integer numbers of a size of 2 bytes (16 bits). Because of its size, it can store values from -32,768 to 32,767.

Int32—This type is for integer numbers of a size of 4 bytes (32 bits). Because of its size, it can store values from -2,147,483,648 to 2,147,483,647.

Int64—This type is for integer numbers of a size of 8 bytes (64 bits). Because of its size, it can store values from -9,223,372,036,854,775,808 to 9,223,372,036,854,775,807.

If we check the size of each type presented so far and calculate the possible combinations of bits, we will discover that the maximum values are not right. For example, an `Int8` uses 1 byte, which means it is composed of 8 bits, and for this reason it should be able to store numbers from 0 to 255 (256 possible combinations). The reason why an `Int8` has a positive limit of 127 is because it only uses 7 bits to store its value, the first bit on the left is reserved to indicate the sign (positive or negative). Although these limits are not restrictive, the language also provides the unsigned versions of these types in case we need to store larger positive values.

UInt—This is the same as `Int` but for unsigned values. Because it does not reserve a bit for the sign, in 64-bit systems it can store values from 0 to 18,446,744,073,709,551,615.

The specific types for `UInt` are `UInt8`, `UInt16`, `UInt32`, and `UInt64`. These types work exactly like their equivalents for `Int`, but they are intended to store only positive numbers.

Although all these types are very useful, they are only good for storing binary values that can be used to represent integer numbers. Arithmetic operations also require the use of real numbers (e.g., 3.14 or 10.543). Computers cannot reproduce these types of values, but they can work with an approximation called floating-point numbers. The following are the floating-point data types defined in the Swift language.

Float—This type is for 32 bits floating-point numbers. It has a precision of 6 decimal digits.

Double—This type is for 64 bits floating-point numbers. It has a precision of at least 15 decimal digits.

Floating-point types can handle huge numbers using scientific notation, but because of their precision, it is recommended to declare a variable of type **Double** when performing calculations and use **Float** for minor tasks such as storing coordinates to position graphics on the screen.

Declaration and Initialization

If we want to store data in memory, the first thing we need to do is to select the right type from the data types provided by the language and then create a variable of that type. This action is called *Declaration*, and it is done using the **var** instruction and the syntax **var name : type**.

```
var mynumber : Int
```

Listing 2-2: Declaring variables

The example of Listing 2-2 creates a variable called **mynumber** of type **Int**. When the system reads this statement, it reserves a space in memory of 8 bytes long (64 bits) and assigns the name **mynumber** to that space. After the execution of this statement, we can use the variable **mynumber** to store in memory any integer value from -9,223,372,036,854,775,808 to 9,223,372,036,854,775,807.

Introduction to Swift

IMPORTANT: According to the official specification, you can use almost any character you want to declare the name of a variable, except for spaces, mathematical symbols, and a few special Unicode characters. Also, they cannot start with a number. If you declare a variable with an illegal name, Xcode will show you an error. There are two things you should always remember: Swift distinguishes between lowercase and uppercase characters (**MyInt** is considered a different variable than **myint**), and also that to avoid conflict with reserved words you should declare complex names or define the names with a combination of two or more words (for example, **myint** instead of **int**).

The Basics: The spaces between the name, the type, and the colon are recommended but not required. You can write the instruction of Listing 2-2 without spaces or just a space on one side of the colon (e.g., **var myvariable: Int**).

Memory is a reusable resource. The space we reserve for a variable may have been used before by another variable that was deleted, or pieces of functional code could have been stored in that place, leaving incomprehensible data in the same space of memory we are now trying to use for the new variable. For this reason, after the declaration of a variable we always have to store a value in it. This action is called *Initialization*.

```
var mynumber: Int
mynumber = 5
```

Listing 2-3: *Initializing variables*

In the new example of Listing 2-3, we first declare the variable as we did before, and then initialize it with the value 5 (we store the number 5 in the space of memory reserved for this variable). To store the value, we use the = (equal) symbol and the syntax **name = value**, where **name** is the name of the variable and **value** is the value we want to store (once the variable was already declared, we do not have to use the **var** instruction or specify its type anymore).

Most of the time, we know what the variable's initial value will be right away. In cases like this, Swift allows us to declare and initialize the variable in just one line of code.

```
var mynumber: Int = 5
```

Listing 2-4: *Declaring and initializing variables in the same statement*

Although this code does not perform any other task than storing the value 5 in memory, we can use a Playground's feature to check the current value stored in the variable. To do this, we just have to write the name of the variable in a new statement and the current value will be shown on the Results Side Bar (this is only available on Playground).

```
var mynumber: Int = 5
mynumber  // 5
```

Listing 2-5: *Reading variables*

Do It Yourself: If you haven't done it yet, create a new Playground file with the Blank template. When the interface is opened, replace all the statements of the Xcode's template by the code of Listing 2-5 and press the Play button. You should see the value 5 on the Results Side Bar. Repeat this process for the following examples. Each example in this chapter replaces the previous one.

The Basics: The text added at the end of the last statement of Listing 2-5 is a comment used to show the value produced by the statement. Comments are ignored by the compiler but useful for programmers to remember vital information that could help in further reviews of the code. They are introduced after the characters // (e.g., // `comment`) or in between the characters /* */ (e.g., /* `comment` */). The compiler ignores everything written on the right side of //, and everything between /* and */. You can also use these characters to comment lines of code you do not want to use at the moment. Xcode actually offers a shortcut to comment code. You have to select the lines of code you want to comment and press the keys Command and /.

Variables are called variables because their values are not constant. We can change them any time we want. To store a new value in the space of memory reserved for a variable, we have to implement the same syntax used for initialization.

```
var mynumber: Int = 5
mynumber = 87
```

Listing 2-6: Assigning a new value to a variable

The process of storing a new value is called *assignment*. In these terms, we can say that in the example of Listing 2-6 we "assign the value 87 to the variable `mynumber`". This value replaces the old one in memory. After that second statement is executed, every time we read the `mynumber` variable it will return the value 87 (unless another value is assigned to the variable later).

 IMPORTANT: Once a variable is declared, the values stored in that variable have to be of the same type. If we declare a variable of type `Int`, we cannot store floating-point values in it (e.g. 14.129).

Of course, we can create all the variables we want and of any type we need.

```
var mynumber: Int = 5
var myfavorite: Float = 14.129
```

Listing 2-7: Declaring variables of different types

The first statement of Listing 2-7 declares an integer variable and initializes it with the value 5. The second statement does the same but for a floating-point variable. When the values are of a clear type, Swift can infer them. If this is the case, the syntax may be simplified, as in the following example.

```
var mynumber = 5
var myfavorite = 14.129
```

Listing 2-8: Declaring variables without specifying the type

Swift infers the variable's type from the value we are trying to assign to it. In this last example, the value 5 is clearly an integer and the value 14.129 is clearly a floating-point value, so Swift creates the variable `mynumber` of type `Int` and the variable `myfavorite` of type `Double` (it selects the most comprehensive type).

 IMPORTANT: When the type is not clear, we have to declare it explicitly. For example, if we are initializing a variable with the value 8, but we want to assign floating-point numbers to this variable in the future, we have to declare it as `Float` or `Double` (as we did in Listing 2-7), otherwise Swift will infer an `Int`.

The Basics: Xcode offers a tool we can use to confirm the data type assigned to a variable and get additional information. All you have to do is click on the name of the variable while holding down the Option key on your keyboard. This opens a popup window with the full declaration of the variable, including its data type, and any information we may need to identify the function of the code. As we will see later, this not only works with variables but also constants and any type of instruction, including functions, properties, methods, etc.

An important feature of variables is that the value of one may be assigned to another.

```
var mynumber = 5
var myfavorite = mynumber
```

Listing 2-9: Assigning variables to variables

The second statement of Listing 2-9 reads the value of the **mynumber** variable and assigns it to the **myfavorite** variable. The type of **myfavorite** is inferred to be **Int** (the same of **mynumber**). After this code is executed, we have two integer variables, each with its own space in memory and the value 5 stored in them.

Arithmetic Operators

Storing values in memory is what variables allow us to do, but those values do not have to be declared explicitly, they can also be the result of arithmetic operations. Swift supports the five basic arithmetic operations: + (addition), – (subtraction), * (multiplication), / (division) and % (remainder or modulus).

```
var mynumber = 5 + 10   // 15
```

Listing 2-10: Assigning the result of an operation to a variable

When the system reads the statement of Listing 2-10, it adds 10 to 5 and assigns the result to **mynumber** (15). Of course, we can use variables of any data type we need and perform any of the operations available.

```
var mynumber = 2 * 25   // 50
var anothernumber = 8 - 40 * 2   // -72
var myfraction = 5.0 / 2.0   // 2.5
```

Listing 2-11: Performing operations in variables of different type

The first two statements of Listing 2-11 are easy to read. They perform arithmetic operations over integer numbers that produce an integer value as result, so the variables **mynumber** and **anothernumber** will be of type **Int**. The problem arises when we work with operations that may produce floating-point numbers. That is why for the third statement we specifically declared the values as floating-point numbers (adding the .0 at the end). This forces Swift to infer the variable's type as **Double**.

The Basics: Arithmetic operations are executed following an order of precedence determined by the operators. For example, multiplication and division have more precedence over addition and subtraction. This means that the multiplications and divisions will be performed before the additions and subtractions. If you want to change the order, you have to enclose the values between parentheses (e.g., **var number = (8 − 40) * 2**).

When the compiler finds an operation with two or more numbers and has to infer the type of the result, it converts the number of the less comprehensive type to the most comprehensive type. For example, when we declare an **Int** and a **Double** in the same operation (e.g., 5 + 2.0), the **Int** value is converted and processed as **Double**, and therefore the result will also be **Double**. On the other hand, if all the values are integers, then the result will be an integer (unless the variable is explicitly declared as **Float** or **Double**).

```
var myfraction1 = 5.0 / 2.0  // 2.5
var myfraction2 = 5 / 2.0  // 2.5
var myfraction3 = 5 / 2  // 2
```

Listing 2-12: *Inferring the type from an operation*

Listing 2-12 declares and initializes three variables. In the first statement both numbers were declared as floating-point values, so the compiler infers a **Double** and creates the **myfraction1** variable of that type. In the second statement, we have an integer value and a floating-point value. Because of the floating-point value, the compiler interprets the integer (5) as a **Double** (5.0) and creates the **myfraction2** variable of type **Double**. But in the last statement there is no clear floating-point value. Both numbers were declared as integers (with no decimals). In this case, the compiler does not know what we want to do, so it interprets both numbers as integers and creates the **myfraction3** variable of type **Int**. When an operation produces a result that is expected to be an integer, any fractional part is discarded. In this example, the system gets rid of the decimal 5 from the result and only assigns the integer 2 to the variable. If we do not want to lose the fractional part, we don't have to let the compiler infer the type of the variable and declare it ourselves as **Float** or **Double** (e.g., **var myfraction3: Double = 5 / 2**).

 IMPORTANT: When we work with numbers, we can declare the type explicitly by adding the decimal part, but when working with variables, they are already of a specific type, so they must be converted. There is a process called *casting* that allows us to convert a variable of one data type to another. We will study this process in Chapter 3.

Dividing integer numbers may be pointless most of the time, except in some circumstances when we need to know the remainder. The remainder is the amount left over by a division between two numbers and it is calculated using the % symbol.

```
var remainder1 = 11 % 3  // 2
var remainder2 = 20 % 8  // 4
var remainder3 = 5 % 2  // 1
```

Listing 2-13: *Calculating the remainder*

Listing 2-13 shows three examples of how to calculate the remainder of a division. Each statement calculates the remainder of dividing the first number by the second number and assigns the result to the variable. For instance, the first statement produces the remainder 2. The system divides 11 by 3 and finds a quotient of 3. Then, to get the remainder, it calculates 11 minus the multiplication of 3 times the quotient (**11 — (3 * 3) = 2**).

The second statement produces a remainder of 4 and the third statement produces a remainder of 1. This last statement is particularly useful because it allows us to determine whether a value is odd or even. When we calculate the reminder of an integer number divided by 2, we get a result according to its parity (odd or even). If the number is even, the remainder is 0, and if the number is odd, the remainder is 1 (or -1 for negative numbers).

Performing arithmetic operations becomes useful when instead of numbers we use variables.

```
var mynumber = 5
var total = mynumber + 10   // 15
```

Listing 2-14: *Adding numbers to variables*

The example of Listing 2-14 declares the **mynumber** variable and initializes it with the value 5. In the next statement, the **total** variable is declared and initialized with the result of the addition of the number 10 plus the current value of **mynumber** (5 + 10).

In Listing 2-14 we used a new variable to store the result of the operation, but when the old value is not important anymore, we can store the result back into the same variable.

```
var mynumber = 5
mynumber = mynumber + 10   // 15
```

Listing 2-15: *Performing operations on the variable's current value*

In this example, the current value of **mynumber** is added to 10 and the result is assigned to the same variable. After the execution of the second statement, the value of **mynumber** is 15.

 IMPORTANT: As in mathematics, the – sign may be used before the name of a variable to toggle its sign and get the opposite value. If the current value is positive, the result will be negative, and vice versa. For example, assuming that the current value of **mynumber** is 20, the statement **var result = – mynumber** will assign the value -20 to **result**. Another useful application of this technique is to change the current sign of the value of a variable assigning to the variable its own value preceded by the – sign (e.g., **mynumber = – mynumber**).

Working with values previously stored in a variable allows our program to evolve and adapt to new circumstances. For example, this is a good way to create a counter. We could add 1 to the current value of a variable and store the result in the same variable. Every time a statement like this is executed, the value of the variable is incremented by one unit. Recurrent increments and decrements of the values of variables are actually very important in computer programming. Because of this, Swift supports operators that were specifically designed for this purpose.

- **+=** is a shorthand for **variable = variable + number**, where **number** is the value we want to add to the variable's current value.
- **-=** is a shorthand for **variable = variable – number**, where **number** is the value we want to subtract to the variable's current value.

With these operators, we can easily add or subtract a value to the current value of the variable and assign the result back to the same variable.

```
var mynumber = 5
mynumber += 4   // 9
```

Listing 2-16: *Modifying the variable's value using incremental operators*

The process generated by the code of Listing 2-16 is straightforward. After the value 5 is assigned to the **mynumber** variable, the system reads the second statement, gets the current value of the variable, adds 4 to that value, and stores the result back to **mynumber** (9).

As we explained before, the possible values to store in an integer variable are limited by their data type. If we perform an operation that assigns to an integer variable a result out of the range of values it can handle, the application crashes. This is called *overflow* and Swift offers additional operators to avoid it. These operators are called *Overflow Operators* and are declared as normal operators but prefixed by the pound character (**&+**, **&-**, **&***, **&/** and **&%**).

```
var mynumber: Int8 = 120
mynumber = mynumber &+ 10   // -126
```

Listing 2-17: *Operations with Overflow Operators*

An overflow operator performs the calculation until it reaches the limit of the possible range and then keeps calculating from the other side of the range. For example, the minimum and maximum values a variable of type **Int8** can handle are -128 and 127. If we assign to a variable of this type an operation that produces a result higher than 127, the operator adds the remainder of the operation to the number -128, keeping the result inside the range of values -128 and 127. The variable in the example of Listing 2-17 is initialized with a value of 120 and then an operation adds 10 to that number. For a normal operator, the result would be 130, which is out of the range of the variable and would crash the app, but since we are working with an overflow operator, the addition returns the value -126. The operator adds the units to the value until it reaches the maximum limit of the range (127) and then keeps adding the rest of the units to the minimum value the variable can handle (-128), getting the final result (-126).

 IMPORTANT: Overflow operators are useful when we think that an operation could overflow a variable, but most of the time is more practical to just check the value and perform the operation only when the result is within the possible range. In Chapter 3 we will study properties available for integer types that report the minimum and maximum values in real time to prevent overflow.

Constants

As mentioned before, the memory of a computer is a sequence of switches. There are millions and millions of switches, one after another, with no clear delimitations. To be able to know where the space occupied by a variable starts or ends, the system has to use addresses. These addresses are just consecutive numbers that correspond to each byte of memory. For example, if one byte is at the address 000000, the next byte will be at the address 000001, the next one at 000002, and so on. If we declare a variable of 4 bytes, the system has to reserve the four consecutive bytes and remember where they are so as not to overwrite them with the value of another variable. The task is easy when working with primitive types because their sizes are always the same, but the size of variables of more complex or custom data types depends on the values we assign to them. For example, the space in memory required to store the text "Hello" is smaller than the space required for the text "Hello World". A variable will occupy less space with the first value and more with the second one. Managing the memory for data of inconsistent size takes more time and consumes more resources than working with fixed sizes. This is one of the reasons why Swift includes the concept of constants.

Constants are exactly the same as variables, but their values cannot change. Once a constant is declared and initialized, we cannot change its value. In fact, we will get an error if our code tries to do it, so we will know we made a mistake even before running our app. Constants provide a safe way to store a value and help the system to manage the memory, improving the performance of our application and ensuring that a value is not going to change over time.

To declare a constant, we have to apply the same syntax used for a variable but replace the **var** keyword by the **let** keyword.

```
let mynumber = 5
```

Listing 2-18: Declaring and initializing a constant

All the rules for variables also apply to constants; with the exception that we cannot assign a new value after the constant was already initialized. We can declare the constant first, specifying its type, and initialize it later, but we cannot assign new values to it. The **mynumber** constant declared in Listing 2-18 will always have the value 5.

 IMPORTANT: When to use constants or variables depends on your application. As guidance, you can follow what Apple recommends: if a stored value in your code is not going to change, always declare it as a constant with the **let** keyword. Use variables only for storing values that need to be able to change.

2.3 Data Types

Besides the primitive types already studied, Swift defines additional data types to allow us to work not only with numbers but also more complex values such as logical values (true or false), characters, or text.

Characters

Because of their nature, computers cannot store decimal numbers, characters, or text. As we have seen in the previous section, the computer memory is only capable of storing 1s and 0s (switches on and off), but they can work with more complex values using tables that contain the information necessary to represent those values (numbers, letters, symbols, etc.). What the system stores in memory is not the character but the value corresponding to the index of the character on the table. For example, if we use the letter A, the value stored in memory will be the decimal number 65 (in its binary representation) because that's the position of the letter A on the table used by Swift to define these characters. When the value is stored, the system not only stores the value but also a reference to indicate that it represents a character and not just a number. This way, when we get the value back, the system reads the number 65, searches for the character in that position on the table and returns the letter or shows it on the screen.

There are several standard tables of characters available. Swift is compliant with a table called *Unicode*. This is a very comprehensive table that includes every character from almost any language in the world, and also special characters, such as emoticons. Due to its broad range, the space in memory required to store a single character varies from one character to another. For this reason, Swift provides the **Character** type to store these values.

```
var myletter: Character = "A"
```

Listing 2-19: Declaring and initializing a Character *variable*

A character is declared using the **Character** type and initialized with the value between double quotes. In Listing 2-19, we assign the character A to the **myletter** variable.

 The Basics: To be able to interact with a computer, we create layers of abstraction, one on top of another, until we obtain something similar to what we are used to working with in the real world. Represent a character through an index stored in memory as a series of switches on and off may be considered the first layer. Organizing those characters to create instructions the computer can follow would be the second layer. As we will see in further chapters, the organization of those instructions into structures and objects represent new layers of abstraction. Each layer adds more functionality with the final purpose of creating something useful for the real world. To learn how to program an app, we have to understand the tools created by these layers and how to use them. We will go through this process in the rest of the book.

Strings

In a program, we barely work with individual characters, we usually need to store a string of characters. The **String** type was created for this purpose.

```
var mytext: String = "My name is John"
```

***Listing 2-20:** Declaring and initializing a* String *variable*

A string is actually a sequence of **Character** values. It is declared with the **String** type and its value between double quotes. These types of variables are very flexible; we may replace the string by another one of different length, concatenate two or more, or even modify parts of them. Concatenation is a common operation and it is done with the **+** and **+=** operators.

```
var mytext = "My name is "
mytext = mytext + "John"   // "My name is John"
```

***Listing 2-21:** Concatenating strings*

In Listing 2-21, the **mytext** variable is created with the value "My name is " and then the string "John" is added at the end of the current value to get the string "My name is John". The **+=** operator works in a similar way, and we can also combine them to get the string we want.

```
let exclamation = "!"
var mytext = "My name is "
mytext += "John" + exclamation   // "My name is John!"
```

***Listing 2-22:** Concatenating strings with the + and += operators*

The example of Listing 2-22 uses the **+=** operator to add a string at the end of the current value of the **mytext** variable. The final value is "My name is John!". Notice that the **exclamation** variable is considered by Swift to be a **String** value, not a **Character** value (as always, Swift selects the most comprehensive type).

With the **+** and **+=** operators we can only concatenate strings with strings. To concatenate strings with characters and numbers we have to use a procedure called *String interpolation*. The variables have to be included inside the string and wrapped by parentheses prefixed with a backslash.

```
var age = 44
var mytext = "I am \(age) years old"   // "I am 44 years old"
```

***Listing 2-23:** Including variables in strings*

In the code of Listing 2-23, the **age** variable is read, and its current value is added to the string. The string "I am 44 years old" is then assigned to **mytext**. Using this method, we can insert any variable we want inside a string, including **Character** and **String** variables, as well as the result of arithmetic operations. In the following example, the value of **age** is multiplied by 12 and the result is included in the string.

```
var age = 44
var mytext = "I am \(age * 12) months old"   // "I am 528 months old"
```

Listing 2-24: Performing operations inside strings

 IMPORTANT: Processing strings of characters is probably the most important task of any program. Text is the tool used by the application to communicate with the user. For this reason, Swift includes a series of functions we can use to manipulate and work with strings. We will study these functions in Chapter 3.

Booleans

Boolean variables are a type of variables that can only store two possible values: **true** or **false**. These variables are particularly useful when we want to execute an instruction or a set of instructions only in certain conditions. To declare a Boolean variable, we can specify the type as **Bool** or let Swift infer the type from its value, as in the following example.

```
var valid = true
```

Listing 2-25: Declaring a Boolean variable

The purpose of these variables is to simplify the process of identifying a condition. If we use an integer variable to indicate the state of a condition, we have to remember which numbers we decided to use for the valid and the invalid states. Using a Boolean variable instead, we just have to check whether the value is equal to **true** or **false**.

 IMPORTANT: Booleans become useful when we use them along with instructions that allow us to perform a task or repetitive tasks according to a condition. We will study Conditionals and Loops later in this chapter.

Optionals

As we mentioned before, after a variable is declared, we have to provide its initial value. We cannot use a variable if it was not initialized. This means that a variable has a valid value all the time. But this is not always appropriate. Sometimes we do not have an initial value to assign to the variable during development or we need to indicate the absence of a value because the current one becomes invalid. For these situations, Swift defines a modifier that turns every data type into an optional type. This means that the variable marked as optional may have a value or be empty. To declare an optional, we just have to add a question mark after the type's name.

```
var mynumber: Int?
```

Listing 2-26: Declaring an optional variable of type Int

New values are assigned as we do with normal variables.

```
var mynumber: Int?
mynumber = 5
```

Listing 2-27: Assigning new values to optional variables

The empty state is represented by the keyword **nil**. Therefore, when an optional variable is declared but not initialized, as in previous examples, Swift assigns to the variable the **nil** keyword to indicate the absence of a value. If later we need to empty the variable, we can assign the keyword **nil** to it.

```
var mynumber: Int?
mynumber = 5
mynumber = nil
```

Listing 2-28: Using nil *to empty a variable*

The code of Listing 2-28 declares an optional integer, assigns the value 5 to it, and then declares the variable as empty with the keyword **nil**. Although optionals seem to work like regular variables, they do not expose their values. To read the value of an optional, we have to unwrap it by adding an exclamation mark at the end of the name.

```
var mynumber: Int?
mynumber = 5
var total = mynumber! * 10   // 50
```

Listing 2-29: Unwrapping an optional variable

The last statement of Listing 2-29 unwraps **mynumber** to get its value, multiplies this value by 10, and assigns the result to the **total** variable. This is only necessary when we need to use the value. If we just want to assign an optional to another optional, the process is as always.

```
var mynumber: Int?
mynumber = 5
var total = mynumber
```

Listing 2-30: Assigning an optional to another optional

In this last example, the system infers the type of the **total** variable to be an optional of type **Int** and assigns the value of **mynumber** to it. If we want to read the value of **total** later, we have to unwrap it as we did with **mynumber** before.

 IMPORTANT: Before unwrapping an optional, we have to be sure it contains a value (it is not **nil**). If we try to unwrap an empty optional, the app will return an error and crash. Later in this chapter we will learn how to use conditional statements to check this condition.

There are times when we know that an optional will always have a value, but we do not know what the initial value is. For example, we could have a variable that receives a value from the system as soon as the application is executed. When the variable is declared in our code, we do not have a value to assign to it, but we know that the variable will have a value as soon as the user runs the app. For these situations, Swift provides the possibility to declare *implicitly unwrapped optionals*. These are optional variables declared with the exclamation mark instead of the question mark. The system reads these variables as optionals until it is forced to unwrap the value with another exclamation mark (as we did before for normal optionals) or because the variable is used in an operation, as in the following example.

Introduction to Swift

```
var mynumber: Int!
mynumber = 5
var total = mynumber * 10   // 50
```

Listing 2-31: Declaring implicitly unwrapped optionals

In Listing 2-31, the **mynumber** variable was declared as an implicitly unwrapped optional and it was later initialized with the value 5. Notice that it was not necessary to write the exclamation mark when reading its value anymore. The system unwraps the **mynumber** variable automatically to be able to use its value in the multiplication.

Tuples

A tuple is a type of variable that contains a group of one or more values of equal or different type. It is useful when we need to store values that are somehow related to each other. Tuples are declared with their values and types separated by a comma and enclosed between parentheses.

```
var myname: (String, String) = ("John", "Doe")
```

Listing 2-32: Declaring a tuple with two values

In this example, the **myname** variable is declared to be a tuple that contains two **String** values. The values of this tuple are of the same type, but we can use any combination of values we want and also let Swift infer their types.

```
var myname = ("John", "Doe", 44)
```

Listing 2-33: Declaring a tuple with values of different type

To be able to read the values later, an index is automatically assigned to each of the values of the tuple. Indexes start at the value 0, so the first value will be at index 0, the second at index 1, and so on. Using the corresponding index and dot notation we can access the value we want.

```
var myname = ("John", "Doe", 44)
var mytext = "\(myname.0) is \(myname.2) years old" // "John is 44 years
old"
```

Listing 2-34: Reading a tuple

In Listing 2-34 we read the values of the **myname** tuple at index 0 and 2 to include them in a new string and assign the string to **mytext**. The same syntax may be used to modify a value.

```
var myname = ("John", "Doe", 44)
myname.0 = "George"
var mytext = "\(myname.0) is \(myname.2) years old"
```

Listing 2-35: Changing the value of a tuple

The second statement of Listing 2-35 assigns a new string to the first value of the tuple. The new value has to be of the same type as the old one. If we had tried to assign an integer instead, we would have received an error. After the code is executed, the value of **mytext** will be "George is 44 years old".

Indexes are a quick way to access the values of a tuple, but they do not help us remember what the values represent. To facilitate the identification of the values in a tuple, we can assign a name to each one of them. The name has to be declared before the value and separated with a colon, as shown next.

```
var myname = (name: "John", surname: "Doe", age: 44)
var mytext = "\(myname.name) is \(myname.age) years old"
```

Listing 2-36: Declaring names for the values of a tuple

Sometimes the values are required more than once, and the dot notation may not be practical. For these situations, Swift provides a way to copy the values of the tuple into independent variables.

```
var myname = ("John", "Doe", 44)
var (name, surname, age) = myname
var mytext = "\(name) \(surname) is \(age) years old"
```

Listing 2-37: Creating multiple variables from the values of a tuple

The names of the variables are declared between parentheses and the tuple is assigned to this construction. The values are assigned to the variables in the same order they have inside the tuple. These variables may be used later as we would do with any other variable. If only some of the values are required, the rest may be ignored writing an underscore in their place.

```
var myname = ("John", "Doe", 44)
var (name, _, age) = myname
var mytext = "\(name) is \(age) years old"
```

Listing 2-38: Ignoring some of the values of a tuple

Only the variables **name** and **age** are used in this last example (notice the underscore in the place of the second variable). The string assigned to **mytext** is "John is 44 years old".

 IMPORTANT: Tuples are particularly useful when working with functions, as we will see later. The use of tuples is only recommended when we need to share information between different pieces of code, but not to store persistent data. To store complex data structures, you should use collections (such as arrays or dictionaries). We will study collections next and functions in Chapter 3.

2.4 Collections

Most of the time, instead of independent units of information, programs require lists of related values. These lists are called *collections*. From the options of a menu to the books in a library, any useful information in the real world may be organized as a collection of values. Swift provides three generic types of collections: Arrays, Sets and Dictionaries.

Arrays

Arrays are variables that contain an ordered list of values. They have the capacity to store all the values we want, but they all have to be of the same type. For example, if we create an array of type **Int**, we will only be able to store values of type **Int**. The declaration of an array includes the type and the values enclosed in square brackets.

Introduction to Swift

```
var list: [Int] = [15, 25, 35]
```

Listing 2-39: Declaring arrays

Again, Swift may infer the type from the values.

```
var list = [15, 25, 35]
```

Listing 2-40: Declaring arrays with type inference

The **list** array declared in these examples was initialized with three integer values, 15, 25 and 35. The values of an array are usually called *elements* or *items*. On these terms, we can say that the code of Listing 2-40 declares an array of three elements of type **Int**.

An index is assigned to each of the values automatically, starting from 0, but arrays do not use the dot notation applied to tuples, the index of the element we want to read has to be declared after the array's name, enclosed in square brackets.

```
var list = [15, 25, 35]
list[1]   // 25
```

Listing 2-41: Reading the array's elements

The last statement of Listing 2-41 shows the value of the second element of the **list** array (the element at index 1) on the Results Side Bar. We can also use indexes to modify the values of an array, as we did with tuples.

```
var list = [15, 25, 35]
list[0] = 400
list   // [400, 25, 35]
```

Listing 2-42: Assigning a new value to an element

Assigning new values is only possible for elements that already exist in the array. To add a new element, or several, we can use the **+=** operator.

```
var list = [15, 25, 35]
list += [45, 55]
list   // [15, 25, 35, 45, 55]
```

Listing 2-43: Adding new elements to an array

The **+=** operator adds an array at the end of another array. In Listing 2-43 we use it to add two more elements to the array declared in the first statement. The final array contains the values 15, 25, 35, 45, and 55, in that order.

 IMPORTANT: The elements added to the array have to be of the same type of the original array (in this last example, they have to be of type **Int**). If you try to add elements of different type, Xcode will show you an error.

What the **+=** operator actually does is to concatenate two arrays and assign the result back to the same variable. If we want to use two or more arrays to create a new one, we can apply the **+** operator.

```
var list1 = [15, 25, 35]
var list2 = [45, 55, 65]
var final = list1 + list2   // [15, 25, 35, 45, 55, 65]
```

Listing 2-44: Concatenating two arrays

It is possible to declare arrays of arrays. These types of arrays are called multidimensional arrays. Arrays inside arrays are listed separated by comma.

```
var list: [[Int]] = [[2, 45, 31], [5, 10], [81, 12]]
```

Listing 2-45: Creating multidimensional arrays

The example of Listing 2-45 creates an array of arrays of integers (notice the declaration of the array **[Int]** inside another array **[[Int]]**). To access the values, we have to declare the indexes of each level between square brackets, one after another. The following example returns the first value (index 0) of the second array (index 1). The instruction searches for the array at index 1 and then looks for the number at index 0.

```
var list: [[Int]] = [[2, 45, 31], [5, 10], [81, 12]]
list[1][0]   // 5
```

Listing 2-46: Reading values from a multidimensional array

To create a new empty array or remove all its elements, we can assign square brackets with no values to the variable.

```
var list = [15, 25, 35]
list = []
```

Listing 2-47: Removing the elements of an array

If we use empty square brackets to declare a new array, we have to specify the element's data type (e.g., **var list: [Int] = []**). Another way to create an empty array is to declare the value of the variable as the data type followed by parentheses, as in **var list = [Int]()**. Elements may be added later using the **+=** operator (see Listing 2-43) or applying any of the functions available for this purpose (we will study functions and **Array** functions in Chapter 3).

 The Basics: There is a low-level definition for arrays that requires the keyword **Array** and the data type between angle brackets. The syntax to create an array is **Array<Type>**, where **Type** is the data type of the elements of the array. For example, to create an empty array of integers we write **var myarray = Array<Int>()**. If the types are defined explicitly, we can just use the empty parentheses, as in **var myarray: [Int] = Array()**.

Sets

If we store two elements in an array, one element will automatically receive the index 0 and the other the index 1. This correlation between indexes and values never changes, allowing elements to be listed always in the right order and also have elements with the same value at different indexes. Sets are similar to arrays, but they do not assign an index to their values and therefore

Introduction to Swift

there is no order and no duplicated values. This makes accessing values in sets much faster than arrays, but also makes them only useful in very specific circumstances.

The declaration of sets is similar to arrays, but we have to specify the type as **Set**.

```
var ages: Set = [15, 25, 35, 45]
```

Listing 2-48: *Creating a set of integers*

The set's data type is inferred by Swift from the values assigned to it. If we need to declare the type, for example, to create an empty set, we have to use the set's low-level definition that includes the **Set** keyword followed by the data type between angle brackets.

```
var ages: Set<Int> = []
```

Listing 2-49: *Creating an empty set of integers*

 IMPORTANT: Because the set's elements are not associated to an index, there is not much we can do with the set alone. Later in this chapter we will see how to interact through a collection with loops, and in Chapter 3 we will learn more about sets and how we can read and process their values.

Dictionaries

There is only one way to access the elements of an array and that is through their numeric indexes. Dictionaries offer a better alternative. With dictionaries, we can define the indexes ourselves using any custom value we want. Each index has to be explicitly declared along with its associated value. In the declaration, we have to specify the data type of both the indexes and their values. Listing 2-50 shows the required syntax.

```
var list: [String: String] = ["First": "Apple", "Second": "Orange"]
```

Listing 2-50: *Declaring a dictionary*

Of course, if the indexes and the values are of a clear type, Swift can infer them.

```
var list = ["First": "Apple", "Second": "Orange"]
```

Listing 2-51: *Declaring a dictionary with type inference*

As with arrays, if we want to read or replace a value, we just have to declare its index in square brackets after the name of the dictionary.

```
var list = ["First": "Apple", "Second": "Orange"]
list["Second"] = "Banana"
```

Listing 2-52: *Assigning a new value to an element of a dictionary*

The second statement of Listing 2-52 assigns a new value to the element identified with the keyword "Second". Now the dictionary contains two elements with the values "Apple" and "Banana". If the keyword used to assign the new value exists, the system updates the value, but if the keyword does not exist, a new element is created, as shown next.

```
var list = ["First": "Apple", "Second": "Orange"]
list["Third"] = "Banana"
```

Listing 2-53: *Adding a new element to a dictionary*

In this last example, the second statement assigns the value "Banana" to a keyword that does not exist. The system creates the new element with the specified keyword and value. The result is a dictionary containing three values "Apple", "Orange", and "Banana".

Dictionaries return optional values. If we try to read an element with a keyword that does not exist, the value returned is **nil**.

```
var list = ["First": "Apple", "Second": "Orange"]
list["Third"]   // nil
```

Listing 2-54: *Reading an element that does not exist*

The code of Listing 2-54 tries to read a value with the keyword "Third" that does not exist in the **list** dictionary. As a result, the value **nil** is shown on the Results Side Bar. If the element exists and we want to read its value, we have to unwrap it.

```
var list = ["First": "Apple", "Second": "Orange"]
var message = "We have \(list["First"]!) and \(list["Second"]!)"
```

Listing 2-55: *Using the value of an element*

Dictionaries may also contain arrays as values. The declaration is simple, the key is declared as always, and the single value is replaced by an array.

```
var fruits: [String: [String]] = ["A": ["Apple", "Apricot"], "B":
["Banana", "Blueberries"]]
```

Listing 2-56: *Combining dictionaries and arrays*

Reading the values of a dictionary like this is a little bit more complicated. Because dictionaries return optionals, we cannot just specify the indexes as we do for multidimensional arrays (see Listing 2-46). The value returned by the dictionary has to be unwrapped before accessing its values.

```
var fruits: [String: [String]] = ["A": ["Apple", "Apricot"], "B":
["Banana", "Blueberries"]]
let list = fruits["A"]!   // ["Apple", "Apricot"]
list[0]   // "Apple"
```

Listing 2-57: *Reading arrays inside dictionaries*

In Listing 2-57 we create a dictionary with two values. The values are arrays of strings with a string as key. The code gets the array corresponding to the "A" key, unwraps it, and stores it in a constant. Because the **list** constant contains the array assigned to the "A" key, we are able to read its values.

Since dictionary values are treated as optionals, we can also assign the value **nil** to remove an element. The following example removes the element with the keyword "First".

Introduction to Swift

```
var list = ["First": "Apple", "Second": "Orange"]
list["First"] = nil
```

Listing 2-58: Removing an element from a dictionary

As with arrays, to declare a new empty dictionary or remove all its elements, we have to assign to the variable the square brackets with no values (a colon is required for dictionaries).

```
var list = ["First": "Apple", "Second": "Orange"]
list = [:]
```

Listing 2-59: Removing all the elements from a dictionary

If we use empty square brackets to declare a new dictionary, we have to specify the data types for its keywords and values (e.g., **var list: [String: String] = [:]**). Another way to create an empty dictionary is to declare the value of the variable as the data types followed by parentheses (e.g., **var list = [String: String]()**). Elements may be added later by declaring a new keyword (see Listing 2-53) or by applying any of the functions available for this purpose (we will study functions and **Dictionary** functions in Chapter 3).

 The Basics: As with arrays and sets, there is a low-level definition for dictionaries that requires the keyword **Dictionary** and the data types between angle brackets. The syntax to create a dictionary is **Dictionary<Type1, Type2>**, where **Type1** is the data type of the indexes and **Type2** is the data type of the values. For example, to create an empty dictionary of strings we write **var list = Dictionary<String, String>()**. If the types were explicitly defined, we can just use the empty parentheses, as in **var list: [String: String] = Dictionary()**.

2.5 Conditionals and Loops

Up to this point we have been writing instructions in a sequence, one after another. In this kind of program, the system executes each statement once and in the same order they were presented. It starts with the one at the top and goes on until it reaches the end of the list. The purpose of Conditionals and Loops is to break this sequential flow. Conditionals allow us to execute one or more instructions only when a condition is met, and Loops let us execute a group of instructions over and over again until a condition is met.

If and Else

A simple but handful conditional statement available in Swift is **if**. With **if** we can check a condition and execute a group of instructions only when the condition is true. The instructions that are going to be executed have to be declared between braces after the condition.

```
var age = 19
var message = "John is old"
if age < 21 {
    message = "John is young"
}
message   // "John is young"
```

Listing 2-60: Comparing two values with if

Two variables are declared in the code of Listing 2-60. The **age** variable contains the value we want to check, and the **message** variable is the one we are going to modify depending on the state of the condition. The **if** statement compares the value of **age** with the number 21 using the character < (less than). This comparison returns the state of the condition (true or false). If the condition is true (the value of **age** is less than 21), the instruction between braces is executed, assigning a new value to the **message** variable, otherwise the instruction is ignored, and the execution continues with the instructions after the **if** statement.

 The Basics: The instruction between braces in the last example is displaced to the right. The whitespace on the left is used to help us differentiate the statements between braces from the rest of the statements. This whitespace is automatically generated for you by Xcode, but you can do it yourself when necessary pressing the Tab key on your keyboard.

The < symbol we used in the last example to compare values is part of a group of operators called *comparison operators*. The following is the list of comparison operators available in Swift.

- **==** checks whether the value on the left is equal to the value on the right.
- **!=** checks whether the value on the left is different than the value on the right.
- **>** checks whether the value on the left is greater than the value on the right.
- **<** checks whether the value on the left is less than the value on the right.
- **>=** checks whether the value on the left is greater or equal than the value on the right.
- **<=** checks whether the value on the left is less or equal than the value on the right.

All these operators are applied the same way we did in the previous example. For instance, the following code changes the value of **message** when the value of **age** is less or equal than 21.

```
var age = 21
var message = "John is old"
if age <= 21 {
    message = "John is young"
}
message   // "John is young"
```

Listing 2-61: Comparing two values with the <= operator

 The Basics: Braces are applied in many constructions in Swift. They allow us to create independent processing units with their own instructions and variables. These constructions are usually called *blocks*. We will learn more about blocks in this and following chapters.

When only two results are expected, we may define the condition using a Boolean value. These values do not need to be compared; they already return a state (true or false).

```
var underage = true
var message = "John is allowed"
if underage {
    message = "John is underage"
}
message   // "John is underage"
```

Listing 2-62: Conditions with Boolean values

Introduction to Swift

The code of Listing 2-62 checks whether the value of the **underage** variable is **true** or **false**. If it is **true** (which means the condition is true), a new string of characters is assigned to the **message** variable. If, on the other hand, we want to execute the statements when the value is **false**, we have to write an exclamation mark before the condition to toggle its state. The value of the **message** variable in the following example is not modified.

```
var underage = true
var message = "John is underage"
if !underage {
    message = "John is allowed"
}
message  // "John is underage"
```

Listing 2-63: Using logical operators

The exclamation mark is part of a group of logical operators provided by Swift.

- **!** (logical NOT) toggles the state of the condition. If the condition is true, it returns false, and vice versa.
- **&&** (logical AND) checks two conditions and returns true if both are true.
- **||** (logical OR) checks two conditions and returns true if one or both are true.

Logical operators work with any kind of conditions, not only Booleans. To work with complex conditions, it is recommended to enclose the condition between parentheses.

```
var smart = true
var age = 19
var message = "John is underage or dumb"
if (age < 21) && smart {
    message = "John is allowed"
}
message  // "John is allowed"
```

Listing 2-64: Using logical operators to check several conditions

The **if** statement of Listing 2-64 compares the value of the **age** variable with 21 and checks the value of the **smart** variable. If **age** is less than 21 and **smart** is **true**, then the overall condition is true and a new string is assigned to **message**. If any of the individual conditions is false, the overall condition will be false and the block of instructions will not be executed.

 The Basics: Using **&&** (AND) and **||** (OR) you can create a logical sequence. The system evaluates one condition at a time and compares the results sequentially. For example, a set of conditions that evaluate as **true && false || true**, return the value **true**. The first expression is evaluated as **false** (**true && false = false**), but the last value is evaluated against the first result, so the final result is **true** (**false || true = true**). If you want to make sure that the expressions are evaluated in the correct order, you can enclose them between parentheses, as in **(true && false) || true**. The expression between parentheses is evaluated first and the result is then evaluated against the rest of the expression.

Although we can use comparison operators and logical operators in most of the basic data types available, optionals are slightly different. Their values are wrapped, so we cannot compare them with other values or check their state as we do with Booleans. Optionals have to be compared against the keyword **nil** first and then unwrapped before to work with their values.

```
var count = 0
var myoptional: Int? = 5

if myoptional != nil {
    let uvalue = myoptional!
    count = count + uvalue
}
count   // 5
```

Listing 2-65: Checking whether an optional contains a value or not

Listing 2-65 shows the process we must follow to read the value of an optional variable. The optional is checked first against **nil**. If it is different than **nil** (which means it contains a value), we unwrap the optional inside the block of statements using an exclamation mark, assign its value to a constant, and use the constant to perform any operation necessary (in this example, the value of the **count** variable is incremented by the value of the optional).

We always have to make sure that an optional has a value before unwrapping it. Because of this, Swift introduces a better syntax that checks the optional and unwraps its value at the same time. It is called *Optional Binding*.

```
var count = 0
var myoptional: Int? = 5
if let uvalue = myoptional {
    count = count + uvalue
}
count   // 5
```

Listing 2-66: Using optional binding to unwrap an optional variable

This new code is cleaner and easy to read. The optional is unwrapped as part of the condition checked by the **if** statement. If it is different than **nil**, its value is assigned to the **uvalue** constant and the statements in the block are executed.

 IMPORTANT: If we want to unwrap several optionals at the same time using Optional Binding, we have to declare the expressions separated by a comma (e.g., **let value1 = optional1, let value2 = optional2**).

There are times in which instructions have to be executed for either state of the condition (true or false). Swift includes the **if else** construction to help in this situation. The instructions are presented in two blocks. The first block will be executed when the condition is true, and the second block will be executed otherwise.

```
var mynumber = 6
if mynumber % 2 == 0 {
    mynumber = mynumber + 2
} else {
    mynumber = mynumber + 1
}
mynumber   // 8
```

Listing 2-67: Using if else to respond to both states of the condition

The code of Listing 2-67 is a simple example that checks whether a value is odd or even using the remainder operator. The condition gets the remainder of the division between the value of the **mynumber** variable and 2 and compares the result against 0. If true, it means that the value of **mynumber** is even, so the first block is executed. On the other hand, if the value is different than 0 it means that it is odd, so the block corresponding to the **else** instruction is executed instead.

The statements **if** and **else** may be concatenated to check for as many conditions as we need. In the following example, we check the age of a customer. The first condition checks whether its age is less than 21. If this is not true, the second condition checks whether the age is over 21. If this is not true, the final **else** block is executed.

```
var age = 19
var message = "The customer is "
if age < 21 {
   message += "underage"
} else if age > 21 {
   message += "allowed"
} else {
   message += "21 years old"
}
message  // "The customer is underage"
```

Listing 2-68: *Concatenating* if else *instructions*

If all we need is to modify the value of a variable depending on a condition, we can use a shortcut provided by Swift called *ternary operator*. This is a construction composed by the condition and the two values we want to return for each state. The first value must be preceded by the **?** character and the second value by the **:** character, as in the following example.

```
var age = 19
var message = "The customer is "
message += age < 21 ? "underage" : "allowed"
message  // "The customer is underage"
```

Listing 2-69: *Implementing the ternary operator*

The first value is returned if the condition is true and the second value is returned if the condition is false. The advantage of using the ternary operator is that it reduces the code significantly, but the result is the same than using an **if else** statement. In this example, we get again the message "The costumer is underage".

Switch

The **if** and **else** statements may be included as many times as necessary, but soon it might get to a point where the code is impossible to read and maintain. When several conditions have to be checked, it is better to use the **switch** instruction instead. This instruction compares a value against a list of values and executes the instructions corresponding to the value that matches. The possible values are listed between braces using the **case** keyword, as in the following example.

```
var age = 19
var message = ""
```

```
switch age {
   case 13:
      message = "Happy Bar Mitzvah!"
   case 16:
      message = "Sweet Sixteen!"
   case 21:
      message = "Welcome to Adulthood!"
   default:
      message = "Happy Birthday!"
}
message   // "Happy Birthday!"
```

Listing 2-70: Checking conditions with `switch`

The cases have to be exhaustive; every possible value of the variable being checked has to be contemplated. If we do not include a **case** statement for every possible value, we have to add a **default** statement at the end that will be executed when no match is found.

In Listing 2-70, we compare the value of the **age** variable against a small set of values corresponding to special dates. If no **case** matches the value of the variable, the **default** statement is executed and the string "Happy Birthday!" is assigned to **message**.

When we have to execute the same set of instructions for more than one value, we can declare the values separated by comma.

```
var age = 6
var message = "You have to go to "
switch age {
   case 2, 3, 4:
      message += "Day Care"
   case 5, 6, 7, 8, 9, 10, 11:
      message += "Elementary School"
   case 12, 13, 14, 15, 16, 17:
      message += "High School"
   case 18, 19, 20, 21:
      message += "College"
   default:
      message += "Work"
}
message  // "You have to go to Elementary School"
```

Listing 2-71: Checking multiple conditions per case

The use of consecutive values is very common in computer programming. Swift includes two new operators to generate ranges of values and simplify our code.

- **...** (three dots) creates a range from the value on the left to the value on the right, including both values in the range (e.g., 1...4 creates a range that includes the values 1, 2, 3 and 4).
- **..<** (two dots and the less than character) creates a range from the value on the left to the value before the value on the right. This means that only the value on the left is included in the range (e.g., 1..<4 creates a range with the values 1, 2 and 3).

The following example applies range operators to the code of Listing 2-71.

```
var age = 6
var message = "You have to go to "
```

```
switch age {
    case 2...4:
        message += "Day Care"
    case 5...11:
        message += "Elementary School"
    case 12...17:
        message += "High School"
    case 18..<22:
        message += "College"
    case 22...:
        message += "Work"
    default:
        message += "Breastfeeding"
}
message  // "You have to go to Elementary School"
```

Listing 2-72: *Using range operators in a* switch *statement*

Declaring a range like **2...4** is the same as declaring the values 2, 3, 4 separated by commas. If the value of **age** is within one of the ranges, the instructions for that **case** are executed. As illustrated by this example, we can also declare only one side of the range and let the system determine the other. The last case in Listing 2-72 creates a one-sided range from the value 22 to the maximum value allowed for the type.

 IMPORTANT: Ranges can be made from different types of values, not only integers, and are especially useful when working with strings of characters, as we will see later. We will study practical applications of ranges in this and further chapters.

The **switch** statement can also work with more complex data types, such as strings and tuples. In the case of tuples, **switch** provides additional options to build complex matching patterns. For example, the following code checks the second value of a tuple to determine the difference in age.

```
var message = ""
var ages = (10, 30)

switch ages {
    case (10, 20):
        message = "Too close"
    case (10, 30):
        message = "The right age"
    case (10, 40):
        message = "Too far"
    default:
        message = "Way too far"
}
message  // "The right age"
```

Listing 2-73: *Matching a tuple in a* switch *statement*

This example always compares the first value of the tuple against 10 but checks different matches for the second value. If a value does not matter, we can use an underscore on its place to ignore it.

```
var message = ""
var ages = (10, 30)

switch ages {
   case (_, 20):
      message = "Too close"
   case (_, 30):
      message = "The right age"
   case (_, 40):
      message = "Too far"
   default:
      message = "Way too far"
}
message   // "The right age"
```

Listing 2-74: Matching only the second value of a tuple

These examples match only specific values, but we can use range operators to match the value against a range.

```
var message = ""
var ages = (10, 35)

switch ages {
   case (_, 11...20):
      message = "Too close"
   case (_, 21...30):
      message = "The right age"
   case (_, 31...40):
      message = "Too far"
   default:
      message = "Way too far"
}
message   // "Too far"
```

Listing 2-75: Matching values against a range

An alternative offered by a **switch** statement to create complex matching patterns is to capture a value in a constant to be able to access it from the instructions of the **case**.

```
var message = ""
var ages = (10, 20)

switch ages {
   case (let x, 20):
      message = "Too close to \(x)"
   case (_, 30):
      message = "The right age"
   case (let x, 40):
      message = "Too far to \(x)"
   default:
      message = "Way too far"
}
message   // "Too close to 10"
```

Listing 2-76: Capturing values with constants

In the example of Listing 2-76, every time the **switch** statement checks a **case**, it creates a constant called **x** and assigns the tuple's first value to it. Because of this, we can access the value from the statements inside the **case** and use it to perform a customized task (in this example we just add the value to a string).

There is an even more complex matching pattern that involves the use of a clause called **where**. This clause allows us to check additional conditions. In the following example, we capture the values of the tuple with another tuple and compare them against each other.

```
var message = ""
var ages = (10, 20)

switch ages {
    case let (x, y) where x > y:
        message = "Too young"
    case let (x, y) where x == y:
        message = "The same age"
    case let (x, y) where x < y:
        message = "Too old"
    default:
        message = "Not found"
}
message   // "Too old"
```

Listing 2-77: Comparing values with where

Every time the **switch** statement tries to match a **case** in the example of Listing 2-77, it creates a tuple and assigns the values of **ages** to it. The **where** clause compares the values and when the condition returns true it executes the statements in the **case**.

While and Repeat While

The conditionals studied so far execute the statements corresponding to each of the states of the condition only once. Sometimes the program requires executing a block of instructions several times until a condition is satisfied. This is called *loop*. The simplest alternative offered by Swift to create loops is the **while** statement (and its sibling **repeat while**).

The **while** statement checks a condition and executes the statements in its block while the condition is true. The following example initializes a variable with the value 0 and then checks its value in a **while** statement. If the value of the variable is less than 5, the statements inside the block are executed. After this, the condition is checked again. The loop keeps running until the condition becomes false (the value of the **counter** variable is equal or greater than 5).

```
var counter = 0
while counter < 5 {
    counter += 1
}
counter   // 5
```

Listing 2-78: Using while *to create a loop*

If the condition returns false when it is checked for the first time, the statements in the block are never executed. If we want to execute the statements at least once, we have to use the **repeat while** instructions.

```
var counter = 10
repeat {
    counter += 1
} while counter < 5
counter   // 11
```

Listing 2-79: Using repeat while *to create a loop*

In this case, the initial value of the **counter** variable is declared as 10. This is greater than 5, but since we are using **repeat while**, the statements in the block are executed before the condition is checked, so the final value of counter will be 11 (its value is incremented once and then the condition returns false, ending the loop).

For In

The purpose of the **for in** loop is to iterate over collections of elements such as arrays, dictionaries, and also ranges and strings of characters. During the execution of a **for in** loop, the system reads the elements of the collection one by one and assigns their values to a constant that can be processed by the statements inside the block. The condition that has to be satisfied for this loop to be over is reaching the end of the list.

The syntax of a **for in** loop is **for constant in collection {}**, where **constant** is the name of the constant that we are going to use to capture the value of each element, and **collection** is the name of the collection that we want to iterate over (array, dictionary, set, etc.).

```
var fruits = ["Banana", "Orange", "Apple"]
var message = "My fruits:"

for myfruit in fruits {
    message += " " + myfruit
}
message   // "My fruits: Banana Orange Apple"
```

Listing 2-80: Using for in *to iterate over an array*

The code of Listing 2-80 uses an array called **fruits** with three elements and the **myfruit** constant to capture their values. The statement inside the block adds the value of each element to the **message** variable to get the final string "My fruits: Banana Orange Apple".

When the constant is not required inside the block, we can replace it with an underscore.

```
var fruits = ["Banana", "Orange", "Apple"]
var counter = 0
for _ in fruits {
    counter += 1
}
var message = "I have \(counter) fruits"   // "I have 3 fruits"
```

Listing 2-81: Iterating over an array without reading its values

The iteration over dictionaries is a little bit different than arrays. Dictionaries return a tuple containing the index and the value of each element, so we have to apply the same syntax used in Listing 2-37 to store the values of the tuple in multiple constants.

Introduction to Swift

```
var fruits = ["First": "Apple", "Second": "Orange"]
var message = "My fruits:"

for (myindex, myfruit) in fruits {
   message += " \(myindex)-\(myfruit)"
}
message   // "My fruits: First-Apple Second-Orange"
```

Listing 2-82: Using for *in to iterate over a dictionary*

The **for in** loop in Listing 2-82 reads the elements of the **fruits** dictionary one by one, assigns the index and the value of the current element to the **myindex** and **myfruit** constants, and adds their values to the **message** variable.

Besides iterating over arrays, sets and dictionaries, we can also create loops with ranges. This is particularly useful when we need to generate a loop with a specific number of cycles. The following example iterates over a range of integers from 0 to 5, generating a total of 6 cycles.

```
var total = 0
for value in 0...5 {
   total += value
}
total   // 15
```

Listing 2-83: Using for *in to iterate over a range*

Control Transfer Statements

Loops sometimes must be interrupted, independently of the state of the condition. Swift offers multiple instructions to break the execution flow of loops and conditionals, the following are the most frequently used.

continue—This instruction interrupts the current cycle and moves to the next. The system ignores the rest of the statements in the block after the instruction is executed.

break—This instruction interrupts the loop. The rest of the statements in the block and any pending cycles are ignored after the instruction is executed. It is also useful to ignore cases in **switch** statements, as we will see later.

The **continue** instruction is applied when we do not want to execute the rest of the statements in the loop but we want to keep the loop running.

```
let mynumbers = [2, 4, 6, 8]

var total = 0
for number in mynumbers {
   if number == 6 {
      continue
   }
   total += number
}
var message = "The total is: \(total)"   // "The total is: 14"
```

Listing 2-84: Jumping to the next cycle of the loop

The **if** statement inside the **for in** loop of Listing 2-84 compares the value of **number** with the value 6. If the number currently returned by the loop is 6, the **continue** instruction is executed, the last statement inside the loop is ignored, and the loop moves on to the next element in the **mynumbers** array. In consequence, all the numbers of the array are added to the **total** variable except the number 6.

Unlike the **continue** instruction, the **break** instruction interrupts the loop completely, moving the execution flow to the statement after the loop.

```
let mynumbers = [2, 4, 6, 8]

var total = 0
for number in mynumbers {
   if number == 6 {
      break
   }
   total += number
}
var message = "The total is: \(total)"   // "The total is: 6"
```

Listing 2-85: Interrupting the loop

Again, the **if** statement of Listing 2-85 compares the value of **number** with the value 6, but this time it executes the **break** instruction when a match is found. If the number currently returned by the loop is 6, the **break** instruction is executed, and the loop is over, no matter how many elements are left in the array. In consequence, only the values located before the number 6 are added to the **total** variable.

The **break** instruction is also useful to cancel the execution of the **switch** statement. The problem with the **switch** statement in Swift is that the cases have to be exhaustive, which means that every possible value has to be considered and every case has to contain at least one statement to perform the corresponding task, but most of the time this is not possible or necessary. Using the **break** instruction, we can ignore the statements of the cases that are not applicable. For example, we can declare the cases for the values we need and then break the execution in the **default** case for the rest of the values that we do not care about.

```
var message = "Empty"
let fruits = ["Banana", "Orange", "Apple"]
let myfruit = fruits[1]

switch myfruit {
   case "Banana", "Apple":
      message = "You have the right fruit"
   default:
      break
}
```

Listing 2-86: Ignoring values in a switch *statement*

Listing 2-86 includes a **switch** statement to check the value of the **myfruit** constant. If the value does not match any of the values in the **case** statement, the **break** statement stops the execution of **switch** and returns the control to the next statement.

Executing the **break** instruction in the **default** case of a **switch** statement is very common because it allows us to only consider the values we need and ignore the rest.

Guard

The **guard** instruction is similar to the **if** instruction, but it has the purpose to prevent the execution of the code that follows the statement. For example, we can break the execution of a loop when a condition is satisfied, as we do with an **if else** statement.

```
let mynumbers = [2, 4, 6, 8]

var total = 0
for number in mynumbers {
    guard number != 6 else {
        break
    }
    total += number
}
var message = "The total is: \(total)"  // "The total is: 6"
```

Listing 2-87: *Interrupting a loop with* guard

The **guard** instruction works along with the **else** instruction and therefore it is very similar to the **if else** statement, but its code is only executed when the condition is false. In the example of Listing 2-87, the **for in** loop reads the values in the **mynumbers** array one by one. While the numbers are different than 6, they are added to the **total** variable, but when the number is equal to 6, the condition of the **guard** instruction returns false and therefore the **break** instruction is executed, finishing the loop. At the end, the **total** variable contains the result of adding 2 + 4.

 The Basics: The advantage of **guard** over the **if else** statements is that when we use optional binding, the variable or constant defined in the condition outlives the statement, and therefore we can read its value outside the block.

 IMPORTANT: Although you can implement the **guard** instruction to break or continue a loop, the instruction was introduced to work along with the **return** instruction to interrupt the execution of a function. We will study the **return** instruction and functions in the next chapter.

2.6 Enumerations

Enumerations are a way to create custom data types with their own limited set of values. An enumeration type is like a Boolean type but with the possible values defined by the programmer. They are defined with the keyword **enum** and the values between braces. Each value is declared using the **case** keyword.

```
enum Number {
    case one
    case two
    case three
}
```

Listing 2-88: *Defining an enumeration type*

The example of Listing 2-88 defines an enumeration type we call **Number** with three possible values: **one**, **two**, and **three**. We can choose any strings we want for the name and the cases, and the values may be declared in just one **case** statement separated by a comma.

```
enum Number {
    case one, two, three
}
```

Listing 2-89: Declaring the enumeration values in one statement

An enumeration is a custom data type. We cannot do anything with the definition alone, we have to create a variable of this type and assign to that variable one of the possible values using dot notation.

```
enum Number {
    case one, two, three
}
var mynumber: Number = Number.one
```

Listing 2-90: Declaring a variable of type Number

The word **Number** is like the word **Int**, just a name for the data type. Variables declared of this type may only have the values allowed by the type (**one**, **two**, or **three**). To assign a value, we have to use the name of the enumeration and dot notation. The **mynumber** variable declared in Listing 2-90 is of type **Number** and has the value **one**.

Once the type of the variable was already defined, only the dot and the value are necessary to modify its value.

```
enum Number {
    case one, two, three
}
var mynumber = Number.one
mynumber = .two
```

Listing 2-91: Assigning a new value to a variable of type Number

At the end of the example of Listing 2-91, we assign a new value to **mynumber**. The value **.two** may have been written as **Number.two**. Both syntaxes are valid, but Swift infers that the value provided is of the same type as the variable's type, so it is not necessary to declare the data type anymore. Notice that we can also let Swift infer the type when the variable is declared.

Like Booleans, enumeration types may be used as signals to indicate a state that can be checked later to decide whether or not to perform a certain task. Therefore, they are frequently used with conditionals and loops. The following example checks the value of an enumeration variable with a **switch** statement. These statements are particularly useful when working with enumerations. Enumeration types have a limited set of values, making it easy to define a **case** for each one of them.

```
enum Number {
    case one
    case two
    case three
}
var mynumber = Number.two
var message = ""
```

```
switch mynumber {
   case .one:
      message = "The number is 1"
   case .two:
      message = "The number is 2"
   case .three:
      message = "The number is 3"
}
message  // "The number is 2"
```

Listing 2-92: Using `switch` *with an enumeration type*

In Listing 2-92, the enumeration type **Number** is defined first. The **mynumber** variable is declared next to be of this type and the value **two** is assigned to it. Next, a **switch** statement compares the value of this variable with the three possible values of its type and assigns the corresponding string to **message**. Notice again that Swift is capable of inferring the type of the enumeration inside the **switch** statement, so it does not require us to specify the type **Number** every time we use its values.

Associated Values

The members of an enumeration type can also have associated values. These values are assigned to each member as if they were normal variables. The values must be of a type designated during the declaration of the enumeration, as shown next.

```
enum Number: Int {
   case one = 1
   case two = 2
   case three = 3
}
var mynumber = Number.one
```

Listing 2-93: Assigning raw values to enumeration members

If we do not assign the values ourselves, Swift automatically assigns an integer to each member. The numbers start from 0, like the indexes of an array. Of course, values are not restricted to integers. The following example associates the values of **Number** to strings.

```
enum Number: String {
   case one = "Number One"
   case two = "Number Two"
   case three = "Number Three"
}
var mynumber = Number.one
```

Listing 2-94: Assigning strings to enumeration members

 The Basics: Enumerations provide additional functionality, including a property to read associated values, and can also define custom properties and methods to store additional values and perform tasks. We will learn more about enumerations and how to read their values in Chapter 3.

Introduction to Swift

Chapter 3
Swift Paradigm

3.1 Programming Paradigms

Programs wouldn't be very useful if we were only able to write them as a consecutive set of instructions. At first, this was actually the only way to write a program, but soon languages incorporated tools to allow programmers to group instructions together and execute them every time necessary. The way instructions are organized is called *paradigm*. Different paradigms are now available, with the most common being the Object-Oriented Programming paradigm, or OOP. This paradigm emerges from the construction and integration of processing units called *objects*. Swift adopts OOP, but it does not focus as much on objects as other languages do. Instead, it expands other types of processing units called *structures* to conform a new paradigm called *Protocol-Oriented Programing*, where the processing units are independent but associated with each other through blueprints called *protocols*. The Swift paradigm unifies objects, structures, and the enumerations introduced in Chapter 2, through protocols that define how these units will behave and the type of functionality they will have.

 IMPORTANT: This chapter introduces the tools offered by Swift to build professional applications. If you find any of this information difficult to understand, feel free to give it a quick glance and come back later when they are applied in more practical situations.

 Do It Yourself: The examples in this chapter were designed to be tested in Playground. You just have to create a Playground file with a Blank template and then replace the code with the example you want to try.

3.2 Functions

The processing units that define the Swift paradigm, like objects, structures, and enumerations, are capable of encapsulating data along with functionality. The data is stored in the same variables we studied before, but the functionality is provided by functions. Functions are blocks of code delimited by curly braces and identified by a name. The difference between functions and the block of codes used in loops and conditional statements is that there is no condition to satisfy; the statements inside a function are executed every time the function is called (executed). Functions are called by writing their names followed by parentheses. This call may be performed from anywhere in the code and every time necessary, which completely breaks the sequential processing of a program. Once a function is called, the execution of the program continues with the statements inside the function (no matter where it is located in the code), and only returns back to the section of the code that called the function once the execution of the function is over.

Declaration of Functions

Functions are declared using the **func** keyword, a name, parentheses, and the code between braces.

```
var mynumber = 5
func myfunction() {
    mynumber = mynumber * 2
}
myfunction()
mynumber   // 10
```

Listing 3-1: Declaring and calling functions

The code in Listing 3-1 declares the **mynumber** variable, initializes it with the value 5, and then declares a function called **myfunction()**. The statements in a function are only processed when the function is called, so after its declaration we call our function with the instruction **myfunction()**. Every time **myfunction()** is called, it multiplies the current value of **mynumber** times 2 and assigns the result back to the variable. When the processing of the statements inside the function is over, the execution returns to the statement after the call (in this case, the last statement of the code that shows the final value of **mynumber** on the Results Side Bar).

As we already mentioned, once the function is declared, we can call it any time necessary and from anywhere in the program. For example, the following code runs a **for in** loop that calls **myfunction()** a total of 5 times (the range goes from 0 to 4). Every time the function is executed, **mynumber**'s current value is multiplied by 2, getting a result of 160.

```
var mynumber = 5
func myfunction() {
    mynumber = mynumber * 2
}
for _ in 0..<5 {
    myfunction()
}
mynumber   // 160
```

Listing 3-2: Calling functions from a loop

The function in these examples is modifying the value of an external variable (a variable that was not declared inside the function). Creating a function that works with values and variables that do not belong to the function itself could be dangerous; some variables may be modified by accident from other functions, the function may be called before the variables were even declared or initialized, or the variables that the function tries to modify may not be accessible by the function (functions have limited scope, as we will see later). To make sure that a function processes the right values, they have to be sent to the function when it is called. The type of values the function can receive and the names they are going to take are specified within the function's parentheses separated by a comma. When the function is executed, these parameters are turned into constants that we can read inside the function to access their values.

```
func duplicate(number: Int) {
    let total = number * 2
    let message = "Result: \(total)"   // "Result: 10"
}
duplicate(number: 5)
```

Listing 3-3: Sending values to a function

In the example of Listing 3-3 we do not use external variables anymore. The value to be processed is sent to the function when it is called and received by the function through its parameter. The parameters are declared within the function's parentheses with the same syntax used for constants or variables. We have to write the name and the data type separated by a colon. In this example, the function is declared with one parameter of type **Int** called **number**.

The call must include the name of the parameter and the value we want to send to the function. When the function of Listing 3-3 is called, the value between the parentheses of the call (5) is assigned to the **number** constant, the value of the constant is multiplied times 2, and finally the result is included in a string.

 The Basics: The constants declared for the function to receive values are called *parameters*. On the other hand, the values specified in the call are called *attributes*. In these terms, we can say that a function's call has attributes, the values of which are sent to the function and received by its parameters.

Functions may not only be called every time we need them, but also the values we provide to the function in the call may be different each time. This is important because it makes functions reusable.

```
func duplicate(number: Int) {
    let total = number * 2
    let message = "Result: \(total)"
}
duplicate(number: 5)    // "Result: 10"
duplicate(number: 25)   // "Result: 50"
```

Listing 3-4: Sending different values to a function

The constants and variables declared inside a function, like **total** and **message**, are not accessible from other parts of the code (they have different scopes, as we will see in the next section of this chapter). Using parameters, we can allow a function to receive values, but the result produced by the processing of these values is trapped inside the function. To communicate this result to the rest of the code, functions can return a value using a special instruction called **return**. The **return** instruction finishes the processing of the function, so we have to declare it at the end of the function or after all the statements required have been processed, as in the following example.

```
func duplicate(number: Int) -> Int {
    let total = number * 2
    return total
}
let result = duplicate(number: 25)
let message = "The result is \(result)"   // "The results is 50"
```

Listing 3-5: Returning the result from a function

When we create a function that returns a value, the type of the value returned has to be specified in the declaration after the parentheses with the syntax **-> Type**, where **Type** is just the data type of the value that is going to be returned by the function. The function can only return values of the type indicated in its definition. The example of Listing 3-5 can only return integer values because we declared the returned type as **Int** (**-> Int**).

In this example, the **duplicate()** function was modified to be able to return an integer containing the result of the multiplication. The value returned takes the place of the call, so we can assign it to a variable or use it in a statement. This example declares the function first, then declares the **result** variable and assigns to this variable a call to the **duplicate()** function with the value 25. The system does not really assign the call of the function to the **result** variable; what it does is to execute the function right away and assign the value returned by the function to the variable (the instruction **duplicate(number: 25)** is executed first and then the value returned by the function is assigned to **result**).

The values received and returned by a function may be of any available type. The following is a similar example that takes an array of integers, adds the values to another variable, and returns the result (notice that this time we do not assign the result to a variable, we include the call directly in a string).

```
func sumup(list: [Int]) -> Int {
    var total = 0
    for number in list {
        total = total + number
    }
    return total
}
var numbers = [1, 2, 3, 4, 5]
var message = "The result is: \(sumup(list: numbers))" // 15
```

Listing 3-6: *Sending an array to a function*

The **sumup()** function receives the **numbers** array, assigns it to the **list** constant (declared as an array of integers) and then it iterates over the array to add the values of its items to the **total** variable. At the end, the value of **total** is returned and included in the string.

That last example is expanded next to return a tuple containing two integers that represent the number of elements in the array and the result of the addition of their values.

```
func totalelements(list: [Int]) -> (Int, Int) {
    var counter = 0
    var total = 0
    for number in list {
        total = total + number
        counter += 1
    }
    return (counter, total)
}
var numbers = [1, 2, 3, 4, 5]
var (amount, result) = totalelements(list: numbers)
var message = "Addition of \(amount) elements = \(result)"
```

Listing 3-7: *Returning a tuple*

Similar to the **sumup()** function declared before, the **totalelements()** function of Listing 3-7 receives an array (**list: [Int]**), but this time it returns a tuple containing two integers (**-> (Int, Int)**). The function not only adds the value of the elements in the array but also counts how many elements are added and returns a tuple with both values. At the end, the values of the tuple are assigned to the variables **amount** and **result** and then incorporated into a string.

Another important aspect of the definition of a function are the parameter's names. When we call a function, we have to declare the names of the parameters. For example, the function **duplicate()** of previous examples includes a parameter called **number**. Every time we call this function, we have to include the name of the parameter in the call (e.g., **duplicate(number: 50)**). The names in the call are called *argument labels*. Swift automatically generates argument labels for every parameter using the parameters' names. Sometimes the names we assign to the parameters of a function may be descriptive enough for the statements of the function but may

Swift Paradigm

be confusing when we perform the call. For cases like these, Swift allows us to define our own argument labels in the function's definition; we just have to declare them before the name of the parameter separated by a space.

```
func duplicate(years number: Int) -> Int {
    let total = number * 2
    return total
}
let result = duplicate(years: 8)
let message = "The result is \(result)"   // "The results is 16"
```

Listing 3-8: Declaring argument labels

The **duplicate()** function of Listing 3-8 declares an argument label called **years** for the **number** parameter. From now on, the name of the parameter (**number**) is the one used by the statements of the function to access the value received from the call, while the argument label (**years**) is used when calling the function to identify the value.

If what we want instead is to remove an argument label, we have to define the argument label as an underscore.

```
func multiply(number1: Int, _ number2: Int) -> Int {
    let total = number1 * number2
    return total
}
let result = multiply(number1: 25, 3)
let message = "The result is \(result)"   // "The result is 75"
```

Listing 3-9: Removing argument labels

In this example, we preserved the behaviour by default for the first parameter and removed the argument label for the second parameter. Now the call only has to include the argument label of the first parameter (**multiply(number1: 25, 3)**).

Every function we have defined so far requires the values to be specified in the call. We cannot omit any of the values that the function expects to receive, but Swift lets us declare a default value for any of the function's parameters and avoid this requirement.

```
func sayhello(name: String = "Undefined") -> String {
    let text = "Your name is " + name
    return text
}
let message = sayhello()   // "Your name is Undefined"
```

Listing 3-10: Declaring default values for parameters

The code of Listing 3-10 declares the function **sayhello()** with one parameter of type **String** called **name** and with the string "Undefined" as its value by default. When the function is called without a value, the string "Undefined" is assigned to **name**.

Generic Functions

Although creating multiple functions with the same name is not allowed, we can do it if their parameters are not the same. Functions with equal names but different parameters are considered by Swift to be different functions. This allows us to define multiple functions with the same name that process different types of values.

```
func getDescription(value: Int) -> String {
    let message = "The value is \(value)"
    return message
}
func getDescription(value: String) -> String {
    let message = "The value is \(value)"
    return message
}
let result1 = getDescription(value: 3)   // "The value is 3"
let result2 = getDescription(value: "John")   // "The value is John"
```

Listing 3-11: Declaring different functions with the same name

The functions in Listing 3-11 have the same name but one receives an integer and the other a string. When we call the **getDescription()** function, Swift selects the function to execute depending on the value provided in the attributes (when we call the function with an integer, the first function is executed, and when we do it with a string, the second function is executed).

The advantage of creating functions with the same name is that there is only one name to remember. We call the function and Swift takes care of executing the right one depending on the values assigned to the attributes in the call. But when the functions perform the same task and only differ in the type of value received, they become redundant. In the example of Listing 3-11, we have two functions that return a message with the value received. They are exactly the same with the exception that one receives an integer and the other a string. In cases like this, we can replace both functions with a generic function using a generic data type.

Generic data types are placeholders for real data types. When the function is called, the generic data type is turned into the data type of the values received. If we send an integer, the generic data type turns into an **Int** data type. To define a generic function, we have to declare the generic data type using a custom name between angle brackets after the function's name, as in the following example.

```
func getDescription<T>(value: T) -> String {
    let message = "The value is \(value)"
    return message
}
let result1 = getDescription(value: 3.5)   // "The value is 3.5"
let result2 = getDescription(value: "George")   // "The value is George"
```

Listing 3-12: Defining generic functions

The function of Listing 3-12 is a generic function. The generic data type was called T (this is a standard name for a generic data type, but we can use any name we want). The function performs the same task and is called the same way as the two functions from the previous example, but now we have reduced the amount of code in our program. When the function is called, the **T** generic data type is converted into the data type received and the value is processed (the first time the function is called in our example, **T** is turn into a **Double** and the second time into a **String**).

 IMPORTANT: Although we can send any value of any type we want to a generic function, the operations we can perform on them are very limited due to the impossibility of the compiler to know the nature of the values received. For example, we can add two integers, but we can't add two Boolean values. To solve these issues, we can constraint the data types with protocols. We will study how to define protocols and how to use them later in this chapter.

The Basics: In our example, both parameters are of type **T** and therefore both must be of the same data type, but we can declare two or more generic data types separated with commas if necessary (e.g., **<T, X>**).

Standard Functions

The main advantage of functions is that we can call them from any part of the program that has access to them and they will always perform the same operations. We do not even need to know how the function does it, we just have to send to the function the values we want to be processed and read the result. Their statements can be modified, improved, or we can even completely change the operations they perform, without affecting the rest of the code. The only thing the rest of the code needs to know is what values the function can receive and what kind of values it returns, but how those values are processed inside the function becomes irrelevant. This characteristic allows programmers to share functions and also use pre-programmed functions provided by frameworks to incorporate additional functionality that would take them too long to develop themselves.

Every feature of the Swift language we have implemented so far is included in a library called *Standard Library*. The standard library includes everything from operators to primitive types and even functions. These functions are accessible from everywhere in our code and perform basic but useful operations. The following is a list of the most frequently used.

print(String**)**—This function prints a string on the Xcode's console.

abs(Value**)**—This function returns the absolute value of an integer (inverts negative values to always get a positive number). The value may be a number of any primitive data type.

max(Value, Value, ...**)**—This function compares two or more values and returns the largest.

min(Value, Value, ...**)**—This function compares two or more values and returns the smallest.

assert(Condition, String**)**—This function stops the execution of the application if the condition defined by the first attribute is false, and prints the message provided by the second attribute on the Xcode's console. The first attribute is any condition capable of returning true or false (or the Boolean values **true** or **false**).

stride(from: Value, **through:** Value, **by:** Value**)**—This function returns a sequence of values from the value specified by the **from** attribute to the value specified by the **through** attribute in intervals specified by the **by** attribute. The value of the attributes may be of any of the numerical data types available in Swift. The Standard Library also includes the **stride(from: Value, to: Value, by: Value)** function to generate a sequence that does not include the last value. We will see an example of how to use these functions in Chapter 24, Listing 24-9.

 IMPORTANT: The list of functions included in the Swift standard library is extensive. For a complete list visit our website and follow the links for this chapter.

Of all the functions in this list, **print()** is probably the most useful. Its purpose is to print temporary values of variables on the Xcode's console that may help us solve the errors in our code, as in the following example.

```
var absolutenumber = abs(-25)
print("The number is: \(absolutenumber)")    // "The number is: 25"
```

Listing 3-13: Printing values on the console with `print()`

The code of Listing 3-13 also implements the **abs()** function to get the absolute value of the number provided between parentheses. The last statement prints a string on the console with the result (see Chapter 2, Figure 2-2).

Scopes

The conditionals, loops, and functions we have studied in this chapter have a thing in common: they all use blocks of code (statements between braces) to enclose their functionality. Blocks are independent processing units; they contain their own statements and variables. To preserve their independence and avoid conflicts between these units and the rest of the code, their variables and constants are isolated. Variables and constants declared inside a block are not accessible from other parts of the code; they can only be used inside the block they were created.

The space in the code where a variable is accessible is called *scope*. Swift defines two types of scopes: the global scope and the local scope. The variables and constants outside a block have global scope, while those declared inside a block have local scope. The variables and constants with global scope are accessible from any part of the code, while those with local scope are only accessible from the statements inside the block in which they were created (and also the statements from blocks created inside their block). For better understanding, here is a practical example.

```
var sum = 0.0
var myarray = [10.0, 20.0, 30.0, 40.0, 50.0]

func first() {
    let multi = 10.0
    sum += myarray[1] * multi
}
func second() {
    var myarray = [1.0, 2.0, 3.0, 4.0, 5.0]
    let multi = 3.5
    sum += myarray[2] * multi
}
first()
second()

print("Total: \(sum)")    // "Total: 210.5"
```

Listing 3-14: Using variables and constants of different scopes

This example declares two variables in the global space, **sum** and **myarray**, and then two functions with some local constants and variables. As we explained before, the constants and variables declared in the global space have global scope, and therefore they are accessible from anywhere in the code, but those declared inside functions or blocks of code have local scope and they are only accessible from the space in which they were created. Therefore, the **multi** constant declared inside the **first()** function is only accessible from this function (neither the statements in the global space nor other blocks outside **first()** have access to it), but the global variable **sum** used in the next statement to store the result of the multiplication has global scope, so its value will be available everywhere.

The next function, **second()**, declares a new variable called **myarray**. This variable has the same name as **myarray** declared before in the global space, but they have different scopes and therefore they are two different variables. When we read the **myarray** variable in the **second()** function to add a new value to the **sum** variable, the variable accessed is the one declared inside the function because in that space this new variable has precedence over the global variable with the same name.

 Do It Yourself: Replace the code in your Playground file with the code of Listing 3-14. Check the values on the Results Side Bar to understand how the variables are accessed and which variable is used each time.

As demonstrated by the last example, we can declare variables with the same name as long as they have different scopes. Another example is the **multi** constant declared inside the **second()** function. This constant has the same name as the one declared in the **first()** function, but it has a different scope and therefore it is a different constant.

Blocks of code, including those used to create functions, conditionals, and loops, have their own scope and know the variables that are available to them. Because of this, we can generate independent processing units that do not interfere with the operations of other units but are still connected to the space in which they were declared. This characteristic is so important in computer programming that an additional tool called *Closures* was included in Swift to take advantage of it.

As well as conditionals and loops, functions may also be declared inside other functions. Functions declared inside functions are called *nested functions*. Here is an example.

```
func first() -> Int {
    var counter = 0

    func second() -> Int {
        counter += 1
        return counter
    }
    return second()
}
let total = first()
print("The count is \(total)")   // "The count is 1"
```

Listing 3-15: Declaring nested functions

There are two functions in Listing 3-15, but the **second()** function was declared inside the **first()** function. The **counter** variable is declared first, and then the **second()** function is declared and executed. The statements in the **second()** function increment the value of **counter** by 1 and return the result. The **first()** function takes this value and also returns it. In the last statement on the global space, the value returned by **first()** is assigned to the **total** variable and printed on the console.

The variables and constants declared inside a function are created and then destroyed when the execution of the function is over. The values returned by functions are just copies of the values of the variables. In the example of Listing 3-15, the value returned by both functions is just a copy of the final value of the **counter** variable. The variable is destroyed as soon as the last statement of the **first()** function is executed. And here is when nested functions become useful. If instead of the value returned by the function we return the function itself, what is returned is a reference to the function. This means that the function is not destroyed. Since the function is not destroyed, it preserves all the variables in its scope, and therefore we can keep accessing these variables, modifying their values, etc.

The syntax required to return a function from another function is a little bit different from what we have seen so far. The possibility of a function to receive or return another function has to be specified in its parameters and return type. The syntax of a function type is **(parameters) -> Type**. In the following example, we create a function called **first()** that returns another function called **second()**. The function returned does not receive any value and returns an integer, so the return type of the **first()** function is declared as **() -> Int** (this construction replaces the simple **Int** returned by the same function in the previous example).

```
func first() -> () -> Int {
   var counter = 0

   func second() -> Int {
      counter += 1
      return counter
   }
   return second
}
let incrementor = first()
print("The count is \(incrementor())")   // "The count is 1"
```

Listing 3-16: Returning functions

In the code of Listing 3-16, the **second()** function is declared inside the **first()** function as we did before, but instead of executing the **second()** function and returning the value it produces, we return the function itself declaring only its name without parentheses (**return second**). In the global space, the function returned by **first()** is assigned to the **incrementor** variable, and this variable is used later to call the **second()** function.

The function returned keeps a reference to the **counter** variable. Because of this, the **counter** variable still exists and is accessible by the function assigned to **incrementor**. Every time we call the function using the instruction **incrementor()**, the **counter** variable is incremented by 1. After the **second()** function is returned, the variables of the **first()** function are not accessible anymore (because the execution of the **first()** function is over), but the **second()** function can remember these variables and still have access to them. It is said that the variables are closed inside the function returned.

 IMPORTANT: Every time the **first()** function is executed, it creates a new **counter** variable and a new **second()** function. This means that you can use the **first()** function to create all the copies of the **second** function you need. Each function returned by the execution of **first()** will have its own scope and its own copy of the **counter** variable.

 The Basics: Functions are called using their names and the attributes between parentheses. We always have to write the parentheses when we want to execute a function and process its statements, even when no attributes are required, but when we want to reference a function, we only have to use its name.

Closures

The process of closing the variables and constants of a function is so useful that Swift offers a specific construction called *Closure* for this purpose. Closures are simple blocks of code with the syntax **{ (parameters) -> Type in statements }**. They are similar to functions (functions are actually closures with a name), but everything goes between the braces and the **in** instruction is included to separate the closure's data types from the statements.

```
func first() -> () -> Int {
    var counter = 0

    return { () -> Int in
        counter += 1
        return counter
    }
}
let incrementor = first()
print("The count is \(incrementor())")   // "The count is 1"
```

Listing 3-17: Using closures

The example of Listing 3-17 demonstrates how easy it is to create a closure and how they simplify our code. Instead of declaring a function inside another function, as we did in previous examples, we declare a closure as the value to be returned by the function. Since functions and closures are basically blocks of code, they behave the same way, only the syntax changes. The rest of the code follows the same pattern as before: the closure returned is assigned to **incrementor** and it is executed through this variable every time we want to increment the value of **counter** by 1.

Of course, a closure can also receive values. As functions, the closure's attributes are declared between the parentheses.

```
func first() -> (Int) -> Int {
    var counter = 0

    return { (number: Int) -> Int in
        counter += number
        return counter
    }
}
let incrementor = first()
print("The count is \(incrementor(10))")   // "The count is 10"
```

Listing 3-18: Defining closures with attributes

The new closure of Listing 3-18 receives an integer value and adds it to the **counter** variable. Thanks to this, now **counter** is not incremented by a specific number but by the number provided every time the closure is executed (**incrementor(10)**). Notice that the attribute is declared in the closure's definition, but it also has to be specified in the function's return type (**(Int) -> Int**).

In this and previous, examples we assigned the function or closure returned by the **first()** function to the **incrementor** variable. What is assigned to the variable is actually a reference to the function or closure, and this is why we can execute the function or the closure later using the variable. The variable becomes the name for that specific block of code. This is common practice and can be applied anywhere in the code. For example, we could have assigned the closure to a variable inside the function and then return the value of that variable instead.

```
func first() -> (Int) -> Int {
    var counter = 0
    let process = { (number: Int) -> Int in
        counter += number
        return counter
    }
```

```
      return process
}
let incrementor = first()
print("The count is \(incrementor(10))")   // "The count is 10"
```

Listing 3-19: Assigning closures to constants and variables

A great advantage of being able to assign closures to constants or variables is the possibility to initialize them with the result of complex processes or operations. The closure is assigned to the constant or variable and executed right away adding parentheses at the end of the declaration. When the system reads the statement, it executes the closure and assigns the value returned by it to the constant or variable.

```
let fruits = ["Apple", "Orange", "Banana", "Apple"]
let process = { () -> Int in
   var counter = 0
   for fruit in fruits {
      if fruit == "Apple" {
         counter += 1
      }
   }
   return counter
}()
print("There are \(process) apples")   // "There are 2 apples"
```

Listing 3-20: Initializing constants and variables with closures

The closure declared in Listing 3-20 counts the number of values in the array that are equal to the string "Apple" and returns the result (notice the parentheses at the end that tell the compiler to execute the closure right away). The task performed in this example is simple, but the technique is usually applied to more complex processes such as loading content from a file or opening a database.

If the closure does not receive any parameter, as in the last example, we can simplify its syntax declaring the type of the constant or variable and letting Swift infer the type of the value returned. Notice that when the closure doesn't receive a value, we can also remove the **in** keyword.

```
let fruits = ["Apple", "Orange", "Banana", "Apple"]
let process: Int = {
   var counter = 0
   for fruit in fruits {
      if fruit == "Apple" {
         counter += 1
      }
   }
   return counter
}()
print("There are \(process) apples")   // "There are 2 apples"
```

Listing 3-21: Simplifying the syntax of closures

 IMPORTANT: Closures can be sent or returned from functions and used the same way as any other value. In the next section of this chapter, we will study some of these alternatives and implement them in practical situations.

Swift Paradigm

If the closure doesn't return any value, the return type has to be declared with the **Void** keyword. We usually find this kind of situation when we want to pass a closure to a function. For example, we may need to create a function that receives and executes different types of closures.

```
let process = {
    print("Hello")
}
func first(myclosure: () -> Void) {
    myclosure()
}
first(myclosure: process)
```

Listing 3-22: Passing a closure to a function

In this example, we create a simple closure called **process** that prints a string. The function was declared with the name **first** and only one statement in charge of executing the closure received. At the end, we call this function with the value of **process**. The system calls the function, the function receives the closure, and executes it, printing the word "Hello" on the console.

Because passing a closure to a function is common practice in Swift, the language offers a shortcut. Whenever we want to call a function that receives a closure, we can declare the closure at the end of the call, as in the following example.

```
func first(myclosure: () -> Void) {
    myclosure()
}
first() {
    print("Hello")
}
```

Listing 3-23: Declaring the closure in the call

This code works exactly the same way as the previous one, the function receives the closure and executes it, printing the word "Hello" on the console, but the closure is not assigned to a variable, we just declare it at the end of the call.

These types of closures are called *Trailing Closures*. The closure declared after the parenthesis is considered to be the last argument of the function (Notice that when we pass the closure this way, the call does not include the attribute **myclosure** anymore).

 IMPORTANT: If you want to execute the closure received by the function from outside the function, you have to declare it as an *escape* closure. Escape closures are closures that remain in memory after the function is executed. They are declared by preceding them with the keyword **@escaping**. We will see some examples in Chapter 23. For more information, read Apple's guide "The Swift Programming Language". The link is available on our website.

3.3 Structures

Structures are the essential part of the organizational paradigm proposed by Swift. They are custom data types that include not only the data but also the code in charge of processing that data. When we define a structure, what we are doing is declaring a data type that may contain variables and constants (called *properties*) and also functions (called *methods*). Later we can declare variables and constants of this type to store information with the characteristics defined by the structure. These values (called *instances*) will be unique, each one with its own properties and methods.

Definition of Structures

To define a new structure, we have to use the **struct** keyword and enclose the data and functionality between braces.

```
struct Item {
    var quantity: Double = 0
    var name: String = "Not defined"
    var price: Double = 0
}
```

Listing 3-24: *Declaring a structure type*

Listing 3-24 defines a structure called **Item** with three properties: **quantity**, **name**, and **price**. The definition by itself does not create anything; it is just delineating the elements of the type (also called *members*), like a blueprint used to create the real structures. What we have to do to store values of this new data type in memory, as we would do with any other data type, is to declare a variable or constant of this type. The declaration is done as before, but the type is the name of the structure and the initialization value is a special constructor, usually called *initializer*, with the syntax **Name()** (where **Name** is, again, the name of the structure).

```
struct Item {
    var quantity: Double = 0
    var name: String = "Not defined"
    var price: Double = 0
}
var purchase: Item = Item()
```

Listing 3-25: *Declaring a variable of type* Item

The code of Listing 3-25 creates a variable of type **Item** that stores an instance of the **Item** structure containing the properties **quantity**, **name**, and **price**. The instance is created by the **Item()** initializer and then assigned to the **purchase** variable.

 The Basics: It is advisable to write the names of custom data types, such as structures and classes, capitalized (e.g., **Item**, **TheItem**, **TheRedItem**, etc.). This technique is often called Camel Case and helps us differentiate the name of data types from other elements such as functions and variables.

The properties of a new instance always take the values declared in the structure's definition (**0**, **"Not Defined"** and **0**), but we can change them as we do with any other variable. The only difference is that the properties are inside a structure, so every time we want to access them we have to mention the structure they belong to. The syntax uses dot notation, as in **variable.property**, where **variable** is the name of the variable that contains the instance of the structure and **property** is the name of the property we want to access.

```
struct Item {
   var quantity = 0.0
   var name = "Not defined"
   var price = 0.0
}
var purchase = Item()

purchase.quantity = 2
purchase.name = "Lamps"
purchase.price = 10.50

var total = purchase.quantity * purchase.price
print("Invoice: \(purchase.quantity) \(purchase.name) $ \(total)")
```

Listing 3-26: Assigning new values to the properties of a structure

In Listing 3-26 the structure and **purchase** variable are declared as before, but this time we let Swift infer their types. After the instance is created, new values are assigned to its properties using dot notation. Dot notation is not only used to assign new values but also to read the current ones. In the last statements, the value of the **quantity** property is multiplied by the value of **price** to get the total money spent, and then everything is printed on the console ("Invoice: 2.0 Lamps $ 21.0").

 Do It Yourself: Replace the code in your Playground file with the code of Listing 3-26. Create another variable after **total** and assign to this variable the initializer of the **Item** structure to create another instance. Assign different values to the properties of each instance to learn how to work with different copies of the same structure.

Structures may be instantiated inside other structures, as many times as necessary, in an unlimited chain. The dot notation is extended in these cases to reach every element in the hierarchy.

```
struct Price {
   var USD = 0.0
   var CAD = 0.0
}
struct Item {
   var quantity = 0.0
   var name = "Not defined"
   var price = Price()
}
var purchase = Item()

purchase.quantity = 2
purchase.name = "Lamps"
purchase.price.USD = 10.50
```

Listing 3-27: Structures inside structures

Listing 3-27 defines two structures: **Price** and **Item**. The **price** property of the **Item** structure was now defined as a property of type **Price**. Instead of storing a single value, now it can store a structure with two properties, **USD** and **CAD**, for American and Canadian dollars. When the **Item** structure is created and assigned to the **purchase** variable, the **Price** structure for the **price** property is also created with its values by default. By concatenating the names of the variables and properties containing these structures we can reach and modify any value we want. For example, the last statement in the code of Listing 3-27 accesses the **USD** property of the **price** structure inside the **purchase** structure to assign a new price to the item in American Dollars (**purchase.price.USD = 10.50**).

Methods

If we could only store properties, structures would be just a complex data type, like a tuple, but as we mentioned before, code may also be defined as part of the structure. This is done through functions. Functions inside structures are called *methods*, but their syntax is exactly the same.

```
struct Item {
    var quantity = 0.0
    var name = "Not defined"
    var price = 0.0
    func total() -> Double {
       let cost = quantity * price
          return cost
    }
}
var purchase = Item()
purchase.quantity = 2
purchase.name = "Lamp"
purchase.price = 10.50
print("Total cost: \(purchase.total())")   // "Total cost: 21.0"
```

Listing 3-28: Defining methods

In Listing 3-28, a method was declared as part of the definition of the **Item** structure. The method calculates the total money spent in the transaction multiplying the value of the **quantity** property times the value of **price**. This is the same operation we have done before through an independent statement, but now it is part of the structure, ensuring that it is always accessible and produces always the right result (we do not have to write the operation over and over again, it is always part of the instance we are working with).

The dot notation also applies to methods. The syntax to execute a method is **variable.method()**, where **variable** is the name of the variable that contains the instance of the structure and **method** is the name of the method we want to call inside that structure.

Since methods are functions, they can receive and return values. In the example of Listing 3-28, the **total()** method returns a value of type **Double** corresponding to the total cost of the transaction.

A method can read the values of the instance's properties but cannot assign new values to them. If we want a method to be able to modify the values of the properties of its own instance, we have to use a special keyword called **mutating**. The **mutating** keyword has to be placed before the **func** keyword in the method's definition.

```
struct Item {
    var quantity = 0.0
    var name = "Not defined"
    var price = 0.0
    mutating func total() {
       let cost = quantity * price
       name += " $ \(cost)"
    }
}
```

```
var purchase = Item()
purchase.quantity = 2
purchase.name = "Lamp"
purchase.price = 10.50

purchase.total()
print("Your purchase: \(purchase.name)")   // "Your purchase: Lamp $ 21.0"
```

Listing 3-29: Assigning new values to properties from inside the structure

The **total()** method of the **Item** structure in Listing 3-29 is declared as a mutating method to be able to assign a new value to the **name** property from its statements. Now the structure not only calculates the total amount of the transaction but also adds it to the name of the item. The last statements of this example call the **total()** method to prepare the string for **name** and then print the result on the screen.

Initialization

Every instance we create from the structure's definition has the purpose to store and process specific data. For example, we can create multiple instances of the **Item** structure defined in previous examples to store information about several products. Each product will have its own name and price, so the properties of each instance have to be initialized with the proper values. The initialization of an instance is a very common process, and it is difficult to do if we have to assign the values one by one after the instances are created. For this reason, Swift provides different alternatives to initialize values. The most convenient is called *memberwise initializer.*

Memberwise initializers detect the properties of the structure and declare their names as argument labels. By declaring these argument labels, we can provide the values for initialization between the parentheses of the initializer. The following code implements the memberwise initializer to initialize an instance of the **Item** structure declared in previous examples.

```
struct Item {
    var quantity = 0.0
    var name = "Not defined"
    var price = 0.0
}
var purchase = Item(quantity: 2, name: "Lamp", price: 10.50)

var total = purchase.quantity * purchase.price
print("Invoice: \(purchase.quantity) \(purchase.name) $ \(total)")
```

Listing 3-30: Initializing properties

Memberwise initializers reduce the amount of code and simplify initialization. Also, if we use the memberwise initializer, we can ignore the values by default declared in the definition.

```
struct Item {
    var quantity: Double
    var name: String
    var price: Double
}
var purchase = Item(quantity: 2, name: "Lamp", price: 10.50)

var total = purchase.quantity * purchase.price
print("Invoice: \(purchase.quantity) \(purchase.name) $ \(total)")
```

Listing 3-31: Using memberwise initializers to provide the initial values of a structure

The two forms of initialization we have seen so far are not customizable enough. Some structures may have multiple properties to initialize or even methods that have to be executed right away to get the proper values for the instance to be ready. To add more alternatives, Swift provides a method called `init()`. The `init()` method is called as soon as the instance is created, so we can use it to assign values to the properties or perform operations and initialize the properties with the results.

```
struct Price {
   var USD: Double
   var CAD: Double

   init() {
      USD = 5
      CAD = USD * 1.29
   }
}
var myprice = Price()
```

Listing 3-32: Initializing properties from the `init()` method

When the instance is generated by the initializer, the properties are created first and then the `init()` method is executed. Inside this method we can perform any operation we need to get the properties' initial values. In the example of Listing 3-32, we assign an initial value of 5 to the **USD** property and then multiply this value by the corresponding exchange rate to get the value of the **CAD** property (the same price in Canadian dollars).

As well as any other method or function, the `init()` method may include parameters. These parameters are added to be able to specify initial values from the initializer.

```
struct Price {
   var USD: Double
   var CAD: Double

   init(americans: Double) {
      USD = americans
      CAD = USD * 1.29
   }
}
var myprice = Price(americans: 5)
```

Listing 3-33: Declaring the `init()` method with parameters

This is similar to what Swift creates for us in the background when we use memberwise initializers, but the advantage of declaring the `init()` method ourselves is that we can specify only the parameters we need (as in the last example) or even declare multiple `init()` methods to present several alternatives for initialization, as shown next.

```
struct Price {
   var USD: Double
   var CAD: Double

   init(americans: Double) {
      USD = americans
      CAD = USD * 1.29
   }
```

Swift Paradigm

```
    init(canadians: Double) {
        CAD = canadians
        USD = CAD * 0.7752
    }
}
var myprice = Price(canadians: 5)
```

Listing 3-34: Declaring multiple `init()` *methods*

As we mentioned when we were studying functions, Swift identifies each function by its name and parameters, so we can declare several functions with the same name as long as they have different parameters. Of course, this also applies to methods, including the `init()` method. In the example of Listing 3-34, two `init()` methods were declared to initialize the instance of the structure. The first method receives a **Double** value with the name **americans** and the second method also receives a **Double** value but with the name **canadians**. The right method will be executed according to the attribute included in the initializer. In this example, we use the attribute **canadians** with the value 5, so the instance is initialized by the second method.

Property Keywords

Swift defines keywords (also called *modifiers*) that can be applied to properties to confer them special attributes. There are several keywords available, but two are particularly useful when working with properties: **lazy** and **private**. The **lazy** keyword defines a property whose initial value is not assigned until the property is used for the first time, and the **private** keyword defines a property that is only accessible from the methods of the structure it belongs to.

The **lazy** keyword is used when the property's value may take time to be determined and we do not want the initialization of the structure to be delayed. For example, we may have a property that stores a currency rate retrieved from a server. This is an intensive task that we should perform when the value is required and not every time a structure from this definition is initialized.

```
struct Price {
    var USD: Double
    lazy var rate: Double = {
        return 1.29
    }()
    init(money: Double) {
        USD = money
    }
}
var purchase = Price(money: 3.5)
```

Listing 3-35: Defining `lazy` *properties*

The **Price** structure of Listing 3-35 defines two properties: **USD** and **rate**. The **USD** property is a **Double** value that we use to store the price, and **rate** is a lazy property that returns the current currency rate. A closure is assigned to the **rate** property to get the current rate and return it, but because we declared the property as **lazy**, the closure will only be executed when we try to read the property's value (in this example the value 1.29 is not assigned to the **rate** property because the property has not been used).

This is a simple example that returns a fixed value, but in practice the closure may include code that retrieves the current exchange rate from a server, which takes time and consumes resources. If we only need instances to store the price, it does not make sense to load the rate from the web every time an instance is created, and therefore we should declare the property as **lazy**. This keyword is not only useful when we load resources from the Internet but also when the property values are obtained from files or databases.

Another important keyword that applies to properties is **private**. This keyword makes the properties only accessible by methods of the structure. A normal property may be accessed from outside the structure using dot notation, as we did in previous examples. If we want to make sure that a property can only be accessed and modified by the methods of its structure, we can declare it as private. For instance, we can set the **rate** property of our **Price** structure to be private so only the methods can modify its value.

```
struct Price {
    var USD: Double
    private var rate = 1.29

    init(money: Double) {
        USD = money
    }
    func getCAD() -> Double {
        let total = USD * rate
        return total
    }
}
var purchase = Price(money: 3.5)
```

Listing 3-36: Declaring private *properties*

The code of Listing 3-36 defines the **rate** property as private and adds a method called **getCAD()** to use the property's value. If we try to access this property from outside the structure using dot notation, Xcode will return an error (**purchase.rate**).

Computed Properties

The properties we have declared up to this point are called *Stored Properties*. Their function is to store a value in memory. But there is another type of property called *Computed Properties*. These properties do not store a value of their own, instead they have access to the rest of the properties of the structure and can perform operations to set and retrieve their values.

Two special methods were included for computed properties to be able to set and retrieve a value: **get** and **set**. These methods are also called *getter* and *setter* and are declared between braces after the property's name. Although both methods are useful, only the **get** method is mandatory. Here is a simple example.

```
struct Price {
    var USD: Double
    var ratetoCAD: Double

    var canadians: Double {
        get {
            let price = USD * ratetoCAD
            return price
        }
    }
}
```

```
var purchase = Price(USD: 11, ratetoCAD: 1.29)
print("Price in CAD: \(purchase.canadians)")  // "Price in CAD: 14.19"
```

Listing 3-37: Declaring computed properties

The structure defined in Listing 3-37 contains a stored property called **USD** to store the price in American dollars, a stored property called **ratetoCAD** to store the exchange rate for Canadian dollars, and a computed property called **canadians** that converts the US dollars into Canadian dollars and returns the result. Computed properties are similar to methods, they calculate the value every time the property is read. No matter if a process changes the value of the **ratetoCAD** property, the **canadians** property will return the right price in Canadian dollars.

Including the **set** method for the **canadians** property we can, for example, set a new price using the same currency.

```
struct Price {
    var USD: Double
    var ratetoCAD: Double
    var ratetoUSD: Double

    var canadians: Double {
        get {
            return USD * ratetoCAD
        }
        set {
            USD = newValue * ratetoUSD
        }
    }
}
var purchase = Price(USD: 11, ratetoCAD: 1.29, ratetoUSD: 0.7752)

purchase.canadians = 500
print("Price: \(purchase.USD)")  // "Price: 387.6"
print("Price in CAD: \(purchase.canadians)")  // "Price in CAD: 500.004"
```

Listing 3-38: Adding the set method to set a new value

The new structure defined in Listing 3-38 can retrieve and also set a price in Canadian dollars. When we set a new value for the **canadians** property, the value is stored in a constant called **newValue** (the constant is created automatically for us). Using this constant, we can process the value received and perform the operations we need. In this example, the value of **newValue** is multiplied by the exchange rate to turn the price in Canadian dollars into American dollars. The price is always stored in American dollars but using the **canadians** property we can set it and retrieve it in Canadian dollars.

If we want to use a different name for the new value, we can set the parameter's name between parentheses. In the following example the parameter was called **CAD** and used instead of **newValue** to calculate the value for the **USD** property.

```
struct Price {
    var USD: Double
    var ratetoCAD: Double
    var ratetoUSD: Double

    var canadians: Double {
        get {
            return USD * ratetoCAD
        }
```

```
        set(CAD) {
            USD = CAD * ratetoUSD
        }
    }
}
var purchase = Price(USD: 11, ratetoCAD: 1.29, ratetoUSD: 0.7752)

purchase.canadians = 500
print("Price: \(purchase.USD)")   // "Price: 387.6"
print("Price in CAD: \(purchase.canadians)")   // "Price in CAD: 500.004"
```

Listing 3-39: Using a different name for the parameter of the set method

Type Properties and Methods

The properties and methods declared above are accessible on the instances created from the definition of the structure. This means that we have to create an instance of the structure to be able to access its properties and methods. But there are times when being able to execute properties and methods from the definition make sense. We might need, for example, to get some information that affects all the instances, set some values to create instances with a specific configuration, or call methods to create instances with standard values. In Swift, this is possible by declaring type properties and methods (properties and methods accessible from the type, not the instance).

Type properties and methods for structures are declared adding the **static** keyword to their definition. Once a property or method is declared with this keyword, they are only accessible from the definition itself. In the following example, we include the **currencies** type property to inform how many currencies the structure can handle.

```
struct Price {
    var USD: Double
    var CAD: Double

    static var currencies = 2
}
print(Price.currencies)   // 2
```

Listing 3-40: Defining type properties

As illustrated by the code of Listing 3-40, there is no need to create an instance to access a type property or method. After the definition, the **currencies** property is read using the name of the structure and dot notation (**Price.currencies**). If we create an instance from this definition, the only properties accessible from the instance will be **USD** and **CAD**. The **currencies** property is a type property, only accessible from the type itself. The same happens with methods.

```
struct Price {
    var USD: Double
    var CAD: Double

    static func reserve() -> Price {
        let instance = Price(USD: 10.0, CAD: 11.0)
        return instance
    }
}
```

```
var reserveprice = Price.reserve()
print("Price in USD: \(reserveprice.USD) CAD: \(reserveprice.CAD)")
```

Listing 3-41: Defining type methods

The example of Listing 3-41 adds a type method called **reserve()** to the structure's definition. The method creates and returns an instance of the structure it belongs to with standard values. This is a common procedure and another way to create our own initializer. If we use the initializer by default, the values have to be provided every time the instance is created, but with a type method the only thing we have to do is call the method on the type to get in return an instance already configured with specific values. In our example, the values correspond to a reserved price. We call the **reserve()** method on the **Price** type, the method creates the instance with the values 10.0 and 11.0, and then the instance returned is assigned to the **reserveprice** variable. At the end, the values of both properties are printed on the console to confirm that their values were defined by the **reserve()** method (again, the method is not accessible from the instance, only from the type).

Primitive Type Structures and Casting

Including several properties and methods inside a structure and then assigning an instance of that structure to a variable is a simple way to wrap data and functionality together in a single portable unit of code. Structures are usually used this way, as practical wrappers of code, and Swift takes advantage of this feature extensively. In fact, all the primitive data types defined in Swift are structures. The syntax **variable: Int = value**, for example, is a shortcut provided by Swift for the initializer **variable = Int(value)**. Every time we assign a new value to a primitive variable we are assigning a structure that contains that value (all the conversions are done for us in the background). The following are the initializers of some of the primitive types studied in Chapter 2.

Int(Value**)**—This is the initializer of the **Int** data type. The attribute is the value we want to assign to the instance. If no value is provided, the value 0 is assigned by default. Initializers for similar types are also available (**Int8()**, **Int16()**, **Int32()**, and **Int64()**).

UInt(Value**)**—This is the initializer of the **UInt** data type. The attribute is the value we want to assign to the instance. If no value is provided, the value 0 is assigned by default. Initializers for similar types are also available (**UInt8()**, **UInt16()**, **UInt32()**, and **UInt64()**).

Float(Value**)**—This is the initializer of the **Float** data type. The attribute is the value we want to assign to the instance. If no value is provided, the value 0.0 is assigned by default.

Double(Value**)**—This is the initializer of the **Double** data type. The attribute is the value we want to assign to the instance. If no value is provided, the value 0.0 is assigned by default.

The structures for these types were already defined for us in the Swift's standard library. All we have to do to get an instance is to call its initializer with the value we want to store.

```
var mynumber = Int(25)
var myprice = Double(4.99)
```

Listing 3-42: Initializing variables with initializers

The variables **mynumber** and **myprice**, declared in Listing 3-42, are inferred to be of type **Int** and **Double**. The initializers create a structure for each value and assign the instances to the variables. This is the same as assigning the values directly to the variable (e.g., **var myprice =**

4.99). There is no advantage in the use of initializers for primitive types except when the value provided is of a different data type. The definitions of these structures include several initializers that convert the value to the corresponding type. This is usually called *casting*, and we can use it to turn a variable of one type into another when required. For example, when we divide numbers, the system converts those numbers to the right type and performs the operation, but variables are already of a specific type and therefore they have to be explicitly converted before the operation is performed or we get an error (The process does not really convert the variable; it just creates a new value of the right type).

```
var number1 = 10
var number2 = 2.5
var total = Double(number1) / number2  // 4.0
```

Listing 3-43: Casting a variable

The variables **number1** and **number2** of Listing 3-43 are of type **Int** and **Double**. To perform a division between these two variables we have to cast one of them to the data type of the other (arithmetic operations cannot be performed on values of different type). Using the **Double()** initializer, we create a new value of type **Double** from the value of **number1** and perform the operation (the value 10.0 created by the initializer is divided by the value 2.5 of **number2** to get the result 4.0). The process is described as "casting the **number1** variable to a **Double**".

These initializers are also useful when working with **String** values. Sometimes the characters of a string represent numbers that we need to process. The problem is that strings cannot be processed as numbers. We cannot include a string in an arithmetic operation without first converting the string into a value of a numeric data type. Fortunately, the initializers for numeric types such as **Int** and **Double** can convert a value of type **String** into a number. If the operation cannot be performed, the constructor returns **nil**, so we can treat it as an optional value. In the following example, we convert the string "45" into the integer 45 and add it to the value 15.

```
var units = "45"

if let number = Int(units) {
   let total = number + 15
   print("The total is \(total)")   // "The total is 60"
}
```

Listing 3-44: Extracting numbers from strings

Just as any other structure, the structures defined for primitive types also have their own properties and methods. This includes type properties and methods. For instance, the following are the most frequently used properties and methods provided by the structures that process integer values, such as **Int** or **Int8**.

min—This type property returns the minimum value the type can handle.

max—This type property returns the maximum value the type can handle.

random(in: Range)—This type method returns a random number. The value is calculated from a range of integers provided by the **in** attribute.

negate()—This method inverts the sign of the value.

The **random(in:)** method is probably the most useful. With it we can get a random number from a range of values.

```
var mynumber: Int = 0
var attempts = 0

while mynumber != 5 {
    mynumber = Int.random(in: 1...10)
    attempts += 1
}
print("It took \(attempts) attempts to get the number 5")
```

Listing 3-45: Calculating random numbers

The code of Listing 3-45 calculates random numbers inside a **while** loop with the **random(in:)** method. The condition stops the loop when the number returned by the method is equal to 5. Inside the loop, we also increment the value of the **attempts** variable to calculate the number of cycles required for the **random(in:)** method to return our number.

 Do It Yourself: Replace the code in your Playground file with the code of Listing 3-45. You should see a text on the console describing how many attempts it took to the **random(in:)** method to get the number 5. Press the Stop and Play buttons at the button of the Playground's window to execute the code again. The number of attempts should change every time.

Another useful contribution of the integer data types are the **min** and **max** properties. These properties may be used to determine whether an operation might overflow the variable (produce a result that is greater or smaller than the minimum and maximum allowed).

```
var mynumber: Int8 = 120
let increment: Int8 = 10

if (Int8.max - mynumber) >= increment {   // (127 - 120) >= 10
    mynumber += increment
}
print(mynumber)   // "120"
```

Listing 3-46: Checking the maximum possible value for the Int8 *type*

The code of Listing 3-46 takes advantage of the **max** property to make sure that incrementing the value of a variable will not produce overflow (the result will not be greater than the maximum the variable can handle). The code starts by defining a variable of type **Int8** to store the result of the operation and another to store the number we want to add. Then, we calculate how far the current value of **mynumber** is from the maximum value admitted by an **Int8** type variable (**Int8.max — mynumber**) and compare this result with the value of **increment**. If the number of units we have left is greater or equal than the value of **increment**, we know that the operation can be performed without going over the limit (in this example the operation is not performed because the addition of 120 + 10 produces a result greater than the limit of 127 admitted by the **Int8** data type).

 Do It Yourself: Replace the code in your Playground file with the code of Listing 3-46. Read the **min** and **max** properties of other integer types, such as **Int16**, **Int32**, and **Int64** to see their limitations.

The type **Double** also includes its own selection of properties and methods.

pi—This type property returns the value of the constant Pi.

infinity—This type property returns an infinite value.

minimum(Double, Double)—This type method compares the values provided by the attributes and returns the minimum.

maximum(Double, Double)—This type method compares the values provided by the attributes and returns the maximum.

random(in: Range)—This type method returns a random number. The value is calculated from a range of values of type `Double` provided by the `in` attribute.

negate()—This method inverts the sign of the value.

squareRoot()—This method returns the square root of the value.

remainder(dividingBy: Double)—This method returns the remainder produced by dividing the value by the value specified by the `dividingBy` attribute.

rounded(FloatingPointRoundingRule)—This method returns the value rounded according to the rule specified by the attribute. The attribute is an enumeration with the values `awayFromZero`, `down`, `toNearestOrAwayFromZero`, `toNearestOrEven`, `towardZero` and `up`.

In this case, the most useful method is probably `rounded()`. With this method, for instance, we can round a floating-point value to the nearest integer.

```
var mynumber: Double = 2.890
mynumber = mynumber.rounded(.toNearestOrAwayFromZero)
print("The round number is \(mynumber)")   // "The round number is 3.0"
```

Listing 3-47: Rounding floating-point values

Of course, Boolean values are also structures. The `Bool` data type offers the following methods.

toggle()—This method toggles the value. If the value is `true`, it becomes `false` and vice versa.

random()—This type method returns a random `Bool` value.

The following example checks the current value of a variable and changes the value to `false` if it is `true`.

```
var valid: Bool = true
if valid {
    print("It is Valid")
    valid.toggle()
}
print(valid)   // false
```

Listing 3-48: Changing the value of a `Bool` variable

String Structures

Not only primitive data types are structures, but so are the rest of the data types defined in the Swift's standard library, including the `String` data type. As we have seen in Chapter 2, we can initialize a `String` structure by simply assigning a string (a text between double quotes) to a constant or a variable. This is another shortcut. In the background, instances of the `String` structure are created from the initializer included in the structure's definition.

String(Value)—This initializer creates a string from the value provided by the attribute. The **String** structure defines multiple versions of this initializer to create strings from different types of values, including other strings, characters, and numbers.

Most of the time, we will assign a string directly to a variable as we have done so far, but the **String()** initializer may be useful when we need to convert values of other data types into a string.

```
var age = String(44)
var mytext = "My age is " + age   // "My age is 44"
```

Listing 3-49: Converting a number into a string

Once the string is created, we can manipulate it with the properties and methods provided by the **String** structure. The following are the most frequently used.

isEmpty—This property returns a Boolean value that indicates whether the value is an empty string or not. This is the same as comparing the string against an empty string (**string == ""**).

count—This property returns the total number of characters in the string.

first—This property returns the first character in the collection (the first character of the string).

last—This property returns the last character in the collection (the last character of the string).

lowercased()—This method returns a copy of the string in lowercase letters.

uppercased()—This method returns a copy of the string in uppercase letters.

hasPrefix(String)—This method returns a Boolean value that indicates whether the string begins with the text specified by the attribute or not.

hasSuffix(String)—This method returns a Boolean value that indicates whether the string ends with the text specified by the attribute or not.

append(String)—This method adds a character or a string of characters at the end of the original string. This is the same as concatenating strings with the + operator.

contains(Character)—This method returns a Boolean value that indicates whether the character specified by the attribute exists in the string or not.

An important characteristic of Swift's strings is that they are composed of Unicode characters. The particularity of these types of characters is that they can occupy different amounts of space in memory, even when the characters are visually the same. Because of this, it is not possible to establish the position of a character using integer values. The index of the first character is always 0, but the index of the consecutive characters depends on the size of their predecessors. Swift solved this problem adding a new data type called **Index**. This is another structure defined inside the **String** structure specifically designed to manage string indexes. The **String** structure includes properties and methods to work with these indexes and access the characters. The following are the most frequently used.

startIndex—This property returns the index value of the first character of the string.

endIndex—This property returns the index value of one position after the last character of the string. It is useful to manipulate range of characters, as we will see later.

index(of: Character)—This method returns the index where the character specified by the **of** attribute appears for the first time in the collection.

insert(Character, **at:** Index)—This method inserts into the string the character provided by the first attribute at the position determined by the **at** attribute.

insert(contentsOf: String, **at:** Index)—This method inserts into the string the value of the **contentsOf** attribute at the position determined by the **at** attribute.

remove(at: Index)—This method removes and returns the character at the position determined by the **at** attribute.

prefix(through: Index)—This method returns a string created from the first character of the original string to the character at the index indicated by the **through** attribute.

prefix(upTo: Index)—This method returns a string created from the first character of the original string to the character at the index indicated by the **upTo** attribute, but without including this last character.

replaceSubrange(Range, **with:** String)—This method replaces the characters in the position determined by the range provided as the first attribute with the string provided by the **with** attribute.

removeSubrange(Range)—This method removes the characters in the positions determined by the range specified by the attribute.

Because a string is a collection of **Character** values we can process it as we do with any other collection type. For instance, we can create a **for in** loop to process each character.

```
var text = "Hello World"
var counter = 0

for letter in text {
    if letter == "l" {
        counter += 1
    }
}
print("The text has \(counter) letters L")   // "The text has 3 letters L"
```

Listing 3-50: Iterating over the characters in a string

The loop of Listing 3-50 reads each character in the **text** variable and stores it in the **letter** constant. Inside the loop, the value of the **counter** variable is incremented every time the value of **letter** is equal to the letter L (lowercase).

In this example, we used the loop to count characters, but if we want to count all the characters in the string, there is a simpler way. Strings include the **count** property for this purpose. The property returns an integer that represents the total amount of characters in the string.

```
var text = "Hello World"
let total = text.count   // 11
print("Total characters in the string: \(total)")
```

Listing 3-51: Counting the characters in a string

Strings also include several properties and methods to access the characters individually. Two of those properties are **startIndex** and **endIndex**. From the values returned by these

Swift Paradigm

properties we can get the **Index** values for the first and last characters, calculate specific positions, and process the characters we want. For example, we can access the character associated to an index by declaring the index between square brackets after the name of the string, as we do with arrays.

```
var text = "Hello World"
if !text.isEmpty {
   let start = text.startIndex
   let firstCharacter = text[start]

   print("First character is \(firstCharacter)")  // "First character is
H"
}
```

Listing 3-52: Processing the string's characters

The first thing we do in the example of Listing 3-52 is to check the value of the **isEmpty** property to make sure the string is not empty and there are characters to read (notice the **!** character to invert the condition). Once we know we can proceed, we get the index of the string's first character from the **startIndex** property and read the character in that position using square brackets.

If we want to access a character in a different position, we have to increment the value returned by **startIndex**. The trick is that, since **Index** values are not integers, we cannot add a simple number to them. Instead, we have to use the following methods provided by the **String** structure.

index(after: Index)—This method increments the index specified by the **after** attribute one unit and returns a new **Index** value with the result.

index(before: Index)—This method decrements the index specified by the **before** attribute one unit and returns a new **Index** value with the result.

index(Index, **offsetBy:** Int)—This method increments the index specified by the first attribute the amount of units specified by the **offsetBy** attribute and returns a new **Index** value with the result.

The following example advances the initial index 6 positions to get a different character.

```
var text = "Hello World"
if text != "" {
   let start = text.startIndex
   let newIndex = text.index(start, offsetBy: 6)

   print("The character is \(text[newIndex])")  // "The character is W"
}
```

Listing 3-53: Calculating a specific index

The **index()** method applied in Listing 3-53 takes an integer to calculate the new index. The original index is increased the number of units indicated by the integer and the resulting **Index** value is returned. With this index, we get the character at the position 6 (indexes start from 0).

If we wanted to get the previous index, we could have specified a negative number of units for the offset value, but another way to move forward and backward is to implement the other versions of the **index()** method. The following example gets the next index after the initial index and prints the corresponding character on the screen.

```
var text = "John"
let start = text.startIndex
var next = text.index(after: start)

print("Second letter is \(text[next])")  // "Second letter is o"
```

Listing 3-54: Getting the next index

Once the right index is calculated, we can call some of the **String** methods to insert or remove characters. The **insert()** method, for instance, inserts a single character at the position indicated by its second attribute. In the following example, we call it with the value of the **endIndex** property to add a character at the end of the string (**endindex** points to the position after the last character).

```
var text = "Hello World"
text.insert("!", at: text.endIndex)

print("New string is \(text)")  // "New string is Hello World!"
```

Listing 3-55: Inserting a character in a string

If we do not know exactly where the character we are looking for is located, we can find a specific index with the **index()** method. The value returned by this method is an optional containing the **Index** value of the first character that matches its attribute or **nil** in case of failure. In the following example, we implement this method to find the first space character and remove it with the **remove()** method.

```
var text = "Hello World"
var findIndex = text.index(of: " ")

if let index = findIndex {
    text.remove(at: index)
    print("New string is \(text)")  // "New string is HelloWorld"
}
```

Listing 3-56: Removing a character

If we want to work with groups of characters, we have to use ranges of **Index** values. We studied ranges before in Chapter 2. They are made using the **...** and the **..<** operators. In the examples of that chapter we used them to create ranges of integers, but the operators can take any type of values we need, including **Index** values.

```
var text = "Hello World"
var start = text.startIndex
var findIndex = text.index(of: " ")

if let end = findIndex {
    print("First word is \(text[start..<end])")  //"First word is Hello"
}
```

Listing 3-57: Getting a range of characters

The **index()** method in Listing 3-57 looks for a space character and returns its index. With this value, we can now create a range from the first character to the first space character and get the string's first word. But we have to be careful because the **end** index is pointing to the space

```
```

character, not to the last character of the word. If we create a range between these two values, the space character will be included at the end. To create a range that does not include this character, we have to use the **..<** operator. This operator generates a half-open range that runs from one value to another but does not include the value on the right.

We can also use ranges to replace or remove parts of the text. The **String** structure offers the **replaceSubrange()** and **removeSubrange()** methods for this purpose.

```
var text = "Hello World"
var start = text.startIndex
var findIndex = text.index(of: " ")

if let end = findIndex {
   text.replaceSubrange(start..<end, with: "Goodbye")   // "Goodbye World"
}
findIndex = text.index(of: " ")
if let start = findIndex {
   text.removeSubrange(start...)   // "Goodbye"
}
```

Listing 3-58: Working with ranges of characters

Listing 3-58 implements both methods. The **replaceSubrange()** method replaces the characters from the beginning of the string up to the character before the space character (the word "Hello") with the string "Goodbye", getting the sentence "Goodbye World", and the **removeSubrange()** method uses an open range to remove the characters of this sentence from the space character to the end of the string (" World"), getting the final string "Goodbye". Notice that after applying the methods over the same string, the indexes are lost and therefore we have to calculate them again. That is why before calling the **removeSubrange()** method we search for the position of the space character once more and update the **findIndex** variable.

The rest of the methods provided by the **String** structure are straightforward. The following example implements some of them to check if a string contains the word "World" at the end and converts all the letters into uppercase letters.

```
let text = "Hello World"
if text.hasSuffix("World") {
   print(text.uppercased())   // "HELLO WORLD"
}
```

Listing 3-59: Implementing String methods

Array Structures

Arrays are also implemented as structures, and they include all the necessary properties and methods to add, insert, or delete elements. Here is a list of the most frequently used.

> **count**—This property returns the total number of elements in the array.
>
> **isEmpty**—This property returns a Boolean value that indicates if the array is empty.
>
> **first**—This property returns the first element of the array or **nil** if the array is empty.
>
> **last**—This property returns the last element of the array or **nil** if the array is empty.
>
> **append(**Element**)**—This method adds the value specified by the attribute at the end of the array.

append(contentsOf: Array**)**—This method adds the array specified by the **contentsOf** attribute at the end of the array.

insert(Element, **at:** Int**)**—This method adds a new element in a specific position of the array. The first attribute is the value we want to assign to the new element, and the **at** attribute represents the position of the array in which we want to insert the element.

insert(contentsOf: Array, **at:** Int**)**—This method adds the array provided by the **contentsOf** attribute to the original array. The **at** attribute determines the position where the array is added.

remove(at: Int**)**—This method removes an element from the array in the index specified by the **at** attribute.

removeFirst()—This method removes the first element of the array. It returns the value of the element deleted.

removeLast()—This method removes the last element of the array. It returns the value of the element deleted.

removeAll()—This method removes all the elements in the array. This is the same as assigning the value [ ] to the variable.

removeAll(where: Block**)**—This method removes the elements in the array that meet the condition established by the closure assigned to the **where** attribute.

removeSubrange(Range**)**—This method removes a range of elements from the array. The attribute is a range of integers representing the indexes of the elements to remove.

replaceSubrange(Range, **with:** Array**)**—This method replaces a range of elements with the elements of the array provided by the **with** attribute. The first attribute is a range of integers corresponding to the indexes of the elements we want to replace.

dropFirst(Int**)**—This method removes the number of elements specified by the attribute from the beginning of the array. If no amount is declared, the method removes only the first element.

dropLast(Int**)**—This method removes the number of elements specified by the attribute from the end of the array. If no amount is declared, the method removes only the last element.

min()—This method compares the values of the elements in the array and returns the smallest.

max()—This method compares the values of the elements in the array and returns the largest.

sort()—This method sorts the elements in the array in ascending order.

sort(by: Block**)**—This method sorts the elements in the array in the order determined by the attribute. The attribute is a block of code (closure or function) that determines the order.

sorted()—This method returns a new array with the elements of the original array sorted in ascending order.

sorted(by: Block**)**—This method returns a new array with the elements of the original array in the order determined by the attribute. The attribute is a block of code (closure or function) that determines the order.

randomElement()—This method randomly selects an element from the array and returns it. If the array is empty, the value returned is `nil`.

shuffled()—This method returns an array with the elements of the original array in random order.

reversed()—This method returns a new array with the elements of the array in reverse order.

enumerated()—This method is used to iterate over the elements of the array. It returns a tuple containing the index and the value of the current element.

joined(separator: String)—This method returns a string that includes all the values in an array of strings joined by the string specified by the **separator** attribute.

filter(Block)—This method filters an array and returns another array with the values that passed the filter. The attribute is a block of code (closure or function) that process the elements one by one.

map(Block)—This method returns a new array containing the results of processing each of the values of the array. The attribute is a block of code (closure or function) that process the elements one by one.

contains(where: Block)—This method returns a Boolean value that determines if the array contains an element that meets the condition in the closure specified by the **where** attribute.

We have seen how to iterate over the elements of an array with the **for in** loop in Chapter 2, but that iteration only returns the value of the element, not its index. An alternative is provided by the **enumerated()** method, designed to work with these types of loops. Each cycle returns a tuple with the index and the value of the current element.

```
let fruits = ["Banana", "Orange", "Apple"]
var message = "My fruits:"

for (myindex, myfruit) in fruits.enumerated() {
   message += " \(myindex + 1)-\(myfruit)"
}
print(message)   // "My fruits: 1-Banana 2-Orange 3-Apple"
```

Listing 3-60: Reading indexes and values of an array

The example of Listing 3-60 uses the variables **myindex** and **myfruit** to capture the values produced by the **enumerated()** method and generate a string (since the array's indexes start from 0, we added 1 to **myindex** to start counting from 1).

The methods to add and remove elements from an array are straightforward. The following example illustrates how to implement them.

```
var fruits = ["Banana", "Orange", "Apple"]
if !fruits.isEmpty {
   fruits.removeLast()   // ["Banana", "Orange"]
   fruits.insert("Pear", at: 1)   // ["Banana", "Pear", "Orange"]
   fruits.removeAll()   // []
   fruits.append("Peach")   // ["Peach"]
   fruits.insert(contentsOf: ["Cherry"], at: 1)   // ["Peach", "Cherry"]
}
```

Listing 3-61: Adding and removing elements

The Basics: Every time an array is modified, its indexes are reassigned. For instance, if you remove the first element of an array of three elements, the index 0 is reassigned to the second element and the index 1 to the third element. The system makes sure that the indexes of every array are always consecutive and start from 0.

A more complex method is **removeAll(where:)**. This method allows us to remove several elements of the array at once, but only those that meet a condition. The condition is established by a closure that processes each of the values in the array and returns **true** or **false** depending on whether the value meets the condition or not. In the following example, we compare each value with the string "Orange" and therefore all the values "Orange" are removed from the array.

```
var fruits = ["Banana", "Orange", "Apple", "Orange"]
fruits.removeAll(where: { (value) in
    return value == "Orange"
})
print(fruits)   // ["Banana", "Apple"]
```

Listing 3-62: Removing all the elements that meet a condition

Another method that can receive a closure to determine a condition is **contains(where:)**. In the following example, we use this method to determine whether an array contains a value greater than 60 or not.

```
var fruits = [55, 12, 32, 5, 9]
let found = fruits.contains(where: { (value) in
    return value > 60
})
print(found)   // false
```

Listing 3-63: Finding if an element meets a condition

As explained in Chapter 2, the values of an array are accessible through their index. We can read a value by adding the square brackets after the array's name with the index's number of the value we want to read (e.g., **fruits[1]**), but we can also select a random value with the **randomElement()** method. This method selects a value from the array and returns it. The value returned in this case is an optional, so we have to compare it against **nil** or use optional binding before processing it, as in the following example.

```
let fruits = ["Banana", "Orange", "Apple"]
if let randomValue = fruits.randomElement() {
    print("The selected value is: \(randomValue)")
}
```

Listing 3-64: Selecting a random value from an array

Another random operation is performed by the **shuffled()** method. With this method we can order the elements of an array randomly.

```
var fruits = ["Banana", "Orange", "Apple"]
fruits = fruits.shuffled()
print(fruits)   // e.g.: ["Orange", "Apple", "Banana"]
```

Listing 3-65: Changing the order of the elements of an array

Swift Paradigm

Besides working with all the elements of an array, we can do it with a range of elements. Ranges work with arrays the same way they work with strings. They offer an easy way to create new arrays with some of the elements of another.

```
var fruits = ["Banana", "Orange", "Apple", "Cherry"]
var someFruits = fruits[0..<2]  // ["Banana", "Orange"]

print("The new selection has \(someFruits.count) fruits")
```

Listing 3-66: Reading a range of elements

The code of Listing 3-66 gets the elements at the indexes 0 and 1 from the **fruits** array and assigns them to the new **someFruits** array. Now we have two arrays: **fruits** with 4 elements and **someFruits** with 2.

Arrays created from a range of indexes are of type **ArraySlice**. This is a special type provided by Swift to store temporary arrays that are composed of elements taken from other arrays. We can iterate over these types of arrays with a loop or read its elements as we do with normal arrays, but if we want to assign them to other array variables or use them for persistent storage, we have to cast them as **Array** types using the **Array()** initializer. The initializer takes the values of the **ArraySlice** variable and returns a normal array. The following example uses the initializer to cast the **someFruits** array created before.

```
var fruits = ["Banana", "Orange", "Apple", "Cherry"]
var someFruits = fruits[0..<2]  // ["Banana", "Orange"]
var newArray = Array(someFruits)
```

Listing 3-67: Casting arrays of type ArraySlice

The **Array** structure also offers the **removeSubrange()** and **replaceSubrange()** methods to remove and replace a range of elements.

```
var fruits = ["Banana", "Orange", "Apple", "Banana", "Banana"]
fruits.removeSubrange(1...2)
fruits.replaceSubrange(0..<3, with: ["Cherry", "Cherry", "Cherry"])

print("The new array has \(fruits.count) fruits")
```

Listing 3-68: Removing and replacing elements

In Listing 3-68 we call the **removeSubrange()** method to remove the range of elements from index 1 to index 2, getting an array filled with the value "Banana", and then we call the **replaceSubrange()** method to replace the elements from index 0 to index 2 with another array filled with "Cherries". This is just a simple example that helps us understand how the methods work, but it shows a recurrent situation in app development where sometimes we need to fill a collection with elements of the same value. When working with arrays, this is simple to achieve. The **Array** structure includes a practical initializer that takes two attributes called **repeating** and **count** and generates an array filled with the number of elements indicated by **count** and with the value indicated by **repeating**.

```
var fruits = ["Banana", "Orange", "Apple"]

let total = fruits.count
let newArray = Array(repeating: "Cherry", count: total)
fruits.replaceSubrange(0..<total, with: newArray)
```

```
print("The new array has \(fruits.count) fruits")
```

Listing 3-69: Initializing an array with elements of the same value

The advantage of this initializer is that we do not have to know how many elements we need during development. We can calculate the number during execution and create an array filled with all the elements we need and values by default. In the example of Listing 3-69, we create an array with the same amount of elements as the **fruits** array and then use the **replaceSubrange()** method to replace every single element with a new one.

The methods to remove and replace elements of an array are not selective enough; they affect the elements in a specific index or a range of indexes without considering their values. If we want to perform a more specific job, we have to use the **filter()** method. This method takes a function or a closure as an attribute, iterates over the array, and sends each element to the block of code for processing. If the function or closure returns **true**, the element is included in the new array, otherwise it is ignored. Therefore, the function or closure has to be able to receive a value of the same data type as the array and return a Boolean value to indicate whether or not the value should be part of the new array. For the following example we decided to call the **filter()** method with a function called **myfilter()**. What the function does is to return **true** if the value received is different than the string "Grape". As a result, the new array returned by **filter()** will contain only the elements "Apple" and "Banana".

```
var fruits = ["Apple", "Grape", "Banana", "Grape"]

func myfilter(fruit: String) -> Bool {
   if fruit != "Grape" {
      return true
   } else {
      return false
   }
}
var filteredArray = fruits.filter(myfilter)   // ["Apple", "Banana"]
```

Listing 3-70: Filtering the elements of an array

If we prefer, instead of a function we can provide a closure as the attribute and include the whole code in just one single statement.

```
var fruits = ["Apple", "Grape", "Banana", "Grape"]

var filteredArray = fruits.filter({ (fruit: String) -> Bool in
   if fruit != "Grape" {
      return true
   } else {
      return false
   }
})
filteredArray   // ["Apple", "Banana"]
```

Listing 3-71: Using a closure to filter the array

Since the filter was made by just one instruction that already returns **true** or **false**, we can simplify the code returning the instruction itself.

```
var fruits = ["Apple", "Grape", "Banana", "Grape"]

var filteredArray = fruits.filter({ (fruit: String) -> Bool in
    return fruit != "Grape"
})
```

Listing 3-72: Optimizing the closure

This makes the code concise and easy to read, but the advantage of using closures is that we can simplify the instruction even more. First, there is type inference. The closure is provided as the argument of a method that belongs to a generic structure (a structure that can handle different data types), therefore Swift can infer the data type of its parameter. But that is not all. From the **return** instruction, Swift can also infer the data type of the value to be returned by the closure. Because of this, the only thing left is the name we want to use for the parameter.

```
var fruits = ["Apple", "Grape", "Banana", "Grape"]
var filteredArray = fruits.filter({ (fruit) in return fruit != "Grape" })
```

Listing 3-73: Inferring the data types in the closure

Since we only have one statement to generate the value returned, the closure can be simplified even more by ignoring the **return** instruction.

```
var fruits = ["Apple", "Grape", "Banana", "Grape"]
var filteredArray = fruits.filter({ (fruit) in fruit != "Grape" })
```

Listing 3-74: Simplifying closures

 IMPORTANT: Closure's syntax may be simplified to the point of providing only the statement that processes the values received. It is not the purpose of this book to explore all the possibilities and tools provided by the Swift language. For more information, visit our website and follow the links for this chapter.

When it comes to sorting the elements of an array, there are three options available: **reversed()**, **sort()** (and its variant **sort(by:)**), and **sorted()** (and its variant **sorted(by:)**). The **reversed()** method takes the elements of an array and returns a new array with the same elements in reversed order. The value returned by the method is stored in a structure of type **ReversedRandomAccessCollection**. As we did before with the **ArraySlice** types, we can cast these values as **Array** structures with the **Array()** initializer.

```
var fruits = ["Apple", "Blueberry", "Banana"]
var array = Array(fruits.reversed())  // ["Banana", "Blueberry", "Apple"]
```

Listing 3-75: Reversing the elements of an array

The **sort()** and **sorted()** methods sort the array in ascending order. The difference between these methods is that **sort()** stores the values in the same array, while **sorted()** generates and returns a new array with the values in order.

```
var fruits = ["Blueberry", "Apple", "Banana"]
fruits.sort()   // ["Apple", "Banana", "Blueberry"]
```

Listing 3-76: Sorting the elements of an array

If we want to sort the elements in a custom order, we have to use the methods
sort(by:) or **sorted(by:)**. These methods work in a similar fashion to the **filter()**
method studied before. They take a function or a closure that receives the value of two
elements and return **true** if the first element should appear before the second element, or
false otherwise. From this value, the methods establish the order of the elements and
generate the new array.

```
var fruits = ["Apple", "Raspberry", "Banana", "Grape"]
var newArray = fruits.sorted(by: { (value1, value2) in value1 > value2 })
print(newArray[0])   // "Raspberry"
```

Listing 3-77: Sorting the elements of an array in a custom order

The closure provided to the **sorted()** method in Listing 3-77 receives two values we called
value1 and **value2** and returns a Boolean value. If **value1** is greater than **value2**, the closure
returns **true**, otherwise it returns **false**. When the **sorted()** method is executed, it performs
a loop. On each cycle, two values of the **fruits** array are sent to the closure. The closure
compares the values and returns **true** or **false** accordingly. This indicates to the **sorted()**
method which value should appear before the other in the new array, effectively sorting the
elements.

Unlike the example we programmed for the **filter()** method, this one does not
compare the attribute against a specific value. This allows us to order arrays of any data type.
For example, we can use the same closure to sort an array of integers.

```
var numbers = [55, 12, 32, 5, 9]
var newArray = numbers.sorted(by: {(value1, value2) in value1 < value2})
print(newArray[0])   // 5
```

Listing 3-78: Sorting an array of integers

If we decide to work with specific data types, we can perform custom tasks. For example,
we can process **String** values to count the characters and order the strings according to
their length.

```
var fruits = ["Apple", "Blueberry", "Banana", "Grape"]
var newArray = fruits.sorted(by: { (value1, value2) in value1.count <
value2.count })
print(newArray)   // ["Apple", "Grape", "Banana", "Blueberry"]
```

Listing 3-79: Sorting strings according to the number of characters

Collections like arrays also include two powerful methods to compare elements: **min()** and
max(). These methods compare the values and return the smallest or largest, respectively.

```
let ages = [32, 540, 12, 27]
```

```
if !ages.isEmpty {
    if let older = ages.max() {
        let digits = String(older)
        print("The maximum age is \(digits.count) digits long")
    }
}
```

Listing 3-80: Getting the largest element

The code of Listing 3-80 takes the largest value from an array of integers and counts the number of digits in the value returned. Because the **max()** method returns an error if the collection is empty, we check this condition with the **isEmpty** property first. The rest of the code unwraps the value returned by the **max()** method, turns it into a string, and counts its characters to print the number of digits on the console.

Besides selecting the largest or smallest value with the **max()** and **min()** methods, we can also fetch values from the array using the **first** and **last** properties.

```
let ages = [32, 540, 12, 27]
if let firstAge = ages.first {
    print("The first person is \(firstAge) years old")
}
```

Listing 3-81: Getting the first value of an array

The value returned by the **first** property is an optional. That is why we use optional binding to get the value and store it in the **firstAge** constant. The **first** and **last** properties only get the first and last value, respectively. To search for any value in the array or its index, the **Array** structure offers the following methods.

index(of: Element)—This method performs a search from the beginning of the array and returns the index of the first element found that is equal to the value of the **of** attribute.

lastIndex(of: Element)—This method performs a search from the end of the array and returns the index of the first element found that is equal to the value of the **of** attribute.

firstIndex(where: Block)—This method returns the index of the first value that meets the condition in the closure assigned to the **where** attribute.

lastIndex(where: Block)—This method returns the index of the last value that meets the condition in the closure assigned to the **where** attribute..

first(where: Block)—This method returns the first value that meets the condition in the closure assigned to the **where** attribute.

last(where: Block)—This method returns the last value that meets the condition in the closure assigned to the **where** attribute.

If we only need the index of a particular element, we can use the **index(of:)** method. For instance, the following example looks for the first appearance of the number 540 in the **ages** array and prints its index.

```
let ages = [32, 540, 12, 27, 54]
if let index = ages.index(of: 540) {
    print("The value is at the position \(index)")   // 1
}
```

Listing 3-82: Getting the index of a specific value

If what we need instead is to get the index of a value that meets certain condition, we can use methods like `firstIndex(where:)` or `lastIndex(where:)` depending whether we want to search from the beginning or the end of the array.

```
let ages = [32, 540, 12, 27, 54]
let first = ages.firstIndex(where: { (value) in
    return value < 30
})
if first != nil {
    print("The first value is at index \(first!)")   // 2
}
```

Listing 3-83: Getting the index of a value that meets a condition

In the example of Listing 3-83, we look for the index of a value that is smaller than 30. The `firstIndex(where:)` method reads every value of the array from the beginning and sends them to the closure assigned to the **where** attribute. This closure assigns the current value to the **value** constant and compares it against the number 30, if the value is greater than 30, the closure returns **false**, otherwise it returns **true** and the index of that value is assigned to the **first** variable. In this case, the first number in the array smaller than 30 is 12, and therefore the index assigned to the variable is 2.

Set Structures

Sets are also implemented as structures and, because their elements are not associated with an index, the properties and methods they offer are the only way we have to process their values. The following are the most frequently used.

count—This property returns the total number of elements in the set.

isEmpty—This property returns a Boolean value that indicates whether the set is empty or not.

contains(Element**)**—This method returns a Boolean value that indicates whether or not there is an element in the set with the value specified by the attribute.

contains(where: Block**)**—This method returns a Boolean value that determines if the set contains an element that meets the condition in the closure specified by the **where** attribute.

min()—This method compares the elements in the set and returns the smallest.

max()—This method compares the elements in the set and returns the largest.

sorted()—This method returns an array with the elements of the set sorted in ascending order.

sorted(by: Block**)**—This method returns an array with the elements of the set in the order determined by the block specified by the **by** attribute.

randomElement()—This method randomly selects an element from the set and returns it. If the set is empty, the value returned is **nil**.

shuffled()—This method returns an array with the elements of the set in random order.

insert(Element**)**—This method inserts a new element in the set with the value provided by the attribute.

union(Collection**)**—This method returns a new set created with the values of the original set plus the values provided by the attribute. The attribute may be an array or another set.

Swift Paradigm

subtract(Collection**)**—This method returns a new set created by subtracting the elements provided by the attribute to the original set. The attribute may be an array or another set.

intersection(Collection**)**—This method returns a new set created with the values of the original set that coincide with the values provided by the attribute. The attribute may be an array or another set.

remove(Element**)**—This method removes from the set the element with the value provided by the attribute.

removeAll()—This method removes all the elements in the set. This is the same as assigning the value `[]` to the variable.

isSubset(of: Set**)**—This method returns a Boolean value that indicates whether or not the set is a subset of the set specified by the **of** attribute.

isSuperset(of: Set**)**—This method returns a Boolean value that indicates whether or not the set is a superset of the set specified by the **of** attribute.

isDisjoint(with: Set**)**—This method returns a Boolean value that indicates whether or not the original set and the set specified by the **with** attribute have elements in common.

Because elements in a set are not associated with an index, if we want to know whether an element exists or not, we have to search for its value. The `Set` structures provide the `contains()` method for this purpose.

```
var fruits: Set = ["Apple", "Orange", "Banana"]
if fruits.contains("Apple") {
   print("Apple exists!")
}
```

Listing 3-84: Searching for an element

To insert a new element we just have to execute the **insert()** method.

```
var fruits: Set = ["Apple", "Orange", "Banana"]
if !fruits.contains("Grape") {
   fruits.insert("Grape")
}
print("The set has \(fruits.count) elements")   // 4
```

Listing 3-85: Inserting a new element

In listing 3-85 we use the **contains()** method again to check if an element with the value "Grape" already exists in the array. If no element is found, we insert the element with the **insert()** method. Checking the value is not necessary; if the value is already part of the set, the **insert()** method does not perform any action.

To remove an element we have to call the **remove()** method.

```
var fruits: Set = ["Apple", "Orange", "Banana"]
if fruits.remove("Banana") != nil {
   print("The element was removed")
}
```

Listing 3-86: Removing an element

The **remove()** method removes the element which value matches the value of its attribute or returns **nil** in case of failure. In the code of Listing 3-86, we compare the value returned by the method to **nil** and print a message if the element was successfully removed.

Sets are collections without order. Every time we read a set, the order in which its values are returned is not guaranteed, but we can use the **sorted()** method to create an array with the values of the set in order. The following example sorts the elements of the **fruits** set in alphabetical order, creating a new array we called **orderFruits**.

```
var fruits: Set = ["Apple", "Orange", "Banana"]
var orderFruits = fruits.sorted()
print(orderFruits[0])   // "Apple"
```

Listing 3-87: Sorting the elements of a set

The application of the rest of the methods available to manipulate the set is straightforward. The following example joins two sets with the **union()** method and then subtracts elements from the result with the **subtract()** method.

```
var fruits: Set = ["Apple", "Orange", "Banana"]

var newSet = fruits.union(["Grapes"]) //
"Apple","Grapes","Orange","Banana"
newSet.subtract(["Apple", "Banana"])   // "Orange", "Grapes"
```

Listing 3-88: Combining sets

The **Set** structures also offer methods to compare sets. We can determine if a set is a subset or a superset of another set with the **isSubset()** and **isSuperset()** methods or check if two sets have elements in common with the **isDisjoint()** method. The following example implements the **isSubset()** method to check if the fruits in a basket come from the store. The code checks if the elements in the **basket** set are found in the **store** set and returns **true** in case of success.

```
var store: Set = ["Banana", "Apple", "Orange", "Pear"]
var basket: Set = ["Apple", "Orange"]

if basket.isSubset(of: store) {
    print("The fruits in the basket are from the store")
}
```

Listing 3-89: Comparing sets

The Basics: Use a set instead of an array every time you do not need an ordered list of elements and you are worried about performance. Sets are faster than arrays and dictionaries, and that is usually the only advantage they have to offer.

Dictionary Structures

Dictionaries are implemented as structures as well. Here is a list of their most useful properties and methods.

count—This property returns the total number of elements in the dictionary.

isEmpty—This property returns a Boolean value that indicates if the dictionary is empty.

keys—This property returns a collection with the keys of the elements in the dictionary. It is of type `LazyMapCollection`, a collection structure.

values—This property returns a collection with the values of the elements in the dictionary. It is of type `LazyMapCollection`, a collection structure.

sorted(by: Block**)**—This method returns an array of tuples containing each element of the dictionary (key and value) in the order determined by the block specified by the **by** attribute.

randomElement()—This method randomly selects an element from the dictionary and returns a tuple with its key and value. If the dictionary is empty, the value returned is `nil`.

shuffled()—This method returns an array of tuples containing the keys and values of each element of the dictionary in random order.

updateValue(Value, **forKey:** Key**)**—This method updates the value of an element with the value and key specified by its attributes. If the key does not exist, the method creates a new element. It returns the previous value when the key already exists or `nil` otherwise.

removeValue(forKey: Key**)**—This method removes the element with the key equal to the value of the **forKey** attribute. It returns an optional containing the value of the deleted element or `nil` if no element with the specified key was found.

removeAll()—This method removes all the elements in the dictionary. This is the same as assigning the value `[:]` to the variable.

contains(where: Block**)**—This method returns a Boolean value that determines if the dictionary contains an element that meets the condition in the closure specified by the **where** attribute.

Some of the methods provided by the **Dictionary** structure are similar to those included in the **Array** and **Set** structures, but others are more specific. For example, the **updateValue()** and **removeValue()** methods require the element's key to perform their task.

```
var fruits = ["one": "Banana", "two": "Apple", "three": "Pear"]
fruits.updateValue("Banana", forKey: "three")
fruits.removeValue(forKey: "one")   // ["three": "Banana", "two": "Apple"]
```

Listing 3-90: Adding and removing elements from a dictionary

The **updateValue()** method updates the value of an element when there is already an element with that key or creates a new one if the key does not exist. This is the same as assigning a value directly to an element (Chapter 2, Listings 2-52 and 2-53), but the method returns the previous value, which may be useful sometimes.

As sets, dictionaries are an unordered collection of values, but we can create an array with their elements in a specific order using the **sorted()** method. The method processes and returns the values as tuples, with the element's key as the first value of the tuple and the element's value as the second value of the tuple, and it assigns to the attribute the names **key** and **value** (see Listing 2-36).

```
var fruits = ["one": "Banana", "two": "Apple", "three": "Pear"]
var list = fruits.sorted(by: { (value1, value2) in value1.1 < value2.1 })
print("The key of the second element is \(list[0].key)")   // "two"
print("The value of the second element is \(list[0].value)")   // "Apple"
```

Listing 3-91: Sorting the values of a dictionary

The code of Listing 3-91 compares the values at index 1 to sort the **fruits** dictionary by its values in alphabetical order (**value1.1 < value2.1**). The array returned is a collection of tuples, with every element containing the keys and values of the original dictionary (**[(key: "two", value: "Apple"), (key: "one", value: "Banana"), (key: "three", value: "Pear")]**).

We have already seen how to iterate over the elements of a dictionary with a **for in** loop in Chapter 2 (see Listing 2-82). The loop gets each element and generates a tuple with the key and value. There are times when we only need the element's key or the element's value. To help us with this, the **Dictionary** structure provides two properties: **keys** and **values**. The properties return a collection containing only the keys or the values of the elements, respectively.

```
var fruits = ["one": "Banana", "two": "Apple", "three": "Pear"]
for key in fruits.keys {
   if key == "two" {
      print("We have an element with the key 'two'")
   }
}
```

Listing 3-92: Iterating over the dictionary's keys

The collections returned by the **keys** and **values** properties are structures of a collection type called **LazyMapCollection**. As we did before with other types, to work with the values of a **LazyMapCollection** collection we have to turn it into an array with the **Array()** initializer.

```
var fruits = ["one": "Banana", "two": "Apple", "three": "Pear"]
let keys = Array(fruits.keys)
print("The first key in the array is \(keys[0])")  // "one"
```

Listing 3-93: Reading a dictionary key

 IMPORTANT: The order in which the elements of a dictionary are stored and returned is not guaranteed. The **for in** loop and the **keys** and **values** properties may return the values in a different order than the one they were declared. If you need an ordered list, use an array or turn the dictionary into an array with the **sorted()** method.

Range Structures

The **...** and **..<** operators implemented in this and the previous chapter to create ranges are shortcuts for the creation of structures that represent a range. Swift defines five structures to create ranges from these operators: **Range**, **ClosedRange**, **CountableRange**, **CountableClosedRange**, and **CountablePartialRangeFrom**. When we declare a range using any of the operators, Swift creates the proper structure according to the operator and the type of values in the range. These structures provide common properties and methods to work with the range. The following are the most frequently used.

lowerBound—This property returns the range's lower value (the value on the left).

upperBound—This property returns the range's upper value (the value on the right). This property is not available for partial ranges.

contains(Element)—This method returns a Boolean value that determines if the value specified by the attribute is inside the range.

clamped(to: Range)—This method compares the original range with the range specified by the **to** attribute and returns a new range with the part of the ranges that overlap.

Ranges defined with complex values, like the **Index** values used to manage strings, generate structures of type **Range** or **ClosedRange** (always depending on the operator, ..< or ...), ranges defined with integers generate structures of type **CountableRange** or **CountableClosedRange**, and partial ranges created with the ... operator, as in 5..., generate structures of type CountablePartialRangeFrom. The advantage of the **CountableRange** and **CountableClosedRange** structures is that they are implemented as collections and therefore have access to properties and methods of collections, such as the **reversed()** method to reverse the range.

```
var message = ""
var range = 0..<10

for item in range.reversed() {
   message += "\(item) "
}
print(message)  // "9 8 7 6 5 4 3 2 1 0 "
```

Listing 3-94: Inverting a CountableRange *range*

The code of Listing 3-94 creates a **CountableRange** with the **..<** operator and then calls the **reversed()** method to invert the range. The values are stored in the **message** variable to check that the range was effectively reversed.

3.4 Enumerations

Enumerations behave pretty much like structures. We can define our own properties and methods inside an enumeration, and they also include initializers, properties and methods by default. The most useful property is called **rawValue**, which lets us read the values associated with each **case**. As we learned in Chapter 2, the values of an enumeration may have associated values. These values are called *raw values* and are accessible from this property. Raw values are usually used as a description, as in the following example.

```
enum Number: String {
   case one = "Number 1"
   case two = "Number 2"
   case three = "Number 3"
}
var mynumber = Number.one
print("The value is \(mynumber.rawValue)") // "The value is Number 1"
```

Listing 3-95: Reading raw values

Enumeration types include a member initializer to create an instance from a raw value. Instead of declaring the variable using the name of the member (**one**), as we did in Listing 3-95, we can use the initializer and the raw value. The initializer includes the **rawValue** attribute to specify the value used to create the instance.

```
enum Number: String {
   case one = "Number 1"
   case two = "Number 2"
   case three = "Number 3"
}
var mynumber = Number(rawValue: "Number 2")
```

```
if mynumber == .two {
    print("Correct Value")
}
```

Listing 3-96: Creating an enumeration from its initializer

In Listing 3-96 we create an instance of **Number** with the value "Number 2" and then check that the variable contains the proper member value with an **if** statement. We can compare the member value or the raw value to identify an instance of an enumeration type. It does not really matter what value we use as long as we know what we are looking for.

What makes enumerations part of the programming paradigm proposed by Swift is not their capacity to store different types of values but the possibility to include custom methods and also computed properties. The following example adds a method to our **Number** enumeration that prints a message depending on the current value.

```
enum Number: Int {
    case one = 1
    case two = 2
    case three = 3

    func printMessage() -> String {
        switch self {
            case .one:
                return "We are the best"
            case .two:
                return "We have to study more"
            case .three:
                return "This is just the beginning"
        }
    }
}
var mynumber = Number(rawValue: 2)

if mynumber != nil {
    print(mynumber!.printMessage())   // "We have to study more"
}
```

Listing 3-97: Adding methods to an enumeration

When we need to check the current value of the instance from inside the method, we have to use the **self** keyword. This keyword refers to the instance where the method is being executed (in our case, **mynumber**), and this is how we can check for the instance's current value and return the right message (we will learn more about the **self** keyword next).

 IMPORTANT: Enumeration types can be turned into complex processing units, combining multiple methods, properties, and data types. It is not the purpose of this book to show you every possible alternative. For more information, visit our website and follow the links for this chapter.

3.5 Objects

Objects are also data types that encapsulate data and functionality in the form of properties and methods, but unlike the structures and enumerations introduced before they are stored by reference, which means that more than one variable can refer to the same object. This makes objects suitable for situations where the same piece of data has to be shared by different parts of the code.

IMPORTANT: Although Swift introduces its own paradigm based on structures and protocols, most of the frameworks provided by Apple are still programmed in Objective-C with classes (the blueprints for objects) and therefore we have to work with objects and implement the Object-Oriented Programming paradigm to create our apps. At this moment, Apple's advice is to work with objects when necessary and apply structures and protocols in our own code every time we deem it appropriate. We will study protocols and the Protocol-Oriented Programming paradigm later.

Definition of Objects

Like structures and enumerations, objects are defined first and then instances are created from their definition. The definitions of objects are called *classes*, and what we called objects are actually the instances created from those classes. Classes are declared the same way as structures or enumerations, but instead of the **struct** or **enum** keywords we have to use the **class** keyword.

```
class Employee {
   var name = "Undefined"
   var age = 0
}
```

Listing 3-98: Defining a class

The code of Listing 3-98 defines a simple class called **Employee** with two properties: **name** and **age**. As always, this does not create anything, it is just defining a new custom data type. To store data in memory in this format, we have to declare a constant or a variable of this type and assign to it an instance of the class created by an initializer.

```
class Employee {
   var name = "Undefined"
   var age = 0
}
let employee1: Employee = Employee()
```

Listing 3-99: Creating an object from a class

In Listing 3-99, the **Employee()** initializer creates a new instance of the class **Employee**. Since the words instance and object are synonyms, we can say that we have created a new object called **employee1** containing two properties: **name** and **age**. To access the properties of the **employee1** object we can use dot notation.

```
class Employee {
   var name = "Undefined"
   var age = 0
}
let employee1 = Employee()
employee1.name = "John"
employee1.age = 32
```

Listing 3-100: Assigning new values to the object's properties

Another way to modify the values of the properties of an object is from its methods. In contrast to structures, methods that belong to objects can modify the properties of their own object without adding anything to the definition (they do not need to be declared as **mutating**).

```
class Employee {
    var name = "Undefined"
    var age = 0

    func changename(newname: String, newage: Int) {
        name = newname
        age = newage
    }
}
let employee1 = Employee()
employee1.changename(newname: "Martin", newage: 32)
```

Listing 3-101: Modifying properties from the object's methods

In Listing 3-101, the **changename()** method is added to the **Employee** class to modify the values of its properties. The last statement of this example calls this method in the **employee1** object to assign the values "Martin" and 32 to the **name** and **age** properties, respectively.

 IMPORTANT: As well as structures, we can create all the objects we need from the same definition (class). Each object will have its own properties, values, and methods.

Property Observers

Properties are accessible from every part of the code that has access to the structures or objects they belong to. Therefore, they may be modified at any moment by different processes, such as in response to user interaction or events produced by the system. To inform the instance of a structure or a class that one of its stored properties was modified, Swift introduces Property Observers.

Property Observers are special methods (like the **init()** method introduced before in this chapter) that can be added to a property to execute code before and after a new value is assigned to it. The methods are called **willSet()** and **didSet()**, and are declared between braces after the properties declaration.

```
class Employee {
    var name = "Undefined"
    var state = "Active"
    var difference = 0

    var age: Int = 0 {
        willSet {
            if newValue > 65 {
                state = "Retired"
            }
        }
        didSet {
            difference = age - oldValue
        }
    }
}
let employee1 = Employee()
employee1.age = 66
print(employee1.state)   // "Retired"
```

Listing 3-102: Adding observers to a property

Swift Paradigm

The **Employee** class of Listing 3-102 contains a total of four properties (**name**, **state**, **difference**, and **age**). Property Observers were declared for the **age** property. Every time a new value is assigned to this property, the **willSet()** and **didSet()** methods are executed. The **willSet()** method is called before the new value is assigned to the property and the **didSet()** method is called after the value was assigned. Swift automatically creates a parameter called **newValue** for the **willSet()** method to provide access to the value that is going to be assigned to the property. In our example, when this method is executed, the value of **newValue** is compared to the number 65 and, if the condition is true, the value of the **state** property is changed to "Retired". Something similar happens with the **didSet()** method. Swift automatically creates a parameter called **oldValue** to provide access to the property's old value after the new value is assigned. We subtract this value to the current value to get the difference between the old and the new age and then assign the result to the **difference** property.

We can change the names of the methods' parameters by declaring our own names between parentheses. In the following example, the names provided by Swift are replaced by **newage** and **previousage,** respectively.

```swift
class Employee {
   var name = "Undefined"
   var state = "Active"
   var difference = 0

   var age: Int = 0 {
      willSet(newage) {
         if newage > 65 {
            state = "Retired"
         }
      }
      didSet(previousage) {
         difference = age - previousage
      }
   }
}
let employee1 = Employee()
employee1.age = 66
print(employee1.state)   // "Retired"
```

Listing 3-103: Providing our own names for the parameters of the observers

 IMPORTANT: Property Observers can be used in structures but are particularly useful with objects. As we will see next, there are different programming patterns that allow us to connect objects with other objects and delegate work. Property Observers are the best way to inform an object that its properties were modified, so it can update the rest of its data and adapt to the new situation when necessary (see Chapter 14, Listing 14-12).

Type Properties and Methods

We have studied type properties and methods before for structures. These are properties and methods that are accessible from the data type (the class) and not from the instances created from that type. They work in classes the same way as in structures, but instead of the **static** keyword we have to use the **class** keyword.

```
class Employee {
    var name = "Undefined"
    var age = 0

    class func description() {
        print("This class stores the name and age of an employee")
    }
}
Employee.description()
```

Listing 3-104: Declaring a type method for a class

The code of Listing 3-104 defines a simple **Employee** class with two properties: **name** and **age**. The type method declared next is just describing the purpose of the class. Every time the **description()** method is executed, the description of the class is printed on the console. Again, we do not have to create an instance of the class because the method is executed on the class itself.

Optional Chaining

As well as structures, objects can contain other objects, and their values are accessible through dot notation. Listing 3-105, next, shows an example with two classes: **Salary** and **Employee**.

```
class Salary {
    var money = 0.0
}
class Employee {
    var name = "Undefined"
    var age = 0
    var salary = Salary()
}
let employee1 = Employee()

employee1.name = "George"
employee1.age = 34
employee1.salary.money = 55000
```

Listing 3-105: Creating objects inside objects

This is a similar example to the one programmed before to connect structures (Listing 3-27). The **Employee** class includes a property called **salary** that contains an object of the **Salary** class. When a new instance of the **Employee** class is created, the **Salary()** initializer creates an instance of the **Salary** class and assigns the object to **salary**. Dot notation is used later to concatenate the values and access the properties of each object.

In this example, the **salary** object is created during instantiation, but this is not usually the case. Sometimes the values of the properties containing objects are defined after the instance is created and therefore those properties have to be declared as optionals. The problem with optionals is that we always have to check whether the variable or property has a value before we use it. One way to do it is to compare the optional against **nil** or use Optional Binding (studied in Chapter 2), but when we have one object inside another in a long chain, and more than one component of that chain is an optional, the code gets messy. To simplify this task, Swift introduces Optional Chaining.

Optional Chaining is a simple tool to access objects, properties and methods in a hierarchical chain that contains optional components. As always, the access to these components is done through dot notation, but a question mark is added to the names of the variables and properties that have optional values. When the system finds an optional, it checks whether or not it contains a value and continues only in case of success. Here is the same example, but with the **salary** property turned into an optional.

```
class Salary {
    var money = 0.0
}
class Employee {
    var name = "Undefined"
    var age = 0
    var salary: Salary?
}
let employee1 = Employee()

employee1.name = "George"
employee1.age = 34
employee1.salary?.money = 55000   // returns nil
```

Listing 3-106: Accessing optional properties

The **salary** property in the code of Listing 3-106 is an optional (its initial value is not defined). Every time we need to read this property we have to unwrap its value, but if we use Optional Chaining, we just have to concatenate the values with dot notation and add a question mark after the name of the optional. The system reads every component in the instruction and checks their values. If any of the optionals have no value, it returns **nil**, but when all the optionals have values, the instruction performs the task (in this case, assigning the number 55000 to **money**).

Reference Types

The data types we have studied before, including structures and enumerations, are value types. This means that every time we assign a variable of any of these types to another variable, the value is copied. For example, if we create an instance of a structure and then assign that instance to another variable, the instance is actually copied, and we end up with two instances of the same structure (two copies in memory). Here is an example.

```
struct Employee {
    var name = "Undefined"
}
var employee1 = Employee()

var employee2 = employee1
employee2.name = "George"
print("Employee1 Name: \(employee1.name)")   // "Undefined"
```

Listing 3-107: Creating a copy of an instance

The code of Listing 3-107 defines a simple structure called **Employee** with just one property called **name**. After the definition, a new instance is created with the **Employee()** initializer and assigned to the **employee1** variable. Next, the **employee1** variable is assigned to a new variable called **employee2**. At this moment, the system makes a copy of the structure contained in the **employee1** variable and assigns that copy to **employee2**. Both variables, **employee1** and **employee2**, have a copy of the structure. Therefore, when we assign the value "George" to the property of the instance in the **employee2** variable, the value of the property in **employee1** is still "Undefined". The following figure illustrates this process.

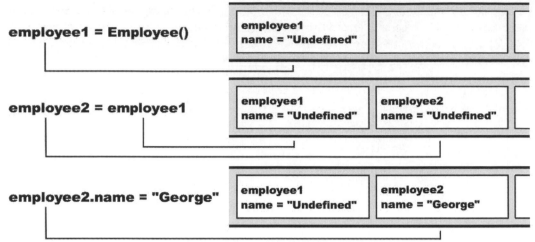

Figure 3-1: Value types stored in memory

Figure 3-1 shows how two different copies of the **Employee** structure, one referenced by the **employee1** variable and the other referenced by the **employee2** variable, are stored in memory. Any modification to the values of one of the instances will not affect the other, because they occupy different spaces in memory.

Objects, on the other hand, are passed by reference. This means that when we assign an existing object to a constant or a variable, a reference to the object is assigned to it, not a copy of the object. Here is the same example, this time applied to objects.

```
class Employee {
    var name = "Undefined"
}
let employee1 = Employee()
let employee2 = employee1
employee2.name = "George"
print("Employee1 Name: \(employee1.name)")  // "George"
```

Listing 3-108: Creating a new reference to an object

The object in **employee2** is exactly the same as the object in **employee1**. Any change in the **name** property is reflected in the other because both point to the same object in memory (they refer to the same instance). Figure 3-2 next illustrates this process.

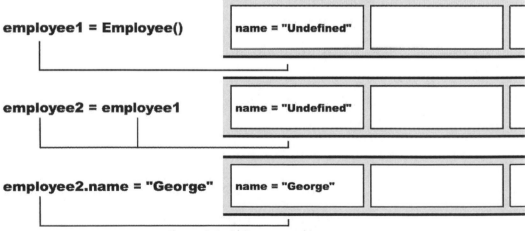

Figure 3-2: Objects stored in memory

Swift Paradigm

Constants or variables that were assigned an object do not store the object; they actually store the value of the memory address where the object is located. When a constant or variable containing this address is assigned to another constant or variable, only the address is copied, and this is why the object is not duplicated. This is the most important characteristic of objects, and what makes them suitable for situations in which data in memory has to be accessed and shared by different parts of the code. A common example is when we need to define a data type to control the device's screen. The screen is only one, so we shouldn't generate multiple copies of the data that controls it. Instead, we create an object and pass the reference of that object to the rest of the code. Each part of the code accesses exactly the same object and works with the same properties and methods. Every change on its properties is always reflected on the screen.

 IMPORTANT: Because constants and variables store a reference to an object (a memory address), you may have two variables in your code that reference the same object. If you need to know whether this is the case, you can compare the variables with the operators **===** (identical to) and **!==** (not identical to) provided by Swift. If what you need is to know whether two separate objects contain different information, you can use the basic operators **==** and **!=**, but you can only do this when the objects conform to the **Equatable** protocol; a protocol that determines how the objects will be compared. We will study protocols and the **Equatable** protocol later in this chapter.

 The Basics: When you modify the properties of an object, its properties are modified but not its reference. This is why objects are usually stored in constants and only their properties are defined as variables. Unless we plan to replace one object by another later, it is always recommended to store objects in constants.

Using references is one of the characteristics that make objects unique and useful, but objects are always passed by reference, even when they are sent to a function or method. Sometimes this is not ideal. While developing our application we will find that there are times when several copies of the same object are required to produce what we want (e.g., to create different buttons on the screen). In cases like this, we can create multiple instances from the same class.

```
class Employee {
    var name = "Undefined"
}
let employee1 = Employee()
let employee2 = Employee()
employee2.name = "George"
print("Employee1 Name: \(employee1.name)")   // "Undefined"
```

Listing 3-109: Creating several objects from the same class

Two different objects are created by the code of Listing 3-109. Both objects, **employee1** and **employee2**, are independent instances and occupy a different space in memory. Assigning a new value to the **name** property in the **employee2** object does not affect the value of the same property in the **employee1** object (the **name** property on this object still has the value "Undefined").

Because the same object may be referenced by multiple constants or variables, every language that works with objects offers a way for the object to reference itself. In Swift this is done automatically, but there are situations in which this reference has to be declared explicitly. For this purpose, Swift defines a special keyword called **self**. We have introduced this keyword earlier in this chapter to be able to read the current value of an enumeration from inside the instance (see Listing 3-97). In objects, the **self** keyword works exactly the same way; it references the object that belongs to.

The most common situations in which the use of this keyword is required is when we need to declare the names of the parameters of a method equal to the names of the object's properties. If the names are the same, the system does not know whether we are referring to the property or the parameter. The **self** keyword clarifies the situation.

```
class Employee {
    var name = "Undefined"

    func changename(name: String) {
        self.name = name
    }
}
let employee1 = Employee()
employee1.changename(name: "Martin")

print("Name: \(employee1.name)")   // "Name: Martin"
```

Listing 3-110: *Referring to the object with* self

The **self** keyword in the **changename()** method of Listing 3-110 represents the object created from the **Employee** class and helps the system understand what we are referring to when we use the word **name**. When we call the **changename()** method in the **employee1** object, the value of the **name** parameter is assigned to the **name** property (**self.name**) of the object. The **self** keyword in this example is a reference to the object stored in the **employee1** variable. This would be the same as declaring **employee1.name**, but since we do not know the name of the variable that is going to store the instance when the class is defined, we have to use **self** instead.

Memory Management

Because objects are stored by reference, they can be referenced by several variables at the same time. If a variable is erased, the object it references cannot be erased from memory because another variable could still be using it. This creates a situation where we can end up with objects that are not required anymore filling up the device's memory. One approach to solve this problem was to provide the tools for programmers to erase the objects themselves. Having the proper tools was one step forward, but most programmers struggled to find the right place in the code to erase the object, figure out when the object was no longer being referenced by any variable, or remember to do it, delivering apps that after extended use would fill the memory and crash. The final solution was to create an automatic system that counts the number of variables referencing an object and only removes the object from memory when all the references were erased (all the variables were erased, set to **nil**, or they were assigned a reference to another object). The system was called *ARC* (Automatic Reference Counting) and it was integrated into Objective-C and now Swift. Thanks to ARC, we do not have to worry about the memory anymore; the objects are automatically erased when there is no longer a constant, variable or property containing a reference to that space in memory.

In an ideal scenario, this system works like magic, counting how many references we create to the same object and erasing that object when none of those references exist anymore. But there are situations in which we can create something called a *Strong Reference Cycle*. This happens when two objects have a property that references the other object.

```
class Employee {
    var name: String?
    var location: Department?
}
class Department {
    var area: String?
    var person: Employee?
}
var employee: Employee? = Employee()
var department: Department? = Department()
```

Listing 3-111: Creating objects with strong references

The code of Listing 3-111 defines two classes: **Employee** and **Department**. Both classes contain a property that references an object of the other class. After the definition, objects of each class are created and stored in the **employee** and **department** variables. In this example, we did not assign any value to their properties, therefore the only references we have created are the references stored in the variables, as illustrated in the following figure.

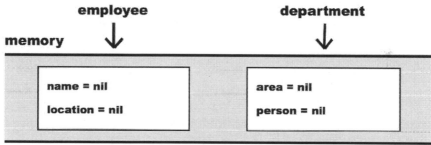

Figure 3-3: Objects referenced only by variables

In this case, if the variables are erased or their values are modified, the corresponding objects are erased as well because they are only referenced by the **employee** and **department** variables. But everything changes when we reference the objects from their own properties.

```
class Employee {
    var name: String?
    var location: Department?
}
class Department {
    var area: String?
    var person: Employee?
}
var employee: Employee? = Employee()
var department: Department? = Department()

employee?.name = "John"
employee?.location = department
department?.area = "Mail"
department?.person = employee
```

Listing 3-112: Referencing one object from another

In the code of Listing 3-112, new values are assigned to the objects' properties. The reference in the **department** variable is assigned to the **location** property of the **employee** object, and the reference in the **employee** variable is assigned to the **person** property of the **department** object. Now each object contains a reference to the other. The result is illustrated in Figure 3-4.

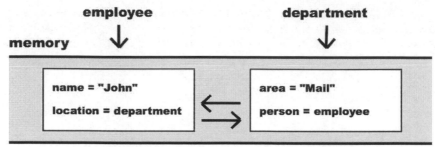

Figure 3-4: Objects referencing each other

At this point, each object is referenced by a variable and also a property. The object of the **Employee** class is referenced by the **employee** variable and the **person** property, and the object of the **Department** class is referenced by the **department** variable and the **location** property. If for some reason we do not need to access these objects from our code anymore and erase or modify the values of the **employee** and **department** variables, ARC will not erase the objects from memory because their properties still have a reference that keeps them alive. This is illustrated in Figure 3-5.

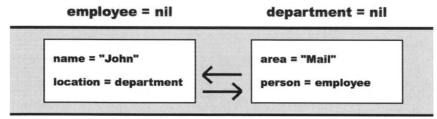

Figure 3-5: Objects preserved in memory

This example assigns **nil** to the **employee** and **department** variables, and in consequence the old objects are not accessible from our code anymore, but they are preserved in memory because ARC has no way to know that they have become useless to our program.

Swift has solved this problem classifying the references into three categories: strong, weak, and unowned. Normal references are considered to be strong; they are always valid and the objects they point to are preserved in memory as long as they exist. These are the kind of references we have been using so far, and that is why the cycle created by our example is called Strong Reference Cycle. The solution to break this cycle is to define one of the references as **weak** or **unowned**. When ARC encounters one of these types of references to be the last reference to an object, the object is erased from memory as if the reference had never existed.

```
class Employee {
    var name: String?
    var location: Department?
}
class Department {
    var area: String?
    weak var person: Employee?
}
var employee: Employee? = Employee()
var department: Department? = Department()
employee?.name = "John"
employee?.location = department
department?.area = "Mail"
department?.person = employee
```

Listing 3-113: Assigning weak references

Swift Paradigm

In the code of Listing 3-113, the **person** property was declared as **weak**. Now, when the references from the variables are erased, the object created from the **Employee** class is erased from memory because the only reference it has left is the weak reference from the **person** property. After this object disappears, the object created from the **Department** class does not have any other strong reference either, so it is also erased from memory.

What the weak reference does is to reference an object without affecting ARC's counting. Weak references are not considered by ARC to determine whether an object should be erased or not. The unowned reference works the same way, but it differs with the weak reference on the type of values it applies to. Weak references apply to variables and properties with optional values (they can be empty at some point) and unowned references apply to non-optional values (they always have a value).

 IMPORTANT: The use of weak and unowned references is not frequent, except for the construction of the user's interface, as we will see in Chapter 5. There are more complex situations in which these types of references become useful, but the topic is beyond the scope of this book. For more information, visit our website and follow the links for this chapter.

Inheritance

One of the main purposes of structures and objects is to define pieces of code that can be copied and shared. The code is defined once and then instances (copies) of that code are created every time they are required. This programming pattern works well when we define our own code but presents some limitations when working with code programmed by other developers and shared through libraries and frameworks. The programmers creating the code for us cannot anticipate how we are going to use it and all the possible variations required for every specific app. To provide a solution to this problem, classes incorporate inheritance. A class can inherit properties and methods from another class and then incorporate improvements adding some properties and methods of its own. This way, programmers can share their classes and developers can adapt them to their own needs.

To illustrate how inheritance works, the following examples present a situation in which a class has to be expanded to contain additional information that was not initially contemplated.

```
class Employee {
   var name = "Undefined"
   var age = 0
   func createbadge() -> String {
      return "Employee \(name) \(age)"
   }
}
```

Listing 3-114: Defining a basic class

The **Employee** class declared in Listing 3-114 is a normal class, similar to those we have defined before. It has two properties and a method called **createbadge()** that returns a string containing the values of those properties. This class would be enough to create objects that generate the string of text necessary to print a badge for every employee showing its name and age. But for the sake of argument, let's say that some of the employees require a badge that also displays the department they work in. One of the options is to define another class with the same properties and methods and add what we need, but this produces redundant code and it is not possible when the class was taken from a library (we usually do not have access to the definition of the classes provided by other developers or they are too complex to modify or duplicate). The solution is to create a new class that inherits the characteristics of the basic class and adds its own properties and methods to satisfy the new requirements. To indicate that a class inherits from another class, we have to write the name of the basic class after the name of the new class separated by a colon.

```
class Employee {
    var name = "Undefined"
    var age = 0
    func createbadge() -> String {
        return "Employee \(name) \(age)"
    }
}
class OfficeEmployee: Employee {
    var department = "Undefined"
}
```

Listing 3-115: Inheriting properties and methods from another class

The **OfficeEmployee** class added to our code in Listing 3-115 only has one property called **department**, but it inherits the **name** and **age** properties, and also the **createbadge()** method from the **Employee** class. All these properties and methods are available in any of the objects created from the **OfficeEmployee** class, as shown next.

```
class Employee {
    var name = "Undefined"
    var age = 0

    func createbadge() -> String {
        return "Employee \(name) \(age)"
    }
}
class OfficeEmployee: Employee {
    var department = "Undefined"
}
let employee = OfficeEmployee()
employee.name = "George"
employee.age = 25
employee.department = "Mail"

var badge = employee.createbadge()
print("Badge: \(badge)")   // "Badge: Employee George 25"
```

Listing 3-116: Creating objects from a subclass

A class like **Employee** is called *superclass*, and a class that inherits from another class is called *subclass*. In these terms, we can say that the **OfficeEmployee** class is a subclass that inherits the properties and methods of its superclass **Employee**. A class can inherit from a superclass that already inherited from another superclass in an infinite chain. When a property is accessed, or a method is called, the system looks for it on the object's class and, if it is not there, it keeps looking in the superclasses up the hierarchical chain until it finds it.

 IMPORTANT: Inheritance does not work the other way around. For example, considering the code of Listing 3-116, objects created from the class **OfficeEmployee** have access to the **department** property of this class and also the properties and methods of the **Employee** class, but objects created from the **Employee** class do not have access to the **department** property.

Because of this hierarchical chain, sometimes a method does not have access to all the properties available for the object. For example, the **createbadge()** method called on the **employee** object created in Listing 3-116 have access to the properties declared on the **Employee** class but not to those declared in the **OfficeEmployee** class. If we want the method to also print the value of the **department** property, we have to implement it again in the **OfficeEmployee** class with the appropriate modifications. To overwrite a method of a superclass, we have to prefix it with the **override** keyword.

```
class Employee {
   var name = "Undefined"
   var age = 0
   func createbadge() -> String {
      return "Employee \(name) \(age)"
   }
}
class OfficeEmployee: Employee {
   var department = "Undefined"
   override func createbadge() -> String {
      return "Employee \(department) \(name) \(age)"
   }
}
let employee = OfficeEmployee()
employee.name = "George"
employee.age = 25
employee.department = "Mail"
var badge = employee.createbadge()
print("Badge: \(badge)")  // "Badge: Employee Mail George 25"
```

Listing 3-117: Overwriting an inherited method

The new **OfficeEmployee** subclass of Listing 3-117 overwrites the **createbadge()** method of its superclass to generate a string that includes the value of the **department** property. Now, when the method is executed from an object of this class, the method called is the one declared in **OfficeEmployee** (the old method from the superclass is ignored), and the badge generated includes the values of the three properties.

Using inheritance, we have created a new class without modifying previous classes or duplicating any code. The **Employee** class can create objects to store the name and age of an employee and generate a badge with this information, and the **OfficeEmployee** class can create objects to store the name, age, and also the department of the employee and generate a more complete badge with the values of all these properties.

As we explained before, when we call the **createbadge()** method on the **employee** object created from the **OfficeEmployee** class in Listing 3-117, the method executed is the one defined in the **OfficeEmployee** class. If we want to execute the method on the superclass instead, we have to use a special keyword called **super**. The **super** keyword is similar to the **self** keyword, but instead of referring to the object, **super** refers to the superclass. It is often used when we have overwritten a method, but we still need to execute the method of the superclass. Here is an example.

```
class Employee {
   var name = "Undefined"
   var age = 0
   func createbadge() -> String {
      return "Employee \(name) \(age)"
   }
}
```

```
class OfficeEmployee: Employee {
    var department = "Undefined"
    override func createbadge() -> String {
        let oldbadge = super.createbadge()
        return "\(oldbadge) \(department)"
    }
}
let employee = OfficeEmployee()
employee.name = "George"
employee.age = 25
employee.department = "Mail"

var badge = employee.createbadge()
print("Badge: \(badge)")    // "Badge: Employee George 25 Mail"
```

Listing 3-118: Calling a method from the superclass

This is the same as the previous example, but now, when the **createbadge()** method of an object created from the **OfficeEmployee** class is called, the method calls the **createbadge()** method of the superclass first and assigns the result to the **oldbadge** constant. The value of this constant is later added to the value of the **department** property to generate the final string.

Type Casting

Inheritance not only transfers functionality from one class to another but also connects the classes together. The superclasses and their subclasses are linked together in a hierarchical chain. Because of this, whenever we declare a variable of the type of the superclass, objects of the subclasses can be assigned to that variable too. This is a very important feature that allows us to do things like creating arrays of objects that are of different classes but belong to the same class hierarchy.

```
class Employee {
    var name = "Undefined"
    var age = 0
}
class OfficeEmployee: Employee {
    var deskNumber = 0
}
class WarehouseEmployee: Employee {
    var area = "Undefined"
}
var list: [Employee] = [OfficeEmployee(), WarehouseEmployee(),
OfficeEmployee()]
```

Listing 3-119: Creating an array of objects from different subclasses

The code of Listing 3-119 defines a basic class called **Employee** and then two subclasses that inherit from **Employee** called **OfficeEmployee** and **WarehouseEmployee**. The purpose is to have the common information for every employee in one class and then have classes for specific types of employee. This allows us to create objects that only carry the information they need. For instance, an employee working at the warehouse doesn't need the **deskNumber** property, because he doesn't work on a desk, and an employee working at the office doesn't need the **area** property because he doesn't work on a specific area, he works on his desk. Following this organization, we can create objects that only contain the **name**, **age**, and **deskNumber** properties to represent employees working at the office and objects that only contain the **name**, **age**, and **area** properties to represent employees working at the warehouse.

No matter the differences between one object and another, they all represent employees of the same company, so sooner or later we will have to include them on the same list. The class hierarchy allows us to do that. We can declare a collection, such as an array, of the data type of the superclass and then store objects of the subclasses in it. In Listing 3-119 we did exactly that with the **list** array.

This is all good until we try to read the array. The elements of the array are all considered to be of type **Employee**, so we cannot access all of their properties, only the ones defined in the **Employee** class. Also, there is no way to know what type of object each element is. We could have an **OfficeEmployee** object at index 0 and later replace it by a **WarehouseEmployee** object. The indexes and the array itself do not provide any clue to identify the objects. Swift solves both problems with the **is** and **as** operators.

is—This operator returns a Boolean value that indicates if the value is of a certain data type.

as—This operator converts a value of one class to another class when possible.

Identifying an object is easy with the **is** operator. This operator returns a Boolean value that we can use in an **if** statement to check the object's class.

```
var countOffice = 0
var countWarehouse = 0

for obj in list {
    if obj is OfficeEmployee {
        countOffice += 1
    } else if obj is WarehouseEmployee {
        countWarehouse += 1
    }
}
print("We have \(countOffice) employees working at the office")   //2
print("We have \(countWarehouse) employees working at the warehouse") //1
```

Listing 3-120: Identifying the object's data type

In Listing 3-120, we create the **list** array again with objects from the same classes defined in the previous example, but this time we add a **for in** loop to iterate over the array and count how many objects of each class we have found. The **if** statement inside the loop uses the **is** operator to check if the current object stored in the **obj** constant is of type **OfficeEmployee** or **WarehouseEmployee** and increments the counter respectively (**countOffice** or **countWarehouse**). At the end, the values of the counters are printed on the screen to show how many objects of each class are in the array.

 Do It Yourself: The example of Listing 3-120 and the following examples, omit the definitions of the structures and the **list** array introduced in Listing 3-119. If you want to test these examples, you have to include those definitions in your code.

Counting objects is not really what these operators are all about. The idea is to figure out the type with the **is** operator and then convert the object with the **as** operator to be able to access their properties and methods. The **as** operator converts a value of one type to another. The conversions are not always guaranteed, and that is why this operator comes in two more forms: **as!** and **as?**. These versions of the **as** operator work in a similar way to optionals. The **as!** operator forces the conversion and returns an error if the conversion is not possible, and the **as?** operator tries to convert the object and returns an optional with the new object or **nil** in case of failure.

```
for obj in list {
    if obj is OfficeEmployee {
        let temp = obj as! OfficeEmployee
        temp.deskNumber = 100
    } else if obj is WarehouseEmployee {
        let temp = obj as! WarehouseEmployee
        temp.area = "New Area"
    }
}
```

Listing 3-121: Casting an object

When we use the **as!** operator we are forcing the conversion, so we have to make sure that the conversion is possible or otherwise the app will crash (this is the same that happens when we unwrap optionals with the exclamation mark). In the code of Listing 3-121, we only use this operator after we have already checked with the **is** operator that the object is of the right class. Once the object is casted (converted) into its real type, we can access its properties and methods. In this example, the objects returned by the **as!** operator are stored in the **temp** constant and then new values are assigned to the **deskNumber** and **area** properties, respectively.

Checking for the type before converting is a little bit redundant. To simplify this code, we can use the **as?** operator. Instead of forcing the conversion and crashing our app in case of failure, this particular version of the **as** operator tries to perform the conversion and returns an optional reflecting the result of the operation.

```
for obj in list {
    if let temp = obj as? OfficeEmployee {
        temp.deskNumber = 100
    } else if let temp = obj as? WarehouseEmployee {
        temp.area = "New Area"
    }
}
```

Listing 3-122: Casting an object with the as? *operator*

In this new example, we use optional binding to cast the object and assign the result to the **temp** constant. First, we try to cast **obj** as an **OfficeEmployee** object. If we are successful, we assign the value 100 to the **deskNumber** property, but if the value returned is **nil**, then we try to cast the object to the **WarehouseEmployee** class to modify its **area** property.

Casting can also be performed on the fly if we are sure that the conversion is possible. The statement to cast the object is the same, but we have to declare it between parentheses.

```
let myarea = (list[1] as! WarehouseEmployee).area
print("The area of employee 1 is \(myarea)")   // "Undefined"
```

Listing 3-123: Casting an object on the fly

In this example, we do not assign the object to any variable; we just cast the element of the **list** array at index 1 as a **WarehouseEmployee** object inside the parentheses and then access its **area** property. The value of this property is stored in the **myarea** constant and then printed on the console. Remember that conversions performed with the **as!** operator are only possible when we are sure it is going to be successful (in this case we have to know for sure that the element of the array at index 1 is a **WarehouseEmployee** object).

Swift Paradigm

IMPORTANT: The `as!` operator is applied when the conversion is guaranteed to be successful, and the `as?` operator is used when we are not sure about the result. But it is also possible to use the basic `as` operator when the Swift compiler can verify that the conversion will be successful. There are two circumstances when this is possible: when we are converting an object of a subclass into its superclass and when we are casting some primitive data types. We will see an example in Chapter 4, when we study how to convert `String` values into `NSString` objects.

Any and AnyObject

The `as` operator works on objects that belong to the same class hierarchy. Because sometimes the objects that require casting are not in the same hierarchy, Swift defines several generic data types to represent values of any kind. The most frequently used are `Any` and `AnyObject`. The `Any` type has the purpose to represent instances of any data type, while the `AnyObject` type was designed to represent only objects. The values of these types are related to others, as if they would belong to the same hierarchy. Taking advantage of these generic types, we can create collections with values that are not associated with each other.

```
class Employee {
    var name = "Undefined"
}
class Department {
    var area = "Undefined"
}
var list: [AnyObject] = [Employee(), Department(), Department()]

for obj in list {
    if let temp = obj as? Employee {
        temp.name = ""
    } else if let temp = obj as? Department {
        temp.area = ""
    }
}
```

Listing 3-124: Working with objects of `AnyObject` *type*

The `list` array declared in Listing 3-124 is of type `AnyObject` and therefore it can contain objects of any type (any class). To populate the array, we created two simple and independent classes: `Employee` and `Department`. A few objects are created from these classes and included into the array. The objects are later casted by the `as?` operator inside a `for in` loop and their corresponding properties are modified following the same procedure used in previous examples.

Initialization

We have been initializing the properties during definition in every class declared so far. This is because classes do not provide member initializers as structures do. The properties of a class have to be initialized explicitly in the definition or during instantiation by the `init()` method. This is the same method previously introduced for structures and we can use it in our classes to create our own initializers.

```
class Employee {
    var name: String
    var age: Int
```

```
    init(name: String, age: Int) {
       self.name = name
       self.age = age
    }
}
let employee1 = Employee(name: "George", age: 28)
```

Listing 3-125: Declaring a Designated Initializer

The `init()` method declared for the **Employee** class in Listing 3-125 initializes every property of the class with the values specified in the **Employee()** initializer. This type of initializer is called *Designated Initializer* and its purpose is to prepare the properties of the object that has been created.

When we declare a Designated Initializer, we have to make sure all the properties are initialized. If we know that in some circumstances our code will not be able to provide all the values during initialization, we can also declare a Convenience Initializer. A Convenience Initializer is an initializer that offers a convenient way to initialize an object with default values for some or all of its properties. It is declared as an `init()` method but preceded by the **convenience** keyword. A Convenience Initializer always calls the Designated initializer of the same class with the corresponding values.

```
class Employee {
   var name: String
   var age: Int

   init(name: String, age: Int) {
      self.name = name
      self.age = age
   }
   convenience init() {
      self.init(name: "Undefined", age: 0)
   }
}
let employee1 = Employee()
```

Listing 3-126: Declaring a Convenience Initializer

When we create an instance of **Employee**, the system detects the number and type of attributes provided and executes the corresponding initializer. For example, if we provide the values for the **name** and the **age** parameters in the code of Listing 3-126, the system executes the Designated Initializer because this is the initializer that contains the necessary parameters to receive those values, but if the initialization does not include any attribute, as in this example, the Convenience Initializer is executed instead and then the Designated Initializer is called with values by default ("Undefined" for the **name** parameter and 0 for the **age** parameter).

This process is similar to what we have done with structures. The difference is inheritance. Classes can inherit properties and methods from other classes, and this includes the `init()` method. When a subclass does not provide its own Designated Initializer, the initializer of its superclass is executed.

```
class Employee {
   var name: String
   var age: Int
```

```
    init(name: String, age: Int) {
        self.name = name
        self.age = age
    }
}
class OfficeEmployee: Employee {
    var department: String = "Undefined"
}
let employee1 = OfficeEmployee(name: "George", age: 29)
```

Listing 3-127: Inheriting the Designated Initializer

The code of Listing 3-127 defines the subclass **OfficeEmployee** that inherits from the **Employee** class. The **OfficeEmployee** class does not provide any initializer, so the only initializer available is the one provided by its superclass. This initializer only initializes the properties **name** and **age** of the superclass. The **department** property of **OfficeEmployee** is explicitly initialized with the value "Undefined" (every object created from this class has this value by default). To provide an initializer that also includes this property, we have to declare a new Designated Initializer in the **OfficeEmployee** class.

```
class Employee {
    var name: String
    var age: Int
    init(name: String, age: Int) {
        self.name = name
        self.age = age
    }
}
class OfficeEmployee: Employee {
    var department: String
    init(name: String, age: Int, department: String) {
        self.department = department

        super.init(name: name, age: age)
    }
}
let employee1 = OfficeEmployee(name: "John", age: 24, department: "Mail")
```

Listing 3-128: Declaring a Designated Initializer for the subclass

The Designated Initializer of a subclass has to initialize the properties of its own class first and then call the initializer of its superclass. This is done by calling the **init()** method on **super**. The **super** keyword refers to the superclass, so when the system executes the **super.init()** statement in the code of Listing 3-128, the **init()** method of the superclass is executed and the **name** and **age** properties of this class are initialized.

 IMPORTANT: If you need to declare the same initializer of the superclass in the subclass, you have to overwrite the initializer in the subclass with the **override** keyword, as in **override init()**, and call the initializer of the superclass with **super** (e.g., **super.init()**).

 The Basics: There are different ways to combine Designated and Convenience initializers. The possibility of classes to inherit from other classes in an unlimited chain can turn initialization into a very complex process. This book does not explore all the possibilities provided by Swift for initialization. For more information, visit our website and follow the links for this chapter.

Deinitialization

There is a counterpart of the initialization process called *Deinitialization*. Despite its name, this process is not directly related to the initialization process but rather to the ARC system. ARC, as we studied previously in this chapter, is an automatic system adopted by Swift to manage memory. Letting the system manage the memory and take care of removing the objects our program doesn't need anymore presents a huge advantage, but it also means that we do not always know when an object is going to be removed. There are times when an object is using resources that have to be closed, information that has to be stored, or we just have to report to other objects that the object is not available anymore. Swift offers the **deinit** method to execute any last-minute instructions we need before the object is erased from memory.

```
class Item {
   var quantity = 0.0
   var name = "Not defined"
   var price = 0.0
   deinit {
      print("this instance was erased")
   }
}
var purchase: Item? = Item()
purchase = nil
```

Listing 3-129: Declaring a deinitializer

The code of Listing 3-129 defines a simple class with a deinitializer. The object is created and assigned to an optional variable. Right after that, the **nil** value is assigned to the same variable to erase the reference and test the **deinit** method. In this example, we just print a message on the console. Deinitialization is usually required for complex objects in charge of managing files or other resources, but the declaration of the **deinit** method is the same.

3.6 Protocols

The two main characteristics of classes and objects are the capacity to encapsulate data and functionality and the possibility to improve code through inheritance. This introduced a huge advantage over previous paradigms and turned Object-Oriented Programming into the standard. But that changed with the introduction of structures in Swift. Swift's structures not only can encapsulate data and functionality, just like objects, but thanks to the adoption of protocols they can also share code. Figure 3-6 illustrates the differences between these two paradigms.

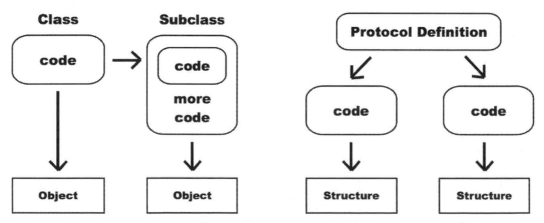

Figure 3-6: Object-Oriented Programming versus Protocol-Oriented Programming

Swift Paradigm

In OOP, the code is implemented inside a class and then objects are created from that class. If we need to create objects with additional functionality, we define a subclass that inherits the code from the superclass and adds some of its own. Protocols offer a slightly different approach. The properties and methods we want the structures to have in common are defined in the protocol and then implemented by the structures' definitions. This lets us associate different structures together through a common pattern. The code implemented by each structure is unique, but they follow a blueprint set by the protocol. If we know that a structure uses a protocol, we can always be sure that besides its own definitions, it will also include the properties and methods defined by the protocol. In addition, protocols can be extended to provide their own implementations of the properties and methods we want the structures to have in common, allowing the paradigm to completely replace classes and objects and offer a more intuitive way to create our programs.

IMPORTANT: The Swift paradigm is built from the combination of structures and protocols, but protocols may also be adopted by enumerations and classes. For instance, Objective-C and the frameworks programmed in this language use protocols to offer a programming pattern called *Delegation*. We will study how to conform to protocols from classes and how to implement delegation later in this chapter.

The Basics: When a data type adopts a protocol, we say that the data type *conforms* to that protocol.

Definition of Protocols

Protocols are defined with the **protocol** keyword followed by the name and the list of properties and methods between braces. No values or statements are assigned or declared inside a protocol, only the names and the corresponding types; the structure that conforms to the protocol is in charge of the implementation. Because of this, methods are defined as always, but they omit the braces and the statements, and properties have to include the **get** and **set** keywords between braces to indicate whether they are read-only properties, or we can read and also assign values to them (see Listing 3-38 for an example of getters and setters). The adoption of the protocol by the structure is declared including the protocol's name after the structure's name separated by a colon, as shown in the following example.

```
protocol Printer {
   var name: String { get set }
   func printdescription()
}
struct Employees: Printer {
   var name: String
   var age: Int
   func printdescription() {
      print("Description: \(name) \(age)")
   }
}
let employee1 = Employees(name: "John", age: 32)
employee1.printdescription()   // "Description: John 32"
```

Listing 3-130: Defining protocols

The protocol is only a blueprint; it tells the structure what properties and methods are required, but the structure has to provide its own implementations. In the example of Listing 3-

130, we define a protocol called **Printer** that includes the **name** property and the **printdescription()** method. The **Employees** structure defined next conforms to this protocol, and along with the protocol's property and method it also implements its own property called **age**. Although this property was not defined in the protocol, we can read it inside the **printdescription()** method and print its value.

The advantage of this practice is evident when structures of different types conform to the same protocol, as shown in the following example.

```
protocol Printer {
    var name: String { get set }
    func printdescription()
}
struct Employees: Printer {
    var name: String
    var age: Int
    func printdescription() {
        print("Description: \(name) \(age)")
    }
}
struct Offices: Printer {
    var name: String
    var employees: Int
    func printdescription() {
        print("Description: \(name) \(employees)")
    }
}
let employee1 = Employees(name: "John", age: 32)
let office1 = Offices(name: "Mail", employees: 2)
office1.printdescription()   // "Description: Mail 2"
```

Listing 3-131: Defining multiple structures that conform to the same protocol

Although the structures created in Listing 3-131 from the **Employees** and **Offices** definitions are different (they have different properties), they both conform to the **Printer** protocol and provide their own implementation of the **printdescription()** method. The common functionality defined by the protocol assures us that no matter what type of structure we are working with, it will have an implementation of the **printdescription()** method.

 IMPORTANT: When a structure conforms to a protocol, it has to implement its properties and methods. If you forget to implement any property or method defined in the protocol, Xcode will show you an error. If you need to declare them as optionals, you can prefix them with the **optional** keyword. Properties and methods declared as optionals do not have to be implemented by the class that conforms to the protocol (they can be implemented only when we need them). At this moment, protocols in Swift have to be converted to Objective-C protocols prefixing the definition with the **@objc** attribute to be able to support optionals.

Protocols not only act as blueprints, they are also considered to be data types. We can treat a structure as if it is of the data type of the protocol it conforms to. This lets us associate structures by their common functionality.

```
let employee1 = Employees(name: "John", age: 32)
let office1 = Offices(name: "Mail", employees: 2)
```

```
var list: [Printer] = [employee1, office1]
for element in list {
   element.printdescription()
}
```

Listing 3-132: Using protocols as data types

Listing 3-132 uses the same protocol and structures defined in the previous example, but this time it stores the instances in an array. The type of the array was defined as **Printer**, which means the array may contain structures of any type as long as they conform to the **Printer** protocol. Because of this, no matter the element's data type (**Employees** or **Offices**) we know that they always have an implementation of the **name** property and the **printdescription()** method.

Because protocols are data types, we can use them as any other type, define variables, send and receive them from functions, etc. The following example declares a function that returns a value of type **Printer**.

```
func getFile(type: Int) -> Printer {
   var data: Printer!
   switch type {
      case 1:
         data = Employees(name: "John", age: 32)
      case 2:
         data = Offices(name. "Mail", employees: 2)
      default:
         break
   }
   return data
}
let file = getFile(type: 1)
file.printdescription()  // "Description: John 32"
```

Listing 3-133: Returning values of a protocol data type

The **getFile()** function of Listing 3-133 creates an instance of a structure depending on the value received. If the **type** parameter is equal to 1, it returns an instance of **Employees**, but if the value is equal to 2, it returns an instance of **Offices**. But because the value returned by the function is of type **Printer** we know it will always include the **printdescription()** method.

When we process a structure as a protocol type, we can only access the properties and methods defined by the protocol. If we need to access the properties and methods defined by the structure, we have to cast it using the **is** and **as** operators studied before (see Listing 3-121).

```
let employee1 = Employees(name: "John", age: 32)
let office1 = Offices(name: "Mail", employees: 2)

var list: [Printer] = [employee1, office1]
for element in list {
   if element is Employees {
      let employee = element as! Employees
      print(employee.age)  // "32"
   }
   element.printdescription()
}
```

Listing 3-134: Accessing the properties defined in the Employees *structure*

Once we cast the element to the original data type, we can access its own specific properties and methods. In Listing 3-134, we check the type of the element with the **is** operator, and if the element is of type **Employees**, we cast it with the **as!** operator and read its **age** property.

 Do It Yourself: The last three examples use the protocol and structures defined in Listing 3-131. Copy the definitions of Listing 3-131 in your Playground file and add the code of the example you want to try.

Swift Protocols

The Swift language makes use of protocols extensively. Almost every API includes protocols that define common features and behaviour for their data types, including enumerations, structures and classes. But there are also important protocols defined in the Swift standard library that we can use to improve our custom data types. The following are some of the protocols provided by Swift to define basic behavior.

Equatable—This protocol defines a data type which values can be compared with other values of the same type using the operators == and !=.

Comparable—This protocol defines a data type which values can be compared with other values of the same type using the operators >, <, >=, and <=.

Numeric—This protocol defines a data type that only works with values that can participate in arithmetic operations.

Hashable—This protocol defines a data type that provides the hash value required for the value to be included in sets and as index of dictionaries.

CaseIterable—This protocol defines a data type, usually an enumeration without associated values, that provides a property called **allCases** that contains the collection of all the cases included in the type.

These protocols are part of elemental processes performed by the system and the Swift language. For example, when we compare two values with the == or != operators, the system checks whether the values conform to the **Equatable** protocol and then calls a type method in the values' data types to compare them and solve the condition (true or false, depending on whether the values are equal or not). Because these operations are fairly common, by default, Swift primitive data types conform to the **Equatable** protocol and implement its methods, but we can also implement them in our own data types to compare their values. For this purpose, we have to declare that the data type conforms to the protocol and implement the methods required by it. The **Equatable** protocol requires only one method called == to check for equality (the system infers that if two values are not equal, they are different, and therefore the method for the != operator is optional). This method must have a name equal to the operator (==), receive the two values we have to compare, and return a Boolean value to communicate the result of the comparison. For instance, we can make our **Employees** structure conform to the **Equatable** protocol and implement a method with the name == to be able to compare two different instances of the same structure.

```
struct Employees: Equatable {
   var name: String
   var age: Int
   static func == (value1: Employees, value2: Employees) -> Bool {
      return value1.name == value2.name
   }
}
```

```
let employee1 = Employees(name: "George", age: 32)
let employee2 = Employees(name: "George", age: 55)

if employee1 == employee2 {
   print("Equal")   // "Equal"
} else {
   print("Different")
}
```

Listing 3-135: Conforming to the Equatable *protocol*

In this example, we compare the values of the **name** properties and therefore the structures are going to be equal when the names of the employees are equal. If what we want is to compare each of the properties in the structure, then we can omit the method. When we conform to the **Equatable** protocol, the compiler automatically generates the method for us to compare all the values of the structure (in this case, **name** and **age**).

```
struct Employees: Equatable {
    var name: String
    var age: Int
}
let employee1 = Employees(name: "George", age: 32)
let employee2 = Employees(name: "George", age: 55)

if employee1 == employee2 {
    print("Equal")
} else {
    print("Different")   // "Different"
}
```

Listing 3-136: Letting the compiler create the protocol methods for us

Because we did not declare the **==** method in the example of Listing 3-136, the system creates the method for us and compares the values of both properties. As a result, the objects are considered to be different (the names are the same, but the ages are different).

Of course, we could have compared the properties directly (**employee1.name == employee2.name**) but being able to compare the objects instead simplifies the code and allow us to use our structures (or objects) in APIs that require the values to be comparable. For example, when we created a generic function earlier in this chapter, we could not perform any operations on the values received by the function (see Listing 3-12). Because the data type we use in those functions is generic (it can be turned into any other data type), Swift is incapable of knowing the capabilities of the data type and therefore Xcode will return an error if we try to perform operations on the values, but we can easily change the situation by making the generic type conform to a protocol. This feature is called *type constraint* because it constraints the generic type to a data type with certain capabilities. For instance, the function in the following example receives two generic values, but only of a data type that conforms to the **Equatable** protocol, and therefore we can compare the values inside the function.

```
struct Employees: Equatable {
    var name: String
    var age: Int
}
func compareValues<T: Equatable>(value1: T, value2: T) -> String {
    var message: String!
    if value1 != value2 {
        message = "The values are different"
```

```
    } else {
        message = "The values are equal"
    }
    return message
}
let employee1 = Employees(name: "George", age: 55)
let employee2 = Employees(name: "Robert", age: 55)

let result = compareValues(value1: employee1, value2: employee2)
print(result)   // "The values are different"
```

Listing 3-137: Adding a type constraint to a generic function

As we did before, we let the compiler generate the protocol's function for us, so both properties in the **Employees** structures will be compared. In this case, the ages of the employees are the same (55), but the names are different ("George" and "Robert"), and therefore the system considers the structures to be different.

Another protocol used as a type constraint is **Numeric**. This protocol determines that the data types of the values received by the function or method have to support arithmetic operations.

```
func calculateResult<T: Numeric>(value1: T, value2: T) {
    print(value1 + value2)   // 7.5
}
calculateResult(value1: 3.5, value2: 4)
```

Listing 3-138: Using the Numeric *protocol to set a type constraint*

The **calculateResult()** function of Listing 3-138 is a generic function and therefore it can receive any value of any type, but because we set a type constraint with the **Numeric** protocol, the function can only receive values of data types that can participate in arithmetic operations.

Besides comparing for equality with the **Equatable** protocol, we can also compare magnitudes with the **Comparable** protocol. This protocol is similar to **Equatable**, but the system does not offer a default implementation of the type methods, so we have to implement them ourselves. The protocol requires four methods to represent the operations >, <, >= and <=. In the following example, we compare the ages of the employees.

```
struct Employees: Comparable {
    var name: String
    var age: Int

    static func > (value1: Employees, value2: Employees) -> Bool {
        return value1.age > value2.age
    }
    static func < (value1: Employees, value2: Employees) -> Bool {
        return value1.age < value2.age
    }
    static func >= (value1: Employees, value2: Employees) -> Bool {
        return value1.age >= value2.age
    }
    static func <= (value1: Employees, value2: Employees) -> Bool {
        return value1.age <= value2.age
    }
}
let employee1 = Employees(name: "George", age: 32)
let employee2 = Employees(name: "Robert", age: 55)
```

```
if employee1 > employee2 {
    print("\(employee1.name) is older")
} else {
    print("\(employee2.name) is older")   // "Robert is older"
}
```

Listing 3-139: *Conforming to the* Comparable *protocol*

This protocol works in a similar way than the **Equatable** protocol. When we compare two instances of the **Employees** structure, the system calls the corresponding type method and the method returns **true** or **false** according to the values of the **age** properties of each instance. Because in this example the value of **age** in the **employee1** structure is not greater than the value of **age** in the **employee2** structure, we get the message "Robert is older".

Another useful protocol is **Hashable**. Every time we include a structure or an object in a set or use them as the index of a dictionary, the system requires the data type to provide a hash value that can be used to uniquely identify each item. This is a random integer that is created based on the values of the properties. The function of the **Hashable** protocol is to define properties and methods to handle this value. Most of the data types defined by Swift conform to this protocol and that is why we do not have any problems when including these values in a set or as the index of dictionaries, but for custom structures and objects we have to provide the hash value ourselves. Fortunately, as well as with the **Equatable** protocol, if we do not need a specific property to be used to create the hash value, we just have to conform to the protocol and the system creates the value for us. The following example makes the **Employees** structure conform to the **Hashable** protocol, so we can include the instances in a set.

```
struct Employees: Hashable {
    var name: String
    var age: Int
}
let employee1 = Employees(name: "John", age: 32)
let employee2 = Employees(name: "Robert", age: 55)

let list: Set<Employees> = [employee1, employee2]
for item in list {
    print(item.name)
}
```

Listing 3-140: *Conforming to the* Hashable *protocol*

Hash values are random integers but are created based on the values of the properties. If we just conform to the protocol, the system used the values of all the properties in the instance to create it, but we can declare a specific property to be included by implementing a method defined by the protocol. The protocol defines a method to set the value and a property to read it.

hashValue—This property returns the instance's hash value. It is of type **Int**.

hash(into: inout Hasher)—This method defines the properties that are going to be included in the hasher to create the hash value.

To calculate the hash value, the Swift standard library includes a structure called **Hasher**. This is the structure received by the **hash(into:)** method and it contains a method called **combine()** to tell to the hasher which properties should be fed to the hasher to create the value. The following example illustrates how to implement the **hash(into:)** method and call the **combine()** method on the hasher to create a hash value from the **name** property.

```
struct Employees: Hashable {
    var name: String
    var age: Int
    func hash(into hasher: inout Hasher) {
        hasher.combine(name)
    }
}
let employee = Employees(name: "George", age: 32)
print(employee.hashValue)   // e.g., -7722685913545470055
```

Listing 3-141: Defining our own hash value

At the end of the code of Listing 3-141, we print the value of the **hashValue** property. Because the resulting value is always an integer that is calculated randomly every time the app is executed, we won't notice any difference from when both properties were used to create it, but this procedure may be useful for applications that manage sensitive information or share data online.

The last protocol mentioned above is called **CaseIterable**. This is a simple protocol that defines a property called **allCases** to store a collection with all the cases in an enumeration. Again, the system automatically initializes this property, so all we have to do is to declare that the enumeration conforms to the protocol. In the following example, we define an enumeration with three cases and then iterate through the collection in the **allCases** property to print their names.

```
enum Departments: CaseIterable {
    case mail
    case marketing
    case managing
}
var message = ""
for department in Departments.allCases {
    message += "\(department) "
}
print(message)   // "mail marketing managing "
```

Listing 3-142: Conforming to the CaseIterable protocol

Extensions

Protocols only define the properties and methods that the data types are going to have in common, but they do not include any implementation. However, we can implement properties and methods that will be common to all the data types that conform to the protocol by taking advantage of a feature of the Swift language called *extensions*. Extensions are special declarations that add functionality to an existent data type. We can use them with structures, enumerations, and classes, but they are particularly useful with protocols because this is the way protocols can provide their own functionality. The syntax includes the **extension** keyword followed by the name of the data type we want to extend. The following example recreates the **Printer** protocol we used in previous examples and extends it with a method called **printdescription()**.

```
protocol Printer {
    var name: String { get set }
}
```

```swift
extension Printer {
    func printdescription() {
        print("The name is \(name)")
    }
}
struct Employees: Printer {
    var name: String
    var age: Int
}
struct Offices: Printer {
    var name: String
    var employees: Int
}
let employee1 = Employees(name: "John", age: 45)
let office1 = Offices(name: "Mail", employees: 2)

office1.printdescription()   // "The name is Mail"
```

Listing 3-143: Extending the protocol

In the example of Listing 3-143, we define a **Printer** protocol with just the **name** property and then extend it to include a common implementation of the **printdescription()** method. Now, the **Employees** and **Offices** structures in our example share the same implementation and produce the same result when their **printdescription()** methods are executed.

As we mentioned, extensions are not only available for protocols but also for any other data type. We can use them to extend structures, enumerations, or classes. This is particularly useful when we do not have access to the definitions of the data types and we need to add some functionality (like when they are part of a library or framework). In the following example, we extend the **Int** structure to provide a method that prints a description of its value.

```swift
extension Int {
    func printdescription() {
        print("The number is \(self)")
    }
}
let number = 25
number.printdescription()   // "The number is 25"
```

Listing 3-144: Extending other data types

The **Int** type is a structure defined in the Swift standard library. We cannot modify its definition, but we can extend it to add more functionality. In this last example, we add a method called **printdescription()** to print a message with the current value (notice the use of the **self** keyword to refer to the instance). This method is not included in the original definition, but it is now available for our code.

Delegates

As we have already seen, a structure can also be assigned to another structure's property. For example, we could have an instance of a structure called **Employees** with a property that contains an instance of a structure called **Offices** to store information about the office where the employee works. This opens the door to new programming patterns where structures adopt different roles. The most useful pattern is called *delegation*. A structure or object delegates responsibility for the execution of certain tasks to another structure or object.

```
struct Salary {
   func showMoney(name: String, money: Double) {
      print("The salary of \(name) is \(money)")
   }
}
struct Employees {
   var name: String
   var money: Double

   var delegate: Salary

   func generatereport() {
      delegate.showMoney(name: name, money: money)
   }
}
let salary = Salary()
var employee1 = Employees(name: "John", money: 45000, delegate: salary)

employee1.generatereport()   // "The salary of John is 45000.0"
```

Listing 3-145: Delegating tasks

The **Employees** structure of Listing 3-145 contains three properties. The properties **name** and **money** are in charge of the employee's data, while the **delegate** property stores the instance of the **Salary** structure in charge of printing that data. The code creates the **Salary** instance first and then uses it to create the **Employees** instance. When we call the **generatereport()** method on the **employee1** structure at the end, the method calls the **showmoney()** method on **delegate**, effectively delegating the task of printing the data to this structure.

This pattern presents two problems. First, the structure that is delegating has to know the data type of the structure that is going to become the delegate (in our example, the **delegate** property had to be declared of type **Salary**). Following this approach, not every structure can be a delegate, only the ones specified in the definition (only structures of type **Salary** can be delegates of structures of type **Employee**). The second problem is related to how we know which are the properties and methods that the delegate has to implement. If the structure is too complex or is taken from a library, we could forget to implement some methods or properties and get an error when the structure tries to access them. Both problems are solved by protocols. Instead of declaring a specific structure as the delegate, we define a protocol and declare the **delegate** property to be of that type, as shown in the following example.

```
protocol SalaryProtocol {
   func showMoney(name: String, money: Double)
}
struct Salary: SalaryProtocol {
   func showMoney(name: String, money: Double) {
      print("The salary of \(name) is \(money)")
   }
}
struct Employees {
   var name: String
   var money: Double

   var delegate: SalaryProtocol

   func generatereport() {
      delegate.showMoney(name: name, money: money)
   }
}
```

Swift Paradigm

```
let salary = Salary()
let employee1 = Employees(name: "John", money: 45000, delegate: salary)

employee1.generatereport()   // "The salary of John is 45000.0"
```

Listing 3-146: Delegating with protocols

The advantage of protocols is that we can use structures of different types to perform the task. It doesn't matter what type they are as long as they conform to the delegate's protocol and implement its properties and methods. For example, we could create two different structures to print the data of our last example and assign to the delegate one instance or another depending on what we want to achieve at that particular time.

```
protocol SalaryProtocol {
    func showMoney(name: String, money: Double)
}
struct Salary: SalaryProtocol {
    func showMoney(name: String, money: Double) {
        print("The salary of \(name) is \(money)")
    }
}
struct BasicSalary: SalaryProtocol {
    func showMoney(name: String, money: Double) {
        if money > 40000 {
            print("Salary is over the minimum")
        } else {
            print("The salary of \(name) is \(money)")
        }
    }
}
struct Employees {
    var name: String
    var money: Double
    var delegate: SalaryProtocol

    func generatereport() {
        delegate.showMoney(name: name, money: money)
    }
}
let salary = Salary()
var employee1 = Employees(name: "John", money: 45000, delegate: salary)

employee1.delegate = BasicSalary()
employee1.generatereport()   // "Salary is over the minimum"
```

Listing 3-147: Using different delegates

The **BasicSalary** structure added in Listing 3-147 conforms to the **SalaryProtocol** protocol and implements its **showMoney()** method, but instead of printing a single message it produces two different results depending on the current employee's salary. The output produced by the execution of the **generatereport()** method now depends on the type of structure we previously assigned to the **delegate** property.

 The Basics: Swift proposes a new paradigm that integrates structures with protocols, but most of the frameworks provided by Apple are still programmed in Objective-C using classes. The delegate pattern is extensively used with classes in these frameworks to communicate objects and make them work together. Later, we will see more examples of their application in practical situations.

Chapter 4
Frameworks

4.1 iOS SDK

The programming tools studied in previous chapters are not enough to build a useful application. Creating an app requires accessing intricate features and technologies and also performing complex tasks that usually involve hundreds or sometimes thousands of lines of code. Because the tasks are similar in every application, developers usually have to program the same code over and over again. Considering this situation, systems always provide pre-programmed code that perform common tasks, allowing developers to focus on more meaningful goals. These pieces of code (classes, structures, etc.) are organized according to their purpose in frameworks.

Apple has been building frameworks to help developers create professional applications since the production of the first personal computer. These frameworks were developed in different languages and through a long period of time, resulting in a very diverse set of tools, with old and new frameworks that sometimes overlap and even replace one another. They conform what is now known as the iOS SDK (Software Development Kit) that is included in the package we get along with Xcode.

What the frameworks do is to give us definitions of structures and classes that we instantiate to get the blocks of code our application needs to work. To learn how to program applications, we have to learn what these frameworks provide and how to implement them in our code.

 IMPORTANT: In this chapter, we will study basic aspects of some of the frameworks that you will use extensively in your applications. We only explain the features that are considered essential for app development and those that you need to know to understand the rest of the examples of this book. For a complete list, read the official references at **developer.apple.com/reference** or visit our website and follow the links for this chapter. As recommended in previous chapters, if you find any of this information difficult to understand, feel free to give it a quick glance and come back later when you find them applied in more practical situations.

Importing Frameworks

The standard libraries included with the Swift language are automatically loaded for us, but when our code requires the use of external frameworks we have to indicate it to the system. This is done by adding the **import** instruction at the beginning of each file followed by the name of the framework we want to include (e.g., **import Foundation**). Once the framework is imported, it is automatically included in our file, giving us access to all the structures, classes, functions and any of the values defined in its code.

4.2 Foundation

Foundation is probably one of the first frameworks provided by Apple. It was written in Objective-C and developed by Steve Jobs's second company NeXT. The framework was created to manage basic tasks but also to store data. Data storage is actually one of its most important functions. Foundation provides its own data types (structures and classes) to store numbers and strings of characters, to create arrays and dictionaries, and even a primary class called **NSObject** with basic behaviour that every other class inherits from. Most of these definitions are now obsolete, replaced by Swift's data types, but others remain useful, as we will see next.

More Standard Functions

No matter the language, there are simple operations that are always required by any program. The codes to perform tasks such as calculate the power of a number or generate a random value were always provided through elemental libraries. Objective-C took advantage of these libraries and Swift is no exception, but the language makes them available through diverse paths. Some functions are provided by the Swift's standard library, as we have seen in Chapter 2, while others are loaded from old libraries by frameworks like Foundation. The libraries automatically loaded by the Foundation framework include generic functions that we can use to perform basic operations. The following are the most frequently used.

pow(Float, Float)—This function returns the result of raising the first value to the power of the second value. The attributes may be numbers of type `Float` or `Double`.

sqrt(Float)—This function returns the square root of the value of its attribute. The attribute may be a number of type `Float` or `Double`.

log(Float)—This function returns the natural logarithm of the value of its attribute. Other related functions are `log2()`, `log10()`, `log1p()`, and `logb()`. The attribute may be a number of type `Float` or `Double`.

sin(Float)—This function returns the sine of the value of its attribute. Other related functions are `asin()`, `sinh()`, and `asinh()`. The attribute may be a number of type `Float` or `Double`.

cos(Float)—This function returns the cosine of the value of its attribute. Other related functions are `acos()`, `cosh()`, and `acosh()`. The attribute may be a number of type `Float` or `Double`.

tan(Float)—This function returns the tangent of the value of its attribute. Other related functions are `atan()`, `atan2()`, `tanh()`, and `atanh()`. The attribute may be a number of type `Float` or `Double`.

The application of these functions is straightforward, as shown in the following example.

```
import Foundation

let square = sqrt(4.0)
let power = pow(2.0, 2.0)
let maximum = max(square, power)

print("The maximum value is \(maximum)")   // "The maximum value is 4.0"
```

Listing 4-1: Applying math functions

The first thing we do in the code of Listing 4-1 is to import the Foundation framework. After this, we can implement any of the tools defined inside the framework, including the generic functions introduced before. This example gets the square root of 4.0, calculates 2.0 to the power of 2.0, and then compares the results using the `max()` function from the Swift's standard library.

Strings

Swift data types usually overwrite old data types defined in Objective-C. One of these data types is `String`. There is a class in the Foundation framework called `NSString` that was used to store and manage strings in codes programmed in Objective-C. The `String` structure adopts most of its functionality, turning the class obsolete, but because Swift has to coexist with old frameworks, **NSString** objects are still required in some circumstances. The **NSString** class includes several Initializers to create these objects. The one usually implemented in Swift takes an attribute called **string** with the string of characters we want to assign to the object.

```
import Foundation

var text: NSString = NSString(string: "Hello")
```

Listing 4-2: Creating an NSString *object*

If we already have a **String** value in our code, we can cast it into an **NSString** object with the **as** operator.

```
import Foundation

var text = "Hello World"
var newText = text as NSString
```

Listing 4-3: Casting a String *value into an* NSString *object*

As we mentioned, most of the properties and methods defined in the **NSString** class are available from **String** values. This also includes some of its initializers. For instance, the following is a very useful initializer we can use to format strings.

String(format: String, **arguments:** Array)—This initializer creates a string from the string provided by the **format** attribute and the array of values provided by the **arguments** attribute. The **format** attribute is a template used to create the string, and the **arguments** attribute is an array with the values we want to include in the string.

Although we can incorporate values into strings with string interpolation (see Chapter 2, Listing 2-23), there are some limitations, especially when working with old frameworks. The **String(format:, arguments:)** initializer is used to create more complex formats. The initializer takes a string and replaces the placeholders inside the string with values from the array. The placeholders are declared with the % symbol followed by a character that represents the type of value we want to include. For example, if we want the placeholder to be replaced by an integer, we have to use the characters %d.

```
import Foundation

var age = 44
var mytext = String(format: "My age is %d", arguments: [age])
```

Listing 4-4: Creating a formatted string

The code of Listing 4-4 replaces the %d characters in the string with the value of the **age** variable and stores the resulting string in the **mytext** variable. The final string reads "My age is 44".

There are different placeholders available. The most frequently used are %d for integers, %f for floating-point numbers, and %@ for objects and structures. We can use any of these characters and as many times as we need. All we have to remember is to select the characters according to the type of value we want to insert and respect the order.

```
import Foundation

var age = 44
var mytext = String(format: "My %@ is %d", arguments: ["age", age])
```

Listing 4-5: Formatting a string with multiple values

The code of Listing 4-5 replaces the placeholders in the string with two values: a string and an integer. The string stored in the **mytext** variable will be "My age is 44". This is straightforward and very similar to what we would obtain with string interpolation, but there are things we cannot do with other methods. For example, there is a syntax for the %f placeholder that may be useful when working with floating-point numbers. This placeholder can include the number of decimal digits we want to consider. For example, the characters %.2f are replaced by a **Float** or a **Double** value with only two digits after the decimal point.

```
import Foundation

var length = 12.3472
var mytext = String(format: "%.2f meters", arguments: [length])   // 12.35
```

Listing 4-6: Formatting a string with floating-point values

As we have seen in Chapter 3, **String** structures can handle strings very efficiently, but there are still a few properties and methods defined in the **NSString** class that can simplify our work.

capitalized—This property returns a string with the first letter of every word in uppercase.

length—This property returns the number of characters in the string of an **NSString** object (If the string was created as a **String** value, we should use the **count** property instead).

contains(String**)**—This method returns a Boolean value that indicates whether or not the string specified by the attribute was found inside the original string.

compare(String, **options:** CompareOptions, **range:** Range?, **locale:** Locale?**)**—This method compares the original string with the string provided by the first attribute and returns an enumeration of type **ComparisonResult** with a value corresponding to the lexical order of the strings. The **orderedSame** value is returned when the strings are equal, the **orderedAscending** value is returned when the original string precedes the value of the first attribute, and the **orderedDescending** value is returned when the original string follows the value of the first attribute. The **options** attribute is a property of the **CompareOptions** structure. The properties available are **caseInsensitive** (it considers lowercase and uppercase letters to be the same), **literal** (performs a byte-to-byte comparison), **diacriticInsensitive** (ignores diacritic marks such as the visual stress on vowels), **widthInsensitive** (ignores the width difference in characters that occurs in some languages), and **forcedOrdering** (the comparison is forced to return **orderedAscending** or **orderedDescending** values when the strings are equivalent but not strictly equal). The **range** attribute defines a range that determines the portion of the original string we want to compare. Finally, the **locale** attribute is a **Locale** structure that defines localization (we will study internationalization and localization in Chapter 28). Except for the first attribute, the rest of the attributes are optional.

caseInsensitiveCompare(String**)**—This method compares the original string with the string provided by the attribute. It works exactly like the **compare()** method but with the option **caseInsensitiveSearch** set by default.

These methods may be used to search for a value inside a string, but the **NSString** class offers a more specific method to do it.

range(of: String, **options:** CompareOptions, **range:** Range?, **locale:** Locale?)—This method searches for the string specified by the first attribute and returns a range to indicate where the string was found or **nil** in case of failure. The **options** attribute is a property of the **CompareOptions** structure. The properties available for this method are the same we have for the **compare()** method, with the difference that we can specify three more: **backwards** (searches from the end of the string), **anchored** (matches characters only at the beginning or the end, not in the middle), and **regularExpression** (searches with a regular expression). The **range** attribute defines a range that determines the portion of the original string where we want to search. Except for the first attribute, the rest of the attributes are optional.

We can call these methods from **String** values, but because they are bridged to **NSString** methods, we still have to import the Foundation framework to be able to use them. Some of them perform operations that are similar to those offered by the **String** structure, but with these methods we get a more comprehensive result. For example, the **compare()** method compares two strings the same way we do with the **==** operator, but the value returned is not just **true** or **false**.

```
import Foundation

var string = "Orange"
var search = "Apple"

var result = string.compare(search)
switch result {
   case .orderedSame:
      print("String and Search are equal")
   case .orderedDescending:
      print("String follows Search")
   case .orderedAscending:
      print("String precedes Search")
}
```

Listing 4-7: Comparing String *values*

The **compare()** method takes a string, compares it to the original string, and returns a value of the **ComparisonResult** enumeration type to indicate the order. The **ComparisonResult** enumeration contains three values: **orderedSame**, **orderedDescending**, and **orderedAscending**. After comparing the values of the **string** and **search** variables in Listing 4-7, the **result** variable contains one of these values according to the lexical order of the strings. In this example, the value "Orange" assigned to **string** is bigger (follows) the value "Apple" assigned to **search**, so the value returned is **orderedDescending** (the order is descending from **string** to **search**). We check this value with a **switch** statement and print a message according to the result.

The **compare()** method implemented in Listing 4-7 and the **==** operator studied in Chapter 2 consider a lowercase string different than an uppercase string. Adding an option to the **compare()** method we can compare two strings without considering lower or uppercase letters.

```
import Foundation

var string = "Orange"
var search = "ORANGE"
```

```
var result = string.compare(search, options: .caseInsensitive)
switch result {
   case .orderedSame:
      print("String and Search are equal")
   case .orderedDescending:
      print("String follows Search")
   case .orderedAscending:
      print("String precedes Search")
}
```

Listing 4-8: Comparing String *values with options*

The strings stored in the **string** and **search** variables in Listing 4-8 are different, but because of the **caseInsensitive** option, they are considered equal. This type of comparison is very common, which is why the class includes the **caseInsensitiveCompare()** method that all it does is call the **compare()** method with the **caseInsensitive** option already set.

Despite this being the most common scenario, we can perform more precise comparison by providing a range to the **compare()** method. The option specifies the range of characters in the original string we want to compare.

```
import Foundation

var string = "905-525-6666"
var search = "905"
var start = string.startIndex
var end = string.index(of: "-")

if let endIndex = end {
   let result = string.compare(search, options: .caseInsensitive, range:
start..<endIndex)
   if result == .orderedSame {
      print("String and Search are equal")
   } else {
      print("String and Search are different")
   }
}
```

Listing 4-9: Comparing only a range of characters

The example of Listing 4-9 compares only the initial characters of a string to check the area code of a phone number. The code defines a range that goes from the first character of the **string** variable to the position before the – character. This range is provided to the **compare()** method and in consequence the value of the **search** variable is compared only against the first three characters of the **string** variable.

Besides comparing strings we can also search for strings using the **range()** method. This method searches for a string inside another string and returns a range that determines where the string was found.

```
import Foundation

var string = "The Suitcase is Black"
var search = "black"

var range = string.range(of: search, options: .caseInsensitive)
if let rangeToReplace = range {
   string.replaceSubrange(rangeToReplace, with: "Red")
```

```
} else {
    print("Not Found")
}
```

Listing 4-10: Searching and replacing characters in a string

The **range()** method returns an optional value that contains the range where the string was found or **nil** in case of failure. In Listing 4-10, we search for the value of the **search** variable inside the **string** variable and check the optional value returned. When we have a range to work with (which means that the value was found) we use it to call the **replaceSubrange()** method (introduced in Chapter 3). This method replaces the characters inside the range by the string "Red".

Ranges

Although Swift includes range structures to store ranges of values, some frameworks programmed in Objective-C still implement an old Foundation class called **NSRange**. The **NSRange** class is slightly different than the Swift's **Range** structure. Instead of storing the initial and final values of the range, **NSRange** objects store the initial value and the length of the range. The following are the initializers each data type includes to convert one value to another.

NSRange(Range)—This initializer creates an **NSRange** object from a **Range** value.

NSRange(Range, in: String)—This initializer creates an **NSRange** object to represent a **Range** structure with string indexes.

Range(NSRange)—This initializer creates a **Range** structure from an **NSRange** value.

Range(NSRange, in: String)—This initializer creates a **Range** structure to represent an **NSRange** object with string indexes.

The **NSRange** class also includes two properties to retrieve its values: **location** and **length**. The following example initializes an **NSRange** object from a Swift range and prints its values.

```
import Foundation

let range = NSRange(4..<10)
print("Initial: \(range.location)")   // "Initial: 4"
print("Length: \(range.length)")   // "Length: 6"
```

Listing 4-11: Creating and reading an NSRange value

The initializer implemented in this example is for countable ranges. If we work with string indexes, we have to use the initializer defined for strings. This is because the **String** structure works with Unicode characters while **NSString** objects work with a more specific character encoding called *UTF-16*. Working with different character encodings means that the space the characters occupy in memory varies. A range that represents a series of characters in a **String** value may differ from a range that represents the same series of characters in an **NSString** value. To solve this problem, we have to implement the other initializer that includes an additional attribute to show Swift the string the range is associated with.

```
import Foundation

let text = "Hello World"
if let start = text.index(of: "W") {
    let newRange = NSRange(start..., in: text)
    print("Initial: \(newRange.location)")   // "Initial: 6"
    print("Length: \(newRange.length)")   // "Length: 5"
}
```

Listing 4-12: Converting a range of string indexes

The example of Listing 4-12 gets the index of the letter W, creates a range from this index to the end of the string, and converts the range into an **NSRange** value with the appropriate **NSRange** initializer. At the end, we just print the values of the **NSRange** object on the console, but these types of values are usually required by old frameworks, as we will see later.

Numbers

Foundation offers a class called **NSNumber** to represent and store different types of numbers. This was, along with the primitive types offered by the C language, the default tool to store and work with numbers before Swift. With the inclusion of the Swift's primitive types, the use of this class is no longer necessary, but there are a few old frameworks programmed in Objective-C that still require these types of values. To create an **NSNumber** object from a Swift data type, we have to use the following initializer.

NSNumber(value: Value)—This initializer creates an **NSNumber** object with the value specified by the **value** attribute. The attribute may be a value of any of the data types available in Swift for numbers.

The class also provides properties to perform the opposite operation, getting Swift data types from **NSNumber** objects. The following are the most frequently used.

intValue—This property returns an **Int** value with the object's number.

floatValue—This property returns a **Float** value with the object's number.

doubleValue—This property returns a **Double** value with the object's number.

The following example shows how to create **NSNumber** objects and how to get them back as Swift data types to perform operations.

```
import Foundation

var number = NSNumber(value: 35)
var duplicate = number.doubleValue * 2   // 70
```

Listing 4-13: Working with NSNumber objects

As well as Swift primitive data types, **NSNumber** objects use the maximum number of digits allowed for the type. Every time we print one of these values, all the digits are shown on the screen, including all the decimal digits. Earlier in this chapter we showed how to customize the number of digits presented for a number with a **String** initializer and placeholders (e.g., **%.2f**), but this is not customizable enough. To provide a better alternative, Foundation offers the **NumberFormatter** class. This class allows us to create strings that contain numbers in a specific format. The class offers properties and methods to work with standard formats or create our own.

numberStyle—This property sets or returns a value that determines the style used to format the number. It is an enumeration of type **Style** with the values **none** (default), **decimal**, **currency**, **percent**, **scientific**, and **spellOut**.

roundingMode—This property sets or returns the rounding mode. It is an enumeration of type **RoundingMode** with the values **ceiling**, **floor**, **down**, **up**, **halfEven** (default), **halfDown**, and **halfUp**.

minimumIntegerDigits—This property sets or returns an integer value that determines the minimum number of digits included in the number's integer part.

maximumIntegerDigits—This property sets or returns an integer value that determines the maximum number of digits included in the number's integer part.

minimumFractionDigits—This property sets or returns an integer value that determines the minimum number of digits included after the decimal point.

maximumFractionDigits—This property sets or returns an integer value that determines the maximum number of digits included after the decimal point.

string(from: NSNumber)—This method returns a string that includes the number provided by the **from** attribute in the format specified by the properties of the object.

The default configuration of a **NumberFormatter** object sets the style as **none** and the rounding mode as **halfEven**, which means that the string produced by the **string()** method will be composed of a number with the decimal part rounded to the nearest integer, but we can change this behaviour assigning new values to the object's properties.

```
import Foundation

var money = NSNumber(value: 5.6897)

let format = NumberFormatter()
format.numberStyle = .currency
format.roundingMode = .floor

var price = format.string(from: money)  // $5.68
```

Listing 4-14: Formatting a number to represent money

To format a number, we first have to create the **NumberFormatter** object with the **NumberFormatter()** initializer, then configure its properties, and finally execute the **string()** method to get the formatted number in a string. In the example of Listing 4-14, we create a **NumberFormatter** object and then set its style as **currency** and its rounding mode as **floor**. The number stored in the **money** variable is sent to the **string()** method of this object to get the string in the specified format. The final result is a string with the currency symbol and the number of decimal digits corresponding to the device's configuration. For example, if the device was set in the United States, the string produce by this example will be "$5.68".

If we want to format a number with a specific number of digits, we can take advantage of the **minimumFractionDigits** and **maximumFractionDigits** properties.

```
import Foundation

var money = NSNumber(value: 5.68)

let format = NumberFormatter()
format.numberStyle = .decimal
```

```
format.minimumFractionDigits = 3
format.maximumFractionDigits = 3
var price = format.string(from: money)   // $ 5.680
```

Listing 4-15: Specifying the number of digits

Once the **NumberFormatter** object is created, it can be used to format all the numbers we want. In the following example, we create two strings to represent the price and total price of a transaction. Notice that, to be able to perform operations with the numbers, this time we use Swift data types and convert them to **NSNumber** objects at the end.

```
import Foundation

var money = 5.6897
var total = money * 4

let format = NumberFormatter()
format.numberStyle = .currency
format.roundingMode = .ceiling

var price = format.string(from: NSNumber(value: money))   // $5.69
var result = format.string(from: NSNumber(value: total))   // $22.76
```

Listing 4-16: Formatting multiple values

We can also change the style and the rounding mode to get the format we need. The most common styles are **currency** to represent money, **percent** to represent percentages, and **spellOut** to represent the number in words ("five point six eight nine seven"). The rounding modes used more often are **ceiling**, **floor**, and **halfEven**, to round the last digit up, down, or to the closest integer.

 IMPORTANT: Besides the standard configurations, the **NumberFormatter** class offers multiple properties to set any custom format necessary. For example, instead of relying on the system to provide the symbol for the currency, you can specify it explicitly by assigning a new value to the **currencySymbol** property. To see all the properties available, visit our website and follow the links for this chapter.

With the **NumberFormatter** class, we can round and format the numbers that are going to be shown on the screen, but sometimes the operations performed to get those numbers require a specific number of decimal digits to produce the right result. This is especially true when working with numbers that represent money. The numbers have to be rounded all the way through, usually to only two decimals. Foundation offers the **NSDecimalNumber** and the **NSDecimalNumberHandler** classes to produce and format decimal numbers. The classes include the following initializers.

NSDecimalNumber(value: Value)—This initializer creates an **NSDecimalNumber** object with the value specified by the **value** attribute. The attribute is a value of any of the data types available in Swift for numbers.

NSDecimalNumberHandler(roundingMode: RoundingMode, **scale:** Int16, **raiseOnExactness:** Bool, **raiseOnOverflow:** Bool, **raiseOnUnderflow:** Bool, **raiseOnDivideByZero:** Bool)—This initializer creates an **NSDecimalNumberHandler** object that defines the format and behaviour of an **NSDecimalNumber** object. The **roundingMode** attribute is an enumeration of type **RoundingMode** with the values **plain**, **down**, **up** and **bankers** that define the rounding mode. The **scale** attribute defines the number of digits allowed for the number after the decimal point. The rest of the attributes define what the object should do when it finds problems with the number (exactness, overflow, underflow, or if the number is divided by zero).

Before working with **NSDecimalNumber** objects we have to configure their behaviour with an object of the **NSDecimalNumberHandler** class. This object may be assigned to each **NSDecimalNumber** object through its methods or we can use a type property called **defaultBehavior** to configure the class itself. This way, every object created from that moment on will share the same behaviour. The following example implements this last approach to create two **NSDecimalNumber** objects with the same characteristics.

```
import Foundation

let roundup = NSDecimalNumberHandler(roundingMode: .plain, scale: 2,
raiseOnExactness: false, raiseOnOverflow: false, raiseOnUnderflow: false,
raiseOnDivideByZero: true)
NSDecimalNumber.defaultBehavior = roundup

var money = NSDecimalNumber(value: 35.5761)
var quantity = NSDecimalNumber(value: 3.20)
```

Listing 4-17: Defining the behaviour of the NSDecimalNumber *objects*

The example of Listing 4-17 creates an **NSDecimalNumberHandler** object with the rounding mode defined as **plain**, the scale as **2** (the numbers will not have more than two decimal digits) and configured to only check for errors when the number is divided by zero. Next, we assign this object to the **NSDecimalNumber** class with the property **defaultBehavior**. This type property sets the configuration of the class and therefore all the **NSDecimalNumber** objects created from that moment on will share that behaviour.

Notice that the two **NSDecimalNumber** objects created at the end of Listing 4-17 are not immediately formatted according to the behaviour established by the **NSDecimalNumberHandler** object. This is because the configuration is applied when the numbers are used in operations. The class offers several methods to perform mathematic operations with **NSDecimalNumber** values. The following are the most frequently used.

adding(NSDecimalNumber)—This method adds the number of the object to the number provided by the attribute and returns a new **NSDecimalNumber** object with the result.

subtracting(NSDecimalNumber)—This method subtracts the number provided by the attribute to the number of the object and returns an **NSDecimalNumber** object with the result.

multiplying(by: NSDecimalNumber)—This method multiplies the number of the object times the number of the **by** attribute and returns an **NSDecimalNumber** object with the result.

dividing(by: NSDecimalNumber)—This method divides the number of the object by the number provided by the **by** attribute and returns an **NSDecimalNumber** object with the result.

raising(toPower: NSDecimalNumber)—This method raises the number of the object to the power provided by the **toPower** attribute and returns a new **NSDecimalNumber** object with the result.

multiplying(byPowerOf10: NSDecimalNumber)—This method multiplies the number of the object to the number 10 raised by the number provided by the **byPowerOf10** attribute and returns a new **NSDecimalNumber** object with the result.

The following example shows how to perform an operation on two **NSDecimalNumber** objects. The values are multiplied by the **multiplying()** method and the **NSDecimalNumber** object returned with the result is stored in another variable called **total**. Notice that now the result contains only two decimal values, as specified by the configuration.

```
import Foundation

let roundup = NSDecimalNumberHandler(roundingMode: .plain, scale: 2,
raiseOnExactness: false, raiseOnOverflow: false, raiseOnUnderflow: false,
raiseOnDivideByZero: true)
NSDecimalNumber.defaultBehavior = roundup
var money = NSDecimalNumber(value: 35.5761)
var quantity = NSDecimalNumber(value: 3.20)
var total = money.multiplying(by: quantity)   // 113.84
```

Listing 4-18: Performing operations with NSDecimalNumber *objects*

Do It Yourself: Copy the code of Listing 4-18 in your Playground file. Replace the **multiplying()** method by any of the methods provided by the class to check how they work.

IMPORTANT: An **NSDecimalNumber** object does not prepare the number to be shown to the user. For example, the number 3.20 is shown as 3.2. To show all the digits on the screen, you have to format the value of the **NSDecimalNumber** object with the **NumberFormatter** class.

Dates

Often, multiple structures and classes are implemented together to achieve a common purpose. We have seen this pattern in the classes studied above, and Foundation also uses it to work with dates and times. The framework defines multiple classes and structures to create and process dates, including **Date**, **Calendar**, **DateComponents**, **DateInterval**, **DateFormatter**, **Locale**, and **TimeZone**. The data type that creates the structure to store the actual date is **Date**. The following are some of its initializers.

Date()—This initializer creates a **Date** structure with the system's current date.

Date(timeIntervalSinceNow: TimeInterval**)**—This initializer creates a **Date** structure with a date calculated from the addition of the current date plus the time specified by the **timeIntervalSinceNow** attribute. The attribute is a value of type **TimeInterval** (a type alias of **Double**) that indicates how many seconds the date is from the initial date.

Date(timeInterval: TimeInterval, **since:** Date**)**—This initializer creates a **Date** structure with a date calculated from the addition of the date specified by the **since** attribute plus the time specified by the **timeInterval** attribute. The attribute is a value of type **TimeInterval** (a type alias of **Double**) that indicates how many seconds the date is from the initial date.

The following example shows different ways to initialize a date.

```
import Foundation

var currentdate = Date()
var nextday = Date(timeIntervalSinceNow: 24 * 60 * 60)
var tendays = Date(timeInterval: -10 * 24 * 3600, since: nextday)
```

Listing 4-19: Storing dates with Date *structures*

Frameworks

If the initializer requires an interval, the value is specified in seconds. An easy way to calculate the seconds is multiplying every component. For example, the date for the **nextday** object created in Listing 4-19 is calculated adding 1 day to the current date. The number of seconds in 1 day are calculated multiplying the 24 hours of the day times the 60 minutes in an hour times the 60 seconds in a minute (24 * 60 * 60). There are 86400 seconds in a day, but it is much easier to get them by multiplying the components. For the **tendays** object, we apply the same technique. The initializer used to get this object adds the interval to a specific date (**nextday**). The seconds are calculated by multiplying the components, albeit this time it multiplies the previous result by -10 to get a date 10 days previous to **nextday** (we will see better ways to add components to a date later).

 IMPORTANT: These methods require a value of type **Double** to declare the interval in seconds, but instead of **Double** the framework calls it **TimeInterval**. This is a type alias (an alternative name for an existing type). Once defined, aliases are used exactly like regular data types. To create your own type aliases, you can use the instruction **typealias** (e.g., **typealias myinteger = Int**).

Besides these initializers, the class also includes two type properties that return special dates. These properties produce values that are useful to set limits and order lists, as we will see later.

distantFuture—This type property returns a **Date** structure with a value that represents a date in a distant future.

distantPast—This type property returns a **Date** structure with a value that represents a date in a distant past.

The **Date** structure also includes properties and methods to calculate and compare dates. The following are the most frequently used.

timeIntervalSinceNow—This property returns a **TimeInterval** value representing the difference in seconds between the date in the **Date** structure and the current date.

compare(Date**)**—This method compares the date in the **Date** structure with the date specified by the attribute and returns an enumeration of type **ComparisonResult** with a value corresponding to the temporal order of the dates. The possible values are **orderedSame** (the dates are equal), **orderedAscending** (the date is earlier in time than the value of the attribute), and **orderedDescending** (the date is later in time than the value of the attribute).

timeIntervalSince(Date**)**—This method compares the date in the **Date** structure with the date specified by the attribute and returns the interval between both dates in seconds. The value returned is of type **TimeInterval**.

addingTimeInterval(TimeInterval**)**—This method adds the seconds specified by the attribute to the date in the **Date** structure and returns a new **Date** structure with the result.

addTimeInterval(TimeInterval**)**—This method adds the seconds specified by the attribute to the date in the **Date** structure and stores the result in the same structure.

Comparing dates and calculating the intervals between dates is a constant requirement in app development. The following example compares the current date with a date calculated from a specific number of days. If the resulting date is later in time than the current date, the code prints a message on the console to show the time remaining in seconds.

```
import Foundation

var days = 7

var today = Date()
var event = Date(timeIntervalSinceNow: Double(days) * 24 * 3600)

if today.compare(event) == .orderedAscending {
   let interval = event.timeIntervalSince(today)
   print("We have to wait \(interval) seconds")
}
```

Listing 4-20: Comparing two dates

The dates in **Date** structures are generic and therefore they do not have an associated calendar. This means that to be able to interpret the components in a date (year, month, day, etc.) we have to decide first in the context of which calendar the date is going to be interpreted. The calendar for a date is defined by a structure called **Calendar**. This structure provides properties and methods to process a date according to a specific calendar (Gregorian, Buddhist, Chinese, etc.). To initialize a **Calendar** structure, we have the following initializer and type property.

Calendar(identifier: Identifier**)**—This initializer creates a **Calendar** structure with the calendar specified by the attribute. The **identifier** attribute is a property of a structure called **Identifier** defined inside the **Calendar** structure. The properties available are **gregorian, buddhist, chinese, coptic, ethiopicAmeteMihret, ethiopicAmeteAlem, hebrew, ISO8601, indian, islamic, islamicCivil, japanese, persian, republicOfChina, islamicTabular** and **islamicUmmAlQura**.

current—This type property returns a structure with the current calendar set in the system.

A **Calendar** structure includes the following properties and methods to manage the calendar and also to get and set new dates.

identifier—This property returns the value that identifies the calendar.

locale—This property sets or returns the **Locale** structure used by the **Calendar** structure to process dates. The value by default is the **Locale** structure defined by the system.

timeZone—This property sets or returns the **TimeZone** structure used by the **Calendar** structure to process dates. The value by default is the **TimeZone** structure defined by the system.

dateComponents(Set, from: Date**)**—This method returns a **DateComponents** structure with the components indicated by the first attribute from the date indicated by the **from** attribute. The first attribute is a set with properties of a structure called **Unit** that represent each component. The most frequently used are **year, month, day, hour, minute,** and **second**.

dateComponents(Set, from: Date**, to:** Date**)**—This method returns a **DateComponents** structure with the components indicated by the first attribute, which values represent the difference between the dates specified by the **from** and **to** attributes. The first attribute is a set with properties of a structure called **Unit** that represent each component. The most frequently used are **year, month, day, hour, minute,** and **second**.

date(byAdding: DateComponents, **to:** Date)—This method returns a **Date** structure with the value obtained by adding the components indicated by the **byAdding** attribute to the date indicated by the **to** attribute.

date(from: DateComponents)—This method returns a date created from the components provided by the **from** attribute. The value returned is a **Date** structure.

The **Calendar** structure works along with the **DateComponents** structure to read and return components from a date. The objects created from the **DateComponents** structure include the following properties to read and set the values of the components.

year—This property sets or returns an integer that represents the number of the year.

month—This property sets or returns an integer that represents the number of the month.

day—This property sets or returns an integer that represents the number of the day.

hour—This property sets or returns an integer that represents the number of hours.

minute—This property sets or returns an integer that represents the number of minutes.

second—This property sets or returns an integer that represents the number of seconds.

weekday—This property sets or returns an integer that represents the number of the day in the week. In the Gregorian calendar, the values are assigned from Sunday, starting by 1.

The example of Listing 4-21, next, combines all these elements together to get the year of the current date.

```
import Foundation

var today = Date()
let calendar = Calendar.current
var components = calendar.dateComponents([.year], from: today)
print("The year is \(components.year!)")
```

Listing 4-21: Extracting components from a date

In Listing 4-21, a reference to the calendar set in the system is obtained by calling the **current** property and then the **dateComponents()** method is executed to get the year.

Several components may be fetched at the same time declaring more values in the set. The following example gets the year, month and day of the current date.

```
import Foundation

var today = Date()
let calendar = Calendar.current
var components = calendar.dateComponents([.year, .month, .day], from:
today)
print("Today \(components.day!)-\(components.month!)-
\(components.year!)")
```

Listing 4-22: Extracting multiple components from a date

The **DateComponents** structures are used to retrieve the components of existing dates and also to set the values for new dates. In the following example, a new **Date** structure is created from the values of a **DateComponents** structure.

```
import Foundation

let calendar = Calendar.current
var components = DateComponents()
components.year = 1970
components.month = 8
components.day = 21

var birthday = calendar.date(from: components)   //"Aug 21,1970, 12:00 AM"
```

Listing 4-23: Creating a new date from components

The **date(from:)** method of the **Calendar** structure returns a new date with the values provided by the **DateComponents** structure. The components which values are not explicitly defined take values by default (e.g., 12:00 AM).

Generating a new date demands the use of a specific calendar. For example, in the code of Listing 4-23, the values of the components are declared with the format established by the Gregorian calendar. In this case, we relied on the calendar returned by the system, but if we want to use the same calendar no matter where the app is executed, we have to set it ourselves from the **Calendar** initializer.

```
import Foundation

let id = Calendar.Identifier.gregorian
let calendar = Calendar(identifier: id)

var components = DateComponents()
components.year = 1970
components.month = 8
components.day = 13
var birthday = calendar.date(from: components)
```

Listing 4-24: Using a Gregorian calendar

Declaring a specific calendar is not only recommended when creating new dates but also when calculating dates by adding components, as in the following example.

```
import Foundation

let id = Calendar.Identifier.gregorian
let calendar = Calendar(identifier: id)
var components = DateComponents()
components.day = 120

var today = Date()
var appointment = calendar.date(byAdding: components, to: today)
```

Listing 4-25: Adding components to a date

The **date()** method implemented in Listing 4-25 adds components to a date and returns a new **Date** structure with the result. In this example, the component **day** was set to a value of 120. The **date()** method takes this value and adds it to the date in the **today** structure (the current date).

A common task when working with multiple dates is getting the lapse of time between dates, such as the hours remaining for a process to be finished or the days left to an event. The **Calendar** structure includes a version of the **dateComponents()** method that allows us to compare two dates and get the difference expressed in a specific component.

Frameworks

```
import Foundation

let calendar = Calendar.current
var components = DateComponents()
components.year = 1970
components.month = 8
components.day = 21

var today = Date()
var birthday = calendar.date(from: components)
if let olddate = birthday {
   var components = calendar.dateComponents([.day], from: olddate, to:
today)
   print("Days between dates: \(components.day!)")
}
```

Listing 4-26: Comparing dates

This example calculates the days between a birthday and the current date. The value returned by the **date()** method used to generate the birthday's date returns an optional. If the method is not able to calculate a date from the provided components, the value returned will be **nil**. Because of this, before calculating the days between the dates, we have to unwrap this value. In Listing 4-26, the value of the **birthday** structure is unwrapped and assigned to the **olddate** constant. This date is compared to the current date in the **today** structure and the number of days between the dates is returned and printed on the console.

Another way to specify intervals between dates is with the **DateInterval** structure. This structure allows us to create an interval with **Date** values. The following are its initializers.

DateInterval(start: Date, **end:** Date)—This initializer creates **DateInterval** structure with an interval created from the **Date** values provided by the **start** and **end** attributes.

DateInterval(start: Date, **duration:** TimeInterval)—This initializer creates a **DateInterval** structure with an interval created from the date specified by the **start** attribute and the date calculated from the addition of the time specified by the **duration** attribute.

The **DateInterval** structure also offers the following properties and methods to access the values of the interval.

start—This property sets or returns the initial **Date** of the interval.

end—This property sets or returns the final **Date** of the interval.

duration—This property sets or returns the duration of the interval in seconds.

contains(Date)—This method returns a Boolean value that indicates whether or not the date specified by the attribute is inside the interval.

intersects(DateInterval)—This method returns a Boolean value that indicates if the interval intersects with the interval specified by the attribute.

intersection(with: DateInterval)—This method returns a **DateInterval** value with the interval in which the original interval and the interval provided by the **with** attribute overlap.

A typical use of the **DateInterval** structure is to create an interval from two dates and check if a specific date falls inside the interval, as in the following example.

```
import Foundation

let calendar = Calendar.current

var components = DateComponents()
components.year = 1970
components.month = 8
components.day = 21
var birthday = calendar.date(from: components)

components.year = 2020
components.month = 8
components.day = 21
var future = calendar.date(from: components)

if birthday != nil && future != nil {
   let today = Date()
   let interval = DateInterval(start: birthday!, end: future!)
   if interval.contains(today) {
      print("You still have time")
   }
}
```

Listing 4-27: Finding a date in an interval

The code of Listing 4-27 creates two dates, **birthday** and **future**, and then generates an interval from one date to another. The **contains()** method is used next to check whether the current date is inside the interval or not.

Printing independent components, as we did in previous examples, is not a problem because they are just integer values, but a complete date requires a format that will vary depending on the requirements of the app. For example, sometimes the limited space available on the screen to print the date demands expressing it just with basic values, but in other circumstances the application may require a full description, including the names of the month and the day of the week. Foundation provides the **DateFormatter** class to produce a textual representation of dates and times. The class includes several properties and methods to configure the object and generate the string.

dateStyle—This property sets or returns the style of the date. It is an enumeration of type **Style** with the values **none**, **short**, **medium**, **long**, and **full**.

timeStyle—This property sets or returns the style of the time. It is an enumeration of type **Style** with the values **none**, **short**, **medium**, **long**, and **full**.

dateFormat—This property sets or returns a custom format for the date and time. Its value is a string with characters that specify the position of the components of the date.

monthSymbols—This property returns an array of strings with the names of the months in correlative order (index 0 returns "January", index 1 "February", and so on). Other related properties are **shortMonthSymbols** (returns an abbreviation of the names) and **veryShortMonthSymbols** (returns the initials).

locale—This property sets or returns the **Locale** structure used by the **DateFormatter** object to process the date. The value by default is the **Locale** structure defined by the system.

timeZone—This property sets or returns the **TimeZone** structure used by the **DateFormatter** object to process the date. The value by default is the **TimeZone** structure defined by the system.

Frameworks

string(from: Date)—This method returns a string with the date provided by the **from** attribute in the format specified by the properties of the object.

date(from: String)—This method interprets the value of the **from** attribute as a date and returns a **Date** structure containing the value or **nil** when no date is found in the string.

The process to format a date is simple. The **DateFormatter** object is created first, then the **dateStyle**, **timeStyle**, or **dateFormat** properties are initialized to set the format we want, and the **string()** method is called at the end to get the string.

```
import Foundation

var today = Date()
let formatter = DateFormatter()
formatter.dateStyle = DateFormatter.Style.medium
formatter.timeStyle = DateFormatter.Style.medium

var mydate = formatter.string(from: today) // "Aug 30, 2018, 12:20:59 PM"
```

Listing 4-28: Formatting dates

In the code of Listing 4-28 the style is declared as **medium** for both date and time, but we can specify other values to produce a different result. If only the date or the time are required, we can declare the style **none** for the one we want to hide or leave the property with the value by default, as in the following example.

```
import Foundation

var today = Date()
let formatter = DateFormatter()
formatter.dateStyle = DateFormatter.Style.full
var mydate = formatter.string(from: today) //"Wednesday, August 30, 2018"
```

Listing 4-29: Formatting only the date

The **string()** method in Listing 4-29 returns a string containing the full date without the time (the style for the time was not declared). The full date includes the names of the day and the month. If we want to design our own format, we can take advantage of the **dateFormat** property.

```
import Foundation

var today = Date()
let formatter = DateFormatter()
formatter.dateFormat = "(yyyy) MM dd"
var mydate = formatter.string(from: today) // "(2018) 08 30"
```

Listing 4-30: Defining our own format

The **dateFormat** property uses characters to represent date components. The **string()** method replaces those characters by the values of the date and returns the formatted string.

 Do It Yourself: Replace the code in your Playground file with the codes of Listings 4-28, 4-29, or 4-30. Try different values and combinations for the **dateStyle**, **timeStyle**, and **dateFormat** properties to see the strings they produce.

IMPORTANT: In the example of Listing 4-30, we used the characters for the year (**yyyy**) the month (**MM**), and the day (**dd**) to define the format, but there are also characters available for the hour (**HH**), minutes (**mm**), seconds (**ss**), and more. For a complete list, visit our website and follow the links for this chapter.

The **Calendar** structure and **DateFormatter** class process dates according to local conventions, including the language, symbols, etc. This means that the components of a date are going to be interpreted according to the conventions currently set on the device. For example, the same date will look like this "Friday, September 18, 2018" for a user in the United States and like this "2018年9月18日 星期五" for a user in China. How dates are going to be processed is determined by an object of the **Locale** structure. Every device has a **Locale** structure assigned by default, and our code will work with it unless we determine otherwise. To get a reference to the current structure or create a new one, the **Locale** structure includes the following initializer and type property.

Locale(identifier: String)—This initializer creates a **Locale** structure configured for the region determined by the value of the attribute. The attribute is a string that represents a language and a region (e.g., en_US for the United States, zh_CN for China).

current—This type property returns the **Locale** structure assigned by default to the device or defined by the user in the Settings app.

The structure also offers properties to get information from an instance or the class itself. The following are the most frequently used.

identifier—This property returns a string with the locale's identifier.

languageCode—This property returns a string with a code that identifies the locale's language.

regionCode—This property returns a string with a code that identifies the locale's region.

calendar—This property returns a **Calendar** structure with the locale's calendar.

decimalSeparator—This property returns a string with the locale's decimal separator.

currencyCode—This property returns a string with a code that identifies the locale's currency.

currencySymbol—This property returns a string with the symbol that represents the locale's currency.

usesMetricSystem—This property returns a Boolean value that determines whether or not the locale is using the metric system.

availableIdentifiers—This type property returns an array of strings with the locale identifiers available in the system.

preferredLanguages—This type property returns an array with the languages preferred by the user.

Although it is recommended to use the **Locale** structure set by the system and keep the values by default, there are times when our application has to present the information with a specific configuration. For example, we may need to create an application that always shows dates formatted in Chinese, no matter where the user is located. We can do this by assigning a new **Locale** structure to the **locale** property of the **DateFormatter** object used to format the date.

```
import Foundation
var today = Date()
let formatter = DateFormatter()
formatter.dateStyle = DateFormatter.Style.full

let chinaLocale = Locale(identifier: "zh_CN")
formatter.locale = chinaLocale
let displayDate = formatter.string(from: today) // "2018年8月30日 星期三"
```

Listing 4-31: Defining a different Locale *structure*

The code of Listing 4-31 creates a new **Locale** structure with the zh_CN identifier, which corresponds to China and the Chinese language, and assigns it to a **DateFormatter** object. Now, every string generated by this object will contain a date formatted according to Chinese conventions.

 IMPORTANT: The list of identifiers you can use to create a **Locale** structure is extensive. You can read the type property **availableIdentifiers** on the **Locale** structure to get an array with the values available.

 The Basics: The **Locale** structure is not only used to define date formats but also multiple linguistic and cultural norms that apply to a particular region. For this reason, the class is used to prepare the app for international distribution; a process called Internationalization. We will study Internationalization in Chapter 28.

The date stored in a **Date** structure is not a date but the number of seconds between the date represented by the object and an arbitrary date in the past (January 1st, 2001). To process these values and get the actual date, the **Calendar** structure and the **DateFormatter** class need to know the time zone the date belongs to. Foundation includes the **TimeZone** structure to manage time zones. An object is assigned by default to the system containing the time zone where the device is located (this is why when we display a date it coincides with the date on our device), but we can create a different one as we did with the **Locale** structure. To get a reference to the current structure or create a new one, the **TimeZone** structure includes the following initializer and type property.

TimeZone(identifier: String)—This initializer creates a **TimeZone** structure configured for the time zone determined by the value of the **identifier** attribute. The attribute is a string that represents the name of the time zone (e.g., "Europe/Paris", "Asia/Bangkok").

current—This type property returns the **TimeZone** structure assigned by default to the device or defined by the user in the Settings app.

Time zones are a very complex subject, but usually the applications are quite simple. For example, we can calculate the time in different parts of the world from the same date using different **TimeZone** structures.

```
import Foundation

let tokyoTimeZone = TimeZone(identifier: "Asia/Tokyo")
let madridTimeZone = TimeZone(identifier: "Europe/Madrid")

var today = Date()  // "Jul 30, 2018 at 5:35 PM"
let formatter = DateFormatter()
```

```
formatter.dateStyle = DateFormatter.Style.short
formatter.timeStyle = DateFormatter.Style.short
formatter.timeZone = tokyoTimeZone
let tokyoDate = formatter.string(from: today) // "7/31/18, 6:35 AM"
formatter.timeZone = madridTimeZone
let madridDate = formatter.string(from: today)  // "7/30/18, 11:35 PM"
```

Listing 4-32: *Working with different time zones*

The code of Listing 4-32 creates two **TimeZone** structures, one for Tokyo's time zone and another for Madrid's time zone, and then assigns the structures to a **DateFormatter** object to generate the strings from the current date and get the current dates and times in Tokyo and Madrid.

 IMPORTANT: The list of names for the time zones is stored in a database. The **TimeZone** structure offers the **knownTimeZoneIdentifiers** property to get an array with the values available.

Measurements

Other types of data we usually need in our applications are units of measurement, such as pounds, miles, etc. Defining our own units present some challenges, but Foundation includes the **Measurement** structure to simplify our work. This structure includes two properties, one for the value and another for the unit. The initializer requires these two values to create the structure.

Measurement(value: Double, **unit:** Unit)—This initializer creates a **Measurement** structure with the values specified by the **value** and **unit** attributes. The **unit** attribute is a property of a subclass of the **Dimension** class.

The value declared for the **Measurement** structure is the number that determines the magnitude, like 55 in 55 km, and the unit is a property of a subclass of the **Dimension** class that represents the unit of measurement, like km in 55 km. The **Dimension** class contains all the basic functionally required for measurement but is through its subclasses that the units of measurement are determined. Foundation offers multiple subclasses to define units for different types of dimensions. The following are the most frequently used.

UnitDuration—This subclass of the **Dimension** class defines the units of measurement for duration (time). The subclass includes the following properties to represent the units: **seconds**, **minutes** and **hours**, with **seconds** defined as the basic unit.

UnitLength—This subclass of the **Dimension** class defines the units of measurement for length. The subclass includes the following properties to represent the units: **megameters**, **kilometers**, **hectometers**, **decameters**, **meters**, **decimeters**, **centimeters**, **millimeters**, **micrometers**, **nanometers**, **picometers**, **inches**, **feet**, **yards**, **miles**, **scandinavianMiles**, **lightyears**, **nauticalMiles**, **fathoms**, **furlongs**, **astronomicalUnits**, and **parsecs**, with **meters** defined as the basic unit.

UnitMass—This subclass of the **Dimension** class defines the units of measurement for mass. The subclass includes the following properties to represent the units: **kilograms**, **grams**, **decigrams**, **centigrams**, **milligrams**, **micrograms**, **nanograms**, **picograms**, **ounces**, **pounds**, **stones**, **metricTons**, **shortTons**, **carats**, **ouncesTroy**, and **slugs**, with **kilograms** defined as the basic unit.

UnitVolume—This subclass of the **Dimension** class defines the units of measurement for volume. The subclass includes the following properties to represent the units: **megaliters**,

kiloliters, liters, deciliters, centiliters, milliliters, cubicKilometers, cubicMeters, cubicDecimeters, cubicMillimeters, cubicInches, cubicFeet, cubicYards, cubicMiles, acreFeet, bushels, teaspoons, tablespoons, fluidOunces, cups, pints, quarts, gallons, imperialTeaspoons, imperialTablespoons, imperialFluidOunces, imperialPints, imperialQuarts, imperialGallons, and **metricCups**, with **liters** defined as the basic unit.

The **Measurement** structure includes the following properties and methods to access the values and convert them to different units.

value—This property sets or returns the structure's value. It is of type **Double**.

unit—This property sets or returns the structure's unit of measurement. It is represented by a property of a subclass of the **Dimension** class.

convert(to: Unit)—This method converts the values of the **Measurement** structure to the unit specified by the **to** attribute. The attribute is a property of a subclass of the **Dimension** class.

converted(to: Unit)—This method converts the values of the **Measurement** structure to the unit specified by the **to** attribute and returns a new **Measurement** structure with the result. The attribute is a property of a subclass of the **Dimension** class.

The initialization of a **Measurement** structure is simple, we just have to provide the value for the magnitude and the property that represents the unit of measurement we want to use. The following example creates two structures to store a measure of 30 centimeters and another of 5 pounds.

```
import Foundation

var length = Measurement(value: 30, unit: UnitLength.centimeters) // 30.0 cm
var weight = Measurement(value: 5, unit: UnitMass.pounds)   // 5.0 lb
```

Listing 4-33: Initializing Measurement *structures*

If the measures are of the same dimension (e.g., length), we can perform operations with their values. The **Measurement** structure allows the operations +, −, *, /, and also the use of the comparison operators ==, !=, <, >, <=, and >= to compare values. The following example adds two measures in centimeters.

```
import Foundation

var length = Measurement(value: 200, unit: UnitLength.centimeters)
var width = Measurement(value: 800, unit: UnitLength.centimeters)

var total = length + width   // 1000.0 cm
```

Listing 4-34: Adding the values of two Measurement *structures*

If the measures are of different units, the **Measurement** structure returned by the operation is defined with the dimension's basic unit. For example, if we are working with lengths, the basic unit is **meters**.

```
import Foundation

var length = Measurement(value: 300, unit: UnitLength.meters)
var width = Measurement(value: 2, unit: UnitLength.kilometers)
var total = length + width   // 2300.0 m
```

Listing 4-35: Adding two values of different units

The code of Listing 4-35 adds two lengths of different units (meters and kilometers). The system converts kilometers to meters and then performs the addition, returning a **Measurement** structure with a value in meters (2300.0 m).

If we want everything to be performed in the same unit, we can convert a value to a different unit using the **convert()** or **converted()** methods. In the following example, we convert the unit of the **length** variable to kilometers and perform an addition again in kilometers.

```
import Foundation

var length = Measurement(value: 300, unit: UnitLength.meters)
var width = Measurement(value: 2, unit: UnitLength.kilometers)
length.convert(to: UnitLength.kilometers)
var total = length + width   // 2.3 km
```

Listing 4-36: Converting units

The values of a **Measurement** structure are printed as they are stored and with the units they represent, but this is usually not what we need to present to our users. Foundation offers the **MeasurementFormatter** class to format these values. This class works in a similar way than the **DateFormatter** class studied in the previous section. The class can determine how the value and the unit are going to be displayed (e.g., cm, centimeters) and adapt them to the location and configuration of the device (the user's country and language). The following are all the properties and methods available in the **MeasurementFormatter** class to format a value.

unitStyle—This property sets or returns the style used to display the measure. It is an enumeration of type **UnitStyle** defined in a superclass of the **MeasurementFormatter** class. The possible values are **short**, **medium** and **long**.

unitOptions—This property sets or returns options that determine how the values are going to be presented. It is a property of a structure called **UnitOptions** defined inside the **MeasurementFormatter** class. The properties available are **providedUnit** (uses the provided unit instead of the local unit), **naturalScale** (expresses the numbers in a natural format, like in kilometers instead of meters when the numbers are big enough), and **temperatureWithoutUnit** (shows the value of the temperature without the unit).

numberFormatter—This property sets or returns a custom format for the number. It is a value of type **NumberFormatter** (studied before in this chapter to format numbers).

locale—This property sets or returns the **Locale** structure used by the **MeasurementFormatter** object to process the value. The value by default is the **Locale** structure defined by the system.

string(from: Measurement)—This method returns a string with the measure provided by the **from** attribute in the format specified by the properties of the object.

As with the **DateFormatter** class, the **MeasurementFormatter** class has to be initialized first and then configured with the type of format we want to use. The string is finally generated with the **string()** method, as in the following example.

```
import Foundation

var length = Measurement(value: 40, unit: UnitLength.kilometers)

var formatter = MeasurementFormatter()
formatter.unitStyle = MeasurementFormatter.UnitStyle.long
formatter.unitOptions = MeasurementFormatter.UnitOptions.naturalScale

var newValue = formatter.string(from: length)   // "24.855 miles"
```

Listing 4-37: Formatting a measurement

One of the advantages of using a formatter to present a measure is that the value and the unit are automatically adapted to the location and language of the user. If the code is executed in a location where the unit of measurement is miles instead of kilometers, the values of the **Measurement** structure will be converted to miles, as shown in the example of Listing 4-37 ("24.855 miles").

If our application has to present the same unit of measurement independently of the location, we can set a specific locale with the **locale** property, as we did before for dates. The following example formats the measures in Chinese, no matter where the app is executed.

```
import Foundation

var length = Measurement(value: 40, unit: UnitLength.kilometers)

var formatter = MeasurementFormatter()
formatter.unitStyle = MeasurementFormatter.UnitStyle.long
formatter.unitOptions = MeasurementFormatter.UnitOptions.naturalScale
formatter.locale = Locale(identifier: "zh_CN")

var newValue = formatter.string(from: length)   // 40公里
```

Listing 4-38: Formatting a measure for a specific locale

We can also specify a format for the number. The **MeasurementFormatter** class offers the **numberFormatter** property to assign a **NumberFormatter** object to the formatter. For example, we can format the value of a measure to always include 6 digits.

```
import Foundation

var length = Measurement(value: 40, unit: UnitLength.kilometers)

var formatter = MeasurementFormatter()
formatter.unitStyle = MeasurementFormatter.UnitStyle.long
formatter.unitOptions = MeasurementFormatter.UnitOptions.naturalScale

var formatNumber = NumberFormatter()
formatNumber.minimumIntegerDigits = 6
formatter.numberFormatter = formatNumber

var newValue = formatter.string(from: length)   // "000025 miles"
```

Listing 4-39: Formatting the measurement's value

 IMPORTANT: The **Measurement** class also allows you to define your own units of measurement. The topic is beyond the scope of this book. For more information, visit our website and follow the links for this chapter.

4.3 Core Graphics

Core Graphics is an old framework programmed in the C language. It was developed to provide a platform-independent two-dimensional drawing engine for Apple systems. The framework is composed of basic drawing tools, including its own specific data types, and also a complete low-level drawing API known as Quartz 2D. Because of its characteristics, instead of being replaced, the framework was integrated with newer frameworks that came along, and now it is an important piece in the construction of graphic interfaces for mobile applications.

 IMPORTANT: In this chapter, we are going to explore the part of Core Graphics used by modern frameworks to build user interfaces, but the framework is extensive and includes tools for the creation of custom graphics, as we will see in Chapter 24.

Data Types

The most widely adopted feature of Core Graphics is a series of data types defined under the name of **CGGeometry** (CG stands for Core Graphics). In Swift, these data types are implemented as structures, with their own initializers, properties and methods. They are not only used for drawing but also to position graphic elements on the screen, such as buttons, labels, etc.

Every data type defined in this framework stores values that represent attributes, such as position or size. The following is the data type included in the framework to specify these values.

CGFloat—This structure is used to store `Float` type values for drawing purposes.

A more complex structure is `CGSize`, designed to store values that represent dimensions. This data type includes the following initializer, properties and method.

CGSize(width: CGFloat, **height:** CGFloat**)**—This initializer creates a `CGSize` structure with the values specified by the **width** and **height** attributes. The structure defines initializers to create instances from values of type `Int`, `CGFloat`, and `Double`.

zero—This type property returns a `CGSize` structure with its values set to zero.

width—This property sets or returns the structure's width.

height—This property sets or returns the structure's height.

equalTo(CGSize**)**—This method returns a Boolean value that indicates whether the `CGSize` structure is equal to the value of the attribute.

Another structure is `CGPoint`, which is used to define points in a two-dimensional coordinate system. This data type includes the following initializer, properties and method.

CGPoint(x: CGFloat, **y:** CGFloat**)**—This initializer creates a `CGPoint` structure with the coordinates specified by the **x** and **y** attributes. The structure defines initializers to create instances from values of type `Int`, `CGFloat`, and `Double`.

zero—This type property returns a `CGPoint` structure with its values set to zero.

x—This property sets or returns the structure's x coordinate.

y—This property sets or returns the structure's y coordinate.

equalTo(CGPoint**)**—This method returns a Boolean value that determines whether the `CGPoint` structure is equal to the value of the attribute.

There is also a similar structure called **CGVector** to manage a two-dimensional vector. This data type includes the following initializer and properties.

CGVector(dx: CGFloat, **dy:** CGFloat)—This initializer creates a **CGVector** structure with the vector's coordinates specified by the **dx** and **dy** attributes. The structure defines initializers to create instances from values of type **Int**, **CGFloat**, and **Double**.

zero—This type property returns a **CGVector** structure with its values set to zero.

dx—This property sets or returns the structure's x coordinate.

dy—This property sets or returns the structure's y coordinate.

Finally, there is a more complex structure called **CGRect** that we can use to define and work with rectangles. This data type includes the following initializers, properties and methods.

CGRect(origin: CGPoint, **size:** CGSize)—This initializer creates a **CGRect** structure to store the origin and size of a rectangle. The **origin** attribute is a **CGPoint** structure with the coordinates of the rectangle's origin, and the **size** attribute is a **CGSize** structure with the rectangle's width and height.

CGRect(x: CGFloat, **y:** CGFloat, **width:** CGFloat, **height:** CGFloat)—This initializer creates a **CGRect** structure to store the origin and size of a rectangle. The **x** and **y** attributes define the coordinates of the rectangle's origin, and the **width** and **height** attributes its size. The structure defines initializers to create instances from values of type **Int**, **CGFloat**, and **Double**.

zero—This type property returns a **CGRect** structure with its values set to zero.

origin—This property sets or returns a **CGPoint** structure with the coordinates of the rectangle's origin.

size—This property sets or returns a **CGSize** structure with the rectangle's width and height.

minX—This property returns the minimum value of the rectangle's **x** coordinate.

minY—This property returns the minimum value of the rectangle's **y** coordinate.

maxX—This property returns the maximum value of the rectangle's **x** coordinate.

maxY—This property returns the maximum value of the rectangle's **y** coordinate.

midX—This property returns the value of the rectangle's **x** coordinate located at the horizontal center of the rectangle.

midY—This property returns the value of the rectangle's **y** coordinate located at the vertical center of the rectangle.

equalTo(CGRect**)**—This method returns a Boolean value that determines if the **CGRect** structure is equal to the value specified by the attribute.

contains(CGPoint**)**—This method returns a Boolean value that determines if the value specified by the attribute is contained inside the **CGRect** structure. The attribute may be of type **CGPoint** (to detect if a point is inside the rectangle) or **CGRect** (to detect if another rectangle is inside the original rectangle).

intersects(CGRect**)**—This method returns a Boolean value to indicate if the rectangle specified by the attribute intersects with the original rectangle.

intersection(CGRect**)**—This method returns a **CGRect** structure with the coordinates and size of the rectangle formed by the intersection of the original rectangle with the rectangle specified by the attribute.

union(CGRect**)**—This method returns a new **CGRect** structure with the coordinates and size of a rectangle that includes the original rectangle and the rectangle specified by the attribute.

The structures provided by Core Graphics are declared and initialized as any other structures in Swift, but we have to import the Core Graphics framework first for the types to be recognized.

```
import CoreGraphics

var myfloat: CGFloat = 35
var mysize: CGSize = CGSize(width: 250, height: 250)
var mypoint: CGPoint = CGPoint(x: 20, y: 50)
var myrect: CGRect = CGRect(origin: mypoint, size: mysize)
var myvector: CGVector = CGVector(dx: 30, dy: 30)
```

Listing 4-40: Initializing Core Graphics' structures

 The Basics: The values in a coordinate system are identified with the letters **x** and **y**. Core Graphics follows this convention and assigns these names to the parameters of the structures that store coordinate values. We will study coordinates and coordinate systems later in this chapter.

The **CGSize**, **CGPoint**, and **CGVector** structures may be initialized with their member initializers, but the **CGRect** structure provides an additional initializer to create the instance from the values of its internal structures.

```
import CoreGraphics

var myrect = CGRect(x: 30, y: 20, width: 100, height: 200)

print("The origin is at \(myrect.origin.x) and \(myrect.origin.y)")
print("The size is \(myrect.size.width) by \(myrect.size.height)")
```

Listing 4-41: Using the convenience initializer

The **origin** and **size** properties of a **CGRect** value are **CGPoint** and **CGSize** structures, respectively, so they can be copied into other variables or properties as any other values.

```
import CoreGraphics

var myrect = CGRect(x: 30, y: 20, width: 100, height: 200)

var mypoint = myrect.origin
var mysize = myrect.size
print("The origin is at \(mypoint.x) and \(mypoint.y)")
print("The size is \(mysize.width) by \(mysize.height)")
```

Listing 4-42: Accessing the structures inside a CGRect structure

Sometimes our application has to work with Core Graphic's structures, but we do not know the values they are going to require. In cases like this, we can take advantage of the **zero** type property. This property is available in most structures and what it does is to return a structure with its values initialized to 0.

```
import CoreGraphics

var myrect = CGRect.zero
```

```
print("The origin is at \(myrect.origin.x) and \(myrect.origin.y)")
print("The size is \(myrect.size.width) by \(myrect.size.height)")
```

Listing 4-43: Assigning empty structures to a CGRect *variable*

The **myrect** variable of Listing 4-43 is a **CGRect** structure with all its properties initialized with the value 0. Assigning the value of the **zero** property to a variable is the same as using the initializer **CGRect(x: 0, y: 0, width: 0, height: 0)**.

The **CGRect** structure also includes properties to calculate values from its coordinates and size. For example, the **midX** and **midY** properties return the coordinates at the center of each side.

```
import CoreGraphics

var rect = CGRect(x: 0, y: 0, width: 100, height: 100)

print("The horizontal center is \(rect.midX)")   // 50.0
```

Listing 4-44: Calculating the coordinate at the center of the rectangle

The rest of the methods included in the **CGRect** structure are easy to implement as well. The following example creates a rectangle and a point and then checks whether the point is inside the rectangle or not with the **contains()** method.

```
import CoreGraphics

var rect = CGRect(x: 0, y: 0, width: 100, height: 100)
var point = CGPoint(x: 10, y: 50)

if rect.contains(point) {
    print("The point is inside the rectangle")
}
```

Listing 4-45: Detecting if a point is inside a rectangle

4.4 UIKit

UIKit (User Interface Kit) is the framework that defines the elements of the graphic interface for mobile applications. From strings of text to buttons and switches, all the standard elements that users manipulate on the screen to interact with the application are defined by the classes in this framework. Its primary focus is the user's interface, but it also provides elemental classes the application needs to work and connect with the rest of the system.

The application's ecosystem is a very complex mesh of elements that communicate back and forward. To check and respond to messages coming from these systems, including the operative system, the application has to keep calling itself in an infinite loop and at the same time fulfill its own purposes. These complex tasks are simplified by dividing the ecosystem into multiple parts that take care of every piece of the puzzle. The scheme is depicted in Figure 4-1.

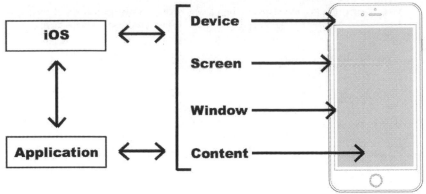

Figure 4-1: App's ecosystem

The app has to read information from the device and the screen, generate the graphics for the window and its content, and also keep the loop running to constantly check for events produced by any of these systems, such as the device informing that a rotation has taken place, a button on the screen reporting that has been tapped, or the system reporting that the app was suspended because of an incoming phone call, to name a few. This is an extremely complex process that demands a deep understanding of the technologies involved. To alleviate the work for developers and let them concentrate on what is really important for their apps, UIKit includes several classes that represent and take care of every part of this system, including `UIApplication`, `UIDevice`, `UIScreen`, and `UIWindow`.

UIApplication

When the app is built, the compiler includes a basic piece of code that is in charge of performing the first steps to initiate and transfer control of the device to our app. One of the tasks of this code is to create an object of the `UIApplication` class. This object generates a loop to process events, prepares the app to work, and also transfers the control to our own code when everything is ready. The `UIApplication` class includes a type property to provide access to this object.

shared—This type property returns the instance of the `UIApplication` class that was created for our app.

Once we get a reference to this object, we can access its properties and methods. The following are the most frequently used.

delegate—This property returns a reference to the object assigned as the delegate of the `UIApplication` object. As we will see later, a delegate object is assigned to the `UIApplication` object to communicate with our code.

windows—This property returns an array with references to the windows created for the app. If the device is not connected to an external screen, this array only contains one element referencing the window assigned to the device's main screen.

keyWindow—This property returns a reference to the active window. Its value is an optional of type `UIWindow` (it returns a `UIWindow` object or `nil` if no window was found).

applicationState—This property returns the current state of the app. It is an enumeration called `State` included in the `UIApplication` class. The values available are `active` (the app is active), `inactive` (the app is running but not active), and `background` (the app is running in the background).

Frameworks

The **UIApplication** object is created for us in the background as soon as the application is executed, but we can read the **shared** property to get a reference to the current object.

```
import UIKit

let app = UIApplication.shared
var state = app.applicationState
switch state {
   case .active:
      print("The application is active")
   case .inactive:
      print("The application is inactive")
   case .background:
      print("The application is in the background")
}
```

Listing 4-46: Accessing the UIApplication *object*

In Listing 4-46, a reference to the **UIApplication** object is stored in the **app** variable. From this variable, we check the app's state and print the corresponding message.

 Do It Yourself: The examples in this chapter were designed for testing on Playground. Playground was developed to learn, practice, and test code, but cannot simulate a system such as a mobile device. Therefore, some of the classes presented in this chapter will produce fake values or generate a simple graphic representation of the result. For example, the **UIApplication** object is not active in Playground and therefore the message printed on the console will be "The application is inactive". This will only work on real applications. We will learn how to create those types of applications in Chapter 5.

UIDevice

The **UIDevice** class was defined to get information from the device where the app is running. The class includes a type property to get a reference to the object that represents the current device and instance properties to configure the object and return the data.

current—This type property returns an instance of the **UIDevice** class that represents the device where the app is currently running.

systemName—This property returns a string with the name of the operative system running in the device (e.g., "iPhone OS").

systemVersion—This property returns a string with the version of the operative system running in the device (e.g., "12.0").

userInterfaceIdiom—This property returns the type of device running the application. The value returned is an enumeration of type **UIUserInterfaceIdiom** with the values **unspecified**, **phone**, **pad**, **TV**, and **carPlay**.

orientation—This property returns a value that determines the current orientation of the device. It is an enumeration of type **UIDeviceOrientation** with the values **unknown**, **portrait**, **portraitUpsideDown**, **landscapeLeft**, **landscapeRight**, **faceUp**, and **faceDown**. This property requires the accelerometer to be enabled to provide accurate information (see the example in Chapter 19, Listing 19-10).

beginGeneratingDeviceOrientationNotifications()—This method enables the accelerometer and begins the process that will deliver notifications to communicate changes in the orientation.

endGeneratingDeviceOrientationNotifications()—This method tells the system that the accelerometer is no longer required and stops the delivery of notifications.

The implementation of this class is simple. We get an instance of the object that represents the current device first and then read its properties. The following example checks whether or not the application is running on an iPhone.

```
import UIKit

let current = UIDevice.current
let device = current.userInterfaceIdiom

if device == .phone {
    print("This is an iPhone")
} else {
    print("This is not an iPhone")
}
```

Listing 4-47: Getting information from the device

 Do It Yourself: Replace the code in your Playground file by the code of Listing 4-47. Again, in Playground this code produces values by default. The only way to get values that are significant to our application is to execute it on a real device. We will learn how to do it in Chapter 5.

UIScreen

The **UIScreen** object allows us to get information that describes the main screen and also external screens connected to the device. The class offers two type properties to get these objects and some instance properties to return information about the screen.

main—This type property returns a **UIScreen** object to manage the main screen.

bounds—This property returns a **CGRect** value with the dimensions of the screen expressed in points. The values vary according to the device's orientation.

nativeBounds—This property returns a **CGRect** value with the dimensions of the screen expressed in pixels. The values are always returned considering a portrait orientation.

scale—This property returns a **CGFloat** value representing the scale of the screen. This is a value that translates between points and real pixels on the screen, as we will see next.

brightness—This property sets or returns a **CGFloat** value that determines the brightness of the screen. It takes values from 0.0 to 1.0.

The screen of a device is composed of a grid of hundreds of dots called *pixels*, ordered in rows and columns. The color of each pixel is established by three values contained within the pixel (four including transparency). The values represent a combination of the colors red, green, and blue. By combining the pixels on the grid and the colors, the screen can display any type of graphics, including buttons, text, pictures, etc.

Frameworks

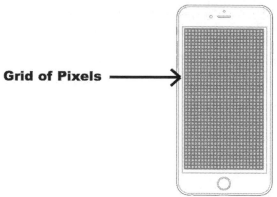

Grid of Pixels ———————→

Figure 4-2: Grid of pixels

The number of pixels varies from one device to another. Anticipating this scenario, Apple adopted the concept of points (sometimes called *logical pixels*). The goal was to have a unit of measurement that is independent of the device and the density of the pixels on the screen. A point occupies a square of one or more pixels, but the developer does not need to know how many, it is all managed by the system.

At this moment, points in Apple mobile devices may represent a square of up to three pixels, depending on the device and the technology. Here is the list of the number of points and the corresponding pixels for every device available at the moment.

- iPhone 3 and older   320 x 480 points   320 x 480 pixels   1x scale
- iPhone 4   320 x 480 points   640 x 960 pixels   2x scale
- iPhone 5   320 x 568 points   640 x 1136 pixels   2x scale
- iPhone 6/7/8   375 x 667 points   750 x 1334 pixels   2x scale
- iPhone 6/7/8 Plus   414 x 736 points   1242 x 2208 pixels   3x scale
- iPhone X   375 × 812 points   1125 × 2436 pixels   3x scale
- iPad, iPad 2 and Mini   768 x 1024 points   768 x 1024 pixels   1x scale
- iPads with Retina   768 x 1024 points   1536 x 2048 pixels   2x scale
- iPad Pro   1366 x 1024 points   2732 x 2048 pixels   2x scale

The difference between points and pixels represents the scale. iPhones 3 and older have a scale of 1 (1 point represents 1 pixel), while iPhones 4, 5, 6, 7 and 8 have a scale of 2 (1 point represents a square of 2 pixels). Some iPhones and iPads share a grid with the same amount of points, independently of the scale, but with the introduction of the iPhones Plus and their larger screens, the scale was expanded to 3 (1 point represents 3 pixels). This allows developers to create graphic interfaces that adapt to every device, no matter how many pixels they have on their screens.

The properties **bound**, `nativeBounds`, and `scale` included in the `UIScreen` class return the values corresponding to the screen of the device where the app is running. The **bound** and `nativeBounds` properties contain `CGRect` structures, while `scale` is just a `CGFloat` value.

```
import UIKit

let screen = UIScreen.main

let pointsWidth = screen.bounds.size.width
let pointsHeight = screen.bounds.size.height
print("Width: \(pointsWidth) x Height: \(pointsHeight)")

let pixelsWidth = screen.nativeBounds.size.width
let pixelsHeight = screen.nativeBounds.size.height
```

```
print("Width: \(pixelsWidth) x Height: \(pixelsHeight)")
print("Scale: \(screen.scale)")
```

Listing 4-48: Getting information from the screen

The native resolution in pixels is always returned considering a portrait orientation, but the size in points is returned according to the current orientation. For example, the dimensions of the iPhone 8's screen are 375 points wide and 667 points tall in portrait, but 667 points wide and 375 points tall in landscape.

UIWindow

Every app generates windows to visually communicate with their users. Desktop applications include several windows, but mobile devices, due to the limited size of their screens, only have one. This window is like a virtual space of the size of the screen, where the visual elements of the app are laid out. UIKit includes the **UIWindow** class to create the object that manages the window for our app. Usually, this object is automatically created as soon as the app is executed, but we can access it from our code reading the **windows** or **keywindow** properties of the **UIApplication** object.

Because of the especial characteristics of mobile devices, once the window is created it never changes. If the graphics or the interface has to be modified, the content of the window is the one replaced, but the window remains the same. For this reason, we barely interact with this object. The following are its most frequently used properties.

screen—This property returns a **UIScreen** object that represents the device's screen. This is the same object returned by the **main** property of the **UIScreen** class.

rootViewController—This property returns a reference to the object controlling the app's initial view.

```
import UIKit

let app = UIApplication.shared

let window = app.keyWindow
if let bounds = window?.screen.bounds {
    print("Size: \(bounds.size.width) x \(bounds.size.height)")
}
```

Listing 4-49: Accessing the UIWindow *object*

This example gets a reference to the **UIWindow** object created for our app, then reads its **screen** property to get a reference to the **UIScreen** object assigned to the application and reads its **bounds** property to print the screen's size on the console. The **keywindow** property returns an optional, so we have to use Optional Chaining and Optional Binding to access the object's properties.

 IMPORTANT: The **rootViewController** property stores a reference to an object that contains the initial view of the interface and is in charge of managing that view. These objects are called *View Controllers*. We will study views next and View Controllers in Chapter 5.

UIView

The window is the space where the graphics are displayed, but it does not generate any visible content by itself. The user's interface is built inside the window from similar containers called *views*. These views are rectangular areas of custom size, designed to display graphics on the screen. Some views are used just as containers while others are improved to present graphic tools, such as buttons and switches, and also graphic content, such as images and text. The views are organized in a hierarchy, one inside another, with a view of the size of the window as the hierarchy's root (usually called *main view* or *container view*).

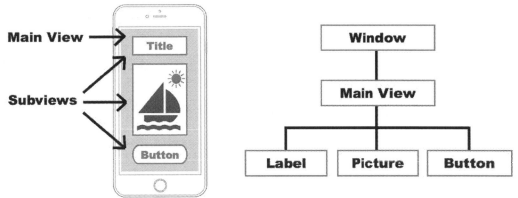

Figure 4-3: Views hierarchy

No matter the purpose of the view (to be a container or to present content), they are all created from objects of the **UIView** class. This is a basic class that is only capable of creating and managing the rectangular area occupied by the view, but subclasses of this class may be defined to add functionality and present any type of content we want. Although the objects created directly from the **UIView** class are very limited, they have an extensive list of properties and methods to configure and draw their views. The following are the most useful initializer, properties, and methods available.

UIView(frame: CGRect)—This initializer creates a **UIView** object in the position and size determined by the **frame** attribute.

frame—This property sets or returns a **CGRect** value that determines the position and size of the rectangular area occupied by the view. The values for the position are determined from the coordinates of the view's container (the window or another view).

bounds—This property sets or returns a **CGRect** value that determines the position and size of the rectangular area occupied by the view inside its own frame. The values for the position are determined from the view's coordinates system.

center—This property sets or returns a **CGPoint** value that determines the coordinates of the center of the view's frame.

backgroundColor—This property sets or returns an object that determines the color of the view's background. The value is an object of the **UIColor** class (introduced next).

alpha—This property sets or returns a **CGFloat** value that determines the view's alpha level (the level of transparency). The property takes values from 0.0 (transparent) to 1.0 (opaque).

isHidden—This property sets or returns a Boolean value that determines whether the view is visible (**false**) or hidden (**true**).

isOpaque—This property sets or returns a Boolean value that determines whether the view is opaque or not.

contentMode—This property sets or returns a value that determines the mode used by the view to lay out its content when its size changes (frequently used with images). It is an enumeration called **ContentMode** included in the **UIView** class. The values available are `scaleToFill`, `scaleAspectFit`, `scaleAspectFill`, `redraw`, `center`, `top`, `bottom`, `left`, `right`, `topLeft`, `topRight`, `bottomLeft`, and `bottomRight`.

clipsToBounds—This property sets or returns a Boolean value that determines whether or not the content of the view is confined to the view's bounds.

isUserInteractionEnabled—This property sets or returns a Boolean value that determines whether or not the view responds to the user's interaction (e.g., a tap of the finger).

isMultipleTouchEnabled—This property sets or returns a Boolean value that determines if the view can handle multiple touch events.

isExclusiveTouch—This property sets or returns a Boolean value that determines whether or not the view delivers to other views the touch events that cannot handle.

superview—This property returns a reference to the **UIVIew** object that is the container of the view. If the view is not inside another view, the value returned is `nil`.

subviews—This property returns an array containing references to the **UIView** objects that are inside the view (subviews).

tag—This property sets or returns an integer value that identifies the view.

viewWithTag(Int)—This method searches for a subview of the view with the tag specified by the attribute. The value returned is an optional containing a **UIView** object or `nil` in case of failure.

The window is positioned inside the screen, while the views are positioned inside the window and inside one another, generating a hierarchical structure (see Figure 4-3). To establish the position of every element in its container, UIKit uses coordinate systems. The next figure illustrates the coordinate system of the screen of an iPhone 8.

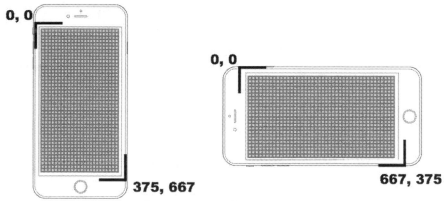

Figure 4-4: Coordinate system

The rows and columns of points are counted from the top-left corner to the bottom-right corner of the container (the values are incremented from left to right and top to bottom). For example, the first point at the top-left corner of the screen is at the position 0, 0 (column 0, row 0), while the point at the bottom-right corner is at the position 375, 667 (667, 375 in landscape orientation). Following standard conventions, the point at the position 0, 0 is called the *origin*, and the values for the positions are identified by the letters **x** and **y** (**x** for columns and **y** for rows).

Frameworks

In UIKit, this same coordinate system is applied to every element of the interface, including the window and the views. The window and the main view occupy the whole screen, and therefore they share the same origin and size. The next example creates a view of 375 points by 667 points to represent the main view that might be contained by a window of an iPhone 8.

```
import UIKit

var mainframe = CGRect(x: 0, y: 0, width: 375, height: 667)
let container = UIView(frame: mainframe)
```

Listing 4-50: Creating a view

The initializer of the **UIView** class takes a parameter called **frame** of type **CGRect** to establish the position and size of the view. The view created by the code of Listing 4-50 will be positioned at the window's coordinates 0, 0 and will have a size of 375 by 667 points, covering the whole screen of an iPhone 8.

 Do It Yourself: Replace the code in your Playground file by the code of Listing 4-50. In the Results Side Bar, click on the Quick Look button corresponding to the line that creates the **container** object to see a representation of the view. At this moment, you will only be able to see a gray rectangle. We will add some color next.

The background color of the **UIView** object is set as transparent by default. If we want to change the color, we have to assign a new value to the **backgroundColor** property of the view. This value has to be provided as an object of the **UIColor** class. The class includes some initializers and properties to create these objects. The following are the most frequently used.

UIColor(red: CGFloat, green: CGFloat, blue: CGFloat, alpha: CGFloat)—This initializer creates a **UIColor** object with a color set by the values of its attributes. It takes values from 0.0 to 1.0. The **red** attribute defines the level of red, **green** the level of green, **blue** the level of blue, and **alpha** defines the alpha level (transparency).

UIColor(patternImage: UIImage)—This initializer creates a **UIColor** object with a color defined as the image provided by the **patternImage** attribute. The image will be replicated as many times as necessary to cover the area where the color is assigned (we will study the **UIImage** class in Chapter 8).

The **UIColor** class also offers an extensive list of type properties that return a **UIColor** object with a predefined color. Some of these properties are **black**, **gray**, **darkGray**, **lightGray**, **white**, **red**, **green**, **blue**, **cyan**, **yellow**, **magenta**, **orange**, **purple**, and **brown**.

The **UIColor** objects are assigned to the views and almost any other element of the user interface to define their colors. They are created from the initializers or type methods listed above and then assigned to the corresponding properties, as in the following example.

```
import UIKit

let container = UIView(frame: CGRect(x: 0, y: 0, width: 375, height:
667))

var color = UIColor(red: 1.0, green: 0.0, blue: 0.0, alpha: 1.0)
container.backgroundColor = color
```

Listing 4-51: Assigning a color to the view

The color for the **UIColor** object created in Listing 4-51 is defined by the attributes of the initializer. The system used in this case is called RGB. The color is constructed by adding the values of every component: Red, Green, and Blue (RGB). In this example, the **red** attribute was set to 1.0 while the rest of the colors were set to 0.0, defining a pure red. Exactly the same object is returned by the type property **red**, implemented in the following example.

```
import UIKit

let container = UIView(frame: CGRect(x: 0, y: 0, width: 375, height:
667))
var color = UIColor.red
container.backgroundColor = color
```

Listing 4-52: Assigning the color red to the view

 Do It Yourself: Replace the code in your Playground file by the code of Listing 4-52. In the Result Side Bar, click on the Show Result button corresponding to the line that assigns the new color to the **backgroundColor** property of the view. You should see a rectangular red view within the Editor Area.

 The Basics: The **UIColor** initializer uses values from 0.0 to 1.0 to determine the levels of red, green, and blue that compose the color, but RGB colors are usually determined with integer values from 0 to 255. If you prefer to work with these values, you can convert them dividing the values by 255.0. For example, if the level of red is 190, you can get the value for the initializer with the formula 190.0 / 255.0.

The user's interface is built by adding views to parent views that work as containers, creating the hierarchical structure introduced in Figure 4-3. The container view is called the *superview* and the views inside are called *subviews*. When a view is added to a superview, the object is stored in the **subviews** property of the superview. This is a property containing an array of views (objects of the **UIView** class or any of its subclasses). To add and manage the views inside this array, the **UIView** class offers the following methods.

addSubview(UIView**)**—This method adds a view at the end of the **subviews** array.

insertSubview(UIView, **at:** Int**)**—This method inserts a view in the **subviews** array at the index indicated by the **at** attribute.

insertSubview(UIView, **aboveSubview:** UIView**)**—This method inserts a view in the **subviews** array above the subview indicated by the **aboveSubview** attribute.

insertSubview(UIView, **belowSubview:** UIView**)**—This method inserts a view in the **subviews** array below the subview indicated by the **belowSubview** attribute.

exchangeSubview(at: Int, **withSubviewAt:** Int**)**—This method exchanges the positions in the **subviews** array of the subviews at the indices indicated by the attributes.

bringSubviewToFront(UIView**)**—This method moves the subview specified by the **toFront** attribute to the end of the **subviews** array (to the front).

sendSubviewToBack(UIView**)**—This method moves the subview specified by the **view** attribute to the beginning of the **subviews** array (to the back).

removeFromSuperview()—This method is called on a subview to remove it from its superview.

The subviews are shown on the screen according to their position on the **subviews** array. The subviews with a lower index are drawn first, so the views with a higher index are shown at the top. This is why the method most frequently used to add a view to another view is **addSubview()**. This method adds the view to the end of the **subviews** array, effectively drawing the view at the top.

```
import UIKit

let container = UIView(frame: CGRect(x: 0, y: 0, width: 375, height: 667))
container.backgroundColor = UIColor.red

let subview1 = UIView(frame: CGRect(x: 20, y: 20, width: 335, height: 300))
subview1.backgroundColor = UIColor.lightGray

let subview2 = UIView(frame: CGRect(x: 20, y: 347, width: 335, height: 300))
subview2.backgroundColor = UIColor.lightGray

container.addSubview(subview1)
container.addSubview(subview2)
```

Listing 4-53: Adding subviews

After creating the **container** view, the code of Listing 4-53 creates two more views and adds them as its subviews with the **addSubview()** method. The **subviews** property of **container** now has two elements: the **subview1** and **subview2** views. These subviews are of different color, creating two smaller rectangles of 335 by 300 points over the main view, as shown in Figure 4-5.

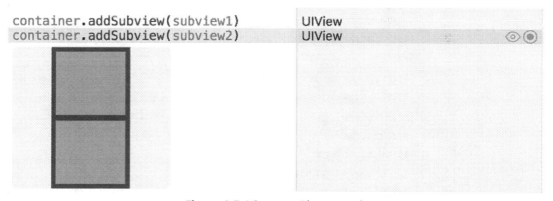

Figure 4-5: Views on Playground

Every subview is attached to its superview and positioned on the screen according to its coordinate system. When we set the values of the **x** and **y** parameters in the **UIView** initializer for every view, we have to consider the coordinates of their superviews, not the screen or other container views up the chain. For example, the position of the **subview1** inside the **container** view is 20, 20, but its own coordinate system starts again from 0, 0 at its top-left corner. The same happens with **subview2**. Any views added to these subviews will have a position according to the coordinates of their superviews and not the coordinates of the **container** view or the window. Figure 4-6 illustrates these views and their coordinate systems.

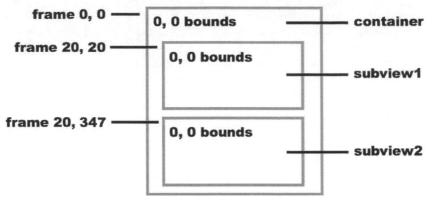

Figure 4-6: Subviews and their coordinates

These values are reflected in the **frame** and **bounds** properties of the **UIView** objects that represent each view. For example, the **x** and **y** values of the **frame** property of **subview1** are 20, 20, but the **x** and **y** values of the **bounds** property of **subview1** are 0, 0, because the **bounds** property refers to the view's internal frame and its own coordinate system.

UIView Subclasses

The views created from the **UIView** class are good as containers and organizers but do not present any content. The content has to be generated by subclasses of **UIView**. These subclasses overwrite some **UIView** methods and also provide their own properties and methods to draw graphics inside the view or respond to the user. Considering how difficult and time consuming it is to create every single element of the interface from scratch, UIKit provides ready to use subclasses of **UIView** for the creation of standard elements. From labels and buttons to images and tables, there is a **UIView** subclass to present on the screen everything our app needs. Figure 4-7 shows a scheme with the **UIView** class and its most important subclasses.

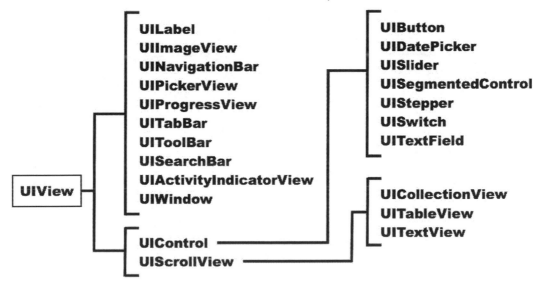

Figure 4-7: UIView *subclasses*

Some classes that add graphic content and process basic user interaction, such as **UILabel** or **UIImageView**, inherit directly from **UIView**, while classes that require more complex functionality, such as **UIButton** or **UITableView**, inherit from intermediate subclasses. The two intermediate subclasses depicted in Figure 4-7, **UIControl** and **UIScrollView**, provide

Frameworks

common functionality for their own subclasses. **UIControl** adds to **UIView** the capacity to respond to user interaction and report events, and **UIScrollView** adds the possibility to create views with scrollable content. The subclasses created from these two classes inherit their characteristics and add more specific functionality. All these subclasses are extremely useful for app development. We will study some of the simple **UIView** subclasses next and explore more complex subclasses in further chapters.

UILabel

The **UILabel** class creates a view that draws one or multiple lines of text that can be used to present information or to identify other elements on the interface. The following are some of the properties defined by the class to configure the view and format the text.

text—This property sets or returns the text displayed by the label.

attributedText—This property sets or returns the formatted text displayed by the label.

font—This property sets or returns the font used to display the label. Its value is an object of the **UIFont** class (we will introduce this class next).

textColor—This property sets or returns the color of the text. It is of type **UIColor**.

textAlignment—This property sets or returns the alignment of the text. It is an enumeration of type **NSTextAlignment** with the values **left** (to the left side of the view), **center** (to the center of the view), **right** (to the right side of the view), **justified** (the last line of the paragraph is aligned), and **natural** (uses the alignment associated with the text).

lineBreakMode—This property sets or returns the mode used to display lines of text that get out of the boundaries of the view. It is an enumeration of type **NSLineBreakMode** with the values **byWordWrapping** (the word that does not fit is moved to the next line), **byCharWrapping** (the character that does not fit is moved to the next line), **byClipping** (characters that does not fit are not drawn), **byTruncatingHead** (the beginning of the text is replaced by ellipsis), **byTruncatingTail** (the end of the text is replaced by ellipsis), **byTruncatingMiddle** (the middle of the text is replaced by ellipsis).

numberOfLines—This property sets or returns the number of lines allowed for the text. If the text requires more lines than those set by this property, it is truncated according to the mode selected by the **lineBreakMode** property. A value of 0 declares a label with unlimited lines.

adjustFontSizeToFitWidth—This property sets or returns a Boolean value that determines whether or not the size of the font has to be reduced to fit the text inside the view. It only works when the **numberOfLines** property is set to 1.

isEnabled—This property sets or returns a Boolean value that determines if the label is enabled. When the value of this property is set to **false**, the text is shown on the screen in a light color, usually light gray.

shadowColor—This property sets or returns the color of the shadow. It is an optional property of type **UIColor**. When its value is **nil**, the text is drawn with no shadow.

shadowOffset—This property sets or returns the offset of the shadow. Its value is a **CGSize** structure that establishes the horizontal and vertical displacement.

The content produced by the **UILabel** class, as any other subclass of **UIView**, is contained inside a view. Therefore, the **UILabel** class implements the **UIView** class initializer to specify the position and size of the view's area.

```
import UIKit

let container = UIView(frame: CGRect(x: 0, y: 0, width: 375, height:
667))

let label = UILabel(frame: CGRect(x: 20, y: 20, width: 150, height: 30))
label.text = "Hello World"

container.addSubview(label)
```

Listing 4-54: Creating a label

Labels, as any other graphic elements generated from subclasses of **UIView**, are inserted in container views to create the user's interface. In Listing 4-54, the container is created first and then a label is added as one of its subviews by the **addSubview()** method. The text for this label is assigned to the **text** property of the **UILabel** object as soon as the object is created. This is an optional property and its value by default is **nil**. This time, we assigned the value before the label view was added to the container, but we could have done it any time. The system updates the views on the screen over and over again after a few milliseconds, so the view will reflect the change right away every time a new value is assigned to this property.

The label is positioned inside the container at the point 20, 20 and has a size of 150 points wide and 30 points tall. These are the measures of the rectangular area occupied by the view, not the size of the text. The size of the text is determined by the font type set by default in the system. If we want to set a different size or font type, we have to assign a new **UIFont** object to the **font** property of the **UILabel** object. **UIFont** objects are not only assigned to labels but also to other elements that present text on the screen. They contain properties and methods to store and manage fonts. The following are the most frequently used initializer and type methods included in the **UIFont** class to create these objects.

UIFont(name: String, **size:** CGFloat)—This initializer creates a **UIFont** object with the font referenced by the **name** attribute and a size determined by the **size** attribute. The **name** attribute is a string with the font's PostScript name.

labelFontSize—This type property returns a **CGFloat** value with the size of the font used by the system to create **UILabel** objects.

buttonFontSize—This type property returns a **CGFloat** value with the size of the font used by the system to create **UIButton** objects (buttons).

systemFontSize—This type property returns a **CGFloat** value with the size of the font used by the system.

preferredFont(forTextStyle: UIFont.TextStyle)—This type method returns a **UIFont** object with the font associated to the style specified by the **forTextStyle** attribute and a size specified by the user in Settings. The attribute is a property of a structure called **TextStyle** included in the **UIFont** class. The properties available are **body, callout, caption1, caption2, footnote, headline, subheadline, largeTitle, title1, title2, title3**.

systemFont(ofSize: CGFloat)—This type method returns a **UIFont** object with the font set by default on the system and a size determined by the **ofSize** attribute.

boldSystemFont(ofSize: CGFloat)—This type method returns a **UIFont** object with the font of type bold set by default on the system and a size determined by the **ofSize** attribute.

italicSystemFont(ofSize: CGFloat)—This type method returns a **UIFont** object with the font of type italic set by default on the system and a size determined by the **ofSize** attribute.

Although we can create a font object with the initializer or any of the methods above, Apple recommends to work only with the **preferredFont()** method. The fonts returned by this method are called *Dynamic Types* because they are selected by the system according to the style specified by the attribute and the size set by the user. The Settings app offers an option to change the font size for all the applications installed on the device. If our application adopts Dynamic Types, it can respond to these changes and show the text on the screen with the size preferred by the user (the option is available in General / Accessibility / Large Text).

To assign a new font to a label, we have to create the **UIFont** object with the styles we want and then assign it to the label's **font** property.

```
import UIKit

var myfont = UIFont.preferredFont(forTextStyle: .headline)
var label = UILabel(frame: CGRect(x: 20, y: 20, width: 150, height: 50))
label.text = "Hello World"
label.font = myfont
```

Listing 4-55: Creating dynamic font types

The code of Listing 4-55 creates a **UILabel** object with the text "Hello World" and a font determined by the **headline** style. This is the style used for titles and headers, but we can define any style we want depending on the purpose of the text. For example, for long texts and content the preferred style is **body**. Every style uses different font types and they may look different, but the size is always determined by the system or the user from the Settings app.

Hello World

Figure 4-8: Label with `headline` *style*

 IMPORTANT: Fonts with dynamic types automatically adapt their size to the size determined by the user from Settings (General / Accessibility / Large Text), but if changes are performed after the app was installed and launched, we have to listen to notifications from the system to force the app to adapt the fonts to the new size. We will learn more about labels in Chapter 5 and how to listen to system notifications in Chapter 19.

 The Basics: The example of Listing 4-55 does not add the label to a container view. Playground lets you check the result of executing your code independently of the context. When testing code on Playground, you can click on the Show Result button to see a representation of the views and their content on the screen without the need to create a proper structure. In a real application though, every view has to be added as a subview of another view.

If we do not want to use Dynamic Types, we can create the font object with a specific family type and size using the **UIFont** initializer. The following example creates the **UIFont** object with a font called *Georgia-Italic* and a size of 30 points. Notice that because the size of this font is bigger than a normal font, we incremented the size of the label's frame to fit the text.

```
import UIKit

var myfont = UIFont(name: "Georgia-Italic", size: 30)

var label = UILabel(frame: CGRect(x: 20, y: 20, width: 300, height: 50))
```

```
label.text = "Hello World"
label.font = myfont
```

Listing 4-56: Creating a specific font

Hello World

Figure 4-9: Label with custom font and size

 IMPORTANT: We always have to make sure that the size of the label's view is big enough to fit all the text or at least that the text will not be truncated in a way that becomes unintelligible for the user. In Chapter 6 we will study ways to set the system to ignore the width and height and expand the view automatically.

 The Basics: The font names for the **UIFont** initializer are the PostScript names of the fonts. To find these names, open the Font Book application from your Applications folder, go to the View menu, and select the option Show Font Info. On the right column of the window you will see the information for the selected font, starting by its PostScript name. Select the font you would like to include in your app to get its name. Most of the font types in your computer are available in iOS, but you can also add your own fonts to the project. For more information, visit our website and follow the links for this chapter.

We can also use fonts set by default on the system that were carefully selected to optimize the design and produce a pleasant experience for the user. The **UIFont** class includes several type methods to get an object with these settings.

```
import UIKit

var myfont = UIFont.systemFont(ofSize: 30)

var label = UILabel(frame: CGRect(x: 20, y: 20, width: 300, height: 50))
label.text = "Hello World"
label.font = myfont
```

Listing 4-57: Using the system's standard font

The **systemFont()** method applied in Listing 4-57 returns a **UIFont** object with the standard system font but the size specified by the attribute.

Hello World

Figure 4-10: Label with system font

This time we declared a fix value of 30, but we can take advantage of some of the type methods of the **UIFont** class to set the size as some of the values by default defined by the system.

```
import UIKit

var size = UIFont.buttonFontSize
var myfont = UIFont.systemFont(ofSize: size)
```

Frameworks

```
var label = UILabel(frame: CGRect(x: 20, y: 20, width: 300, height: 50))
label.text = "Hello World"
label.font = myfont
```

Listing 4-58: Getting the font size used by default for buttons

This last example reads the **buttonFontSize** property to get the size by default of the font used by the system to write the text inside buttons and assign it as the size of the **myfont** object. This is helpful when we want to present text along with some buttons and we have to keep everything in proportion (we will study buttons later).

So far, we have been working with short texts and making sure that the size of the label's view is big enough to display the whole text on the screen. This is not always possible. Sometimes the size of the label's view is permanent or there is not enough room on the interface to expand it, but the text may need more space. The **UILabel** class provides the **lineBreakMode** property to establish how the text is going to be processed when it is longer than the size of its view. The value by default is **byTruncatingTail**, which means the characters at the end of the text that do not fit inside the view are going to be replaced by ellipsis. Other frequent values are **byTruncatingMiddle**, to truncate the middle of the text, or **byClipping**, to hide the characters that exceed the view's boundaries. The following example assigns a longer text to the **text** property to see the effects of the line break modes applied to the label.

```
import UIKit

var myfont = UIFont.systemFont(ofSize: 30)

var label = UILabel(frame: CGRect(x: 20, y: 20, width: 150, height: 30))
label.text = "This is a Beautiful Life"
label.lineBreakMode = .byClipping
```

Listing 4-59: Clipping the label's text

This is a Beautiful Li

Figure 4-11: Label clipped

 Do It Yourself: Replace the code in your Playground file by the code of Listing 4-59. Click the Show Result button corresponding to the last statement to see the label in the editor. Try every possible value for the **lineBreakMode** property to see how they work.

The **UILabel** class includes more properties to customize the text, including changing its color by assigning a **UIColor** object to the **textColor** property, or even generating a shadow with the **shadowColor** and **shadowOffset** properties, as shown next.

```
import UIKit

var color = UIColor.blue
var shadow = UIColor.lightGray
var myfont = UIFont.systemFont(ofSize: 30)

var label = UILabel(frame: CGRect(x: 20, y: 20, width: 150, height: 30))
label.text = "Hello World"
```

```
label.textColor = color
label.shadowColor = shadow
label.shadowOffset = CGSize(width: 2, height: 2)
```

Listing 4-60: Customizing the label's text

Hello World

Figure 4-12: Label with shadow

These properties assign the styles to the whole text. Every time a new font, size or color is assigned to the **UILabel** object, all the characters are affected. If we want some parts of the text to have a different style, we have to create a separate label or assign the text to the **attributedText** property instead. This property takes a value of type **NSAttributedString**. The **NSAttributtedString** class is a subclass of the **NSString** class defined to manage text with attributes (styles) that are assigned to an individual character or a range of characters. The **NSAttributedString** class includes the properties and methods to store an attributed string and return information about it, but it is through its **NSMutableAttributedString** subclass that we can assign attributes to a selected range of characters. The following list includes the initializer, properties and methods to create attributed text with this subclass.

NSMutableAttributedString(string: String)—This initializer creates an **NSMutableAttributedString** object with the text specified by the **string** attribute.

string—This property returns a **String** value with the text managed by the object.

length—This property returns the number of characters in the string.

setAttributes(Dictionary, **range:** NSRange)—This method assigns attributes to a range of characters (previous attributes are removed). The first attribute is a dictionary containing properties that describe the attributes and the values for the corresponding styles (font, color, etc.), and the **range** attribute defines the range of characters to be affected.

addAttributes(Dictionary, **range:** NSRange)—This method adds attributes to a range of characters. The new attributes are added to the attributes already assigned to the characters in the range. The first attribute is a dictionary containing properties that describe the attributes and values for the corresponding styles (font, color, etc.), and the **range** attribute defines the range of characters to be affected.

addAttribute(NSAttributedString.Key, **value:** Any, **range:** NSRange)—This method adds a single attribute to a range of characters. The new attribute is added to the attributes already assigned to the characters in the range. The first attribute is the property that describes the attribute, the **value** attribute is the value of the corresponding style (font, color, etc.), and the **range** attribute defines the range of characters to be affected.

removeAttribute(NSAttributedString.Key, **range:** NSRange)—This method removes an attribute previously assigned to a range of characters. The first attribute is the property that describes the attribute, and the **range** attribute is an **NSRange** object defining the range of characters to be affected.

The attributes assigned to an attributed text are identified with the properties of a structure called **Key** included in the **NSAttributedString** class. The list of properties is extensive, with the most frequently used being **font** (font), **foregroundColor** (color of the text), **strokeColor** (color of the stroke), **strokeWidth** (width of the stroke), and **shadow** (shadow).

The first step we have to perform to show attributed text on the screen is to create the **NSMutableAttributedString** object, then assign the attributes from the object's methods, and finally assign the object to the label's **attributedText** property. One of the most common methods used to add attributes is **addAttribute()**.

```
import UIKit

let myfont = UIFont.systemFont(ofSize: 30)
let myrange = NSRange(0..<5)

var mytext = NSMutableAttributedString(string: "Hello World")
mytext.addAttribute(NSAttributedString.Key.font, value: myfont, range:
myrange)
var label = UILabel(frame: CGRect(x: 20, y: 20, width: 150, height: 30))
label.attributedText = mytext
```

Listing 4-61: Adding attributes one by one to a range of characters

The **addAttribute()** method requires the property of the **NSAttributedString.Key** structure that represents the attribute we want to add to the text, the value for the attribute, and an **NSRange** object to determine the range of characters we want to affect. In Listing 4-61, we use the **font** property to assign a system font of size 30 to the first five characters of the string (the word "Hello").

Hello World

Figure 4-13: Different attributes for the same label

Most of the **NSAttributedString.Key** properties require values of types we already know, such as **UIFont** (applied in the previous example) or **UIColor**, but some require more specific types. For example, the **shadow** property requires an object of the **NSShadow** class. This is a simple class with a few properties to configure the characteristics of a shadow.

shadowColor—This property defines the color of the shadow. It takes a value of type **UIColor**.

shadowOffset—This property defines the offset of the shadow. It takes a value of type **CGSize** to determine the horizontal and vertical displacement.

shadowBlurRadius—This property defines the shadow's blur effect. It takes a value of type **CGFloat**.

Effects like shadows are noticeable when they are applied to big fonts. This requires us to assign multiple attributes to the same string. Although we can add all the attributes we need one by one with the **addAttribute()** method, the class offers a better method called **setAttributes()**. This method takes a dictionary with the properties and their values and assigns the attributes all at once.

```
import UIKit

let myfont = UIFont.systemFont(ofSize: 30)
let myrange = NSRange(0..<5)
let color = UIColor.red

let shadow = NSShadow()
shadow.shadowColor = UIColor.black
shadow.shadowOffset = CGSize(width: 2, height: 2)
```

```
let attributes = [NSAttributedString.Key.font: myfont,
NSAttributedString.Key.foregroundColor: color,
NSAttributedString.Key.shadow: shadow]

var mytext = NSMutableAttributedString(string: "Hello World")
mytext.setAttributes(attributes, range: myrange)

var label = UILabel(frame: CGRect(x: 20, y: 20, width: 150, height: 30))
label.attributedText = mytext
```

Listing 4-62: Adding multiple attributes

In the code of Listing 4-62, several attributes are assigned to the string all at once. Besides changing the font, as we did before, now we assign a new color to the text and a shadow. The values are defined first, including the object for the shadow, and then the **attributes** dictionary is created to include every property and value that correspond to the attributes we want to assign to the text. Finally, the **setAttributes()** method takes this dictionary and assigns the attributes to the characters inside the **myrange** range.

Figure 4-14: Multiple attributes for the same label

UIProgressView

The **UIProgressView** class provides properties and methods to create and define the style of a progress bar. This control was designed to depict the progress of a task over time. The class includes its own initializer and also a property and a method to set and read the progress.

UIProgressView(progressViewStyle: UIProgressView.Style)—This initializer creates a **UIProgressView** object with values by default and the style set by the attribute. The attribute is an enumeration called **Style** included in the **UIProgressView** class. The values available are **default** (standard progress bar) and **bar** (progress bar for Toolbars).

progress—This property sets or returns the current progress. The possible values are between 0.0 and 1.0. The value by default is 0.0.

setProgress(Float, **animated:** Bool)—This method sets the value of the **progress** property. The first attribute is a value between 0.0 and 1.0, and the **animated** attribute indicates if the transition will be animated.

The Progress View has a size by default, but it adapts to the size of its view. Using the frame property inherited from **UIView** we can resize the bar to our liking.

```
import UIKit

var progressbar = UIProgressView(progressViewStyle: .default)
progressbar.frame = CGRect(x: 50, y: 50, width: 200, height: 0)
progressbar.progress = 0.6
```

Listing 4-63: Creating a progress bar

The bar is drawn with a standard height, so the **height** property of the **CGRect** value is ignored. Figure 4-15 illustrates the bar created by the code of Listing 4-63.

Figure 4-15: Progress View

The class also includes the following properties to configure the bar.

progressTintColor—This property sets or returns the color of the part of the progress bar that is filled. It is an optional of type `UIColor`.

trackTintColor—This property sets or returns the color of the part of the progress bar that is not filled. It is an optional of type `UIColor`.

progressImage—This property sets or returns the image used to illustrate the part of the progress bar that is filled. It is an optional of type `UIImage`.

trackImage—This property sets or returns the image used to illustrate the part of the progress bar that is not filled. It is an optional of type `UIImage`.

```
import UIKit

var progressbar = UIProgressView(progressViewStyle: .default)
progressbar.progress = 0.2
progressbar.tintColor = UIColor.red
progressbar.trackTintColor = UIColor.blue
```

Listing 4-64: Customizing the progress bar

UIActivityIndicatorView

The `UIActivityIndicatorView` class provides properties and methods to create a spinning wheel that indicates that a task is in progress. Unlike the progress bar studied before, this type of indicator has no implicit limitations. The class includes its own initializer.

UIActivityIndicatorView(style: UIActivityIndicatorView.Style)—This initializer creates a `UIActivityIndicatorView` object with the style set by the attribute. The attribute is an enumeration called **Style** included in the `UIActivityIndicatorView` class. The values available are **whiteLarge** (large white indicator), **white** (standard white indicator), and **gray** (standard gray indicator).

color—This property sets or returns the color of the indicator. It takes a value of type `UIColor`.

hidesWhenStopped—This property sets or returns a Boolean value that determines if the indicator is going to be hidden when the animation stops.

isAnimating—This property returns a Boolean value that determines whether the indicator is animating or not.

startAnimating()—This method starts the animation.

stopAnimating()—This method stops the animation.

```
import UIKit

var progress = UIActivityIndicatorView(style: .gray)
progress.frame.origin = CGPoint(x: 50, y: 50)
progress.color = UIColor.red
progress.startAnimating()
```

```
if progress.isAnimating {
    print("In Progress")
}
```

Listing 4-65: Creating an Activity Indicator

The code of Listing 4-65 creates a standard gray indicator, but it changes its color to red. After the indicator is created, the **startAnimating()** method has to be called to start the animation. The code also checks the value returned by the **isAnimating** property to confirm the indicator is animating. Figure 4-16 illustrates how a working indicator looks like.

Figure 4-16: Activity Indicator

 IMPORTANT: The Show Result button generates a window with a capture of the image produced by the control. Starting or stopping the wheel has no effect on this image. To see the indicator at work you have to include it in a real application.

UIControl

Some of the most valuable subclasses of **UIView** are actually subclasses of an intermediate subclass called **UIControl** (see Figure 4-7). The **UIControl** subclass includes things like properties to determine the current state of the control (selected, disabled, etc.) and also methods to respond to user interaction. The following are the most frequently used.

isEnabled—This property sets or returns a Boolean value indicating whether the element is enabled or not.

isSelected—This property sets or returns a Boolean value indicating whether the element is selected or not.

isHighlighted—This property sets or returns a Boolean value indicating whether the element is highlighted or not.

addTarget(Any?, **action:** Selector, **for:** UIControl.Event**)**—This method sets a responder to an event. The first attribute is a reference to the object that responds to the event (usually **self**), the **action** attribute is a selector (a reference to a method) indicating the method in the target object that is going to be executed when the event takes place, and the **for** attribute is a property of a structure called **Event** included in the **UIControl** class that determines the type of event the target will respond to. The most frequently used properties are **touchDown**, **touchDragEnter**, **touchDragExit**, **touchUpInside**, **touchCancel**, and **valueChanged**.

removeTarget(Any?, **action:** Selector?, **for:** UIControl.Event**)**—This method removes a responder for an event. The values of the attributes must be the same assigned to the **addTarget()** method.

The **UIControl** class does not create any control by itself but serves as the basis for the construction of more complex classes that define visual controls capable of processing user interaction, like buttons or sliders.

Frameworks

UIButton

Probably the simplest but most useful subclass of **UIControl** is **UIButton**. This subclass creates a button composed of a text or an image that can execute an action when the user taps on it. There are different kinds of buttons defined by the class, as illustrated in Figure 4-17.

Figure 4-17: Button types

The DetailDisclosure, InfoLight, and InfoDark buttons produce the same graphic, but the InfoLight button looks better on dark background and the InfoDark button looks better on light background. On the other hand, the System and Custom buttons were designed to show text, similar to a web link, but the Custom button can also present images and a custom appearance. To create a button, the **UIButton** class includes the following initializer.

UIButton(type: UIButton.ButtonType)—This initializer creates a **UIButton** object configured according to the type specified by the **type** attribute. The attribute is an enumeration called **ButtonType** included in the **UIButton** class. The values available are **custom**, **system**, **detailDisclosure**, **infoLight**, **infoDark**, and **contactAdd**.

The simplest buttons to implement are ContactAdd, DetailDisclosure, InfoLight, and InfoDark. These buttons are shown on the screen with a predefined image. The following example creates a button of type ContactAdd (see Figure 4-17).

```
import UIKit

let button = UIButton(type: .contactAdd)
```

Listing 4-66: Creating a button of type ContactAdd

 Do It Yourself: Replace the code in your Playground file by the code of Listing 4-66. In the Results Side Bar, click on the Show Result button to see a representation of the button. As other controls, buttons are not functional in Playground.

These types of buttons are not used very often. Text and image buttons are more frequent and for that we have the System and Custom types. These buttons can show a title and also images and backgrounds that are fully customizable. Also, different values can be assigned to different states and therefore the buttons will change according to their present condition. For example, if the button is pressed, the state changes to Highlighted and the attributes associated to that state are assigned to the button. The states are defined by properties of a structure called **State** included in the **UIControl** class. The properties available are **normal** (the initial state), **highlighted** (the button was touched), **disabled** (the button was disabled), **selected** (the button was selected), and **focused** (the focus is on the button). The **UIButton** class include the following properties and methods to modify the characteristics of the button for each of these states.

titleLabel—This property returns a `UILabel` object with the text of the button. The **font** property of this object can be modified to assign a new font to the text.

setTitle(String, for: UIControl.State**)**—This method sets the text of the button to the value specified by the first attribute and for the state specified by the **for** attribute.

setAttributedTitle(NSAttributedString, **for:** UIControl.State**)**—This method sets the text of the button to the value specified by the first attribute and for the state specified by the **for** attribute.

setTitleColor(UIColor, **for:** UIControl.State**)**—This method sets the color of the text to the value specified by the first attribute and for the state specified by the **for** attribute.

setImage(UIImage, **for:** UIControl.State**)**—This method sets the image of the button to the one specified by the first attribute and for the state specified by the **for** attribute.

setBackgroundImage(UIImage, **for:** UIControl.State**)**—This method sets the background image of the button to the one specified by the first attribute and for the state specified by the **for** attribute.

Custom buttons are usually implemented when we want to use images (we will study how to work with images in Chapter 8), but System buttons are more popular because they include built-in functionality, like transitions between states. The following example illustrates how to create and configure these buttons.

```
import UIKit

let view = UIView(frame: CGRect(x: 0, y: 0, width: 200, height: 200))

let button = UIButton(type: .system)
button.frame = CGRect(x: 50, y: 50, width: 100, height: 32)
button.titleLabel?.font = UIFont.systemFont(ofSize: 25)
button.setTitle("Tap Here", for: .normal)
button.setTitleColor(UIColor.blue, for: .normal)
view.addSubview(button)
```

Listing 4-67: Customizing a text button

In Listing 4-67, the title and the color were assigned for the normal state (**normal**). This is the only one required. If no styles are specified for other states, the system defaults to normal. We also changed the label's font. This affects every state. Notice that the **titleLabel** property returns an optional that we have unwrapped with Optional Chaining.

UISegmentedControl

The **UISegmentedControl** class provides properties and methods to create a series of synchronized buttons (if one button is pressed, the other buttons are deactivated). Its initializer takes an array of strings or images to define the buttons.

UISegmentedControl(items: [Any]?**)**—This initializer creates a **UISegmentedControl** object with buttons generated from the strings or images provided by the **items** attribute. The attribute is an array of **String** values or **UIImage** objects.

Each button of the segment is identified by an index starting from 0. The properties and methods in the class use this index to modify a specific button.

numberOfSegments—This property returns the number of buttons in the control.

selectedSegmentIndex—This property sets or returns the selected button in the control.

setTitle(String, forSegmentAt: Int**)**—This method sets the title for the button at the index specified by the **forSegmentAt** attribute.

setImage(UIImage, forSegmentAt: Int**)**—This method sets the image for the button at the index specified by the **forSegmentAt** attribute.

insertSegment(withTitle: String, **at:** Int, **animated:** Bool**)**—This method inserts a button with the title specified by the **withTitle** attribute at the index specified by the **at** attribute. The **animated** attribute indicates if the process will be animated.

insertSegment(with: UIImage, **at:** Int, **animated:** Bool**)**—This method inserts a button with the image specified by the **with** attribute at the index specified by the **at** attribute. The **animated** attribute indicates if the process will be animated.

removeSegment(at: Int, **animated:** Bool**)**—This method removes the button at the index specified by the **at** attribute. The **animated** attribute indicates if the process will be animated.

setEnabled(Bool, forSegmentAt: Int**)**—This method sets the condition of the button at the index specified by the **forSegmentAt** attribute. The first attribute determines whether the button is enabled (`true`) or disabled (`false`).

In a Segmented Control, only one button can be selected at a time. When the user taps on a button, the button tapped is selected and the rest are deselected. The change can also be performed from the code assigning a new value to the `selectedSegmentIndex` property. The following example creates a Segmented Control with two buttons, Yes and No, and sets the last button as selected.

```
import UIKit

let segment = UISegmentedControl(items: ["Yes", "No"])
segment.frame.origin = CGPoint(x: 50, y: 50)
segment.selectedSegmentIndex = 1
```

Listing 4-68: Creating a Segmented Control

The size of the control is determined automatically by the title of its buttons, the size of its view and the size of its superview. Figure 4-18 illustrates the Segmented Control generated by the code of Listing 4-68 in two states, with none of the buttons selected and with the No button selected.

Figure 4-18: Segmented Control

The buttons and their titles are set by the initializer. They are created based on the number of elements in the array and their values. Sometimes, the options available change and the control has to adapt to the new situation. The `setTitle()` method lets us assign a new title to a specific button after the control was already created.

```
import UIKit

let segment = UISegmentedControl(items: ["Yes", "No"])
segment.frame = CGRect(x: 50, y: 50, width: 200, height: 30)
segment.setTitle("Agree", forSegmentAt: 0)
```

Listing 4-69: Modifying a Segmented Control

Besides changing the titles we can also insert new buttons after the control was already created with the **insertSegment()** methods. These methods take the title or image for the new button, the index where the button should be placed, and a Boolean value to determine if the process should be animated.

```
import UIKit

let segment = UISegmentedControl(items: ["Yes", "No"])
segment.frame = CGRect(x: 50, y: 50, width: 200, height: 30)
segment.insertSegment(withTitle: "Not Sure", at: 2, animated: false)
```

Listing 4-70: Adding new buttons to a Segmented Control

UISwitch

The **UISwitch** class provides properties and methods to create a switch to select between two possible values (**true** or **false**). The user selects the current value by swiping a round button to one side or another, turning the switch on and off. The class uses the **UIView** initializer to declare the area of the view, but the **size** component is ignored because the switch always has a size by default.

```
import UIKit

let myswitch = UISwitch(frame: CGRect(x: 50, y: 50, width: 0, height: 0))
```

Listing 4-71: Creating a switch

Switches are turned on and off by the user, but the class includes some tools to modify the state from code.

isOn—This property sets or returns the state of the switch. It is a Boolean value that determines the state of the switch; on (**true**) or off (**false**).

setOn(Bool, animated: Bool)—This method sets the state of the switch. The first attribute sets the switch on (**true**) or off (**false**), and the **animated** attribute determines if the transition will be animated.

```
import UIKit

let myswitch = UISwitch(frame: CGRect(x: 50, y: 50, width: 0, height: 0))
if !myswitch.isOn {
   myswitch.setOn(true, animated: true)
}
```

Listing 4-72: Switching the switch on

The code of Listing 4-72 reads the **isOn** property to check the state of the switch first, and if it is off it turns it on. Figure 4-19 illustrates the two possible states.

Figure 4-19: Switch on and off

When the switch is turned on, its background color changes. We can modify this color, the color of the border and the button using the following properties.

onTintColor—This property sets or returns the color of the switch's background when it is turned on. It is an optional of type **UIColor**.

tintColor—This property sets or returns the color of the switch's border when it is turned off. It is an optional of type **UIColor**.

thumbTintColor—This property sets or returns the color of the switch's button. It is an optional of type **UIColor**.

```
import UIKit

var colorBackground = UIColor(red: 0.9, green: 0.9, blue: 1.0, alpha:1.0)
var colorButton = UIColor(red: 0.5, green: 0.5, blue: 1.0, alpha: 1.0)

let myswitch = UISwitch(frame: CGRect(x: 50, y: 50, width: 0, height: 0))
myswitch.onTintColor = colorBackground
myswitch.tintColor = colorBackground
myswitch.thumbTintColor = colorButton
```

Listing 4-73: Changing the colors of the switch

In this last example, the colors are declared first and then assigned to the corresponding properties. This time we used RGB colors to paint the switch with different tones of blue.

UISlider

The **UISlider** class provides properties and methods to create a control that lets the user select a value from a range of values. The control is presented as a horizontal bar with a round indicator that points to the selected value. The class uses the **UIView** initializer to set the view. The control adapts its size to the size of the view, but we must set minimum values for the graphics to fit inside.

```
import UIKit

let slider = UISlider(frame: CGRect(x: 50, y: 50, width: 200, height:31))
```

Listing 4-74: Creating a Slider

By default, Sliders are created with a range of values from 0.0 to 1.0 and the indicator pointing at the value 0.0. To adapt the control to our needs, we have to modify its properties.

value—This property sets or returns the selected value. When the value is set, the indicator is moved to the corresponding position. It takes a value of type **Float**.

minimumValue—This property sets or returns the minimum value for the Slider. It takes a value of type **Float**.

maximumValue—This property sets or returns the maximum value for the Slider. It takes a value of type `Float`.

setValue(Float, animated: Bool)—This method sets the selected value as the value specified by the first attribute and moves the indicator to the corresponding position. The **animated** attribute is a Boolean value to specify if the indicator will be animated or not.

```
import UIKit

let slider = UISlider(frame: CGRect(x: 50, y: 50, width: 200, height:31))

slider.minimumValue = 0.0
slider.maximumValue = 10.0
slider.value = 6.0
```

Listing 4-75: Setting the values for the Slider

The code of Listing 4-75 sets the minimum value at 0.0, the maximum value at 10.0, and the selected value as 6.0. The result is shown in Figure 4-20.

Figure 4-20: Slider

The class also provides properties and methods to customize the Slider, changing colors and adding images on the sides to represent minimum and maximum values.

minimumTrackTintColor—This property sets or returns the color of the bar on the left side of the indicator. It is an optional of type `UIColor`.

maximumTrackTintColor—This property sets or returns the color of the bar on the right side of the indicator. It is an optional of type `UIColor`.

minimumValueImage—This property sets or returns the image that represents the minimum value. It is an optional of type `UIImage`.

maximumValueImage—This property sets or returns the image that represents the maximum value. It is an optional of type `UIImage`.

```
import UIKit

let slider = UISlider(frame: CGRect(x: 50, y: 50, width: 200, height:31))
slider.minimumValue = 0.0
slider.maximumValue = 10.0
slider.value = 9.0

slider.minimumTrackTintColor = UIColor.red
slider.maximumTrackTintColor = UIColor.blue
```

Listing 4-76: Changing the colors of the Slider

Frameworks

UIStepper

The **UIStepper** class provides properties and methods to create a set of two buttons with the minus and plus symbols that allow users to increment or decrement a value. The class uses the **UIView** initializer to declare the area of the view, but the **size** component is ignored, and the control is always drawn with a size by default.

```
import UIKit

let stepper = UIStepper(frame: CGRect(x: 50, y: 50, width: 0, height: 0))
```
Listing 4-77: *Creating a Stepper*

Figure 4-21: *Stepper*

The initializer used in the code of Listing 4-77 returns a Stepper with values by default. The minimum value is set to 0.0, the maximum value is set to 100.0, the initial value is set to 0.0, and the incremental value is set to 1.0. We can adapt the control to our needs from its properties.

value—This property sets or returns the current value of the Stepper.

minimumValue—This property sets or returns the minimum value. It takes a value of type **Double**.

maximumValue—This property sets or returns the maximum value. It takes a value of type **Double**.

stepValue—This property sets or returns the number by which the current value of the Stepper will be incremented or decremented. It takes a value of type **Double**.

The class also includes properties to configure the behaviour and appearance of the control.

autorepeat—This property sets or returns a Boolean value that indicates if the value is incremented automatically. If it is set to **true**, the value of the Stepper is incremented repeatedly when the user presses and holds down the button.

isContinuous—This property sets or returns a Boolean value that indicates whether the updated values are reported during the user interaction or only when the user interaction ends.

wraps—This property sets or returns a Boolean value that determines how the value is processed when it reaches the minimum or maximum values allowed. If **true**, when the value goes beyond the limit the opposite limit is assigned to it and the value keeps decrementing or incrementing in a loop. On the other hand, when the property is **false**, the value stops decrementing or incrementing when a limit is reached.

tintColor—This property sets or returns the color of the control.

```
import UIKit

let stepper = UIStepper(frame: CGRect(x: 50, y: 50, width: 0, height: 0))
stepper.value = 4.0
stepper.minimumValue = 1.0

stepper.maximumValue = 9.0
stepper.stepValue = 0.5
```

Listing 4-78: Setting the values for the Stepper

 The Basics: Although you can create the controls programmatically, as we have done in this chapter, the interfaces of professional applications are created visually with the tools provided by Xcode, but any change required later has to be done in code and that is why it is important to know and understand the objects behind them. We will learn how to create these elements visually and how to take advantage of the Xcode interface in the next chapter.

Frameworks

Chapter 5
Building Applications

5.1 The Interface

Up to this point we have been working with a simplified interface called Playground. Playground is a recent addition to Xcode designed to reduce the learning curve and simplify testing. It is good for learning, but to build full applications we have to move to the Xcode's main interface. This is a toolset that comprises an editor, a visual interface, resource managers, configuration panels, and debugging tools, all integrated into a single working space where we can create and modify our applications.

Xcode Projects

Applications are built from several files and resources, including our own codes, frameworks, images, databases, etc. Xcode organizes this information in projects. An Xcode project comprises all the information and resources necessary to create one application. The welcome window, illustrated in Figure 1-2, presents a button called *Create a new Xcode project* to initiate a project. When we click on this button, a new window lets us choose the template we want to use to create our project.

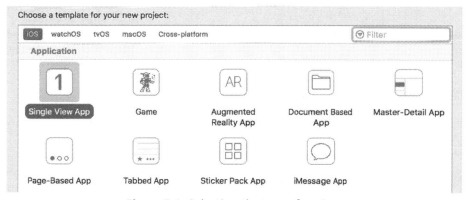

Figure 5-1: *Selecting the type of project*

The selection screen organizes all the options in several categories, iOS, watchOS, tvOS, and macOS (OS X), representing each operative system Apple has to offer (shown at the top). To develop applications for iPhones and iPads, we have to select the options under the iOS category.

Xcode provides templates to give us something to start with. There are several templates available for every platform and different types of projects, such as 2D and 3D video games, single or multiple views, etc. Templates include basic files with pre-programmed code that help us organize our own code. The following are some of the options available to create applications.

Single View App—This option creates a basic template with only one view. It is a very basic template, but more views may be added later according to our needs.

Master-Detail App—This option creates the structure of views necessary to divide the screen into two parts, the Master view (to contain menus or options) and the Detail view (to contain the most relevant information). This is a very useful template for iPad applications, but can also be used for iPhones.

Tabbed App—This option creates a container view with other views inside and a bar with navigation buttons. The buttons allow users to select the view they want to see.

After selecting a template, the next step is to insert information about the project. The information required depends on the type of template selected. Figure 5-2 shows what we see if we select the Single View Application option for the iOS system (the one selected in Figure 5-1).

Product Name:	Test
Team:	Add account...
Organization Name:	John D Gauchat
Organization Identifier:	com.formasterminds
Bundle Identifier:	com.formasterminds.Test
Language:	Swift
	☐ Use Core Data
	☐ Include Unit Tests
	☐ Include UI Tests

Figure 5-2: Project configuration window

This window asks for some basic information like the name of the project (it could be any name we want), the programming language we are going to use (Swift or Objective-C), and the name of the Organization (our name or the name of our company). Most of this is personal information that does not present any challenge, but there are two values that require some consideration, the Team and the Organization Identifier. The Team is our developer account (or our team developer account if we work in a company). This is the account we have to create at developer.apple.com to be able to develop and publish our apps. Although this information is required to test the application in mobile devices or publish the app, Xcode allows us to select it here by clicking on the Add account button or do it later from the Xcode's Preferences menu, as we will see later. On the other hand, the Organization Identifier is mandatory and has to be unique. This is the reason why Apple recommends using an inverted domain. In the example of Figure 5-2 we inserted the inverted domain com.formasterminds as our Organization Identifier. This value is applied automatically along with the app's name to create the Bundle identifier (com.formasterminds.Test). Using the inverted domain ensures that the Bundle identifier (our project's identifier) will be unique.

IMPORTANT: Although it's not mandatory, you should get your own domain and website. Apple not only recommends the use of an inverted domain to generate the Bundle Identifier, but at the time of submitting your app to the App Store you will be asked to provide the web page used for promotion and where the users should go for support. We will study how to submit an app in Chapter 30.

The Basics: There are additional options at the bottom that we can check to prepare our template to work with complementary systems like Unit Testing and Core Data. For most projects, these options are not required, but we will explore some of these alternatives in following chapters (see Core Data in Chapter 22).

After all the values were provided, we have to press the Next button and select the folder to store the project. Xcode creates a folder for each project, so we only need to designate the destination folder where we are going to store all of our projects and everything else is generated for us.

Xcode Tools

Once the project is created, Xcode generates the initial files according to the selected template and presents the main interface on the screen. Figure 5-3, next, shows what this interface looks like.

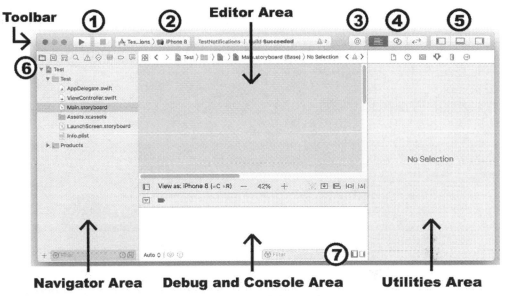

Figure 5-3: *Xcode's interface*

Like the Playground interface, the Xcode's main window is organized in several areas. There is a Toolbar at the top with configuration buttons, an area for edition at the center called *Editor Area*, and three removable panels on the sides and bottom called *Navigator Area*, *Debug and Console Area*, and *Utilities Area*. Although we will study each tool later at the moment they are required, it is a good idea to get familiar with the main parts of the Xcode's interface before working on our first project.

Toolbar—This is a horizontal bar at the top that lets us control the appearance of the rest of the interface and keeps us informed about warnings, errors, and the app's status during execution. It provides two buttons to run and stop the app (Figure 5-3, number 1), a display to show the status of the app (Figure 5-3, number 2), a button that opens a popup window with tools to create the user interface (Figure 5-3, number 3), three buttons to split the Editor Area (Figure 5-3, number 4), and another three buttons at the top right corner to show or hide the removable areas of the interface (Figure 5-3, number 5).

Navigator Area—This is a removable area that provides information related to the files that comprise the application and also tools for debugging (identify and remove errors in the code). From here, we can select the files to edit, create groups to organize those files, add resources, check for errors, etc. In addition to the files, this area shows an option at the top to configure the app (Figure 5-3, number 6).

Editor Area—This is the only non-removable area and is the one where we will do much of the work. The content of the files is displayed here and also the app's configuration.

Debug and Console Area—This is a removable area that splits into two sections that can be shown or hidden by the buttons at the bottom (Figure 5-3, number 7). The section on the left provides information for debugging, while the section on the right is a console to display the results of the execution of our code, including warnings and errors.

Utilities Area—This is a removable area that provides additional information about the files and their content. From here, we can edit the configuration of the interface and its elements.

 Do It Yourself: Open Xcode and select the option *Create a new Xcode project* from the welcome window (Figure 1-2). On the template window, select the iOS tab and the option *Single View Application* (Figure 5-1). Insert the information for your project as shown in Figure 5-2 (remember to set the language as "Swift"). Select the folder to store the project and click Create. You should see a window similar to Figure 5-3.

Running the Project

Xcode offers two ways to run our application: the simulator or a real device. The buttons to select these options, execute, and stop the app are at the left-hand side of the Toolbar.

Figure 5-4: Buttons to execute the app

Applications are always executed on a specific destination. This destination could be different things, from real devices to windows or simulators, and have different configurations, including settings like the region where the device is located, and the human language used by the app to display the information on the screen. Xcode lets us define and configure the possible destinations for our app using an arrangement called *Scheme*. When a project is created, a Scheme is automatically generated for us with options that are according to the type of project we are creating and our local settings (region and language set on the computer). For example, the default Scheme of a project for a mobile application includes several iOS simulators and offers access to the devices currently connected to the computer. The Scheme is selected from the button on the left of the Scheme section and the destination is selected from the button on the right (Figure 5-4, right). When the destination button is clicked, we can see a list with devices and simulators we can choose from.

Figure 5-5: Options available to run the app

During development, the most common destination is the simulator. The simulator is a program included in the Xcode's package that reproduces a specific device in a separate window. It is a very practical tool because it is fast, reproduces almost every feature of a real device, and can run fully functional applications. When we want to run the app, all we have to do is to select the simulator from the Scheme and then click Play. Figure 5-6 shows the simulator configured as an iPhone 8, running the app created by the Single View Application template.

Building Applications

Figure 5-6: iPhone simulator running an empty template

 The Basics: When a project is created from the Single View Application template, the user's interface is declared as an empty view. That is why the simulator of Figure 5-6 only shows the status bar and an empty screen. The template leaves everything ready for us to start adding graphic elements and writing our code.

To run the app on the simulator, we just have to select the type of device to simulate and press play, but to do it on a real device we have to register our developer account with Xcode. This is the account we have to create at developer.apple.com to be able to run our apps in a device and publish them later in the App Store. If we did not do it by clicking the Add Account button when the project was created (Figure 5-2), we have to do it from Xcode's configuration panel. The panel is accessible from the Xcode menu at the top of the screen. We have to select the option Preferences and then select the Accounts tab, as shown in Figure 5-7, number 1.

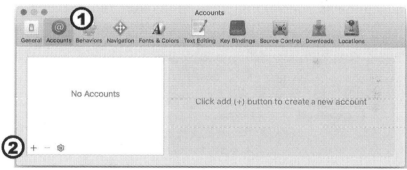

Figure 5-7: Xcode Preferences window

The Accounts tab offers buttons to add and remove accounts (Figure 5-7, number 2). To add our account, we have to click the plus button and select the option Apple ID from the popup menu. The next window presents a form with fields to insert our email and password.

Figure 5-8: Registering our Apple ID in Xcode

Once we insert this information, the account is added to the list and configured to work with this copy of Xcode. Xcode automatically generates all the certificates and provisioning profiles required to run our app in a device.

IMPORTANT: Certificates and provisioning profiles are also necessary to publish the application in the App Store. If you find problems running your app or want to learn more about how to create certificates and provisioning profiles, read Chapter 30.

 Do It Yourself: If you haven't done it yet, create a new Single View Application project following the steps described in the previous section. With the project opened, press the Scheme button (Figure 5-4) and select one of the iPhone's simulators. Press the Play button to run the app. You should see the simulator's window on the screen (Figure 5-6). Insert your account information as explain above, connect your device to the computer, select it from the Scheme, and run the app again.

 The Basics: Pressing the Play button on the toolbar executes the app on the simulator or a device, but we can also build our code without running the app. This is useful when we want to check if the code contains errors. The option to build the app is available in the Product menu at the top of the window. You can also start this process by pressing the keys Command + B.

5.2 Templates

Templates are a simple way to start building our application. They include files with basic code to let us concentrate on what is important for our app right from the beginning. But to take advantage of these files we have to understand first how Xcode suggests applications should be built and the tools it provides for this purpose.

MVC

Xcode proposes an architectural paradigm that divides the application in three interconnected parts, the Model, the View, and the Controller (called MVC for short). Every part of the code performs a specific task and communicates to the other parts only the information strictly necessary. Figure 5-9 illustrates the elements involved.

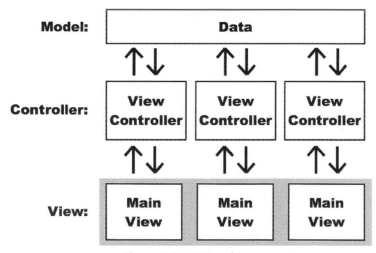

Figure 5-9: MVC architecture

The Model is the data the app has to process, the View is the user's interface, composed of the window and its views, and the Controller are the objects in charge of reading and processing the data and also updating and receiving the input from the views. The objects managing the data and the views are not connected with each other, they send the information to the controller and this code decides what to do with it. This allows reusability. We can use the same code to control different views or replace the user's interface entirely without having to change a line of code in the rest of the program. As long as they know what to do with the information received from other objects and return the right values in response, each part remains independent.

This structure is created from several objects. The interface is created from the **UIView** objects introduced in Chapter 4, these objects are connected to controller objects (one for each main view in the interface), and the controller objects are connected to the objects that manage the app's data. Along with these objects, there is also the **AppDelegate** object, used by the **UIApplication** object to communicate with our code.

The application loop and the window are created directly from the **UIApplication** and **UIWindow** classes studied in Chapter 4, but the rest of the objects are created from the files provided by the templates and our own code. Figure 5-10 shows the Navigator Area with the list of files generated by the Singe View Application template.

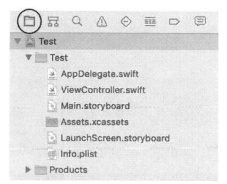

Figure 5-10: *Template's basic files*

 The Basics: Xcode organizes the files in groups. Groups are not real directories. All the files for our app are stored in the same directory, but they are organized in groups to help us find them on the Navigator Area. If you cannot see the files, click on the first button of the Toolbar at the top of the Navigator Area (circled in Figure 5-10) or go to the View menu at the top of the screen, select the option Navigators, and click on Show Project Navigator.

An app requires at least three files. There is a file defining the delegate of the **UIApplication** object that is going to establish the communication between the application loop and our code (AppDelegate.swift), a file defining the object that will control the initial main view and its content (ViewController.swift), and a file defining the objects that will create the views and represent every screen of the interface (Main.storyboard).

Application Delegate

One of the files available in every template is called AppDelegate.swift. This file defines a class called **AppDelegate** to create an object that will be the delegate of the **UIApplication** object. Once created, the **AppDelegate** object is assigned to the **delegate** property of the **UIApplication** object and becomes the connection between this object and our code. The code generated by the template for this file contains a property called **window** and a few empty methods. The property is just a reference to the **UIWindow** object created for our app, and the methods are some of the methods defined by the **UIApplicationDelegate** protocol that this class conforms to.

There are different states associated with an application. At a certain moment, the application may be running in the foreground, active, inactive, or running in the background. For example, when the user taps on the app's icon, the application is loaded and becomes Active, but if the user later presses the Home button to open a different application, the app's state changes to Background. Every time the state of the application changes, the `UIApplication` object calls a method on the `AppDelegate` object to let us know what happened. The following are some of these methods, defined by the `UIApplicationDelegate` protocol.

application(UIApplication, **didFinishLaunchingWithOptions:** Dictionary**)**—This is the first method to be executed. It is called to let us know that the basic objects were already instantiated and the app is ready to work. We can write inside this method all the code we need to prepare our app, such as declaring initial values, creating or opening a database, checking the current settings, etc.

applicationWillResignActive(UIApplication**)**—This method is called when the app becomes inactive, usually due to an incoming call or message.

applicationDidEnterBackground(UIApplication**)**—This method is called when the app is closed (it moves to the background).

applicationWillEnterForeground(UIApplication**)**—This method is called before the app becomes active again.

applicationDidBecomeActive(UIApplication**)**—This method is called when the app is launched and also when it comes back from the inactive state.

applicationWillTerminate(UIApplication**)**—This method is called before the app is terminated. This state usually occurs when the system decides to terminate the app because it needs the memory for other applications or the app is terminated by the user.

All the methods in the `UIApplicationDelegate` protocol are optional. This means that we can implement only the methods our application needs. For example, some simple applications only implement the `application(UIApplication, didFinishLaunchingWithOptions: Dictionary)` method to initialize the application, as in the following example.

```
import UIKit

@UIApplicationMain
class AppDelegate: UIResponder, UIApplicationDelegate {
   var window: UIWindow?
   var basicSalary: Double?

   func application(_ application: UIApplication,
didFinishLaunchingWithOptions launchOptions:
[UIApplication.LaunchOptionsKey : Any]? = nil) -> Bool {
      basicSalary = 30000.0
      return true
   }
}
```

Listing 5-1: Defining our own AppDelegate.swift file

The main purpose of the `AppDelegate` class is to give us a chance to react every time the state of the app changes, but because the application's delegate is accessible from every part of the code through the `delegate` property of the `UIApplication` object, it is common practice to use this object to declare values that will be required by different parts of the code and also to initialize data containers such as databases or files. To illustrate this process, in the example of Listing 5-1 we have declared a single property called `basicSalary`. The system creates an instance of the `AppDelegate` object first, including its properties, and as soon as the app is ready to work, the **UIApplication** object calls the **application(UIApplication, didFinishLaunchingWithOptions:)** method to let us perform the tasks required to initialize our app (in this case, we just assign the value 30000.0 to the property).

 Do It Yourself: Click on the AppDelegate.swift file in the Navigator Area to see its content in the Editor Area. The code generated by the template includes all the methods listed above with comments explaining what the methods should be used for. Erase every one of them except the **application(UIApplication, didFinishLaunchingWithOptions:)** method and add the declaration and initialization of the **basicSalary** property, as shown in Listing 5-1. We will work with this property later.

Storyboard

The user interface is built with views inside a single window. One view, usually called *main view* or *container view*, is responsible for organizing all the graphic elements on the screen. Several main views put together simulate virtual screens. This is how the app manages different graphic screens and expands the interface. The main views replace one another inside the same window to give the impression of having more space than a single screen can offer.

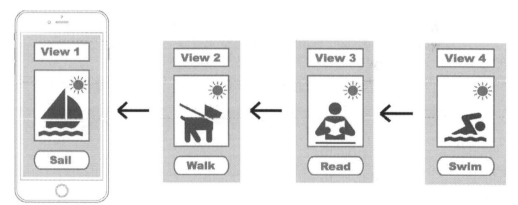

Figure 5-11: Multiple main views to expand the interface

Creating and organizing these views and their content from code could demand hours of meticulous work. It is very difficult to achieve the desired design and functionality for the user interface when we have to program every single element the way we did in Chapter 4. This is why Xcode introduces a graphic tool called *Storyboard*. The Storyboard produces a result similar to Figure 5-11. It lets us organize the main views and their content visually. Every component of the interface is displayed in the Editor Area, and we can drag and connect everything without writing a single line of code. All the information for the views created in the Storyboard is stored in an XML file. When the app is executed, this XML code is interpreted, the real objects are instantiated, and the views are drawn on the screen.

 The Basics: An XML file is just a text file written in a language called *XML* that is easy to read for humans and machines. These files are used to transfer information from one server to another, but because of its characteristics it was adopted by Xcode to represent objects. We will learn more about XML in Chapter 27.

The files that store the information for the Storyboard have the **storyboard** extension. Templates always include a storyboard file with a few initial views. Figure 5-12 shows what we see on the Editor Area when we click on the Main.storyboard file included in the Single View Application template.

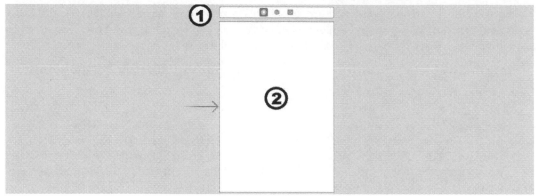

Figure 5-12: Main view in the Storyboard

The box shown in Figure 5-12 is called *Scene*. The Storyboard uses these boxes to represent main views. A Scene contains the main view where the interface is created (Figure 5-12, number 2) and a small bar at the top with options to configure the Scene and the controller for the view (Figure 5-12, number 1). Clicking on the main area selects the main view and clicking on the bar selects the Scene. The controller for the view may also be selected from the buttons shown on the bar when we click on it (Figure 5-13 below). The button on the left represents the controller object responsible for the view, the button at the middle provides options to configure the element designated as first responder (studied in Chapter 7), and the button on the right lets us connect main views together (studied in Chapter 13).

Figure 5-13: Buttons to configure the Scene

The initial shape of the Scenes resembles an iPhone, but we can change it anytime we want from the toolbar at the bottom of the Editor Area.

Figure 5-14: Editor Area's toolbar

The toolbar contains several buttons to help us configure the Storyboard and its content.

Document Outline (1)—This button opens a panel on the left side of the Editor Area with a list of the Scenes, their main views, content, and other components of the Storyboard. From this list, we can select the elements, edit their names or change their order.

Device Configuration (2)—This button displays a list of available devices and configurations that we can select to change the appearance of the Scenes in the Storyboard.

Zoom (3)—These buttons allow us to zoom the Storyboard in and out.

Auto Layout (4)—These buttons open popup windows to create, configure, and resolve issues with constraints (we will study constraints and Auto Layout in Chapter 6).

The Basics: When we start a new project, Xcode automatically opens the Document Outline panel. The panel partially covers the Editor Area and reduces the working space. To close this panel, click on the Document Outline button in the Editor Area's toolbar (Figure 5-14, number 1).

Building Applications

From the Device Configuration button, we can select the device we want the Scenes to represent and also their orientation. Figure 5-15, below, shows the initial options available.

Figure 5-15: *Selecting the device we want to represent in the Storyboard*

When we select an option, all the Scenes in the Storyboard change to represent the new configuration, allowing us to design the interface for every device available. If we select an iPad, more options are added to include split views that let us prepare the interface for these special conditions (iPads can split the screen in two to open two applications simultaneously).

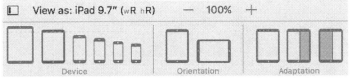

Figure 5-16: *Selecting the adaptation for iPads*

 The Basics: You can select a different device or configuration any time you want, and also zoom in or out with the zoom button to reduce or expand the size of the Scenes for better visualization.

Every time an element in the Storyboard is selected (either a Scene, a main view or its content), the Utilities Area (the removable panel on the right) shows a series of panels for configuration. The panels are selected from the buttons at the top of the area. The most useful are the Attributes Inspector panel and the Size Inspector panel. From the Attributes Inspector panel, we can modify properties related to the attributes of the selected element, and from the Size Inspector panel we can change its size and position. Figure 5-17 shows how to open these panels and some of the properties they include when the main view is selected.

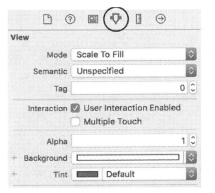 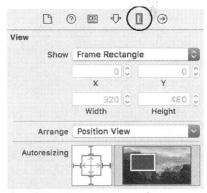

Figure 5-17: *Attributes Inspector panel and Size Inspector panel*

The values on each panel of Figure 5-17 correspond to the same properties studied in Chapter 4 for **UIView** objects. For example, if we change the value of the Background field in the Attributes inspector panel (see Figure 5-17, left), the selected value will be assigned to the **backgroundColor** property of the **UIView** object created to represent the main view. The same happens with the rest of the properties displayed on the panels. All the values defined on these panels will be assigned to the corresponding properties of the object created later to represent the element. From here, we can visually modify all the values and configure the elements in the Storyboard without writing a single line of code.

Do It Yourself: Click on the Main.storyboard file in the Navigator Area to see its content in the Editor Area. You should see something similar to Figure 5-12. Click on the main view to see the configuration options in the Utilities Area. Select a new color in the Background option to change the color of the view (Figure 5-17, left).

View Controllers

Each main view in the Storyboard is responsible for showing its content on the screen and adapting to new circumstances. With the purpose of controlling each view and performing any standard function they require, the UIKit framework includes the **UIViewController** class. This is a basic class with properties and methods to manage a single view and its content, and also respond to changes on its state. Although it provides everything we need to control a particular main view, we do not work directly with objects created from this class. Instead, we define a subclass of **UIViewController** for every main view in the Storyboard and add our own properties and methods to perform the tasks that are specific for that view and our app.

Most templates follow this pattern and always include files with subclasses of the **UIViewController** class to control the views they provide. For example, the ViewController.swift file created by the Single View Application template declares a class called **ViewController** that inherits from the **UIViewController** class and is in charge of controlling the single main view included by the template in the Storyboard. The initial file is mostly empty but it has two overwritten methods of its superclass: **viewDidLoad()** and **didReceiveMemoryWarning()**. These are methods of the **UIViewController** class that are executed to report changes in the condition of the view. We have to overwrite these methods in our subclass if we want to program our own response. Along with these two, the class includes a few more methods to report each state.

viewDidLoad()—This method is called after the main view and its content is loaded in memory. It is the first method called on the object to indicate that the main view is ready to be shown on the screen.

viewWillAppear()—This method is called after the **viewDidLoad()** method and before the main view is shown on the screen.

viewDidAppear()—This method is called after the main view is shown on the screen.

viewWillDisappear()—This method is called before the main view is removed from the screen.

viewDidDisappear()—This method is called after the main view has been removed from the screen.

didReceiveMemoryWarning()—This method is called when the app receives a memory warning from the system. It is used to free memory and avoid our app being terminated.

Usually we do not need other methods than **viewDidLoad()** to set up the view and the **didReceiveMemoryWarning()** to take care of memory. This is why these are the only methods declared by the template. The following example modifies the **ViewController** class provided by the Single View Application template to read the property we added to the **UIApplication** delegate in Listing 5-1 and print its value on the console as soon as the main view controlled by this object is loaded.

```
import UIKit
class ViewController: UIViewController {
    override func viewDidLoad() {
        super.viewDidLoad()

        let app = UIApplication.shared
        let mydelegate = app.delegate as! AppDelegate
        if let salary = mydelegate.basicSalary {
            print("Basic Salary is \(salary)")
        }
    }
}
```

Listing 5-2: Adding our own code to the ViewController.swift file

The first thing we do inside the **viewDidLoad()** method of Listing 5-2 is call the same method in the superclass (see **super** in Chapter 3). When a method Is overwritten, the original method is not executed anymore. Some classes, like the **UIViewController** class, include methods that perform essential tasks necessary for the app to work properly. If we do not call them, those tasks are never performed.

After the method is called in the superclass, we can include our own code. In this example, we get a reference to the **UIApplication** object to read the properties of its delegate. First, we obtain the reference by reading the **shared** property of the class. Next, we read the object's **delegate** property and assign it to the **mydelegate** constant (this is the object created from the class declared in the AppDelegate.swift file). Notice that we have to cast this object as **AppDelegate** with the **as!** operator because the **AppDelegate** object is a subclass of the **UIResponder** class (a basic class in UIKit) and the **delegate** property returns a value of this type. Finally, we use Optional Binding to read the **basicSalary** property of the delegate and print its value on the console ("Basic Salary is 30000.0").

When this app is executed, the system creates all the basic objects, including the **UIApplication** object and its delegate, and then calls the **application(UIApplication, didFinishLaunchingWithOptions:)** method of the **AppDelegate** object. In this method, we define and initialize the **basicSalary** property (see Listing 5-1). When the execution of this method is over, the system looks for the main view that has to show first and calls the **viewDidLoad()** method of its view controller. In this method, we get the value of the **basicSalary** property defined in the delegate object and print it on the console.

 Do It Yourself: The last example assumes that you have already declared the **basicSalary** property in the app's delegate, as shown in Listing 5-1. Replace the code in your ViewController.swift file by the code of Listing 5-2. Select an iPhone simulator and press the Play button to execute the app (Figure 5-4). The value of the **basicSalary** property is printed on the console at the bottom of the Xcode's interface (Figure 5-3, Debug and Console Area). If you cannot see the console, press the middle button on the right-hand side of Xcode's Toolbar (Figure 5-3, number 5) or the buttons at the bottom of the panel (Figure 5-3, number 7).

 IMPORTANT: The main views defined in the Storyboard conform a path the user may follow to achieve a goal (e.g., access information, find a picture, etc.). The starting point of the path is determined by assigning the view controller object that controls the initial main view to a property of the **UIWindow** object called **rootViewController** (see **UIWindow** in Chapter 4). This may be done programmatically, but you can also do it from the Storyboard. All you have to do is point the arrow on the screen to the main view you want to show first (Figure 5-12). If the arrow is not visible, you can specify the Scene you want to show first from the Utilities Area. Select the Scene in the Storyboard (click on the bar at the top), go to the Utilities Area, open the Attributes Inspector panel (Figure 5-17), and activate the option *Is Initial View Controller*.

A **UIViewController** object not only manages the main view but also its content. The class includes the **view** property to store a reference to the main view controlled by the object. After the main view associated with the view controller is created from the Storyboard, a reference is assigned to its **view** property. Using this property, we can manage the views' content, add subviews, etc. The following example adds a **UILabel** view to the main view created by the template.

```
import UIKit

class ViewController: UIViewController {
    override func viewDidLoad() {
        super.viewDidLoad()

        let app = UIApplication.shared
        let mydelegate = app.delegate as! AppDelegate

        if let salary = mydelegate.basicSalary {
            let title = UILabel(frame:CGRect(x:20, y:20, width:300,
height:50))
            title.text = "Basic Salary is \(salary)"
            view.addSubview(title)
        }
    }
}
```

Listing 5-3: Adding a subview to the main view from the ViewController *object*

This new version of our **ViewController** class creates a **UILabel** view with a string that includes the value of the **basicSalary** property defined in the application's delegate. The label is added to the main view next by calling its **addSubview()** method. Remember that the **view** property of every view controller has a reference to the main view in the Storyboard, so we can add anything we want to the view from this property and this way modify the user interface.

Figure 5-18: Label added to the initial view

 Do It Yourself: Replace the code in your ViewController.swift file by the code of Listing 5-3. Select an iPhone simulator and press the Play button to execute the app. You should see the text "Basic Salary is 30000.0" at the top of the screen.

 IMPORTANT: The **viewDidLoad()** method is called after the views are loaded in memory and before they are shown on the screen. This means that all the code defined inside this method is executed before the user is able to see the view. If the code takes time to finish, the user may have the impression that the application crashed. To avoid this situation, sometimes it is better to also implement the `viewDidAppear()` method and move some of the initialization code to this method. The method is called after the main view and its content is shown on the screen, and therefore, from the user's perspective, there is no lag or interruption. In further chapters, we will see when the use of this and other initialization methods may be appropriate.

5.3 Interface Builder

Creating the initial interface by adding subviews to the main view from our code, as we did in the last example, may be appropriate for very small applications, but as the interface grows and new elements and functionality are introduced, the code becomes difficult to develop and maintain. This is especially true with mobile applications, where we not only have to define the initial interface but also adapt it to new conditions produced by the rotation of the screen or the app running on different devices. This problem was solved by Xcode with the introduction of Interface Builder.

Interface Builder was actually the first visual tool introduced by Xcode. At the beginning, we were able to design the user's interface one main view at a time. Later, Storyboards were introduced to let us connect the main views together and develop the whole interface in one place. Nowadays, we use the Storyboard to create and connect the main views and Interface Builder to generate their content.

Object Library

Interface Builder is an integral part of Xcode. All we have to do to take advantage of this tool is to click on the storyboard file and start dragging elements inside the views. The elements, including views, main views (also called view controllers), and all the `UIView`'s subviews studied in Chapter 4, are listed in a popup window that opens when we press the Library button on the right side of the toolbar (Figure 5-3, number 3). The window is called the Object Library. We can scroll down the list to see familiar elements like labels and buttons or use the search field at the top to quickly find an element.

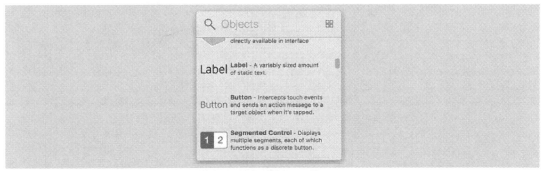

Figure 5-19: Object Library

The elements in the Object Library are incorporated into the view by dragging and dropping, as illustrated in Figure 5-20 below. If we want to drag more than one element, we can press and hold down the Option key to keep the window open.

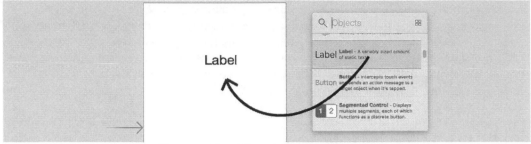

Figure 5-20: Adding elements to the view

Once the element is dropped inside the view it becomes the selected element. Selected elements are surrounded by little squares that we can drag to change the size of their views. We can also drag the element to a new position and select another element by clicking on it. Several elements may be selected at the same time by pressing and holding down the Shift key on the keyboard. Some elements, such as labels and buttons, allow us to double click on them to edit their content.

The element dropped inside a view becomes one of its subviews. It is the same process performed by the **addSubview()** method of the **UIView** object, with the difference that this time everything is done visually. All the views and subviews generated by this tool are stored as XML code in the storyboard file and then the real objects are reconstructed when the application is executed.

Guide Lines

While the element is being dragged over a view, Xcode shows guide lines to help us find the right place to drop it. There are lines that determine the horizontal and vertical center of the view, the superior, inferior and lateral margins, and also the position of one element relative to another. Figure 5-21 shows what we see when we drag a new label to the corner of the main view.

Figure 5-21: View guide lines

These lines become visible again when we drag the elements inside the view to find the right location and when we expand the area of the element's view by dragging the little squares around it.

 Do It Yourself: Drag some of the elements you already know to the view in your Storyboard and increment the size of their views, position them side by side, or move them close to the border to understand how the guide lines work and how they can help you build your interface.

Properties

As well as the main view, the elements in the interface may be selected and configured from the panels in the Utilities Area. Most of the properties studied in Chapter 4 are available from these panels. Figure 5-22 shows what the Attributes Inspector panel and the Size Inspector panel look like after a label is selected.

Building Applications

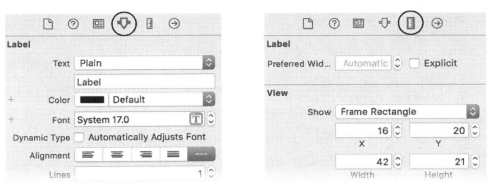

Figure 5-22: Editing the properties of a label from the Utilities Area

Most of the elements' properties are available from this panel. For example, we can modify the text, color, and font of a label, and also the styles for Dynamic Type fonts studied in Chapter 4 (Body, Headline, etc.), so we can create labels with a specific style that adapt to the size determined by the user.

Classes like **UILabel** are subclasses of the **UIView** class. Other similar classes like **UIButton**, for example, are subclasses of **UIControl**, which is a subclass of **UIView**. Therefore, they not only have access to their own properties, but also to other important properties they inherit from their superclasses, such as the **backgroundColor** property of the **UIView** class, used to set the element's background color, or the **isEnabled** property of the **UIControl** class, used to enable or disable the element. All these options are available on the Attributes Inspector panel under the sections Control and View.

 Do It Yourself: Drag and drop several labels from the Library to the view. Select the labels one at a time and modify their values from the Utilities Area (Figure 5-22, left). When the text inserted for the label is longer than the size of its view, it gets truncated. If you want to show the whole text, you have to expand the label's view dragging the little squares around it or modifying the values in the Size Inspector panel (Figure 5-22, right).

5.4 Connections

As we already mentioned, the elements generated in the Storyboard and Interface Builder, including views, subviews, and their properties, are stored as XML code in the storyboard file. Right after the app is executed, the objects for the main views and their content are created from this code. The **UIView** objects that represent the main views are connected to their view controllers through the **view** property, but the objects that represent the subviews inside these main views (labels, buttons, etc.) are not connected to our code. They did not exist when we were programming our app (they were just XML code in the storyboard file), and therefore we cannot reference these objects from our code. To solve this problem, Xcode introduces the concepts of Outlets and Actions.

Outlets

An Outlet is a property referencing an object of the user interface. These are normal properties but prefixed by the **@IBOutlet** attribute to indicate to Xcode that they are related to an element in the Storyboard. When the app is executed, the objects are created from the Storyboard and then assigned to their Outlets in our code. It is through these Outlets that we can access the objects from code and read and set the values of their properties.

There are different ways to create an Outlet and generate the code for the connection. The simplest is to drag a line from the element in the Storyboard to our view controller and let Xcode generate the codes on both ends. For this, we need to divide the Editor Area in two parts by clicking the Assistant Editor button (Figure 5-3, number 4). Figure 5-23, next, illustrates what the Editor Area looks like after we open the storyboard file and click this button.

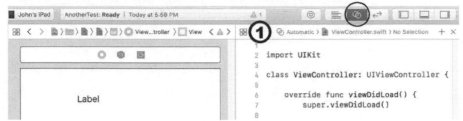

Figure 5-23: Assistant Editor

When we click the Assistant Editor button (circled at the top of Figure 5-23), the Editor Area is divided in two parts to show additional content on the right. This new area can show the content of a file related to the file opened on the left, or any other file we want. The option to select the file to be shown is at the top of the Assistant Editor (Figure 5-23, number 1). If the option is set to Automatic, Xcode shows the file associated to the file in the Editor Area (e.g., the view controller of the selected Scene), but if the option is set to Manual, the file shown is the last file selected. If the corresponding view controller is not shown on the right when a Scene is selected, we have to click on this button and change the option to Automatic.

The connection between the elements in the main view on the left and our code on the right is established by dragging a line from the element to the class while pressing and holding down the Control key on the keyboard. Xcode generates a blue line on the screen to show the connection that is being created and to indicate where the property is going to be placed in our code when the mouse's button is released. The figure below is a capture of this process.

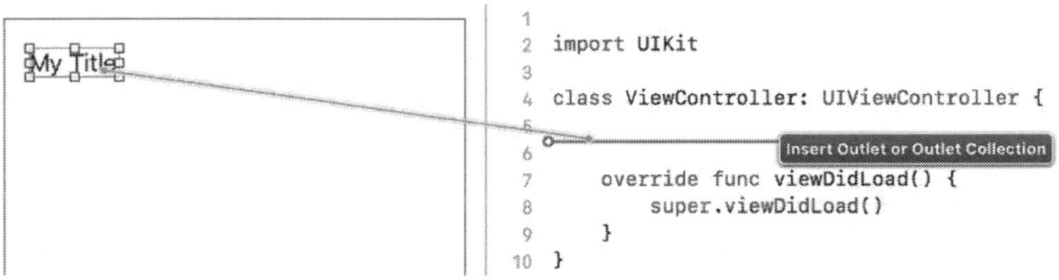

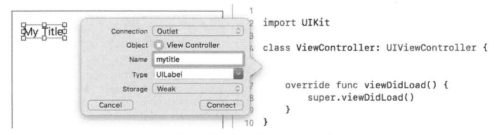

Figure 5-24: Connection between a label and its view controller

Outlets, as well as properties, should always be created at the beginning of the class. When we reach this place and release the mouse's button, Xcode shows a popup window to configure the connection.

Figure 5-25: Configuring a connection

The window asks for the type of the connection (Outlet or Action) and additional information to generate the code. To create an Outlet, we have to select the option Outlet in the Connection field, insert the name we want to assign to the property, its data type, and the value that

Building Applications

determines how the memory is going to be managed. The latter is usually specified as **weak**, because its container (the **UIView** object that represents the main view) already has a strong reference to the object (see Memory Management in Chapter 3).

In the example depicted in Figures 5-24 and 5-25, a label with the text My Title was added to the main view and then connected to the view controller with an Outlet called **mytitle**. When we click the Connect button in the popup window, Xcode generates the code for the Outlet. The following example shows what the code looks like when the Outlet is added to an empty view controller class.

```
import UIKit

class ViewController: UIViewController {
    @IBOutlet weak var mytitle: UILabel!

    override func viewDidLoad() {
        super.viewDidLoad()
    }
}
```

Listing 5-4: Adding an Outlet for a label to the view controller

 Do It Yourself: Drag and drop a label from the Object Library into the view in the Storyboard. Double-click the label to change its text to "My Title" and expand the label's view size if necessary to fit the text. Click on the button to open the Assistant Editor (Figure 5-23). Position the mouse over the label and press and hold down the Control key on your keyboard. Press the mouse's button and drag a line from the label to the beginning of the **ViewController** class. Release the mouse's button when you see something similar to Figure 5-24. A popup window similar to Figure 5-25 will open. Define the Connection as Outlet, the name as **mytitle**, the type as **UILabel**, and the Storage as **weak**. Click the Connect button to generate the code. Your view controller should look like Listing 5-4.

 IMPORTANT: There are some names that are already in use by the UIKit classes or are reserved by the Swift language and we cannot use in our own properties or methods. For example, you cannot give a property the name **title** because the **UIViewController** class already defines a stored property with that name. Every time there is a conflict with the name of a property or a method, Xcode will show you an error. To avoid these conflicts, always use more descriptive names such as **homeTitle** or **titleLabel**.

Notice that the properties for Outlets are declared as implicitly unwrapped optionals. We studied these types of optionals in Chapter 2. They are useful when we do not have the initial value for the variable or the property during development, but we know that once the value is assigned, they will never be empty again. This fits perfectly into the methodology applied to the creation of views and subviews. The objects that represent these views do not exist during development (they are just XML code), but they are created later and assigned to the Outlets as soon as the app is executed. The reason why we used these types of optionals instead of regular optionals (declared with the question mark) is because we do not want to have to unwrap their values every time we have to use them. This is demonstrated in the following example where we access the **mytitle** property as if it were a normal **UILabel** property to change its color to red.

```
import UIKit

class ViewController: UIViewController {
   @IBOutlet weak var mytitle: UILabel!

   override func viewDidLoad() {
      super.viewDidLoad()
      mytitle.textColor = UIColor.red
   }
}
```

Listing 5-5: Modifying the label's properties

When this app is executed, the objects from the Storyboard are created and a reference to the **UILabel** object that represents the label is assigned to the **mytitle** property. As soon as the main view and the label are loaded into memory, the **viewDidLoad()** method is called. Inside this method we use the **mytitle** property to access the **textColor** property of the **UILabel** object and change the label's color to red.

Connections in the Storyboard

When an Outlet is created, Xcode generates code in our view controller and also in the storyboard file. A common mistake we have to be aware of is to think that deleting the code for an Outlet in the view controller is enough to break the connection. This only deletes the connection in our code, but it does nothing to the XML code in the storyboard file. To also erase the connection in the storyboard, we have to click the mouse's right button (Secondary click) when the pointer is over an element to open a popup window where we can edit the element's configuration, as shown in Figure 5-26.

Figure 5-26: Popup window to manage connections in the Storyboard

The popup window shows all the connections created for the selected element. The name of the property is on the left and the name of the object is on the right. The name of the object includes a small x on the left that is highlighted by a circle when we hover the mouse over. Clicking on this x erases the corresponding XML code in the storyboard file and completely breaks the connection (we can also erase the element if we do not need it anymore, and the connections are erased with it).

Actions

Some elements of the interface are not limited to show graphics on the screen; they can also process user interaction. We have studied some of them in Chapter 4. Buttons, Switches, Segmented Controls, and others are designed to respond to the user and also fire an event to report the situation to the application. The way they do the latter is through a process called *target-action*. This is a programming pattern that allows an object to call a method on another object when a specific event occurs (e.g., a button is pressed, a switch is turned off, etc.). For this purpose, these elements implement a method inherited from the **UIControl** class called **addTarget()** (see **UIControl** class in Chapter 4).

The **addTarget()** method adds to its object a target and an action for a specific event. The action is the method to be called when the event occurs, the target is the object that the method belongs to, and the event is a specific type of activity that the user performs on the element (pressing a button, incrementing a value, etc.).

The implementation of this pattern requires an element that can perform an action (such as a button), an Outlet connected to that element (or a reference if the element is created programmatically), and a custom method to process the response. As an example, we are going to insert a label and a button in our view using Interface Builder and declare a method in our view controller called **showCounter()** to count and print the times the button is pressed. Figure 5-27 shows what the view looks like after the addition of the label and the button.

Figure 5-27: *Interface to test Actions*

The text for the label and the title of the button were changed to "Pressed: 0" and "Press Here", respectively. We can do this by double-clicking the elements or selecting each element and modifying their properties from the Attributes inspector panel in the Utilities Area (Figure 5-22). After adding the elements, they have to be connected to Outlets in our view controller, as shown next.

```
import UIKit

class ViewController: UIViewController {
   @IBOutlet weak var counterLabel: UILabel!
   @IBOutlet weak var pressHere: UIButton!
   var counter: Int = 0

   override func viewDidLoad() {
      super.viewDidLoad()
      pressHere.addTarget(self, action: #selector(showCounter(sender:)),
for: UIControl.Event.touchUpInside)
   }
   @objc func showCounter(sender: UIButton) {
      counter += 1
      counterLabel.text = "Pressed: \(counter)"
   }
}
```

Listing 5-6: *Adding a target-action to a button*

The initial statements of the **ViewController** class of Listing 5-6 declare the Outlets for the label and the button with the names **counterLabel** and **pressHere**. Right after that, we define a property of type **Int** called **counter** to keep track of the times the button is pressed. Finally, inside the **viewDidLoad()** method, the **pressHere** property is used to add a target and an action to the button with the **addTarget()** method. The syntax for this method is **addTarget(target, action, event)**. The target in this example was declared as **self** (the **ViewController** object), the action was declared as the **showCounter()** method defined below, and the event was specified as **touchUpEvent** (this event is fired after the button is pressed and released).

To declare the method that we want to execute when the action is performed, we have to use selectors. Selectors are a feature that Swift takes from Objective-C. They are declared with the instruction `#selector(method)` and the syntax for the method must include the names of its parameters followed by a semicolon, as in `#selector(showCounter(sender:))`. Because this is an old Objective-C feature, it also requires the methods to be declared as Objective-C methods. In Swift, this is done by prefixing the name of the method with the keyword `@objc`, as we did in our example.

What the `addTarget()` method is doing is to ask the `UIButton` object that represents the button on the screen to call the `showCounter()` method in the `ViewController` object when it is pressed and released. When this happens, the `showCounter()` method increments the value of the `counter` property by 1 and assigns to the label a string composed of the text "Pressed: " plus the current value of the `counter` property.

 Do It Yourself: Delete all the elements you have added to your view by selecting them one by one and pressing the Delete key on your keyboard. Clean the code in your view controller, including the Outlets. Drag and drop a label and a button from the Object Library into the view. Double-click the label and the button to change their text and title (see Figure 5-27). Create Outlets for both elements with the names `counterLabel` and `pressHere`. Copy the rest of the code of Listing 5-6 into the `ViewController` class. Run the application in the simulator. Every time the button is pressed you should see the number on the label incremented by one unit.

As illustrated by the code of Listing 5-6, to add a target and respond to an event the view controller has to include an Outlet for the control, call the `addTarget()` method to set the target for the object, and define the method that responds to the action. This protocol is always the same, only the method that processes the response changes. This is the reason why Xcode introduces Actions. Actions are connections between the elements in the Storyboard and our code, but unlike Outlets, they connect the elements to methods, not properties. The purpose is to move the definition of the action and the target to the Storyboard. When a control is connected to our code by an Action, the definition of the `addTarget()` method is automatically performed in the Storyboard, so the only thing left to do in our code is to define the method that will respond to the event.

Adding an Action for an element is similar to adding an Outlet. We have to drag a line from the control to the view controller class while pressing and holding down the Control key and then provide the information for the connection.

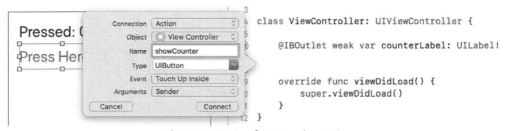

Figure 5-28: Configuring the Action

The first thing we have to do in the popup window is to select the type of the connection as Action. The options to configure the Action are similar to those defined for the `addTarget()` method. We must insert the name of the method, the type of the object, and the type of event that will trigger the action. The last option, Arguments, determines the values we want to send to the method. The option includes three possible values: None (no value is sent to the method), Sender (a reference to the object that represents the control is sent to the method), and Sender

Building Applications

and Event (a reference to the object that represents the control and also information about the event that triggered the action are sent to the method). By default, this value is set to Sender, which will create a parameter for the method called **sender** to receive a reference to the object.

 IMPORTANT: Selecting the data type of the object is important when we need to access the object's properties and methods. If you set this value as **Any**, multiple elements can be connected to the same Action, but Swift may not be able to find the properties and methods of specific types like **UIButton**.

After all the information is declared, Xcode generates the codes in both ends. The declaration of the method in our view controller is similar to the method in the previous example, but this time it is prefixed by the **@IBAction** attribute to establish its relationship with the element in the Storyboard.

```
import UIKit

class ViewController: UIViewController {
   @IBOutlet weak var counterLabel: UILabel!
   var counter: Int = 0

   @IBAction func showCounter(_ sender: UIButton) {
      counter += 1
      counterLabel.text = "Pressed: \(counter)"
   }
}
```

Listing 5-7: Defining an Action for the button

From this example, we can clearly see the advantage of using Actions. The code of Listing 5-7 has been greatly simplified. This time the objects in the Storyboard take care of defining the action and the target, and we only have to declare the method that is going to be executed when the event occurs. The process produced by this code is exactly the same as the previous example. When the button is pressed, the **UIButton** object created from the Storyboard calls the **showCounter()** method in our view controller and the text in the **counterLabel** label is updated.

 Do It Yourself: Delete the elements inside the view by selecting them one by one and pressing the Delete key on your keyboard. Clean the code in your view controller, including the Outlets. Drag and drop a new label and a button from the Object Library into the view (Figure 5-26). Double-click the label and the button to change their text and title (see Figure 5-27). Create an Outlet for the label called **counterLabel** and an Action for the button with the name **showCounter()**, the event Touch Up Inside, and the rest of the values by default. Complete the **ViewController** class with the code of Listing 5-7. Run the application in the simulator. Every time the button is pressed you should see the number on the label incremented by one unit.

Actions are the best way to prepare our code to process user interaction. Every control defined in UIKit can process this type of connection, although the events fired are not always the same. For example, the Segmented Control fires an event called *Value Changed* every time the user selects a new segment. Figure 5-29, next, shows an interface that includes this type of control.

Figure 5-29: Segmented Control with two options

The Segmented Control used in this example was defined with two segments (buttons) with the titles Black and Red, representing colors for the label. This is the number of segments presented by default, but we can add more from the Attributes inspector panel in the Utilities Area.

As we have seen in Chapter 4, the way this control works is by keeping track of which segment is currently selected. An index value is assigned to each segment in correlative order starting from 0. When a new segment is selected, the value of its index is assigned to the **selectedSegmentIndex** property of the **UISegmentedControl** object that represents the element and the Value Changed event is fired. By creating an Action that responds to this event, we can check the **selectedSegmentIndex** property and execute the corresponding code according to its value.

```
import UIKit

class ViewController: UIViewController {
   @IBOutlet weak var mytitle: UILabel!

   @IBAction func selectColor(_ sender: UISegmentedControl) {
      if sender.selectedSegmentIndex == 0 {
         mytitle.textColor = .black
      } else if sender.selectedSegmentIndex == 1 {
         mytitle.textColor = .red
      }
   }
}
```

Listing 5-8: Responding to the Value Changed event of a Segmented Control

The **ViewController** class of Listing 5-8 defines a method called **selectColor()** that is assigned as the Action for the Segmented Control illustrated in Figure 5-28. When the user selects a new segment by pressing the button, the Value Changed event is fired and the **selectColor()** method is executed. Inside this method, we check the value of the **selectedSegmentIndex** property of the **sender** object and change the color of the label accordingly (black for the segment at index 0 and red for the segment at index 1).

 Do It Yourself: Delete the elements inside the view and clean the code in your view controller, including the Outlets and the Actions. Drag and drop a label and a Segmented Control from the Object Library into the view in the Storyboard (as illustrated in Figure 5-29). Double-click on the label and each segment to change the text and the titles. Create an Outlet for the label called **mytitle** and an Action for the control. In the popup window for the Action, select the type Action, define the name for the method as **selectColor**, select the type for the value to be sent to the method as **UISegmentedControl**, and select the Value Changed event and the Sender argument for the last two options. Click the Connect button to generate the connection and copy inside the method the statements presented in Listing 5-8. Execute the application. You should be able to change the color of the label by pressing the buttons.

A similar procedure can be performed by the Switch control. This type of control has always two positions: on or off. By checking the value of its **isOn** property, we can determine the current state and perform the operations we want. In the following example, if the **isOn** property is **true**, the color of the label is changed to black, otherwise it is changed to red.

Figure 5-30: Switch in the Storyboard

```
import UIKit

class ViewController: UIViewController {
   @IBOutlet weak var mytitle: UILabel!

   @IBAction func switchColor(_ sender: UISwitch) {
      if sender.isOn {
         mytitle.textColor = .black
      } else {
         mytitle.textColor = .red
      }
   }
}
```

Listing 5-9: Changing the color with a switch

 Do It Yourself: Delete the elements inside the view and clean the code in your view controller, including the Outlets and the Actions. Drag and drop a label and a Switch from the Object Library into the view in the Storyboard (as illustrated in Figure 5-30). Create an Outlet for the label called **mytitle** and the Action for the switch. In the popup window for the Action, select the type Action, define the name for the method as **switchColor**, select the type for the value to be sent to the method as **UISwitch**, and select the Value Changed event and the Sender argument for the last two options. Click the Connect button to generate the connection and copy inside the method the statements presented in Listing 5-9. Run the application. Turning the switch on and off should change the color of the label.

Other controls that fire the Value Changed event to perform an Action are the Stepper (**UIStepper**) and the Slider (**UISlider**). The Stepper lets the user increment or decrement a value by a specific number of units in a predetermined range. The following example adds a Stepper to the view and a label to show the current value.

Figure 5-31: Stepper in the Storyboard

As with any other element, the values of the Stepper's properties may be modified from the Attribute inspector panel. By default, the range goes from 0 to 100, it starts counting from 0 and the value is incremented by 1. For this example, we leave the values by default and define an Action that assigns the current value of the **value** property of the **UIStepper** object to the label.

```
import UIKit

class ViewController: UIViewController {
   @IBOutlet weak var counterLabel: UILabel!

   @IBAction func increment(_ sender: UIStepper) {
      counterLabel.text = String(sender.value)
   }
}
```

Listing 5-10: Incrementing or decrementing a value with a Stepper

 Do It Yourself: Delete the elements inside the view and clean the code in your view controller, including the Outlets and the Actions. Drag and drop a new label and a Stepper from the Object Library into the view in the Storyboard. Double-click the label to change its text to "0.0", as illustrated in Figure 5-31. Create an Outlet for the label called **counterLabel** and an Action for the Stepper called **increment()** with the same options used before. Click the Connect button to generate the connection and copy inside the method the statement presented in Listing 5-10. Run the application. The value in the label should be incremented or decremented every time you press the buttons of the Stepper. If the values are truncated, it is a sign that the label's view is not big enough to display large numbers. Increment the size of the label's view and try again.

The Slider is slightly similar to the Stepper, but its value is incremented or decremented according to how far the indicator is displaced. This type of control is usually applied to analog systems where a specific value is not required (e.g., volume control, brightness, etc.). For this example, we use a Progress View element to show the values selected from the Slider in a progress bar.

Figure 5-32: Progress View and Slider in the Storyboard

```
import UIKit

class ViewController: UIViewController {
   @IBOutlet weak var progress: UIProgressView!

   @IBAction func updateProgress(_ sender: UISlider) {
      progress.progress = sender.value
   }
}
```

Listing 5-11: Incrementing or decrementing a value with a Slider

When the user moves the pointer of the Slider, the value in its **value** property changes and the method assigned as the Action is executed. In the example of Listing 5-11, we called this method **updateProgress()**. Inside the method, the value of the **value** property is assigned to the **progress** property of the **UIProgressView** object to update the progress bar.

Building Applications

Do It Yourself: Delete the elements inside the view and clean the code in your view controller, including the Outlets and the Actions. Drag and drop a Progress View and a Slider from the Object Library into the view in the Storyboard (as illustrated in Figure 5-32). Create an Outlet for the progress bar called **progress** and an Action for the Slider called **updateProgress()**. Copy inside the method the statement presented in Listing 5-11. The progress bar should change according to the position of the Slider.

 The Basics: The Progress View and the Slider work by default with the same range of values (0.0 to 1.0). If you change the range for the Slider you will have to adapt the number returned by this element to the Progress View range to be able to show the correct level of progress.

Outlet Collections

An Outlet Collection is a type of Outlet that can reference one or more elements. It is helpful when several elements of the interface have to be modified at the same time. The property created for the Outlet is an array containing references to each element. Iterating over the array, we can reach every element connected to the Outlet and access their properties.

The following example presents an interface with three buttons. The Say Hello and Say Goodbye buttons print messages on the console and the Disable button is used to disable the first two.

Say Hello

Say Goodbye

Disable

Figure 5-33: Interface to test Outlet Collections

To create the functionality for this interface, we have to define an Action for every button and an Outlet Collection for the first two. The Outlet Collection is created by control-dragging a line from the first element to the view controller, as we did before, but this time the Connection has to be set as Outlet Collection. The subsequent connections can be created by control-dragging a line from the indicator on the left of the Outlet to the next element of the list, as shown in Figure 5-34.

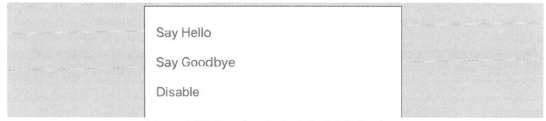

Figure 5-34: Connecting multiple elements to the same Outlet

After the Outlet Collection is defined and the first two buttons are connected, we have to create the Actions. Listing 5-12, next, shows the view controller with the connections and all the Actions required for this example.

```
import UIKit

class ViewController: UIViewController {
    @IBOutlet var buttons: [UIButton]!

    @IBAction func sayHello(_ sender: UIButton) {
        print("Hello!")
    }
    @IBAction func sayGoodbye(_ sender: UIButton) {
        print("Goodbye!")
    }
    @IBAction func disableButtons(_ sender: UIButton) {
        for button in buttons {
            button.isEnabled = false
        }
    }
}
```

Listing 5-12: Implementing an Outlet Collection

The methods for the Say Hello and Say Goodbye buttons (**sayHello()** and **sayGoodbye()**) print messages on the console, but the method for the Disable button (**disableButtons()**) takes advantage of the **isEnabled** property inherited by the **UIButton** class from the **UIControl** class to deactivate the other two buttons (see **UIControl** in Chapter 4). To access the property of every button, we iterate over the **buttons** array produced by the Outlet Collection. When the Disable button is pressed, the **disableButtons()** method assigns the value **false** to the **isEnabled** property of the buttons referenced by the Outlet Collection and in consequence the first two buttons are disabled (they are shown in color gray and do not respond to the user anymore).

 Do It Yourself: Delete previous elements and code in your project. Drag and drop three buttons to the view to create the interface of Figure 5-32. Control-drag a line from the first button to the code and create an Outlet Collection called **buttons** (the type of the connection has to be selected as Outlet Collection in the popup window). Control-drag a line from the indicator on the left side of the Outlet to the second button to add that button to the collection. Create the Actions for every button and complete the methods with the code of Listing 5-12. Every time you press any of the first two buttons, a message is printed on the console, but when you press the third button, the other buttons are disabled.

Real-Life Application

The same way there are Outlet Collections to connect several elements to the same Outlet, there is also the possibility to connect several elements to the same Action (the same method). The following example builds a calculator to demonstrate how to implement these types of Actions and how to program an application with the features studied so far.

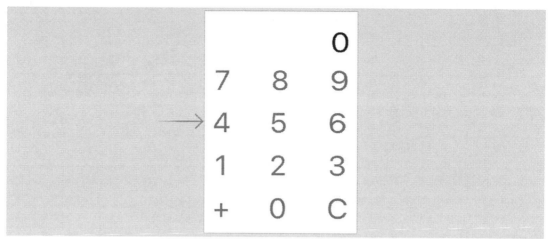

Figure 5-35: *Interface for a basic calculator*

Our calculator's interface is depicted in Figure 5-35 above. We need one label at the top to represent the display (to show the input and the results), and also 12 buttons to let the user insert new numbers, add the values, and clean the display (our calculator only adds integers). The label's view was extended to the sides of the main view to let the user insert up to 8 digits and the text for both, the label and the buttons, was set to 60 points. This makes the elements big enough to occupy most of the screen of a regular iPhone.

 Do It Yourself: Delete any element in your view and the code in your **ViewController** class from previous examples. Drag and drop a label and all the buttons necessary to get the design illustrated in Figure 5-35. Expand the label's view until you reach the guide lines on each side of the view, change its text to "0", and align it to the right from the Attributes Inspector panel. Change the font size of the label and buttons to 60 points.

 The Basics: The Storyboard allows you to copy and paste elements in the view. To create the buttons for the calculator, you can add a button, change the title to the corresponding number, and then copy and paste the button (pressing Command + C and Command + V on your keyboard). Position the new button at the right place, change its title and repeat the process until you have created all the buttons you need. You can also drag an element while holding down the Option key on your keyboard to create a duplicate and select multiple elements to move them around.

The buttons for the numbers (0 to 9) are all going to be connected to one single Action we call **addNumber()**. We have to create this Action from one button and then drag the line from the rest of the buttons to this same method (the whole method turns blue to indicate the connection). The challenge presented by various buttons calling the same method is how to identify which button performed the call. There are at least two ways to do this. We could read the **currentTitle** property of the **sender** parameter (the **UIButton** object) and check its value to detect which button was pressed, or we can use the **tag** property. Every subclass of **UIView** inherits the **tag** property from its superclass. This property stores a value of type **Int** to identify the view. Assigning an integer value to this property, we are able to identify the view later. For this purpose, we have to set the value of the **tag** property of each button from the Attributes Inspector panel, as shown in Figure 5-36.

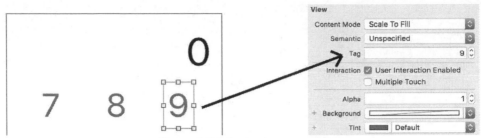

Figure 5-36: Button's properties

This process is only required for the buttons with numbers, the rest of the buttons (+ and C) are going to be connected to their own Actions. Listing 5-13, next, presents the view controller with the necessary Outlets, Actions, and code to control the whole process.

```
import UIKit

class ViewController: UIViewController {
    @IBOutlet weak var display: UILabel!

    var current: Double = 0
    var total: Double = 0
    let digits = 8
    var format = NumberFormatter()

    @IBAction func addNumber(_ sender: UIButton) {
        let number = Double(sender.tag)
        let text = display.text!
        if current == 0 {
            current = number
        } else if text.count < digits {
            current = (current * 10) + number
        }
        display.text = format.string(from: NSNumber(value: current))
    }
    @IBAction func calculate(_ sender: UIButton) {
        total += current
        display.text = format.string(from: NSNumber(value: total))
        current = 0
    }
    @IBAction func clean(_ sender: UIButton) {
        current = 0
        total = 0
        display.text = "0"
    }
}
```

Listing 5-13: Programming the calculator's view controller

The code starts by defining the necessary properties to store the numbers and show them on the display. The **current** property stores the current value typed by the user (one digit at a time), the **total** property stores the result of the last operation, the **digits** property indicates the maximum number of digits available on the display, and the **format** property is a **NumberFormatter** object we use to format the numbers that are going to be shown on the screen.

Building Applications

The view controller is completed by the **display** Outlet of the label and three Actions: **addNumber()**, **calculate()**, and **clean()**. The **addNumber()** method adds the number of the button pressed by the user to the value of the **current** property, the **calculate()** method adds the number inserted by the user to the previous result, and the **clean()** method cleans the display and the values of the properties to start again from scratch.

The calculator adds a new integer number to the previous result. This only presents one small complication. The number inserted by the user is not always the final value. This is because the number is inserted in sequence and it may be composed of more than one digit. For example, when the user presses the button 5 and afterwards the button 4, the value to be processed is 54. We have to add the number 4 to the number 5 as a new digit to get the final number. The **addNumber()** method achieves this by calculating and storing the total value in the **current** property. First, it reads the value of the **tag** property, converts it to a **Double** type, and stores it in the **number** constant (**let number = Double(sender.tag)**). The conversion is necessary because the **tag** property returns an integer value and we are working with properties of type **Double** (operations can only be performed on values of the same type). The **number** constant is used next to calculate the total value inserted by the user. If the value of **current** is equal to 0, the number is assigned directly to the **current** property; otherwise we have to check if the digits already inserted are not over the limit. This limit is defined by the **digits** property. We count the number of digits in the display using the **count** property and compare it with the value of **digits** (**text.count < digits**). If the current number of digits is less than the limit, we add the value of the **number** property as a new digit of the **current** property (the new digits are added by multiplying the current value times 10 (**current = (current * 10) + number**). At the end, the new value of the **current** property is processed by the **string()** method of the **format** object to eliminate the decimal numbers, and the string returned is assigned to the label to show the final value on the display.

The Basics: The **format** object was configured with values by default. This configuration rounds the decimal number to the nearest integer and returns a string containing an integer value. For more information on **NumberFormatter**, see Chapter 4.

The codes for the **calculate()** and **clean()** methods are simpler. The **calculate()** method is executed when the **+** button is pressed to perform the addition. This method adds the value of the **current** property to the value of the **total** property and shows it on the calculator's display. After that, it assigns the value 0 to the **current** property to get it ready to receive new values. On the other hand, the **clean()** method is executed when the **C** button is pressed. All we have to do here is to clean the display and the properties to start all over again.

Do It Yourself: Connect the label to an Outlet called **display** and the buttons to their corresponding Actions. The buttons with numbers must be all connected to the same Action called **addNumber()**, the button with the + character has to be connected to an Action called **calculate()**, and the button with the letter C has to be connected to an Action called **clean()**. Select the buttons with numbers one by one and change the value of their **tag** property from the Attributes Inspector panel to match the numbers of their titles (Figure 5-36). Complete the **ViewController** class with the code of Listing 5-13. Run the application. Every time you want to add a new value or see the result you have to press the + button.

Taking advantage of what we already know, we can modify the elements to get a more professional design. For example, the design shown in Figure 5-37 below was achieved by adding a few extra views with backgrounds of different colors to delimit the display and the whole calculator.

Building Applications

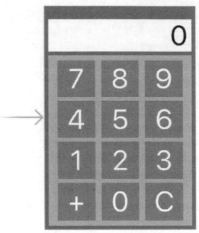

Figure 5-37: A better design for the calculator

This design includes three empty views: one with a dark background to represent the calculator's box, another with a lighter background to delimit the area of the buttons, and a smaller one to represent the display. The label and the buttons were added as subviews of the smaller views, and the smaller views were added as subviews of the view representing the calculator's case. The color for the titles of the buttons was changed to white and their background color to gray. All the properties to apply these styles are available in the Attributes Inspector panel.

Empty views are included in the list of elements offered by the Object Library, as shown in Figure 5-38 below. When a new view is dragged to the Storyboard, it has a size by default, but we can easily change it by dragging the little squares around it.

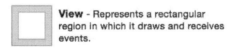

Figure 5-38: Views in the Object Library

 IMPORTANT: All the projects presented in this book are available in our website. Go to www.formasterminds.com and click on the option Sample Codes.

Building Applications

Chapter 6
Adaptivity

6.1 Adaptivity

Adaptivity is a term that describes the capacity of the interface to adapt to changes in the size of the screen, either because the app is running on devices with different screens, the space available changes, or the device is rotated. Adaptivity is just an idea, accomplished by the combination of two technologies called *Auto Layout* and *Size Classes*. Combining these tools, we are able to develop different versions of the interface for every device and orientation.

6.2 Auto Layout

When a view is added to a Scene, we have to specify the values of its `frame` property to determine the view's position and size (see `UIView` in Chapter 4). This is an intuitive way to organize the interface but presents the problem that the values do not adapt to changes in the space available, as illustrated in Figure 6-1.

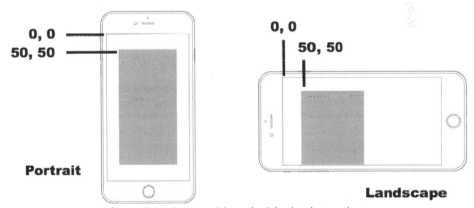

Figure 6-1: View positioned with absolute values

This example shows what happens when we determine the position and size of a view in portrait mode and then rotate the device. In landscape mode, half of the gray box generated by the view disappears at the bottom of the screen because there is not enough vertical space available to show it all. Although we could solve this problem by assigning new values to the element's `frame` property every time the space changes, this approach presents a difficult challenge. All the values for every view in the interface have to be modified, not only when the screen is rotated but also for every type of screen available. And the list of possible scenarios grows every time a new device enters the market or new features are introduced, like the split-screen mode in iPads that allow users to run two apps simultaneously. The solution is provided by Auto Layout.

Auto Layout is a system that uses a set of rules to organize the elements of the user interface. The rules establish the relationship between elements and between the elements and their containers. These rules are simple statements that determine things like how far a view should be from another view, or how a set of views should be aligned. As an example, Figure 6-2, next, presents a container with a button in a position and with a size determined by four rules. These specific rules tell the system how far the button should be from the sides of its container. The example on the left is what we would see during implementation, when all the rules are assigned to the element. The illustration on the right represents the same element during execution, when the position and size of the button have already been modified to abide to those rules.

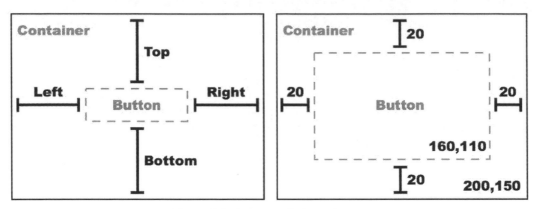

Figure 6-2: Rules applied to a button

The rules applied to the button of Figure 6-2 are saying things like "this button always has to be 20 points from the top of its container" and "this button always has to be 20 points from the left side of its container". Every rule determines one aspect of the relationship between the button and its container to help the system determine the position and size of the button every time the space available changes. Because of this, we no longer have to declare explicit values to lay out the elements; they are calculated by the system after all the rules have being considered.

 IMPORTANT: When we use Auto Layout, the values assigned to the `frame` property of every view in the Storyboard are not considered by the system anymore. Assigning new values to this property has no effect on the position and size of the element on the screen, but there are situations in which the values of this property are still useful. We will see some examples in further chapters.

Constraints

Computers cannot understand human expressions like "position the view 50 points from the edge of the container". For this reason, Auto Layout defines a set of specific rules that we can configure and combine to organize the interface. Auto Layout's rules are called *Constraints*, and they are comprehensive enough to let us create any design we want.

There are two main groups of constraints: Pin constraints and Align constraints. Pin constraints define space, such as the space between a view and the edge of its container, while Align constraints define how the views should be aligned with respect to other views or their containers. The following list describes the Pin constraints available.

Top Space—This constraint defines the space between the top of the element and its nearest neighbour or the top edge of the container (superview).

Bottom Space—This constraint defines the space between the bottom of the element and its nearest neighbour or the bottom edge of the container (superview).

Leading Space—This constraint defines the space between the left side of the element and its nearest neighbour or the left edge of the container (superview).

Trailing Space—This constraint defines the space between the right side of the element and its nearest neighbour or the right edge of the container (superview).

Width—This constraint defines the width of the element.

Height—This constraint defines the height of the element.

Aspect Ratio—This constraint defines the aspect ratio of the element.

Equal Widths—This constraint declares that two elements will have the same width. If the width of one of the elements changes, the same value is assigned to the other element affected by the constraint.

Equal Heights—This constraint declares that two elements will have the same height. If the height of one of the elements changes, the same value is assigned to the other element affected by the constraint.

The following are the constraints for alignment:

Horizontal in Container—This constraint aligns the center of the element with the center of its container in the horizontal axis.

Vertical in Container—This constraint aligns the center of the element with the center of its container in the vertical axis.

Leading Edges—This constraint aligns two elements to their left side.

Trailing Edges—This constraint aligns two elements to their right side.

Top Edges—This constraint aligns two elements to their top edge.

Bottom Edges—This constraint aligns two elements to their bottom edge.

Horizontal Centers—This constraint aligns two elements to their horizontal center.

Vertical Centers—This constraint aligns two elements to their vertical centers.

Baselines—This constraint aligns two elements to their baselines.

Most of these constraints are straightforward, but some of them adapt to the circumstances. For example, the constraints that affect the left or right side of the elements are called *Leading* and *Trailing* because they are applied to a side according to the language set in the system. In Arabic languages, for example, the leading space is on the right side of the element and the trailing space is on the left.

Assigning Constraints

Every element on the interface requires constraints to define its position and size. Xcode offers a series of buttons at the bottom of the Storyboard to add and manage constraints.

Figure 6-3: Buttons to work with constraints

These buttons have different functions, from adding constraints to helping us solve the issues that arise along the way. The button on the left (1) updates the values of the view's frame if they do not match the values of the constraints, the next button (2) embeds the view in a Stack View to lay it out with other views in columns or rows, the following button (3) opens a menu with options to add constraints for alignment (Align menu), the next one (4) opens a menu to add constraints for space (Pin menu), and the last button on the right (5) opens a menu with options to help us solve issues with constraints or let the system place the constraints for us.

To add a constraint to an element, we first have to select the element in the Scene and then click the button to open the Align or Pin menus, as illustrated by Figure 6-4.

Figure 6-4: Align and Pin menus

These menus list all the constraint types described above, but they adjust the options to the types and number of elements selected. For example, those constraints that require two elements are disabled when only one element is selected. After we activate the constraint we want to add, the Add Constraints button at the bottom of the menu is highlighted. Clicking this button, adds the constraint to the view. Figure 6-5 shows the process of adding a Top Space constraint to a view.

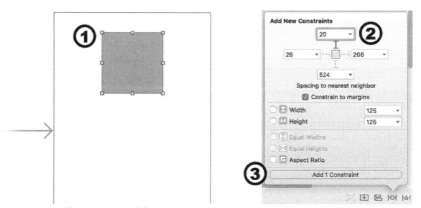

Figure 6-5: Adding a Top Space constraint to a single view

Space constraints are added from the Pin menu. We have to select the view (Figure 6-5, number 1), click the Pin button at the bottom of the Editor Area to open the Pin menu (Figure 6-3, number 4), activate the constraint we want to add (Figure 6-5, number 2), and press the Add Constraint button to add the constraint to the view (Figure 6-5, number 3). Space constraints are selected by clicking the red line between their value and the small square in the middle that represents the view, as shown in Figure 6-6.

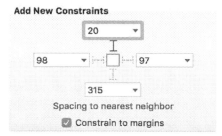

Figure 6-6: *Tool to add Space constraints*

The value for the constraint is set by default as the value defined in the Storyboard, but we can change it to any value we want. In our example, we have activated the Top Space constraint with a value of 20. This means that when the system reads this constraint it will position the top of the view 20 points from its nearest neighbour. If there are no other elements at the top, the distance is determined from the top of the element to the top edge of its container.

After the constraints have been selected and configured, we have to press the Add Constraints button at the bottom of the menu to effectively add the constraints to the view. The menu is closed and Xcode shows lines in the Storyboard representing the constraints. Every time an element is selected, the lines that represent its constraints are shown on the screen, as illustrated in Figure 6-7.

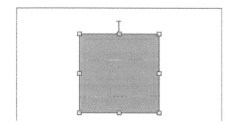

Figure 6-7: *View with a Top Space constraint*

 Do It Yourself: Create a new Single View Application project. Click in the storyboard file to show the Storyboard in the Editor Area. Drag an empty view from the Object Library to the main view. Assign a background color, a size, and a position similar to the view depicted in Figure 6-5. With the view selected, open the Pin menu and add a Top Space constraint (Figure 6-5). Keep the value of the constraint as suggested by Xcode. You should see the line representing the constraint as shown in Figure 6-7.

 The Basics: The Pin and Align menus allow the addition of multiple constraints at the same time. The title of the Add Constraints button is automatically updated to reflect the number of constraints selected. When you press this button, all the selected constraints are added at once.

Although a constraint determines a specific rule, one constraint alone cannot provide enough information for the system to determine the position and size of the element. When this happens, Xcode shows the constraint in the Storyboard in color red. The color indicates that the constraints assigned to the element are ambiguous or insufficient. There is a total of three colors: blue, orange and red. The constraints are shown in blue when the system has enough information to display the element, orange when the constraint establish different values than those currently used on the screen to display the element, and red when there are not enough constraints or some are in conflict (the system cannot satisfy all the constraints at the same time).

In our example, the constraint is red because the system knows about the vertical position of the view (the value of the y coordinate), but we did not specify yet how it should be positioned horizontally and how its size should be determined. There are several options available, depending on what we want to do. For instance, if we want to position the view at the center of the main view, we have to add a Horizontal alignment constraint.

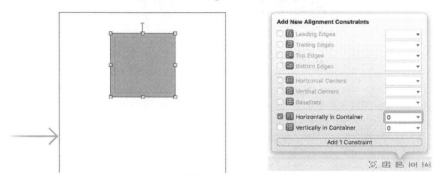

Figure 6-8: *Adding an alignment constraint*

These types of constraints are added from the Align menu, as illustrated in Figure 6-8. The constraints available for single elements are the Horizontal in Container (to center the element horizontally) and the Vertical in Container (to center the element vertically). The rest of the options are only available for multiple elements. All the options on this menu also have a value that determines the offset of the constraint. By default, the value is 0, but we can change it to displace the view to the left of the center (positive values) or the right (negative values). In this example, we have selected the Horizontal in Container constraint with an offset value of 0 to center the view horizontally and right in the middle of its container (the main view).

Now, the view is centered on the screen, but the constraints are still red. The two constraints we have added so far (the Top Space constraint and the Horizontal in Container constraint) tell the system that the top of the view has to be 20 points from the top of the container and aligned with its horizontal center. This is enough to establish the position, but we still have to provide more information for the size. The box could expand or contract to always be at a certain distance from the sides of the container, as we did with the button in Figure 6-2, or it could have a specific size. For this example, we have decided to give our view a specific size of 125 by 125.

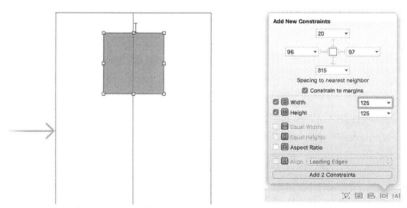

Figure 6-9: *Adding the Width and Height constraints*

The Width and Height constraints tell the system that the view always has to have a specific width and height. The size is determined by the values declared for each constraint in the Pin menu, as shown in Figure 6-9. By default, the menu shows the current values defined in the Storyboard, but we can change them to declare the size we want. Figure 6-10 illustrates our view with all of its constraints.

Adaptivity

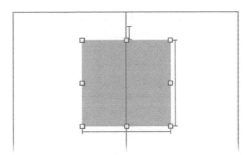

Figure 6-10: View with all the necessary constraints

All the constraints are now blue because the system has enough information to draw the view. The Top Space and Horizontal in Container constraints establish the position while the Width and Height constraints determine the size. No matter what the orientation or the size of the screen are, our view will be drawn at 20 points from the top margin of the main view, in the center of the screen, and with a size of 125 by 125 points.

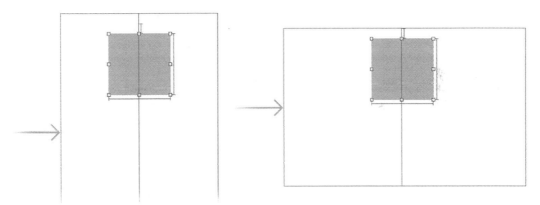

Figure 6-11: Interface in portrait and landscape

 Do It Yourself: Add to the view the Horizontal in Container constraint as shown in Figure 6-8 and the Width and Height constraints as shown in Figure 6-9. Click on the Device Configuration button and select the Landscape orientation (Figure 5-15). You should see something similar to Figure 6-11.

Unless we have a good reason to set a specific size, we should always let the size of the elements be determined by the relation between the element and its siblings or the container. For instance, if we want the view of our example to always be at the center of the screen, it is better to set Leading and Trailing constraints to define the space on the sides and let the system determine its width, as illustrated in Figure 6-12.

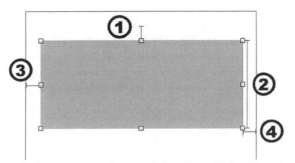

Figure 6-12: Space constraints to define the width of the element

In this example, the position and size of the view are determined by the Top Space (1), Height (2), Leading Space (3), and Trailing Space (4) constraints. The Leading Space and Trailing Space constraints tell the system that the view has to be at a certain distance from the edge of the container and it should be shrunk or stretched to always be at that distance.

The view of Figure 6-12 has an absolute height determined by the Height constraint, but we could also change that assigning a Bottom space constraint or an Aspect Ratio constraint, as in the following example.

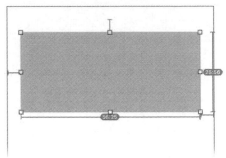

Figure 6-13: *Aspect Ratio constraint*

The example of Figure 6-13 uses an Aspect Ratio constraint to determine the height of the view. The width is determined by the Leading Space and Trailing Space constraints, and the height is defined to be proportional to the current width by the Aspect Ratio constraint. When the view gets wider because of the Space constraints on the sides, it also gets proportionally taller. Because of these constraints, the view always has the same rectangular shape.

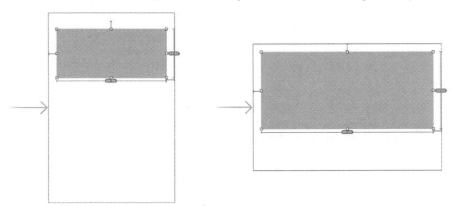

Figure 6-14: *Same aspect ratio in portrait and landscape*

 Do It Yourself: Select and erase the view on your Storyboard to start all over from scratch. Add a rectangular view at the center of the main view, similar to the one shown in Figure 6-13. Assign a background color to be able to see it. Open the Pin menu and add a Top constraint of 20 points, a Leading constraint of 20 points and a Trailing constraint of 20 points (remember to click on the red lines to activate the constraints, Figure 6-6). Click on the Aspect Ratio constraint on this same menu to also add it to the view. Change the orientation from the Device Configuration panel, as shown in Figure 6-14.

 The Basics: The aspect ratio is a value that determines how many points on one side correspond to the points on the other side. For example, a ratio of 1:2 determines that for each point on one side, the other side should have two points. The Aspect Ratio constraint sets this value according to the current aspect ratio of the view. Next, we will see how to modify this value and specify a custom ratio.

Adaptivity

Editing Constraints

Every constraint has associated values to determine its properties, such as the distance, the width of the element, etc. Assigning new values to the constraints changes how they affect the elements and how the interface is built. The Align and Pin menus only allow us to add new constraints, not to edit the ones already created. Xcode offers different alternatives to access and edit the constraints. The simplest is to select the element and open the Size Inspector panel in the Utilities Area (Figure 5-22, right). The constraints associated with the element are listed at the bottom, as shown next.

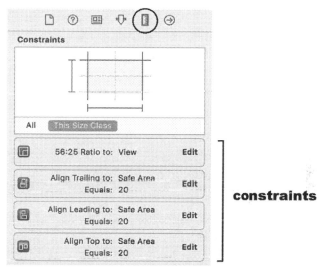

Figure 6-15: *List of constraints on the Size Inspector panel*

The constraints are listed like buttons at the bottom of the panel. Figure 6-15 shows the four constraints added to the view of our last example (Aspect Ratio, Trailing Space, Leading Space, and Top Space, in that order). Each constraint on the list presents an Edit button to edit its values. Figure 6-16, below, shows the small window that opens when we click on this button. Changing the values in this window automatically modifies the constraint (this menu also opens if we double-click the constraint in the Storyboard).

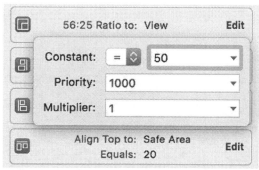

Figure 6-16: *Popup window to edit the values of a constraint*

There are different options available to configure a constraint. The option that determines the value of the constraint, such as the distance or the width, is called *Constant*. We will study the rest later in this chapter.

Do It Yourself: Select the view in the Storyboard. Click on the button to show the Size Inspector panel (circled in Figure 6-15). Click on the Edit button of any of the constraints to change its value. Try, for example, to assign a value of 50 to the Top Space constraint, as we did in Figure 6-16. The changes will be immediately reflected in the Storyboard when possible.

Constraints have their own panel with more configuration options. To open this panel, we can double click the constraint on the Size Inspector panel (Figure 6-15), select the constraint from the Storyboard, or click on the item that represents the constraint inside the Document Outline panel (see Figure 5-14, number 1). When a constraint is selected, its values are shown in the Utilities Area. Figure 6-17 is a capture of this panel after the Top Space constraint of the view from our example was selected. From this panel, we can change all the constraint's values and also some of the aspects of the elements it is connected to, as we will see next.

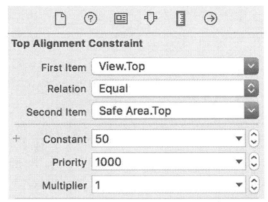

Figure 6-17: Constraint editor in the Utilities Area

Safe Area

The system defines a layout guide called *Safe Area* where we can place the content of our interface. This is the area determined by the space remaining inside the view after all the toolbars and special views are displayed by the system. For example, in a Single View application, the system creates a status bar at the top of the screen. This size of this bar may be adapted to different devices and orientations or being completely removed at any time. To make sure that our content never overlaps with this bar, we can pin it to the edges of the Safe Area.

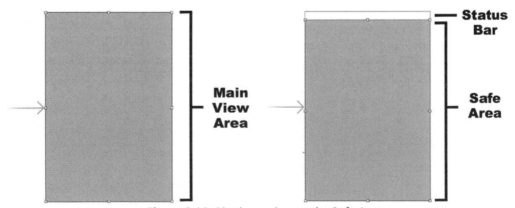

Figure 6-18: Pinning a view to the Safe Area

In Figure 6-18, the view on the left was pinned to the top edge of the main view and therefore it will be covered by the status bar. On the other hand, the view on the right was pinned to the top edge of the Safe Area and therefore it will never overlap with the status bar or any other toolbar introduced by the system or the view controllers. If the bar is removed, as it happens in some devices when the screen is in landscape mode, the Safe Area is extended, and the view automatically occupies the area left by the bar.

By default, pin constraints are attached to the Safe Area. This is the reason why the Top Space constraint of our previous example was separated from the top edge of the main view in Portrait mode (see Figure 6-7). If instead we want our view to be pinned to the top edge of the main view, we have to change the constraint's configuration from the Size Inspector panel (Figure 6-17).

When we select a constraint, the Size Inspector panel shows the two elements the constraint is attached to. For example, the Top Space constraint added to our view in previous examples is connected to the top edge of the view and the top edge of the Safe Area. If we want the constraint to be connected to the top of the main view instead, we have to change the second item of the relationship to Superview, as shown in Figure 6-19.

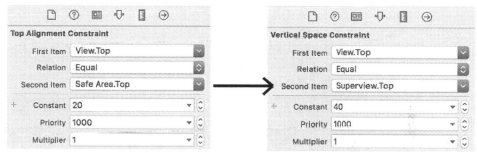

Figure 6-19: *Pinning the view to its superview*

Figure 6-20, next, shows what we see in the Storyboard when we change the relationship. The system extends the constraint to consider the space occupied by the status bar.

Figure 6-20: *View pinned to the Safe Area or the superview*

The option to select the element to which the constraint is going to be connected is also available in the Pin menu. When we select a Space constraint to add it to a view, we can click on the arrow on the right-hand side of the value and select the destination view, as shown next.

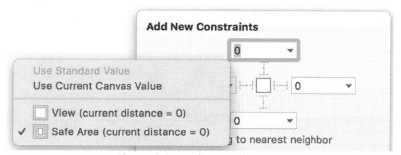

Figure 6-21: *Selecting the view*

The menu displays a list of the elements available to attach to the constraint. In this example, only the Safe Area and the main view are available, but there may be others, as we will see later.

Standard Values

The system defines standard values for the distance between views and between the views and their container to help us organize the interface. These are the same values used by the guide lines that help us position the elements inside the main view. We do not have to use them, but their use is recommended because they are adapted to each device according to styles defined by Apple.

There are different ways to insert these values. An alternative is provided by the Pin menu. When we add a Space constraint between a view and its container view, we can set the constraint to be between the element and the margins by selecting the option *Constrain to margins* (the option is displayed below the Space constraints in the Pin menu, as shown in Figure 6-6). Figure 6-22 shows what we see when we pin our gray view to the main view instead of the Safe Area with the option Constrain to margins activated and deactivated (the margins are not assigned when we pin the view to the Safe Area, only when we pin it to its container).

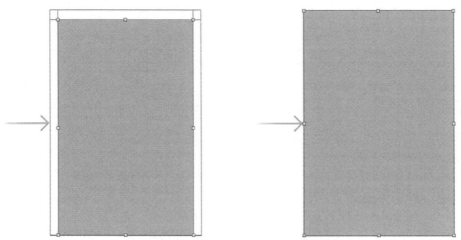

Figure 6-22: Constraints added with the Constrain to margins option activated and deactivated

The view on the left side of Figure 6-22 was connected to the main view with Space constraints of value 0, but with the Constrain to margins option activated. Therefore, the view is positioned a few points away from the edge of the main view. The view on the right was affected by the same constrains but now with the Constrain to margins option deactivated. Because of this, the sides of the view reach the edge of the container (no margin is generated).

 Do It Yourself: Erase the view in your Scene and create a new one or clean the constraints of the one you already have. Select the view and open the Pin menu. If necessary, click on the option Constrain to Margins to activate it. Click on the arrows on the right-hand side of the Space constraints' values and select the main View as the destination for every side (Figure 6-21). Assign a value of 0 to each constraint and press the Add Constraints button. You should see something similar to Figure 6-22, left.

When we use the Constrain to margins option of the Pin menu, the constant value of the constraint determines the distance from the margin, not from the edge of the container. For example, if we declare a value of 20 for the constant and the margin is set as 16 points by the system, the distance between the elements will be 36 points. If we want one of the constraints to consider only the constant value, we have to select it and remove the value of the margin from the constraint's panel in the Utilities Area.

Adaptivity

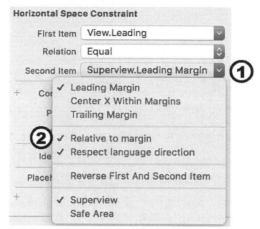

Figure 6-23: Constraint's configuration

The panel shows the two elements associated with the constraint and their relation. The element on the side of the constraint that considers the margin includes the word Margin in the description (Figure 6-23, number 1). If we click the arrow in this field, Xcode opens a menu with an option called Relative to margin activated (Figure 6-23, number 2). If we deactivate this option, the constraint does not consider the margin anymore. Figure 6-24 shows what happens with the interface of our previous example after the Relative to margin option is deactivated for the Leading constraint.

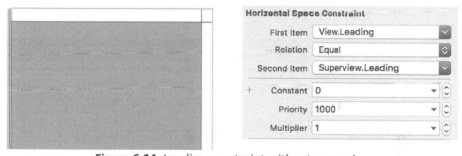

Figure 6-24: Leading constraint without a margin

 The Basics: It is recommendable to always pin the elements to the Safe Area and use margins only when we want to have absolute control on the position and size of the elements. This is the reason why the Safe Area is the option activated by default.

Resolving Auto Layout Issues

As we mentioned before, Xcode shows the constraints in different colors depending on the information they provide. We have seen the lines in red when there were not enough constraints to position or size the element, and blue when the system had all the information it needed to place the element on the screen. But there is another situation. Sometimes the constraints are enough but Xcode cannot determine the position and size of the views in the Storyboard and therefore there is a mismatch between what we see in the Storyboard and what we will see after the constraints are applied. This situation may occur because Xcode decides that it is better to show the view in the current position and with the current size to make easy for us to edit the interface, or it just cannot determine the new position and size under the present conditions. To help us identify the problem, Xcode shows the constraints in orange and includes dashed lines demarking the area where the view should be.

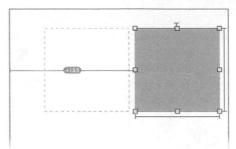

Figure 6-25: Element in the wrong position

The example of Figure 6-25 presents a simple view with a Top Space constraint and Width and Height constraints to determine its size. The horizontal position was specified by a Leading Space constraint, but the view was moved to the right and therefore it is shown by Xcode in its original place and dashed lines are displayed demarking the position in which it should be according to the constraints. This is just an indication and we could keep adding or modifying the constraints until the design is over, but if we need the Storyboard to represent the final interface, we have to solve the issue. One option is to update the view's frame to match the constraints' values. This is done by selecting the view and clicking on the Update Frames button at the bottom of the Editor Area (Figure 6-3, number 1). Once we press this button, the values of the view's frame are updated, and the view is positioned in the place determined by the constraints.

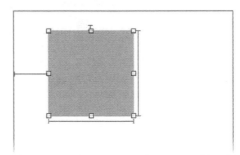

Figure 6-26: Element in the position determined by the constraints

For more complex issues, Xcode offers the Resolve Auto Layout Issues menu (Figure 6-3, number 5).

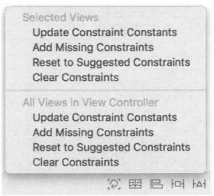

Figure 6-27: Resolve Auto Layout Issues

The Resolve Auto Layout Issues menu not only allows us to solve problems with the constraints, but it can also help us determine what the right constraints are for our interface. The following are the options available (the options are available twice, one for the selected views and another for all the views inside a Scene).

Adaptivity

Update Constraints Constants—This option updates the values of the constraints to match the current position and size of the view.

Add Missing Constraints—This option adds the constraints for us. Xcode guesses what the constraints should be according to the current position and size of the views in the Storyboard and automatically adds those constraints. It is useful as a starting point.

Reset to Suggested Constraints—This option modifies the constraints we have created to take them back to the state established by Xcode when the suggested constraints were generated.

Clear Constraints—This option erase the constraints. We can select this option when the constraints are not working, and we have decided to start all over again from scratch, but it is also useful when working with different Size Classes, as we will see later.

 Do It Yourself: Erase all the views in your main view. Add a new view similar to Figure 6-27 at the center of the main view. Assign a Top Space constraint of 20 points and also the Width and Height constraints to set its size. Finally, add a Leading Space constraint of 20 points and drag the view to a new position. Because the current position is not the one determined by the constraints, Xcode will show dashed lines to indicate the final position and a value on the line representing the difference between the current distance and the real one. Press the button Update Frames or select the option Update Constraints Constants from the Resolve Auto Layout Issues menu to update the interface. As with any other software, you can always press the Command + Z keys to undo what you did and try again.

Xcode offers tools with more specific information to help us identify and solve complex problems with constraints. An easy way to get this information is from the Error button at the top of the Editor Area (Figure 6-28, number 1).

Figure 6-28: Errors and Warnings

This button displays a list of the errors and warnings that are currently affecting our application. Figure 6-29 shows the warning displayed when a view is not in the position determined by the constraints.

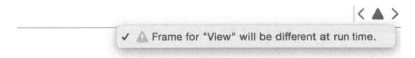

Figure 6-29: Current issues with constraints

Another way to get a detailed explanation of the issues regarding our constraints is from the Document Outline panel (Figure 5-14, number 1). This panel displays a list of the elements and constraints in the interface and also a small button at the top right corner whenever there is an issue with the constraints (Figure 6-30, number 1).

Figure 6-30: *Getting the list of issues from the Document Outline panel*

When we click this button, the list of views and constraints is replaced by the list of issues our interface currently has.

Figure 6-31: *List of issues in the Document Outline panel*

The issues are listed one over another with detailed information, such as the current and expected values, the constraints needed, etc. Every item of the list also includes another button (Figure 6-31, number 1) to open a popup menu with suggestions and solutions.

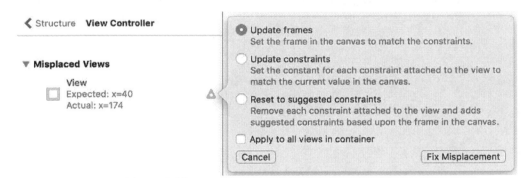

Figure 6-32: *Automatic solutions for constraint issues*

Some of the options in this menu are available in the Resolve Auto Layout Issues menu, but they are adapted to the issue we are dealing with.

Intrinsic Content Size

Some elements like labels and buttons generate their own content. This content defines a minimum size that the element's view adopts when no size is determined by the constraints. For example, the intrinsic content size of a label is determined by the size of its text. Because of this property, sometimes all we need for an element is to declare enough constraints to determine its position.

Adaptivity

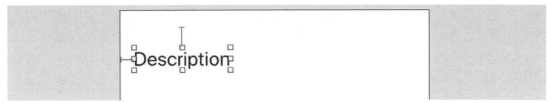

Figure 6-33: Label defined with intrinsic content size

The label of figure 6-33 has only two constraints, Top Space of 16 points and Leading Space of 30 points. There are no requirements for its size. If no constraints are defined, the label automatically adopts the size of its text.

 The Basics: Elements with intrinsic content size always adopt the size of their content when they are created. If, for some reason, we modify their content or their frame, we can go to the Editor menu at the top of the screen and select the option *Size to Fit Content* to force the view to go back to its intrinsic content size.

If we need to know what the current intrinsic content size of a view is, the **UIView** class includes the following property to return this value.

intrinsicContentSize—This property returns a **CGSize** value with the element's intrinsic content size.

The following example connects a label with an Outlet called **mytitle**, assigns a new text to it, and prints the new values of its intrinsic content size on the console.

```
import UIKit

class ViewController: UIViewController {
   @IBOutlet weak var mytitle: UILabel!

   override func viewDidLoad() {
      super.viewDidLoad()

      mytitle.text = "Description: My New Label"
      let labelSize = mytitle.intrinsicContentSize
      print("New Width: \(labelSize.width)")
      print("New Height: \(labelSize.height)")
   }
}
```

Listing 6-1: Reading the intrinsic content size

 Do It Yourself: Erase the views in the main view and any previous code in the view controller. Add a new label to the main view with a Top Space and a Leading Space constraint to define its position (see Figure 6-33). Create an Outlet for the label called **mytitle**. Copy and paste the code in Listing 6-1 into your view controller and run the application. The label's text is modified as soon as the app is executed, and the new values of its intrinsic content size are printed on the console.

Multiple Views Constraints

The Pin and Align menus add the constraints to every selected element, but do not include options to add constraints between elements. Xcode provides an additional way to add constraints that makes it easy to connect elements with each other. It requires the same procedure we use to create Outlets and Actions, but instead of pressing the Control key and dragging the line to the view controller we do it to another view, as shown in Figure 6-34.

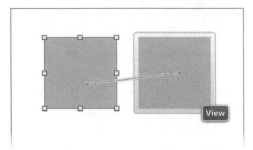

Figure 6-34: *Control-drag to add a constraint*

When the mouse button is released, Xcode shows a popup menu over the target to select the constraint we want to add.

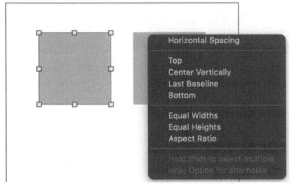

Figure 6-35: *Quick menu to add constraints*

The menu shows multiple options depending on what Xcode thinks we are trying to do. For example, when we control-drag a horizontal line from one view to another, the menu shows the Horizontal Spacing option at the top to let us add a Space constraint between the views.

Although this technique is useful to connect views together, we can also use it to add all the same constraints applied before. For example, control-dragging a line from a view to its superview we can add a Top Space constraint.

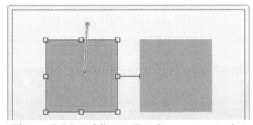

Figure 6-36: *Adding a Top Space constraint*

 The Basics: If you hold down the Command key or the Shift key when the menu is open, you can select multiple constraints. After all the constraints are selected, press the Enter key to add them to the views.

When we drag and drop a line inside the same view, the menu displayed by Xcode includes options like Width, Height, and also Aspect Ratio. Figure 6-37 shows the options available after a horizontal line is dragged from and into the view on the left.

Adaptivity

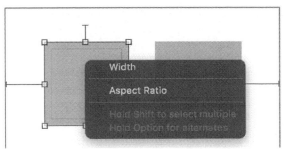

Figure 6-37: Popup menu to add a Width constraint

When working with two views connected with each other, we have to make sure that the constraints provide enough information for the system to position and size both views, but there are different options available, depending on what we want to achieve. For instance, we can define the width for only one view and let the system determine the width of the other. In the example of Figure 6-38, next, we pinned the views to the sides and with each other, but only added a Width constraint for the view on the left.

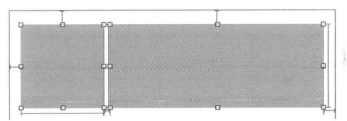

Figure 6-38: Adapting multiple views to the space available

Because we defined a fixed width for the left view only, that view is always of the same size while the view on the right extends or contracts to fill the space available. If we had defined both views with a fixed size, the system would not have been able to adapt the interface to the size of the screen and it would have produced an error message.

 Do It Yourself: Delete the views in your Storyboard. Add two square views as in Figure 6-34. Control-drag from the left view to the right view to add a Space constraint (the option is called Horizontal Spacing, see Figures 6-34 and 6-35). Control-drag from the left view to the top of the main view to add a Top Space constraint (the option is called Top Space to Safe Area). Repeat the process for the right view. Control-drag from the left view to the left side of the main view to create a Leading Space constraint (called Leading Space to Safe Area). Repeat the process with the view on the right to create a Trailing Space constraint (called Trailing Space to Safe Area). Control-drag a horizontal line inside the view on the left to create a Width constraint (Figure 6-33). Control-drag a vertical line inside each view to create Height constraints. Select the landscape mode from the bottom panel (see Figure 5-15). You should see something similar to Figure 6-38.

Another problem that arises when working with multiple views is how to align them to a single point. A common solution involves the use of invisible views to help us organize the rest of the views in the interface. The following example centers two labels in the main view, using a third view as a separator.

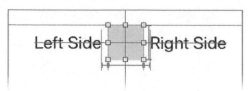

Figure 6-39: Labels centered with an invisible view

The view is centered in the main view and it has a fixed width and height, and the labels are pinned to the sides of the view and also centered to the view with Vertical Center constraints. The result is that the labels are always oriented towards the center of the main view.

To hide the view, we can select the option Hidden from the Attributes Inspector panel or assign the value `true` to the view's `isHidden` property from code. This property makes the view visible during development, but it hides it when the app is executed.

Do It Yourself: Delete the previous views in the Storyboard. Add a square view at the center of the main view with a Top Space constraint, a Horizontal in Container constraint and the Width and Height constraints shown in Figure 6-39. Add two labels on each side of the view. Control-drag lines from each label to the view to add a Space constraint (Horizontal Spacing) and a Vertical Center constraint (Center Vertically). Select the view and mark the option Hidden from the Attributes Inspector panel. Change the orientation of the Scene to see how the labels adapt to the space available.

Besides the Vertical Center constraint applied in the last example to center the labels vertically with the view, there are other alignment constraints available to align two or more elements together. These types of constraints are added from the Align menu and their application is straightforward, as shown in Figure 6-40.

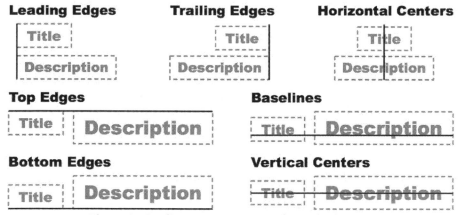

Figure 6-40: Alignment constraints for multiple views

These types of constraints provide the alternative to build more complex layouts. For example, they can help us determine the size of an element according to the space occupied by two or more elements. Figure 6-41 illustrates this situation.

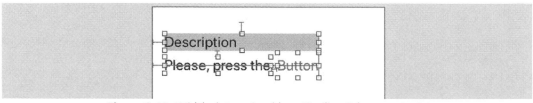

Figure 6-41: Width determined by a Trailing Edge constraint

Adaptivity

This example includes two labels with the text "Description" and "Please, Press the", and a button with the title "Button". All the elements have Space constraints to the margins of the container and between them to establish their positions. Their sizes are determined by their intrinsic content size, except for the label at the top. The width of this label is determined by a Trailing Edge constraint connected to the button (called *Trailing* on the quick menu). Because of this, the label at the top always extends to reach the right side of the button, independently of the size of the rest of the elements.

Relations and Priorities

The constraints we have defined so far are constant. This means that their values do not change, and the system has to satisfy every one of them or return an error in case of failure. But some interfaces require more flexibility. Sometimes constraints need only an approximate value or they are not required all the time. For these situations, constraints include two more configuration values called *Relation* and *Priority*. The Relation determines the relationship between the constraint and its constant value, while the priority determines which constraint is more important. Important constraints are satisfied first and then the system tries to satisfy the rest as close as possible. The possible relations are the following:

- **Equal** determines that the constraint's value must be equal to the constant value. This is the relation by default.
- **Less Than or Equal** determines that the constraint's value can be equal or less than the constant value.
- **Greater Than or Equal** determines that the constraint's value can be equal or greater than the constant value.

On the other hand, the priorities are defined by an integer value between 1 and 1000. For common situations, Xcode declares three predefined states:

- **Low (250)** determines a low priority.
- **High (750)** determines a high priority.
- **Required (1000)** determines that the constraint is required.

There are multiple situations in which these values become useful. For example, we may have a label that we want to be of a specific size, but that we also want to adapt if new text is assigned to it.

The following interface includes a label and a view. The label was defined with a Width constraint of 100, a Leading Space constraint that pins it to the left side of the main view and a Vertical Center constraint that keeps it vertically centered with the view. The view has a Height constraint to define its height and Space constraints to define its position and the distance between its left side and the label, but its width is determined by the space available. The result is that the view extends or contracts, but the label has always the same width (100 points).

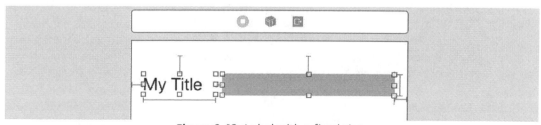

Figure 6-42: Label with a fixed size

The problem arises when a text longer than 100 points is assigned to the label. Because the Width constraint determines a fixed size of 100 points, the new text is clipped. Figure 6-43 shows what happens when we assign a longer text to the label of our example from the Attribute Inspector panel.

Figure 6-43: *Longer text gets clipped*

What we want is for the label to stay at a size of 100 points but to grow when the space is not enough to show the full text. We need the value of the Width constraint to be Greater Than or Equal to 100 points. To change the relation, we have to select the constraint, click the button on the right side of the Relation value (Figure 6-44, number 1), and select the option from the quick menu (Figure 6-44, number 2).

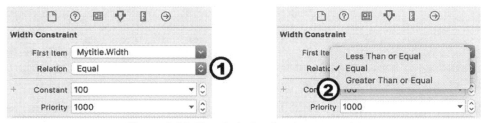

Figure 6-44: *New Relation for the constraint*

After the Greater Than or Equal relation is selected, the system tries to keep the label's width at 100 points whenever possible, but it lets the label expand if necessary. Now the text is not clipped when it is longer than 100 points and the view only fills the remaining space.

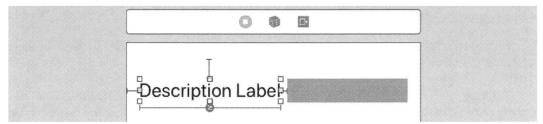

Figure 6-45: *The label expands to display the full text*

Do It Yourself: Delete the previous views in the Scene. Add a label on the left side of the main view with the text "My Title" and a size of 24 points. Insert a long view on the right with a gray background, as shown in Figure 6-42. Add a Leading Space constraint and a Trailing Space constraint to the label. Add a Width constraint to the label with a value of 100. Add a Top Space constraint and a Trailing Space constraint to the view. Add a Height constraint to the view to define its height. And lastly, add a Vertical Center constraint between the label and the view. You should see something similar to Figure 6-42. Assign the text "Description Label" to the label from the Attributes Inspector panel. You should see something similar to Figure 6-43. Select the label's Width constraint and change its relationship to Greater Than or Equal, as shown in Figure 6-44. You should see something similar to Figure 6-45.

Adaptivity

There are times when two or more constraints have to be constant, but they cannot be always satisfied. In cases like this, the system needs to know which one is more important. In the interface of Figure 6-46 below, two views are on the sides of a label. The views expand to occupy the space around the label, but they cannot reduce their sizes further than 50 points.

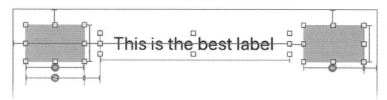

Figure 6-46: *Testing conflicting constraints*

In our example, the label was defined with a Width constraint equal to 250 points. The views are pinned to the main view and to the label by Space constraints and they also have a Width constraint but this time Greater Than or Equal to 50 (the views are connected to each other by an Equal Width constraint to make their widths equal all the time). This means that the label will always have the same size, but the views will extend or contract to fill the space available. When there is plenty of space, the constraints work as expected. The views expand from the label to the margins of the main view to fill the space available (Figure 6-47, right). The problem emerges when there is not enough space to simultaneously satisfy all the Width constraints. The label has to always be 250 points wide and the views' width cannot be less than 50 points. As we can see from Figure 6-47 below, the constraints are fine when there is enough space (landscape mode), but when there is no room for all the element, the constraints are shown in red (portrait mode).

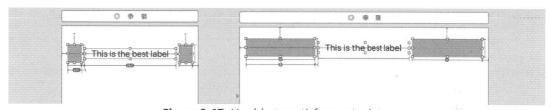

Figure 6-47: *Unable to satisfy constraints*

 IMPORTANT: In these situations, the app will not crash but the system will print an error on the console with the message "Unable to simultaneously satisfy constraints" followed by a list of all the constraints that couldn't be satisfied.

We have defined the Width constraints for the views to be Greater Than or Equal to 50 because it is important for us that they are never smaller than 50 points, but all the Width constraints are defined by default with a priority of 1000. For the system, the Width constraint of the label is equally important than the Width constraints of the views and it does not know what to do when there is not enough space to satisfy all of them. The solution is simple. We have to tell the system that it is important for us that the width of the views is never less than 50 points, but we do not care as much about the width of the label. This is achieved by reducing the priority of the label's width.

The constraints with a higher-priority value are satisfied first, and then the system tries to satisfy the rest as close as possible. Figure 6-48 shows what we see if we assign a priority of, for example, 750 to the label's Width constraint. Now the label's width is reduced to make room for the views and the constraint that is not satisfied is shown with a dashed line.

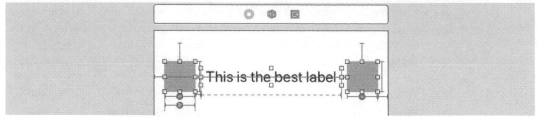

Figure 6-48: Label's Width constraint with a lower priority

 IMPORTANT: Besides Constant, Relation, and Priority, there is an additional value available to configure constraints called *Multiplier*. The multiplier is multiplied by the value of the constant to get a proportional value. For example, when the Multiplier value of an Equal Width constraint is set to 2, the element will be twice as big as the original. The system also uses the Multiplier to set the value for the Aspect Ratio constraint.

There are two more types of priorities that are useful for elements with intrinsic content size, such as labels and buttons. They are called *Content Hugging* priority and *Content Compression Resistance* priority. Figure 6-49 shows the controls available on the Size Inspector panel to modify their values.

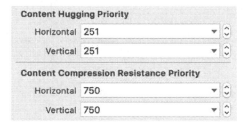

Figure 6-49: Options to modify content priorities

The Content Hugging priority determines how much the element wants to stay of the size of its content and avoid extending (it hugs its content). On the other hand, the Content Compression Resistance priority determines how much the element wants to stay of the size of its content and avoid contracting (resist compression). Figure 6-50 presents an example of two labels with a visible background to demonstrate how this works.

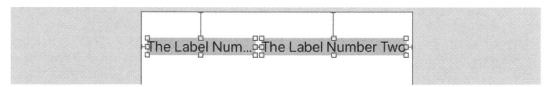

Figure 6-50: Interface to test content priorities

The labels are pinned to the main view and to each other with Space constraints. Their widths were not defined, so they will extend or contract according to the space available. Which label extends, and which one contracts is decided by the system considering their priorities. For this example, we have decided to assign to the label on the right higher values for its priorities. Its horizontal Content Hugging priority was declared as 750 and its Content Compression Resistance priority was declared as 1000. This will not let the label on the right extend or contract, so it is always the label on the left that adapts to the space available.

Adaptivity

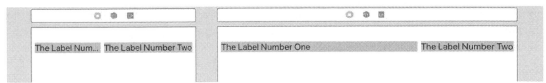

Figure 6-51: Labels with different content priorities

If, for example, we want the label on the right to contract when there is not enough space, we can change its Content Compression Resistance priority to a value smaller than the value of the label on the left. Figure 6-52 shows the effect of assigning a value of 250 to the Content Compression Resistance priority for the label on the right and a value of 750 for the label on the left. The label on the left keeps expanding when there is more space available, but now is the label on the right who contracts to make some room when the space is not enough to fit both.

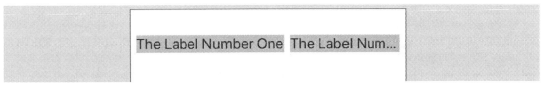

Figure 6-52: Labels with different compression values

 The Basics: The priorities can be set for both the horizontal and vertical axis. The horizontal values usually apply to elements like labels and buttons, while the vertical values are frequently used with Text Fields and images.

Stack Views

Constraints were developed to affect single properties, such as a specific dimension of an element or the distance from one element to another. Because of this, designing an interface, even a simple one, requires an intricate network of constraints interconnecting the elements together. Fortunately, this elaborated system can be simplified by including our views inside other views that act as containers, which distributes the constraints in different hierarchy levels.

In the following example, we have positioned a view in the center of our main view and added a label inside. The constraints for the view are connected to the main view, but the constraints for the label are connected to the view (the label's superview).

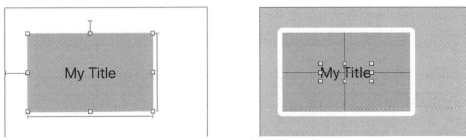

Figure 6-53: Views inside views

Figure 6-53 shows the constraints for the view and the label. The view has a Width and a Height constraint to define its size and a Top and a Leading Space constraint to determine its position. The label, on the other hand, has Horizontal and Vertical alignment constraints to determine its position inside the view. Because of this distribution, the view adapts to the space available on the screen, but the label is always at the center of its container.

The height of the container view in Figure 6-53 was determined by a Height constraint, but we can also define it with the constraints assigned to its content. The trick is to assign Space constraints at the top and the bottom of the elements. The system calculates the height of the content from these constraints and extends or contracts the container to fit its content. In the following example, the horizontal position of the label is defined with a Horizontal alignment constraint, as before, but the vertical position is defined with Top and Bottom Space constraints. From these constraints and the intrinsic size of the label, the system is able to calculate the height of the container view and therefore we no longer need the Height constraint for this view.

Figure 6-54: Height of the container defined by the content

Using views as containers is a common practice. They create a hierarchy of constraints that simplify our work, but they still present a challenge. Every time we have to modify the interface, adding or removing elements from these containers, we still have to deal with their constraints. Considering that containers usually display their content in columns or rows of views, UIKit introduces the `UIStackView` class to simplify this work. This class creates a special view that manages a horizontal or vertical stack of views and all their constraints. This means that using a Stack View to contain our views, we do not have to worry about their constraints anymore; all we have to do is to add or remove the views we want to be included in the stack and the Stack View takes care of assigning all the necessary constraints to place them horizontally or vertically. The following is one of the initializers provided by the class to create these kinds of container views.

UIStackView(arrangedSubviews: [UIView]**)**—This initializer creates a Stack View that contains the views declare by the attribute. The **arrangedSubviews** attribute is an array with references to all the views we want to include in the stack.

As always, the Object Library offers the options to add them to our interface.

Figure 6-55: Horizontal and Vertical Stack Views in the Object Library

The class provides the following properties and methods to organize the views and the space available inside the Stack View.

arrangedSubviews—This property returns an array with references to the views managed by the Stack View.

axis—This property sets or returns a value that defines the Stack View's axis (the orientation in which the views are going to be laid out). It is an enumeration called **Axis** included in the `UILayoutConstraint` class. The values available are `horizontal` and `vertical`.

alignment—This property sets or returns a value that determines how the views inside the Stack View are going to be aligned. It is an enumeration called **Alignment** included in the `UIStackView` class. The values available are `fill`, `leading`, `center`, and `trailing`.

distribution—This property sets or returns a value that determines how the views are going to be distributed along the Stack View's axis. It is an enumeration called **Distribution** included in the `UIStackView` class. The values available are `fill` (the views are resized according to their index), `fillEqually` (the views are equally resized),

fillProportionally (the views are resized proportionally according to their intrinsic content size), **equalSpacing** (the space between the views is distributed equally), and **equalCentering** (the space between the center of the views is equal).

spacing—This property sets or returns a **CGFloat** value that defines the space between views.

addArrangedSubview(UIView)—This method adds a view to the end of the Stack View.

insertArrangedSubview(UIView, at: Int)—This method adds a view to the Stack View at the index specified by the **at** attribute.

removeArrangedSubview(UIView)—This method removes a view from the Stack View.

To include a Stack View in our interface, we just have to drag the option from the Object Library to the Scene. The Stack View is represented by a white rectangle that we can pin to the main view, the Safe Area, or other views. Once the Stack View is in place, we can add all the subviews we want, as show in Figure 6-56.

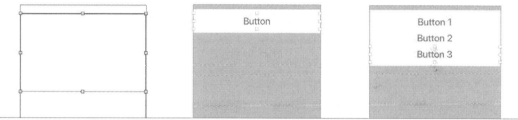

Figure 6-56: Buttons inside a Stack View

In this example, we pinned the Stack View with Space constraints to the top and the sides of the Safe Area and then dragged three buttons inside. Notice that we did not define the view's height because the system can determine the size from the size of the content. Every time we add or remove a view from the stack, the Stack View's height is updated (see Figure 6-56, right).

Once the content of the Stack View is defined, we can determine how the views are going to be aligned. By default, the **alignment** property is set to **fill**, which means that the views are going to be expanded to occupy all the space available, but we can also align them to the center, left or right by changing the Stack View's configuration, as shown in Figure 6-57 (we assigned a gray background to the buttons to be able to see the space occupied by their views).

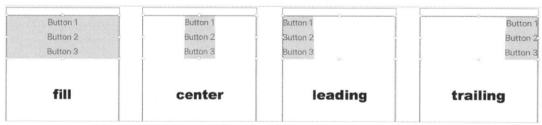

Figure 6-57: Views inside a Stack View with different alignments

The value of the property may be defined from code through an Outlet connected to the Stack View, or from the Attributes Inspector panel. To see the values, we have to select the Stack View from the Document Outline panel or by holding down the Shift key and clicking the mouse's right button over the Stack View's content. The options include the values for alignment, distribution, and spacing. The latter generates a space between the views.

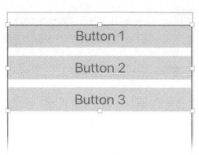

Figure 6-58: Space between views

In this example, we assigned a value of 15 to the `spacing` property. We can also change the distribution to define how the space between views is distributed. In the following example, we pinned the Stack View to the bottom of the Safe Area and apply some of the values of the `distribution` property to it (Fill, Fill Equally, and Equal Spacing, in that order).

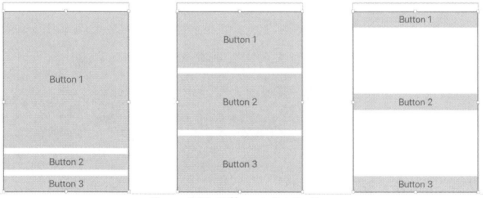

Figure 6-59: Different distributions

Stack Views can only manage one row or one column of views (horizontal or vertical), but they can be nested, providing an alternative for the creation of more complex arrangement. For example, we can add a horizontal Stack View on top of the buttons to show images.

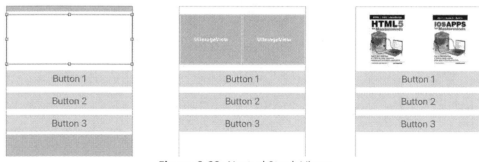

Figure 6-60: Nested Stack Views

In Figure 6-60, we added a horizontal Stack View with a `fill` alignment on top of the buttons (left), then we added two Image Views to this Stack View, and finally assigned the images with an Aspect Fit content mode.

 IMPORTANT: The Image View adopts the height of the image assigned to it. In our example, the images are of the right size, but you can add Height constraints to the Image Views if you have to define a different size.

Adaptivity

The Basics: The advantage of using Stack Views to organize the interface is clear, we just have to define the constraints to place the Stack View and then the view takes care of assigning the constraints for its content. Depending on your design, you may use Stack Views to organize most of your app's interface or just work with single constraints, as we did so far.

Document Outline Panel

As we already mentioned, the Document Outline panel is an additional panel that opens on the left side of the Editor Area when we click on the button at the bottom-left corner (see Figure 5-14, number 1). It offers a quick access to all the elements and constraints in the Storyboard and allows us to select them, connect them to Outlets and Actions in our code, change their names to make them easy to find, move them up or down in the hierarchy, delete them, and also create new constraints. As always, the constraints are created holding down the Control key and dragging a line between the elements we want to connect, but Instead of control-dragging a line from one element to another in the Storyboard, we can do it from one item to another inside this panel.

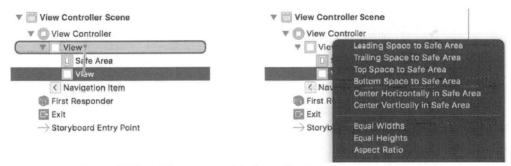

Figure 6-61: Adding constraints from the Document Outline panel

The same result is produced when we control-drag a line from an element in the Storyboard to an item in the panel. This technique is particularly useful when some of the elements are not visible. A very common scenario is to have a view as the background of our interface that covers the main view's area but contains some elements that need to be pinned to the main view (e.g., an image used as a background). Figure 6-62 illustrates how we would create a constraint between a label inside a view and the main view.

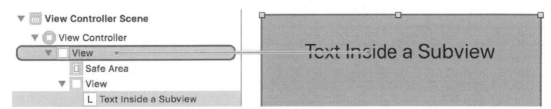

Figure 6-62: Constraints between elements and items in the Document Outline panel

Another useful feature of this panel is the possibility to change the place of an element in the hierarchy. For instance, the label in Figure 6-62 is a subview of a view inside the main view. If we want to position this label over the view but not inside, we can change its place in the hierarchy by dragging it to a new location on the list, as illustrated in Figure 6-63.

Figure 6-63: *The views hierarchy was modified*

Now, the label is inside the main view instead of the subview. But there is still a problem. Views are drawn in the order they are presented in the Document Outline panel. In the example of Figure 6-63, the label will be drawn first and the subview next. This means that the subview will cover the label. For the user to see the label, we have to move it down the list by dragging its item again, as shown in Figure 6-64. After we perform this change, the main view is drawn first, then the subview, and finally the label.

Figure 6-64: *The view's place was modified*

When working with elements and constraints inside the Document Outline panel it is difficult to remember which item corresponds to an element in the Storyboard. To simplify our work, we can change the names of the items by selecting them and pressing the Enter key. For instance, in our example, we added two constraints to the label, a Top Space and Horizontal in Container constraints, to position the label at the top and in the center of the main view. Xcode uses the text on the label to name these constraints. The names are so long that they don't even fit inside the panel. Figure 6-65 shows what they look like after shorting their names.

Figure 6-65: *New names for the constraints*

Constraint Objects

The information for the constraints is stored as XML code in the Storyboard's file along with the rest of the information for the interface. Once the application is executed, objects that represent the constraints are created. These objects are instances of the **NSLayoutConstraint** class. The objects defined in the Storyboard are automatically created from this class, but we can also use it to create our own constraints from code. The class includes the following initializer to create these objects.

NSLayoutConstraint(item: Any, **attribute:** Attribute, **relatedBy:** Relation, **toItem:** Any?, **attribute:** Attribute, **multiplier:** CGFloat, **constant:** CGFloat**)**— This initializer creates a **NSLayoutConstraint** object from the information provided by the attributes. The **item** and **toItem** attributes are the elements affected by the constraint, the

attribute attributes specify the type of constraint on each side of the connection, and the **relatedBy**, **multiplier**, and **constant** attributes provide the constraint's values.

This initializer takes all the necessary values to configure the constraint, including the views involved, the value of the Relation, Multiplier and Constant properties, and the attributes of the views that are going to be controlled by the constraint, such as the side, dimension, etc. The `NSLayoutConstraint` class includes the following enumerations to set the attributes and the relation.

Attribute—This enumeration defines the part of the object that should be used to set the constraint. The possible values are `left`, `right`, `top`, `bottom`, `leading`, `trailing`, `width`, `height`, `centerX`, `centerY`, `baseline`, and `notAnAttribute`.

Relation—This enumeration defines the relation between the first and the second attributes. The possible values are `lessThanOrEqual`, `equal`, and `greaterThanOrEqual`.

The `NSLayoutConstraint()` initializer returns `NSLayoutConstraint` objects but do not add the constraints to the view. The constraints are added and managed by the following methods of the `UIView` class.

constraints—This property returns an array with the `NSLayoutConstraint` objects that represent the constraints managed by the view.

addConstraint(NSLayoutConstraint**)**—This method adds a constraint to the view.

addConstraints([NSLayoutConstraint]**)**—This method adds an array of constraints to the view.

removeConstraint(NSLayoutConstraint**)**—This method removes the constraint referenced by the attribute from the view.

removeConstraints([NSLayoutConstraint]**)**—This method removes the constraints referenced by the attribute from the view.

The `NSLayoutConstraint` initializer takes one or two views, depending on the type of constraint, the attributes we want to associate to the constraint, and its values. The following example applies a Top Space, a Width, and a Horizontal in Container constraints to a label.

```
import UIKit

class ViewController: UIViewController {
    override func viewDidLoad() {
        super.viewDidLoad()

        let mylabel = UILabel(frame: CGRect.zero)
        mylabel.text = "Hello World"
        mylabel.textAlignment = .center
        mylabel.translatesAutoresizingMaskIntoConstraints = false
        view.addSubview(mylabel)

        let constraint1 = NSLayoutConstraint(item: mylabel,
attribute: .top, relatedBy: .equal, toItem: view, attribute: .top,
multiplier: 1, constant: 50)
        let constraint2 = NSLayoutConstraint(item: mylabel,
attribute: .width, relatedBy: .equal, toItem: nil,
attribute: .notAnAttribute, multiplier: 1, constant: 200)
        let constraint3 = NSLayoutConstraint(item: mylabel,
attribute: .centerX, relatedBy: .equal, toItem: view,
attribute: .centerX, multiplier: 1, constant: 0)
```

```
    view.addConstraints([constraint1, constraint2, constraint3])
    }
}
```

Listing 6-2: Laying out elements with constraints defined in code

When elements are introduced to the interface without constraints, Xcode uses an old system called *Autoresizing* to position and size them. The information generated by this system is later applied to create constraints for the elements and present the interface on the screen. If the constraints are added from code though, the system doesn't know that there are constraints available and try to create its own. To tell the system that we are going to define the constraints ourselves, we have to set the view's `translatesAutoresizingMaskIntoConstraints` property to `false`. Assigning the value `false` to this property avoids the creation of automatic constraints and ensures that those we define in code will not be in conflict with those defined by the system. We have to declare this property for every view we want to add to the interface.

The example of Listing 6-2 adds the label to the main view and then defines its constraints. The Top Space constraint is added by establishing a relation between the label's **top** attribute and the main view's **top** attribute. The Width constraint, on the other hand, only affects one element. In situations like this, the values for the second element and its attribute are not necessary, so they are declared as null with the values **nil** and **notAnAttribute**, respectively.

Constraints created from code may be added or removed. The following example takes advantage of the `removeConstraint()` method of the **UIView** class to change the position of a label when a button is pressed.

```
import UIKit

class ViewController: UIViewController {
    var mylabel: UILabel!
    var constraintLeft: NSLayoutConstraint!
    var constraintRight: NSLayoutConstraint!
    var constraintCenter: NSLayoutConstraint!

    override func viewDidLoad() {
        super.viewDidLoad()

        mylabel = UILabel(frame: CGRect.zero)
        mylabel.text = "Center"
        mylabel.translatesAutoresizingMaskIntoConstraints = false
        view.addSubview(mylabel)

        let constraintLabel = NSLayoutConstraint(item: mylabel,
attribute: .top, relatedBy: .equal, toItem: view, attribute: .top,
multiplier: 1, constant: 50)
        view.addConstraint(constraintLabel)

        constraintLeft = NSLayoutConstraint(item: mylabel,
attribute: .left, relatedBy: .equal, toItem: view, attribute: .left,
multiplier: 1, constant: 20)
        constraintRight = NSLayoutConstraint(item: mylabel,
attribute: .right, relatedBy: .equal, toItem: view, attribute: .right,
multiplier: 1, constant: -20)
        constraintCenter = NSLayoutConstraint(item: mylabel,
attribute: .centerX, relatedBy: .equal, toItem: view,
attribute: .centerX, multiplier: 1, constant: 0)
        view.addConstraint(constraintCenter)
```

```
        let button = UIButton(type: .system)
        button.setTitle("Move Label", for: .normal)
        button.translatesAutoresizingMaskIntoConstraints = false
        button.addTarget(self, action: #selector(moveLabel),
for: .touchUpInside)
        view.addSubview(button)

        let constraintButton1 = NSLayoutConstraint(item: button,
attribute: .top, relatedBy: .equal, toItem: mylabel, attribute: .bottom,
multiplier: 1, constant: 30)
        let constraintButton2 = NSLayoutConstraint(item: button,
attribute: .centerX, relatedBy: .equal, toItem: view,
attribute: .centerX, multiplier: 1, constant: 0)
        view.addConstraints([constraintButton1, constraintButton2])
    }
    @objc func moveLabel() {
        let text = mylabel.text!
        switch text {
            case "Right":
            view.removeConstraint(constraintRight)
            view.addConstraint(constraintLeft)
            mylabel.text = "Left"
        case "Left":
            view.removeConstraint(constraintLeft)
            view.addConstraint(constraintCenter)
            mylabel.text = "Center"
        case "Center":
            view.removeConstraint(constraintCenter)
            view.addConstraint(constraintRight)
            mylabel.text = "Right"
        default:
            break
        }
    }
}
```

Listing 6-3: Removing constraints

The code of Listing 6-3 creates a label and a button. The button always has to be at the center of the screen, so we added a permanent Horizontal in Container constraint setting the **centerX** attributes of the button and the main view as **equal**, but the label will move every time the button is pressed. To achieve this, we have defined three properties that store the necessary constraints: **constraintLeft**, **constraintRight**, and **constraintCenter**. After the constraints for the button are defined, these three constraints are also defined and the **constraintCenter** constraint is added to the label to establish its initial position at the center. Because of this, the initial interface positions both elements at the center of the screen. But this changes when the user presses the button and the **moveLabel()** method is executed. This method checks the current text assigned to the label and compares it to the strings "Right", "Left", and "Center" to establish the current position. Then, it removes and adds the constraints to move the label to the next place. For example, if the current value is "Right", it means that the label is at the right side of the main view and we have to move it to the left. The code removes the **constraintRight** constraint, adds the **constraintLeft** constraint, and changes the label's text to "Left". Figure 6-66 illustrates the three different configurations we see in the simulator after the button is pressed.

Figure 6-66: *Different constraints for a label*

Besides adding and deleting constraints, we can also edit their values. For this purpose, the **NSLayoutConstraint** class offers the following properties.

firstItem—This property sets or returns a reference to the first element associated with the constraint. It is an optional of type **AnyObject**.

secondItem—This property sets or returns a reference to the second element associated with the constraint. It is an optional of type **AnyObject**.

firstAttribute—This property sets or returns the value of the first element's attribute. It is an **NSLayoutConstraint.Attribute** enumeration value.

secondAttribute—This property sets or returns the value of the second element's attribute. It is an **NSLayoutConstraint.Attribute** enumeration value.

priority—This property sets or returns the constraint's priority value. It is a structure of type **UILayoutPriority** with the properties **required**, **defaultHigh**, **defaultLow**, and **fittingSizeLevel**.

relation—This property sets or returns the constraint's relation value. It is an **NSLayoutConstraint.Relation** enumeration value.

multiplier—This property sets or returns the constraint's multiplier value. It is a **CGFloat** value.

constant—This property sets or returns the constraint's constant value. It is a **CGFloat** value.

The following example creates a button in the middle of the screen that extends or contracts when it is pressed. The first group of constraints determine its vertical position (50), horizontal position (**centerX**), and height (50), while the last constraint determines its width. The value of the Width constraint is changed by the **expandButton()** method along with the button's text every time the button is pressed.

```
import UIKit

class ViewController: UIViewController {
    var button: UIButton!
    var constraintWidth: NSLayoutConstraint!

    override func viewDidLoad() {
        super.viewDidLoad()

        button = UIButton(type: .system)
        button.setTitle("Expand", for: .normal)
        button.backgroundColor = UIColor.lightGray
        button.translatesAutoresizingMaskIntoConstraints = false
        button.addTarget(self, action: #selector(expandButton),
for: .touchUpInside)
        view.addSubview(button)
```

Adaptivity

```
        let constraintButton1 = NSLayoutConstraint(item: button,
attribute: .top, relatedBy: .equal, toItem: view, attribute: .top,
multiplier: 1, constant: 50)
        let constraintButton2 = NSLayoutConstraint(item: button,
attribute: .height, relatedBy: .equal, toItem: nil,
attribute: .notAnAttribute, multiplier: 1, constant: 50)
        let constraintButton3 = NSLayoutConstraint(item: button,
attribute: .centerX, relatedBy: .equal, toItem: view,
attribute: .centerX, multiplier: 1, constant: 0)
        view.addConstraints([constraintButton1, constraintButton2,
constraintButton3])

        constraintWidth = NSLayoutConstraint(item: button,
attribute: .width, relatedBy: .equal, toItem: nil,
attribute: .notAnAttribute, multiplier: 1, constant: 150)
        view.addConstraint(constraintWidth)
    }
    @objc func expandButton() {
        if constraintWidth.constant < 280 {
            button.setTitle("Contract", for: .normal)
            constraintWidth.constant = 280
        } else {
            button.setTitle("Extend", for: .normal)
            constraintWidth.constant = 150
        }
    }
}
```

Listing 6-4: Updating constraints

 The Basics: We cannot only modify the constraints added from code but also those created in the Storyboard. All we have to do is control-drag a line from the constraint to the view controller and create an Outlet. This Outlet is similar to any other we have created so far, but instead of referencing a view it references the **NSLayoutConstraint** object that represents the constraint.

Creating one constraint at a time with **NSLayoutConstraint** objects takes time and requires multiple lines of code. Apple provides two solutions to this problem that involves the implementation of a visual format language to obtain multiple objects at once, or the use of layout anchors that allow us to attach a constraint to anchors assigned to each view or layout guide. The latter is the most popular because it adds the constraints from one view to another using properties. The following are the properties provided by the **UIView** class for this purpose.

topAnchor—This property returns an object that represents the view's top edge.

bottomAnchor—This property returns an object that represents the view's bottom edge.

leadingAnchor—This property returns an object that represents the view's leading edge.

trailingAnchor—This property returns an object that represents the view's trailing edge.

widthAnchor—This property returns an object that represents the view's width.

heightAnchor—This property returns an object that represents the view's height.

centerXAnchor—This property returns an object that represents the view's horizontal center.

centerYAnchor—This property returns an object that represents the view's vertical center.

leftAnchor—This property returns an object that represents the view's left edge.

rightAnchor—This property returns an object that represents the view's right edge.

firstBaselineAnchor—This property returns an object that represents the baseline of the top line of text in the view.

lastBaselineAnchor—This property returns an object that represents the baseline of the last line of text in the view.

These properties contain objects defined by subclasses of the `NSLayoutAnchor` class called `NSLayoutXAxisAnchor`, `NSLayoutYAxisAnchor`, and `NSLayoutDimension`. The following are the most frequently used methods included in these classes to add the constraints.

constraint(equalTo: NSLayoutAnchor, **constant:** CGFloat)—This method returns a `NSLayoutConstraint` object with a constraint that defines one anchor as equal to the other anchor, and with an offset determined by the **constant** attribute.

constraint(greaterThanOrEqualTo: NSLayoutAnchor, **constant:** CGFloat)—This method returns a `NSLayoutConstraint` object with a constraint that defines one anchor as greater than or equal to the other anchor, and with an offset determined by the **constant** attribute.

constraint(lessThanOrEqualTo: NSLayoutAnchor, **constant:** CGFloat)—This method returns a `NSLayoutConstraint` object with a constraint that defines one anchor as less than or equal to the other anchor, and with an offset determined by the **constant** attribute.

constraint(equalTo: NSLayoutDimension, **multiplier:** CGFloat)—This method returns a `NSLayoutConstraint` object with a constraint that defines the size attribute of the view equal to the specified anchor multiplied by the value of the **multiplier** attribute (used to defined equal widths and heights or to create Aspect Ratio constraints).

constraint(equalToConstant: CGFloat)—This method returns a `NSLayoutConstraint` object with a constraint that defines the size attribute of the view equal to the value of the attribute.

constraint(greaterThanOrEqualToConstant: CGFloat)—This method returns a `NSLayoutConstraint` object with a constraint that defines the size attribute of the view greater than or equal to the value of the attribute.

constraint(lessThanOrEqualToConstant: CGFloat)—This method returns a `NSLayoutConstraint` object with a constraint that defines the size attribute of the view less than or equal to the value of the attribute.

Depending on the types of constraints we need, we may use one method or another. For example, the following view controller creates a view and implements the `constraint(equalTo:, constant:)` method to add Space constraints on its sides.

```
import UIKit

class ViewController: UIViewController {
    override func viewDidLoad() {
        super.viewDidLoad()

        let grayView = UIView(frame: CGRect.zero)
        grayView.backgroundColor = UIColor.lightGray
        grayView.translatesAutoresizingMaskIntoConstraints = false
        view.addSubview(grayView)
        let constraint1 = grayView.leadingAnchor.constraint(equalTo:
view.leadingAnchor, constant: 0)
```

Adaptivity

```
        let constraint2 = grayView.trailingAnchor.constraint(equalTo:
view.trailingAnchor, constant: 0)
        let constraint3 = grayView.topAnchor.constraint(equalTo:
view.topAnchor, constant: 0)
        let constraint4 = grayView.bottomAnchor.constraint(equalTo:
view.bottomAnchor, constant: 0)
        view.addConstraints([constraint1, constraint2, constraint3,
constraint4])
    }
}
```

Listing 6-5: Attaching constraints to the view's anchors

The constraints in this example are created from the Leading anchor of our view to the Leading anchor of the main view. The same for the Trailing anchor, the Top anchor and the Bottom anchor. Finally, the constraints are added to the view with the `addConstraints()` method, as we did before. Because we use a constant of value 0, the view is expanded to occupy the whole are of the main view.

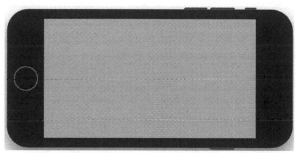

Figure 6-67: View pinned from its anchors

The **NSLayoutConstraint** class offers a Boolean property called **isActive** to activate or the deactivate a constraint. Using this property, we can tell the system which constraints are going to affect the layout, and because the process of activating or deactivating a constraint automatically calls the **addConstraint()** and **removeConstraint()** methods we don't have to call these methods anymore, as shown in the following example.

```
import UIKit

class ViewController: UIViewController {
    override func viewDidLoad() {
        super.viewDidLoad()

        let grayView = UIView(frame: CGRect.zero)
        grayView.backgroundColor = UIColor.lightGray
        grayView.translatesAutoresizingMaskIntoConstraints = false
        view.addSubview(grayView)

        grayView.centerXAnchor.constraint(equalTo: view.centerXAnchor,
constant: 0).isActive = true
        grayView.centerYAnchor.constraint(equalTo: view.centerYAnchor,
constant: 0).isActive = true
        grayView.widthAnchor.constraint(equalToConstant: 125).isActive =
true
        grayView.heightAnchor.constraint(equalToConstant: 125).isActive =
true
    }
}
```

Listing 6-6: Adding constraints with the isActive property

In this example, we assign the value `true` to the `isActive` property of each constraint using dot notation. The `NSLayoutConstraint` object is created first with the `constraint()` method and then the value `true` is assigned to the property, activating the constraint. The code creates two Alignment constraints to position the view at the center of the main view and Width and Height constraints to determine its size. The result is shown in Figure 6-68.

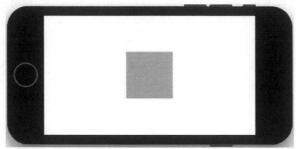

Figure 6-68: *Constraints activated with the* `isActive` *property*

The constraints not only can be attached to the anchors of the views but also to the anchors of layout guides like the Safe Area. The `UIView` class includes the following properties to access the layout guides available.

safeAreaLayoutGuide—This property returns a `UILayoutGuide` object with anchor properties we can use to define constraints between the views and the Safe Area.

layoutMarginsGuide—This property returns a `UILayoutGuide` object with anchor properties we can use to define constraints between the views and their superview's margins.

readableContentGuide—This property returns a `UILayoutGuide` object with anchor properties we can use to define constraints between the views and the readable area of their superviews (the area in which the lines of text are short enough to make it readable).

The `UILayoutGuide` objects include the same properties than `UIView` objects to define the anchors and therefore we can use them to create the constraints. The following example creates constraints between a view and the main view's margins.

```
import UIKit

class ViewController: UIViewController {
    override func viewDidLoad() {
        super.viewDidLoad()
        let grayView = UIView(frame: CGRect.zero)
        grayView.backgroundColor = UIColor.lightGray
        grayView.translatesAutoresizingMaskIntoConstraints = false
        view.addSubview(grayView)

        let marginsGuide = view.layoutMarginsGuide
        grayView.leadingAnchor.constraint(equalTo:
marginsGuide.leadingAnchor, constant: 0).isActive = true
        grayView.trailingAnchor.constraint(equalTo:
marginsGuide.trailingAnchor, constant: 0).isActive = true
        grayView.topAnchor.constraint(equalTo: marginsGuide.topAnchor,
constant: 0).isActive = true
        grayView.bottomAnchor.constraint(equalTo:
marginsGuide.bottomAnchor, constant: 0).isActive = true
    }
}
```

Listing 6-7: Attaching constraints to the Layout Margins Guide

Adaptivity

The code of Listing 6-7 defines a constant called `marginsGuide` to store a reference to the Layout Margins Guide, and then defines the constraints between the view's anchors and the anchors of the guide. The result is shown in Figure 6-69.

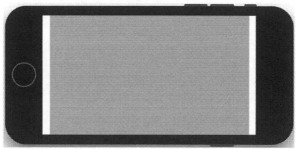

Figure 6-69: Constraints between a view and the Layout Margins Guide

Updating Frames

Usually, the views are updated automatically in every drawing cycle (an automatic cycle that updates the screen several times per second), but sometimes we may need to get the current position or size of an element before this process takes place (e.g., read the `frame` property of a view modified by a constraint). To make sure that we get the current values, we have to ask the system to update the interface. The `UIView` class includes the following methods for this purpose.

setNeedsLayout()—This method informs the system that the current layout is invalid and it should be updated in the next drawing cycle.

layoutIfNeeded()—This method forces the system to update the layout immediately.

These methods must be called on the `view` property of the view controller one after another. First we call the `setNeedsLayout()` method to tell the system that the current layout is invalid and then the `layoutIfNeeded()` method to force it to refresh the interface. After the methods are executed, we can read any of the element's properties, such as `frame`, and we will get values that reflect what the user sees on the screen (for an example, see Chapter 11, Listing 11-5).

Real-Life Application

The basic calculator developed in Chapter 5 was designed with absolute values. When an app like that is executed, Xcode uses a system called *Autoresizing* to automatically generate constraints based on the position and size of the elements defined in the Storyboard. This allows us to see the interface on the screen, but the elements do not adapt to the space available and therefore they always look the same. Taking advantage of Auto Layout, we can now design our calculator to adapt to every device and orientation.

To create a calculator with Auto Layout, we have to start by creating a new Single View Application project and add a view to the main view with a dark background color. This view represents the calculator's box, so we have to make it of the size of the screen adding Space constraints with a value of 0 to each side of the Safe Area.

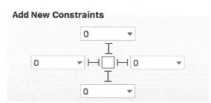

Figure 6-70: Space constraints for the calculator's box

After updating the frames, the view should look like Figure 6-71 below.

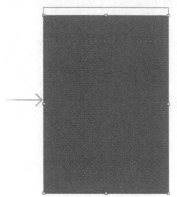

Figure 6-71: Box defined with space constraints

To create the display and the buttons, we have to add two more views inside the view already in the Storyboard. We have to give the views a shape that resembles a display and a keypad, and a background color that delineates the area, as shown in Figure 6-72.

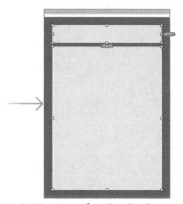

Figure 6-72: Views for the display and buttons

These views are pinned to the sides of their container and between each other with Space constraints and standard values. We also have to add an Aspect Ratio constraint to the view for the display to let it extend or contract but always preserving the same rectangular shape.

To create the real display, we have to add a label to the display view and pin it to the sides of the view with Space constraints and a value of 8 points to give it a little margin. The label's text has to be aligned to the right and have the value "0", as shown in Figure 6-73.

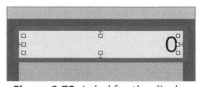

Figure 6-73: Label for the display

The last step is to create the buttons. We have to add them one by one, as we did in Chapter 5. In our example, the buttons have a gray background and a white title.

Adaptivity

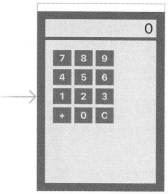

Figure 6-74: Configuring the buttons

There are different ways to organize the buttons and their constraints. For this example, we have decided to assign Space constraints to every button and let them extend or contract all together according to the space available. To add these constraints, we have to select all the buttons (pressing the Shift key), open the Pin menu, mark all the Space constraints, insert a value of 8 for each one of them, and activate the Equal Width and Equal Height constraints, as illustrated in Figure 6-75.

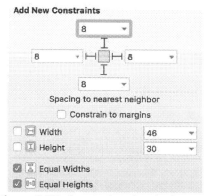

Figure 6-75: Constraints for the buttons

This generates Space constraints for every button between each other and between the buttons and the container. The Equal Width and Equal Height constraints are added to define their sizes. Because of these constraints, the buttons will extend or contract, but will always be of the same size, as shown in Figure 6-76.

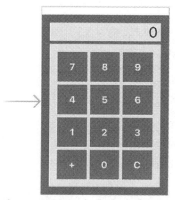

Figure 6-76: Calculator's final design

The interface is ready. Now all we have to do is assign the value of the buttons to their `tag` property from the Attributes Inspector panel, as shown in Figure 5-36, connect the Outlets and Actions as we did in Chapter 5, and copy the code from Listing 5-13 into our view controller. The application works exactly the same way as before, but now the interface adapts to the size of the screen and its orientation.

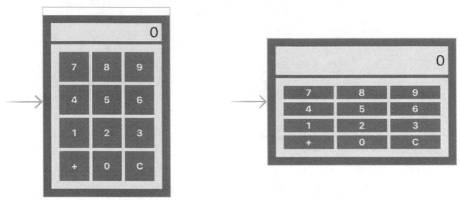

Figure 6-77: Calculator in portrait and landscape

Auto Layout can adapt the interface, resizing and adjusting the elements to fit the space available, but it cannot modify every property or rearrange the elements to meet new requirements. If we use Auto Layout alone to design our interface, we will soon be restricted by its limitations. For example, the display of our calculator looks fine in portrait mode, but it gets too big and the digits too small in landscape mode (Figure 6-77, right). On an iPad, the label will actually look too small for a device of that size, and at the same time the buttons on an iPhone in landscape mode look squashed. Solving these issues requires coding complex routines to change not only the elements' properties but probably also restructure every single constraint on the interface or even delete or replace some of the elements. To simplify our work, Xcode defines Size Classes.

6.3 Size Classes

The way Auto Layout organizes the interface is by telling the system how every element should be laid out. In practice, this is only useful when the space available preserves its original proportions. For example, the screen of an iPhone X in portrait mode is slightly higher than the screen of an older iPhone in the same orientation, but the proportions between width and height are similar. Adapting the interface to these variations only requires simple transformations, such as extending or contracting the elements. Things change when we compare devices with very different screens, such as an iPhone and an iPad, or the same device in different orientations. In these disparate conditions, the interface has to adapt in a way Auto Layout cannot handle. To get the design we want in every possible configuration, the values of the elements and constraints have to be drastically modified, and some of them have to be removed or added. To know when to perform these changes, the system uses values that represent the relative size of the space in which the interface is being presented. The classification is made based on the magnitude of the horizontal and vertical dimensions of the space. The size is called *Regular* if it is big enough to fit a regular interface or *Compact* otherwise. This classification is, of course, arbitrary. Apple's developers decided what should be considered Compact and what Regular based on the screen's sizes of the devices currently available in the market.

The Compact and Regular values conform a unit of measurement used to identify the horizontal and vertical space available called *Size Classes* (this has nothing to do with the classes defined to create objects). Because of the rectangular shape of the screen, the interface is

Adaptivity

defined by two Size Classes, one for the horizontal space and another for the vertical space. For example, the Size Classes defining the space available for iPhones in portrait mode are Compact for their horizontal space and Regular for their vertical space because in this orientation the screen's width is constrained but its height has enough space to display a normal user interface. Every device is assigned different Size Classes, depending on the size of their screens and orientations, as illustrated by Figure 6-78.

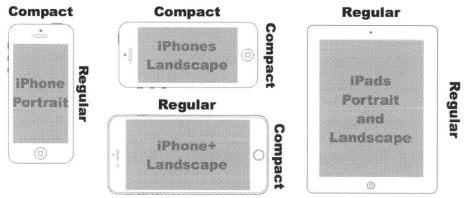

Figure 6-78: Size Classes assigned to mobile devices

The combinations presented in Figure 6-78 are actually the only four possible combinations of Size Classes: Compact width and Regular height, Compact width and Compact height, Regular width and Compact height, and Regular width and Regular height. By selecting the appropriate Size Classes for the width and height, it is possible to adapt our interface to any space available.

Adapting Properties

Xcode offers tools to introduce modifications for specific Size Classes. For example, we can add a label to an interface for the Size Classes Compact width and Regular height and the label will be shown only on iPhones in portrait mode (see Figure 6-78, left). With these tools, we cannot only add or remove elements but also modify some properties and add, remove or modify constraints for any combination of Size Classes we want.

The simplest change we can perform for a Size Class is to modify the value of a property. Some attributes like the background color or the font size can be changed from the Attributes Inspector panel. When an element on the interface is selected, this panel shows the values of its properties. The properties that can be adapted to a specific Size Class include a + button on the side. Figure 6-79 shows the button available for the Font field when a label is selected.

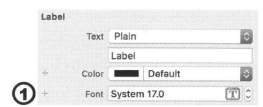

Figure 6-79: Adapting a font from the Attributes Inspector panel

When we click on the + button to add a font for a Size Class, Xcode shows a popup menu to select the combination of Size Classes we want to associate with the font.

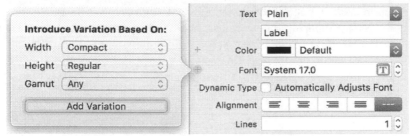

Figure 6-80: *Menu to select a combination of Size Classes*

 IMPORTANT: The menu includes an additional option at the end called Gamut. This is a range used to represent colors. In most devices, colors are represented by a system called RGB (also called sRGB, where the s stands for standard), but recently Apple made available an additional system called P3. The option you choose depends on the type of color system you want to implement in your application. Most applications work with sRGB, but you can also select the option Any if your application implements both systems.

After we select the combination of Size Classes we want to associate with the new font and press the Add Variation button, a new Font field is added to the Attributes Inspector panel. Figure 6-81 shows what we see when a font is added for the Size Classes Compact width and Regular height.

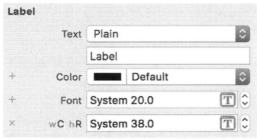

Figure 6-81: *New font size for a label in Compact width and Regular height*

In the example of Figure 6-81, we have defined the font size for the label as 38 points when the interface is presented on iPhones in portrait mode (Compact width and Regular height). The label is displayed with a size of 38 points in this configuration and with a size of 20 points anywhere else.

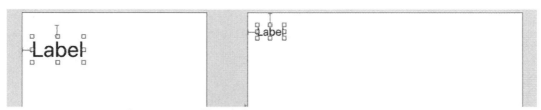

Figure 6-82: *Different font size in portrait and landscape*

In this example, we have selected a specific combination of Size Classes to affect only one type of device and orientation (iPhones in portrait), but the system also contemplates the possibility of adapting the interface for the Size Class corresponding to only one dimension (horizontal or vertical) without considering the other. The option is called *Any* and it is available from the Size Classes menu. For example, we can select the Size Classes Regular width and Any height to affect only iPads, iPhones Plus and X in landscape orientation (see Figure 6-78).

Adaptivity

The Basics: The configuration by default is considered to be for the Size Classes Any width and Any height, which means it will be applied to any configuration of Size Classes unless another value has been provided for a specific Size Class, as we did in the example of Figure 6-81.

Adapting Constraints

There are three things we can do with constraints: modify their values, deactivate them, and add new ones. The values are actually not modified; instead, new values are added for a specific configuration. For example, if we want our label to be 50 points from the top when the interface is presented in iPhones in portrait orientation, we can select the label's Top Space constraint and add a new value for the Size Classes Compact width and Regular height from the Size Inspector panel.

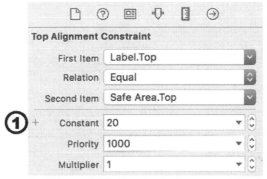

Figure 6-83: Constraint's properties

Figure 6-83 shows the Size Inspector panel after the Top Space constraint for our label is selected. To add an additional value for a specific configuration of Size Classes, we have to follow the procedure explained before. For example, if we want to move down the label when the interface is displayed on an iPhone in portrait orientation, we have to add a value for the Size Classes Compact width and Regular height, as in the following example.

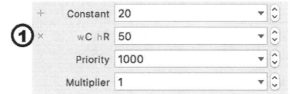

Figure 6-84: Different value for the constraint in Compact width and Regular height

Any value we insert in this field will be applied to the constraint when the interface is shown in a space with that specific configuration. The change is also reflected in the Storyboard as soon as the new value is inserted. From now on, both values are shown in the Size Inspector panel, no matter what configuration or orientation is selected, but each value only affects the constraint in its own configuration.

 The Basics: The Size Inspector panel shows an **x** button on the left side of every additional value to remove it. When a value is removed, the constraint takes back the value defined for the Size Classes Any width and Any height.

Modifying values of constraints for specific Size Classes is similar to what we have done so far with Auto Layout. To perform more drastic changes, we have to remove and add constraints. The constraints are not really removed but rather uninstalled. We install a constraint for specific Size Classes and uninstall it for others. For example, if we want our label to be pinned to the left side of the main view in iPhones in portrait mode but to appear at the center of the screen when the device is in landscape mode, we have to uninstall the Leading Space constraint for Compact width and Compact height and install a Horizontally in Container constraint.

Constraints are uninstalled from the Size Inspector panel. The following figure shows this panel after the Leading Space constraint assigned to the label in our example is selected.

Figure 6-85: Installed option

The option to uninstall the selected constraint is shown at the bottom of the panel (Figure 6-85, number 1). The option available by default corresponds to Any width and Any height, which means that the constraint is applied to any combination of Size Classes. To uninstall this constraint, we first have to add the option for a specific configuration clicking the + button on the left, as we do in the following example (Compact width and Compact height).

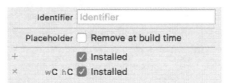

Figure 6-86: Adding the Installed option for a specific configuration

Once the new option is added, we have to uninstall the constraint by clicking the checked button.

Figure 6-87: Uninstalling a constraint for Compact width and Compact height

The constraint still exists, but it is not functional in Compact width and Compact height. This means that in that configuration (iPhones in landscape mode), the label now needs new constraints. The new constraints are added as we did before from the Auto Layout buttons, but we have to install them only for the Size Classes Compact width and Compact height to affect the label only on that configuration. After adding a Horizontally in Container constraint to center the label, we have to add the Installed option for Compact width and Compact height and uninstall the constraint for all the rest of the configurations, as shown in Figure 6-88.

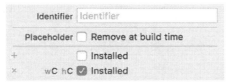

Figure 6-88: Horizontally constraint installed only for Compact width and Compact height

Adaptivity

Now, there is a Leading Space constraint that is installed for the label in any configuration except Compact width and Compact height, and a Horizontally in Container constraint (Center X) that is installed only in Compact width and Compact height. The result is shown in Figure 6-89; the label is always pinned to the left side except in iPhones in landscape mode.

Figure 6-89: Different constraints applied to the same label

Do It Yourself: This example assumes that you have created the previous example with a single label and added the Top and Leading Space constraints shown in Figure 6-82. Click on the Device Configuration button, select a small iPhone, and change the orientation to landscape (Figure 5-15). Select the label's Leading Space constraint. In the Size Inspector panel, click the + button of the Installed option and add a new option for the Compact width and Compact height (Figure 6-86). Click on the option to deactivate it (Figure 6-87). Select the label (use the Document Outline panel if it is not visible) and add a Horizontally in Container constraint (Figure 6-89, right). Install this constraint for the Size Classes Compact width and Compact height and uninstall it for the rest (Figure 6-88). The label should be displayed on the left in any device and orientation except for regular iPhones in landscape.

The procedure we have described above may be applied to single constraints, but it is not appropriate to develop complex interfaces. Manually installing and uninstalling constraints for every combination of Size Classes is a time-consuming activity and error prone. For this reason, Xcode provides a button in the Device Configuration panel called *Vary for Traits* that allows us to select which Size Classes we want to modify, and all the changes performed from that moment on will only affect those specific Size Classes.

Figure 6-90: Vary for Traits button

When we click the Vary for Traits button, a popup menu opens up to let us select which Size Class we want to modify, horizontal or vertical (Width or Height). After we select an option, the changes are applied to the Size Classes established by the current configuration of the Scenes. For example, if the configuration we see on the screen is of a regular iPhone in landscape orientation and we select both options, Width and Height, the modifications will be applied to the Size Classes Compact width and Compact height (small iPhones in landscape).

As soon as an option is selected, Xcode shows in the panel a list of the devices that present that configuration and will be affected by the changes. Figure 6-91 shows what the panel looks like after we select the Width and Height options with the Scenes set as an iPhone 4s in landscape mode. From that moment, we can erase the constraints we don't want for that configuration and add new ones, Xcode will take care of install and uninstall them for us.

Figure 6-91: *Vary for Traits activated for Compact width and Compact height*

Once we finish our work, we have to press the Done Varying button to indicate that we are no longer introducing modifications for those Size Classes.

 The Basics: If the design requires multiple constraints to be removed and replaced, we can select all the views involved and click on the option Clear Constraints for the selected views in the Resolve Auto Layout Issues menu (Figure 6-3, number 5).

Adapting Elements

The process to add or remove an element is the same we used for constraints, we have to select the element and install it or uninstall it for the configuration of Size Classes we want to affect, although now the option is not available from the Size Inspector panel but from the Attributes Inspector panel.

Figure 6-92: *Installed option for views*

As we did for constraints, we can use the Vary for Traits button to simplify our work. Using these tools, we cannot only adapt the interface and make our app look better in every configuration but also add new functionality according to the space available.

Trait Collection Objects

Every time the interface is displayed, each part of it receives a Trait Collection object with information about its own space on the screen, including the horizontal and vertical Size Classes, and this is how we can recognize the current Size Classes from code. The objects are created from the **UITraitCollection** class. The instantiation of these objects is automatic, but we can also create our own using the initializers provided by the class. The most frequently used are those related to Size Classes.

UITraitCollection(horizontalSizeClass: UIUserInterfaceSizeClass**)**—This initializer creates a **UITraitCollection** object with the value specified by its attribute. The attribute is an enumeration with the values **unspecified**, **compact**, and **regular**.

UITraitCollection(verticalSizeClass: UIUserInterfaceSizeClass**)**—This initializer creates a **UITraitCollection** object with the value specified by its attribute. The attribute is an enumeration with the values **unspecified**, **compact**, and **regular**.

Adaptivity

These initializers are useful when we have to set a configuration for a specific Trait Collection from code, as we will see later, but more useful are the properties provided by the class to read the object's values.

horizontalSizeClass—This property returns the value of the horizontal Size Class represented by the **UITraitCollection** object. It is an enumeration of type **UIUserInterfaceSizeClass** with the values **unspecified**, **compact**, and **regular**.

verticalSizeClass—This property returns the value of the vertical Size Class represented by the **UITraitCollection** object. It is an enumeration of type **UIUserInterfaceSizeClass** with the values **unspecified**, **compact**, and **regular**.

userInterfaceIdiom—This property returns a string that represents the device where the app is running. It is an enumeration of type **UIUserInterfaceIdiom** with the values **unspecified**, **phone**, **pad**, **tv**, and **carPlay**.

displayScale—This property returns a **CGFloat** value that represents the scale of the screen.

forceTouchCapability—This property returns a value that determines if 3D touch capability is available on the device. It is an enumeration of type **UIForceTouchCapability** with the values **available**, **unavailable**, and **unknown**.

Views and view controllers adhere to a protocol called **UITraitEnvironment** that defines a property to store the **UITraitCollection** object and a method to report changes.

traitCollection—This property returns a **UITraitCollection** object with the current Trait Collection associated to the view or the view controller.

traitCollectionDidChange(UITraitCollection?**)**—This method is called by views and view controllers that conform to the **UITraitEnvironment** protocol every time their Trait Collection changes. The attribute represents the previous trait collection.

We can access this property and method from every view controller and also our own subclasses of **UIView** (we will learn how to create **UIView** subclasses in Chapter 24). The following example overwrites the **traitCollectionDidChange()** method to print on the console the values of the current Trait Collection.

```
import UIKit

class ViewController: UIViewController {
   override func traitCollectionDidChange(_ previousTraitCollection:
UITraitCollection?) {
      super.traitCollectionDidChange(previousTraitCollection)

      var horizontal: String?
      var vertical: String?
      switch traitCollection.horizontalSizeClass {
         case .regular:
            horizontal = "Regular"
         case .compact:
            horizontal = "Compact"
         default:
            break
      }
      switch traitCollection.verticalSizeClass {
         case .regular:
            vertical = "Regular"
```

```
        case .compact:
           vertical = "Compact"
        default:
           break
      }
      if horizontal != nil && vertical != nil {
         print("The configuration is \(horizontal!) width and
\(vertical!) height")
      }
   }
}
```

Listing 6-8: Detecting changes in the Trait Collection

Every time the Size Classes assigned to the main view change, the system calls the **traitCollectionDidChange()** method on its view controller. From this method, we can read the information of the current trait collection in the **traitCollection** property, as we did in Listing 6-8, or get information about the previous Trait Collection from the **previousTraitCollection** parameter (to know about the previous conditions of the space occupied by the view).

The example of Listing 6-8 reads the **horizontalSizeClass** and **verticalSizeClass** properties of the **UITraitCollection** object and according to their values assigns the strings "Regular" or "Compact" to the corresponding variables (**horizontal** or **vertical**). At the end, we use the values of these variables to print the current configuration on the console, but because sometimes the values of these properties are not defined (their values are **unspecified**), we declared the **horizontal** and **vertical** variables as optionals and compare them against **nil** before printing their values.

 Do It Yourself: Create a new Single View Application project. Complete the **ViewController** class with the code of Listing 6-8 and run the application. As soon as the app is executed and every time the simulator is rotated, the code prints a message on the Xcode's console to report the current Size Classes. You can rotate the simulator from the menu or by pressing the keys Command + left or right arrows.

View controllers also adhere to the **UIContentContainer** protocol that among other methods defines two that report when the trait collection is going to change.

viewWillTransition(to: CGSize, with: UIViewControllerTransition-Coordinator)—This method is called to inform the view controller that its view is going to change size. The **to** attribute specifies the new dimensions of the view, and the **with** attribute is an object that adheres to the **UIViewControllerTransitionCoordinator** protocol, which defines a few methods to let us customize the transition process.

willTransition(to: UITraitCollection, with: UIViewControllerTransition-Coordinator)—This method is called to inform the view controller that the Trait Collection is going to change. The **to** attribute defines the new Trait Collection, and the **with** attribute is an object that adheres to the **UIViewControllerTransitionCoordinator** protocol, which defines a few methods to let us modify the transition process.

The **viewWillTransition()** method is called every time the main view is going to change to a different size, but the **willTransition()** method is only called when the Trait Collection is going to change. For example, when an iPhone rotates from portrait to landscape, both methods are called because the size of the view and the Size Classes change from one orientation to another. But iPads present a different situation. The size of the main view differs

Adaptivity

from portrait to landscape, but the Size Classes are both always Regular (Regular width and Regular height), so the `willTransition()` method is never called. For this reason, it is better to implement the `viewWillTransition()` method every time we need to detect the change in the space available and only use the `willTransition()` method when we have to perform a task that is related to the transition between Trait Collections. The following example implements the `viewWillTransition()` method to detect rotation in any device.

```
import UIKit
class ViewController: UIViewController {
    override func viewWillTransition(to size: CGSize, with coordinator:
UIViewControllerTransitionCoordinator) {
        super.viewWillTransition(to: size, with: coordinator)

        let width = size.width
        let height = size.height
        if width > height {
            print("We are going Landscape")
        } else {
            print("We are going Portrait")
        }
    }
}
```

Listing 6-9: Detecting rotation

The `viewWillTransition()` method includes the `size` parameter with the dimensions the main view is going to take. In the example of Listing 6-9, we get the view's width and height from this parameter and compare their values to determine the orientation. We are going to landscape if the width is greater than the height or to portrait otherwise. In this example we use the `viewWillTransition()` method to report the new orientation, but these methods may be used to perform changes on elements and constraints that are not possible to anticipate in Interface Builder.

The value received by the **with** parameter in both methods is an object that conforms to the **UIViewControllerTransitionCoordinator** protocol. This protocol defines a few methods to let us customize the transition process. The following is the most relevant:

animate(alongsideTransition: Block?, **completion:** Block?**)** —This method executes a closure during the transition process and another after the transition is completed. The **alongsideTransition** and **completion** attributes are the closures we want to execute while the transition occurs or when it is over, respectively.

This method sends an object to the closure with information about the transition that is taking place. This object conforms to the **UIViewControllerTransitionCoordinator-Context** protocol, which defines several methods to get the information. The following are the most relevant.

viewController(forKey: UITransitionContextViewControllerKey)—This method returns a reference to the view controller participating in the transition. The **forKey** attribute is a structure with properties that specify which view controller we want to be returned when two are participating in the transition (one view controller is replacing another). The properties available are **from** (references the view controller that is visible at the beginning of the transition), and **to** (references the view controller that is visible at the end of the transition).

view(forKey: UITransitionContextViewKey**)**—This method returns a reference to the view participating in the transition. The **forKey** attribute is a structure with properties that specify the view we want to be returned when two are participating in the transition (one view is replacing another). The properties available are **from** (references the view that is visible at the beginning of the transition), and **to** (references the view that is visible at the end of the transition).

The **animate()** method must be called on the coordinator object inside the transition methods introduced before every time we want to participate in the transition process. In the following example, we implement this method inside the **viewWillTransition()** method to adapt the size of the label for the display of our calculator to the size of the display.

```
override func viewWillTransition(to size: CGSize, with coordinator:
UIViewControllerTransitionCoordinator) {
    super.viewWillTransition(to: size, with: coordinator)
    coordinator.animate(alongsideTransition: nil, completion: {(context:
UIViewControllerTransitionCoordinatorContext!) in
        let controller = context.viewController(forKey: .from) as!
ViewController
        let display = controller.display!
        let height = display.frame.size.height
        display.font = UIFont.systemFont(ofSize: height)
    })
}
```

Listing 6-10: Calculating the font size for the display

The **viewWillTransition()** method of Listing 6-10 was programmed to work along with the code in the **ViewController** class defined in Chapter 5, Listing 5-13. Inside this method, we call the **animate()** method to perform custom tasks every time the interface is transitioning to a new configuration. There are two things we can do with this method: perform a task during the animation and after completion. The tasks are declared inside closures that include a parameter of type **UIViewControllerTransitionCoordinatorContext** (called **context** by default) that we can use to access the objects participating in the transition. Because our interest is to modify the font size of the display's label to adapt it to the space available and we are only able to know the dimensions of that space after the transition is over, we ignored the first parameter and only provide the closure for **completion**. Inside this closure, we get a reference to our view controller from the **viewController()** method. From this reference, we also get a reference to the **display** property (label's Outlet) and assign it to the **display** constant. This allows us to read the value of the **height** property of the label's frame and assign it as the new font size.

Every time a transition occurs, the **viewWillTransition()** method is called in the **ViewController** object, and then the **animate()** method is executed. When the transition is over, the **completion** closure is executed, and the label's font size is changed. Now, we do not need to declare a font size for every possible configuration from Interface Builder, the label adapts automatically to the space available.

 IMPORTANT: In the closure declared in Listing 6-10, we could have read the **display** property directly from the **ViewController** object using **self** (e.g., **self.display.frame.size.height**), but accessing variables and properties outside the closure from its statements can create strong references cycles and lead to the accumulation of garbage in memory (see Memory Management in Chapter 3). That's the reason why we accessed the **ViewController** object and its properties from the reference returned by the **viewController()** method.

Adaptivity

The Basics: Modifying the interface after the transition is over has its consequences. The most important is that the change is visible to the user. You should always try to determine the right interface for every possible configuration in Interface Builder and apply these methods only when there is no other alternative.

Orientation

Auto Layout and Trait Collections tell the application how the interface is going to be presented on the screen according to the space available and its characteristics (compact or regular), but the app is in charge of determining the orientations available.

The first level of control is provided by the app's settings. Xcode includes an entry at the top of the Navigator Area to access an editor where we can configure our app (Figure 5-3, number 6). When we click this entry, a project editor is shown in the Editor Area. The editor is divided in panes, with each pane allowing the configuration of different aspects of the application, including basic things like setting the possible orientations to instructions on how the code should be compiled. Figure 6-93 shows some of the panes available.

Figure 6-93: Configuration panes

The pane we will probably use the most is the General pane (Figure 6-93, number 1). Here, we can set the app's version, declare the oldest iOS version our app supports, and also control the orientations available, among other things. Figure 6-94 illustrates the section of this pane where we can activate and deactivate the orientations.

Figure 6-94: Orientations allowed

The pane shows the four options available (Portrait, Portrait Upside Down, Landscape Left, and Landscape Right). If any of these options is deactivated, the interface of our app does not change when the device rotates to that orientation. The options are pre-set by Xcode according to the device selected (iPhone, iPad, or Universal for apps that run in both devices). All the orientations are automatically activated for iPad and Universal, but the Upside Down orientation is deactivated if we are creating a project for iPhones. This is to avoid the user making the mistake of answering a call with the phone upside down.

These options affect the entire app. The rotation of the initial view controller and every view controller we add later to the Storyboard will be limited to the options activated in this pane. If we want to define the orientation for each view controller, we have to specify it in the definition of our subclass. The **UIViewController** class includes the following properties for this purpose.

---

shouldAutorotate—This computed property returns a Boolean value that indicates whether we want the view to autorotate or not.

supportedInterfaceOrientations—This computed property returns a value that determines the orientations supported by the view controller. It returns a property of the **UIInterfaceOrientationMask** structure. The properties available are **portrait**, **landscapeLeft**, **landscapeRight**, **portraitUpsideDown**, **landscape**, **all**, and **allButUpsideDown**.

These are computed properties that only return a value, but we can overwrite them in our view controller and make them return a different value to specify the behaviour we want.

```
import UIKit

class ViewController: UIViewController {
    override var shouldAutorotate: Bool {
        return false
    }
}
```

Listing 6-11: Deactivating rotation for a view controller

The **shouldAutorotate** property indicates whether or not the main view should respond to the device's rotation. When we return the value **true** from this property, the main view is rotated in any of the orientations available (those activated in the app's settings), but when we return **false**, as we do in Listing 6-11, the main view is presented in the current orientation and then never rotated.

Another way to tell the system if the main view should rotate or not is by overwriting the **supportedInterfaceOrientations** property. With this property, we can select exactly the orientations available for each view controller by returning a value or a set of values of type **UIInterfaceOrientationMask**.

```
import UIKit

class ViewController: UIViewController {
    override var supportedInterfaceOrientations:
UIInterfaceOrientationMask {
        return .landscape
    }
}
```

Listing 6-12: Allowing only landscape orientation

In this example, we return the value **landscape** to let the interface adapt to any of the landscape orientations (left or right). The main view of this view controller will only adapt when the device is in landscape mode. If we want to specify two or more possible orientations, we have to declare them as elements of a set (e.g., **[.portrait, .landscapeLeft]**).

 IMPORTANT: The settings defined on the General pane have precedence over the view controllers. If we deactivate the landscape modes from the pane, for example, those orientations will not be available in any view controller, no matter the values returned by their methods.

Adaptivity

7.1 Input and Output

Up to this point we have been working with the **UILabel** class to print text on the screen. Although this class can manage any type of text we want, and even create labels with multiple lines of text, it cannot take input from the user and it is not efficient when it comes to presenting extensive content. Considering these limitations, the UIKit framework includes two more classes to complement it: **UITextField** and **UITextView**.

Text Field

The **UITextField** class provides properties and methods to create a field where the user can type text. This is a rectangular box on the screen that activates the keyboard to let the user type characters or paste text in it. The class uses the **UIView** initializer to create the object.

UITextField(frame: CGRect)—This initializer creates an object of the **UITextField** class with a position and size determined by the **frame** attribute.

Of course, if we are creating our interface in Interface Builder using Auto Layout, it is more convenient to add the Text Field from the Object Library. Figure 7-1 shows what the option looks like.

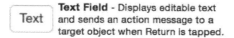

Figure 7-1: *Text Field option in the Object Library*

The following are the most frequently used properties included in the class.

text—This property sets or returns the text inside the field. It is an optional of type **String**.

placeholder—This property sets or returns the message that is displayed while the field is empty. It is an optional of type **String**.

font—This property sets or returns the font used by the Text Field to show the text. It is an optional of type **UIFont**.

textColor—This property sets or returns the color of the text. It is an optional of type **UIColor**.

textAlignment—This property sets or returns the text's alignment. It is an enumeration of type **NSTextAlignment** with the values **left**, **center**, **right**, **justified**, and **natural**.

adjustFontSizeToFitWidth—This property sets or returns a Boolean value that indicates whether or not the size of the font should be reduced to fit the size of the field. Its value is **false** by default. If we set it to **true**, we also have to set a minimum size with the **minimumFontSize** property.

minimumFontSize—This property sets or returns the minimum size allowed for the font. It is of type **CGFloat** with a value of 0.0 by default.

clearsOnBeginEditing—This property sets or returns a Boolean value that determines whether or not the text inside the field should be erased when the user begins editing.

borderStyle—This property sets or returns the value of the style for the field's border. It is an enumeration called `BorderStyle` included in the `UITextField` class. The values available are `none` (no border), `line` (single line around the field), `bezel` (single line with shadows), and `roundedRect` (lines with round corners).

background—This property sets or returns the image for the field's background. It is an optional value of type `UIImage`. The image replaces the border defined by the `borderStyle` property.

clearButtonMode—This property sets or returns a value that determines when the button to clear the text should be displayed. It is an enumeration called `ViewMode` included in the `UITextField` class. The values available are `never`, `whileEditing`, `unlessEditing`, and `always`.

The `UITextField` class also conforms to a protocol called `UITextInputTraits` that defines a set of properties to configure the input produced by the keyboard and the keyboard itself.

autocapitalizationType—This property sets or returns a value that determines when the Shift key will be automatically pressed to insert uppercase letters. It is an enumeration of type `UITextAutocapitalizationType` with the values `none` (Shift is never activated), `words` (Shift is activated to capitalize each word), `sentences` (Shift is activated to capitalize sentences), and `allCharacters` (Shift is always activated).

autocorrectionType—This property sets or returns a value that determines whether or not auto-correction is enabled while typing. It is an enumeration of type `UITextAutocorrectionType` with the values `default`, `no`, and `yes`.

spellCheckingType—This property sets or returns a value that determines whether or not spell checking is enabled while typing. It is an enumeration of type `UITextSpellCheckingType` with the values `default`, `no`, and `yes`.

keyboardType—This property sets or returns a value that determines what type of keyboard should be shown when the Text Field is tapped. It is an enumeration of type `UIKeyboardType` with the values `default`, `asciiCapable`, `numbersAndPunctuation`, `URL`, `numberPad`, `phonePad`, `namePhonePad`, `emailAddress`, `decimalPad`, `twitter`, and `webSearch`.

keyboardAppearance—This property sets or returns a value that determines the appearance of the keyboard. It is an enumeration of type `UIKeyboardAppearance` with the values `default`, `dark`, and `light`.

returnKeyType—This property sets or returns a value that determines the title of the Return key. It is an enumeration of type `UIReturnKeyType` with the values `default`, `go`, `google`, `join`, `next`, `route`, `search`, `send`, `yahoo`, `done`, and `emergencyCall`.

enablesReturnKeyAutomatically—This property sets or returns a Boolean value that determines whether or not the Return key is enabled when the user begins typing. The value by default is `false`, which indicates that the key is always enabled.

isSecureTextEntry—This property sets or returns a Boolean value that determines whether or not the text should be hidden (used to hide passwords). The value by default is `false`.

All these properties are also available from the Attributes Inspector panel. As with any other element, we can setup the Text Field, assign the initial values for its properties from Interface Builder, and later change some aspects, read its values, and control the field from code. The following example includes a Text Field in the Storyboard with the placeholder "Insert title here" and the rest of the values by default. The purpose of this app is to replace the text on the label with the one provided by the user when the Save button is pressed.

Title

Insert Title Here   Save

Figure 7-2: Interface to receive user's input

As we do with any other element in the interface, to access the text inserted by the user and modify the characteristics of the Text Field from our code, we have to create an Outlet. The example of Figure 7-2 requires two Outlets, one for the label and another for the Text Field, and also an Action for the Save button to process the text.

```
import UIKit

class ViewController: UIViewController {
    @IBOutlet weak var titleLabel: UILabel!
    @IBOutlet weak var titleInput: UITextField!

    @IBAction func changeTitle(_ sender: UIButton) {
        if titleInput.text != "" {
            titleLabel.text = titleInput.text
            titleInput.text = ""
        }
    }
}
```

Listing 7-1: Processing user's input

The code of Listing 7-1 does not introduce anything new, but thanks to the Text Field we are now able to process the user's input. When the user taps on the Save button, the **changeTitle()** method is executed and the label's text is replaced with the text inserted by the user. The first thing we do is to confirm that the Text Field is not empty comparing its **text** property with an empty string (**titleInput.text != ""**). When there is a text to process, the value of this property is assigned to the label's **text** property (**titleLabel.text = titleInput.text**), effectively replacing the text on the screen with the text inserted by the user. Finally, the Text Field is cleared to receive a new entry.

Do It Yourself: Create a new Single View Application project. Add a label with the word "Title", a Text Field with the placeholder "Insert title here", and a button called "Save" to the main view, as shown in Figure 7-2. Add the necessary constraints to pin the elements to the sides of the view and with each other. To expand the Text Field and keep the button at its minimum size, select the button and assign a Content Hugging Priority of 750 to it. Create Outlets for the label and the Text Field called **titleLabel** and **titleInput**, respectively. Create an Action for the Save button called **changeTitle()**. Complete the view controller with the code of Listing 7-1. Run the application.

In the example of Listing 7-1, we compare the value inserted by the user with an empty string. If the string is not empty, we process the full string, with all the characters inserted by the user. But sometimes users unintentionally add space characters at the beginning or the end of the string. To make sure that only the relevant characters are processed, we have to trim the string, eliminating any unwanted character at the beginning or the end. The **String** structure includes a convenient method defined specifically for this purpose.

trimmingCharacters(in: CharacterSet)—This method erases the characters indicated by the **in** attribute at the beginning and end of the string and returns a new string with the result. The attribute is a **CharacterSet** structure with the set of characters we want to erase.

The **trimmingCharacters()** method takes a structure of type **CharacterSet** to know what to remove. This structure creates sets of characters for searching operations. The definition includes a few type properties to create structures with standard sets. The most useful are **whitespaces** and **whitespacesAndNewlines**, which return sets that contain invisible characters, like spaces, tabulations, or characters that represent new lines. The following example implements the **whitespaces** property to remove the space characters at the beginning and the end of the string inserted by the user. If the user inserts only space characters, the string returned by the method will be empty and therefore the label will not be modified.

```
import UIKit

class ViewController: UIViewController {
    @IBOutlet weak var titleLabel: UILabel!
    @IBOutlet weak var titleInput: UITextField!

    @IBAction func changeTitle(_ sender: UIButton) {
        var text = titleInput.text!
        text = text.trimmingCharacters(in: .whitespaces)

        if text != "" {
            titleLabel.text = text
            titleInput.text = ""
        }
    }
}
```

Listing 7-2: Trimming text

The **UITextField** class, as well as other classes that create visual controls on the screen, is a subclass of the **UIControl** class and the **UIControl** class is a subclass of the **UIView** class, therefore, **UITextField** objects have access to all their properties and methods, such as the **backgroundColor** property to change the color of their background or the **isEnabled** property to activate or deactivate the field (see Chapter 4, Figure 4-7). The following example modifies the **isEnabled** property to disable the Text Field after the first input.

```
import UIKit

class ViewController: UIViewController {
    @IBOutlet weak var titleLabel: UILabel!
    @IBOutlet weak var titleInput: UITextField!

    @IBAction func changeTitle(_ sender: UIButton) {
        if titleInput.text != "" {
            titleLabel.text = titleInput.text
            titleInput.text = ""
```

Text

```
        titleInput.placeholder = "Text Field Disabled"
        titleInput.isEnabled = false
      }
    }
}
```

Listing 7-3: Disabling the Text Field

The **changeTitle()** method of Listing 7-3 assigns the new text to the label as before, but now it also modifies the **isEnabled** property to disable the field and shows a new placeholder to report the situation to the user. Once the Text Field is disabled, the user cannot type anymore.

These properties provide some level of customization, but they are not enough to control the user's input. Sometimes we need to determine what the user is allowed to insert or how the Text Field should respond. For this purpose, the **UITextField** class includes the **delegate** property to designate a delegate to the Text Field. The **UITextField** object calls methods on this delegate object to report the state of the process. The object assigned as the Text Field's delegate must conform to the **UITextFieldDelegate** protocol, which includes the following methods.

textFieldShouldBeginEditing(UITextField**)**—This method is called by the Text Field on the delegate object to know if edition should be allowed. The method must return a Boolean value that indicates if edition is allowed or not.

textFieldDidBeginEditing(UITextField**)**—This method is called by the Text Field on the delegate object when the user begins editing its content.

textFieldShouldEndEditing(UITextField**)**—This method is called by the Text Field on the delegate object when the user tries to switch focus to another element. The method must return a Boolean value that indicates if edition should stop or not.

textFieldDidEndEditing(UITextField**)**—This method is called by the Text Field on the delegate object after the element loses focus.

textField(UITextField, **shouldChangeCharactersIn:** NSRange, **replacementString:** String**)**—This method is called by the Text Field on the delegate object every time the user inserts or deletes a character or a string of characters. The **shouldChangeCharactersIn** attribute determines the range of characters on the field affected by the operation, and the **replacementString** attribute is the new character or string of characters inserted by the user. The method must return a Boolean value that indicates whether the text should be replaced or not.

textFieldShouldClear(UITextField**)**—This method is called by the Text Field on the delegate object to know if the Text Field should be cleared when the Clear button is pressed. The method must return a Boolean value that indicates whether the Text Field should be cleared or not.

textFieldShouldReturn(UITextField**)**—This method is called by the Text Field on the delegate object when the user taps the Return key on the keyboard. The method must return a Boolean value that indicates if the action should be considered or not.

Usually, the object assigned as the Text Field's delegate is the same view controller that controls the main view in which the Text Field was inserted. In the following example, the **ViewController** object is assigned to the **delegate** property of the Text Field and then the **textFieldShouldBeginEditing()** method is implemented. This method is another way to enable or disable a Text Field. The **UITextField** object calls it as soon as the user taps on the Text Field. If the value returned by the method is **false**, the user is not allowed to insert text.

Text

```
import UIKit

class ViewController: UIViewController, UITextFieldDelegate {
   @IBOutlet weak var titleLabel: UILabel!
   @IBOutlet weak var titleInput: UITextField!

   override func viewDidLoad() {
      super.viewDidLoad()
      titleInput.delegate = self
   }
   @IBAction func changeTitle(_ sender: UIButton) {
      if titleInput.text != "" {
         titleLabel.text = titleInput.text
         titleInput.text = ""
      }
   }
   func textFieldShouldBeginEditing(_ textField: UITextField) -> Bool {
      return false
   }
}
```

Listing 7-4: Assigning a delegate to the Text Field and declaring its methods

The first thing we need to do in our view controller is to declare that the class conforms to the **UITextFieldDelegate** protocol, so the **UITextField** object knows that this object implements the **UITextFieldDelegate** protocol's methods. This is done by adding the name of the protocol after the name of the class, separated by a comma (see Protocols and Delegates in Chapter 3). Next, we have to declare the view controller object as the delegate of the Text Field, so the **UITextField** object knows what is the object that implements the protocol's methods. This is part of the Text Field's configuration, so it has to be done before anything else, and that is why we assign the **self** keyword to the **delegate** property inside the **viewDidLoad()** method (**self** is a reference to the object that the code belongs to, in this case, the **ViewController** object). After the **viewDidLoad()** method is executed and **self** is assigned to the **delegate** property, the **UITextField** object can use this property to access our view controller object and report changes in the state of the Text Field by calling the corresponding methods. For example, when the user taps on the Text Field to start writing on it, the **UITextField** object calls the **textFieldShouldBeginEditing()** method on our view controller object to know if the user should be allowed to type on it (in our example, this method returns the value **false**, indicating that the user is not allowed).

The methods of the **UITextFieldDelegate** protocol are optional, which means we only have to implement the ones we need. If the method does not exist inside the delegate, the Text Field uses the values by default. For example, if we do not declare the **textFieldShouldBeginEditing()** method, as we did in Listing 7-4, the Text Field considers the value to be **true** and allows the user to edit the field.

The **textFieldShouldBeginEditing()** method is a very simple method, but we can declare others to control more aspects of the interaction between the user and the Text Field. For example, if we want to control what the user is allowed to insert, we can implement the **textField(UITextField, shouldChangeCharactersIn:, replacementString:)** method. Every time the user types a character or pastes text inside the Text Field, the **UITextField** object calls this method on its delegate to know whether it should include the entry or not. Implementing this method, we can process the input while it is entered.

```
import UIKit

class ViewController: UIViewController, UITextFieldDelegate {
    @IBOutlet weak var titleLabel: UILabel!
    @IBOutlet weak var titleInput: UITextField!

    override func viewDidLoad() {
        super.viewDidLoad()
        titleInput.delegate = self
    }
    @IBAction func changeTitle(_ sender: UIButton) {
        if titleInput.text != "" {
            titleLabel.text = titleInput.text
            titleInput.text = ""
        }
    }
    func textField(_ textField: UITextField, shouldChangeCharactersIn
range: NSRange, replacementString string: String) -> Bool {
        if let text = textField.text {
            let total = text.count + string.count - range.length
            if total > 10 {
                return false
            }
        }
        return true
    }
}
```

Listing 7-5: Determining the amount of characters allowed

The **textField(UITextField, shouldChangeCharactersIn:, replacement-String:)** method receives three values from the Text Field: a reference to the **UITextField** object, an **NSRange** value that represents the range of characters in the Text Field that are going to be replaced by the new entry, and a **String** value with the new entry. Based on these values, we have to determine if the entry should be included in the field or not and return a Boolean value to indicate our decision. For example, a common procedure is to limit the number of characters allowed in the field. We add the amount of characters currently stored in the **text** property to the number of characters the user wants to introduce minus the length of the range and return **false** if the value exceeds the maximum allowed. This procedure is followed in the example of Listing 7-5. We count the characters in the **text** property and the **string** parameter, add both values, subtract the length of the array, which represents the number of characters currently selected by the user, and finally store the total in the **total** constant. The value of **total** is then compared against 10 (the maximum number of characters allowed) and the value **false** is returned If **total** is greater than this number, rejecting the new entry.

The possibilities of control are limitless. We can filter the input in any way we want. For instance, we could let the user insert only numbers.

```
func textField(_ textField: UITextField, shouldChangeCharactersIn range:
NSRange, replacementString string: String) -> Bool {
    if (Int(string) != nil && textField.text != "0") || string == "" {
        return true
    }
    return false
}
```

Listing 7-6: Allowing only numbers

Text

To determine if the user inserted a number we use the `Int()` initializer. If the value returned by `Int()` is not `nil`, it means that the **string** parameter contains a number. But there are a few other things we have to contemplate to create this filter. The first is that, although the number 0 is a valid integer number, an integer number of two digits or more cannot begin with 0. Therefore, we have to validate the entry only if the current value in the Text Field is not equal to 0. These two values, the value created by the initializer and the current value of the **text** property, determine two of the conditions we need to check to validate the entry, but there is one more. When the user presses a key that does not produce any character, such as the Delete key, the value assigned to the **string** parameter is an empty string and therefore we also need to check this value to determine if the entry is valid or not. Inside the method of Listing 7-6, we create a logical sequence to check all these conditions. If **string** contains a number and the current value of the **text** property is different than 0, or the value of **string** is an empty string, then the whole logical sequence evaluates to true and the entry is validated.

 Do It Yourself: Replace the `textField(UITextField, shouldChange-CharactersIn:, replacementString:)` method of Listing 7-5 by the method of Listing 7-6. Run the application. You should only be allowed to type numbers in the field. If you type the number 0 first, the system will not let you insert any additional number.

Another useful method of the **UITextFieldDelegate** protocol is **textFieldShould-Return()**. This method is called every time the user presses the Return key on the keyboard. As an example, we can use it to perform the same action as the Save button.

```
import UIKit

class ViewController: UIViewController, UITextFieldDelegate {
    @IBOutlet weak var titleLabel: UILabel!
    @IBOutlet weak var titleInput: UITextField!

    override func viewDidLoad() {
        super.viewDidLoad()
        titleInput.delegate = self
    }
    @IBAction func changeTitle(_ sender: UIButton) {
        assignTitle()
    }
    func textFieldShouldReturn(_ textField: UITextField) -> Bool {
        assignTitle()
        return true
    }
    func assignTitle() {
        if titleInput.text != "" {
            titleLabel.text = titleInput.text
            titleInput.text = ""
        }
    }
}
```

Listing 7-7: Responding to the Return key

Because we are performing the same action for both, the Save button and the Return key, we move the statements to a new method called **assignTitle()** and then call this method every time the button or the key are pressed. When the user presses the Return key, the **textFieldShouldReturn()** method is called. This method executes the **assignTitle()** method to replace the label's text and then returns the value **true**. The value returned by the method tells the system whether it should implement the default behaviour after the Return key is pressed or not (usually declared as **true**), but the statements inside the method are executed anyway, no matter what value is returned.

Other methods of the **UITextFieldDelegate** protocol are called when the edition of the Text Field begins or ends. For example, we can implement the **textFieldDidBeginEditing()** method to highlight the active Text Field. The following example changes the Text Field's background color to a light gray when the user taps on it to start typing.

```
func textFieldDidBeginEditing(_ textField: UITextField) {
   textField.backgroundColor = UIColor.lightGray
}
```

Listing 7-8: Highlighting the Text Field

 Do It Yourself: Add the method of Listing 7-8 to the **ViewController** class of Listing 7-7 and run the application. The Text Field's background color should change as soon as you tap on it.

If our interface includes two or more Text Fields, we can take advantage of other methods like **textFieldDidEndEditing()**. Instead of performing a task when the Text Field is tapped, with this method we can do it when the Text Field loses focus (the user taps somewhere else). For example, if we expand our interface to include another Text Field, we can highlight only the one currently selected. Figure 7-3 shows what an interface like this would look like.

Figure 7-3: Interface with two Text Fields

In this example, the original Text Field is used to introduce the title and the new Text Field is used for the subtitle. The Save button still performs the same task, but the view controller has to be updated with another Outlet and an improved Action to process the values of both fields.

```
import UIKit

class ViewController: UIViewController, UITextFieldDelegate {
   @IBOutlet weak var titleLabel: UILabel!
   @IBOutlet weak var titleInput: UITextField!
   @IBOutlet weak var subtitleInput: UITextField!

   override func viewDidLoad() {
      super.viewDidLoad()
      titleInput.delegate = self
      subtitleInput.delegate = self
   }
   @IBAction func changeTitle(_ sender: UIButton) {
      if titleInput.text != "" && subtitleInput.text != "" {
         titleLabel.text = titleInput.text! + " - " + subtitleInput.text!
         titleInput.text = ""
         subtitleInput.text = ""
      }
   }
}
```

```
    func textFieldDidBeginEditing(_ textField: UITextField) {
        textField.backgroundColor = UIColor.lightGray
    }
    func textFieldDidEndEditing(_ textField: UITextField) {
        textField.backgroundColor = UIColor.white
    }
}
```

Listing 7-9: Highlighting two Text Fields

In the view controller of Listing 7-9, we call the new Outlet **subtitleInput**. This new property is later used in the **viewDidLoad()** method to assign the **ViewController** object as the delegate of the second Text Field. Now, every time something happens in any of the Text Fields in our interface, they both call the protocol's methods in our view controller. In this example, we have implemented the **textFieldDidBeginEditing()** and the **textFieldDidEndEditing()** methods to change the background colors. When the user taps on one of the Text Fields to start typing, its background becomes gray, as it did in the previous example, but now when the user taps on the other Text Field, the first one loses focus and it calls the **textFieldDidEndEdition()** method to report what happened to the delegate. From this method, we change the Text Field's background color back to white to reflect the new state.

 Do It Yourself: Add a new Text Field to the interface, as shown in Figure 7-3. Connect this element to the view controller with an Outlet called **subtitleInput**. Update the **ViewController** class with the code of Listing 7-9. Run the application and tap on one Text Field and then the other to see how their background colors change.

Working with two or more Text Fields in the same view and connected to the same delegate presents a challenge. The methods called on the delegate are always the same, no matter which Text Field performed the call. This is the reason why all the methods defined in the **UITextFieldDelegate** protocol include a parameter with a reference to the **UITextField** object that performed the call. We can use this reference to modify the object, as we did before, but also to identify the Text Field we are working with. One simple way to do this is to assign a value to the object's **tag** property. We used this property before for the buttons of the calculator developed in Chapter 5. A different value is assigned to the **tag** property of every Text Field from the Attributes Inspector panel and then the property is read from code to know which Text Field called the method. For example, the following view controller implements the **textField(UITextField, shouldChangeCharactersIn:, replacementString:)** method to establish different limits to the number of characters the user can type on each field. To know which limit to apply, the method identifies the field reading its **tag** property.

```
import UIKit

class ViewController: UIViewController, UITextFieldDelegate {
    @IBOutlet weak var titleLabel: UILabel!
    @IBOutlet weak var titleInput: UITextField!
    @IBOutlet weak var subtitleInput: UITextField!

    override func viewDidLoad() {
        super.viewDidLoad()
        titleInput.delegate = self
        subtitleInput.delegate = self
    }
```

Text

```
@IBAction func changeTitle(_ sender: UIButton) {
    if titleInput.text != "" && subtitleInput.text != "" {
        titleLabel.text = titleInput.text! + " - " + subtitleInput.text!
        titleInput.text = ""
        subtitleInput.text = ""
    }
}
}
func textField(_ textField: UITextField, shouldChangeCharactersIn
range: NSRange, replacementString string: String) -> Bool {
    var maximum = 0
    if textField.tag == 1 {
        maximum = 10
    } else {
        maximum = 15
    }
    if let text = textField.text {
        let total = text.count + string.count - range.length
        if total > maximum {
            return false
        }
    }
    return true
}
}
```

Listing 7-10: Identifying Text Fields

This example assumes that the values of the Text Fields' **tag** properties were defined as 1 and 2, respectively. The **textField(UITextField, shouldChangeCharactersIn:, replacementString:)** method checks this value to know which field is making the call (**textField.tag == 1**), sets the value of the **maximum** variable, and then compares the result against the total amount of characters allowed to validate the entry (**total > maximum**).

 Do It Yourself: Select each Text Field in the Storyboard and assign the corresponding values to their **tag** properties from the Attributes Inspector panel, as shown in Figure 5-36 (1 for the title and 2 for the subtitle). Update the **ViewController** class with the code of Listing 7-10. Run the application. The title should be limited to 10 characters and the subtitle to 15.

Text View

The **UITextView** class provides properties and methods to create a scrollable view that can be used to present long texts. The element can display text and also receive input from the user. If the size of the text surpasses the size of the view, the view allows the user to scroll its content. The class uses the **UIView** initializer to create the object.

UITextView(frame: CGRect**)**—This initializer creates an object of the **UITextView** class with a position and size determined by the **frame** attribute.

Again, if we are creating our interface in Interface Builder, we can add the Text View from the option in the Object Library.

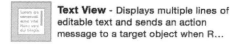

Text View - Displays multiple lines of editable text and sends an action message to a target object when R...

Figure 7-4: Text View option in the Object Library

The following are the most frequently used properties included in this class.

text—This property sets or returns the text in the view. It is an optional of type `String`.

font—This property sets or returns the font used by the Text View to display the text. It is an optional of type `UIFont`.

textColor—This property sets or returns the color of the text. It is an optional of type `UIColor`.

textAlignment—This property sets or returns the text's alignment. It is an enumeration of type `NSTextAlignment` with the values `left`, `center`, `right`, `justified`, and `natural`.

textStorage—This property returns an object that represents the attributed text in the Text View. The object is of a subclass of `NSMutableAttributedString` called `NSTextStorage`. The code provided by the `NSMutableAttributedString` class allows us to edit the text's attributes and the code provided by the `NSTextStorage` class notifies the changes to the Text View as soon as they are made.

isEditable—This property sets or returns a Boolean value that determines whether the user is allowed to edit the text inside the Text View or not.

isSelectable—This property sets or returns a Boolean value that determines whether the user is allowed to select text inside the Text View or not.

selectedRange—This property sets or returns the range of the text selected inside the Text View. It is of type `NSRange`.

scrollRangeToVisible(NSRange**)**—This method scrolls the view to show on the screen the text that corresponds to the range specified by the attribute.

The `UITextView` class can also designate a delegate to report the state of the process. The object assigned as the Text View's delegate must conform to the `UITextViewDelegate` protocol, which includes the following methods.

textViewShouldBeginEditing(UITextView**)**—This method is called by the Text View on the delegate object to know if edition should be allowed. The method returns a Boolean value that indicates if edition is allowed or not.

textViewDidBeginEditing(UITextView**)**—This method is called by the Text View on the delegate object when the user begins editing its content.

textViewShouldEndEditing(UITextView**)**—This method is called by the Text View on the delegate object when the user tries to switch focus to another element. The method returns a Boolean value that indicates if edition should stop or not.

textViewDidEndEditing(UITextView**)**—This method is called by the Text View on the delegate object when the element loses focus.

textView(UITextView, **shouldChangeTextIn:** NSRange, **replacementText:** String**)**—This method is called by the Text View on the delegate object every time the user inserts or deletes a character or a string of characters. The **shouldChangeTextIn** attribute determines the range of characters on the view affected by the operation, and the **replacementText** attribute is the new character or string inserted by the user. The method returns a Boolean value that indicates whether the text should be replaced or not.

textViewDidChange(UITextView**)**—This method is called by the Text View on the delegate object when the user changes the text or any of its attributes.

textViewDidChangeSelection(UITextView**)**—This method is called by the Text View on the delegate object when the user selects text.

As always, we can provide the values for all the properties from the Attributes Inspector panel, including the text to show inside the view. When a Text View is selected, the panel includes an option at the top to indicate the type of text we want to assign to the view: Plain or Attributed. If we select the Attributed option, additional buttons are incorporated to the panel to assign the attributes.

Figure 7-5: Attributed text for the Text View

From the Attributes Inspector panel, we can change every aspect of the whole text or part of it, but this only sets the Text View's initial value. If we want to modify the view's content or replace it when the app is running, we have to do it from code. The **UITextView** class offers two properties to access the object's content: **text** and **attributedText**. With the **text** property, we can set plain text with general attributes, and with the **attributeText** property we can assign attributed text to the view. These properties store different types of texts but are connected with each other. If a value is assigned to one property, the text on the other property is automatically modified. This allows us to use the Text View to display any type of text we want at any moment. If we want to display plain text, we assign a **String** value to the **text** property, but if we want to display text that presents ranges of characters with different attributes, we assign an **NSAttributedString** object to the **attributedText** property.

The problem with this approach is that the **NSAttributedString** class creates immutable objects, which means that every time we want to change any of the attributes in the attributed text we have to create and assign a new object. This issue was solved with the definition of an additional property called **textStorage**. This property stores an object of the **NSMutableAttributedString** class (see Chapter 4). The advantage of using this property is that we can modify the attributes on the same object and the changes performed are automatically reflected in the Text View.

The Basics: The **textStorage** property is of type **NSTextStorage**, a subclass of **NSMutableAttributedString**, that was defined to make it easy to handle and update attributed text.

The following example introduces a new interface with a button and a Text View. The purpose of the button is to assign new attributes to the characters selected by the user.

Figure 7-6: Text View with plain text

The view controller for this interface is very simple, we just need an Outlet to reference the Text View and an Action for the button. Because we want to modify the attributes of the text (change the color of the characters selected by the user) we have to access the **textStorage** property and call its **addAttribute()** method.

```
import UIKit

class ViewController: UIViewController {
   @IBOutlet weak var message: UITextView!

   @IBAction func selection(_ sender: UIButton) {
      let attributedText = message.textStorage
      attributedText.addAttribute(.foregroundColor, value: UIColor.red,
range: message.selectedRange)
   }
}
```

Listing 7-11: Adding attributes to the attributed text of a Text View

The **addAttribute()** method is one of the methods offered by the **NSMutableAttributedString** class to add attributes to an attributed text (see Chapter 4). Because we want to modify the color of the text selected by the user, we declare the property **foregroundColor** and a **UIColor** object with the values for the color we want to assign. The range of characters to modify in this example is the range of characters currently selected. This value is provided by the Text View's **selectedRange** property. Every time the user selects text in the Text View, the value of this property changes to reflect the location of the selected characters. The **selection()** method of Listing 7-11 calls the **addAttribute()** method with all these values to change the color of the selected text to red.

 Do It Yourself: Create a new Single View Application project. Add a button called Change Color at the top of the view, a Text View, and all the necessary constraints to get an interface similar to Figure 7-6. Connect the Text View to your view controller with an Outlet called **message** and the button with an Action called **selection()**. Complete your view controller with the code of Listing 7-11. Run the application in the simulator, double click a word to select it, and press the Change Color button to change its color to red.

Of course, we don't always have to affect the selected characters; we can specify any range of characters we want. For example, we could search for specific words in the text and change the attributes for only those characters. In the following example, we look for the first occurrence of the word "John" and change the color of its characters to blue.

```
import UIKit

class ViewController: UIViewController, UITextViewDelegate {
    @IBOutlet weak var message: UITextView!
    override func viewDidLoad() {
        super.viewDidLoad()
        message.delegate = self
    }
    @IBAction func selection(_ sender: UIButton) {
        let attributedText = message.textStorage
        attributedText.addAttribute(.foregroundColor, value: UIColor.red,
range: message.selectedRange)
    }
    func textViewDidChange(_ textView: UITextView) {
        let text = textView.text!
        if let range = text.range(of: "John", options: .caseInsensitive) {
            let attributedText = textView.textStorage
            attributedText.addAttribute(.foregroundColor, value:
UIColor.blue, range: NSRange(range, in: text))
        }
    }
}
```

Listing 7-12: *Adding attributes to a range of characters*

The code of Listing 7-12 uses the same interface, but this time we assign the view controller as the Text View's delegate to implement the **textViewDidChange()** method. The method is called by the **UITextView** object every time the content of the Text View changes. This way, when the user types or erases a character, our code is aware of it and can process the new value. In this example, we search for the word "John" and change the color of the characters to blue if we find it (Notice that the **addAttribute()** method takes an **NSRange** value, so we had to convert the range to an **NSRange** object using the **NSRange** initializer studied in Chapter 4).

 The Basics: The rest of the **UITextViewDelegate** protocol's methods are similar to the methods studied before for the **UITextField** class, except for how the Return key is handled. The **UITextViewDelegate** protocol does not have a method to process the Return key because the key is used to generate new lines of text.

7.2 Keyboard

iOS has a particular way to control the keyboard. It does not consider the keyboard as a tool, but rather as a way to detect events produced by the user, and therefore it keeps it on screen as long as the element that made it appear is still capable of processing the input. To dismiss the keyboard, we have to tell the system that the element is no longer in charge of processing its events, and this is done by altering the chain of response.

When an event occurs, such as a tap on the screen, the system has to determine which element is going to process the event. The position of the graphics on the screen does not always reflects this responsibility. For example, we could have two views that overlapped but only the view on the back is capable of processing touch events. If we let the view on the front get the events, the view on the back will never know that the user tapped the screen. To solve this problem, the system considers the elements hierarchy and creates a virtual chain in which some elements in certain positions, called *Responders*, receive the event and then decide whether to process it or deliver it to the next element in the chain. Some events, like key events, are sent to specific elements called *First Responders*.

First Responders are designated by the system or our code. This is actually what the system does when the user taps on a Text Field or a Text View: it declares the element as the First Responder, so all the events are first sent to it. And this is also how the system manages the keyboard. The keyboard is opened when an element that is capable of handling key events becomes the First Responder, and it is closed when the element ceases to be the First Responder (it resigns as First Responder).

The UIKit framework defines the **UIResponder** class to manage First Responders and respond to events. The following are its most frequently used properties and methods.

isFirstResponder—This property returns a Boolean value that indicates whether the element is the current designated First Responder or not.

becomeFirstResponder()—This method designates the element as the First Responder.

resignFirstResponder()—This method notifies the element that it has to resign its condition of First Responder.

touchesBegan([UITouch], with: UIEvent?)—This method is called by the system in responder objects (views and view controllers) when the user starts touching the screen.

touchesMoved([UITouch], with: UIEvent?)—This method is called by the system in responder objects (views and view controllers) when the finger touching the screen moves.

touchesEnded([UITouch], with: UIEvent?)—This method is called by the system in responder objects (views and view controllers) when the user stops touching the screen.

touchesCancelled([UITouch], with: UIEvent?)—This method is called by the system in responder objects (views and view controllers) when a touch event is cancelled by the system.

The **UIResponder** class is a basic class that most of the classes inherit from. Because of this, all the elements created from UIKit classes have access to its properties and methods and are capable of handling events. If we need to open the keyboard, we just have to call the **becomeFirstResponder()** method on an element capable of handling key events (which produces the same effect as the user tapping on the element). Closing the keyboard is as simple as calling the **resignFirstResponder()** on the element currently assigned as First Responder. The following example shows how to implement these two methods. This view controller assumes that we have an interface with a Text Field, a label, and a button (see Figure 7-2).

```
import UIKit

class ViewController: UIViewController {
    @IBOutlet weak var titleLabel: UILabel!
    @IBOutlet weak var titleInput: UITextField!

    @IBAction func changeTitle(_ sender: UIButton) {
        if titleInput.text != "" {
            titleLabel.text = titleInput.text
            titleInput.text = ""
            titleInput.resignFirstResponder()
        } else {
            titleInput.becomeFirstResponder()
        }
    }
}
```

Listing 7-13: Opening and closing the keyboard from code

Text

This example is similar to the one presented before in Listing 7-1. We have an Outlet for the label and another for the Text Field. When the user presses the Save button, the `changeTitle()` method checks the content of the Text Field as before, but this time it performs an action either if the text is empty or not. If something was inserted into the field, the method assigns that value to the label and then executes the `resignFirstResponder()` method to force the Text Field to resign its condition as First Responder. When the system detects that there is no First Responder that can handle key events, it closes the keyboard. On the other hand, if the `changeTitle()` method cannot find any text inside the Text Field, it executes the `becomeFirstResponder()` method, turning the Text Field into the First Responder and compelling the system to open the keyboard.

 Do It Yourself: Create an interface similar to the one presented in Figure 7-2. Connect the label, the Text Field and the button with the corresponding Outlets and Action, as we did for the example of Listing 7-1. Complete your view controller with the code of Listing 7-13. Run the application in the simulator and click the Save button. The keyboard will pop up and the Text Field will show the cursor. Write something in the Text Field and press the Save button again. The keyboard should be dismissed.

 The Basics: The simulator includes the same keyboard of a real device, but it can also work with the computer's keyboard. To select one keyboard or another, open the Hardware menu at the top of the screen, go to Keyboard and select the option of your preference.

The `becomeFirstResponder()` method is not always necessary. Usually the user taps on the element when it needs to type something on it and this action automatically makes the element the First Responder, compelling the system to open the keyboard. But the execution of the `resignFirstResponder()` method is required every time we want to dismiss the keyboard because there is no automatic action to do it. In our previous example, we called this method when the Save button was pressed, but a more intuitive interface will also close the keyboard when the user taps somewhere else on the screen. These types of events are detected by the event-handling methods included in the `UIResponder` class, as shown next.

```
import UIKit

class ViewController: UIViewController {
    @IBOutlet weak var titleLabel: UILabel!
    @IBOutlet weak var titleInput: UITextField!

    @IBAction func changeTitle(_ sender: UIButton) {
        if titleInput.text != "" {
            titleLabel.text = titleInput.text
            titleInput.text = ""
        }
    }
    override func touchesBegan(_ touches: Set<UITouch>, with event:
UIEvent?) {
        super.touchesBegan(touches, with: event)
        titleInput.resignFirstResponder()
    }
}
```

Listing 7-14: Dismissing the keyboard when the user touches the screen

The **touchesBegan()** method implemented in Listing 7-14 is called on the view controller when the user touches the screen. We overwrite this method in our view controller to perform custom tasks. In this case, we use it to call the **resignFirstResponder()** method on the Text Field to dismiss the keyboard. As a result, the keyboard is opened when the user taps on the Text Field and closed when the user taps somewhere else (except on the Save button, because the button provides its own response to the event).

Calling the **resignFirstResponder()** method on an element only removes the status of First Responder for that element. If we have several elements that can become First Responders, such as the multiple Text Fields we had in the example of Figure 7-3, we have to call the method on each one of them. To simplify our work, the **UIView** class includes a special method that looks at the view and its subviews to find the current First Responder and ask it to resign.

endEditing(Bool**)**—This method looks for the First Responder in a view and its subviews and asks it to resign its condition. The attribute indicates if the element should be forced to resign or not.

```
import UIKit

class ViewController: UIViewController {
    @IBOutlet weak var titleLabel: UILabel!
    @IBOutlet weak var titleInput: UITextField!

    @IBAction func changeTitle(_ sender: UIButton) {
        if titleInput.text != "" {
            titleLabel.text = titleInput.text
            titleInput.text = ""
        }
    }
    override func touchesBegan(_ touches: Set<UITouch>, with event:
UIEvent?) {
        super.touchesBegan(touches, with: event)
        view.endEditing(true)
    }
}
```

Listing 7-15: Finding the First Responder

This example uses the same view controller of Listing 7-14 but instead of calling the **resignFirstResponder()** method on each Text Field it calls the **endEditing()** method on the main view (the **view** property). This method finds the current First Responder inside the view and forces it to resign its condition. It is the same process, but now we do not have to call the **resignFirstResponder()** method for every Text Field in the view.

 IMPORTANT: The UIKit framework provides the **UIGestureRecognizer** class and several subclasses to control typical events and recognize complicated gestures, such as a swipe, a rotation of the finger, a pinch, etc. Except for specific cases like those studied in this chapter, you will barely use the **UIResponder** event-handling methods. We will study the **UIGestureRecognizer** class in Chapter 12.

Chapter 8
Images and Icons

8.1 Images

Images are used for everything in mobile applications, from backgrounds and patterns to the creation of customized controls. Adding images to our iOS project is very simple, the files have to be dragged from Finder to the Navigator Area in the Xcode's interface and then included in the Storyboard or loaded from code, but there is one important issue we have to consider first: images are stored in files with a resolution in pixels, while our interface is defined in points.

The screens of Apple devices have different resolutions and scales. In some devices, one point represents one pixel and in others more. At this moment, three scales have been defined: 1x, 2x, and 3x (see Chapter 4). The 1x scale defines one point as one pixel, the 2x scale defines 1 point as a square of 2 pixels, and the 3x scale defines one point as a square of three pixels. Because of this, every time we want to introduce images in our interface we have to consider the conversion between pixels and points. For example, if we have an image of 300 pixels wide and 400 pixels tall, in a device with a scale of 1x the image will almost occupy the whole screen, but in a device with a scale of 2x the image will look half its size. The image is actually occupying the same space, 300 by 400 pixels, but because of the higher resolution this number of pixels represents a smaller area on the screen in devices with scales of 2x or 3x, as shown in Figure 8-1.

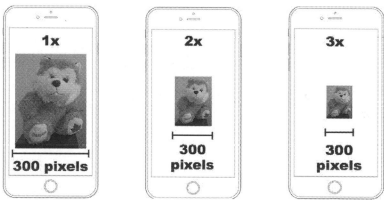

Figure 8-1: Same image in devices with different scale

There are multiple solutions to this problem. The simplest are to scale up a small image in devices with higher resolution or scale down a big image in devices with lower resolution (these are the solutions used by default). For example, we can expand an image of 300 x 400 pixels to 600 x 800 pixels and make it look like the same size in a screen with a scale of 2x (a space of 300 x 400 points represents 600 x 800 pixels at this scale), or we could start with an image of 600 x 800 pixels and reduce it to 300 x 400 pixels for devices with half the scale. One way or another, we have a problem. If we expand a small image to fit a bigger screen, it loses quality, and if we reduce it, it occupies unnecessary space in memory because the image is never shown in its original size. Fortunately, there is a more efficient solution. It requires us to include in our project three versions of the same image, one for every scale. Considering the image of our example, we will need one picture of the husky in a size of 300 x 400 pixels for devices with a scale of 1x, another of 600 x 800 pixels for devices with a scale of 2x, and a third one of 900 x 1200 for devices with a scale of 3x. When we take this approach, the images can be shown in the same size and with the same quality no matter the device, as illustrated in Figure 8-2.

Figure 8-2: Different images for specific scales

Providing the same image in different resolutions solves the problem but introduces some complications. We have to create three versions of the same image and then select which one is going to be shown depending on the scale of the device. To help us select the right image, the iOS system was designed to detect the scale that corresponds to the image by reading a suffix on the file's name. What we have to do is to provide three files with the same name but with suffixes that determine the scale they correspond to. The file containing the image for the 1x scale (300 x 400 pixels in our example) only requires the name and the extension (e.g., **husky.png**), the name of the file with the image for the 2x scale (600 x 800) has to contain the suffix @2x (e.g., **husky@2x.png**), and the name of the file with the image for the 3x scale (900 x 1200) has to contain the suffix @3x (e.g., **husky@3x.png**). Every time the interface requires an image, the system reads the suffixes and loads the file corresponding to the scale of the screen.

The Basics: There is a very useful app available on the App Store for Mac computers called Prepo that can take an image of one size and expand it or reduce it to generate the images required for the rest of the scales. It can also help you generate the icons for your app. To edit the images, you can use any image editor available on the market, such as Pixlr (www.pixlr.com).

To incorporate the images to the project, we have to drag the files from Finder to the Navigator Area. Figure 8-3 shows how this action looks like.

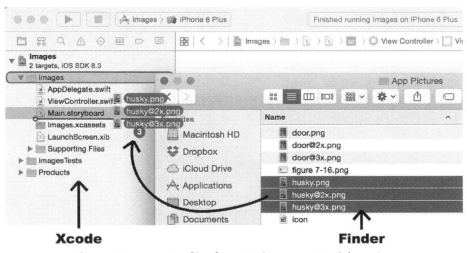

Figure 8-3: Dragging files from Finder to our Xcode's project

When we drop the files into our Xcode's project, a window asks for information about the destination and the target. If we want the files to be copied to the project's folder

Images and Icons

(recommended), we have to activate the option *Copy items if needed*, as shown in Figure 8-4 below. We also have to indicate that the files are going to be added to our project by selecting the project's name in the *Add to targets* option (the project used in Figure 8-4 was called *Test*).

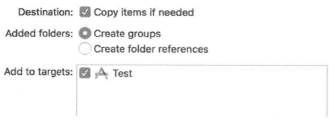

Figure 8-4: *Options to add files to the project*

Once we select these options and click the Finish button, Xcode adds the files to our project.

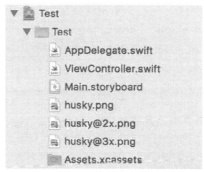

Figure 8-5: *Files in our project*

When we select the option to copy the files into our project's folder, we end up with two copies of the same files, one in the original folder and another in our project's folder. If we modify the original files and try to add them again to the project, instead of overwriting the files Xcode shows an error. To add the updated files to our project, we first have to remove the old ones by selecting the files in the Navigator Area and pressing the Delete key on the keyboard. Xcode asks if we want to remove the reference or remove the files. Selecting the option *Move to Trash*, the files are completely removed from the project and we can add them again.

 The Basics: All the project's files are stored in the same physical folder, but you can create groups on the Xcode's interface to organize them. New groups are created from the File menu. Select the option New / Group, write the name of the group, and then drag the files inside.

Images and Image Views

Because the purpose of images is not only to be presented on the screen but also to be used in the construction of patterns and customized controls, the UIKit framework provides a class called **UIImage** to load the images and then a separate class called **UIImageView** to present them on the screen. Objects created from the **UIImage** class load one image at a time and have its data ready for other objects to use. The class includes multiple initializers to create these objects from a variety of sources. The following are the most frequently used.

UIImage(named: String)—This initializer creates an object that contains the image from the file specified by the **named** attribute. The attribute is a string with the name of the file (for PNG images, the extension is not required).

UIImage(contentsOfFile: String)—This initializer creates an object that contains an image generated from the file indicated by the **contentsOfFile** attribute. The attribute is a string with a path that determines the location of the file.

UIImage(data: Data, **scale:** CGFloat)—This initializer creates an object that contains an image generated from the data provided by the **data** attribute and with an associated scale specified by the **scale** attribute. If the scale is 1, the last attribute may be ignored.

A `UIImage` object includes properties and methods to get information about the image and process it. The following are the most frequently used.

size—This property returns a `CGSize` value with the size of the image.

scale—This property returns a `CGFloat` value with the scale of the image.

imageOrientation—This property returns a value that identifies the orientation of the image. It is an enumeration called `Orientation` included in the `UIImage` class. The values available are **up**, **down**, **left**, **right**, **upMirrored**, **leftMirrored**, and **rightMirrored**.

cgImage—This property returns the image in the Core Graphic format. It is of type `CGImage`, a Core Graphic data type.

ciImage—This property returns the image in the Core Image format. It is of type `CIImage`, a Core Image data type.

pngData()—This method converts the image into raw data in the PNG format and returns a `Data` structure with it.

jpegData(compressionQuality: CGFloat)—This method converts the image into raw data in the JPEG format and returns a `Data` structure with it. The **compressionQuality** attribute is a value between 0.0 and 1.0 that determines the level of compression.

Loading images from our code is very simple. The following example loads a file called oranges.png that contains a pattern and uses it to provide a background to our main view. The example assumes that we have created and incorporated to our project the files oranges.png, oranges@2x.png, and oranges@3x.png (the files are available on our website).

```
import UIKit

class ViewController: UIViewController {
    override func viewDidLoad() {
        super.viewDidLoad()
        if let mypattern = UIImage(named: "oranges") {
            view.backgroundColor = UIColor(patternImage: mypattern)
        }
    }
}
```

Listing 8-1: Adding a background pattern to the main view

The `UIImage()` initializer implemented in Listing 8-1 looks for a PNG file with the name "oranges" and returns a `UIImage` object if the file is found and successfully loaded, or the value `nil` otherwise. In this example, we use the image to create a background pattern. The image is provided as the attribute of the `UIColor` initializer and the color is assigned to the `backgroundColor` property of the main view. When we initialize a `UIColor` object with an image, the object takes that image and prints it over and over again to fill the area (see `UIColor` in Chapter 4). The result is illustrated in Figure 8-6.

Images and Icons

Figure 8-6: Main view with a background pattern
Pattern Copyright by Natalia de Frutos Ramos (nataliafrutos.wordpress.com)

 Do It Yourself: Create a new Single View Application project. Download the three oranges.png files from our website (www.formasterminds.com) or provide your own. Drag the files to your project, as shown in Figure 8-3. Update the **ViewController** class with the code of Listing 8-1. Run the application. You should see something similar to Figure 8-6.

As shown in Listing 8-1, every time we need to load a PNG image we only have to provide the name of the file. The system searches for files with that name and loads the one corresponding to the scale of the device's screen (if the right file cannot be found, the system uses the file with lower resolution and expand it to fill the space).

Some elements, such as buttons, use **UIImage** objects to customize their appearance. Once the images are added to the project, we can assign them to the element from the Attributes Inspector panel. The following example shows how to create a custom button using an image.

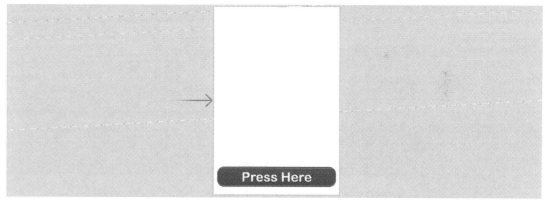

Figure 8-7: Custom button

To create this button, we have to add a normal button to the main view and then modify its properties from the Attributes Inspector panel. As shown in Figure 8-8 below, the type has to be set as Custom (number 1), the title has to be erased (number 2), and the image has to be selected from the Image field (number 3). This example uses the images buttonnormal.png, buttonnormal@2x.png, and buttonnormal@3x.png, available on our website.

As we did from code, we only have to select the file's original name; the files with suffixes are automatically loaded if necessary according to the scale of the device's screen.

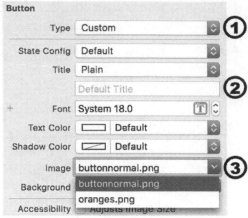

Figure 8-8: Configuring the button from the Attributes Inspector panel

Buttons can present more images depending on their state (see `UIButton` in Chapter 4). If, for example, we want the button to show a different image when it is pressed, we have to add it for the Highlighted state, as shown in Figure 8-9 below (number 1). Once this option is selected, the Image field is emptied to let us pick the new image for that particular state. This example uses the images buttondown.png, buttondown@2x.png, and buttondown@3x.png, available on our website.

Figure 8-9: Adding an image for the Highlighted state

When the app is executed, the `UIImage` objects that represent the images we have added for the button in the Storyboard are recreated and the images are shown on the screen. The interface shows the button with the image defined for the Default state and changes it to the second image when the button is pressed, as illustrated in Figure 8-10.

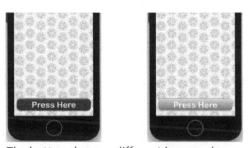

Figure 8-10: The button shows a different image when pressed (right)

Images and Icons

Do It Yourself: Add a button from the Object Library to the main view of the project created for the previous example. Add constraints to pin it to the bottom and the horizontal center of the view. Download the three buttonnormal.png files and the three buttondown.png files from our website (www.formasterminds.com). Drag the files to your project, as shown in Figure 8-3. Select the button in the Storyboard and modify its properties, as shown in Figures 8-8 and 8-9. Run the application. When you press the button, the image should change, as illustrated in Figure 8-10 (right).

 The Basics: If you add the image before erasing the button's title, or accidentally expand the view, the view's size will not match the size of the image. The best way to correct this problem is to select the button and then click on the option *Size to Fit Content* from the Editor menu at the top of the screen, as we did before for labels.

The `UIImage` objects may be added to views, buttons, or other elements to create customized controls, but if we just want to show the image on the screen, we have to create a `UIImageView` object. The `UIImageView` class includes the following initializers.

UIImageView(image: UIImage?)—This initializer creates a `UIImageView` object with the image provided by the **image** attribute. The view's frame is defined at the position 0, 0 and with the size of the image.

UIImageView(image: UIImage?, **highlightedImage:** UIImage?)—This initializer creates a `UIImageView` object with two images, one for the normal state and another for the highlighted state. The view's frame is defined at the position 0, 0 and with the size of the image for the normal state.

Of course, the `UIImageView` objects can also be incorporated to the Storyboard from the option in the Object Library.

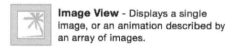

Figure 8-11: Image View option in the Object Library

The class includes properties to retrieve the images and configure the view.

image—This property sets or returns the image for the normal state. It is an optional of type `UIImage`.

highlightedImage—This property sets or returns the image for the highlighted state. It is an optional of type `UIImage`.

isUserInteractionEnabled—This property sets or returns a Boolean value that determines if the Image View responds to user events. By default, it is set to `false`.

isHighlighted—This property sets or returns a Boolean value that determines whether the Image View is highlighted or not.

The class also includes properties and methods to create animations.

isAnimating—This property returns a Boolean that indicates if the animation is running.

animationImages—This property sets or returns an array of `UIImage` objects to be used in the animation.

highlightedAnimationImages—This property sets or returns an array of `UIImage` objects to be used in the animation when the state of the Image View is highlighted.

animationDuration—This property sets or returns a value that determines the number of seconds it takes for the animation to be over. It is of type `TimeInterval`.

animationRepeatCount—This property sets or returns an integer value that determines how many times the animation should be repeated. The value by default is 0, which means the animation will repeat indefinitely.

startAnimating()—This method starts the animation.

stopAnimating()—This method stops the animation.

Image Views are views that contain images. They are shown in the Storyboard as squared areas that we can drag and then position with constrains, as any other view.

Figure 8-12: Adding an Image View to our interface

 The Basics: When you combine two views that can change in size, such as an Image View and a button, the system does not know which one to expand to occupy the space available. To help the system decide, you have to set a higher value for the Content Hugging and Content Compression Resistance priorities of one of the views involved (see Figure 6-49).

To assign an image to the view, we can modify its `image` and `highlightedImage` properties from code or from the Attributes Inspector panel, as we did for the button before. The Attributes Inspector panel shows the values of these two properties at the top, including the + buttons to assign different images for other combinations of Size Classes. The image assigned to the `image` property is shown by default and the one assigned to the `highlightedImage` property is shown when the view is highlighted (the value of its `highlighted` property is `true`).

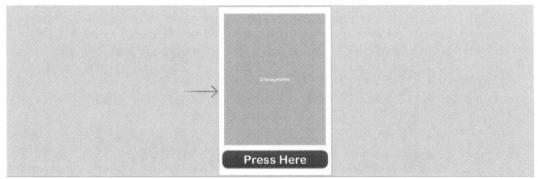

Figure 8-13: Assigning images to the Image View

Image Views have their own size, independent of the size of the image they contain. When we load an image, we have to tell the system how it has to accommodate the image inside the view through the `contentMode` property that the view inherits from the `UIView` class (see `UIView` class in Chapter 4). This property can take several values, with the most useful being Scale to Fill, Aspect Fit, and Aspect Fill. Scale to Fill expands or contracts the image to fit the size of the view, Aspect Fit scales the image to fit the size of the view, keeping its aspect ratio, and

Images and Icons

Aspect Fill scales the image to always fill the view but also keeping its aspect ratio, which means some parts of the image may lay outside the boundaries of the view and, depending on the configuration, they may be hidden. Figure 8-14 shows what the image of the husky looks like when the view is set to different modes. The Image View is always the same size, but the image is adapted to occupy the space available according to the selected mode.

Figure 8-14: Different modes applied to the same Image View

 Do It Yourself: Add a `UIImageView` from the Object Library to the main view of the project created for the previous examples. Add Top, Leading, and Trailing Space constraints to pin it to the top, left, and right side of the main view and also a Bottom constraint to pin it to the top of the button. Assign a value of 750 to the vertical Content Hugging priority and a value 1000 to the vertical Content Compression Resistance priority for the button to not let it expand or shrink (the Image View will always occupy the space available between the main view's top margin and the button). Download the husky.png, husky@2x.png and husky@3x.png files from our website and drag them to your project. Select the Image View and assign the husky.png image to it from the Attributes Inspector panel (Figure 8-13). Try different modes to see how the image is affected.

 IMPORTANT: When we select the mode Aspect Fill, the parts of the image that are outside the boundaries of the view are shown unless we activate the option *Clip to Bounds* from the Attribute Inspector panel. This is the option corresponding to the `UIView` property `clipsToBounds`, a Boolean property that indicates whether or not the content of the view should be clipped when it is outside its boundaries.

Scale to Fill is the mode by default, but it is usually not the one we need. We always have to set how the view is going to show the image, especially with Auto Layout that modifies the view's size to the space available. What mode we should use depends on the purpose of the image. For instance, if we want to show the entire picture of the husky in its original aspect ratio, we have to set the Image View in the Aspect Fit mode. With this configuration, no matter what the space available and the size of the view are, we will always see the entire picture in its original aspect ratio, as shown in Figure 8-15.

Figure 8-15: Image View in Aspect Fit mode

Although the Aspect Fit mode looks fine in this application, it may not be the right one if we want the image to be the background of our interface. In this case, the Image View has to occupy the entire screen and its image always has to fill the view without losing its aspect ratio, therefore the Aspect Fill mode would be more appropriate. Figure 8-16 shows how this mode adapts a background image to fill the view.

Figure 8-16: Background image resized to cover the entire screen

Creating this background is simple. We have to add a new **UIImageView** on the back, pin it with Space constraints to each side of the main view, and set its mode to Aspect Fill.

Figure 8-17: Image View in the background

The Basics: As we explained in Chapter 6, new elements are added at the bottom of the hierarchy, which means they are going to be shown over the previous elements. To move an element to the back, you can use the options from the Editor menu at the top of the screen. Select the element, click to open the Editor menu, click on Arrange, and select the right option to get the element in the position you want. You can also modify the order of the elements from the Document Outline panel (see Figures 6-63 and 6-64).

Because of its constraints, the new **UIImageView** added in Figure 8-17 always occupies the entire screen, and because of the Aspect Fill mode its image always fills the entire area, preserving its quality and aspect ratio.

Figure 8-18: Background image in Aspect Fill mode

Images and Icons

Do It Yourself: Add a new **UIImageView** to the previous example. Add Space constraints to pin the view to each side of the main view. Move the element to the back from the Editor menu or the Document Outline panel. Download the three background.png files from our website and drag them to your project. Assign the image to the Image View and set its mode to Aspect Fill. Run the application. You should see something similar to Figure 8-18.

Image Views, as any other element, may be connected to the view controller with Outlets and then modified from code. For example, we could show a different image when the button is pressed.

```
import UIKit

class ViewController: UIViewController {
   @IBOutlet weak var pictureView: UIImageView!
   let door = UIImage(named: "door")

   @IBAction func changePicture(_ sender: UIButton) {
      pictureView.image = door
   }
}
```

Listing 8-2: Replacing the picture when the button is pressed

Since we now have a background image, the new view controller of Listing 8-2 does not add the background pattern to the main view as we did before. For this example, we only need an Outlet for the Image View and an Action for the button. The Outlet was called **pictureView** and the Action **changePicture()**. We first create a new **UIImage** object with an image called door.png (the three files are available on our website) and then assign this object to the **image** property of the Image View inside the **changePicture()** method to show the door.png image on the screen when the button is pressed.

If we want to switch between the husky.png and the door.png images, we have to create two **UIImage** objects and assign the corresponding object to the **image** property in every turn. In the following example, we create these two objects and add a variable called **current** to know what image is currently being shown. The value 1 corresponds to the husky and 2 to the door.

```
import UIKit

class ViewController: UIViewController {
   @IBOutlet weak var pictureView: UIImageView!
   var current = 1
   let husky = UIImage(named: "husky")
   let door = UIImage(named: "door")

   @IBAction func changePicture(_ sender: UIButton) {
      if current == 1 {
         pictureView.image = door
         current = 2
      } else {
         pictureView.image = husky
          current = 1
      }
   }
}
```

Listing 8-3: Switching pictures

The **UIImage()** initializer returns an optional value, but the **image** property of the **UIImageView** object is an optional too, so we don't need to unwrap them. The result is shown next. Every time the button is pressed, the image on the screen changes.

Figure 8-19: Different images for the same Image View

In this example, we are switching the images with a button, but they could be automatically replaced using the animation features provided by the **UIImageView** class. The following example creates an animation with both images that starts when the button is pressed.

```
import UIKit

class ViewController: UIViewController {
    @IBOutlet weak var pictureView: UIImageView!
    let husky = UIImage(named: "husky")
    let door = UIImage(named: "door")

    override func viewDidLoad() {
        super.viewDidLoad()
        pictureView.animationImages = [door!, husky!]
        pictureView.animationDuration = 4
    }
    @IBAction func changePicture(_ sender: UIButton) {
        pictureView.startAnimating()
    }
}
```

Listing 8-4: Animating images inside an Image View

The animation has to be configured before it is executed. In Listing 8-4 we do it inside the **viewDidLoad()** method. The images we want to include in the animation are assigned to the **animationImages** property of the Image View and the duration of every cycle of the animation is set to 4 seconds. Notice that this time we had to unwrap the **UIImage** objects before to include them in the array because the **animationImages** property is not an optional type.

Once the button is pressed, the **startAnimating()** method of the Image View is executed and the images are automatically replaced over and over again. If we want the animation to stop, we can assign the total number of cycles to the **animationRepeatCount** property or called the **stopAnimating()** method at some point of the execution of the app, as shown next.

```
@IBAction func changePicture(_ sender: UIButton) {
    if pictureView.isAnimating {
        pictureView.stopAnimating()
    } else {
```

Images and Icons

```
        pictureView.startAnimating()
    }
}
```

Listing 8-5: Controlling the animation

The new **changePicture()** method of Listing 8-5 checks if the view is animating with the **isAnimating** property and starts or stops the animation depending on the value returned.

 Do It Yourself: The examples of Listings 8-2, 8-3, and 8-4 use the same interface than before, but incorporate the door.png image that you can download from our website. Copy the images to your project and update the **ViewController** class with the code you want to try. Run the application and press the button to see how they work. Replace the **changePicture()** method in Listing 8-4 with the one in Listing 8-5. Now the animation starts and stops every time the button is pressed.

The array of images assigned to the **animationImages** property does not replace the **UIImage** object assigned to the **image** property of the **UIImageView** object. This means that when the animation is over, the **UIImageView** object shows the image stored in the **image** property again. We can use this feature to improve our example, for instance adding an image to ask the user to press the button to start the animation. In the following example, instead of assigning husky.png as the Image View's initial image, we assign the image sign.png (the files are available on our website). This image is now shown as soon as the app is executed, but it is replaced when the animation begins.

Figure 8-20: Initial image for the Image View

 Do It Yourself: Download the sign.png images from our website and drag them to your project. Select the Image View and assign the sign.png image to it. Run the application and press the button. This image should be replaced by the animation and shown back when the animation is over.

Using images, we can customize our interface and create a unique design. We can also make it more functional. For example, we could change the images for the button when the animation is running to say Stop instead of Press Here. The following example uses the images buttonstopnormal.png and buttonstopdown.png that are available on our website.

```
import UIKit

class ViewController: UIViewController {
    @IBOutlet weak var pictureView: UIImageView!
    @IBOutlet weak var pressButton: UIButton!
```

```
let husky = UIImage(named: "husky")
let door = UIImage(named: "door")
let buttonnormal = UIImage(named: "buttonnormal")
let buttondown = UIImage(named: "buttondown")
let buttonstopnormal = UIImage(named: "buttonstopnormal")
let buttonstopdown = UIImage(named: "buttonstopdown")

override func viewDidLoad() {
   super.viewDidLoad()
   pictureView.animationImages = [door!, husky!]
   pictureView.animationDuration = 4
}
@IBAction func changePicture(_ sender: UIButton) {
   if pictureView.isAnimating {
      pressButton.setImage(buttonnormal, for: .normal)
      pressButton.setImage(buttondown, for: .highlighted)
      pictureView.stopAnimating()
   } else {
      pressButton.setImage(buttonstopnormal, for: .normal)
      pressButton.setImage(buttonstopdown, for: .highlighted)
      pictureView.startAnimating()
   }
}
}
```

Listing 8-6: Modifying the button's images to reflect the state of the animation

The code of Listing 8-6 adds more functionality but follows the same procedure than the previous example. To modify the images associated with every state of the button, we added an Outlet for it called **pressButton**. When the button is pressed, the **changePicture()** method is executed and the images are assigned to the button through its **setImage()** method (for more information about the **setImage()** method see **UIButton** in Chapter 4).

Figure 8-21: Button adapts to the situation

 Do It Yourself: Download the buttonstopnormal.png and buttonstopdown.png images from our website and drag them to your project (your project has to contain all the images we have been using so far to work properly). Copy the code of Listing 8-6 into your view controller. Run the application. You should see the image of the button changing accordingly to the state of the animation.

Visual Effects

Modern versions of iOS extensively use transparency in their interfaces, and Apple encourages developers to also adopt transparency in their own apps. The purpose is to produce a sense of depth and make the user feel like the content extends beyond the screen. One of the tricks used to achieve this effect is blurriness. When elements overlap, images and other elements behind are blurred, producing the feeling that they are far away. The UIKit framework includes the **UIVisualEffectView** class to help us add this effect to our images and our interface. The class includes an initializer with an attribute to define the effect.

UIVisualEffectView(effect: UIVisualEffect?**)**—This initializer creates a **UIVisualEffectView** object with the effect set by the **effect** attribute.

The framework currently offers two subclasses of the **UIVisualEffect** class to define the effect: **UIBlurEffect** and **UIVibrancyEffect**. The following are the initializers to create these objects.

UIBlurEffect(style: Style**)**—This initializer creates a **UIBlurEffect** object with the style defined by the **style** attribute. The attribute is an enumeration called **Style** included in the **UIBlurEffect** class. The values available are **extraLight**, **light**, and **dark**.

UIVibrancyEffect(blurEffect: UIBlurEffect**)**—This initializer creates a **UIVibrancyEffect** object to add vibrancy to the effect. The vibrancy is used to highlight a view inside a blur view.

The Object Library includes options to add an effect view with a blur effect to the Storyboard.

 **Visual Effect View with Blur -** Provides a blur effect

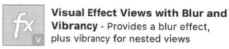 **Visual Effect Views with Blur and Vibrancy -** Provides a blur effect, plus vibrancy for nested views

Figure 8-22: Visual Effect View options in the Object Library

The options create a view that we have to expand to cover the area we want to blur. For example, we can add a Visual Effect View with Blur over a background image to give the sense of depth to the interface. We add the Image View first, then the effect view, and finally the rest of the interface. The Attributes Inspector panel includes the option to select the style of the blur. The value defines different levels of opacity. In the following interface, we used a light effect.

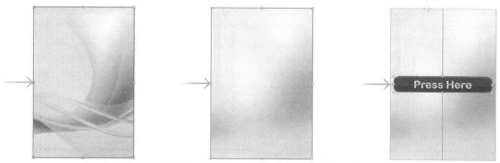

Figure 8-23: Interface with a Visual Effect View

If we want the blur effect to be temporal, we can create the Visual Effect View from code. The following view controller contains an Action for the button included in the interface of Figure 8-23 that adds or removes a Visual Effect View when the button is pressed.

```
import UIKit

class ViewController: UIViewController {
   @IBOutlet weak var backgroundImage: UIImageView!
   var visualEffect: UIVisualEffectView!
```

```
    override func viewDidLoad() {
        super.viewDidLoad()
        let blur = UIBlurEffect(style: UIBlurEffect.Style.light)
        visualEffect = UIVisualEffectView(effect: blur)
        visualEffect.translatesAutoresizingMaskIntoConstraints = false
    }
    @IBAction func addEffect(_ sender: UIButton) {
        if visualEffect.superview == nil {
            view.insertSubview(visualEffect, aboveSubview: backgroundImage)
            visualEffect.leadingAnchor.constraint(equalTo:
view.leadingAnchor, constant: 0).isActive = true
            visualEffect.trailingAnchor.constraint(equalTo:
view.trailingAnchor, constant: 0).isActive = true
            visualEffect.topAnchor.constraint(equalTo: view.topAnchor,
constant: 0).isActive = true
            visualEffect.bottomAnchor.constraint(equalTo: view.bottomAnchor,
constant: 0).isActive = true
        } else {
            visualEffect.removeFromSuperview()
        }
    }
}
```

Listing 8-7: Adding a Visual Effect View over the background image from code

The code of Listing 8-7 defines a property called **visualEffect** to store a reference to the effect view and creates the object as soon as the main view is loaded. We have to create the **UIBlurEffect** object first with the style we want (**light** in this example) and then include it in the initializer of the **UIVisualEffect** class to get the desired effect. Because we are adding the view from code, we also have to program the constraints for it, so we have to set its **translatesAutoresizingMaskIntoConstraints** property to **false** to not let the system define its own constraints (see Chapter 6, Listing 6-2). Also, because in this example we use the same button to add and remove the effect view from the interface, we check if the view was already added or not. There are different ways to achieve this, but for this example we have decided to read the view's **superview** property. When the view is removed from the interface, this property returns **nil**. If the value is different from **nil**, we add the Visual Effect View to the main view with the **insertSubview(UIView, aboveSubview:)** method of the **UIView** class. This method inserts the first view over the second view, and this is what we want this time because we need the Visual Effect View to be over the background image but below the button. After this, the constraints are defined to pin the Visual Effect View to the sides of the main view (the constraints can only be assigned after the view is added to the superview).

 Do It Yourself: Create a new Single View Application project. Add the background.jpg and buttonnormal.png images from the previous example to the project. Add an Image View, pin it to the edges of the main view with Space constraints, and assign the background.jpg image to it. Add a button with the image buttonnormal.png and set Alignment constraints to keep it at the center of the screen. Create an Outlet called **backgroundImage** to connect the background image to the view controller and an Action for the button called **addEffect()**. Complete the **ViewController** class with the code of Listing 8-7. Run the application. Press the button to add and remove the blur effect.

Assets Catalog

Applications usually require dozens or even hundreds of images. No matter how many groups we create in the Navigator Area to organize these files, it will still be very difficult to identify them or remember what they are for just from looking at their names. The UIKit framework defines a class called **UIImageAsset** with the purpose of creating a container that offers a better alternative. The object created from this class is called Assets Catalog and it can work as a container for regular images and icons. The images are added to the Assets Catalog and then we have to ask for the one we want by mentioning its name. This is similar to what we have done so far, but the advantage is that Xcode provides a visual interface to manage the catalog, so we can see a quick preview of the image, load and organize the versions for each scale, and even create different sets of images for each combination of Size Classes.

An Assets Catalog is automatically created for our app and included in the project along with the rest of the files. To open the interface, we have to click on the item called Assets.xcassets in the Navigator Area. The Editor Area shows an interface similar to Figure 8-24.

Figure 8-24: Empty Assets Catalog

The interface includes two columns: the column on the left presents a list of sets of images and the column on the right displays the content of the selected set. A set is composed of the three versions of an image, one for each scale, and also additional images that we want to present in different Size Classes. The list also includes a permanent set called AppIcon that contains the images for the icons necessary to publish our app in the App Store.

New sets can be added from the Editor menu at the top of the screen. If we open the Editor menu and click on the option Add Assets / *New Image Set*, a new empty set is created.

Figure 8-25: New set of images

The name of the set is the name we have to use to get the image from code. Xcode calls the new set *Image* but we can click on it and change it any time we want. Once the set is created, we can drag the file to the corresponding squares on the right column of the interface. For example, the file husky.png from our previous example goes inside the 1x square, the file husky@2x.png goes inside the 2x square, and the file husky@3x.png goes inside the 3x square. Figure 8-26 shows the Editor Area after the images are dragged from Finder to the Assets Catalog and the name of the set is changed to "husky".

Figure 8-26: Husky set is ready

Images and Icons

Once the images are loaded to the catalog, the set is ready to use. We do not need to copy the files to the project's folder anymore or anything like it. All we have to do is to load the image from our app using the name defined for the set (in this case, "husky"). But this process is still a little bit tedious. An easy way to create a new set is to drag the three images for the set to the Assets Catalog. Xcode creates a new set with the images and assigns their names as the name of the set. For instance, we can drag the files door.png, door@2x.png, and door@3x.png of our example and Xcode takes care of creating the set, assigning each image to the corresponding scale, and give it the name "door".

Figure 8-27: New door set

The creation and configuration of the set is done automatically when we drag the files and drop them inside the Assets Catalog. In fact, we can drag several files together and Xcode takes care of extracting the information and creating all the sets. Figure 8-28 illustrates the Assets Catalog after we drag all the files necessary for the application created from previous examples.

Figure 8-28: Assets Catalog with all the image sets for our application

Besides the possibility of including a version of the image for every scale, we can also add versions for different devices and Size Classes. When a set is selected, the Attributes Inspector panel on the right shows a list of properties, including Devices and Size Classes assigned to the set. By default, the set is shown in any device (Universal) and in the Size Classes Any width and Any height, but we can change it by modifying the values of these properties. For example, if we select the iPad from the list of devices, new placeholders are added to the interface.

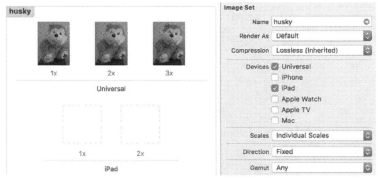

Figure 8-29: Set for specific devices

The same happens when we select different Size Classes. New squares are added at the bottom of the set to allow us to incorporate the corresponding files. For example, if we select

Images and Icons

Any & Compact from the Width Class option, Xcode adds placeholders for the images we want to display when the horizontal Size Class is Compact.

Figure 8-30: Set for specific Size Classes

Now, every time we load the image from the application, the system selects the appropriate version according to the scale, the device, and the Size Class.

 IMPORTANT: The `UIImageAsset` class provides methods to add and remove images to the catalog from code. The `UIImage` class also includes an initializer to create an image for a specific Trait Collection and add it to the catalog. For more information, visit our website and follow the links for this chapter.

Icons

Icons are the little images that the user can tap to launch the app. As we already mentioned, the Assets Catalog includes a set called *AppIcon* to manage the icons we must provide for the application. The set includes placeholders for every icon we need and for every scale to cover all the devices and screens available. It even includes information about their size in points that we can use to design the images. The sizes required depend on the versions of the system and the type of devices our app is prepared for.

As any other image, the icons may be created from any image edition software available in the market. A file has to be created for every size required. For example, the first two placeholders require images of 20 points, which means that we have to create an image of a size of 40 pixels for the 2x scale and an image of a size of 60 pixels for the 3x scale. After all the images are created, we have to drag them to the interface. Figure 8-31 shows what the AppIcon set may look like once all the images are added (sample files are available on our website).

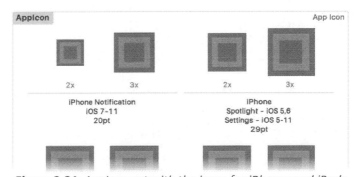

Figure 8-31: AppIcon set with the icons for iPhones and iPads

Launching Image

The launching image is the image that is shown as soon as the app is executed. No matter how small the app is, it always takes a few seconds to load and be responsive the first time it is launched. These images are necessary to show the user that the app is responding to the action of tapping its icon and also to give the impression that the app is executed instantly. Xcode provides an additional file with a single Scene to create an image that adapts to every device using Auto Layout. This file is called LaunchScreen.storyboard, and it is included in the Navigator Area along with the rest.

Apple's guidelines recommend creating a launching image that gives the user the impression that the app is already running. For example, we can add a **UIImageView** pinned to the edges of the main view with an image that simulates the app's interface. Figure 8-32 shows a possible launching screen for the app created in our last example. We added an Image View to the main view with space constraints and the background.png image set in the Aspect Fill mode. Because of the constraints the image will adapt to the space available, and because we use the same image for our app's background, the transition between this image and the app's interface will look smooth to the user.

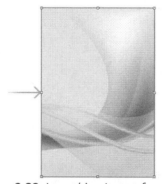

Figure 8-32: *Launching Image for our app*

 IMPORTANT: If you don't want the system to show the status bar, there is an option in the General pane in Settings to hide it. Another alternative is to add the keyword "Status bar is initially hidden" with the value YES to the info.plist file to hide the bar when the app is launched. We will see how to work with this file in Chapter 25 (see Figure 25-5).

 The Basics: Although we could add any element from the Object Library to the main view, only some of them are appropriate. Remember that the content of this view is shown before the app is launched, so there is no code we can process at that moment.

Chapter 9
Pickers

9.1 Listing Values

Something that users require from an application is to be able to select values from a list. In desktop applications, there are several tools available to perform this task, but due to the reduced size of the screens, UIKit had to include a specific type of control for mobile applications. The control is called *Picker*, and what it does is to show a list of values in a graphic that simulates a spinning wheel. The values are presented in rows as if they were printed on the wheel, and the users can select the value they want by rotating it. The framework includes a class to create general-purpose pickers called **UIPickerView** and another for dates called **UIDatePicker**.

Picker View

The **UIPickerView** class provides properties and methods to create a general-purpose picker and manage its values. The values are organized in rows and components (columns). Each component represents a list of values and each row represents an individual value. The components are rotated independently. Figure 9-1 illustrates a picker with two components, one for the city and another for the year, each with multiple rows (values).

Figure 9-1: *Picker View with two components*

To identify each row and component, the picker creates indexes starting from 0. The first value of a row will be at index 0, the second at index 1, and so on. The items in a picker are organized this way so we can associate it with arrays in our code and easily present and retrieve values. The class defines the following properties and methods to interact with the picker.

numberOfComponents—This property returns a value of type **Int** that represents the number of components in the picker.

numberOfRows(inComponent: Int)—This method returns a value of type **Int** that represents the number of rows in a component. The attribute indicates the index of the component we want to access.

selectedRow(inComponent: Int)—This method returns a value of type **Int** that represents the index of the selected row in the component specified by the **inComponent** attribute.

reloadAllComponents()—This method forces the picker to update the values of its components.

reloadComponent(Int**)**—This method forces the picker to update the values of a component. The attribute is a value of type `Int` that indicates the index of the component we want to update.

selectRow(Int, **inComponent:** Int, **animated:** Bool**)**—This method selects the row with the index specified by the first attribute in the component specified by the **inComponent** attribute. The `animated` attribute determines whether the selection should be animated or not. The method rotates the wheel until the selected row is positioned at the center.

The `UIPickerView` class also defines two properties, `delegate` and `dataSource`, to assign delegate objects that will be in charge of configuring the picker and providing the values for the rows. The object assigned to the `delegate` property must conform to the `UIPickerViewDelegate` protocol, which includes the following methods.

pickerView(UIPickerView, **titleForRow:** Int, **forComponent:** Int**)**—This method is called by the `UIPickerView` object on the delegate when it needs a value for the row indicated by the **titleForRow** attribute in the component indicated by the **forComponent** attribute. The method must return a string with the value for the row.

pickerView(UIPickerView, **attributedTitleForRow:** Int, **forComponent:** Int**)**— This method is called by the `UIPickerView` object on the delegate when it needs a value for the row indicated by the **attributedTitleForRow** attribute in the component indicated by the **forComponent** attribute. The method must return an optional of type `NSAttributedString`.

pickerView(UIPickerView, **didSelectRow:** Int, **inComponent:** Int**)**—This method is called by the `UIPickerView` object on the delegate when the user selects a row (moves the wheel to get a new value at the center). The **didSelectRow** and **inComponent** attributes contain the indexes of the selected row and component.

On the other hand, the object assigned to the `dataSource` property must conform to the `UIPickerViewDataSource` protocol, which includes the following methods.

numberOfComponents(in: UIPickerView**)**—This method is called by the `UIPickerView` object on the data source delegate to know the numbers of components it has to display. The method must return a value of type `Int` with the number of components we want.

pickerView(UIPickerView, **numberOfRowsInComponent:** Int**)**—This method is called by the `UIPickerView` object on the data source delegate to know how many rows to display in a component. The **numberOfRowsInComponent** attribute specifies the component's index (the method is called for every component in the picker).

As with any other view, we can create a Picker View from code using the `UIView` initializer (`var picker = UIPickerView(frame: CGRect)`) or by dragging the element from the Object Library.

Picker View - Displays a spinning-wheel or slot-machine motif of values.

Figure 9-2: Picker View option in the Object Library

Picker Views are usually combined with other controllers to process the values selected by the user. The interface of Figure 9-3, below, includes a picker that we are going to use to show a list of years and a label that is going to display the year currently selected.

Pickers

Figure 9-3: Interface to test a Picker View

When the picker is added to the main view in the Storyboard from the Object Library, Xcode shows it with some values by default, as illustrated in Figure 9-3, but the real values have to be provided by the object assigned to the **dataSource** property. This is a normal delegate, but because its purpose is to provide data it is usually called *data source* (hence the name of the property). As always, the delegates could be any objects we want, but it is common practice to declare the view controller in charge of the picker to be the delegate as well as the data source, as in the following example.

```
import UIKit
class ViewController: UIViewController, UIPickerViewDelegate,
UIPickerViewDataSource {
    @IBOutlet weak var showYear: UILabel!
    @IBOutlet weak var pickerYears: UIPickerView!
    var years: [String]!

    override func viewDidLoad() {
        super.viewDidLoad()
        pickerYears.delegate = self
        pickerYears.dataSource = self
        years = ["1944", "1945", "1946", "1947", "1948", "1949", "1950"]
    }
    func numberOfComponents(in pickerView: UIPickerView) -> Int {
        return 1
    }
    func pickerView(_ pickerView: UIPickerView, numberOfRowsInComponent
component: Int) -> Int {
        return years.count
    }
    func pickerView(_ pickerView: UIPickerView, titleForRow row: Int,
forComponent component: Int) -> String? {
        return years[row]
    }
    func pickerView(_ pickerView: UIPickerView, didSelectRow row: Int,
inComponent component: Int) {
        let year = years[row]
        showYear.text = "The Year is: \(year)"
    }
}
```

Listing 9-1: Providing values for the picker

The view controller of Listing 9-1 defines Outlets for the label and the Picker View, and also an array called **years** to store the values we want to assign to the picker. In the **viewDidLoad()** method, we use the Outlet to declare the view controller as the picker's delegate and data source, and also initialize the **years** array with a list of values.

After the properties are initialized, we have to configure the picker and load the data from the delegate and data source methods. We first implement the **numberOfComponents()** method to tell the picker how many components we want. In this case, we return the value 1 because we only need one component to show the list of years (one column). The next method, **pickerView(UIPickerView, numberOfRowsInComponent:)**, performs a similar function, but this time for the rows. Inside this method, we count how many values are in the **years** array and return that number to indicate how many rows we need to show them all. Next is the **pickerView(UIPickerView, titleForRow:, forComponent:)** method, called by the picker to get the value for each row. The first call will be for the row at index 0, then for the row at index 1, and so on. Using the number of the row, we get the corresponding value from the **years** array and return it. Notice that this method can only return a **String** value. If we had an array of integers, for example, before returning each value we would have to convert it to a **String** using string interpolation or the **String()** initializer (e.g., **String(number)**). The last method, **pickerView(UIPickerView, didSelectRow:, inComponent:)**, is called by the picker when the user rotates the wheel and selects a new value. The index value of the selected row is reported by the method through its **didSelectRow** attribute. Using this index value, we can retrieve the value from the array and assign it to the label.

 Do It Yourself: Create a new Single View Application project. Add a Picker View and a label to the main view, as shown in Figure 9-3. Define constraints to keep them at the top of the screen. Connect the label and the picker to Outlets called **showYear** and **pickerYears**, respectively. Complete your code with the code of Listing 9-1 and run the application. Every time you rotate the wheel, the number selected should be shown on the label.

The **pickerView(UIPickerView, didSelectRow:, inComponent:)** method lets us get the value as soon as it is selected, but we can also read the selected value any time we want with the **selectedRow()** method. To test it, we can add a button to the interface and an Action to the view controller to change the value of the label every time the button is pressed.

Figure 9-4: Interface to get the value currently selected

In this example, the method for the action replaces the **pickerView(UIPickerView, didSelectRow:, inComponent:)** method, but they could work together if necessary.

```
import UIKit

class ViewController: UIViewController, UIPickerViewDelegate,
UIPickerViewDataSource {
   @IBOutlet weak var showYear: UILabel!
   @IBOutlet weak var pickerYears: UIPickerView!
   var years: [String]!
```

```
override func viewDidLoad() {
    super.viewDidLoad()
    pickerYears.delegate = self
    pickerYears.dataSource = self
    years = ["1944", "1945", "1946", "1947", "1948", "1949", "1950"]
}
func numberOfComponents(in pickerView: UIPickerView) -> Int {
    return 1
}
func pickerView(_ pickerView: UIPickerView, numberOfRowsInComponent
component: Int) -> Int {
    return years.count
}
func pickerView(_ pickerView: UIPickerView, titleForRow row: Int,
forComponent component: Int) -> String? {
    return years[row]
}
@IBAction func getYear(_ sender: UIButton) {
    let row = pickerYears.selectedRow(inComponent: 0)
    showYear.text = "The Year is: \(years[row])"
}
}
```

Listing 9-2: Getting the selected value

The **getYear()** method of Listing 9-2 is in charge of getting the current selected value. In this method, we call the **selectedRow()** method to get the index of the selected row. The value 0 between parentheses corresponds to the index of the component (we only have one component in our picker). The value of the **row** constant is used next to retrieve the year from the array and assign it to the label.

Besides the user rotating the wheel, there is also a method that allows us to select a value from code. This is particularly useful when we want to show a suggested value on the picker or just initiate the picker in a specific position. The following example initializes the picker in the year 1945.

```
override func viewDidLoad() {
    super.viewDidLoad()
    pickerYears.delegate = self
    pickerYears.dataSource = self
    years = ["1944", "1945", "1946", "1947", "1948", "1949", "1950"]

    if let index = years.index(of: "1945") {
        pickerYears.selectRow(index, inComponent: 0, animated: false)
    }
}
```

Listing 9-3: Selecting the initial value

Because we want the value to be the initial selected value, we have to call the method from the **viewDidLoad()** method. In Listing 9-3, we search for the value "1945" in the array with the **index()** method and then select the row using the index returned. The value for the **animated** attribute was set to **false** because we want the picker to rotate and show the right value as soon as it is displayed, but we can take advantage of this attribute to create a smooth transition when the selection has to be done after the picker was already shown to the user.

Do It Yourself: Replace the `viewDidLoad()` method in the previous example by the one in Listing 9-3 and run the application. The initial selected value in the picker should be "1945".

With a few modifications, we can easily create a picker with more than one component. The following example includes two components to let the user select a year and a city.

```swift
import UIKit

class ViewController: UIViewController, UIPickerViewDelegate,
UIPickerViewDataSource {
    @IBOutlet weak var showYear: UILabel!
    @IBOutlet weak var pickerYears: UIPickerView!
    var cities: [String]!
    var years: [String]!

    override func viewDidLoad() {
        super.viewDidLoad()
        pickerYears.delegate = self
        pickerYears.dataSource = self
        cities = ["Mountain View", "Sunnyvale", "Cupertino", "Santa Clara"]
        years = ["1944", "1945", "1946", "1947", "1948", "1949", "1950"]
    }
    func numberOfComponents(in pickerView: UIPickerView) -> Int {
        return 2
    }
    func pickerView(_ pickerView: UIPickerView, numberOfRowsInComponent
component: Int) -> Int {
        if component == 0 {
            return cities.count
        } else {
            return years.count
        }
    }
    func pickerView(_ pickerView: UIPickerView, titleForRow row: Int,
forComponent component: Int) -> String? {
        if component == 0 {
            return cities[row]
        } else {
            return years[row]
        }
    }
    @IBAction func getYear(_ sender: UIButton) {
        let rowCity = pickerYears.selectedRow(inComponent: 0)
        let rowYear = pickerYears.selectedRow(inComponent: 1)
        showYear.text = "The Year is: \(years[rowYear]) in
\(cities[rowCity])"
    }
}
```

Listing 9-4: Creating a picker with multiple components

The view controller of Listing 9-4 provides values for two components. The first thing we need to do is to add a new array for the values of the second component. We called it **cities**. To tell the picker that we want two components, the value 2 was returned from the **numberOfComponents()** method. From this point on, we have to consider the component every time we interact with the picker. If the index of the component is 0, we work with the **cities** array, and when the index is 1 we work with the **years** array. The **getYear()** method was also expanded to read the selected value from each component and assign them to the label. The final application is shown in Figure 9-5 below.

Figure 9-5: Picker with two components

Date Picker

The **UIDatePicker** class is a subclass of **UIPickerView** designed to simplify the creation of pickers for dates and times. From this class, we can create objects that show dates, dates and times, and even create a countdown timer. This picker can be created from code, using the **UIView** initializer (**var picker = UIDatePicker(frame: CGRect)**) or by dragging the element from the Object Library.

Date Picker - Displays multiple rotating wheels to allow users to select dates and times.

Figure 9-6: Date Picker option in the Object Library

The class provides the following properties to configure the picker.

datePickerMode—This property sets or returns the picker's mode. It is an enumeration called **Mode** included in the **UIDatePicker** class. The values available are **time**, **date**, **dateAndTime**, and **countDownTimer**.

maximumDate—This property sets or returns the maximum date the picker can show. It is a conditional of type **Date**.

minimumDate—This property sets or returns the minimum date the picker can show. It is a conditional of type **Date**.

date—This property sets or returns the selected date. It is of type **Date**.

minuteInterval—This property sets or returns an integer value that determines the interval at which the minutes should be shown (1 by default).

countDownDuration—This property sets or returns a value of type **TimeInterval** that indicates the seconds from which the timer counts down.

setDate(Date, animated: Bool)—This method selects a new date. The first attribute is a **Date** value that specifies the date we want to select, and the **animated** attribute is a Boolean value that determines whether we want the selection to be animated or not.

The class also includes three properties to determine the type of data to show. If the properties are not defined, they take the values by default set on the device.

calendar—This property sets or returns the calendar to use by the picker. It is an optional of type `Calendar`.

locale—This property sets or returns the locale (regional information) to use by the picker. It is an optional of type `Locale`.

timeZone—This property sets or returns the time zone of the date shown by the picker. It is an optional of type `TimeZone`.

As with any other element, the properties of a Date Picker added to the Storyboard may be configured from the Attributes Inspector panel. Depending on the selected mode, some values are considered and others ignored. For example, the Date and Date and Time modes consider the minimum and maximum dates but ignore the Interval value. To set the minimum and maximum dates, we have to select the option and then specify the value, as shown in Figure 9-7.

Figure 9-7: Date Picker properties

A Date Picker does not work with delegates, we interact with the picker directly through its properties and methods, but there is no difference in how it presents the values and how the user selects them. Therefore, we can work with an interface similar to the one used for Picker Views. For our example, we use a Date Picker, a label, and a button, as illustrated in Figure 9-8.

May	30	2016
June	31	2016
July	1	2017
August	**2**	**2018**
September	3	2019
October	4	2020
November	5	2021

Date:

Show Date

Figure 9-8: Interface to test Date Pickers

The purpose of this interface is to learn how to get and process the values selected in the Date Picker. Because of this, the view controller only needs to include the Outlets for the picker and the label, and the Action for the button.

```
import UIKit

class ViewController: UIViewController {
    @IBOutlet weak var picker: UIDatePicker!
    @IBOutlet weak var showDate: UILabel!
```

```
@IBAction func getDate(_ sender: UIButton) {
    let selectedDate = picker.date
    let format = DateFormatter()
    format.dateStyle = DateFormatter.Style.medium
    showDate.text = "Date: \(format.string(from: selectedDate))"
}
}
```

Listing 9-5: Printing the selected date

Getting the date selected on the picker is as simple as reading its **date** property. This property is of type **Date**, which means that we have to create a **DateFormatter** object to format the value before presenting it on the screen (see Dates in Chapter 4). The entire process is done inside the **getDate()** method, executed when the button is pressed. The **DateFormatter** object is created with the **medium** style, the string is generated with the **string()** method, and finally the value is assigned to the label to show it on the screen.

As well as with **UIPickerView** objects, we can also declare an initial value for Date Pickers. The value may be assigned directly to the **date** property or by calling the **setDate()** method. The only difference is that with the method we have the chance to animate the selection. The **viewDidLoad()** method below initializes the picker with the date 08-13-2010.

```
override func viewDidLoad() {
    super.viewDidLoad()
    let calendar = Calendar.current
    var components = DateComponents()
    components.year = 2010
    components.month = 8
    components.day = 13

    if let newDate = calendar.date(from: components) {
        picker.date = newDate
    }
}
```

Listing 9-6: Setting the initial selected date

The code of Listing 9-6 uses a **DateComponents** structure and the **date()** method of the **Calendar** structure to create a date. Because the **date()** method returns an optional, we have to unwrap it before assigning it to the **date** property. Once we add the **viewDidLoad()** method to the previous example, the initial values of the picker will be August 13, 2010.

 Do It Yourself: Create a new Single View Application project. Add a Date Picker, a label, and a button to the main view, as shown in Figure 9-8. Select the mode Date for the picker from the Attributes Inspector panel. Define constraints to keep them at the top of the screen. Connect the label and the picker to Outlets called **showDate** and **picker**, respectively. Connect the button to an Action called **getDate()** and complete the method with the code of Listing 9-5. You can also add the **viewDidLoad()** method of Listing 9-6 to define an initial value. Run the application, select a date, and press the button to assign it to the label.

 IMPORTANT: The **UIDatePicker** class does not provide the functionality to create a countdown timer. When the picker is set with the Count Down Timer mode, it shows hours and minutes to let the user select a starting time, but then is up to us to create the timer and display the time on the screen. We will study the **Timer** class to create these timers in the next chapter.

Pickers

10.1 Timer

Timers are objects created from the **Timer** class that perform an action after a specific period of time. There are two types of timers: repeating and non-repeating. Repeating timers perform the action and then reschedule themselves to do it again in an infinite loop. Non-repeating timers, on the other hand, perform the action once and then invalidate themselves. The class includes the following properties and methods to create and manage timers.

isValid—This property returns a Boolean value that indicates if the timer can still be fired or it was invalidated.

fireDate—This property sets or returns the date in which the timer is going to be fired. It is a value of type **Date**.

timeInterval—This property returns the time interval in seconds for repeating timers. It is a value of type **TimeInterval**.

userInfo—This property returns the object set by the timer to provide additional information.

tolerance—This property sets or returns a period of tolerance in seconds to provide the system with more flexibility. It is a value of type **TimeInterval**. The value by default is 0.

scheduledTimer(timeInterval: TimeInterval, **target:** Any, **selector:** Selector, **userInfo:** Any?, **repeats:** Bool)—This type method returns repeating and non-repeating timers depending on the values of its attributes. The **timeInterval** attribute represents the seconds the timer has to wait before performing the action, the **target** attribute is the object where the action is going to be performed, the **selector** attribute is the method that is going to be executed when the time runs out, the **userInfo** attribute is a custom object with additional information, and the **repeats** attribute indicates the type of timer we want to create (repeating or non-repeating).

fire()—This method fires the timer without considering the time remaining.

invalidate()—This method invalidates the timer (stops the timer).

The **scheduledTimer()** method creates a timer according to the value of its attributes and automatically adds it to an internal loop that will process it when the time runs out. The following example shows how to create a repeating timer.

```
import UIKit

class ViewController: UIViewController {
    var counter: Int = 1
    var timer: Timer!

    override func viewDidLoad() {
        super.viewDidLoad()
        timer = Timer.scheduledTimer(timeInterval: 1.0, target: self,
selector: #selector(report), userInfo: nil, repeats: true)
    }
```

```
@objc func report(sender: Timer) {
    print("\(counter) times")
    counter += 1
    if counter > 10 {
        timer.invalidate()
    }
}
}
```

Listing 10-1: Creating a repeating timer

The code of Listing 10-1 creates the timer as soon as the view is loaded. This timer executes the **report()** method every second until it is invalidated. The **report()** method keeps track of the number of times it was called with the **counter** property. When the value of this property is greater than 10, it calls the **invalidate()** method on the timer to stop it.

The method designated as the action for the timer receives a reference to the timer object that we can use to access the timer's properties or invalidate it, but in this example, we have decided to assign the timer to a property called **timer** in case later we want to stop it from another method.

In the last example, we just printed a message on the console, but timers may be implemented along with other objects in more practical situations. The following example updates the date on the screen combining a timer with a Date Picker.

```
import UIKit

class ViewController: UIViewController {
    @IBOutlet weak var dates: UIDatePicker!

    override func viewDidLoad() {
        super.viewDidLoad()
        Timer.scheduledTimer(timeInterval: 60.0, target: self, selector:
#selector(update), userInfo: nil, repeats: true)
    }
    @objc func update(sender: Timer) {
        dates.date = Date()
    }
}
```

Listing 10-2: Updating a Date Picker with a timer

Listing 10-2 assumes that we have added a Date Picker to the Scene, set its mode to Time, and connected it to the view controller with an Outlet called **dates**. The timer for this example performs its action every 60 seconds (1 minute). The method executed by the timer creates a new **Date** structure with the current date and assigns it to the picker's **date** property to update the value.

 Do It Yourself: Create a new Single View Application project. Add a Date Picker to the main view. Select its mode to Time. Connect the picker to the view controller with an Outlet called **dates**. Complete the view controller with the code of Listing 10-2. Run the application and wait a minute to see the timer updating the time on the screen.

 IMPORTANT: The **scheduledTimer()** method adds the timer to the main loop, but the system can work with multiple loops at a time. The **Timer** class also includes initializers to create independent timers that you can add to any loop you want. For more information, visit our website and follow the links for this chapter.

11.1 Scroll Views

Scroll Views are views that display content larger than the area they cover. They incorporate functionality to let the user scroll the content or zoom in and out any part of it. The UIKit framework provides the **UIScrollView** class to create these types of views. A few classes inherit from **UIScrollView** to take advantage of its capabilities, like the **UITextView** class studied in Chapter 7, but Scroll Views can manage any type of content we need. Figure 11-1 illustrates what the user sees when scrolling within a picture that is larger than the Scroll View's area.

Figure 11-1: *User scrolling through the Scroll View's content area*

The content of a Scroll View is inside a delimited area called *content area*. This area is like a canvas and the Scroll View like a window that lets us see one part of the canvas at a time. Therefore, there are two areas to define: the area of the Scroll View and the area of its content. The area occupied by the Scroll View is usually defined in the Storyboard with constraints, as any other view, but its content area has to be defined in coordinates from the view controller. The following are the most frequently used properties and methods included in the **UIScrollView** class to manage the view and its content.

contentSize—This property sets or returns the size of the content area. It is a structure of type **CGSize**.

contentOffset—This property sets or returns the **x** and **y** coordinates that determine the positions of the piece of image the Scroll View is currently showing on the screen. It is a structure of type **CGPoint**, with a value by default of 0, 0.

contentInset—This property sets or returns the content's padding. This is the space between the edges of the Scroll View and its content. It is a structure of type **UIEdgeInsets** with the properties **top**, **left**, **bottom**, and **right**, and a value by default of 0, 0, 0, 0.

isScrollEnabled—This property is a Boolean value that determines if scrolling is enabled.

isPagingEnabled—This property is a Boolean value that determines whether the Scroll View considers its content as pages or not.

showHorizontalScrollIndicator—This property is a Boolean value that determines whether the horizontal scroll indicator is visible or not.

showVerticalScrollIndicator—This property is a Boolean value that determines whether the vertical scroll indicator is visible or not.

zoomScale—This property sets or returns the current scale of the content. It is of type `CGFloat` with a default value of 1.0.

maximumZoomScale—This property sets or returns the maximum possible scale for the content. It is of type `CGFloat` with a default value of 1.0.

minimumZoomScale—This property sets or returns the minimum possible scale for the content. It is of type `CGFloat` with a default value of 1.0.

zoom(to: CGRect, **animated:** Bool)—This method zooms the content to make visible the area specified by the **to** attribute. The `animated` attribute indicates if the process will be animated or not.

scrollRectToVisible(CGRect, **animated:** Bool)—This method scrolls the content to make visible the area specified by the first attribute. The `animated` attribute indicates if the process will be animated or not.

Scroll Views can also designate a delegate for configuration and to report changes on their state. The delegate must conform to the `UIScrollViewDelegate` protocol and implement its methods. The following are the most frequently used.

viewForZooming(in: UIScrollView)—This method is called by the Scroll View on its delegate to know which view on its content is going to be zoomed in or out.

scrollViewDidScroll(UIScrollView)—This method is called by the Scroll View on its delegate when the user scrolls the content.

scrollViewDidZoom(UIScrollView)—This method is called by the Scroll View on its delegate when the user zooms the content.

Scroll Views are no more than normal views with additional functionality. In the storyboard, they look like a normal view and may occupy the whole area of the main view or share the screen with other views, depending on what we want for our interface. They may be created from code with the `UIView` initializer or added to the Storyboard from the Object Library.

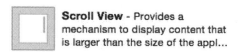

Figure 11-2: *Scroll View option in the Object Library*

Scrolling

Once a Scroll View is added to the Scene, we have to connect it to the view controller and manage its content from code. The following example connects a Scroll View to the `ViewController` class with an Outlet called `mainScroll`, defines the size of its content area, and adds an image to it.

```
import UIKit

class ViewController: UIViewController {
   @IBOutlet weak var mainScroll: UIScrollView!

   override func viewDidLoad() {
      super.viewDidLoad()
      let imgView = UIImageView(image: UIImage(named: "doll"))
      let imgWidth = imgView.frame.size.width
      let imgHeight = imgView.frame.size.height
```

Scroll Views

```
    mainScroll.contentSize = CGSize(width: imgWidth, height: imgHeight)
    mainScroll.addSubview(imgView)
  }
}
```

Listing 11-1: Configuring the Scroll View

The content area of a Scroll View is defined with coordinates, starting from the top-left corner (coordinates 0, 0) and ending at the bottom-right corner (coordinates of which are determined by the size of the area). Every time a Scroll View is included in the interface, we have to declare the size of its content area, otherwise the system will not know how far the user can go. The content is created from other views, such as Image Views or controls, and the views are added to the content area as subviews of the Scroll View. The position of the views in the content area is not determined by constraints but by the values of their **frame** properties.

The example of Listing 11-1 creates the Image View to add to the content area and then declares the size of the area as the size of the image (we did not have to declare the frame of the Image View because the initializer takes the values from the image and automatically assigns them to the **frame** property). After the content area is ready, the Image View is added as a subview of the Scroll View with the **addSubview()** method (see Chapter 4, Listing 4-53). Because the size of the content area is the same as the size of the image it contains, the user can scroll the content and see the whole image, as illustrated in Figure 11-1.

 Do It Yourself: Create a new Single View Application project. Add a Scroll View to the main view and pin it to the Safe Area. Create an Outlet for the Scroll View called **mainScroll** and complete your view controller with the code of Listing 11-1. Download the image doll.jpg from our website and add it to the Assets Catalog. Run the application and scroll the image.

The content area of a Scroll View may contain as many views as we want. The following example includes a second image with a logo at the top-left corner of the area (the image is called logo.png and is available on our website).

```
import UIKit

class ViewController: UIViewController {
    @IBOutlet weak var mainScroll: UIScrollView!

    override func viewDidLoad() {
        super.viewDidLoad()
        let imgView = UIImageView(image: UIImage(named: "doll"))
        let imgWidth = imgView.frame.size.width
        let imgHeight = imgView.frame.size.height
        mainScroll.contentSize = CGSize(width: imgWidth, height: imgHeight)
        mainScroll.addSubview(imgView)
        let logoView = UIImageView(frame: CGRect(x: 25, y: 25, width: 249,
height: 249))
        logoView.image = UIImage(named: "logo")
        mainScroll.addSubview(logoView)
    }
}
```

Listing 11-2: Adding more views to the content area

The example of Listing 11-2 creates the Image View for the logo with a frame in the position 25, 25, and then adds it to the Scroll View. Because the image with the logo is added after the image with the doll, it is shown at the top, but it is fixed at the position 25, 25 in the content area and therefore it scrolls along with the rest of the content, as shown in Figure 11-3.

Figure 11-3: Two images in the content area

As we mentioned, the area occupied by the Scroll View on the interface may be different from the area occupied by its content. If we know the size of the content area, we can position and size content using coordinates, as we did in the previous example, but this is something difficult to do when the content has to be positioned and sized relative to the sides of the content area or to the sides of the Scroll View. For these situations, the `UIScrollView` class offers two layout guides that allow us to set constraints between the views and the content area or between the views and the Scroll View. The following are the properties included in the class to access these guides.

frameLayoutGuide—This property returns a layout guide that represents the frame of the Scroll View.

contentLayoutGuide—This property returns a layout guide that represents the frame of the content area.

Using these guides, we can integrate the content of the Scroll View with the rest of the interface. For instance, we can position the logo of our previous example relative to the sides of the Scroll View, which will keep it fixed in place.

```
import UIKit
class ViewController: UIViewController {
   @IBOutlet weak var mainScroll: UIScrollView!

   override func viewDidLoad() {
      super.viewDidLoad()
      let imgView = UIImageView(image: UIImage(named: "doll"))
      let imgWidth = imgView.frame.size.width
      let imgHeight = imgView.frame.size.height
      mainScroll.contentSize = CGSize(width: imgWidth, height: imgHeight)
      mainScroll.addSubview(imgView)

      let logoView = UIImageView(image: UIImage(named: "logo"))
      logoView.translatesAutoresizingMaskIntoConstraints = false
      mainScroll.addSubview(logoView)

      logoView.topAnchor.constraint(equalTo:
mainScroll.frameLayoutGuide.topAnchor, constant: 25).isActive = true
      logoView.leadingAnchor.constraint(equalTo:
mainScroll.frameLayoutGuide.leadingAnchor, constant: 25).isActive = true
   }
}
```

Listing 11-3: Pinning content to the frame of the Scroll View

The example of Listing 11-3 adds the images of the doll and the logo to the Scroll View, as we did before, but instead of declaring the position and size of the logo with a `CGRect` value, we do it with constraints. We define two constraints to pin the view to the top-left corner of the Scroll

Scroll Views

View, one from the Top anchor of the view to the Top anchor of the Frame layout guide, and another from the Leading anchor of the view to the Leading anchor of the Frame layout guide. Because the image is pinned to the sides of the Scroll View, it always keeps its initial position and does not scroll with the rest of the content anymore, as illustrated in Figure 11-4.

Figure 11-4: Content pinned to the Scroll View

Zooming

Setting the size of the content area gives enough information to the Scroll View to let the user scroll the content, but to zoom in and out we have to define the maximum and minimum scales allowed with the **minimumZoomScale** and **maximumZoomScale** properties, and also conform to the **UIScrollViewDelegate** protocol and implement its **viewForZooming()** method to declare which view is going to participate in the process.

```
import UIKit

class ViewController: UIViewController, UIScrollViewDelegate {
    @IBOutlet weak var mainScroll: UIScrollView!
    var imgView: UIImageView!

    override func viewDidLoad() {
        super.viewDidLoad()
        mainScroll.delegate = self
        imgView = UIImageView(image: UIImage(named: "doll"))
        let imageWidth = imgView.frame.size.width
        let imageHeight = imgView.frame.size.height

        mainScroll.minimumZoomScale = 1.0
        mainScroll.maximumZoomScale = 4.0
        mainScroll.contentSize = CGSize(width: imageWidth, height:
imageHeight)
        mainScroll.addSubview(imgView)
    }
    func viewForZooming(in scrollView: UIScrollView) -> UIView? {
        return imgView
    }
}
```

Listing 11-4: Allowing zooming

The view controller of Listing 11-4 conforms to the **UIScrollViewDelegate** protocol and declares itself as the delegate of the **mainScroll** view. It also declares a minimum scale of 1.0 and a maximum scale of 4.0, and stores a reference to the Image View in the **imgView** property to be able to return it from the **viewForZooming()** method. When the Scroll View detects that the user is trying to zoom in or out, it calls this method on its delegate to know which view in the content area is going to be affected by the action and begins to zoom until a limit is reached.

The zoom scale is considered to be 1.0 at the initial state. If we set absolute values for the **minimumScale** and **maximumScale** properties when the initial image is bigger than the area of the Scroll View, as in the previous example, the user will not be able to zoom out enough to see the whole image on the screen. There are different ways to accommodate these values, depending on the effects we want to achieve in our application. For instance, the following example calculates the minimum scale from the initial size of the image.

```
import UIKit

class ViewController: UIViewController, UIScrollViewDelegate {
    @IBOutlet weak var mainScroll: UIScrollView!
    var imgView: UIImageView!

    override func viewDidLoad() {
        super.viewDidLoad()
        mainScroll.delegate = self

        view.setNeedsLayout()
        view.layoutIfNeeded()

        imgView = UIImageView(image: UIImage(named: "doll"))
        let imageWidth = imgView.frame.size.width
        let imageHeight = imgView.frame.size.height
        let scrollWidth = mainScroll.frame.size.width
        let scrollHeight = mainScroll.frame.size.height

        let minScale = min(scrollWidth / imageWidth, scrollHeight / imageHeight)
        let maxScale = max(minScale * 4.0, 1.0)
        mainScroll.minimumZoomScale = minScale
        mainScroll.maximumZoomScale = maxScale

        mainScroll.contentSize = CGSize(width: imageWidth, height: imageHeight)
        mainScroll.addSubview(imgView)
    }
    func viewForZooming(in scrollView: UIScrollView) -> UIView? {
        return imgView
    }
}
```

Listing 11-5: Calculating the minimum and maximum scales

To calculate what should be the minimum scale so the user can zoom out to see the whole image on the screen, we need to obtain the current values of the Scroll View's **width** and **height** properties. The problem is that the values of these properties are not updated when the interface is presented on the screen but during the system's updating cycles. To force the system to update the values at the time we need them, we have to call the main view's **setNeedsLayout()** and **layoutIfNeeded()** methods (see Chapter 6). If we do not execute these methods before reading the view's **frame** property, the values returned might be those defined in the Storyboard (this is not always required, it depends on when in the process we try to read the frames).

The minimum scale is calculated in Listing 11-5 by dividing one of the Scroll View's dimensions by the same dimension of the Image View. For example, if we divide the width of the Scroll View by the width of the Image View, we get the scale necessary to let the user zoom out until the whole width of the image is visible. But because we want the user to be able to see the whole image, we have to calculate the scale for both dimensions and get the smaller value. We do this comparing the result of both formulas with the **min** function (**min(scrollWidth / imageWidth, scrollHeight / imageHeight)**). This will be our minimum scale. From this value we get the maximum scale multiplying it by 4.

The Basics: If you want the image to be presented from the beginning at the minimum scale, you can set the initial zoom scale with the `zoomScale` property. Insert the statement `mainScroll.zoomScale = minScale` at the end of the `viewDidLoad()` method of Listing 11-5.

Pages

The `UIScrollView` class includes functionality to split the content area into pages. The size of the pages is determined by the size of the Scroll View, so when the user swipes his finger on the screen, the current visible portion of the content area is completely replaced by the part that represents the next page. To activate this mode, we have to assign the value `true` to the `isPagingEnabled` property (or activate the option in the Attributes Inspector panel) and configure the content to represent the virtual pages. The following is a simple example that presents three images, spot1.png, spot2.png, and spot3.png, one per page.

```
import UIKit

class ViewController: UIViewController {
    @IBOutlet weak var mainScroll: UIScrollView!

    override func viewDidLoad() {
        super.viewDidLoad()
        let images = ["spot1", "spot2", "spot3"]
        mainScroll.isPagingEnabled = true

        view.setNeedsLayout()
        view.layoutIfNeeded()
        let scrollWidth = mainScroll.frame.size.width
        let scrollHeight = mainScroll.frame.size.height

        var posX: CGFloat = 0
        for img in images {
            let imgView = UIImageView(frame: CGRect(x: posX, y: 0, width:
scrollWidth, height: scrollHeight))
            imgView.image = UIImage(named: img)
            imgView.contentMode = .scaleAspectFill
            imgView.clipsToBounds = true

            mainScroll.addSubview(imgView)
            mainScroll.contentSize = CGSize(width: scrollWidth *
CGFloat(images.count), height: scrollHeight)
            posX = posX + scrollWidth
        }
    }
}
```

Listing 11-6: Organizing the content area in pages

The Image Views have to be created of the size of the Scroll View and positioned side by side to represent the pages. This is why in Listing 11-6 we declare the frame of every Image View. The values for the frame's **width** and **height** properties are determined by the size of the Scroll View (**scrollWidth** and **scrollHeight**), and the coordinates for the position are calculated according to the page the view represents. The first Image View is added at the coordinate 0, 0, but the second Image View is displaced to the right a distance determined by the width of the Scroll View. To calculate this value, we use the **posX** variable. In every cycle of the loop, the variable is incremented with the value of the **scrollWidth** property to establish the horizontal position of the next view. As a result, the images are positioned on the content area one after another, from left to right.

In this example, we also set the **contentMode** of each Image View to **scaleAspectFill** to fill the entire Image View with the picture and the **clipsToBounds** property to **true** to make sure that the image will never be drawn outside its boundaries.

 Do It Yourself: Create a new Single View Application project. Add a Scroll View to the initial view from the Object Library and pin it to the Safe Area. Create an Outlet for the Scroll View called **mainScroll**. Complete your view controller with the code of Listing 11-6. Download the images spot1.png, spot2.png, and spot3.png from our website and add them to the Assets Catalog. Run the application. When you scroll the content, the interface should transition from right to left or left to right, jumping from one image to another.

The UIKit framework includes a special type of control called Page Control that is particularly useful in these kinds of applications. The control displays dots on the screen that represent each page available and changes their colors according to the page selected or visible. There is an option available in the Object Library to add a Page Control to the Storyboard.

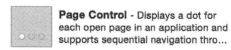

Figure 11-5: Page Control option in the Object Library

The control is created from the **UIPageControl** class. The class provides the following properties for configuration.

currentPage—This property sets or returns the number of the current page.

numberOfPages—This property sets or returns the number of pages represented by the control (the number of dots shown on the screen). It is of type **Int**.

hidesForSinglePage—This property is a Boolean value that determines whether or not the control should be hidden when there is only one page.

pageIndicatorTintColor—This property sets or returns the color of the dots when the pages they represent are not visible. It is an optional of type **UIColor**.

currentPageIndicatorTintColor—This property sets or returns the color of the dot that represents the visible page. It is an optional of type **UIColor**.

To introduce the Page Control in the interface, we could reduce the size of the Scroll View to make room for it or put the control over the Scroll View. The last option looks modern and may include a translucent bar to improve the appearance.

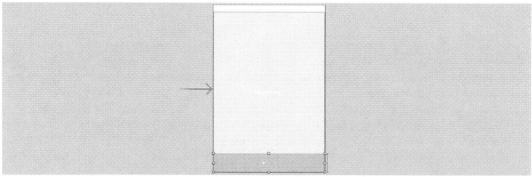

Figure 11-6: Page Control added to the interface

Scroll Views

The interface presented in Figure 11-6 includes a translucent bar at the bottom with the Page Control inside. The bar is created from a simple **UIView** object with a gray background and an Alpha value of 0.7 (to make it translucent), and it is positioned at the top of the Scroll View.

 Do It Yourself: Views that are dragged over a Scroll View become its subviews and therefore part of its content area. This is not the desirable behaviour for the interface of Figure 11-6. What you want is to put the view for the bar over the Scroll View, not inside. To achieve this, you can momentarily reduce the size of the Scroll View, drag the view inside the main view, set its constraints, and then update the frames to move the Scroll View back to its original position, or just uninstall the Scroll View until the bar is added and pinned to the sides. Alternatively, you can drag the view inside the Scroll View and then change its position in the hierarchy from the Document Outline panel (see Figures 6-63 and 6-64). Once the view is ready, change its background color to gray and its alpha value to 0.7 to make it translucent. Finally, add a Page Control at the center of the view with alignment constraints.

The Page Control is configured by default for three pages, but we can change the initial values from the Attributes Inspector panel. This is usually not necessary since the content to display with this type of control is loaded dynamically and its properties are configured from the view controller, as shown in the following example.

```
import UIKit

class ViewController: UIViewController, UIScrollViewDelegate {
    @IBOutlet weak var mainScroll: UIScrollView!
    @IBOutlet weak var pageCounter: UIPageControl!
    var page: Int = 0

    override func viewDidLoad() {
        super.viewDidLoad()
        let images = ["spot1", "spot2", "spot3"]
        pageCounter.numberOfPages = images.count
        pageCounter.pageIndicatorTintColor = UIColor.black
        pageCounter.currentPageIndicatorTintColor = UIColor.white

        mainScroll.delegate = self
        mainScroll.isPagingEnabled = true

        view.setNeedsLayout()
        view.layoutIfNeeded()
        let scrollWidth = mainScroll.frame.size.width
        let scrollHeight = mainScroll.frame.size.height

        var posX: CGFloat = 0
        for img in images {
            let imgView = UIImageView(frame: CGRect(x: posX, y: 0, width:
scrollWidth, height: scrollHeight))
            imgView.image = UIImage(named: img)
            imgView.contentMode = .scaleAspectFill
            imgView.clipsToBounds = true

            mainScroll.addSubview(imgView)
            mainScroll.contentSize = CGSize(width: scrollWidth *
CGFloat(images.count), height: scrollHeight)
            posX = posX + scrollWidth
        }
    }
```

```
func scrollViewDidScroll(_ scrollView: UIScrollView) {
    let pageWidth = mainScroll.frame.size.width
    let getPage = round(mainScroll.contentOffset.x / pageWidth)
    let currentPage = Int(getPage)

    page = currentPage
    pageCounter.currentPage = page
}
}
```

Listing 11-7: Calculating the page

To represent the pages on the screen with the Page Control, we not only have to configure the control but also get the number of the current visible page. The **UIScrollView** class does not offer any property or method to help us get this value; we have to calculate it ourselves. Fortunately, the delegate offers a method called **scrollViewDidScroll()** that is executed every time the user scrolls the content. Also, the system automatically updates the **contentOffset** property with the current displacement of the content area every time a scroll takes place. Implementing these tools, we can calculate the current page. The value is obtained dividing the value of the **x** property of the **contentOffset** structure by the size of the page (the width of the Scroll View). Because the result is a floating-point number, we round it, turn it into an integer, and assign it to the **currentPage** property of the Page Control to show the current page on the screen.

 Do It Yourself: Connect the Page Control to an Outlet called **pageCounter**. Complete your view controller with the code of Listing 11-7 and run the application. The Page Control should indicate the current visible page.

Letting the user zoom in or out the entire content area when the Scroll View is configured to work with pages would defeat the purpose of pages, but it is possible to let the user zoom each page individually. Scroll Views may be created inside other Scroll Views, and we can use this feature to build complex interfaces where a view may have parts of its content presented with vertical scroll and other parts with horizontal scroll. We can also use this feature to allow zooming inside each page of a Scroll View. All we have to do is embed the content of each page inside additional Scroll Views, set their maximum and minimum scales, and implement the **viewForZooming()** method of the **UIScrollViewDelegate** protocol to tell the Scroll Views that zooming is allowed, as we did in the example of Listing 11-5.

```
import UIKit

class ViewController: UIViewController, UIScrollViewDelegate {
    @IBOutlet weak var mainScroll: UIScrollView!
    @IBOutlet weak var pageCounter: UIPageControl!
    var imageViews: [UIImageView] = []
    var page: Int = 0

    override func viewDidLoad() {
        super.viewDidLoad()
        let images = ["spot1", "spot2", "spot3"]
        pageCounter.numberOfPages = images.count
        pageCounter.pageIndicatorTintColor = UIColor.black
        pageCounter.currentPageIndicatorTintColor = UIColor.white

        mainScroll.delegate = self
        mainScroll.isPagingEnabled = true

        view.setNeedsLayout()
        view.layoutIfNeeded()
```

Scroll Views

```
            let scrollWidth = mainScroll.frame.size.width
            let scrollHeight = mainScroll.frame.size.height

        var posX: CGFloat = 0
        for img in images {
            let childScroll = UIScrollView(frame: CGRect(x: posX, y: 0,
width: scrollWidth, height: scrollHeight))
            childScroll.contentSize = CGSize(width: scrollWidth, height:
scrollHeight)
            childScroll.minimumZoomScale = 1.0
            childScroll.maximumZoomScale = 4.0
            childScroll.delegate = self

            let imgView = UIImageView(frame: CGRect(x: 0, y: 0, width:
scrollWidth, height: scrollHeight))
            imgView.image = UIImage(named: img)
            imgView.contentMode = .scaleAspectFill
            imgView.clipsToBounds = true
            imageViews.append(imgView)

            childScroll.addSubview(imgView)
            mainScroll.addSubview(childScroll)
            mainScroll.contentSize = CGSize(width: scrollWidth *
CGFloat(imageViews.count), height: scrollHeight)
            posX = posX + scrollWidth
        }
    }
    func scrollViewDidScroll(_ scrollView: UIScrollView) {
        let pageWidth = mainScroll.frame.size.width
        let getPage = round(mainScroll.contentOffset.x / pageWidth)

        let currentPage = Int(getPage)
        if currentPage != page {
            let scroll = imageViews[page].superview as! UIScrollView
            scroll.setZoomScale(1.0, animated: true)
            page = Int(currentPage)
            pageCounter.currentPage = page
        }
    }
    func viewForZooming(in scrollView: UIScrollView) -> UIView? {
        return imageViews[page]
    }
}
```

Listing 11-8: *Zooming the pages in and out*

On the view controller of Listing 11-8, Scroll Views are created to embed every Image View and then are added as subviews of the **mainScroll** view. Notice that the minimum and maximum scales are set only for the nested Scroll Views, not for the **mainScroll** view, because we only want to make the zoom available for the Scroll Views assigned to every page.

There is also an aesthetic change inside the **scrollViewDidScroll()** method. This method is executed every time the user scrolls the pages, but that scroll does not always cause the current page to be replaced. We check this condition comparing the current page with the previous one and set the zoom scale back to 1.0 if the new page is different. This returns the images to the initial state every time the user moves to another page.

The examples we have studied so far create applications that let the user transition from one image to another with the move of a finger. But this presents a problem. Because the size of the pages is determined from the size of the Scroll View, the application does not work anymore if the device is rotated or the size of the Scroll View changes for some reason. To solve this problem, we have to implement the methods defined for Trait Collections to detect and report changes in size (see Chapter 6, Listing 6-9). The following example implements the **viewWillTransition()** method to update the frames of the Image Views and their Scroll Views when the device is rotated.

```
import UIKit

class ViewController: UIViewController, UIScrollViewDelegate {
    @IBOutlet weak var mainScroll: UIScrollView!
    @IBOutlet weak var pageCounter: UIPageControl!
    var imageViews: [UIImageView] = []
    var page: Int = 0
    var rotating = false

    override func viewDidLoad() {
        super.viewDidLoad()
        let images = ["spot1", "spot2", "spot3"]
        pageCounter.numberOfPages = images.count
        pageCounter.pageIndicatorTintColor = UIColor.black
        pageCounter.currentPageIndicatorTintColor = UIColor.white

        mainScroll.delegate = self
        mainScroll.isPagingEnabled = true
        view.setNeedsLayout()
        view.layoutIfNeeded()

        for img in images {
            let childScroll = UIScrollView(frame: CGRect.zero)
            childScroll.minimumZoomScale = 1.0
            childScroll.maximumZoomScale = 4.0
            childScroll.delegate = self

            let imgView = UIImageView(frame: CGRect.zero)
            imgView.image = UIImage(named: img)
            imgView.contentMode = .scaleAspectFit
            imgView.clipsToBounds = true
            imageViews.append(imgView)
            childScroll.addSubview(imgView)
            mainScroll.addSubview(childScroll)
        }
        updateSize()
    }
    func updateSize() {
        let scrollWidth = mainScroll.frame.size.width
        let scrollHeight = mainScroll.frame.size.height
        var posX: CGFloat = 0
        for imgView in imageViews {
            let scroll = imgView.superview as! UIScrollView
            scroll.frame = CGRect(x: posX, y: 0, width: scrollWidth, height:
scrollHeight)
            scroll.contentSize = CGSize(width: scrollWidth, height:
scrollHeight)
            imgView.frame = CGRect(x: 0, y: 0, width: scrollWidth, height:
scrollHeight)
            posX = posX + scrollWidth
        }
        mainScroll.contentSize = CGSize(width: scrollWidth *
CGFloat(imageViews.count), height: scrollHeight)
        let scrollView = imageViews[page].superview as! UIScrollView
        mainScroll.scrollRectToVisible(scrollView.frame, animated: true)
    }
```

```
func scrollViewDidScroll(_ scrollView: UIScrollView) {
    if !rotating {
        let pageWidth = mainScroll.frame.size.width
        let getPage = round(mainScroll.contentOffset.x / pageWidth)
        let currentPage = Int(getPage)
        if currentPage != page {
            let scroll = imageViews[page].superview as! UIScrollView
            scroll.setZoomScale(1.0, animated: true)
            page = Int(currentPage)
            pageCounter.currentPage = page
        }
    }
}
func viewForZooming(in scrollView: UIScrollView) -> UIView? {
    return imageViews[page]
}
override func viewWillTransition(to size: CGSize, with coordinator:
UIViewControllerTransitionCoordinator) {
    super.viewWillTransition(to: size, with: coordinator)
    rotating = true
    coordinator.animate(alongsideTransition: nil, completion:
{(context: UIViewControllerTransitionCoordinatorContext!) in
        let scroll = self.imageViews[self.page].superview as!
UIScrollView
        scroll.setZoomScale(1.0, animated: true)
        self.updateSize()
        self.rotating = false
    })
}
}
```

Listing 11-9: Adapting the content area to a new orientation

An important change we have to make in this new example is to move the definition of the frames for the Scroll Views and their Image Views to a separate method. This is because every time the size of the **mainScroll** view changes, the code has to update the values of the frames. We still define the pages inside the **viewDidLoad()** method, but we call our **updateSize()** method at the end to define their frames. This method is called again when the user rotates the device. Every time the system detects a rotation or changes on the interface, it calls the **viewWillTransition()** method. In this method we call the **animate()** method of the transition coordinator to update the values of the frames as soon as the transition is over (the statements were declared inside the closure for the completion handler). There are two more important things we do inside this method: we restore the zoom of the current page back to its initial scale and modify the value of a Boolean property called **rotating** to inform the rest of the code that the interface is rotating. This is because we do not want to calculate the number of the current page inside the **scrollViewDidScroll()** method until all the values for the frames are updated. The **updateSize()** method also includes a call to the **scrollRectToVisible()** method of the **mainScroll** view at the end to scroll the content to the right position after the rotation (when the device is rotated, the values of the **contentOffset** property are not updated by the system).

Do It Yourself: The last two examples use the same interface created before. Copy the code you want to try inside your view controller and run the application. In the example of Listing 11-9, we defined the value of the **contentMode** property as **scaleAspectFit** so the user can see the entire images on the screen in any orientation. Try other values to find out which is better for your application.

Scrolling the Interface

Scroll Views let us display any content that does not fit entirely on the screen, including the interface itself. There are times when our interface contains so many elements and controls that there is not enough space to show them all, some get hidden when the device is rotated, or are overlapped by the keyboard. Scroll Views provide the functionality we need to display large interfaces inside a single main view, but they present a challenge. The content area of a Scroll View lays its views using a coordinate system and absolute values, while the interface is organized with constraints. If we add an element to the Scroll View, this element is not incorporated as a subview but as part of its content area and therefore it is positioned and sized according to the values of its **frame** property. Fortunately, there are different ways to connect the content of a Scroll View with the rest of the views on the interface and adapt their size to the space available. An alternative is to create the right constraints to set the size of the content area and report it to the Scroll View. There are different ways to do it, but the simplest is to add a single view inside the Scroll View and then use this view as the container for the rest of the interface. Figure 11-7 illustrates the process. The Scroll View is added to the main view first (left), then a single view is added to the Scroll View (center), and finally the view is extended to occupy the entire area of the Scroll View.

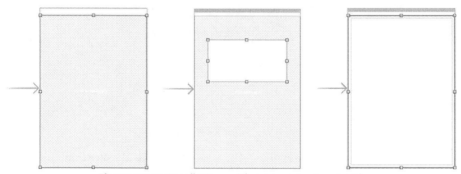

Figure 11-7: Scroll View with an empty view inside

Both views have to be pinned to the edges of their respective containers with Top, Bottom, Leading and Trailing Space constraints. The Scroll View is pinned to the Safe Area and the view inside the Scroll View is pinned to the edges of the Scroll View. Figure 11-8 illustrates all the constraints required.

Figure 11-8: Initial constraints for the views

The constraints for both views are the same, but their purpose is different. The Space constraints for the Scroll View define its size on the interface, but the Space constraints for the container view communicate the size of the view to the Scroll View so that the Scroll View always knows the current size of its content area.

Do It Yourself: Create a new Single View Application project. Add a Scroll View to the main view. Select the Scroll View, open the Pin menu and create Leading, Trailing, Top, and Bottom constraints to pin it to the Safe Area. Add an empty view inside the Scroll View, expand it to occupy the Scroll View's area (Figure 11-7, right), and create Leading, Trailing, Top, and Bottom constraints to pin it to the sides of the Scroll View. You will see that the constraints are shown in color red, because the system does not have enough information to establish the size of the content area yet.

Now that the initial conditions were established, we have to create the constraints necessary to determine the size of the view inside the Scroll View. The vertical size is determined by the elements inside the view and their constraints, but the horizontal size has to be determined by the space available. This requires the creation of two more constraints that pin the container view to the left and right sides of the main view. Figure 11-9 illustrates the process. We have to control-drag a line from the view inside the Scroll View to the main view in the Document Outline panel and create Leading and Trailing constraints with a value of 0.

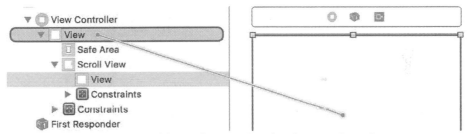

Figure 11-9: *Additional constraints for the container view*

Every time the device is rotated or the space available changes, these constraints change the width of the view inside the Scroll View and this new size is communicated to the Scroll View by the Space constraints added before.

 Do It Yourself: Control-drag a line from the view inside the Scroll View to the item that represents the main view in the Document Outline panel (Figure 11-9). Create a Leading and a Trailing constraint.

So far, we have determined the width of the content area. To determine the height, we have to add the elements of the interface inside the container view and set constraints that link them to each side of the view. In the following example, we have added a Text Field, an Image View, a Text View, and a button. Figure 11-10 shows this interface, including all the constraints. Notice that we have added constraints from the elements to every side of their container view, including the bottom.

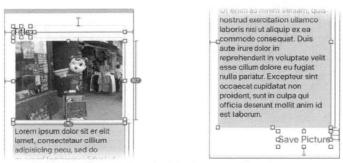

Figure 11-10: *Interface inside the container view*

Scroll Views

These interfaces are usually bigger than the standard size of the Scenes. Xcode offers the alternative to set a specific size for the main view, so we can design longer interfaces in the Storyboard. The tool is called *Simulated Size* and it is available in the Size Inspector panel when the Scene is selected. It includes two options, Fixed and Freeform. When we select Freeform, the panel lets us change the values of the main view's width and height, as shown next.

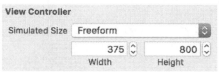

Figure 11-11: *Simulated Size tool*

Once all the elements of our interface are added to the container view and all the constraints for these elements are defined, the Scroll View is ready to determine the size of its content area and let us scroll to see the parts that are not visible. Figure 11-12 shows the application in the simulator.

Figure 11-12: *Scrolling the interface*

Do It Yourself: Select the Scene in the Storyboard. Open the Size Inspector panel and select the Freeform option from the Simulated Size tool. Set the size of the main view to 320 x 800 or any value you want. Expand the Scroll View and the container view to fit the new size. Add the elements shown in Figure 11-10 to the container view, including the Text View with a gray background. Set the proper constraints to pin the elements to each other and to the sides of the view (Figure 11-10). Remember to assign Height constraints to the elements that do not have intrinsic content size, such as the image View and the Text View. Run the application. You should be able to scroll the interface vertically, as shown in Figure 11-12.

Scroll Views are also useful when we need to displace the interface to help the user achieve a purpose or keep an input field visible when the keyboard is activated. The following example scrolls the interface of Figure 11-10 when the Text View is selected.

```
import UIKit

class ViewController: UIViewController, UITextViewDelegate {
    @IBOutlet weak var mainScroll: UIScrollView!
    @IBOutlet weak var descriptionView: UITextView!
```

Scroll Views

```
override func viewDidLoad() {
    super.viewDidLoad()
    descriptionView.delegate = self
}
func textViewDidBeginEditing(_ textView: UITextView) {
    let height = descriptionView.frame.origin.y - 8
    mainScroll.setContentOffset(CGPoint(x: 0, y: height), animated:
true)
}
}
```

Listing 11-10: Scrolling the Text View to the top

To perform the task when the Text View is selected, the view controller has to conform to the **UITextViewDelegate** protocol and implement the **textViewDidBeginEditing()** method (see Chapter 7). Inside this method, we calculate how much we have to scroll the interface to keep the Text View visible when the keyboard is opened. The value is obtained from the distance between the top of the main view and the vertical position of the Text View (**descriptionView.frame.origin.y**). We add 8 to this value to add a padding at the top of the Text View and then use the result to set the new value for the **contentOffset** property. In consequence, when the user taps on the Text View, the **textViewDidBeginEditing()** method is executed and the content of the Scroll View is displaced to show the Text View at the top of the screen.

Figure 11-13: Scrolling the interface when the keyboard is opened

 IMPORTANT: This is a simple approach to deal with the keyboard; it does not contemplate how to revert the situation and it uses approximate values, but it gives you an idea of the things you can do with a Scroll View. In Chapter 19 we will study how to work with keyboard notifications and how to get the right values to position the elements on the screen.

Scroll Views

Chapter 12
Gesture Recognizers

12.1 Gestures

Gestures are actions performed by the user on the screen, such as tapping, swiping, or pinching. These gestures are difficult to detect because all that the screen returns are the position of the fingers, not information on how the fingers were moved. This is why Apple introduced gesture recognizers. A gesture recognizer is an object that performs all the necessary calculations to detect a gesture. The UIKit framework defines a base class called `UIGestureRecognizer` to provide the basic functionality for gesture recognizers and also multiple subclasses with additional properties and methods to create recognizers for specific gestures.

UITapGestureRecognizer—This class creates a gesture recognizer that recognizes single or multiple taps. The class includes the integer properties `numberOfTapsRequired` and `numberOfTouchesRequired` to determine the number of taps that have to occur and the number of fingers that have to tap for the gesture to be recognized.

UIPinchGestureRecognizer—This class creates a gesture recognizer that recognizes a pinching gesture (zoom in or zoom out). The class includes the properties `scale` and `velocity` to set a scaling factor and return the velocity of the pinch. The properties are of type `CGFloat`.

UIRotationGestureRecognizer—This class creates a gesture recognizer that recognizes a rotating gesture. The class includes the properties `rotation` and `velocity` to set the rotation of the gesture in radians and return the velocity in radians per second. They are of type `CGFloat`.

UISwipeGestureRecognizer—This class creates a gesture recognizer that recognizes a swiping gesture. The class includes the properties `direction` and `numberOfTouchesRequired` to set the direction allowed and the number of fingers that must touch the screen for the gesture to be recognized. The `direction` property is a structure (or a set of structures) of type `UISwipeGestureRecognizerDirection` with the properties `right`, `left`, `up`, and `down`.

UIPanGestureRecognizer—This class creates a gesture recognizer that recognizes a panning gesture. The class includes the method `translation(in: UIView?)` to return the current position of the gesture relative to the starting position, the method `velocity(in: UIView?)` to return the velocity of the gesture expressed in points per second, and the properties `maximumNumberOfTouches` and `minimumNumberOfTouches` to set the maximum and minimum number of fingers that must be touching the view for the gesture to be recognized.

UIScreenEdgePanGestureRecognizer—This class creates a gesture recognizer that recognizes a panning gesture that starts near the edge of the screen. The class includes the `edges` property to determine the edges that recognize the gesture. The property is a structure or a set of structures of type `UIRectEdge` with the properties `top`, `left`, `bottom`, `right`, and `all`.

UILongPressGestureRecognizer—This class creates a gesture recognizer that recognizes a long-press gesture (the user presses one or more fingers on the screen for a certain period of time). The class includes the properties `minimumPressDuration` (a

`Double` value to indicate the minimum time the fingers must press the screen), `numberOfTouchesRequired` (the number of fingers that must touch the screen), `numberOfTapsRequired` (the number of taps), and `allowableMovement` (a `CGFloat` value that indicates the maximum movement allowed).

The `UIGestureRecognizer` class provides an initializer to create objects from every subclass and also general properties and methods. The following are the most frequently used.

init(target: Any?, **action:** Selector?**)**—This initializer creates a gesture recognizer configured with the target and the action specified by its attributes. The **target** attribute is the object where the action will be executed, and the **action** attribute is the method to be executed when the gesture is detected.

state—This property returns the current state of the gesture recognizer. It is an enumeration called **State** included in the `UIGestureRecognizer` class. The values available are **possible**, **began**, **changed**, **ended**, **cancelled**, **failed**, and **recognized**.

view—This property returns a reference to the view the gesture recognizer is attached to.

isEnabled—This property sets or returns a Boolean value that determines whether or not the gesture recognizer is enabled.

numberOfTouches—This property returns the number of touches involved in the gesture.

location(in: UIView?**)**—This method returns a `CGPoint` value that indicates the coordinates where the gesture occurred in the view specified by the **in** attribute.

location(ofTouch: Int, **in:** UIView?**)**—This method returns a `CGPoint` value that indicates the coordinates where a touch occurred in the view specified by the **in** attribute. The **ofTouch** attribute is the index of the touch we want to check (touches are stored in an array).

Gesture recognizers may be added to an element from code or in the Storyboard from the Object Library. Figure 12-1 shows the options available.

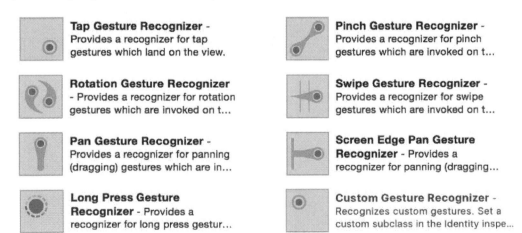

Figure 12-1: Gesture Recognizer options in the Object Library

Although gesture recognizers may be added to any of the views provided by the UIKit framework, not all of them are ready to recognize gestures. The `UIView` class offers two Boolean properties we can modify called `isUserInteractionEnabled` and `isMultipleTouch-Enabled` to activate detection of gestures and multiple touch. If we want to use gestures in a

Gesture Recognizers

view that deactivates these options by default, like an Image View for example, we have to change their values from code or from the Attributes Inspector panel, as shown next.

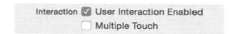

Figure 12-2: *Options to enable interaction*

Gesture recognizers are added to the Storyboard as any other view. All we have to do is to drag the gesture recognizer from the Object Library and drop it on the view we want to recognize the gesture. Xcode adds an icon to the top of the Scene to represent it. Figure 12-3 shows what the Scene looks like after we add a Pan Gesture to an Image View on the interface.

Figure 12-3: *Gesture Recognizer's icon*

For this example, we included an Image View with the picture of the husky (husky.png) that we are going to fade in and out responding to the Pan Gesture.

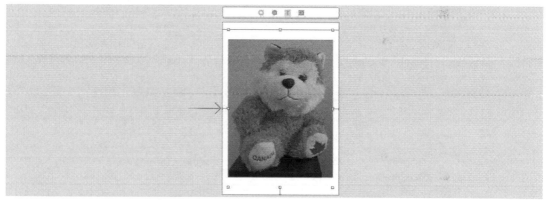

Figure 12-4: *Image View with a Pan Gesture*

The view controller needs an Outlet for the Image View and an Action for the gesture. To create the Action, we have to control-drag a line from the gesture's icon (Figure 12-3) or from the item that represents the gesture in the Document Outline panel.

```
import UIKit

class ViewController: UIViewController {
   @IBOutlet weak var picture: UIImageView!
   var previous: CGFloat = 0

   @IBAction func fadingOut(_ sender: UIPanGestureRecognizer) {
      let translation = sender.translation(in: picture)
      let delta = translation.x - previous
      let width = picture.frame.size.width
      let alpha = picture.alpha + (delta / width)

      if alpha > 0.1 && alpha < 1 {
         picture.alpha = alpha
      }
```

```
        if sender.state == .ended {
            previous = 0
        } else {
            previous = translation.x
        }
    }
}
```

Listing 12-1: Responding to a gesture

Every type of gesture returns different kinds of information. In the case of the pan gesture, the object includes a few methods that calculate and return the current position and velocity of the gesture. Every time a gesture begins, or a change occurs on its state, the object calls the Action method with a reference to itself (**sender: UIPanGestureRecognizer**). From this reference, we can read and process the information provided by the gesture object and perform custom tasks. In Listing 12-1, we call the **translation()** method to get the value of the current position and calculate the difference between the old horizontal position and the new one. From this difference and the width of the image, we can get a proportional value that added to the alpha value lets us associate the movement of the finger with changes in the translucency of the picture on the screen.

Because the limits of the gesture's position may vary, we check that the alpha value obtained from those numbers does not go over 1.0 or below 0.1 (at 0.0 the Image View does not recognize the gesture anymore), and then assign it to the **alpha** property of the Image View to reflect the changes. To keep track of the old position and be able to compare it with the new one, we store it in the **previous** property. Every time the action is called to report changes in the gesture, the new value is stored in this property. But because the position of a pan gesture is considered to be 0 at the point when the gesture begins, we cannot keep using the values of a previous gesture and therefore the value of the **previous** property must return to 0 when the gesture is over. This is detected at the end reading the value of the gesture's **state** property.

Do It Yourself: Create a new Single View Application project. Download the husky.png image from our website and add it to the Assets Catalog. Add an Image View to the main view and assign the image of the husky to it. In the same panel, activate the option called *User Interaction Enabled* for the Image View (Figure 12-2). Drag the option Pan Gesture from the Object Library and drop it over the Image View. You should see the icon pictured in Figure 12-3. Create an Outlet for the image called **picture**. Control-drag a line from the gesture's icon to the view controller to create an Action called **fadingOut()**. Complete the view controller with the code of Listing 12-1 and run the application. The picture should fade in and out when you move your finger left and right.

The Basics: Gesture recognizers cannot be added to different views. If we want to use the same gesture recognizer for different views, we have to create new objects, but several gesture recognizers of the same type may be connected to the same Action.

Gesture recognizers may be added to any view from code. The object is created first with the **UIGestureRecognizer** initializer and then configured and added to the view. The **UIView** class offers the following methods to manage gesture recognizers.

addGestureRecognizer(UIGestureRecognizer)—This method adds a gesture recognizer to the view. The attribute is an object of a **UIGestureRecognizer** subclass.

removeGestureRecognizer(UIGestureRecognizer)—This method removes a gesture recognizer from the view. The attribute is a reference to the gesture added before with the **addGestureRecognizer()** method.

The following example adds a Tap gesture to a Scroll View to zoom in and out to specific points of the image. This code assumes that we have added a Scroll View to the initial Scene and pin it to the Safe Area, as we did for some of the examples in the previous chapter.

```
import UIKit

class ViewController: UIViewController, UIScrollViewDelegate {
    @IBOutlet weak var scroll: UIScrollView!
    var image: UIImageView!
    var zooming = false

    override func viewDidLoad() {
        super.viewDidLoad()
        scroll.delegate = self
        scroll.minimumZoomScale = 1.0
        scroll.maximumZoomScale = 4.0

        image = UIImageView(image: UIImage(named: "doll"))
        scroll.contentSize = CGSize(width: image.frame.size.width, height:
image.frame.size.height)
        scroll.addSubview(image)

        let gesture = UITapGestureRecognizer(target: self, action:
#selector(zoomPicture))
        scroll.addGestureRecognizer(gesture)
    }
    func viewForZooming(in scrollView: UIScrollView) -> UIView? {
        return image
    }
    @objc func zoomPicture(sender: UITapGestureRecognizer) {
        if !zooming {
            let position = sender.location(in: scroll)
            scroll.zoom(to: CGRect(x: position.x, y: position.y, width: 1,
height: 1), animated: true)
            zooming = true
        } else {
            scroll.setZoomScale(1.0, animated: true)
            zooming = false
        }
    }
}
```

Listing 12-2: Adding gestures from code

The **UIGestureRecognizer** initializer requires two values: a reference to the object where the action will be performed and the method that is going to be executed when the gesture is detected. Because we are going to perform all the tasks on the view controller, we declared the target as **self** and created a method called **zoomPicture()** to perform the action.

This example follows the procedure studied in Chapter 11 to configure the Scroll View and allow the user to scroll and zoom the picture. When the Scroll View is ready, the code creates a **UITapGestureRecognizer** object and adds it to the view with the **addGestureRecognizer()** method. In consequence, every time the user taps on the Scroll View, the **zoomPicture()** method is executed. In this method, we zoom in or out, depending on the value of the **zooming** property used as control. To zoom in, the code gets the position of the tap in the view's coordinates from the **location()** method and then zooms in to a rectangle in that position. To zoom out, we just set the scale back to 1.0.

Do It Yourself: Create a new Single View Application project. Add a Scroll View to the main view and pin it to the Safe Area. Connect the Scroll View with an Outlet called **scroll**. Download the doll.jpg image from our website and add it to the Assets Catalog. Complete the view controller with the code of Listing 12-2. Run the application and tap on the image. The image should zoom in where you tapped.

The Basics: New devices incorporate a 3D touch feature that measures the pressure applied to the display. This allows developers to provide new functionality to their applications. Apple offers multiple classes to recognize and respond to 3D gestures. The topic is beyond the scope of this book. For more information, visit our website and follow the links for this chapter.

Gesture Recognizers

13.1 Multiple View Controllers

Apps that only require one main view and a simple interface are very hard to find. Because of the limited amount of space, developing apps for mobile devices demands the creation of multiple Scenes to represent virtual screens that replace one another in response to the user (see Figure 5-11). Practical applications contain multiple Scenes connected with each other following a predetermined path that users can take to navigate and get the information they need.

Xcode templates, like the Single View Application template we have been using so far to create our projects, provide initial Scenes to start from. The rest are added later to the Storyboard as needed from options included in the Object Library. The option to add single Scenes that are controlled by **UIViewController** objects is called *View Controller*.

View Controller - A controller that supports the fundamental view-management model in iOS.

Figure 13-1: View Controller option in the Object Library

Dragging this option to the Storyboard creates a new Scene with its own main view. After the Scenes are added, they can be dragged from the top bar to different positions to represent what users will see when they navigate through the interface. Figure 13-2 shows what the Storyboard looks like after we add a new Scene and move it to the right side of the initial Scene.

Figure 13-2: Second view added to the Storyboard

We can add all the Scenes we need to build our interface. Every Scene represents a new screen and their views will be shown on the device's screen one at a time.

Do It Yourself: Create a new Single View Application project. Drag the View Controller option from the Object Library to the Storyboard (Figure 13-1). Arrange the Scenes to look like Figure 13-2.

The option to add a new Scene to the Storyboard is called View Controller because it creates a main view that is controlled by an object of a subclass of the **UIViewController** class, but this does not mean that the option creates the view controller for the view. Every time we add a new Scene to the Storyboard, we have to create the file for the subclass ourselves. Files are created from the File menu. If we click on the File menu and go over the New option, a submenu shows the option File... Once we click on this option, a window is opened to select the type of file we want to create (we can also use a shortcut pressing the Command + N keys).

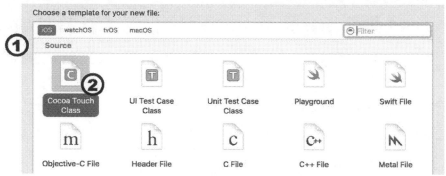

Figure 13-3: Templates for new files

There are several options available in this window. The **UIViewController** class is part of the Cocoa Touch API, therefore to create a file with a **UIViewController** subclass for the new Scene, we have to click on the Cocoa Touch Class option inside the Source panel (Figure 13-3, number 1 and 2). Another window opens up to insert the name and the class we want to create our subclass from.

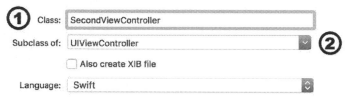

Figure 13-4: Creating the subclass

The first value we have to insert is the name of the class (Figure 13-4, number 1). This value is going to be used as the name of the subclass and also as the name of the new file. It is good practice to start with a word that describes the purpose of the main view and end with the words "ViewController" to reflect the type of class declared inside the file (for this example, we called it *SecondViewController*). The next option is the superclass of our subclass. For Scenes with a single view this is the **UIViewController** class. The last two options are usually left as is; one determines if the process will create a new Scene (this is not necessary because we have already created the Scene in the Storyboard), and the other determines the language Xcode is going to use to create the file (the last language we use is always shown by default). After the options are selected, the file is created and included with the rest of the files in the Navigator Area.

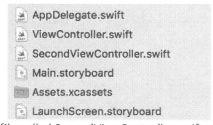

Figure 13-5: New file called SecondViewController.swift added to the project

At this point, we have the Scene in the Storyboard and the file with its view controller, but they are not connected yet. Xcode does not assign the new file to its Scene automatically; we have to do it ourselves from the Identity Inspector panel. This is one of the configuration panels available in the Utilities Area when the Scene is selected. To open the panel, select the Scene and click on the third button at the top of the Utilities Area (circled in Figure 13-6).

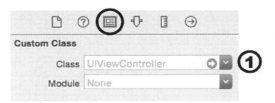

Figure 13-6: Identity Inspector panel

The subclass that controls the view is specified by the first option (Figure 13-6, number 1). We can write the name of the class or select it from the list. Figure 13-6 illustrates what the panel looks like after we select the **SecondViewController** class.

Figure 13-7: Class assigned to the Scene

Now, the second view has its own view controller and we are ready to go. The procedure to create the interface for each view and connect it to our code is the same as before. We have to drag the elements we want to add to each view and then connect them to the code in their respective view controllers (**ViewController** for the view on the left and **SecondViewController** for the view on the right). Xcode simplifies this process by showing the corresponding view controller file in the Assistant Editor area when a Scene is selected in the Storyboard (see Figure 5-23).

 Do It Yourself: Create the subclass for the Scene added before and call it SecondViewController. Select the Scene by clicking on the bar at the top or on the icon that represents the view controller (Figure 5-13). Open the Identity Inspector panel in the Utilities Area (Figure 13-6). Assign the subclass you have just created to the Scene (Figure 13-6, number 1). Open the Assistant Editor (Figure 5-23) and click on the Scenes in the Storyboard to select them. If their corresponding view controller classes are not shown in the Assistant Editor, check that the option at the top is set to Automatic (Figure 5-23, number 1).

Segues

Once we have all the Scenes necessary for our interface we have to connect them together. For this purpose, the UIKit framework introduces the **UIStoryboardSegue** class. From this class, we can create objects called *Segues* that are in charge of connecting the Scenes and transitioning from one view to another. There are different types of Segues available.

Show—This Segue produces a transition from right to left. The view controllers are stored in an array to keep track of the sequence.

Show Detail—This Segue shows a detail view (a second view in the same screen) when there is enough space available (e.g., in iPads), or replaces the current view by the new one like a Show Segue when the space is limited (e.g., in iPhones).

Present Modally—This Segue presents the next view over the current view. The type of transition is set by the **modalTransitionStyle** property of the view controller that triggers the transition. The possible values are **coverVertical** (the view appears from the bottom), **flipHorizontal** (the views are turned around), **crossDissolve** (the views are dissolved), and **partialCurl** (the old view is curled up to reveal the new one).

Present As Popover—This Segue presents a main view as a popover (see Chapter 16).

Custom—This Segue allows developers to provide a custom transition.

Segues are fully integrated to the Storyboard and are created by control-dragging lines between Scenes, as we do to create constraints or Actions and Outlets, but because they are triggered by user interaction they can be created from one Scene to another or from a specific element, such as a button, depending on how we want the user to be able to navigate. The following example uses a simple interface with a list of buttons inside the initial Scene (the Scene pointed by the arrow) and an Image View inside the second Scene. The purpose is to provide buttons in one view the user can tap to select a picture and then transition to a second view that shows the selected picture. The second view also includes a Slider to rate the image, as illustrated in Figure 13-8.

Figure 13-8: Interface with two Scenes

If we run the app at this point, only the initial view is shown on the screen and the buttons do not perform any action. To let the user transition from one view to another, we have to create a Segue from the button Show Husky to the second view. The process is illustrated in Figure 13-9.

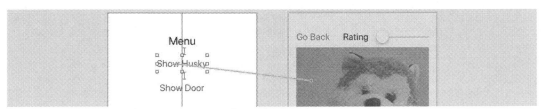

Figure 13-9: Segue from the button to the second view

The line has to be control-dragged from the button to the second view. When the mouse's button is released, Xcode opens a menu to select the type of Segue we want to create.

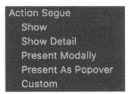

Figure 13-10: Popup menu listing the type of Segues available

Independent view controllers like those implemented in this example can only be connected using a Modal Segue (Present Modally) or a popover Segue (Present As Popover). The Modal Segue opens the destination view over the current view, and the popup Segue shows the destination view partially covering the current view (depending on the space available). What

Segue to implement depends on the requirements of our application and the type of information contained in the view to be presented. For this example, we decided to use the Modal Segue (also known as Presentation or Present Modally).

Figure 13-11: Segue in the Storyboard

After adding the Segue, the Storyboard shows two arrows, one pointing to the view on the left and another connecting both views. The single arrow on the left indicates what view is going to be shown first as soon as the app is executed, and the arrow in the middle is pointing to the view that is going to be shown when the Segue is triggered (the Show Husky button is pressed). The arrows illustrate the path or possible paths the user can follow while interacting with our application. This is the main function of the Storyboard: to help us create a story.

 Do It Yourself: Add the label "Menu" and two buttons called Show Husky and Show Door to the initial view. Add a button called Go Back, the label "Rating", a Slider, and an Image View to the second view. From the Utilities Area, set the value of the Slider to 0, the minimum to 0 as well, and the maximum to 5. Add the image husky.png to the Assets Catalog and assign it to the Image View. Apply all the necessary constraints to get an interface similar to Figure 13-8 (remember to assign higher Content Hugging and Content Compression priorities if necessary). Control-drag a line from the button Show Husky to the second view (Figure 13-9). Select the Segue Present Modally. Run your app and press the Show Husky button. You should see the second view transitioning from the bottom of the screen to the top.

 The Basics: Segues may be deleted and created again to modify the path, and you can also drag the arrow that indicates the initial Scene to another Scene if later you decide the application should start somewhere else.

The Modal Segue was introduced with the purpose to connect single views and present additional information, but still offers a few options for configuration. Among those options is a list of transitions we can choose from. The transition by default is called *Cover Vertical* and it scrolls the destination view from bottom to top, but we can change it from the Utilities Area. When we click on a Segue in the Storyboard (the arrow between views), the Utilities Area presents a configuration panel to edit the Segue.

Figure 13-12: Configuring the Segue

From this panel, we can specify a name to reference the Segue from code, set our own custom Segue, or select the type of transition we want. The picture on the right shows the Transition menu with the types available. Selecting any of these options changes the way the destination view is presented.

 IMPORTANT: Custom transitions may be defined by creating a subclass of the **UIStoryboardSegue** class and overwriting its **perform()** method. The topic is beyond the scope of this book. For more information, visit our website and follow the links for this chapter.

 The Basics: By default, modal views are presented full screen, but Segues include an option called Presentation to select other types of presentation (Figure 13-12). This is particularly useful for iPads. We will study how to create applications for iPads in Chapter 16.

Unwind Segues

Segues allow us to move forward in the Storyboard, from the view the users are seeing on the screen to the view they want to see. The process to move backwards requires a special kind of Segue called *Unwind Segue* that is created following a few unconventional steps. We have to write an Action on the view that triggers the Segue and then connect to that Action the element in the second view that triggers the Unwind Segue. This is because the view controller responsible for transitioning back to the previous view is the one that presented the destination view. In our example, this is the **ViewController** class.

```
import UIKit

class ViewController: UIViewController {
    @IBAction func goBack(_ segue: UIStoryboardSegue) {
    }
}
```

Listing 13-1: Adding the Action for the Unwind Segue

Actions are methods that are executed after the user interacts with an element on the interface. So far, we have taken advantage of Storyboard features to generate the code in our class, but we can also write the Action ourselves and then create the connection. This is the procedure we have to follow to create the Unwind Segue. Listing 13-1 shows an example of how to write the Action in the view controller that presents the destination view. The method can have any name we want but it has to include a parameter of type **UIStoryboardSegue** to provide access to the view controller that is been removed. Once this code is ready, we have to connect the element in the destination view to the Action. This is done by control-dragging a line from the element to an icon at the top of the Scene called *Exit*.

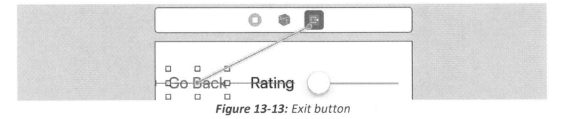

Figure 13-13: Exit button

In Figure 13-13 the Go Back button inside the second view is connected to the Exit icon. When the mouse is released, a menu shows the Actions available in the **ViewController** class.

Navigation

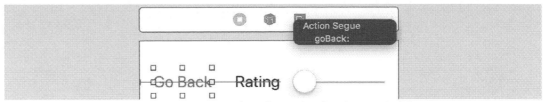

Figure 13-14: Menu to select the Action for the Unwind Segue

Once the `goBack()` Action is selected from this menu, the Go Back button is connected to the Action defined before in the `ViewController` class and the process is over. The system will remove the view every time the button is pressed.

Do It Yourself: Write the Action in your `ViewController` class as shown in Listing 13-1. Control-drag a line from the Go Back button in the second view to the Exit button, as shown in Figure 13-13. Select the `goBack()` action from the menu (Figure 13-14). Run the application and press the Show Husky button to present the second view on the screen. Press the Go Back button to go back to the initial view.

The Action in our `ViewController` class was declared with no statements. This is enough to perform the Unwind Segue, but we can take advantage of this method and its parameter to get information about the view controllers that participate in the transition. The `UIStoryboardSegue` class includes the following properties for this purpose.

source—This property returns a reference to the view controller that is displayed at the beginning of the transition. The value returned is a generic `UIViewController` object that we have to cast to the corresponding type.

destination—This property returns a reference to the view controller that is displayed at the end of the transition. The value returned is a generic `UIViewController` object that we have to cast to the corresponding type.

identifier—This property returns the string we used in Interface Builder to identify the Segue (see Figure 13-12). Using this property, we are able to know what Segue was triggered and get information about the view that is going to be shown on the screen.

The **source** and **destination** properties are required depending on the process. If we want to access the view controller that is going to be removed, we read the **source** property (the origin of the transition), but if we want to access the view controller that is going to be presented on the screen, we access the **destination** (the destination of the transition). To illustrate this process, we are going to add some code to the `SecondViewController` class. This code processes the input from the Slider and adds a property we can read when the Unwind Segue is triggered.

```
import UIKit

class SecondViewController: UIViewController {
    @IBOutlet weak var sliderRating: UISlider!
    var rating: Int = 0

    override func viewDidLoad() {
        super.viewDidLoad()
        sliderRating.value = Float(rating)
    }
    @IBAction func changeRating(_ sender: UISlider) {
        let value = round(sender.value)
```

```
        sliderRating.value = value
        rating = Int(value)
    }
}
```

Listing 13-2: Processing changes in the Slider

The code of Listing 13-2 adds an integer property called **rating** to the **SecondViewController** class to keep track of the rating set by the user. The code also includes an Outlet for the Slider to set its initial value equal to the value of **rating** and an Action to update the value of this property every time the Slider is moved (see **UISlider** in Chapter 4 and Chapter 5, Listing 5-11).

Because the Slider works with consecutive floating-point values and our rating is established by integers between 0 and 5, before to assign the selected value to the **rating** property we have to round the number to the nearest integer with the **round()** function and assign it back to the Slider to reflect the right rating on the screen. This makes the indicator jump from one integer to another, helping the user identify the rating that wants to assign to the picture.

Now that we have the **rating** property, we can read it from the unwind Action in the **ViewController** class.

```
import UIKit

class ViewController: UIViewController {
    var ratingHusky: Int = 0

    @IBAction func goBack(_ segue: UIStoryboardSegue) {
        let controller = segue.source as! SecondViewController
        ratingHusky = controller.rating
    }
}
```

Listing 13-3: Reading properties from the source

Reading the **source** property of the **UIStoryboardSegue** object received by the Action, we can get a reference to the view controller that is being removed and access its properties. In our example, this is the **SecondViewController** class. We get this value, cast it as **SecondViewController**, and store it in the **controller** constant. Now that we have access to the view controller of the second view, we read its **rating** property and store its value in the **ratingHusky** property of the **ViewController** class. Copying the value to a property in the **ViewController** object is necessary because the **SecondViewController** object and all of its properties are destroyed as soon as the view is removed.

This is the first part of the process; we let the user select a rating and when it moves back to the menu, we preserve the selected value in the **ratingHusky** property. If we run the application at this moment and move the Slider to specify a rating, once we go back to the initial view and tap the Show Husky button a second time, the Slider is again in its initial position. This is because the value of the Slider is always set as the value of the **rating** property when the view is loaded. To get the Slider to show the value previously selected, we have to send the value of the **ratingHusky** property in the **ViewController** object back to the **SecondViewController** object every time the Show Husky button is pressed. The **UIViewController** class provides the following methods for this purpose.

prepare(for: UIStoryboardSegue, **sender:** Any?)—This method is called by the system in the view controller object when a Segue is triggered and before the transition is initiated. We can overwrite this method in our view controller to access the destination view controller and modify its properties.

performSegue(withIdentifier: String, **sender:** Any?)—This method triggers a Segue identified with the string specified by the **withIdentifier** attribute. The **sender** attribute is the object that triggers the Segue (usually declared as `self`).

The method we need to implement to send the information to the second view controller is `prepare()`. This is one of those methods that are called by the system in the view controller and can be overwritten to perform custom tasks. In this case, we can overwrite it to access the view controller that is going to be opened and modify its properties before its view is shown on the screen. The following example expands the code in our **ViewController** class to update the value of the `rating` property in the **SecondViewController** class and get the Slider to show the right value.

```
import UIKit

class ViewController: UIViewController {
    var ratingHusky: Int = 0

    @IBAction func goBack(_ segue: UIStoryboardSegue) {
        let controller = segue.source as! SecondViewController
        ratingHusky = controller.rating
    }
    override func prepare(for segue: UIStoryboardSegue, sender: Any?) {
        let controller = segue.destination as! SecondViewController
        controller.rating = ratingHusky
    }
}
```

Listing 13-4: Sending values to the second view controller before its view is loaded

Now the application is complete. The `prepare()` method updates the value of the `rating` property with the value of the `ratingHusky` property before the second view is shown on the screen, and this value is used by the **SecondViewController** object to update the Slider as soon as the view is loaded. When the user presses the Go Back button, the `goBack()` Action is executed in the **ViewController** class and the process is reversed: the `ratingHusky` property is updated with the current value of the `rating` property. In consequence, the rating set by the user is always preserved in the `ratingHusky` property inside the view controller of the initial Scene and used to update the Slider every time the second view is opened.

 Do It Yourself: Copy the code of Listing 13-4 in your **ViewController** class. Create an Outlet called `sliderRating` and an Action called `changeRating()` for the Slider in the second view. Complete the **SecondViewController** class with the code of Listing 13-2. Run the application. The Slider should always reflect the rating previously selected.

 IMPORTANT: Never try to access Outlets of one view controller from another. Always transfer data through normal properties because there is no guarantee that the Outlets will be connected to the objects in the Storyboard until the view is fully loaded. If you have to modify an element directly, declare a property, assign the new value to that property, and then assign the value of that property to the Outlet from any of the methods studied before, such as `viewDidLoad()` or `viewDidAppear()`, as we did in Listing 13-2.

The same procedure can be applied to the second button of the menu to let the user select another image. All we need to do is to add a new Scene to the Storyboard and connect it to the Show Door button using another Modal Segue, as shown in Figure 13-15.

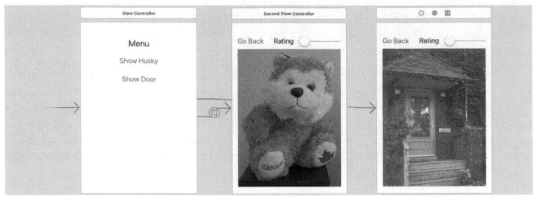

Figure 13-15: Interface with three views

The process to add the Scene is the same as before. We drag the View Controller option to the Storyboard and build the interface. As well as the second view, this view also needs its own view controller. For this example, we called it **ThirdViewController**. Because we use the same types of elements and process the same information, the code for this view controller is the same defined for the **SecondViewController** class in Listing 13-2, including the Outlet and Action for the Slider. What changes is how the **ViewController** class manages the information that is coming from and going to these view controllers. Now we have two Segues, one that opens the view with the husky and another that opens the view with the door, and therefore the code in the **ViewController** class has to recognize the Segue that is being triggered to know how to proceed. This is the reason why the Segue's configuration panel includes a field called *Identifier* (Figure 13-12). The string introduced in this field is assigned to the **identifier** property of the **UIStoryboardSegue** object and that is how we know what Segue was triggered.

As we explained before, to change the Segue's configuration we have to select it and open the Utilities Area (Figure 13-12). For normal Segues it is easy, we just have to select them from the Storyboard and modify their values from the Attributes Inspector panel, but the only way to select an Unwind Segue is from the Document Outline panel. The items that represent the Unwind Segues in this panel are preceded by a small arrow, as illustrated in Figure 13-16 (number 1).

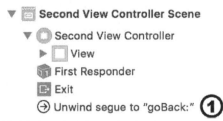

Figure 13-16: Unwind Segue in the Document Outline panel

For our example, we identified the Segues that point to each view with the strings "showHusky" and "showDoor", and the Unwind Segues with the strings "removeHusky" and "removeDoor", respectively. Once we have all the Segues identified, our **ViewController** class can check their values and modify the right properties. The next example shows a possible implementation.

```
import UIKit

class ViewController: UIViewController {
    var ratingHusky: Int = 0
    var ratingDoor: Int = 0
```

```swift
@IBAction func goBack(_ segue: UIStoryboardSegue) {
    if segue.identifier == "removeHusky" {
        let controller = segue.source as! SecondViewController
        ratingHusky = controller.rating
    } else if segue.identifier == "removeDoor" {
        let controller = segue.source as! ThirdViewController
        ratingDoor = controller.rating
    }
}
override func prepare(for segue: UIStoryboardSegue, sender: Any?) {
    if segue.identifier == "showHusky" {
        let controller = segue.destination as! SecondViewController
        controller.rating = ratingHusky
    } else if segue.identifier == "showDoor" {
        let controller = segue.destination as! ThirdViewController
        controller.rating = ratingDoor
    }
}
}
```

Listing 13-5: Processing values according to the Segue

The **prepare()** method is executed every time a normal Segue is triggered. The method in our example compares the value of the **identifier** property of the **segue** object with the strings "showHusky" and "showDoor". If the value is equal to "showHusky", it gets the reference to the **SecondViewController** object and updates the value of its **rating** property with the value of the **ratingHusky** property. If, on the other hand, the value of **identifier** is equal to "showDoor", it gets the reference to the **ThirdViewController** object and updates its **rating** property with the value of the **ratingDoor** property. A similar control is performed for the **goBack** action, although this time we have to check the identifiers for the Unwind Segues ("removeHusky" and "removeDoor").

 Do It Yourself: Add a new Scene to the Storyboard and recreate the same interface of the second view but with the image of the door (you can copy and paste the elements from one view to another). Add a Segue of type Present Modally from the Show Door button to the new Scene. Control-drag a line from the Go Back button to the Exit icon to create the Unwind Segue for the third view. Create a file with a subclass of **UIViewController** called **ThirdViewController** and assign it to the new Scene. Create an Outlet called **sliderRating** and an Action called **changeRating** for the Slider and complete the code of the **ThirdViewController** class with the code of Listing 13-2. Select the Segues in the Storyboard and assign the identifiers "showHusky" and "showDoor", respectively (Figure 13-12). Select the Unwind Segues from the Document Outline panel and assign the identifiers "removeHusky" and "removeDoor", respectively (Figure 13-16). Copy the code of Listing 13-5 in the **ViewController** class. Run the application. The Sliders should always reflect the rating previously selected for each image.

Segues in Code

Of course, implementing the previous technique we could, in theory, build a fully functional interface and a whole application. But designing an application of this kind that contemplates every possible feedback from the user and new information available would be impossible (in our example, we would have to add buttons and views for every new image available). Real applications demand some sort of process in which the content of a view is generated automatically according to the information requested by the user. In this scenario, a view provides an updated list of available options and a single Segue connects this view with the view in charge of presenting the information for every option. The Segue is therefore not triggered by a specific element but from code calling the **performSegue()** method introduced before.

Depending on the amount of values available, the list may be presented with a table, as we will see in Chapter 14, or with simpler controls like a picker. The following example implements a Picker View to present a predefined list of pictures the user can choose from.

Figure 13-17: *Interface to process every option available*

The initial view for this new application contains a Picker View and a button. When the button is pressed, the code for this view controller executes the **performSegue()** method to trigger a Segue that transitions to the second view. There are different ways to create this Segue. The simplest is to control-drag a line from the icon that represents the view controller on the Scene's bar to the second view, as shown in Figure 13-18.

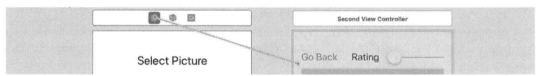

Figure 13-18: *Creating a Segue from one Scene to another*

 IMPORTANT: Segues that are not associated with an element must always have an identifier, so they can be referenced from code (see Figure 13-12).

No matter how the Segue is triggered, the system always calls the **prepare()** method before performing the transition. In the next example, we use this method to report to the second view the item selected on the picker. With this information, the second view loads the corresponding image and sets the Slider to display its rating. The following is the code we need for the **ViewController** class.

```
import UIKit

class ViewController: UIViewController, UIPickerViewDelegate,
UIPickerViewDataSource {
   @IBOutlet weak var pickerPictures: UIPickerView!
   var picturesList: [String]!
   var ratings: [Int]!
   var selectedPicture: Int!

   override func viewDidLoad() {
      super.viewDidLoad()
      pickerPictures.delegate = self
      pickerPictures.dataSource = self
      picturesList = ["Husky", "Door"]
      ratings = [0, 0]
      selectedPicture = 0
   }
```

```
    func numberOfComponents(in pickerView: UIPickerView) -> Int {
        return 1
    }
    func pickerView(_ pickerView: UIPickerView, numberOfRowsInComponent
component: Int) -> Int {
        return picturesList.count
    }
    func pickerView(_ pickerView: UIPickerView, titleForRow row: Int,
forComponent component: Int) -> String? {
        return picturesList[row]
    }
    @IBAction func getPicture(_ sender: UIButton) {
        selectedPicture = pickerPictures.selectedRow(inComponent: 0)
        performSegue(withIdentifier: "showPicture", sender: self)
    }
    override func prepare(for segue: UIStoryboardSegue, sender: Any?) {
        let controller = segue.destination as! SecondViewController
        controller.rating = ratings[selectedPicture]
        controller.picture = picturesList[selectedPicture]
    }
    @IBAction func goBack(_ segue: UIStoryboardSegue) {
        let controller = segue.source as! SecondViewController
        ratings[selectedPicture] = controller.rating
    }
}
```

Listing 13-6: Processing the options available

Most of the code of Listing 13-6 is composed of the delegate methods that configure the picker (see **UIPickerView** in Chapter 9), but we also have the **goBack()** action implemented before for the Unwind Segue and the **prepare()** method to send the information to the second view when the Segue created in Figure 13-18 is triggered. To store the data, we have created three properties: **picturesList**, **ratings**, and **selectedPicture**. The **picturesList** property is an array of strings to store the names of the pictures available, the **ratings** property is an array of integers to store the rating for each picture, and the **selectedPicture** property is a single integer that stores the index of the picture selected from the picker. This last property lets us keep track of the picture we are currently working with. When the **prepare()** method sends the information to the second view, it takes the values from the **picturesList** and **ratings** arrays corresponding to the index determined by the **selectedPicture** property. Likewise, when the **goBack()** method processes the rating set by the user, it stores its value in the position of the **ratings** array also corresponding to the **selectedPicture** property.

The interface includes the Show Picture button to select the picture. This button has been connected with an Action called **getPicture()** that gets the value selected in the picker, assigns it to the **selectedPicture** property, and then executes the **performSegue()** method to trigger the Segue and load the second view (the Segue was identified with the name "showPicture").

Unwind Segues can also be created from the view controller to the Exit button and then triggered by code. To create an Unwind Segue that is not connected to an element, we have to control-drag a line from the icon that represents the view controller at the top of the Scene to the Exit button, as shown in Figure 13-19.

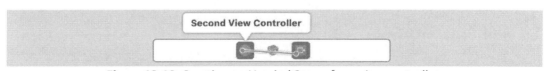

Figure 13-19: Creating an Unwind Segue for a view controller

The view controller for the second view now has to execute the **performSegue()** method to trigger the Unwind Segue and let the user go back to the previous screen. For this purpose, we have included an Action connected to the Go Back button in the **SecondViewController** class (the Unwind Segue was identified with the string "goBack").

```
import UIKit

class SecondViewController: UIViewController {
    @IBOutlet weak var sliderRating: UISlider!
    @IBOutlet weak var pictureView: UIImageView!
    var rating: Int = 0
    var picture: String!

    override func viewDidLoad() {
        super.viewDidLoad()
        sliderRating.value = Float(rating)
        pictureView.image = UIImage(named: picture.lowercased())
    }
    @IBAction func changeRating(_ sender: UISlider) {
        let value = round(sender.value)
        sliderRating.value = value
        rating = Int(value)
    }
    @IBAction func goBack(_ sender: UIButton) {
        performSegue(withIdentifier: "goBack", sender: self)
    }
}
```

Listing 13-7: *Showing the data*

Besides triggering the Unwind Segue, the code of Listing 13-7 also introduces other changes necessary to process the image selected in the initial view. The view controller includes an additional property to store the name of the image selected by the user and load its file. We called this property and the Outlet for the Image View **picture** and **pictureView**, respectively. These properties are used to load the file, create the **UIImage** object, and assign it to the Image View. Notice that the value of the **picture** property was lowercased to match the files' names.

 Do It Yourself: Create a new Single View Application project. Add a second view with a class called **SecondViewController**. Design the interface according to Figure 13-17. The initial view has to include a picker and a button, and the second view's interface is the same implemented for previous examples. Create a Present Modally Segue from the initial view to the second view, as shown in Figure 13-18. Assign the identifier "showPicture" to the Segue. Create an Unwind Segue for the second view as shown in Figure 13-19. Open the Document Outline panel, select this Segue and give it the identifier "goBack" from the Attributes Inspector panel. Copy the code of Listing 13-6 into the ViewController.swift file and the code of Listing 13-7 into the SecondViewController.swift file. Connect the Slider and the Image View to their respective Outlets, and the Slider and the Go Back button to their respective Actions. Run the application. You should be able to select the picture you want to see from the picker and change their ratings.

13.2 Navigation Controllers

The view controllers we used so far are called *Content View Controllers* because they are in charge of managing their own content. They are created from custom subclasses of the

UIViewController class and are focused on presenting and controlling a single main view and its subviews. For this reason, these view controllers are limited when it comes to replacing their own main view by another or providing the means to organize the interface. This is why the UIKit framework includes several subclasses of the **UIViewController** class that include their own functionality and introduce better alternatives to work with multiple views. The view controllers created from these classes are called *Container View Controllers* because they contain other view controllers and organize their views. The most widely used container is the Navigation Controller, created from the **UINavigationController** class. This class creates a container view controller that organizes the views in sequential order and provides the tools to navigate through the hierarchy.

Navigation Controller

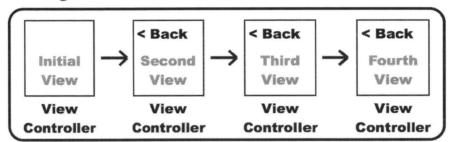

Figure 13-20: View controllers managed by a Navigation Controller

The views managed by a Navigation Controller are presented in sequence. The first view opens the second view, and then the second view opens the third view. When the user decides to go back, the sequence is reversed, the current view is removed, and the previous view is shown on the screen. To keep track of the view controllers in the sequence, the Navigation Controller stores a reference to each one of them in an array called *stack* and then puts or pulls view controllers from the stack every time their views must be presented or removed from the screen. The possible sequences are defined in the Storyboard, but the stack is generated in real time. If we define different paths, as illustrated in Figure 13-21 below, the Navigation Controller only stores in the stack the view controllers on the path the user decides to follow.

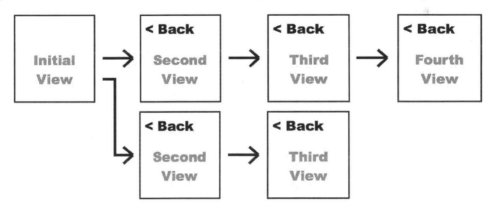

Figure 13-21: Navigation Controller with multiple paths

The difference between building a structure like this with a Navigation Controller rather than the single view controllers and Modal Segues we used before is that Navigation Controllers incorporate additional functionality that makes it easy for us to create a path for the user to navigate through. They use a Segue of type Show that transitions from right to left (or left to right when the view is being removed) reflecting on the screen the sequential order of the views in the stack. They also incorporate bars to identify each view and their predecessors, and properties and methods to control the navigation. The following are the most frequently used.

viewControllers—This property is an array that contains references to the view controllers currently managed by the `UINavigationController` object.

topViewController—This property returns the view controller at the top of the stack (usually the view controller displayed on the screen).

visibleViewController—This property returns the view controller currently shown on the screen. The view controller may belong to the Navigation Controller or to a view opened modally.

popViewController(animated: Bool)—This method removes the top view controller from the stack and makes the previous one active. The **animated** attribute indicates whether the transition will be animated or not.

pushViewController(UIViewController, **animated:** Bool)—This method adds to the stack the view controller referenced by the first attribute. The **animated** attribute indicates whether the transition will be animated or not.

popToRootViewController(animated: Bool)—This method removes all the view controllers from the stack except the initial view controller. The **animated** attribute indicates whether the transition will be animated or not.

Navigation Controllers in the Storyboard

There are two ways to add a Navigation Controller to the Storyboard. If we have already designed the interface, Xcode offers an option to embed the views we already have inside a Navigation Controller. We must select the view that we want to be the initial view for the Navigation Controller and then go to the Editor menu at the top of the screen, open the option Embed In, and then select Navigation Controller (Editor/Embed In/Navigation Controller). The other alternative is to drag the Navigation Controller option from the Object Library. This option creates the Navigation Controller along with its initial view. Figure 13-22 illustrates what the single view of a Single View Application project looks like after it is embedded in a Navigation Controller.

Figure 13-22: Initial view embedded in a Navigation Controller

The view on the left is an empty Scene that represents the Navigation Controller and the view on the right is our initial view. The arrow is now pointing to the Navigation Controller and a Segue connects this controller to the initial view. This Segue is called *Root View Controller* and has the purpose to indicate which is the first view the Navigation Controller has to display. When the app is executed, the system loads the Navigation Controller first and then searches for its root view controller and shows its view on the screen.

IMPORTANT: If you opt for the option to add the Navigation Controller from the Object Library, there is an additional step you have to follow. When the initial view is deleted and a new one is added to the Storyboard, the arrow pointing to the initial view disappears. To get back the arrow and indicate to the system which is the initial view in the Storyboard, you have to select the new Scene (in this case, the Navigation Controller), go to the Attributes Inspector panel, and activate the option *Is Initial View Controller*.

More views may be added to the interface as before, but instead of using the Present Modally Segue to connect the views, we have to create Segues of type Show. Figure 13-23, next, illustrates what we see when we add a second Scene and connect it using this Segue. The initial view includes a label with the text "Root View" and a button with the title "Open Second View". The button was connected to the second view with a Show Segue (the first option of the popup menu). When the user presses the button, the second view is shown on the screen transitioning from right to left.

Figure 13-23: *Navigation stack in the Storyboard*

Do It Yourself: Create a new Single View Application project. Select the Scene, open the Editor menu at the top of the screen, go to Embed In, and select the option Navigation Controller. The Storyboard should look like Figure 13-22. Drag the View Controller option from the Object Library to add another Scene to the Storyboard. Add a label and a button to the initial view and a label to the second view, as illustrated in Figure 13-23. Control-drag a line from the button in the initial view to the second view to create a Segue (Figure 13-9). Select the type Show for the Segue. Create a file with the view controller for the second view called SecondViewController.swift as we did before for previous examples (Figures 13-3, 13-4 and 13-7). Run the application and press the button to see the transition.

Navigation Bar

Besides the new type of Segue and transition, the Navigation Controller introduces a Navigation Bar at the top of every view it manages to help the user navigate. The bar is an object of the **UINavigationBar** class, which includes a few properties and methods for configuration.

barStyle—This property determines the style of the bar. It is an enumeration of type **UIBarStyle** with the values **default**, **black**, **blackOpaque**, and **blackTranslucent**.

barTintColor—This property sets or returns the color applied to the bar's background.

tintColor—This property sets or returns the color applied to the bar's items.

isTranslucent—This property set or returns a Boolean value that determines whether the Navigation Bar is translucent or not.

prefersLargeTitles—This property set or returns a Boolean value that determines whether the title should be displayed in a large format or not.

titleTextAttributes—This property sets or returns the attributes applied to the bar's title. It is a dictionary with the same values used to define the attributes for an `NSMutableAttributedString` object.

largeTitleTextAttributes—This property sets or returns the attributes applied to the large title. It is a dictionary with the same values used to define the attributes for an `NSMutableAttributedString` object.

backIndicatorImage—This property sets or returns the image shown beside the back button. The property works along with the `backIndicatorTransitionMaskImage` to define the new indicator.

setBackgroundImage(UIImage?, **for:** UIBarMetrics**)**—This method assigns an image to the bar's background. The **for** attribute is an enumeration of type `UIBarMetrics` that associates the image with the state of the bar. The possible values for this attribute are `default`, `defaultPrompt`, `compact`, and `compactPrompt`.

The `UINavigationController` class also includes specific properties and methods to access and configure the Navigation Bar.

navigationBar—This property returns a reference to the `UINavigationBar` object that represents the Navigation Bar created for the Navigation Controller.

hidesBarsOnTap—This property takes a Boolean value that indicates whether or not the bars should be hidden when the user taps on the screen.

hidesBarsOnSwipe—This property takes a Boolean value that indicates whether or not the bars should be hidden when the user swipes the finger on the screen.

hidesBarsWhenKeyboardAppears—This property takes a Boolean value that indicates whether or not the bars should be hidden when the keyboard is visible.

hidesBarsWhenVerticallyCompact—This property takes a Boolean value that indicates whether or not the bars should be hidden when the vertical Size Class is Compact.

isNavigationBarHidden—This property returns a Boolean value that indicates if the Navigation Bar is currently hidden.

setNavigationBarHidden(Bool, **animated:** Bool**)**—This method hides or shows the Navigation Bar. The first attribute indicates whether or not the bar will be hidden, and the **animated** attribute determines if the process is going to be animated.

 IMPORTANT: Navigation Bars and their content are positioned by the system at the top of the screen. They do not require constraints, but the rest of the elements in the interface may be pinned with constraints to the Safe Area to not overlap with the bar or the edge of the main view, depending on whether you want to let the content go behind the bar or not.

The Navigation Bar is automatically created by the `UINavigationController` object and stored in its `navigationBar` property, but the bar can be configured from different places in the code. One option is to create a subclass of the `UINavigationController` class (Figures 13-3 and 13-4) and assign it to the Navigation Controller in the Storyboard (Figures 13-6 and 13-7). This is the same procedure used to create the view controller classes for our view controllers, but instead of selecting the `UIViewController` class as the superclass we use the `UINavigationController` class instead.

```
import UIKit

class NavigationViewController: UINavigationController {
    override func viewDidLoad() {
        super.viewDidLoad()
        hidesBarsOnSwipe = true

        let bar = navigationBar
        bar.barTintColor = UIColor(red: 0.9, green: 0.9, blue: 1.0, alpha:
1)
    }
}
```

Listing 13-8: Configuring the Navigation Bar from a subclass of UINavigationController

After the custom class is created, we can configure its bar. The properties of the **UINavigationController** class are accessed directly from the class itself, but to modify the properties of the bar we have to get its reference from the **navigationBar** property. In Listing 13-8, we store this reference in the **bar** constant and then set the bar's background color.

 Do It Yourself: The examples of this section assume that you have created an interface similar to Figure 13-23 and the view controllers **ViewController** and **SecondViewController** were assigned to the initial view and the second view, respectively. Create a new file with a subclass of the **UINavigationController** class called **NavigationViewController**. Assign this new class to the Navigation Controller from the Identity Inspector panel (Figure 13-6). Complete the class with the code of Listing 13-8. Run the application. You should see the Navigation Bar in color violet. Swipe your finger on the screen to hide the bar.

The creation of a subclass of the **UINavigationController** class to configure the Navigation Bar is usually not necessary because the **UIViewController** class offers a property called **navigationController** to get a reference to the Navigation Controller the view controller belongs to. From this reference, we can read the **navigationBar** property of the Navigation Controller to access and configure the bar from any of the view controllers managed by the Navigation Controller. For example, we can do it from the **ViewController** class that controls the initial view.

```
import UIKit

class ViewController: UIViewController {
    override func viewDidLoad() {
        super.viewDidLoad()
        let nav = navigationController!
        nav.hidesBarsOnSwipe = true
        let bar = nav.navigationBar
        bar.barTintColor = UIColor(red: 0.9, green: 0.9, blue: 1.0, alpha:
1)
    }
}
```

Listing 13-9: Configuring the Navigation Bar from the view controller of the initial view

The process is the same as before, but we have to get the reference to the Navigation Controller object from the **navigationController** property first and then read its **navigationBar** property to access the bar.

Do It Yourself: Remove the code from the `NavigationViewController` class and update the `ViewController` class with the code of Listing 13-9. Run the application. Again, you should see a violet Navigation Bar on the screen.

The previous two examples configure the Navigation Bar of a specific Navigation Controller, but our interface may contain several of them. If we want all the Navigation Controllers to share the same configuration, we can take advantage of a method accessible from the `UINavigationBar` class called `appearance()`. This method is defined in the `UIAppearance` protocol and the `UINavigationBar` class conforms to this protocol. From the reference returned by the `appearance()` method, we can change the class' configuration and then every object created from the `UINavigationBar` class will have by default that configuration. Because this procedure modifies the `UINavigationBar` class, we have to perform it before any bar is created. And the best place to do it is from the application's delegate (the AppDelegate.swift file).

```
import UIKit

@UIApplicationMain
class AppDelegate: UIResponder, UIApplicationDelegate {
   var window: UIWindow?

   func application(_ application: UIApplication,
didFinishLaunchingWithOptions launchOptions:
[UIApplication.LaunchOptionsKey : Any]? = nil) -> Bool {
      let bar = UINavigationBar.appearance()
      bar.barTintColor = UIColor(red: 0.9, green: 0.9, blue: 1.0, alpha: 1)
      return true
   }
}
```

Listing 13-10: Configuring all the Navigation Bars from the app's delegate

As we have seen in Chapter 5, any code we want to process right after the application is executed has to be written inside the `application(UIApplication, didFinish-LaunchingWithOptions:)` method of the `AppDelegate` class (see Listing 5-1). In this example, the `appearance()` method is executed first from the `UINavigationBar` class to get a reference to the properties of the Navigation Bar and then the bar is configured as always.

Do It Yourself: Remove the code from the `ViewController` class and update the `AppDelegate` class with the code of Listing 13-10. Run the application. Once more, you should see a violet Navigation Bar on the screen.

The `UIAppearance` protocol also includes a definition of the `appearance()` method that takes a `UITraitCollection` object to configure the Navigation Bars for a specific Trait Collection (see trait Collections in Chapter 6). The syntax is `appearance(for: UITraitCollection)`. The following example assigns a different color for the Navigation Bars when they are presented in Compact or Regular Size Classes.

```
import UIKit

@UIApplicationMain
class AppDelegate: UIResponder, UIApplicationDelegate {
   var window: UIWindow?

   func application(_ application: UIApplication,
didFinishLaunchingWithOptions launchOptions:
[UIApplication.LaunchOptionsKey : Any]? = nil) -> Bool {
```

Navigation

```
        let traitCompact = UITraitCollection(verticalSizeClass: .compact)
        let traitRegular = UITraitCollection(verticalSizeClass: .regular)

        let barCompact = UINavigationBar.appearance(for: traitCompact)
        barCompact.barTintColor = UIColor(red: 0.9, green: 0.9, blue: 1.0,
alpha: 1)
        let barRegular = UINavigationBar.appearance(for: traitRegular)
        barRegular.barTintColor = UIColor(red: 1.0, green: 0.9, blue: 0.9,
alpha: 1)
        return true
    }
}
```

Listing 13-11: Configuring Navigation Bars for a specific Trait Collection

Items

Navigation bars are just empty views, their content is not generated by the bar itself but by objects of the **UINavigationItem** class. In turn, these objects are containers for other views that represent things like the title of the view and buttons. Figure 13-24 illustrates how this structure is organized.

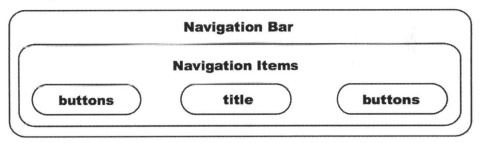

Figure 13-24: Elements of the Navigation Bar

Navigation Items are created automatically by the system along with the Navigation Bar, but the Storyboard only includes the one necessary for the initial view; we have to add the Navigation Items for the rest of the views from the Object Library.

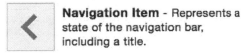

Figure 13-25: Navigation Item option in the Object Library

Navigation items may include a title, a prompt, and buttons on the sides. We can add all the buttons we need (taking into consideration the limited space available), but one button is generated automatically by the Navigation Controller to help the user navigate back to the previous view. By default, this button has the title Back (see Figure 13-24, right), but we can change it, along with the title and prompt, from the Attributes Inspector panel.

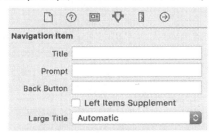

Figure 13-26: Configuring the Navigation Item

The values inserted in the first two fields (Title and Prompt) are shown in the current view, but the value of the third field corresponds to the title of the Back button the system is going to show in the next view. For example, if we select the Navigation Item of the initial view and insert the title "Menu" for the view and the title "Go Back" for the button, we will see something similar to Figure 13-27 below. The title for the view is shown at the center of the Navigation Bar and the Back button in the second view now says "Go Back".

Figure 13-27: Navigation Items in the simulator

As we mentioned, Xcode includes the Navigation Item for the initial view but not for the rest of the views. To add a title and buttons to the second view, we have to drag the Navigation Item option from the Object Library to its Navigation Bar (Figure 13-25). In the interface of Figure 13-27, we added a Navigation Item to the second view and assign the title "Second" to it.

 Do It Yourself: Drag a Navigation Item from the Object Library to the second view. Click on the Navigation Bar of each view and assign them a new title from the Attributes Inspector panel (Figure 13-26).

 IMPORTANT: If a title is provided but no value is defined for the Back button, the button adopts the title of the view it is pointing to (the Back button in our example would have the title "Menu").

Besides the Back button, we can also add custom buttons to the Navigation Bar. These are not regular buttons; they are created from the **UIBarButtonItem** class. The option in the Object Library is called Bar Button Item.

Item	**Bar Button Item** - Represents an item on a UIToolbar or UINavigationItem object.

Figure 13-28: Bar Button Item option in the Object Library

The bar buttons may be added to the left or the right side of the bar, but if we add it to the left in a view that is not the initial view, we have to consider that the button will replace the Back button. Figure 13-29 shows the interface of our example after a Bar Button Item was dragged to the right side of the Navigation Bar in the initial view.

Figure 13-29: Bar Button Item in the Navigation Bar

The title of the button by default is "Item", but we can change it from the Attributes Inspector panel. From this panel, we can also assign a design to the button, custom images for portrait and landscape modes, and a color (the original colors of the images are ignored). Figure 13-30 shows what we see when the Camera option of the System Item property is selected.

Navigation

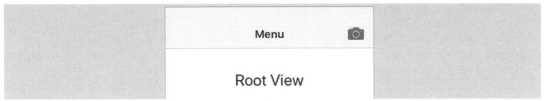

Figure 13-30: *Predefined Bar Button Item*

Bar buttons are created from the **UIBarButtonItem** class instead of the **UIButton** class because they were specifically designed to fit in the limited space of a Navigation Bar or a Toolbar (studied next), but we can connect them to Outlets or Actions in the View Controller as we do with any other button.

Of course, the items of a **UINavigationItem** object may be modified from code. The **UIViewController** class offers a property called **navigationItem** to access the object and its properties. The following are the most frequently used.

title—This property sets or returns the title. It is an optional of type **String**.

prompt—This property sets or returns the prompt. It is an optional of type **String**.

largeTitleDisplayMode—This property sets or returns a value of an enumeration called **LargeTitleDisplayMode** included in the **UINavigationItem** class that determines whether the Navigation Bar is going to show large titles or not. The values available are **automatic** (it is determined by the system depending on the previous view), **always**, and **never**.

backBarButtonItem—This property sets the Back button for the view. It is an optional of type **UIBarButtonItem**.

hidesBackButton—This property is a Boolean value that determines whether or not the Back button is shown. The property must be defined in the view that shows the button.

leftBarButtonItems—This property is an array of **UIBarButtonItem** objects that defines the bar buttons for the left side of the bar.

rightBarButtonItems—This property is an array of **UIBarButtonItem** objects that defines the bar buttons for the right side of the bar.

leftItemsSupplementBackButton—This property is a Boolean value that determines whether the Back button is shown along with the items on the left side of the bar or not. By default, the Back button is not shown when there are custom buttons in its place. We can change this behaviour by setting this property to **true**.

The following example defines the view's title and the title for the Back button from code. The view's title is assigned directly to the **title** property of the **UINavigationItem** object, but there is no property for the title of the Back button; we have to create a new **UIBarButtonItem** object with the title we want and use it to replace the original.

```
import UIKit

class ViewController: UIViewController {
    override func viewDidLoad() {
        super.viewDidLoad()

        let item = navigationItem
        item.title = "First View"
```

```
    let button = UIBarButtonItem()
    button.title = "Close"
    item.backBarButtonItem = button
    }
}
```

Listing 13-12: Configuring the Navigation Item from code

In Listing 13-12, we get the reference to the Navigation Item from the `navigationItem` property of the view controller, define the view's title, and then create the `UIBarButtonItem` object to replace the Back button. The `UIBarButtonItem` class is a subclass of the `UIBarItem` class, which provides properties and methods to configure the buttons. The following are the most frequently used.

title—This property sets or returns the button's title. It is an optional of type `String`.

image—This property sets or returns the image for the button. It is an optional of type `UIImage`.

landscapeImagePhone—This property sets or returns the image for the button that is going to be shown when the device is in landscape mode. It is an optional of type `UIImage`.

tag—This property sets or returns the button's tag value. It is of type `Int`.

In the last example, we used the `title` property to define the button's title. At the end, the button is assigned to the `backBarButtonItem` property of the Navigation Item, effectively replacing the original button by this one. Now, every time we open the second view, the button says "Close".

The button assigned to the `backBarButtonItem` property replaces the Back button and therefore only requires a value for its `title` property (the action to return to the previous view is assigned automatically by the system), but if we want to create custom bar buttons from code, we have to provide more information, such as the method they are going to execute and where that method is located (the target/action mechanism introduced by the `UIControl` class studied in Chapter 4). The `UIBarButtonItem` class includes a few initializers to provide this information.

UIBarButtonItem(barButtonSystemItem: SystemItem, **target:** Any?, **action:** Selector?)—This initializer creates a system button with the target and action defined by its attributes. The first attribute determines the type of button we want to create. It is an enumeration called `SystemItem` included in the `UIBarButtonItem` class. The values available are `done`, `cancel`, `edit`, `save`, `add`, `flexibleSpace`, `fixedSpace`, `compose`, `reply`, `action`, `organize`, `bookmarks`, `search`, `refresh`, `stop`, `camera`, `trash`, `play`, `pause`, `rewind`, `fastForward`, `undo`, `redo`, and `pageCurl`. The `target` and `action` attributes define the target and action, respectively.

UIBarButtonItem(title: String?, **style:** Style, **target:** Any?, **action:** Selector?)— This initializer creates a custom button with the title, target, and action defined by its attributes. The **style** attribute is an enumeration called `Style` included in the `UIBarButtonItem` class. The values available are `plain` (normal button) and `done`. The **target** and **action** attributes define the target and action, respectively.

UIBarButtonItem(image: UIImage?, **landscapeImagePhone:** UIImage?, **style:** Style, **target:** Any?, **action:** Selector?)—This initializer creates a custom button with images for the portrait and landscape mode, and the target and action defined by its attributes. The **style** attribute is an enumeration called `Style` included in the `UIBarButtonItem` class. The values available are `plain` (normal button) and `done`. The **target** and **action** attributes define the target and action, respectively.

The Basics: The `flexibleSpace` and `fixedSpace` values available for system buttons generate empty space to separate the rest of the buttons. These options are also available in the Object Library.

Besides these initializers, we can also use an empty initializer, as we did in Listing 13-12, and define the values later from the properties provided by the class.

style—This property sets the style of the button. It is an enumeration called `Style` included in the `UIBarButtonItem` class. The values available are `plain` (normal button) and `done`.

target—This property sets the target of the action.

action—This property selects the method to be executed when the button is pressed.

The following example implements a `UIBarButtonItem` initializer to add a button on the right side of the bar that adapts to portrait and landscape modes. We also show how to change the colors of the items, and how to apply attributes to the title.

```
import UIKit

class ViewController: UIViewController {
    override func viewDidLoad() {
        super.viewDidLoad()

        let nav = navigationController!
        nav.hidesBarsOnSwipe = true
        let bar = nav.navigationBar
        bar.tintColor = UIColor.black

        let titleFont = UIFont(name: "Verdana-Bold", size: 25.0)
        let color = UIColor.cyan
        let shadow = NSShadow()
        shadow.shadowColor = UIColor.black
        shadow.shadowOffset = CGSize(width: 2, height: 2)

        let attributes = [NSAttributedString.Key.font: titleFont!,
NSAttributedString.Key.foregroundColor: color,
NSAttributedString.Key.shadow: shadow]
        bar.titleTextAttributes = attributes

        let item = navigationItem
        item.title = "Menu"

        let imagePortrait = UIImage(named: "buttonplus")
        let imageLandscape = UIImage(named: "buttonpluslandscape")
        let rightButton = UIBarButtonItem(image: imagePortrait,
landscapeImagePhone: imageLandscape, style: .plain, target: self, action:
#selector(printMessage))
        item.rightBarButtonItems = [rightButton]
    }
    @objc func printMessage() {
        print("Message")
    }
}
```

Listing 13-13: Configuring the Navigation Bar and its items from code

The code of Listing 13-13 defines a few properties and methods of the Navigation Bar we did not use before, such as the `tintColor` property to give a new color to the buttons, and the `titleTextAttributes` property to assign attributes to the bar's title. The latter implements a procedure similar to the one we used before to create attributed text for `NSMutableAttributedString` objects (see Chapter 4). First, we declare the color of the items with the `tintColor` property. Then, we define the values for the attributes, including a `UIFont` object, a color, and a `NSShadow` object for the shadow, create the attributes dictionary, and assign it to the `titleTextAttributes` property of the bar to style the text. And finally, a button is created with two images, one for portrait and another for landscape mode. The result is shown in Figure 13-31.

Figure 13-31: Navigation Bar with a custom style

 Do It Yourself: Erase the button of the camera added before if necessary. Download the buttonplus.png and buttonpluslandscape.png images from our website and add them to the Assets Catalog. Update the `ViewController` class with the code of Listing 13-13. Run the application. You should see something similar to Figure 13-31.

 IMPORTANT: If a Navigation Item does not exist, the system creates one automatically when the `navigationItem` property is accessed for the first time, so you don't have to add the object as you do in the Storyboard.

Navigation Bars offer two formats to display the titles: small and large. Small titles are shown by default, as illustrated by the previous examples, but we can specify our preference using the `prefersLargeTitles` property provided by the `UINavigationBar` class. The following example adds a new statement to our `NavigationViewController` class to style the Navigation Bar with large titles.

```
import UIKit

class NavigationViewController: UINavigationController {
    override func viewDidLoad() {
        super.viewDidLoad()
        navigationBar.prefersLargeTitles = true
    }
}
```

Listing 13-14: Showing large titles

After the property is set to `true`, the Navigation Bars show large titles, as illustrated bellow.

Figure 13-32: Large titles

The option, along with the rest of the properties, is also available from the Attributes Inspector panel when we select the Navigation Bar in the Navigation View Controller.

Navigation

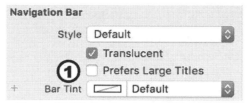

Figure 13-33: Prefers Large Titles option

The **prefersLargeTitles** property activates large titles for every view in the navigation stack, but the **UINavigationItem** class offers the **largeTitleDisplayMode** property to change this behaviour. If we do not want to show large titles on a specific view, we can set this property in the navigation item of the corresponding view controller. For example, we can deactivate large titles in the second view of our example by assigning the value **never** to this property from the **SecondViewController** class.

```
import UIKit

class SecondViewController: UIViewController {
   override func viewDidLoad() {
      super.viewDidLoad()
      navigationItem.largeTitleDisplayMode = .never
   }
}
```

Listing 13-15: Deactivating large titles

Now, the initial view shows large titles, but the second view displays the standard title with a small font.

Figure 13-34: Large and small titles

Tool Bar

Besides the Navigation Bar, UIKit includes another class called **UIToolbar** to add an additional bar at the bottom of the view. Figure 13-35 illustrates the option available in the Object Library.

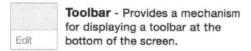

Toolbar - Provides a mechanism for displaying a toolbar at the bottom of the screen.

Figure 13-35: Toolbar option in the Object Library

Toolbars do not require Navigation Items, but they work with **UIBarButtonItem** objects to include buttons. The buttons are added from the Object Library as before and configured from the Utilities Area with the same properties we use for the buttons of a Navigation Bar.

A Toolbar is added from Interface Builder to the main view that requires it. The **UIViewController** class offers the following property and method to manage its buttons.

toolbarItems—This property is an array of **UIBarButtonItem** objects with bar buttons.

setToolbarItems([UIBarButtonItem]?, animated: Bool)—This method assigns the bar buttons provided by the first attribute to the toolbar. The **animated** attribute determines if the process will be animated.

For configuration, the **UIToolbar** class offers the following properties and methods (some of these values are also available from the Attributes Inspector panel).

barStyle—This property determines the style of the bar. It is an enumeration of type **UIBarStyle** with the values **default**, **black**, **blackOpaque**, and **blackTranslucent**.

barTintColor—This property sets or returns the color applied to the bar's background.

tintColor—This property sets or returns the color applied to the bar's items.

isTranslucent—This property is a Boolean value that indicates if the bar is translucent.

setBackgroundImage(UIImage?, **forToolbarPosition:** UIBarPosition, **barMetrics:** UIBarMetrics**)**—This method sets the background image for the bar. The first attribute represents the image, and the **forToolbarPosition** attribute is used to give a hint to the system about where the bar is located. It is an enumeration of type **UIBarPosition** with the values **any**, **bottom**, **top**, and **topAttached**. Finally, the **barMetrics** attribute is an enumeration of type **UIBarMetrics** that associates the image with the state of the bar. The values available are **default**, **defaultPrompt**, **compact**, and **compactPrompt**.

To access the Toolbar from code, we have to create an Outlet. The following example assumes that a Toolbar was added at the bottom of the initial view from Interface Builder and it was connected to the view controller with an Outlet called **myToolbar**. Through this Outlet we access the toolbar and assign a background image to the bar and a color for its buttons.

```
import UIKit

class ViewController: UIViewController {
    @IBOutlet weak var myToolbar: UIToolbar!

    override func viewDidLoad() {
        super.viewDidLoad()
        myToolbar.setBackgroundImage(UIImage(named: "backgroundbar"),
forToolbarPosition: .bottom, barMetrics: .default)
        myToolbar.tintColor = UIColor.white
    }
}
```

Listing 13-16: Configuring the Toolbar from the view controller

Do It Yourself: Drag a Toolbar from the Object Library to the bottom of the initial view. Add the necessary constraints to pin it to the bottom and the sides of the view. Control-Drag a line from the bar to the **ViewController** class to create an Outlet called **myToolbar**. Download the backgroundbar.png files from our website and add them to the Assets Catalog. Update the class with the code of Listing 13-16. Run the application to see what the bar looks like.

IMPORTANT: Unlike Navigation Bars, Toolbars require pin constraints to pin them to the sides of the view, but like Navigation Bars, they are translucent, and the rest of the elements can be pinned to the edge of the view and go behind the bar.

Navigation

The Basics: The `UIToolbar` class also conforms to the `UIAppearance` protocol and therefore it implements its `appearance()` methods, letting us configure all the bars at once from the app's delegate (see Listing 13-10).

Custom Navigation

It is possible to hide the Navigation Bar and provide our own navigation tools. The option is available in the Attributes Inspector panel when the Navigation Controller is selected.

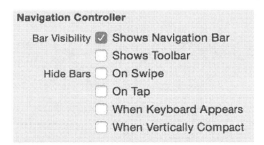

Figure 13-36: Options to show or hide the bars

Clicking on the Shows Navigation Bar option deactivates the bar and removes it from the view controllers in the Storyboard. Once the Navigation Bar is deactivated, it is our responsibility to provide the tools the user needs to navigate.

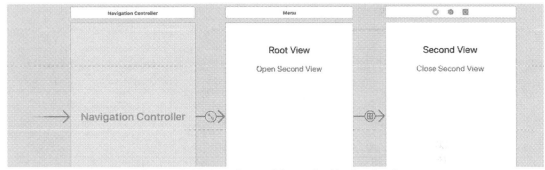

Figure 13-37: Interface without the Navigation Bar

Figure 13-37 introduces a simple interface. With the Navigation Bar removed, we do not have a Back button anymore, so we added a button in the second view called Close Second View to remove it. The class for this view has to include an Action for the button that calls the `popViewController()` method of its Navigation Controller. This method removes the current view and forces the Navigation Controller to show the previous view in the stack.

```
import UIKit

class SecondViewController: UIViewController {
   @IBAction func closeView(_ sender: UIButton) {
      navigationController?.popViewController(animated: true)
   }
}
```

Listing 13-17: Defining our own method to go back

Sharing Data

View controllers managed by a Navigation Controller fulfill a common purpose and therefore they frequently share common data. When working with Navigation Controllers, we should not send information from one view controller to another, as we did before with single view controllers, but instead create a unique source of data. The most frequently used object to store common data is the **AppDelegate** object. The advantage presented by this object is that it is the delegate of the **UIApplication** object created to run the application and therefore it is accessible from anywhere in the code.

As an example, we are going to recreate the application developed at the beginning of this chapter using a Navigation Controller. The interface includes two views embedded in a Navigation Controller, one with the buttons to select the picture and another with an Image View and a Slider to show the picture and rate it.

Figure 13-38: *Picture application created with a Navigation Controller*

The application works as before, the system shows the initial view with the menu first and then when the user clicks on any of the buttons it transitions to the second view to show the selected picture, but because this time we use a Navigation Bar, we do not have to worry about providing a button to go back to the previous view.

 Do It Yourself: Create a new Single View Application project. Embed the initial view in a Navigation Controller. Add a second Scene to the Storyboard. Connect the initial Scene to the second view with a Show Segue (Figure 13-18). Assign the string "showPicture" to the Segue's identifier (Figure 13-12). Create a new file with a view controller called **SecondViewController** and assign it to the second Scene (Figures 13-6 and 13-7). Add a Navigation Item to the Navigation Bar of the second Scene (Figure 13-25). Select the Navigation Items and assign the title "Menu" to the initial view and "Picture" to the second view (Figure 13-26). Add buttons called Show Husky and Show Door to the initial view and assign the values 0 and 1 to their **tag** properties (Figure 5-36). Add an Image View, a label with the text "Rating", and a Slider to the second view. Set a value of 0, a minimum of 0, and a maximum of 5 for the Slider. Select the Prefers Large Titles option in the Attributes Inspector Panel to activate large titles (Figure 13-33). Add the pictures husky.png and door.png to the Assets Catalog. The interface should look like Figure 13-38.

The code is also similar, but the **picturesList**, **ratings**, and **selectedPicture** properties we used before to store the information are going to be defined in the application's delegate, so every time the rating is modified in the second view we do not need to send the data back to the initial view controller; all we have to do is access the app's delegate and change the values of its properties. The following code illustrates how the properties should be declared and initialized in the delegate.

```
import UIKit

@UIApplicationMain
class AppDelegate: UIResponder, UIApplicationDelegate {
    var window: UIWindow?
    var picturesList: [String]!
    var ratings: [Int]!
    var selectedPicture: Int!

    func application(_ application: UIApplication,
didFinishLaunchingWithOptions launchOptions:
[UIApplication.LaunchOptionsKey : Any]? = nil) -> Bool {
        picturesList = ["Husky", "Door"]
        ratings = [0, 0]
        selectedPicture = 0
        return true
    }
}
```

Listing 13-18: Defining common data in the app's delegate

The **picturesList** property is an array with the names of the pictures available, the **ratings** property is another array with the ratings assigned by the user to each picture, and the **selectedPicture** property stores the index of the currently selected picture. The first place where they are required is in the view controller of the initial view. Here, we have to update the **selectedPicture** property every time a button is pressed to communicate to the rest of the code which picture was selected.

```
import UIKit

class ViewController: UIViewController {
    var mydelegate: AppDelegate!

    override func viewDidLoad() {
        super.viewDidLoad()
        let app = UIApplication.shared
        mydelegate = app.delegate as? AppDelegate
    }
    @IBAction func goToPicture(_ sender: UIButton) {
        mydelegate.selectedPicture = sender.tag
        performSegue(withIdentifier: "showPicture", sender: self)
    }
}
```

Listing 13-19: Storing the index of the selected picture

The first thing we do in the **ViewController** class of Listing 13-19 is to get a reference to the application's delegate. The process is the same introduced in Chapter 5 (Listing 5-2). We have to get a reference to the **UIApplication** object created for the application and then read its **delegate** property. The property we need to modify in the delegate is the **selectedPicture** property that stores the index of the selected picture. For this, we have connected both buttons, Show Husky and Show Door, to one Action called **goToPicture()**. When any of the buttons is pressed, we take the value of their **tag** property and assign it to the **selectedPicture** property. At the end, we call the **performSegue()** method to transition to the second view. Notice that this time we do not need to send any value to **SecondViewController** because this view controller also takes the values from the app's delegate, as shown next.

```
import UIKit

class SecondViewController: UIViewController {
    @IBOutlet weak var sliderRating: UISlider!
    @IBOutlet weak var pictureView: UIImageView!
    var mydelegate: AppDelegate!

    override func viewDidLoad() {
        super.viewDidLoad()
        let app = UIApplication.shared
        mydelegate = app.delegate as? AppDelegate

        let selected = mydelegate.selectedPicture!
        let picture = mydelegate.picturesList[selected]
        let rating = mydelegate.ratings[selected]
        sliderRating.value = Float(rating)
        pictureView.image = UIImage(named: picture.lowercased())
    }
    @IBAction func changeRating(_ sender: UISlider) {
        let value = round(sender.value)
        sliderRating.value = value
        let selected = mydelegate.selectedPicture!
        mydelegate.ratings[selected] = Int(value)
    }
}
```

Listing 13-20: Storing the rating in the app's delegate

In the **SecondViewController** class we have to read the three properties of the app's delegate to configure the view. We get the index of the selected picture first and then use it to read the picture's name and rating from the **picturesList** and **ratings** arrays. This information is used next to update the Slider and the Image View before the interface is shown on the screen. The **selectedPicture** and **ratings** properties are also used in the Action connected to the Slider to update the value of the rating with the one selected by the user.

 Do It Yourself: Modify the **AppDelegate** class in the AppDelegate.swift file with the code of Listing 13-18. Connect the Show Husky and Show Door buttons in the initial view to an Action called **goToPicture()**. Complete the **ViewController** class with the code of Listing 13-19. Connect the Slider and the Image View of the second view to Outlets called **sliderRating** and **pictureView**, respectively. Create an Action for the Slider called **changeRating()**. Complete the **SecondViewController** class with the code of Listing 13-20. Run the application and modify the rating of the pictures to verify that the values are preserved.

The use of the app's delegate to store data is only recommended when the amount of data is not significant. For large amounts of data, it is better to create global objects or structures that the application can access every time necessary and where we can safely manage the information available. To do this in Swift is very easy. All the files are considered to be in the global space and are executed as soon as the application is launched. If we want to create a global object or structure that we can access from anywhere in our code, all we have to do is define it and initialize it in a new Swift file.

As any other files, Swift files are created from the File menu or pressing Command + N on the keyboard, but instead of selecting the Cocoa Touch Class option we have to click on the Swift File option (Figure 13-3). The name of the file in this case is just for reference, because except for a few comments and **import** statements, no code is created for the template. Once the file is added to the list of files in our application, we can define our custom classes or structures inside. For our example, we have created a file called ApplicationData.swift and define a structure inside with the same name and all the properties necessary for our application.

```
struct ApplicationData {
    var picturesList: [String]
    var ratings: [Int]
    var selectedPicture: Int

    init() {
        picturesList = ["Husky", "Door"]
        ratings = [0, 0]
        selectedPicture = 0
    }
}
var AppData = ApplicationData()
```

Listing 13-21: Defining a global structure to store common data

 The Basics: The `ApplicationData` structure represents the model in our MVC, or Model-View-Controller (see Chapter 5). In our example, the Views are created from the Storyboard, the Controllers are the view controllers we associate with those views, and the Model is now the `ApplicationData` structure defined in Listing 13-21. This model and the one created with the app's delegate before are suitable for small applications, but there are multiple models and programming patterns available for professional applications (see Chapter 21, Listing 21-21). The topic is beyond the scope of this book. For more information on programming patterns and data management, visit our website and follow the links for this chapter.

The structure declared in Listing 13-21 contains the same information as before, but it provides a unique place to store and manage all the information for our app. Now we can access this data from anywhere in the code by just reading and writing the content of the **AppData** variable. The following example shows how the **ViewController** of our application gets the data from **AppData**.

```
import UIKit

class ViewController: UIViewController {
    @IBAction func goToPicture(_ sender: UIButton) {
        AppData.selectedPicture = sender.tag
        performSegue(withIdentifier: "showPicture", sender: self)
    }
}
```

Listing 13-22: Accessing the global structure from the ViewController *class*

Since we do not have to get a reference to the app's delegate anymore, all we need in the **ViewController** class is the Action for the buttons. When a button is pressed, the **goToPicture()** method is executed as always, but this time instead of accessing the **selectedPicture** property from the app's delegate we do it from the **AppData** structure.

The code for the **SecondViewController** was also simplified. Getting the data from a global structure makes everything easier.

```
import UIKit
class SecondViewController: UIViewController {
    @IBOutlet weak var sliderRating: UISlider!
    @IBOutlet weak var pictureView: UIImageView!

    override func viewDidLoad() {
        super.viewDidLoad()
        let selected = AppData.selectedPicture
        let picture = AppData.picturesList[selected]
        let rating = AppData.ratings[selected]
        sliderRating.value = Float(rating)
        pictureView.image = UIImage(named: picture.lowercased())
    }
    @IBAction func changeRating(_ sender: UISlider) {
        let value = round(sender.value)
        sliderRating.value = value
        let selected = AppData.selectedPicture
        AppData.ratings[selected] = Int(value)
    }
}
```

Listing 13-23: Accessing the global structure from the SecondViewController *class*

 Do It Yourself: Erase the properties in the **AppDelegate** class. Open the File menu, click on New, and select the option File to create a new Swift file. In the next window, click on the Swift File icon and insert the name ApplicationData.swift. Open the new file and replace its code by the code of Listing 13-21. Replace the **ViewController** class by the class of Listing 13-22 and the **SecondViewController** class by the class of Listing 13-23. Run the application. It should work as before but now the data is taken from the **AppData** structure.

13.3 Tab Bar Controllers

A Tab Bar Controller is a simple container view controller that designates two areas on the screen: one for the views and a smaller one at the bottom of the screen for a bar with tabs that users can tap to select the view they want to see. Each tab is associated with only one view and therefore we can use the tabs to move from one view to another.

Figure 13-39: Application based on a Tab Bar Controller

As with Navigation Controllers, there are two ways to add a Tab Bar Controller to the Storyboard. We can embed a view inside a Tab Bar Controller from the Editor menu (Editor/Embed In/Tab Bar Controller) or drag the Tab Bar Controller option from the Object Library to the Storyboard. Figure 13-40 shows what we see when we embed a single view in a Tab Bar Controller.

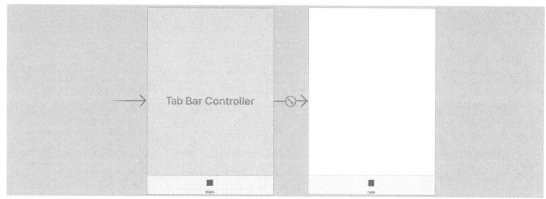

Figure 13-40: Initial view embedded in a Tab Bar Controller

The views managed by the Tab Bar Controller are connected with a Segue called *View Controllers*. To add another view to the Tab Bar Controller, we must insert a Scene in the Storyboard and create a Segue of type View Controllers from the Tab Bar Controller to the view.

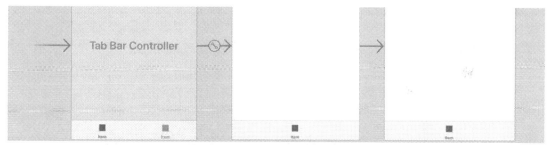

Figure 13-41: Multiple views managed by the Tab Bar Controller

We can add all the views we want. When a view is added to the Tab Bar Controller, the system automatically includes the corresponding tab at the bottom of the view. Then the Tab Bar Controller gets the tabs from the views and generates the bar (Figure 13-41, left). If there is not enough space on the bar to place all the tabs available, the controller adds a tab called *More* that lets the user select the tabs that are not visible.

Tabs

The bar is managed by the Tab Bar Controller, but the tabs are provided by the view controllers they belong to. To change the values and appearance of the tabs, we have to click on each one of them and edit their values from the Attributes Inspector panel.

Figure 13-42: Options to configure the tab

Each tab has a title, image, selected image, and a landscape image to identify the view they represent. There are two alternatives to configure the tab: we can provide a custom name and images, or we can select a tab predefined by the system from the option called *System Item*. If we click on this field, a popup window lists all the tabs available. Figure 13-43 shows what our Tab Bar looks like after the style Favorites and Search were selected for the tabs in our interface.

Figure 13-43: *Tab Bar with tabs defined by the system*

These options define the image and the name. If we want to provide our own name, we have to customize the image as well. The image must be provided with a size of 30 pixels by 30 pixels (60x60 for the 2x scale and 90x90 for the 3x scale) and a transparent background. No colors are necessary because the system uses the image to create a mask and present it with the colors defined by the bar. For our example, we have created the images iconweather.png for the initial view and iconsettings.png for the second view. Figure 13-44 shows what the bar looks like after we modify each tab and give them the names "Weather" and "Settings", respectively.

Figure 13-44: *Tab bar with custom tabs*

 Do It Yourself: Create a Single View Application project and embed the initial view in a Tab Bar Controller (Editor/Embed In/Tab Bar Controller). Add a second view and create a Segue of type View Controllers from the Tab Bar Controller to the new view (Figure 13-41). Download from our website the images iconweather.png and iconsettings.png and add them to the Assets Catalog. Click on the initial view's tab, go to the Bar Item section in the Attributes Inspector panel, and insert the name "Weather" and the image iconweather.png. Repeat the same process with the name "Settings" and the image iconsettings.png for the second view's tab. The bar of the Tab Bar Controller should look like Figure 13-44.

Tabs are created from the **UITabBarItem** class. This is a subclass of the **UIBarItem** class, which is also used to create the buttons for Navigation Controllers (see Listing 13-13). Together, these classes provide the following properties to configure the tab.

title—This property sets or returns the tab's title. It is an optional of type **String**.

image—This property sets or returns the image for the tab's normal state. It is an optional of type **UIImage**.

landscapeImagePhone—This property sets or returns the image for the tab's normal state that is shown when the device is in landscape mode. It is an optional of type **UIImage**.

selectedImage—This property sets or returns the image for the tab's selected state. It is an optional of type **UIImage**.

tag—This property sets or returns the tab's tag value. It is of type **Int**.

badgeValue—This property sets or returns the value of the tab's badge (shown inside a red circle at the top-right corner of the icon). It is an optional of type **String**.

The tabs are configured from the view controllers they belong to. The **UIViewController** class includes the **tabBarItem** property to access the view controller's tab. The next example adds an Action for a button to update the badge when the button is pressed.

Navigation

```
import UIKit
class ViewController: UIViewController {
    var counter = 1
    @IBAction func updateBadge(_ sender: UIButton) {
        let item = tabBarItem
        item?.badgeValue = String(counter)
        counter += 1
    }
}
```

Listing 13-24: Updating the badge from the view controller

The code for the **ViewController** class presented in Listing 13-24 gets a reference to the view's tab from the **tabBarItem** property and then updates its **badgeValue** property with the value of the **counter** property. The counter is incremented every time the button is pressed to illustrate how the badge is modified by the system. Figure 13-45 shows what we see after we run the application and press the button 12 times.

Figure 13-45: Tab with a badge

 Do It Yourself: Add a button to the initial view of the interface of Figure 13-41. Connect the button to an Action called **updateBadge()**. Complete the **ViewController** class with the code of Listing 13-24. Run the application and press the button. You should see something similar to Figure 13-45.

Tab Bar Controller

View controllers are in charge of their own tabs, but the bar and the list of view controllers available is managed by the Tab Bar Controller. The **UITabBarController** class includes the following properties to store the view controllers, keep a reference to the view controller currently selected, and access the bar.

tabBar—This property returns a reference to the **UITabBar** object that represents the bar.

viewControllers—This property sets or returns the view controllers managed by the Tab Bar Controller. It is an array of **UIViewController** objects.

selectedViewController—This property returns a reference to the view controller of the view that is currently being shown on the screen.

selectedIndex—This property returns the index in the **viewControllers** array of the view controller that is currently being shown on the screen. It is a value of type **Int**.

The bar is created from the **UITabBar** class, which offers the following properties for configuration.

barStyle—This property determines the style of the bar. It is an enumeration of type **UIBarStyle** with the values **default**, **black**, **blackOpaque**, and **blackTranslucent**.

barTintColor—This property sets or returns the color applied to the bar's background.

tintColor—This property sets or returns the color applied to the bar's items.

isTranslucent—This property takes a Boolean that determines if the bar is translucent.

backgroundImage—This property sets the background image for the bar. Its value is an optional of type `UIImage`.

selectionIndicatorImage—This property sets the background image for the selected tab. Its value is an optional of type `UIImage`.

itemPositioning—This property sets the positions of the tabs. It is an enumeration called `ItemPositioning` included in the `UITabBar` class. The values available are `automatic` (the tabs are positioned according to the device), `fill` (the tabs are positioned to fill the width of the bar) and `centered` (the tabs are positioned at the center of the bar).

itemSpacing—This property sets the space between tabs when the `itemPositioning` property is set to `centered`. It is a value of type `CGFloat`.

itemWidth—This property sets the width of the tabs when the `itemPositioning` property is set to `centered`. It is a value of type `CGFloat`.

Although the `UITabBar` class also conforms to the `UIAppearance` protocol and implements its `appearance()` method to let us configure the bar by modifying the class, because there is usually only one Tab Bar Controller per application it is better to create a subclass of `UITabBarController` and manage the view controllers and the bar from it. For our example, we have created a file called TabBarController.swift with a subclass of the `UITabBarController` called `TabBarController` and assign it to the Tab Bar Controller of the interface of Figure 13-41.

```
import UIKit

class TabBarController: UITabBarController {
    override func viewDidLoad() {
        super.viewDidLoad()
        let bar = tabBar
        bar.tintColor = UIColor.white
        bar.isTranslucent = true
        bar.backgroundImage = UIImage(named: "tabbar")
    }
}
```

Listing 13-25: Configuring the bar from a subclass of `UITabBarController`

The process is similar to those implemented to configure the bar for Navigation Controllers. In this case, a reference to the bar is obtained from the **tabBar** property provided by the `UITabBarController` class and then the values of its properties are modified.

Do It Yourself: Download the tabbar.png image from our website and add it to your Assets Catalog. Create a new file with a subclass of the `UITabBarController` class called `TabBarController` and assign it to the Tab Bar Controller of Figure 13-41. Complete the subclass with the code of Listing 13-25. The application now shows the bar with a background image.

IMPORTANT: The `UIViewController` class includes a property called `tabBarController` to get a reference to the Tab Bar Controller from its view controllers. It is not recommendable to configure the bar from any of the view controllers because there is no guarantee that the code is going to be processed as soon as the app is executed, but this property may be useful sometimes to get information from the Tab Bar Controller.

Navigation

There are more tasks we can perform from the `UITabBarController` subclass other than configuring the bar. Important things like establishing which view will be shown first or setting the badges for each tab can be done from this subclass. The following example modifies the `selectedIndex` property to declare the second view as the initial view and adds a badge to the Weather's tab.

```
import UIKit

class TabBarController: UITabBarController {
    override func viewDidLoad() {
        super.viewDidLoad()
        let bar = tabBar
        bar.tintColor = UIColor.white
        bar.isTranslucent = true
        bar.backgroundImage = UIImage(named: "tabbar")

        selectedIndex = 1
        let list = viewControllers!
        let controller = list[0] as! ViewController
        let tab = controller.tabBarItem
        tab?.badgeValue = String(20)
    }
}
```

Listing 13-26: Initializing the Tab Bar Controller

The view controllers managed by the Tab Bar Controller are stored in an array called **viewControllers** in the order they were created in the Storyboard. In our example, the view controller for the Weather view was stored at index 0 and the view controller for the Settings view was stored at index 1. This is why we have to assign a value 1 to the **selectedIndex** property to declare the Settings view as the initial view. On the other hand, the view controller of the Weather view is at index 0, and therefore to add a badge to that view's tab we have to get the first element of the **viewControllers** array, cast it as **ViewController** (the array contains elements of type **UIViewController**), and finally access its properties.

 The Basics: Because Tab Bar Controllers are often implemented as the starting point of the application, Xcode offers a template called *Tabbed App* that initializes the Storyboard with a Tab Bar Controller and two views.

Tab Bar Controller Delegate

Tab Bar Controllers can use a delegate object to report when something happened or is about to happen with the tabs. The UIKit framework includes the **UITabBarControllerDelegate** protocol for this purpose. The following are some of the methods defined by the protocol.

tabBarController(UITabBarController, **didSelect:** UIViewController)—This method is called by the **UITabBarController** object when a tab is selected. The **didSelect** attribute is a reference to the view controller of the selected tab.

tabBarController(UITabBarController, **shouldSelect:** UIViewController)—This method is called by the **UITabBarController** object to know whether or not to let the user select a tab. The method returns a Boolean value that indicates the decision made by the code. The **shouldSelect** attribute is a reference to the view controller of the selected tab.

The delegate object may be an external object or the **UITabBarController** subclass that is controlling our Tab Bar Controller. The following example defines our **TabBarController** class as its own delegate to perform a task when a tab is selected.

```
import UIKit

class TabBarController: UITabBarController, **UITabBarControllerDelegate** {
    override func viewDidLoad() {
        super.viewDidLoad()
        **delegate = self**
    }
    func tabBarController(_ tabBarController: UITabBarController,
didSelect viewController: UIViewController) {
        let list = viewControllers!
        let controller = list[1]
        if viewController === controller {
            print("It's Settings")
        }
    }
}
```

Listing 13-27: *Defining the Tab Bar Controller's delegate*

To turn the **TabBarController** class of our example into its own delegate, we have to declare that the class conforms to the **UITabBarControllerDelegate** protocol first, and then assign **self** to its **delegate** property. From that moment on, the **TabBarController** object will call the delegate's methods on itself. In Listing 13-27, we declare the method that is called when the user selects a tab. To check which tab was selected, we compare the value on its **viewController** attribute against the reference stored at index 1 in the **viewControllers** array of the **TabBarController** object. This reference corresponds to the **SecondViewController** object and therefore the task is performed when the Settings view is show on the screen.

There are other ways to detect the type of the selected view controller. For example, we could try to convert it to one of our **UIViewController** subclasses with the **as?** operator and compare the value returned by the conversion against **nil**. If the view controller received by the method is of type **SecondViewController**, the condition will be true, and we can perform the task as we did in Listing 13-27. But following this procedure we could also read the properties of this object, as shown in the following example.

```
import UIKit

class TabBarController: UITabBarController, UITabBarControllerDelegate {
    override func viewDidLoad() {
        super.viewDidLoad()
        delegate = self
    }
    func tabBarController(_ tabBarController: UITabBarController,
shouldSelect viewController: UIViewController) -> Bool {
        **if let controller = viewController as? SecondViewController {**
            **let control = controller.myproperty**
            **if control != 0 {**
                **return false**
            **}**
        **}**
        return true
    }
}
```

Listing 13-28: *Allowing the selection of a tab*

This time, the protocol method implemented is called when a tab is selected but before its view is shown on the screen. We have to return a Boolean value from the method to indicate whether or not the action is valid. To know what value to return, the code of Listing 13-28 detects the tab the user is trying to open by casting the value received from the **viewController** attribute to the class corresponding to the view controller of the Settings view (**SecondViewController**). In case of success, it stores the result in the **controller** constant and uses this reference to access a property called **myproperty**. If the value of this property is different than 0, the code returns **false** and does not let the user select the tab.

 Do It Yourself: Copy the example you want to try in the TabBarController.swift file created before and run the application. The code of Listing 13-28 assumes that you have declared a property called **myproperty** in the **SecondViewController** class and initialize it with an integer.

Real-Life Application

For a better understanding of Tab Bar Controllers and the kind of applications they are suitable for, we are going to finish the Weather application started in previous examples. We need the interface of Figure 13-41 and the tabs of Figure 13-44. The views have to be associated with their respective view controllers (**ViewController** class for the Weather view and **SecondViewController** class for the Settings view).

The app will show the information about the weather in the initial view (Weather) and let the user select the city and the unit of measurement in the second view (Settings). To create the interface for the Weather view, we have to add two big labels at the top for the name of the city and the value of the temperature, and two empty views with a gray background, as shown in the first picture of Figure 13-46 below. The elements have to be pinned to the Safe Area with Space constraints and then the rest of the labels are added inside the gray views (to adjust the height of the gray views to its content, assign Top and Bottom Space constraints to the labels, so the views adapt their heights to the height of their content). We have to create two labels per value, one for the name of the value and another for the value itself. The values we are going to present inside the gray views are Precipitation, Humidity, Wind, Pressure, Visibility, and Feels Like.

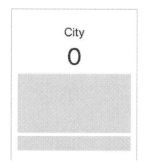  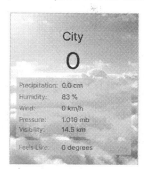

Figure 13-46: Design for the Weather view

To make the app look more professional, we added a background with an Image View (the file for the image is called clouds.jpg and is available on our website). We can add this image first and then the rest of the interface or add it at last and then move it to the back from the Document Outline panel or the Editor menu (Editor/Arrange/Send to Back).

The interface for the Settings view is similar. We have to add two gray views, pin them to the Safe Area, and then incorporate a label and a Segmented Control with two buttons to the view at the top, and a picker to the view at the bottom (center of Figure 13-47). The buttons of the Segmented Control were called Celsius and Fahrenheit to let the user select the preferred unit of measurement. This view was also improved with a background image (the file is called lake.png and is available on our website).

Figure 13-47: *Design for the Settings view*

The next step is to create the model that contains the data that will be presented by the app.

```
struct WeatherData {
   var temperature: Double
   var precipitation: Double
   var humidity: Int
   var wind: Double
   var pressure: Double
   var visibility: Double
   var feels: Double
}
struct ApplicationData {
   var citiesName: [String] = []
   var citiesData: [WeatherData] = []
   var selectedCity: Int
   var celsius: Bool
   init() {
      var cities: [String: [Double]] = [:]
      cities["Toronto"] = [21, 0.0, 83, 0.0, 1.016, 14.5, 24]
      cities["New York"] = [18, 3.0, 95, 12.4, 1.020, 8.5, 15]
      cities["Paris"] = [24, 8.7, 90, 5.4, 1.055, 10.5, 25]
      for (city, data) in cities {
         citiesName.append(city)
         let newData = WeatherData(temperature: data[0], precipitation:
data[1], humidity: Int(data[2]), wind: data[3], pressure: data[4],
visibility: data[5], feels: data[6])
         citiesData.append(newData)
      }
      selectedCity = 0
      celsius = true
   }
}
var AppData = ApplicationData()
```

Listing 13-29: *Preparing the data for the app*

Two structures were defined in Listing 13-29. The **WeatherData** structure stores the data for every city and the **ApplicationData** structure manages the data and the settings for the app. There are four properties in the **ApplicationData** structure: **citiesName**, **citiesData**, **selectedCity**, and **celsius**. The **citiesName** property is an array of strings to store the names of the cities, the **citiesData** property is an array of **WeatherData** structures to store the data for every city, the **selectedCity** property is used to store the index of the city currently selected, and the **celsius** property is a Boolean value that indicates whether the temperature is going to be shown in Celsius or Fahrenheit. When the **ApplicationData** structure is initialized, the information for every city is stored inside a dictionary and then the dictionary is used to initialize the properties. This dictionary has a **String** value for key and an array of **Double** for values, as the dictionaries studied in Chapter 2 (see Listings 2-56 and 2-57).

The Basics: In a real application, this information would be loaded from a server. We will learn how to incorporate data to the app from external sources in Chapter 27.

Now that we have the data, we have to show it on the Weather view. For this purpose, the **ViewController** class have to include Outlets for every label and turn the data of the selected city into **Measurement** values to show it on the screen.

```swift
import UIKit

class ViewController: UIViewController {
    @IBOutlet weak var cityLabel: UILabel!
    @IBOutlet weak var temperatureLabel: UILabel!
    @IBOutlet weak var precipitationLabel: UILabel!
    @IBOutlet weak var humidityLabel: UILabel!
    @IBOutlet weak var windLabel: UILabel!
    @IBOutlet weak var pressureLabel: UILabel!
    @IBOutlet weak var visibilityLabel: UILabel!
    @IBOutlet weak var feelsLabel: UILabel!

    override func viewWillAppear(_ animated: Bool) {
        let selected = AppData.selectedCity
        let cityData = AppData.citiesData[selected]
        var temperature = Measurement(value: cityData.temperature, unit:
UnitTemperature.celsius)
        var feels = Measurement(value: cityData.feels, unit:
UnitTemperature.celsius)
        if !AppData.celsius {
            temperature.convert(to: UnitTemperature.fahrenheit)
            feels.convert(to: UnitTemperature.fahrenheit)
        }
        let precipitation = Measurement(value: cityData.precipitation,
unit: UnitLength.centimeters)
        let wind = Measurement(value: cityData.wind, unit:
UnitSpeed.kilometersPerHour)
        let pressure = Measurement(value: cityData.pressure, unit:
UnitPressure.millibars)
        let visibility = Measurement(value: cityData.visibility, unit:
UnitLength.kilometers)
        let formatter = MeasurementFormatter()
        formatter.unitStyle = MeasurementFormatter.UnitStyle.short
        formatter.unitOptions =
MeasurementFormatter.UnitOptions.providedUnit
        temperatureLabel.text = formatter.string(from: temperature)
        feelsLabel.text = formatter.string(from: feels)
        cityLabel.text = AppData.citiesName[selected]
        precipitationLabel.text = formatter.string(from: precipitation)
        humidityLabel.text = "\(cityData.humidity) %"
        windLabel.text = formatter.string(from: wind)
        pressureLabel.text = formatter.string(from: pressure)
        visibilityLabel.text = formatter.string(from: visibility)
    }
}
```

Listing 13-30: View controller for the Weather view

The code of Listing 13-30 creates all the **Measurement** values required and turn them into strings with the **string()** method before to assign them to the labels. To format the strings, we use the **short** style and the option **providedUnit** so all the units are shown as defined (see the **Measurement** structure in Chapter 4).

IMPORTANT: Tab Bar Controllers load the views once and then keep them in memory. This means that the `viewDidLoad()` method will be executed only once, and any change performed by the user in another view will not be reflected on the screen later. That is why this time we used the `viewWillAppear()` method instead.

The Settings view requires a little work but nothing far from what we have learned so far. We need an Action for the Segmented Control to change the unit of measurement when a button is pressed and the delegate methods to configure the picker and get the selected value.

```
import UIKit

class SecondViewController: UIViewController, UIPickerViewDelegate,
UIPickerViewDataSource {
    @IBOutlet weak var selectTemperature: UISegmentedControl!
    @IBOutlet weak var picker: UIPickerView!

    override func viewDidLoad() {
        super.viewDidLoad()
        picker.delegate = self
        picker.dataSource = self
        picker.selectRow(AppData.selectedCity, inComponent: 0, animated:
false)
        if AppData.celsius {
            selectTemperature.selectedSegmentIndex = 0
        } else {
            selectTemperature.selectedSegmentIndex = 1
        }
    }
    @IBAction func changeTemperature(_ sender: UISegmentedControl) {
        if sender.selectedSegmentIndex == 0 {
            AppData.celsius = true
        } else {
            AppData.celsius = false
        }
    }
    func numberOfComponents(in pickerView: UIPickerView) -> Int {
        return 1
    }
    func pickerView(_ pickerView: UIPickerView, numberOfRowsInComponent
component: Int) -> Int {
        return AppData.citiesName.count
    }
    func pickerView(_ pickerView: UIPickerView, titleForRow row: Int,
forComponent component: Int) -> String? {
        return AppData.citiesName[row]
    }
    func pickerView(_ pickerView: UIPickerView, didSelectRow row: Int,
inComponent component: Int) {
        AppData.selectedCity = row
    }
}
```

Listing 13-31: View controller for the Settings view

The code of Listing 13-31 sets the initial conditions when the view is loaded and then changes those conditions in the `AppData` structure responding to the user. Because the data is stored in a global structure and we used the `viewWillAppear()` method to update the information on the Weather view, the changes performed here are immediately reflected on the screen.

Chapter 14
Table Views

14.1 Tables

One of the basic characteristics of computers is their capacity to process sequential data. Due to their elemental structure, composed of a sequence of switches on and off, computers are experts at organizing information as lists of values. It did not take long for computer systems to adopt the concepts of tables to present this type of information. A table is an organizational system that proposes an arrangement of data in rows and columns. Apple has always provided the tools to create tables on its systems, but because of the small screens of mobile devices, it was compelled to introduce a new version of tables composed of only one column. Despite their simplicity, tables in iOS are very powerful. They provide tools to manage the data, organize it in single lists or sections, and are built inside a Scroll View, allowing the content to be shown with no limitations whatsoever. Figure 14-1 shows two basic configurations. In the table on the left, the items are presented in a single list. On the right, the items are organized in sections.

Figure 14-1: Table Views in Plain style

iOS tables may also adopt two styles: Plain and Grouped. Plain tables display single lists with information of the same type, while the purpose of Grouped tables is to group information of different types. The tables in Figure 14-1 are both Plain, one with a single list and the other organized in sections. Next, we show the same tables but this time with a Grouped style (notice that the version with sections separates the items in categories instead of alphabetically).

Figure 14-2: Table Views in Grouped style

Table Views

Tables are created from the **UITableView** class. The class includes the following properties and methods to create and configure the table.

allowsSelection—This property sets or returns a Boolean value that determines if the user can select a cell or not.

allowsMultipleSelection—This property sets or returns a Boolean value that determines if the user can select multiple cells or not.

isEditing—This property sets or returns a Boolean value that indicates whether the table is in edition mode or not. The edition mode is used to insert, delete, or move rows.

rowHeight—This property sets or returns a **CGFloat** value that determines the cells' height.

estimatedRowHeight—This property sets or returns a **CGFloat** value that determines the approximate size of the cell. It has the purpose to improve performance and it is required when working with variable cell heights.

separatorStyle—This property sets or returns the style for the cells' separators. It is an enumeration called **SeparatorStyle** included in the **UITableViewCell** class. The values available are **none**, **singleLine**, and **singleLineEtched**.

separatorColor—This property sets or returns the color for the cells' separators. It is an optional of type **UIColor**.

separatorInset—This property sets or returns the padding for the cells' separators. It is a structure of type **UIEdgeInsets** with the properties **top**, **left**, **bottom**, and **right** (only the left and right values are considered).

tableHeaderView—This property sets or returns the view that represents the table's header. The value by default is **nil**.

tableFooterView—This property sets or returns the view that represents the table's footer. The value by default is **nil**.

sectionIndexColor—This property sets or returns the color for the Table View's index text. It is an optional of type **UIColor**.

sectionIndexBackgroundColor—This property sets or returns the color for the background of the Table View's index when it is not being touched. It is an optional of type **UIColor**.

sectionIndexTrackingBackgroundColor—This property sets or returns the color for the background of the Table View's index when the user touches it. It is of type **UIColor**.

indexPathForSelectedRow—This property returns an **IndexPath** structure with the location of the currently selected cell.

dequeueReusableCell(withIdentifier: String, **for:** IndexPath)—This method returns a reusable cell with the specified identifier. The first attribute is the string that identifies the cell and the **for** attribute is a structure with the location of the cell.

cellForRow(at: IndexPath)—This method returns a reference to the **UITableViewCell** object of the cell at the index path specified by the **at** attribute.

indexPath(for: UITableViewCell)—This method returns an **IndexPath** structure with the location of a cell. The attribute is a reference to the object that represents the cell.

selectRow(at: IndexPath?, **animated:** Bool, **scrollPosition:** ScrollPosition**)**—This method selects the cell at the location specified by the **at** attribute. The **animated** attribute indicates whether the process is going to be animated or not, and the **scrollPosition** attribute indicates if the table will scroll to the position of the cell and how. It is an enumeration called `ScrollPosition` included in the `UITableView` class. The values available are **none**, **top**, **middle**, and **bottom**.

deselectRow(at: IndexPath, **animated:** Bool**)**—This method deselects the cell at the location specified by the **at** attribute. The **animated** attribute indicates whether the process is going to be animated or not.

scrollToRow(at: IndexPath, **at:** ScrollPosition, **animated:** Bool**)**—This method scrolls the Table View to show on the screen the cell at the position indicated by the **at** attribute. The **position** attribute indicates if the table will scroll to the position of the cell and how. It is an enumeration called `ScrollPosition` included in the `UITableView` class. The values available are **none**, **top**, **middle**, and **bottom**. The **animated** attribute indicates whether the process is going to be animated or not.

setEditing(Bool, **animated:** Bool**)**—This method sets the value of the `isEditing` property. The attribute is the value we want to assign to the property, and the **animated** attribute determines if the change will be animated.

reloadData()—This method forces the Table View to reload the cells and sections.

beginUpdates()—This method indicates that an updating process has begun. It is used to animate the insertion or deletion of multiple cells.

endUpdates()—This method indicates that an updating process has ended. It is used to animate the insertion or deletion of multiple cells.

insertRows(at: [IndexPath], **with:** RowAnimation**)**—This method inserts new cells at the locations indicated by the **at** attribute. The **with** attribute indicates how the insertion is going to be animated. It is an enumeration called `RowAnimation` included in the `UITableView` class. The values available are **fade**, **right**, **left**, **top**, **bottom**, **none**, **middle**, and **automatic**.

deleteRows(at: [IndexPath], **with:** RowAnimation**)**—This method deletes the cells at the locations indicated by the **at** attribute. The **with** attribute indicates how the deletion is going to be animated. It is an enumeration called `RowAnimation` included in the `UITableView` class. The values available are **fade**, **right**, **left**, **top**, **bottom**, **none**, **middle**, and **automatic**.

insertSections(IndexSet, **with:** RowAnimation**)**—This method inserts new sections at the location indicated by the first attribute. The **with** attribute indicates how the insertion is going to be animated. It is an enumeration called `RowAnimation` included in the `UITableView` class. The values available are **fade**, **right**, **left**, **top**, **bottom**, **none**, **middle**, and **automatic**.

deleteSections(IndexSet, **with:** RowAnimation**)**—This method deletes the sections at the location indicated by the first attribute. The **with** attribute indicates how the insertion is going to be animated. It is an enumeration called `RowAnimation` included in the `UITableView` class. The values available are **fade**, **right**, **left**, **top**, **bottom**, **none**, **middle**, and **automatic**.

Table View Cells

Tables present the information in cells, one per row, with each cell in charge of displaying a unique piece of data. Cells are created from the `UITableViewCell` class. The class offers the following properties and methods to create and configure each cell.

textLabel—This property returns the **UILabel** object used to present the primary text of standard cells. The text is modified assigning a new value to its **text** property.

detailTextLabel—This property returns the **UILabel** object used to present the secondary text of standard cells. The text is modified assigning a new value to its **text** property.

imageView—This property returns the **UIImageView** object used to present the image of standard cells. The image is modified assigning a new **UIImage** object to its **image** property.

accessoryType—This property sets or returns the type of the accessory view (a view, usually an icon, displayed on the right side of standard cells). It is an enumeration called **AccessoryType** included in the **UITableViewCell** class. The values available are **none**, **disclosureIndicator**, **detailDisclosureButton**, **checkmark**, and **detailButton**.

selectionStyle—This property sets or returns the style of the cell when it is selected. It is an enumeration called **SelectionStyle** included in the **UITableViewCell** class. The values available are **none**, **blue**, **gray**, and **default**.

contentView—This property returns a reference to the cell's view. From this reference, we can access the rest of the elements in the cell or add new ones.

backgroundView—This property sets or returns the cell's background view.

Table View Protocols

The **UITableView** class defines the properties **delegate** and **dataSource** to assign delegate objects to the table. The delegates will be in charge of providing the data to display and the information required to configure the table. The protocols defined for these delegates are **UITableViewDelegate** and **UITableViewDataSource**. The following are the most frequently implemented methods of the **UITableViewDelegate** protocol.

tableView(UITableView, **heightForRowAt:** IndexPath**)**—This method is called by the table to get the height of the cell at the location indicated by the **heightForRowAt** attribute. The method must return a **CGFloat** value with the height of the cell. When the cells are all of the same height, it is recommendable to use the Table View's **rowHeight** property instead.

tableView(UITableView, **heightForHeaderInSection:** Int**)**—This method is called by the table to get the height of the header for the section at the index indicated by the **heightForHeaderInSection** attribute. The method must return a **CGFloat** value with the height of the header.

tableView(UITableView, **heightForFooterInSection:** Int**)**—This method is called by the table to get the height of the footer for the section at the index indicated by the **heightForFooterInSection** attribute. The method must return a **CGFloat** value with the height of the footer.

tableView(UITableView, **willDisplay:** UITableViewCell, **forRowAt:** Index-Path**)**—This method is called by the table when the cell indicated by the **willDisplay** attribute is about to be presented on the screen. The **forRowAt** attribute indicates the cell's location.

tableView(UITableView, **willDisplayHeaderView:** UIView, **forSection:** Int**)**—This method is called by the table when the header's view of a section is about to be presented on the screen. The **willDisplayHeaderView** attribute is a reference to the header's view and the **forSection** attribute is the index of its section.

tableView(UITableView, **willDisplayFooterView:** UIView, **forSection:** Int**)**—This method is called by the table when the footer's view of a section is about to be presented on the screen. The **willDisplayFooterView** attribute is a reference to the footer's view and the **forSection** attribute is the index of its section.

tableView(UITableView, **didSelectRowAt:** IndexPath**)**—This method is called by the table after the user selects a cell. The **didSelectRowAt** attribute indicates the location of the cell.

tableView(UITableView, **didDeselectRowAt:** IndexPath**)**—This method is called by the table when a cell is deselected. The **didDeselectRowAt** attribute indicates the location of the cell.

tableView(UITableView, **leadingSwipeActionsConfigurationForRowAt:** Index-Path**)**—This method is called by the table to get the actions to display on the left side of each row when they are in edition mode. It must return a `UISwipeActionsConfiguration` object containing the `UIContextualAction` objects that define each action.

tableView(UITableView, **trailingSwipeActionsConfigurationForRowAt:** Index-Path**)**—This method is called by the table to get the actions to display on the right side of each row when they are in edition mode. It must return a `UISwipeActionsConfiguration` object containing the `UIContextualAction` objects that define each action.

And the following are the most frequently implemented methods of the `UITableViewDataSource` protocol.

tableView(UITableView, **numberOfRowsInSection:** Int**)**—This method is called by the table to get the number of cells that have to be created in the section indicated by the **numberOfRowsInSection** attribute. The method must return an integer value with the number of cells in the section.

numberOfSections(in: UITableView**)**—This method is called by the table to get the total number of sections that have to be created. The method must return an integer value with the amount of sections.

tableView(UITableView, **cellForRowAt:** IndexPath**)**—This method is called by the table to get the cell for the location indicated by the **cellForRowAt** attribute. The method must return the `UITableViewCell` object that represents the cell.

tableView(UITableView, **titleForHeaderInSection:** Int**)**—This method is called by the table to get the title for the header of the section indicated by the **titleForHeaderInSection** attribute. The method must return a `String` value with the header's title.

tableView(UITableView, **titleForFooterInSection:** Int**)**—This method is called by the table to get the title for the footer of the section indicated by the **titleForFooterInSection** attribute. The method must return a `String` value with the footer's title.

tableView(UITableView, **commit:** EditingStyle, **forRowAt:** IndexPath**)**—This method is called by the table when the user inserts or deletes a row. It is implemented along with edition tools provided by Table Views. The **commit** attribute is an enumeration called `EditingStyle` included in the `UITableViewCell` class that indicates the type of operation performed. The possible values are `delete` and `insert`.

sectionIndexTitles(for: UITableView**)**—This method is called by the table to get the strings that represent the sections in the table's index. The method must return an array of strings with the values for the indexes.

tableView(UITableView, **sectionForSectionIndexTitle:** String, **at:** Int**)**—This method is called by the table to get the section corresponding to an index title. The method must return an integer value with the section's index. The **sectionForSectionIndexTitle** attribute is a string with the index's title, and the **at** attribute is the position where the title is located on the index.

tableView(UITableView, **moveRowAt:** IndexPath, **to:** IndexPath**)**—This method is called when the user moves a cell to a different position on the table. It is implemented along with edition tools provided by Table Views. The **moveRowAt** attribute is the path in which the cell is currently located and the **to** attribute is the path where the cell is going to be placed.

tableView(UITableView, **canMoveRowAt:** IndexPath**)**—This method is called when the user tries to move a cell to a different position. The method must return a Boolean value to indicate if the action is allowed. The **canMoveRowAt** attribute indicates the cell's current location.

Index Path

Tables identify their sections and rows with consecutive indexes starting from 0. To report these values, the table uses structures of type `IndexPath`. The structure includes the following properties.

section—This property returns the index of the section where the row is located.

row—This property returns the index of the row.

item—This property returns the index of the item in a Collection View (we will study Collection Views in Chapter 15).

The `IndexPath` structures are automatically created and defined by the Table View when it has to establish the order of the cells in the table, but there are situations in which we have to create these structures ourselves. The class includes the following initializers.

IndexPath(row: Int, **section:** Int**)**—This initializer creates an `IndexPath` structure with the values provided by the attributes. It is used with Table Views.

IndexPath(item: Int, **section:** Int**)**— This initializer creates an `IndexPath` structure with the values provided by the attributes. It is used with Collection Views.

Implementing Table Views

The first step to include a table in our interface is to add the Table View to the main view. The `UITableView` class includes an initializer to create Table Views from code.

UITableView(frame: CGRect, **style:** Style**)**—This initializer creates a `UITableView` object with the frame specified by the **frame** attribute. The **style** attribute is an enumeration called `Style` included in the `UITableView` class with the values `plain` and `grouped`.

To insert Table Views in the Storyboard, the Object Library includes the Table View option.

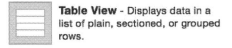

Table View - Displays data in a list of plain, sectioned, or grouped rows.

Figure 14-3: Table View option in the Object Library

Table Views are normal views and therefore they are positioned and sized inside the main view with constraints. Although we can give them any size we want, due to the type of information they manage, they are usually defined of the size of the screen.

    Table Views

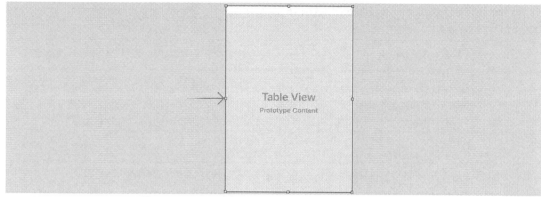

Figure 14-4: Table View pinned to the Safe Area

The **UITableViewCell** class also includes an initializer to create cells.

UITableViewCell(style: Style, **reuseIdentifier:** String?**)**—This initializer creates a **UITableViewCell** object for a cell with the style specified by the **style** attribute. The **style** attribute is an enumeration called **Style** included in the **UITableViewCell** class. The values available are **default**, **value1**, **value2**, and **subtitle**. The **reuseIdentifier** attribute is a string that identifies the cell (to use as a prototype for other cells).

The Object Library provides an option to add a cell to the Table View.

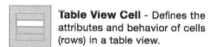

Table View Cell - Defines the attributes and behavior of cells (rows) in a table view.

Figure 14-5: Table View Cell option in the Object Library

Dragging the option of Figure 14-5 to the Table View creates a prototype cell.

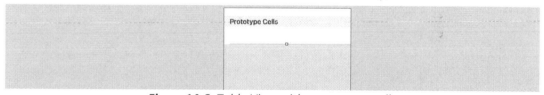

Figure 14-6: Table View with a prototype cell

Cells added to the Table View from the Object Library are prototype cells. When the app is executed, the view controller creates all the cells it needs to show the information on the screen from this prototype. As we do with Segues, prototype cells are identified from code using a string called *Identifier* set from the Attributes Inspector panel (Figure 14-7, number 2).

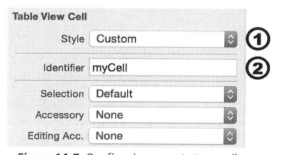

Figure 14-7: Configuring a prototype cell

From this panel, we can also select the style for the cell (Figure 14-7, number 1). There are five options available.

- **Custom** creates a cell with no style and custom content (the cell is empty; no elements are defined by default).
- **Basic (Default)** creates a cell with a single label for the title on the left and an optional Image View.
- **Right Detail (Value1)** creates a cell with a black label for the title on the left and a blue label for the description on the right.
- **Left Detail (Value2)** creates a cell with a blue label for the title on the left and a black label for the description on the right.
- **Subtitle** creates a cell with a black label for the title on top and a gray label for the description below.

The configuration of the table by default is enough to get it working, but the view controller has to conform to the protocols and implement their methods to provide the information the table is going to present. Most of the protocol methods are optional, but there are two of the **UITableViewDataSource** protocol that the table needs to call to know the number of rows it has to present and to get the cells it has to include in each row. The view controller in the following example conforms to the **UITableViewDataSource** protocol, assigns itself as the Table View's data source, and implements these two methods.

```
import UIKit

class ViewController: UIViewController, UITableViewDataSource {
   @IBOutlet weak var myTable: UITableView!
   var items: [String]!

   override func viewDidLoad() {
      super.viewDidLoad()
      items = ["Lettuce", "Tomatoes", "Milk", "Granola", "Donuts",
"Cookies", "Butter", "Cheese", "Lemonade", "Yogurt", "Oatmeal", "Juice",
"Tea", "Coffee", "Bagels", "Brownies", "Potatoes", "Onions"]
      myTable.dataSource = self
   }
   func tableView(_ tableView: UITableView, numberOfRowsInSection
section: Int) -> Int {
      return items.count
   }
   func tableView(_ tableView: UITableView, cellForRowAt indexPath:
IndexPath) -> UITableViewCell {
      let cell = myTable.dequeueReusableCell(withIdentifier: "myCell",
for: indexPath)
      cell.textLabel?.text = items[indexPath.row]
      return cell
   }
}
```

Listing 14-1: Feeding the table with data

The view controller needs an Outlet to access the Table View, but the cell is referenced from its identifier. The code of Listing 14-1 defines an Outlet for the table called **mytable** and then declares a property called **items** to store the array of strings that are going to be shown by it. To feed the table with these values, we have to implement the protocol's methods. The first method required is the **tableView(UITableView, numberOfRowsInSection:)**. From this method, we have to return the number of items we are going to present in every section of the table. By default, tables only have one section, so we just have to count the elements in the **items** array and return the result. The second method, **tableView(UITableView, cellForRowAt:)**, requires a little bit of work. This method is called every time the table is going to draw a row on the screen and needs its cell. Using the value of the index path received by the method, we have to create the cell for that row and return it. Since we have added a prototype cell to the table in the Storyboard, all we have to do to create the cell is to call the table's **dequeueReusableCell()** method with the identifier of the prototype cell ("myCell" in our example). The method returns a **UITableViewCell** object that we have to modify to configure the cell with the right values for the row. For a standard cell (not customized), there are only three properties we can work with: **textLabel** for the title of the cell, **detailTextLabel** for the description, and **imageView** for the image. In our example, we get the element of the **items** array corresponding to the row's index and assign it to the **text** property of the **UILabel** object in the **textLabel** property. As a result, every cell on the table has a title defined with the corresponding value of the **items** array.

 Do It Yourself: Create a new Single View Application project. Add a Table View to the main view and pin it to the edges of the view. Add a Table View Cell to the table. In the Attributes Inspector panel, change the style of the cell to Basic and give it the identifier "myCell" (Figure 14-7). Connect the table to an Outlet called **myTable**. Complete the view controller with the code of Listing 14-1. Run the application. You should see something similar to the left picture of Figure 14-1.

 IMPORTANT: Cells are created from a prototype to improve performance. Using prototypes, the system can create only the cells that are visible and reuse the **UITableViewCell** objects to represent new cells when the user scrolls the table (hence the name *reuse identifier*). You can create as many prototype cells as you want, just remember to give them a different identifier to be able to select the prototype you want to use from code.

We can take advantage of the rest of the elements in a standard cell to present more information. The following example uses a prototype cell with the style Subtitle and three associated arrays to include the title, description, picture, and an accessory for every item on the list (all the images are available on our website).

```
import UIKit

class ViewController: UIViewController, UITableViewDataSource {
    @IBOutlet weak var myTable: UITableView!
    var items: [String]!
    var descriptions: [String]!
    var images: [String]!
    var selected: [Bool]!

    override func viewDidLoad() {
        super.viewDidLoad()

        items = ["Lettuce", "Tomatoes", "Milk", "Granola", "Donuts",
"Cookies", "Butter", "Cheese", "Lemonade", "Yogurt", "Oatmeal", "Juice",
"Tea", "Coffee", "Bagels", "Brownies", "Potatoes", "Onions"]
        descriptions = ["1 lb.", "Sweet tomatoes", "2 lts.", "12 bars", "A
dozen", "Oreos", "2", "Lactose free", "2 lts.", "Strawberrie yogurt", "1
box", "Orange juice", "Green tea", "1 bag of beans", "6", "Chocolate
brownies", "2 lbs.", "1 lb."]
```

```
    images = ["lettuce", "tomato", "milk", "granola", "donuts",
"cookies", "butter", "cheese", "lemonade", "yogurt", "oatmeal", "juice",
"tea", "coffee", "bagels", "brownies", "potato", "onions"]
    selected = [true, true, true, true, true, true, true, true, true,
true, true, true, true, true, true, true, true, true]
    myTable.dataSource = self
}
func tableView(_ tableView: UITableView, numberOfRowsInSection
section: Int) -> Int {
    return items.count
}
func tableView(_ tableView: UITableView, cellForRowAt indexPath:
IndexPath) -> UITableViewCell {
    let cell = myTable.dequeueReusableCell(withIdentifier: "myCell",
for: indexPath)
    let row = indexPath.row
    cell.textLabel?.text = items[row]
    cell.detailTextLabel?.text = descriptions[row]
    cell.imageView?.image = UIImage(named: images[row])

    if selected[row] {
        cell.accessoryType = .checkmark
    }
    return cell
}
}
```

Listing 14-2: Taking advantage of the elements in a standard cell

The view controller of Listing 14-2 uses four properties to store the data for the table. These are associated arrays, which means that the elements of the same index are part of the same unit of information. The element at index 0 of the **items** array contains the name of the first item, the element at index 0 of the **descriptions** array contains the description of the first item, and so on. The **selected** property is an array of Boolean values. When the value of the element is **true**, we show an accessory in that cell. The initial values were all defined as **true**, so the table will look like Figure 14-8.

Figure 14-8: Subtitle cells in the simulator with Checkmark accessories

 The Basics: The arrays combined to store pieces of data that correspond to the same unit of information are called *Parallel Arrays*. Parallel arrays are practical when working with small applications, like the one created in Listing 14-2, but are not recommendable for larger applications. They are error prone and difficult to sort. If we try to order one array alphabetically, for example, the indexes will not match anymore with the rest of the arrays. We will see better forms to organize the model in further examples.

Table Views

Selection

Accessory types like the one implemented in the previous example are used to reflect or propose user interaction. For example, the Disclosure Indicator type is used to indicate to the user that there is more information available for that item. To take advantage of these indicators, we have to let the user interact with the table. The **UITableViewDelegate** protocol offers a few methods for this purpose. In the following example we implement the **tableView(UITableView, didSelectRowAt:)** method to modify the accessory type every time a cell is selected.

```swift
import UIKit

class ViewController: UIViewController, UITableViewDataSource,
UITableViewDelegate {
    @IBOutlet weak var myTable: UITableView!
    var items: [String]!
    var descriptions: [String]!
    var images: [String]!
    var selected: [Bool]!

    override func viewDidLoad() {
        super.viewDidLoad()
        items = ["Lettuce", "Tomatoes", "Milk", "Granola", "Donuts",
"Cookies", "Butter", "Cheese", "Lemonade", "Yogurt", "Oatmeal", "Juice",
"Tea", "Coffee", "Bagels", "Brownies", "Potatoes", "Onions"]
        descriptions = ["1 lb.", "Sweet tomatoes", "2 lts.", "12 bars", "A
dozen", "Oreos", "2", "Lactose free", "2 lts.", "Strawberrie yogurt", "1
box", "Orange juice", "Green tea", "1 bag of beans", "6", "Chocolate
brownies", "2 lbs.", "1 lb."]
        images = ["lettuce", "tomato", "milk", "granola", "donuts",
"cookies", "butter", "cheese", "lemonade", "yogurt", "oatmeal", "juice",
"tea", "coffee", "bagels", "brownies", "potato", "onions"]
        selected = [true, true, true, true, true, true, true, true, true,
true, true, true, true, true, true, true, true, true]
        myTable.dataSource = self
        myTable.delegate = self
    }
    func tableView(_ tableView: UITableView, numberOfRowsInSection
section: Int) -> Int {
        return items.count
    }
    func tableView(_ tableView: UITableView, cellForRowAt indexPath:
IndexPath) -> UITableViewCell {
        let cell = myTable.dequeueReusableCell(withIdentifier: "myCell",
for: indexPath)
        let row = indexPath.row
        cell.textLabel?.text = items[row]
        cell.detailTextLabel?.text = descriptions[row]
        cell.imageView?.image = UIImage(named: images[row])

        if selected[row] {
            cell.accessoryType = .checkmark
        }
        return cell
    }
    func tableView(_ tableView: UITableView, didSelectRowAt indexPath:
IndexPath) {
        let cell = myTable.cellForRow(at: indexPath)
        let row = indexPath.row
```

```
        if selected[row] {
          cell?.accessoryType = .none
          selected[row] = false
        } else {
          cell?.accessoryType = .checkmark
          selected[row] = true
        }
        myTable.deselectRow(at: indexPath, animated: true)
    }
}
```

Listing 14-3: Selecting items

The view controller of Listing 14-3 conforms to the **UITableViewDelegate** protocol to be able to implement the **tableView(UITableView, didSelectRowAt:)** method. This method is called by the Table View every time the user selects a cell. We first use the cell's index path to get a reference to the selected cell with the table's **cellForRow()** method and then use this reference to modify the **accessoryType** property of that cell. If the cell already had a checkmark, we remove it, or put it back otherwise.

Every time a cell is selected, the table highlights the cell with a gray background. The background remains as long as the cell keeps its selected state. This state does not change until the user selects another cell, and therefore it is our responsibility to change it if it is no longer necessary. To deselect the cell, we have to call the table's **deselectRow()** method, as we did in Listing 14-3. Although it is recommended to deselect the cell every time the selection is no longer necessary, we also have the alternative to change the cell's selection style. For example, if we do not want the cell to show a gray background when selected, we can assign the value **none** to the cell's **selectionStyle** property and the selection will not be visible anymore.

 Do It Yourself: Select the prototype cell created in the previous example and change its style to Subtitle. Download the thumbnail images from our website and add them to the Assets Catalog. Replace the code in the view controller with the code of Listing 14-3. Run the application. You should see something similar to Figure 14-8. Tap on the cells to select or deselect an item.

Sections and Indexes

Tables may organize the information in sections. By default, a table only has one section and all the rows belong to the same section, but we may declare more from the **UITableViewDataSource** protocol's methods. The **numberOfSections()** method returns the number of sections available and the **tableView(UITableView, titleForHeaderInSection:)** method provides the title for each section.

```
import UIKit

class ViewController: UIViewController, UITableViewDelegate,
UITableViewDataSource {
    @IBOutlet weak var myTable: UITableView!
    var categories: [String]!
    var items: [[String]]!
    override func viewDidLoad() {
        super.viewDidLoad()

        categories = ["B", "C", "D", "G", "J", "L", "M", "O", "P", "T","Y"]
        items = [["Bagels", "Brownies", "Butter"], ["Cheese", "Coffee",
"Cookies"], ["Donuts"], ["Granola"], ["Juice"], ["Lemonade", "Lettuce"],
```

Table Views

```
["Milk"], ["Oatmeal", "Onions"], ["Potatoes"], ["Tea", "Tomatoes"],
["Yogurt"]]
    myTable.delegate = self
    myTable.dataSource = self
  }
  func tableView(_ tableView: UITableView, cellForRowAt indexPath:
IndexPath) -> UITableViewCell {
    let cell = myTable.dequeueReusableCell(withIdentifier: "myCell",
for: indexPath)
    let row = indexPath.row
    let section = indexPath.section
    cell.textLabel?.text = items[section][row]
    return cell
  }
  func tableView(_ tableView: UITableView, numberOfRowsInSection
section: Int) -> Int {
    return items[section].count
  }
  func numberOfSections(in tableView: UITableView) -> Int {
    return categories.count
  }
  func tableView(_ tableView: UITableView, titleForHeaderInSection
section: Int) -> String? {
    let title = categories[section]
    return title
  }
}
```

Listing 14-4: Defining sections

Like rows, sections are identified with a consecutive index starting from 0, but when working with sections we have to contemplate that the sequence of indexes for rows start from 0 in every section. The data for the table has to observe this pattern, and this is why in the example of Listing 14-4 we use a multidimensional array to store the values (see Chapter 2, Listing 2-46). The first element of the **items** array is an array with the values for the cells of section 0, the second element is an array with the values for the cells of section 1, and so on. This provides a data structure that is easy to associate with the structure of the table. For example, to return the number of rows in a section from the **tableView(UITableView, numberOfRowsInSection:)** method, all we have to do is count the elements in the array corresponding to the section (**items[section].count**). The same happens when we prepare the cell in the **tableView(UITableView, cellForRowAt:)** method. The value for the title of the cell is obtained from the **items** array using the values of the **section** and **row** properties as indexes.

For the titles of every section, we use a separate array called **categories**. Each element in this array corresponds to a section in the **items** array, and therefore we use it to count the sections available in the **numberOfSections()** method. The values of the **categories** array are returned from the **tableView(UITableView, titleForHeaderInSection:)** method to represent the titles for each section. If we don't implement this method, the sections' headers are not shown on the screen.

If we set the style of the table for the previous example as Plain, we will see something similar to the right picture of Figure 14-1, where the headers of each section adopt a size relative to the size of their content. Implementing the **tableView(UITableView, heightForHeaderInSection:)** method of the **UITableViewDelegate** protocol we can specify a custom height.

```
func tableView(_ tableView: UITableView, heightForHeaderInSection
section: Int) -> CGFloat {
    return 50
}
```

Listing 14-5: Assigning a specific height to the headers

 The Basics: By checking the value of the **section** attribute, we can return a specific height for each section. The same may be achieved for the footers and cells implementing the **tableView(UITableView, heightForFooterIn-Section:)** and **tableView(UITableView, heightForRowAt:)** methods.

There are also methods available in the **UITableViewDelegate** protocol to customize the views of headers, footers and cells before they are drawn on the screen. They are used to perform last-minute settings. For example, we may implement the **tableView(UITableView, willDisplay:, forRowAt:)** method to change aspects of the cells, such as the background color. In the following example, we calculate if the row's index of the current cell is odd or even and assign a background color accordingly (see Listing 2-67).

```
func tableView(_ tableView: UITableView, willDisplay cell:
UITableViewCell, forRowAt indexPath: IndexPath) {
    if indexPath.row % 2 == 0 {
        cell.backgroundColor = UIColor(red: 245.0/255.0, green:
245.0/255.0, blue: 245.0/255.0, alpha: 1)
    } else {
        cell.backgroundColor = UIColor.white
    }
}
```

Listing 14-6: Changing the background color of the cells

Figure 14-9, below, shows some examples. The picture on the left illustrates what the table created by Listing 14-3 looks like after the method of Listing 14-6 is added to the view controller, and the picture on the right illustrates what the table created by Listing 14-4 looks like after the height of the headers is incremented with the method of Listing 14-5.

Figure 14-9: Different designs for cells and sections

 Do It Yourself: Add the method in Listing 14-5 to the view controller of the example of Listing 14-4 and the method in Listing 14-6 to the view controller of the example of Listing 14-3. These examples should look like the pictures of Figure 14-9.

Table Views

When working with sections and Plain tables, we can also provide an index on the right to help the user navigate through the items (see right picture in Figure 14-1). The **UITableViewDataSource** protocol includes a method to return an array with the titles for the indexes. Although the indexes titles may be anything from a single letter to a sentence, it is frequently created with single letters to organize the table alphabetically. For example, we can add the following method to the view controller of Listing 14-4 to create an index with the letters assigned to the titles of the headers.

```
func sectionIndexTitles(for tableView: UITableView) -> [String]? {
    return categories
}
```

Listing 14-7: Creating the index

 Do It Yourself: Add the method in Listing 14-7 to the example of Listing 14-4. Run the application. Tap the letters in the index on the right side of the screen. The table should scroll to the selected section.

The previous index contains one item per section, but sometimes what we want is to show a standard index that includes all the possible options, like a consecutive list of numbers or the entire alphabet. In this case, we have to provide a separate array for the index and then tell the table what section corresponds to the selected item in the index with the **tableView(UITableView, sectionForSectionIndexTitle:, at:)** method.

```
import UIKit

class ViewController: UIViewController, UITableViewDelegate,
UITableViewDataSource {
    @IBOutlet weak var myTable: UITableView!
    var indexLetters: [String]!
    var categories: [String]!
    var items: [[String]]!

    override func viewDidLoad() {
        super.viewDidLoad()
        indexLetters = ["#", "A", "B", "C", "D", "E", "F", "G", "H", "I",
"J", "K", "L", "M", "N", "O", "P", "Q", "R", "S", "T", "U", "V", "W",
"X", "Y", "Z"]
        categories = ["B", "C", "D", "G", "J", "L", "M", "O", "P", "T","Y"]
        items = [["Bagels", "Brownies", "Butter"], ["Cheese", "Coffee",
"Cookies"], ["Donuts"], ["Granola"], ["Juice"], ["Lemonade", "Lettuce"],
["Milk"], ["Oatmeal", "Onions"], ["Potatoes"], ["Tea", "Tomatoes"],
["Yogurt"]]
        myTable.delegate = self
        myTable.dataSource = self
        myTable.contentInset = UIEdgeInsets(top: 20, left: 0, bottom: 0,
right: 0)
    }
    func tableView(_ tableView: UITableView, cellForRowAt indexPath:
IndexPath) -> UITableViewCell {
        let cell = myTable.dequeueReusableCell(withIdentifier: "myCell",
for: indexPath)
        let row = indexPath.row
        let section = indexPath.section
        cell.textLabel?.text = items[section][row]
        return cell
    }
```

```
    func tableView(_ tableView: UITableView, numberOfRowsInSection
section: Int) -> Int {
        return items[section].count
    }
    func numberOfSections(in tableView: UITableView) -> Int {
        return categories.count
    }
    func tableView(_ tableView: UITableView, titleForHeaderInSection
section: Int) -> String? {
        let title = categories[section]
        return title
    }
    func sectionIndexTitles(for tableView: UITableView) -> [String]? {
        return indexLetters
    }
    func tableView(_ tableView: UITableView, sectionForSectionIndexTitle
title: String, at index: Int) -> Int {
        if let index = categories.index(of: title) {
            return index
        }
        return 0
    }
}
```

Listing 14-8: Creating a general index

The example of Listing 14-8 creates a new array with the letters of the alphabet to represent every item of the index and implements the **tableView(UITableView, sectionFor-SectionIndexTitle:, at:)** method to let the table know the relation between these items and the sections. The method is called every time the user taps on the index. The letter tapped is assigned to the method's **sectionForSectionIndexTitle** attribute. For example, when the user taps on the letter C, the value of this attribute is "C" and therefore the **index()** method returns the value 1 (the index of the letter C in the **categories** array). The value is returned, and the table scrolls to the section C. If the title does not correspond to any available section, the value return is 0 (the table scrolls to the first section).

The value returned when no section matches the index title depends on what we want for our application. The method could simply return the index corresponding to the first section (as we did in our example), the last section, or it could try to find the nearest section and return its index. The following example presents a method that looks for a section that matches the title and then, if no match is found, keeps comparing previous titles until it finds a match. The method only returns 0 when no match has been found. In consequence, the table always scrolls to the section selected by the user or the previous one if the selected section does not exist.

```
func tableView(_ tableView: UITableView, sectionForSectionIndexTitle
title: String, at index: Int) -> Int {
    let start = indexLetters.index(of: title)
    for counter in (0...start!).reversed() {
        let letter = indexLetters[counter]
        if let index = categories.index(of: letter) {
            return index
        }
    }
    return 0
}
```

Listing 14-9: Finding the nearest section

Table Views

Do It Yourself: Replace the view controller of Listing 14-4 with the view controller of Listing 14-8. Run the application. Tap on the letter in the index. The table scrolls to the section if it exists, or to the section with the index 0 otherwise. Replace the `tableView(UITableView, sectionForSection-IndexTitle:, at:)` method of Listing 14-8 by the method of Listing 14-9. Run the application again. Tap on the index items that do not match any section to see how the table scrolls to the nearest one.

Custom Cells

Sometimes the labels and the Image View included in a standard cell may not be enough to satisfy the requirements of our application. In cases like this, cells may be customized with the elements we need. Designing the cell is easy, we just have to set the style for the cell as Custom, drag the elements we want to include from the Object Library to the prototype cell, and set their constraints. If we need more space, we can drag the little square at the bottom of the cell or set a specific height from the Size Inspector panel.

Figure 14-10: Custom height for prototype cells

For the following example, we set the height of the prototype cell as 120 and added an Image View on the right and a label on the left. The Image View has a height of 100 points, leaving a 10-points margin at the top and the bottom.

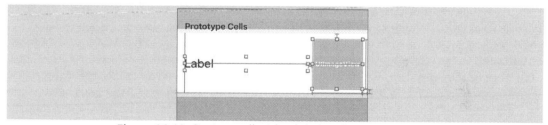

Figure 14-11: Custom cell with a label and an Image View

The height selected from the Size Inspector panel does not determine the height of a custom cell at run time. There are three ways to determine this size. We can set the size of all the cells with the `rowHeight` property of the Table View, define the height of each cell independently with the `tableView(UITableView, heightForRowAt:)` method included in the `UITableViewDelegate` protocol, or use Self-Sizing cells. Self-Sizing cells determine their height from the height of their content. All we have to do is to declare the constraints for top and bottom, as we did in the example of Figure 6-54. For instance, in the interface of Figure 14-11, we have declared Space constraints for the top and bottom of the Image View with a value of 10 and also a Height constraint of 100 points for the same element. From these values, the system determines the cell to be of a height of 120 points.

IMPORTANT: Self-Sizing cells, like the one we have created for this example, adapt their size to the size of their content. This, combined with Dynamic Type fonts, provides an excellent experience for the user (see Chapter 4, Listing 4-55). By assigning top and bottom constraints for a label, you can create cells that adapt their size to the size of the text.

To have access to the elements of a custom cell, we have to create a subclass of **UITableViewCell** and assign it to the cell. The file for the subclass is created as we did before for view controllers (Figures 13-3 and 13-4), only this time we have to select the **UITableViewCell** class as the superclass. As always, there are no requirements for the name, but it is better to give it a name related to the cell (for our example we just called it **FoodCell**). Once the file with the subclass is created, it has to be assigned to the cell from the Identity Inspector panel (Figures 13-6 and 13-7).

The current template generated by Xcode for subclasses of **UITableViewCell** includes the methods **awakeFromNib()** and **setSelected()**. The **awakeFromNib()** method is like the **viewDidLoad()** method for the view controller. It is called as soon as the view is loaded from the Storyboard and it is used to perform any custom initialization we need. The **setSelected()** method, on the other hand, is called when the cell is selected, allowing us to perform custom tasks and manage the selection from inside the cell. These methods are good if we need to perform additional tasks when the cell is created or selected, as we will see in Chapter 15.

 The Basics: The **awakeFromNib()** method is part of a protocol that the objects created from the Storyboard conform to. The method is called as soon as the object is loaded from the file to report its existence. Besides the **UITableViewCell** class, other classes such as the **UIViewController** class also implement this method. In the **UIViewController** class, the method is called before the rest of the methods implemented by the class, such as **viewDidLoad()** or **viewWillAppear()**. You may use it along with these methods or by itself to initialize the view controller.

Once the **UITableViewCell** subclass is created and assigned to the cell, we have to create the Outlets we need to access the elements added to the prototype cell in the Storyboard. Because Xcode not always shows the file in the Assistant Editor when the cell is selected, we have to click on the Automatic option at the top (Figure 5-23, number 1), select Manual, and then navigate the menu to find the file with the **UITableViewCell** subclass we have just created (**FoodCell** in our example). With the file opened in the Assistant Editor we can now control-drag the lines from the elements on the cell to the subclass to create the Outlets. The following example shows what the subclass looks like when the process is over (we have deleted the template methods and created two Outlets called **cellTitle** and **cellImage**).

```
import UIKit

class FoodCell: UITableViewCell {
    @IBOutlet weak var cellTitle: UILabel!
    @IBOutlet weak var cellImage: UIImageView!
}
```

Listing 14-10: Defining a subclass of UITableViewCell *for a custom cell*

 Do It Yourself: Create a new Single View Application project. Add a Table View to the main view. Add a Table View Cell to the table and give it the identifier "myCell". From the Size Inspector panel, click on Custom and insert the value 120 in the Row Height field (Figure 14-10). Add a label and an Image View to the prototype cell, as shown in Figure 14-11. Add the necessary constraints between the elements and the cell, including top and bottom Space constraints for the Image View. Create a new file with a subclass of **UITableViewCell** and call it **FoodCell**. Select the cell, open the Identity Inspector panel and assign the subclass to the cell (Figures 13-6 and 13-7). Open the Assistant Editor, click on Automatic, select Manual, and search for the FoodCell.swift file.

Erase the code inside the class included by the template and create Outlets for the cell's label and Image View called `cellTitle` and `cellImage`, respectively (Listing 14-10).

With the prototype cell ready, it is time to create the view controller. The main difference when working with custom cells is that we do not have access to the standard elements anymore, we have to modify the custom elements we added in the Storyboard from the Outlets created in the `UITableViewCell` subclass (`cellTitle` and `cellImage`).

```
import UIKit

class ViewController: UIViewController, UITableViewDelegate,
UITableViewDataSource {
    @IBOutlet weak var myTable: UITableView!
    var items: [String]!
    var images: [String: String]!

    override func viewDidLoad() {
        super.viewDidLoad()
        items = ["Lettuce", "Tomatoes", "Milk", "Granola", "Donuts",
"Cookies", "Butter", "Cheese", "Lemonade", "Yogurt", "Oatmeal", "Juice",
"Tea", "Coffee", "Bagels", "Brownies", "Potatoes", "Onions"]
        images = ["Lettuce": "lettuce", "Tomatoes": "tomato", "Milk":
"milk", "Granola": "granola", "Donuts": "donuts", "Cookies": "cookies",
"Butter": "butter", "Cheese": "cheese", "Lemonade": "lemonade", "Yogurt":
"yogurt", "Oatmeal": "oatmeal", "Juice": "juice", "Tea": "tea", "Coffee":
"coffee", "Bagels": "bagels", "Brownies": "brownies", "Potatoes":
"potato", "Onions": "onions"]
        items.sort(by: { (value1, value2) in value1 < value2 })
        myTable.dataSource = self
        myTable.delegate = self
    }
    func tableView(_ tableView: UITableView, numberOfRowsInSection
section: Int) -> Int {
        return items.count
    }
    func tableView(_ tableView: UITableView, cellForRowAt indexPath:
IndexPath) -> UITableViewCell {
        let cell = myTable.dequeueReusableCell(withIdentifier: "myCell",
for: indexPath) as! FoodCell
        let row = indexPath.row
        let title = items[row]
        cell.cellTitle.text = title

        if let image = images[title] {
            cell.cellImage.image = UIImage(named: image)
        }
        return cell
    }
}
```

Listing 14-11: Working with custom cells from the view controller

The `dequeueReusableCell()` method returns a `UITableViewCell` object. This is fine when our prototype cell is defined with a standard style, but for custom cells we need the object to be of the type of our subclass. In Listing 14-11, we cast the object as `FoodCell` and then assign the values from the `items` array and the `images` dictionary to the `cellTitle` and `cellImage` properties.

This time, we organized the data for the table combining an array and a dictionary to be able to sort the items in alphabetical order (see the `sort()` method). Combining an array with a dictionary allows us to order the elements of the `items` array in any way we want and still find the right image in the `images` dictionary using the name of the item as key.

Figure 14-12: Table with custom cells

14.2 Table Views in Navigation Controllers

Tables in iOS are meant to work along with other Scenes to provide more functionality. The addition of new rows, for example, requires a separate view to provide the fields and buttons the user needs to insert the information. This is the reason why we frequently see applications with tables embedded in Navigation Controllers. Navigation Controllers present views with a transition that feels more natural to the user and helps establish the relationship between the table and the rest of the views. Figure 14-13 shows what a view with a table looks like after it is embedded in a Navigation Controller.

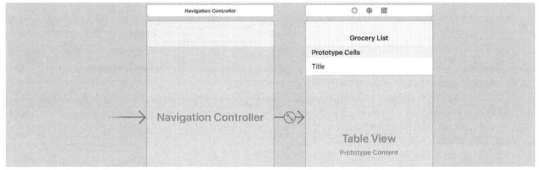

Figure 14-13: Table embedded in a Navigation Controller

 IMPORTANT: When an element that inherits from the `UIScrollView` class, such as a Table View or a Text View, is embedded in a Navigation Controller, its insets are automatically adjusted to place their content inside the Safe Area. Apple wants developers to incorporate transparency into their apps, and therefore Xcode configures the content of the element to be positioned behind the Navigation Bar and let the user see the text through the bar when it is scrolled down. To take advantage of this feature, you have to position the element behind the Navigation Bar and pin it to the top of the main view.

A common function provided by tables is the possibility to select a row to see more information related to the item. For instance, considering the previous examples, we may add a main view that shows the nutritional values associated with an item every time the user taps on its cell.

Table Views

Figure 14-14: Table with a detail view

The view presenting additional information is usually called *Detail View*, because it shows details about the selected item. To create a detail view, we have to add a new Scene to the Storyboard and connect it with a Show Segue (Figure 13-18). For our example, we have added a label, an Image View, and a Text View to the detail view to present the information.

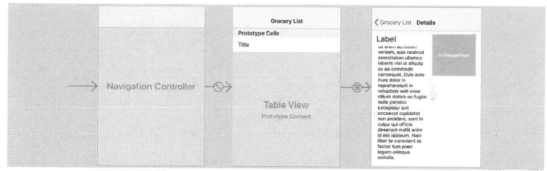

Figure 14-15: Detail view in the Storyboard

A detail view may be used to present additional information for every item on the table. Because the amount of data is significant, we have to manage this information from an external model, as we did in Chapter 13. The following code recreates that model to build the structure we need for the application of Figure 14-14. The **ApplicationData** structure for this example contains two properties: an array called **items** with the names of the items and a dictionary called **details** with the nutritional values of every item. The dictionary has a string as key and an array as value. The dictionary's keys are the values from the **items** array and the dictionary's values are arrays with two elements that represent the name of the image and the nutritional information of each item.

```
struct ApplicationData {
    var items: [String] {
        didSet {
            items.sort(by: { (value1, value2) in value1 < value2 })
        }
    }
    var details: [String: [String]]

    init() {
        items = ["Lettuce", "Tomatoes", "Milk", "Granola", "Donuts",
"Cookies", "Butter"]
        details = ["Lettuce": ["lettuce", "Vitamin A 148%\r\nVitamin C
15%\r\nCalcium 3%\r\nIron 4%\r\nVitamin B-6 5%\r\nMagnesium 3%"],
"Tomatoes": ["tomato", "Vitamin A 16%\r\nVitamin C 22%\r\nCalcium
1%\r\nIron 1%\r\nVitamin B-6 5%\r\nMagnesium 2%"], "Milk": ["milk",
"Calcium 12%\r\nVitamin B-12 8%\r\nMagnesium 2%"], "Granola": ["granola",
"Vitamin C 1%\r\nCalcium 6%\r\nIron 16%\r\nVitamin B-6 5%\r\nMagnesium
```

```
24%"], "Donuts": ["donuts", "Vitamin C 2%\r\nCalcium 2%\r\nIron
22%\r\nVitamin B-12 1%\r\nMagnesium 7%"], "Cookies": ["cookies", "Vitamin
A 1%\r\nCalcium 3%\r\nIron 15%\r\nVitamin D 1%\r\nVitamin B-6
5%\r\nVitamin B-12 1%"], "Butter": ["butter", "Vitamin A 49%\r\nCalcium
2%\r\nVitamin D 15%\r\nVitamin B-12 3%"]]
      items.sort(by: { (value1, value2) in value1 < value2 })
   }
}
var AppData = ApplicationData()
```

Listing 14-12: Building a model with an array for the cells and a dictionary for the details

A great advantage of using an external model to declare the data for the app is that we can manage the data and select what and how it is going to be available. In the example of Listing 14-12, we take advantage of the property's **didSet()** method to sort the elements of the items array in alphabetical order every time a new item is introduced. This alleviates the work of the view controllers that now don't have to worry about how to process the data, they just have to read it from the model and send it to the views.

 The Basics: The nutritional values in the example of Listing 14-12 are separated by the characters **\r\n**. This is a traditional sequence of characters used to indicate a line break. The characters after the sequence are printed on a new line. It is a simple way to create new lines in multiple line elements like labels and Text Views. Swift also offers the alternative of declaring the text between triple quotes (e.g., """My Text"""). This syntax asks the compiler to complete the text with the escape characters required to preserve the original format.

A table inside a Navigation Controller is managed the same way we did before, but because this time we are using a more complex model, instead of reading the **items** property from the view controller we have to read it from the **AppData** structure. Letting the user select a cell and open its detail view also combines techniques implemented before. We have to detect when a cell is selected with the **tableView(UITableView, didSelectRowAt:)** method and trigger the Segue with the **performSegue()** method (see Listing 13-6).

```
import UIKit
class ViewController: UIViewController, UITableViewDelegate,
UITableViewDataSource {
   @IBOutlet weak var myTable: UITableView!

   override func viewDidLoad() {
      super.viewDidLoad()
      myTable.delegate = self
      myTable.dataSource = self
   }
   func tableView(_ tableView: UITableView, numberOfRowsInSection
section: Int) -> Int {
      let data = AppData.items
      return data.count
   }
   func tableView(_ tableView: UITableView, cellForRowAt indexPath:
IndexPath) -> UITableViewCell {
      let data = AppData.items
      let cell = myTable.dequeueReusableCell(withIdentifier: "myCell",
for: indexPath)
      cell.textLabel?.text = data[indexPath.row]
      return cell
   }
```

```
    func tableView(_ tableView: UITableView, didSelectRowAt indexPath:
IndexPath) {
        performSegue(withIdentifier: "showDetails", sender: self)
    }
    override func prepare(for segue: UIStoryboardSegue, sender: Any?) {
        if segue.identifier == "showDetails" {
            let controller = segue.destination as! DetailViewController
            if let path = myTable.indexPathForSelectedRow {
                controller.selected = path.row
            }
        }
    }
    }
}
```

Listing 14-13: Opening the detail view when a cell is selected

The view controller of Listing 14-13 also implements the **prepare()** method to tell the view controller of the detail view what was the row selected by the user (see Listing 13-4). When the user selects a row, the table calls the **tableView(UITableView, didSelectRowAt:)** method. From this method, we execute **performSegue()** to trigger the Segue connected to the detail view (identified in our example with the name "showDetails"). When a Segue is triggered, the system calls the **prepare()** method. In this method, we get a reference to the view controller of the detail view and update the value of its **selected** property with the index path of the selected row (obtained from the Table View's property **indexPathForSelectedRow**).

The view controller for the detail view needs a property called **selected** to store the index of the selected row, and also Outlets for each of the elements on the interface to show the information on the screen. We called this view controller **DetailViewController**.

```
import UIKit

class DetailViewController: UIViewController {
    @IBOutlet weak var titleItem: UILabel!
    @IBOutlet weak var imageItem: UIImageView!
    @IBOutlet weak var nutritionItem: UITextView!
    var selected: Int!

    override func viewDidLoad() {
        super.viewDidLoad()

        if selected != nil {
            let item = AppData.items[selected]
            if let data = AppData.details[item] {
                titleItem.text = item
                imageItem.image = UIImage(named: data[0])
                nutritionItem.text = data[1]
            }
        }
    }
}
```

Listing 14-14: Showing the details for the selected row

The **DetailViewController** class checks whether the **selected** property contains a value or not and then gets the information corresponding to the selected row from the **details** dictionary in the **AppData** structure to show the values on the screen.

Do It Yourself: Create a new Single View Application project. Add a table and a cell to the main view. Identify the cell with the name "myCell" and connect the table to the view controller with an Outlet called `myTable`. Embed the main view in a Navigation Controller. You should see something similar to Figure 14-13. Add another Scene to the Storyboard. Create a Show Segue from the Scene with the table to the second view (Figure 13-18) and identify the Segue with the string "showDetails". Add a label, an Image View and a Text View to the second view to get an interface similar to Figure 14-15. Create a view controller file for the second view called `DetailViewController` (a subclass of `UIViewController`). Create the Outlets for the elements in the view with the names used in Listing 14-14. Create a Swift file called ApplicationData.swift for the `AppData` structure of Listing 14-12. Complete the `ViewController` class with the code of Listing 14-13 and the `DetailViewController` class with the code of Listing 14-14. Download the images for the thumbnails from our website and add them to the Assets Catalog. Run the application and select a row. You should see something similar to Figure 14-14.

Once selected, the rows remain in that state until the user selects another row. This means that when the user comes back from the detail view, the selected row is still selected. As we have seen before, to deselect a row we have to call the Table View's `deselectRow()` method (see Listing 14-3). Where we call this method depends on what we want to achieve with our app. The only thing we have to remember is that once the row is deselected, the `indexPathForSelectedRow` property returns `nil` (because there is no selected row anymore), so we always have to deselect the cell after the value of its row is no longer required. In our example, the best place to call the method would be after the selected row was assigned to the `selected` property of the detail view (`controller.selected = path.row`). A nice effect is achieved by calling the method from the `viewWillAppear()` method. The `viewWillAppear()` method is executed by the system every time the main view is going to be shown on the screen, and therefore we can use it to perform changes on the view when the user comes back from the detail view. The following code shows an implementation of this method that checks if there is a selected row and deselects it.

```
override func viewWillAppear(_ animated: Bool) {
    super.viewWillAppear(animated)
    if let path = myTable.indexPathForSelectedRow {
        myTable.deselectRow(at: path, animated: true)
    }
}
```

Listing 14-15: Deselecting the selected row

Do It Yourself: Add the method of Listing 14-15 to the view controller of Listing 14-13. Run the application and select a row. Go back to the Table View. The selected row should be deselected with an animation.

There is a Segue we may create that simplifies our example a little bit. Instead of connecting the Scene with the table to the detail view, we connect the prototype cell to the detail view, as shown in Figure 14-16 below. The type of Segue is still Show, but the advantage is that the table triggers the Segue as soon as a cell is selected. Because of this, we do not have to call the `performSegue()` method anymore. We can still implement the `tableView(UITableView, didSelectRowAt:)` method to perform any task related to the selection of the cell, but we do not have to trigger the Segue from code anymore.

Table Views

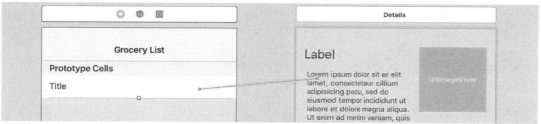

Figure 14-16: *Show Segue connecting the prototype cell with the detail view*

 Do It Yourself: Delete the Segue created before between the initial view and the detail view and create a new Show Segue from the prototype cell to the detail view (Figure 14-16) with the identifier "showDetails". Delete the method `tableView(UITableView, didSelectRowAt:)` in the `ViewController` class. Run the application. Everything should work like before.

Adding Rows

Navigation controllers not only provide a natural transition between views but also a bar where we can put buttons to let the user manage the table and the information it contains. A very common feature added to the table from this bar is a button that opens a view with a form to add new items to the list. There is even a predefined style for Bar Button Items called *Add* that creates a button with a plus sign. Figure 14-17 shows the Add button inserted on the right side of the bar and a new view with an input field to add items to the table. The new view is connected to the Add button with a Show Segue.

Figure 14-17: *View to insert new items*

The addition of new items is very simple, we just have to create a form for the user to insert the data and then store this information in the applications model (the `AppData` structure in our example). For our example, we have created a view with a Text Field and a Save button, as shown in Figure 14-17, right. The view controller class for this view was called `AddItemViewController`. To keep it simple, we have included only a Text Field to let the user insert the name of the item. The rest of the information is filled with placeholders ("noimage" and "Not Defined"). The following is the code for the `AddItemViewController` class.

```
import UIKit

class AddItemViewController: UIViewController {
   @IBOutlet weak var newItem: UITextField!

   @IBAction func saveItem(_ sender: UIButton) {
      var text = newItem.text!
      text = text.trimmingCharacters(in: .whitespaces)
```

```
        if text != "" {
            let lower = text.lowercased()
            let final = lower.capitalized
            AppData.items.append(final)
            AppData.details[final] = ["noimage", "Not Defined"]
            navigationController?.popViewController(animated: true)
        }
    }
}
```

Listing 14-16: Adding items to the `AppData` *structure*

The class includes an Outlet for the Text Field called **newItem** and an Action for the button called **saveItem()**. When the button is pressed, the **saveItem()** method trims the text from the Text Field with the **trimmingCharacters()** method (see Listing 7-2), and then compares it with an empty string. If the user's input is not empty, the code capitalizes the string, adds it to the **items** array with the **append()** method, and uses it as a key for the **details** dictionary.

The process adds the item to the model, but the Table View still does not know that there are more items available. One way to tell the table to update its content is by calling the **reloadData()** method. In our example, the best moment to call this method is when the table is about to be shown on the screen. The following example updates the **viewWillAppear()** method of Listing 14-15 to reload the data every time the user comes back to the table.

```
override func viewWillAppear(_ animated: Bool) {
    super.viewWillAppear(animated)
    if let path = myTable.indexPathForSelectedRow {
        myTable.deselectRow(at: path, animated: true)
    }
    myTable.reloadData()
}
```

Listing 14-17: Updating the table

 Do It Yourself: Add a Bar Button Item to the Navigation Bar over the Table View of our previous example. Add a new Scene to the Storyboard. Connect the bar button to the new view with a Show Segue. Add a label, a Text Field, and a button to the view, as shown in Figure 14-17, right. Create the **AddItemViewController** subclass and assign it to the new Scene. Connect the Text Field to the **AddItemViewController** class with an Outlet called **newItem** and the Save button with an Action called **saveItem()**. Complete this view controller with the code of Listing 14-16. Update the **viewWillAppear()** method of the **ViewController** class with the method of Listing 14-17. Run the application, press the plus button, insert a text, and press the Save button. The new item should be added to the table.

Another alternative to keep the table up to date is to manage the addition of the new item from the table's view controller. This requires us to assign the **ViewController** object of our example as the delegate of the **AddItemViewController** object and implement a method in the **ViewController** class to save the new item and update the table. The advantage of this procedure over updating the table from the **viewWillAppear()** method is that now the table will not reload its data every time it is shown on the screen but only when new items are available. The following is the new code for the **ViewController** class.

Table Views

```
import UIKit

class ViewController: UIViewController, UITableViewDelegate,
UITableViewDataSource {
    @IBOutlet weak var myTable: UITableView!

    override func viewDidLoad() {
        super.viewDidLoad()
        myTable.delegate = self
        myTable.dataSource = self
    }
    override func viewWillAppear(_ animated: Bool) {
        super.viewWillAppear(animated)
        if let path = myTable.indexPathForSelectedRow {
            myTable.deselectRow(at: path, animated: true)
        }
    }
    func tableView(_ tableView: UITableView, numberOfRowsInSection
section: Int) -> Int {
        let data = AppData.items
        return data.count
    }
    func tableView(_ tableView: UITableView, cellForRowAt indexPath:
IndexPath) -> UITableViewCell {
        let data = AppData.items
        let cell = myTable.dequeueReusableCell(withIdentifier: "myCell",
for: indexPath)
        cell.textLabel?.text = data[indexPath.row]
        return cell
    }
    override func prepare(for segue: UIStoryboardSegue, sender: Any?) {
        if segue.identifier == "showDetails" {
            let controller = segue.destination as! DetailViewController
            if let path = myTable.indexPathForSelectedRow {
                controller.selected = path.row
            }
        } else if segue.identifier == "showAddItem" {
            let controller = segue.destination as! AddItemViewController
            controller.delegate = self
        }
    }
    func saveItem(title: String) {
        let lower = title.lowercased()
        let final = lower.capitalized
        AppData.items.append(final)
        AppData.details[final] = ["noimage", "Not Defined"]
        myTable.reloadData()
        navigationController?.popViewController(animated: true)
    }
}
```

Listing 14-18: Storing new items and updating the table from the ViewController *class*

There are two things we have to do in this controller to manage the updates. We have to declare the **ViewController** class as delegate of the **AddItemViewController** class so the **AddItemViewController** object can ask the **ViewController** object to add a new item to the model, and we also have to implement the method that is going to be called to save the item and update the table. The delegate is assigned from the **prepare()** method. In this method, we check when the Segue of the Add button is triggered and then assign **self** (the **ViewController** object) to a property of the **AddItemViewController** class we called **delegate** (the Segue was identified with the string "showAddItem" from the Attributes Inspector panel). The method to store the new item was called **saveItem()**. This method receives the string inserted by the user and follows the same procedure as before to store the item and remove the view from the navigation stack, but this time it also calls the **reloadData()** method at the end to update the table.

In the **AddItemViewController** class we have to declare the **delegate** property and call the delegate's **saveItem()** method when the Save button is pressed. Notice that now the Action only trims the text and checks whether or not it is empty, but the rest of the process is delegated to the **ViewController** object.

```
import UIKit

class AddItemViewController: UIViewController {
    @IBOutlet weak var newItem: UITextField!
    var delegate: ViewController!
    @IBAction func saveItem(_ sender: UIButton) {
        var text = newItem.text!
        text = text.trimmingCharacters(in: .whitespaces)
        if text != "" {
            delegate.saveItem(title: text)
        }
    }
}
```

Listing 14-19: *Calling the* saveItem() *method from the* AddItemViewController *class*

 Do It Yourself: Assign the identifier "showAddItem" to the Segue connected to the Add button. Copy the code of Listing 14-18 inside the **ViewController** class and the code of Listing 14-19 inside the **AddItemViewController** class. Run the application. Everything should work exactly the same way, although this time the table is updated from its own view controller. The **ViewController** class of the example of Listing 14-18 includes all the code generated before in Listing 14-13, including the instructions necessary to open the detail view and show the details of every item, but it does not call the **performSegue()** method anymore because it assumes that you have followed previous instructions to create a Show Segue from the prototype cell to the detail view (see Figure 14-16).

 The Basics: The use of a delegate object usually requires the creation of a protocol that tells you what properties and methods you have to implement. In cases like this, where the connection is established between only two objects, a protocol is not really necessary. You just pass a reference to the object and access its properties and methods.

Deleting Rows

The same way we can add items we can also delete them. The process is as easy as deleting the item from the model and updating the table, but there are infinite possibilities on how to let the user do it. An alternative is to add a button in the Detail view that the user can press to delete the item. In this view, we know what item was selected because we got the index of its row from the table, and the user also knows what item is going to be deleted because it is seeing its data on the screen. Figure 14-18 shows the Detail view of our example modified to include a Delete button below the image.

Table Views

Figure 14-18: Delete button

The Delete button has to be connected to an Action in the **DetailViewController** class to remove the item from the model and close the view.

```
@IBAction func deleteItem(_ sender: UIButton) {
    let title = AppData.items[selected]
    AppData.details.removeValue(forKey: title)
    AppData.items.remove(at: selected)
    navigationController?.popViewController(animated: true)
}
```

Listing 14-20: Removing the selected item

The method of Listing 14-20 reads the value of the selected item, uses this value as a key to remove the corresponding element from the **details** dictionary, and finally deletes the item from the **items** array. When the **popviewController()** method is executed to remove the view from the navigation stack, the view with the table is pushed back to the top of the stack, its **viewWillAppear()** method is executed, and the table is updated with the **reloadData()** method (Of course, we can move this process to the View Controller, as we did before).

Do It Yourself: Add a button called Delete to the detail view of the previous example (Figure 14-18). Connect the button to an Action in the **DetailViewController** class called **deleteItem()**. Complete the method with the code of Listing 14-20. Run the application. Select a row and press the Delete button. The item should be removed from the table (this example assumes that you have a call to the **reloadData()** method in the **viewWillAppear()** method to update the table (see Listing 14-17).

The Basics: The user should be warned every time the code is going to delete data from the model. UIKit offers the **UIAlertController** class to create views for this purpose. We will study how to create Alert Views in Chapter 17.

Besides any custom technique we may develop to let the user remove items, Table Views also provide built-in functionality to do it. The table includes an editing mode that when activated shows a button on the left to delete the item and a button on the right to confirm the action.

Figure 14-19: Table in editing mode

Table Views

The process to activate and deactivate this mode involves the **isEditing** property, the **setEditing()** method (both from the **UITableView** class), and the **tableView(UITableView, commit:, forRowAt:)** method defined in the **UITableViewDataSource** protocol. We first have to provide a way for the user to decide when to activate or deactivate the mode and then process the feedback. For our example, we have added a Bar Button Item to the Navigation Bar called Edit.

Figure 14-20: Edit button

The button has to activate or deactivate the edition mode depending on its current state. To determine the state, we have to read the **isEditing** property, and to set a new state we have to call the **setEditing()** method.

```
@IBAction func editItems(_ sender: UIBarButtonItem) {
   if myTable.isEditing {
      myTable.setEditing(false, animated: true)
   } else {
      myTable.setEditing(true, animated: true)
   }
}
```

Listing 14-21: Activating and deactivating the editing mode

Listing 14-21 shows the Action we need to add to the **ViewController** class of our example to take advantage of the table's editing mode. When the user taps on the Edit button added to the interface in Figure 14-20, the **editItems()** method checks the value of the **isEditing** property and sets the mode to **false** if the property is **true**, or to **true** if the property is **false**. If the **isEditing** value is set to **true**, the table activates the editing mode and shows the edition buttons on the rows (Figure 14-19, left). These buttons do not perform any action but displace the row to the left to uncover a Delete button when pressed. This is the button that actually asks the table to delete the row. When the Delete button is pressed, the table calls the **tableView(UITableView, commit:, forRowAt:)** method to indicate to its delegate that the user wants to delete the row. In this method, we have to remove the item from the model and call the Table View's **deleteRows()** method to delete the row. The following is the implementation of this method required by our example.

```
func tableView(_ tableView: UITableView, commit editingStyle:
UITableViewCell.EditingStyle, forRowAt indexPath: IndexPath) {
   if editingStyle == UITableViewCell.EditingStyle.delete {
      let row = indexPath.row
      let item = AppData.items[row]
      AppData.details.removeValue(forKey: item)
      AppData.items.remove(at: row)
      myTable.deleteRows(at: [indexPath], with: .automatic)
   }
}
```

Listing 14-22: Responding to the Delete button

Table Views

The method of Listing 14-22 removes the item from the model first and then deletes the row. We always have to update the model first or the table will not have enough rows to display the data and will throw an error. Notice that the **deleteRows()** method takes an array of **IndexPath** structures instead of a single one. This is because the method is capable of deleting several rows at a time.

Do It Yourself: Add a Bar Button Item of type Edit to the Navigation Bar at the top of the table's view (Figure 14-20). Connect the button to an Action in the **ViewController** class of our previous example called **editItems()** and complete the method with the code of Listing 14-21. Add the method of Listing 14-22 to the **ViewController** class of Listing 14-18. Run the application and press the Edit button. You should see the edition buttons appear on the left side of the rows (see Figure 14-19). Press one of these buttons. The row should displace to the left and reveal the Delete button. Press it to delete the row.

IMPORTANT: If you have to remove or add several rows at a time, the **UITableView** class includes the **beginUpdates()** and **endUpdates()** methods to animate the changes simultaneously. All you have to do is to call the **beginUpdates()** method before the changes are performed and the **endUpdates()** method after (see Chapter 22, Listing 22-25).

Tables include a hidden feature that simplifies the deletion of rows and the execution of custom tasks. If the **tableView(UITableView, commit:, forRowAt:)** method is implemented, as we did in the previous example, the feature is activated and the user can uncover the Delete button by swiping the row to the left. If you think that this feature is enough for your application, you do not have to add an Edit button to activate or deactivate the editing mode, all you have to do is implement this delegate method. But we can also include our own buttons on the left and right side of the rows implementing the methods **tableView(UITableView, trailingSwipeActionsConfigurationForRowAt:)** and **tableView(UITableView, leadingSwipeActionsConfigurationForRowAt:)** from the **UITableViewDelegate** protocol. These methods are called when the user swipes a row to one side or another and are in charge of defining the buttons the table has to show and the actions they perform. For this purpose, UIKit defines two classes. The **UISwipeActionsConfiguration** class in charge of providing the actions and configuration values, and the **UIContextualAction** class to define each button and action. The following are the initializer and property provided by the **UISwipeActionsConfiguration** class.

UISwipeActionsConfiguration(actions: [UIContextualAction])—This initializer returns an object with the actions provided by the attribute and the configuration defined by its properties.

performsFirstActionWithFullSwipe—This is a Boolean property that defines whether or not the first action included in the object is going to be executed when the user performs a full swipe.

To define the buttons and actions, we have to create an object of the **UIContextualAction** class. The following are its initializer and properties.

UIContextualAction(style: Style, **title:** String?, **handler:** UIContextual-Action.Handler)—This initializer returns a **UIContextualAction** object with the definition of a button. The **style** attribute is an enumeration called **Style** included in the **UIContextualAction** class. The values available are **normal** (color gray) and **destructive** (color red) to define the style of the button. The **title** attribute is a string with the text to be shown on the button, and the **handler** attribute is the closure that is going to be executed when the action is performed. The closure receives three values, a reference to the action, a reference to the button's view, and another closure that takes a Boolean to declare whether the action was successful or not.

title—This property sets or returns a string with the button's title.

backgroundColor—This property sets or returns a **UIColor** object with the button's background color.

image—This property sets or returns a **UIImage** object with the button's image.

If we implement these methods instead of the delegate method implemented in Listing 14-22, the Delete button is replaced by our own buttons. For instance, in the following example we create our own Delete button with a blue background and a different title.

```
func tableView(_ tableView: UITableView,
trailingSwipeActionsConfigurationForRowAt indexPath: IndexPath) ->
UISwipeActionsConfiguration? {
   let button = UIContextualAction(style: .normal, title: "Remove",
handler: { (action, view, completion) in
      let row = indexPath.row
      let item = AppData.items[row]
      AppData.details.removeValue(forKey: item)
      AppData.items.remove(at: row)

      self.myTable.deleteRows(at: [indexPath], with: .automatic)
      completion(true)
   })
   button.backgroundColor = UIColor.blue

   let config = UISwipeActionsConfiguration(actions: [button])
   config.performsFirstActionWithFullSwipe = false
   return config
}
```

Listing 14-23: Creating our own actions

When the user swipes a row to the left, the table calls the method of Listing 14-23 to know what buttons it has to show. In this method, we create an action called **button** with the style **normal**, the title Remove, and a closure that performs the same action as before (it gets the index of the row, it erases the value from the model, and removes the row from the table). Notice that at the end of the closure we have to call the completion handler received by the third attribute with the value **true** to indicate that the action was performed successfully, otherwise the button is not removed. Finally, we create a new **UISwipeActionsConfiguration** object with this action, define its **performsFirstActionWithFullSwipe** property as **false** so the user cannot perform the action with a full swipe, and return it. The result is shown next.

Figure 14-21: Custom actions

Table Views

Do It Yourself: Replace the method introduced in Listing 14-22 by the method of Listing 14-23. Run the application, swipe a row to the left, and press the Remove button. The row should be removed.

Moving Rows

The edition mode also allows users to move cells to a different position on the table. This option is presented as an icon on the right side of the cells. To activate it, we have to implement the **tableView(UITableView, moveRowAt:, to:)** method of the **UITableViewDataSource** protocol. This method is called when a cell is moved to a different position on the table.

The cells are automatically placed in their new position every time the user performs the action, but we have to make sure that the new order of the cells is reflected in the model, so the next time the table loads its content, it shows the cells in the same order the user determined before. The following example shows a possible implementation of the delegate method.

```
func tableView(_ tableView: UITableView, moveRowAt sourceIndexPath:
IndexPath, to destinationIndexPath: IndexPath) {
    let item = AppData.items[sourceIndexPath.row]
    AppData.items.remove(at: sourceIndexPath.row)
    AppData.items.insert(item, at: destinationIndexPath.row)
}
```

Listing 14-24: Reorganizing the model when a cell is moved

In the method of Listing 14-24, we modify the **items** array of our model to change the index of the item that was moved by the user. We first get a reference to the string for the row that is being moved, and then remove the item corresponding to that row and add it again in the new position. Figure 14-21 illustrates what the table looks like after the editing mode is activated.

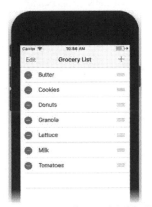

Figure 14-22: Editing mode to move cells

To move a cell, the user has to drag the cell from the icon to the new position. In the example of Figure 14-22, we moved the Cookies cell to the end of the table. When the change is performed, the Table View calls the delegate method of Listing 14-24 and the item corresponding to the cell is moved to an index that reflects its new position on the table.

 Do It Yourself: Add the method of Listing 14-24 to the **ViewController** class of Listing 14-18, run the application, and press the Edit button. You should see the icons to move the cells, as shown in Figure 14-22. Drag a cell to a new position from one of the icons. The table should reorder the cells, as shown in Figure 14-22.

IMPORTANT: The model defined in this chapter automatically organizes the items in alphabetical order (see Listing 14-12). If we want the user to decide the order of the items, we have to use a model that allows it. To test the method of Listing 14-24, you have to delete the `didSet()` method of the `items` property in the `ApplicationData` structure. This makes sure that the model delivers the items in the order they are stored in the array.

14.3 Table View Controller

Table Views that occupy the whole screen are very common in mobile applications. With the intention of simplifying the creation of these tables, the UIKit framework provides a subclass of the `UIViewController` class that includes a full screen table. The class has several advantages over adding the Table View ourselves. For starters, it conforms to the Table View protocols by default, so we do not have to declare it in our subclass and define the values of the table's `delegate` and `dataSource` properties anymore. Also, the controller is fully integrated with the Navigation Controller, so it is easy to create a path for the user to follow. And as if this was not enough, the class offers another type of cells called *Static Cells* that allow us to build static tables, which are tables that always present the cells as they were defined in the Storyboard. The Object Library includes the Table View Controller option to add this view controller to the interface.

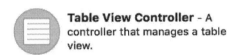

Table View Controller - A controller that manages a table view.

Figure 14-23: Table View Controller option in the Object Library

A Table View Controller looks like any other Scene but with a full-screen table inside. The difference is that the Table View is integrated into the main view and its size cannot be changed.

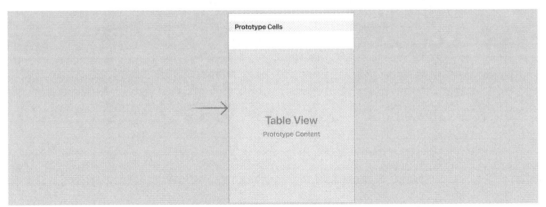

Figure 14-24: Table View Controller in the Storyboard

To manage the Table View, we have to create a subclass of the `UITableViewController` class and assign it to the Scene in the Storyboard. The file is created as any other file with the difference that now we have to select the `UITableViewController` class as the superclass. The template created by Xcode offers most of the delegate methods required for a Table View, but the class works like a normal view controller class. We can delete and add the properties and methods we need. The following example shows a subclass of `UITableViewController` called `MyTableViewController` that we have created to manage the interface of Figure 14-24.

Table Views

```
import UIKit

class MyTableViewController: UITableViewController {
   var items: [String]!

   override func viewDidLoad() {
      super.viewDidLoad()
      items = ["Lettuce","Tomatoes","Milk","Granola","Donuts", "Cookies",
"Butter", "Cheese", "Lemonade", "Yogurt", "Oatmeal", "Juice", "Tea",
"Coffee", "Bagels", "Coffee Filters", "Brownies", "Potatoes", "Onions"]
   }
   override func tableView(_ tableView: UITableView,
numberOfRowsInSection section: Int) -> Int {
      return items.count
   }
   override func tableView(_ tableView: UITableView, cellForRowAt
indexPath: IndexPath) -> UITableViewCell {
      let cell = tableView.dequeueReusableCell(withIdentifier: "myCell",
for: indexPath)
      let row = indexPath.row
      cell.textLabel?.text = items[row]
      return cell
   }
}
```

Listing 14-25: Managing the table from a subclass of the UITableViewController *class*

The **UITableViewController** class conforms to the delegate protocols by default, but it already provides an implementation of the delegate methods, so we have to override those that we want to implement in our subclass. This just means that we have to add the **override** keyword in front of every delegate method we use. The class also includes a property called **tableView** with a reference to the Table View. This saves us from creating the Outlet for the table. The rest of the configuration and codes work exactly the same way as before.

 Do It Yourself: Create a new Single View Application project. Delete the initial Scene and add a Table View Controller from the Object Library (Figure 14-23). Select the Scene, open the Attributes Inspector panel and activate the option Is Initial View Controller to designate it as the initial view. Select the cell, assign the "myCell" identifier to it and change its style to Basic. Create a new file with a subclass of **UITableViewController** called **MyTableViewController** and assign it to the Scene. Complete the class with the code of Listing 14-25. Run the application.

 The Basics: A Table View Controller automatically deselects a cell when the table is shown on the screen. For this reason, we do not have to deselect the cell from the **viewWillAppear()** method anymore, as we did in the example of Listing 14-15. The **UITableViewController** class offers a Boolean property called **clearsSelectionOnViewWillAppear** to activate or deactivate this feature.

Refresh Control

Another advantage of using Table View Controllers is that they include a feature usually provided by modern applications that allow the user to refresh the data by scrolling down the table. When the user keeps scrolling the table, a spinning wheel appears at the top to indicate that the system is refreshing the data. The control may also include text, as shown in Figure 14-25.

Figure 14-25: *Refresh Control*

Although the graphics are created by the Table View Controller, UIKit includes the `UIRefreshControl` class to manage the control. The class includes the following properties and methods to configure the control and report the state of the process.

tintColor—This property sets or returns a `UIColor` value that defines the control's color.

attributedTitle—This property sets or returns the text shown in the control. It is a value of type `NSAttributedString` (defined with an `NSMutableAttributedString` object).

isRefreshing—This is a Boolean property that indicates if the control is in the process of refreshing the data.

beginRefreshing()—This method tells the control that the process of refreshing the data was initiated programmatically.

endRefreshing()—This method tells the control that the process is over.

The `UITableView` class includes the following property to assign the control to the table.

refreshControl—This property sets or returns a reference to the Refresh Control associated to the table.

When the user scrolls down the table, the Table View Controller shows the Refresh Control, but the process of refreshing the data begins when the user lift the finger. At this moment, the control fires a `valueChanged` event to indicate to the code that it should perform the corresponding tasks. Therefore, to respond to the control, we have to add an action for this event with the `addTarget()` method, as shown in the following example.

```
import UIKit

class MyTableViewController: UITableViewController {
    var items: [String]!
    var refresh: UIRefreshControl!

    override func viewDidLoad() {
        super.viewDidLoad()
        refresh = UIRefreshControl()
        refresh.addTarget(self, action: #selector(refreshTable),
for: .valueChanged)
        refresh.attributedTitle = NSMutableAttributedString(string:
"Refreshing Table")
        tableView.refreshControl = refresh
        items = ["Lettuce", "Tomatoes", "Milk", "Granola", "Donuts",
"Cookies", "Butter", "Cheese", "Lemonade", "Yogurt", "Oatmeal", "Juice",
"Tea", "Coffee", "Bagels", "Coffee Filters", "Brownies", "Potatoes",
"Onions"]
    }
    @objc func refreshTable() {
        tableView.reloadData()
        refresh.endRefreshing()
    }
```

```
    override func tableView(_ tableView: UITableView,
numberOfRowsInSection section: Int) -> Int {
        return items.count
    }
    override func tableView(_ tableView: UITableView, cellForRowAt
indexPath: IndexPath) -> UITableViewCell {
        let cell = tableView.dequeueReusableCell(withIdentifier: "myCell",
for: indexPath)
        let row = indexPath.row
        cell.textLabel?.text = items[row]
        return cell
    }
}
```

Listing 14-26: Presenting a Refresh Control

The view controller of Listing 14-26 initializes the control, adds an action to it, and then assigns it to the table. The action is defined as the **refreshTable()** method. When the user uncovers the control and lift the finger, the **valueChanged** event is fired, and the method is executed. In this example, we just reload the data with the **reloadData()** method, but this is where we usually access a server to download information, or read the database to update the data. After the data is updated, we have to call the **endRefreshing()** method to indicate to the control that the process is over.

 Do It Yourself: Update the **MyTableViewController** class from the previous example with the code of Listing 14-26. Run the application and scroll down the table to activate the control. This example defines an attributed text for the control, so you will see something similar to the right picture of Figure 14-25.

Static Tables

As we mentioned before, Table View Controllers offer the possibility to create static tables. Static tables present a fixed number of cells and therefore are particularly useful when we have a limited number of options or predefined data to display. To turn the table of a Table View Controller into a static table, we have to select it and change the Content option in the Attributes Inspector panel to Static Cells, as shown in Figure 14-26.

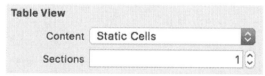

Figure 14-26: Option to change the type of cells

Once the option is selected, the table replaces the prototype cells with three custom cells.

Figure 14-27: Empty static cells

From this point on, the cells and their content are designed as we did before for prototype cells. We may add new cells, delete them, change their size, etc. We can also add more sections modifying the value of the Section option in the Attributes Inspector panel (Figure 14-26). If the main view in the Storyboard is not high enough to fit all the cells we need, we can set a different size from the Simulated Size option in the Size Inspector panel, as we did for Scroll Views in Chapter 11 (Figure 11-11). Figure 14-28 illustrates a possible design. For this example, we changed the table's style to Grouped, use custom cells, and added labels and a section with a single cell to contain an Image View.

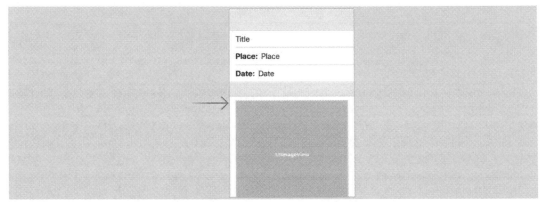

Figure 14-28: *Definition of static cells*

The custom cells for a static table do not need their own **UITableViewCell** subclass; we just have to connect the elements directly to Outlets in the view controller. The following is the code for the **UITableViewController** subclass necessary to control the interface of Figure 14-28.

```
import UIKit

class MyTableViewController: UITableViewController {
    @IBOutlet weak var titleLabel: UILabel!
    @IBOutlet weak var placeLabel: UILabel!
    @IBOutlet weak var dateLabel: UILabel!
    @IBOutlet weak var picture: UIImageView!

    override func viewDidLoad() {
        super.viewDidLoad()
        titleLabel.text = "Toronto's Waterfront"
        placeLabel.text = "Toronto"

        let formatter = DateFormatter()
        formatter.dateStyle = DateFormatter.Style.medium
        dateLabel.text = formatter.string(from: Date())
        picture.image = UIImage(named: "Toronto")
    }
}
```

Listing 14-27: *Defining the content of static cells*

In the view controller for a static table we do not have to declare the number of rows or define the content for each cell because everything has been defined in the Storyboard, but we can assign new values to the elements on each cell. In Listing 14-27, we assign strings to the labels, a date, and an image to the Image View. The result is shown in Figure 14-29.

Table Views

Figure 14-29: Application with a static table

Do It Yourself: Create a new Single View Application project. Download the image Toronto.jpg from our website and add it to the Assets Catalog. Delete the main view and add a Table View Controller from the Object Library (Figure 14-23). Select the Scene, open the Attributes Inspector panel and activate the option Is Initial View Controller. Select the table and change the value of the Content option to Static Cells and the value of the Style option to Grouped. Assign the value 2 to Sections to add another section to the table. Modify the sizes of the cells to fit the elements and add labels to the cells of the first section and an Image View to the cell of the second section, as shown in Figure 14-28. You can also select the sections to change their titles. Create a subclass of **UITableViewController** called **MyTableViewController** and assign it to the view. Complete the class with the code of Listing 14-27 and connect the elements on the cells to the Outlets in the code. Run the application. You should see something similar to Figure 14-29.

14.4 Search

Table Views are capable of managing thousands of rows and sometimes it can be difficult for users to find what they want. For this reason, the UIKit framework defines the **UISearchController** class to create a controller that includes the functionality necessary to let the user search for values in the model and present them on the screen. The controller must be created with the following initializer.

UISearchController(searchResultsController: UIViewController?**)**—This initializer creates a search controller associated with the view controller indicated by the attribute. The attribute is a reference to the view controller where we want to present the information or **nil** if we want to use the current view controller.

The **UISearchController** object creates a search bar with a text field and buttons to let the user perform the search. The following are the properties included in the object to access the bar and configure the controller.

searchBar—This property returns a reference to the **UISearchBar** object created by the controller to present the search bar.

obscuresBackgroundDuringPresentation—This property sets or returns a Boolean that indicates whether the background is obscured during the presentation of the search bar.

hidesNavigationBarDuringPresentation—This property sets or returns a Boolean value that determines whether the Navigation Bar should be hidden during the presentations of the search bar or not.

The controller also includes the `searchResultsUpdater` property to store a delegate object that receives the value introduced by the user, performs the search, and updates the interface. The object assigned to this property must conform to the `UISearchResults-Updating` protocol and implement the following method.

updateSearchResults(for: UISearchController)—This method is called by the search controller to process the value inserted by the user.

To present the search bar, we have to assign the controller to the Navigation Item of the Navigation Bar. The `UINavigationItem` class offers the following properties for this purpose.

searchController—This property sets or returns a reference to the search controller we want to present in the Navigation Bar.

hidesSearchBarWhenScrolling—This property sets or returns a Boolean value that indicates whether the search bar will be hidden when the table is scrolled.

The process is simple. We have to embed a table view in a Navigation Controller, create the search controller with the `UISearchController` initializer, declare the Table View Controller as the delegate, and implement the `UISearchResultsUpdating` protocol's method to process the input. The following is the interface for our example. We embedded a Table View Controller in a Navigation Controller and assigned large titles to the Navigation Bar.

Figure 14-30: Table View Controller embedded in a Navigation Controller

Search controllers provide tools for the user to perform the search, but it is up to us to take this input and select the items in our model that match the term. There are different ways to do this. When working with single arrays, the most simple is to use the **filter()** method studied in Chapter 3. The following example creates a model with a method to filter the data and an additional property to store the items currently selected.

```
struct ApplicationData {
   var items: [String]
   var filteredItems: [String] = []

   init() {
      items = ["Lettuce", "Tomatoes", "Milk", "Granola", "Donuts",
"Cookies", "Butter", "Cheese", "Lemonade", "Yogurt", "Oatmeal", "Juice",
"Tea", "Coffee", "Bagels", "Brownies", "Potatoes", "Onions"]
      filterData(search: "")
   }
   mutating func filterData(search: String) {
      if search == "" {
         filteredItems = items
      } else {
         filteredItems = items.filter({ (item) in
            let value1 = item.lowercased()
            let value2 = search.lowercased()
```

```
            let valid = value1.hasPrefix(value2)
            return valid
        })
    }
    filteredItems.sort(by: { (value1, value2) in value1 < value2 })
    }
}
var AppData = ApplicationData()
```

Listing 14-28: Filtering the data

This model is similar to previous examples, but this time we include a method to filter the items called **filterData()** and a second property called **fileteredItems** to store the items that match the search. The **filterData()** method receives a string with the value the user is looking for. If the value is an empty string, the **items** property is assigned to the **filteredItems** property to show all the original values, otherwise the **items** array is filtered and only the values that match the search are assigned to **filteredItems**. Because the **filterData()** method is going to be called every time the user inserts or deletes a character, we cannot compare entire words, we have to look for values in the **items** array the first letters of which match the characters already inserted by the user. The **hasPrefix()** method introduced in Chapter 3 is perfect for this situation. The method compares two strings and returns **true** if the first string is found at the beginning of the second string (the method distinguishes between lower and uppercase letters, so we have to lowercase both strings before comparing).

Because the model manages the search, the view controller is simple. We just have to create the search controller and conform to the **UISearchResultsUpdating** protocol to process the input.

```
import UIKit

class MyTableViewController: UITableViewController,
UISearchResultsUpdating{
    override func viewDidLoad() {
        super.viewDidLoad()

        let searchController = UISearchController(searchResultsController:
nil)
        searchController.searchResultsUpdater = self
        searchController.obscuresBackgroundDuringPresentation = false
        navigationItem.searchController = searchController
    }
    override func numberOfSections(in tableView: UITableView) -> Int {
        return 1
    }
    override func tableView(_ tableView: UITableView,
numberOfRowsInSection section: Int) -> Int {
        return AppData.filteredItems.count
    }
    override func tableView(_ tableView: UITableView, cellForRowAt
indexPath: IndexPath) -> UITableViewCell {
        let cell = tableView.dequeueReusableCell(withIdentifier: "myCell",
for: indexPath)
        let data = AppData.filteredItems[indexPath.row]
        cell.textLabel?.text = data

        return cell
    }
```

```
func updateSearchResults(for searchController: UISearchController) {
    if let text = searchController.searchBar.text {
        let search = text.trimmingCharacters(in: .whitespaces)
        AppData.filterData(search: search)
        tableView.reloadData()
    }
}
}
```

Listing 14-29: Processing the input from the search controller

The first thing we do in the view controller of Listing 14-29 is to create a search controller. In the initializer, we specify the `nil` value to declare this view controller as the one responsible for showing the results. The view controller is also assigned as the delegate of the search controller through the `searchResultsUpdater` property, and the search controller is finally assigned to the `searchController` property of the Navigation Item to show its search bar on the screen.

When the user inserts a character in the search bar, the search controller calls the `updateSearchResults(for:)` method with a reference to the search controller. From this reference, we can read the value inserted by the user, call the `filterData()` method in the model to perform the search, and update the table. Because `filterData()` stores the results in the `filteredItems` property and the values for the cells are taken from that same property, the results are shown in the table as soon as the user types or deletes a character in the field. The result is shown in Figure 14-31.

Figure 14-31: Search controller in the Navigation Bar

 Do It Yourself: Create a new Single View Application project. Erase the Scene and add a Table View Controller embedded in a Navigation Controller. Select the Navigation Bar and activate the option Prefers Large Titles. Insert the title Groceries for the table view. Select the cell, change its style to Basic, and give it the identifier "myCell". Create a Swift file called ApplicationData.swift with the code of Listing 14-28. Create a subclass of the `UITableViewController` class called `MyTableViewController`. Complete this class with the code of Listing 14-29. Run the application and scroll down the table. You should see the search bar appear at the top. Insert a value. The table should be updated with the items that match the value, as shown in Figure 14-31.

 IMPORTANT: If your view controller is not embedded in a Navigation Controller, you can add the search bar created by the search controller to the table's header. All you have to do is assigned the value of the `searchBar` property to the table's `tableHeaderView` property, as in `tableView.tableHeaderView = searchController.searchBar`.

Table Views

The search bar is hidden until the user scrolls the table, and the Navigation Bar is hidden when the search bar is active, but we can modify this behaviour from the controller's properties. In the example of Listing 14-29, we assigned the value `false` to the `obscuresBackgroundDuringPresentation` property to not let the controller obscure the interface when the bar is selected, but we can also assign the value `false` to the `hidesNavigationBarDuringPresentation` property to keep the Navigation Bar visible, and take advantage of the `hidesSearchBarWhenScrolling` property of the Navigation Item to keep the search bar visible when the table is scrolled up (e.g., `navigationItem.hidesSearchBarWhenScrolling = false`).

Search Bar

The bar created by the controller is an object of the `UISearchBar` class, which includes several methods and properties to configure the bar. In the example of Listing 14-29, we used the `text` property to get the value inserted by the user, but there are more available. The following are the most frequently used.

text—This property sets or returns the text in the field. It is an optional of type `String`.

placeholder—This property sets or returns the placeholder. It is an optional of type `String`.

tintColor—This property sets or returns the color of the bar's elements. It is an optional of type `UIColor`.

 IMPORTANT: The `UISearchBar` class also conforms to the `UITextInputTraits` protocol and implements its properties to configure the keyboard and some features for the Text Field. See `UITextField` in Chapter 7 for more information.

The `UISearchBar` class can also designate its own delegate object to report the state of the bar and feedback from the user. The delegate must conform to the `UISearchBarDelegate` protocol and implement its methods. The following are the most frequently used.

searchBarTextDidBeginEditing(UISearchBar)—This method is called by the bar on its delegate when the edition begins (the user taps on the bar to perform a search).

searchBarTextDidEndEditing(UISearchBar)—This method is called by the bar on its delegate when the edition ends.

searchBarCancelButtonClicked(UISearchBar)—This method is called by the bar on its delegate when the Cancel button is pressed (see Chapter 22, Listing 22-29).

searchBar(UISearchBar, selectedScopeButtonIndexDidChange: Int)—This method is called by the bar on its delegate when a button in the scope bar is pressed. The button's index is provided by the second attribute.

The last method works with a feature provided by search bars called the *Scope Bar* (see Figure 14-32, below). This is an additional bar at the bottom of the search bar with selectable buttons. The buttons work in a similar way as a Segmented Control; when a button is selected, the others are automatically deselected. The `UISearchBar` class includes the following properties to create and configure these buttons.

showsScopeBar—This property is a Boolean value that determines whether or not the scope bar is displayed. When the value is set to `true`, an additional bar is shown at the bottom of the Search Bar with buttons to select the scope of the search.

scopeButtonTitles—This property sets or returns an array of strings with the title for the buttons of the scope bar.

selectedScopeButtonIndex—This property sets or returns the index of the selected button in the scope bar. It is of type `Int`.

The bar assigns an index to every button and then, every time a button is selected, it calls the `searchBar(UISearchBar, selectedScopeButtonIndexDidChange:)` method on its delegate with the value of the button's index. This value may be used to refine the search. For example, we could look for the value in the items' titles or descriptions, depending on which button was selected.

The following is an update to the previous model that includes a dictionary with the calories for every item, so we have different values to search.

```
struct ApplicationData {
    var items: [String]
    var calories: [String: Int]
    var selectedButton: Int
    var filteredItems: [String] = []

    init() {
        items = ["Lettuce", "Tomatoes", "Milk", "Granola", "Donuts",
"Cookies", "Butter", "Cheese", "Lemonade", "Yogurt", "Oatmeal", "Juice",
"Tea", "Coffee", "Bagels", "Brownies", "Potatoes", "Onions"]
        calories = ["Lettuce": 15, "Tomatoes": 18, "Milk": 42, "Granola":
471, "Donuts": 452, "Cookies": 502, "Butter": 717, "Cheese": 402,
"Lemonade": 40, "Yogurt": 59, "Oatmeal": 68, "Juice": 23, "Tea": 1,
"Coffee": 0, "Bagels": 250, "Brownies": 466, "Potatoes": 77, "Onions":
40]
        selectedButton = 0
        filterData(search: "")
    }
    mutating func filterData(search: String) {
        if search == "" {
            filteredItems = items
        } else {
            filteredItems = items.filter({ (item) in
                var valid = false
                if selectedButton == 0 {
                    let value1 = item.lowercased()
                    let value2 = search.lowercased()
                    valid = value1.hasPrefix(value2)
                } else if let maximum = Int(search) {
                    let caloriesItem = calories[item]
                    if caloriesItem! < maximum {
                        valid = true
                    }
                }
                return valid
            })
        }
        filteredItems.sort(by: { (value1, value2) in value1 < value2 })
    }
}
var AppData = ApplicationData()
```

Listing 14-30: Expanding the model to work with a scope bar

Table Views

There are two new properties in this model: **calories** and **selectedButton**. The **calories** property is a dictionary with the names of the items as keys and their calories as values, and the **selectedButton** property keeps track of the scope button selected at the moment. The **filter()** method filters the **items** array according to the value of this property. If the button with the index 0 is selected, **filter()** searches for the string in the items' names, otherwise it turns the string into an integer and looks for the items in the dictionary with a number of calories lower than the current value inserted by the user.

The view controller has to implement the **searchBar(UISearchBar, selectedScopeButtonIndexDidChange:)** method to tell the model what is the button currently selected and adapt the interface.

```
import UIKit

class MyTableViewController: UITableViewController,
UISearchResultsUpdating, UISearchBarDelegate {
    override func viewDidLoad() {
        super.viewDidLoad()

        let searchController = UISearchController(searchResultsController:
nil)
        searchController.searchResultsUpdater = self
        searchController.obscuresBackgroundDuringPresentation = false
        navigationItem.searchController = searchController
        navigationItem.hidesSearchBarWhenScrolling = false

        let searchBar = searchController.searchBar
        searchBar.delegate = self
        searchBar.placeholder = "Search Product"
        searchBar.showsScopeBar = true
        searchBar.scopeButtonTitles = ["Names", "Calories"]
        searchBar.selectedScopeButtonIndex = 0
    }
    override func numberOfSections(in tableView: UITableView) -> Int {
        return 1
    }
    override func tableView(_ tableView: UITableView,
numberOfRowsInSection section: Int) -> Int {
        return AppData.filteredItems.count
    }
    override func tableView(_ tableView: UITableView, cellForRowAt
indexPath: IndexPath) -> UITableViewCell {
        let cell = tableView.dequeueReusableCell(withIdentifier: "myCell",
for: indexPath)
        let data = AppData.filteredItems[indexPath.row]
        cell.textLabel?.text = data
        return cell
    }
    func updateSearchResults(for searchController: UISearchController) {
        if let text = searchController.searchBar.text {
            let search = text.trimmingCharacters(in: .whitespaces)
            AppData.filterData(search: search)
            tableView.reloadData()
        }
    }
    func searchBar(_ searchBar: UISearchBar,
selectedScopeButtonIndexDidChange selectedScope: Int) {
        AppData.selectedButton = selectedScope
        if selectedScope == 0 {
            searchBar.placeholder = "Search Product"
```

```
    } else {
        searchBar.placeholder = "Maximum Calories"
    }
    searchBar.text = ""
    AppData.filterData(search: "")
    tableView.reloadData()
  }
}
```

Listing 14-31: Adding a scope bar

In the code of Listing 14-31, after creating the search controller, we get a reference to its search bar and then modify its properties. We first declare the view controller as the bar's delegate, then assign the string "Search Product" as placeholder, and finally create two buttons called Names and Calories for the scope bar. To respond to the user, we have also implemented the delegate method. When a button is pressed in the scope bar, this method is called, and the index of the button is assigned to the model's `selectedScope` property to notify the model the type of information it has to search. In this method, we also change the bar's placeholder to help the user identify the value it has to insert, clean the bar, and perform an empty search to show all the original values on the screen. In consequence, if the Names button is selected, the model tries to match the value with the names of the items, and when the Calories button is selected, the model compares the value with the number of calories of each item.

Figure 14-32: Scope bar in action

Table Views

15.1 A Collection of Views

With the introduction of the iPad and its larger screen it became evident to Apple that the single column layout provided by Table Views was not enough to create good user interfaces. But adding more columns to the table wouldn't satisfy these new demands either. Developers needed a flexible way to organize data on the screen and that is how Collection Views were born. Collection Views take a list of views (cells) and present them on the screen using a predefined layout. They come with a grid-like layout by default, but we can customize it to present the views any way we want.

Figure 15-1: *Collection Views*

Collection View

Collection Views are created the same way as tables. There is a class to create the view, a class for the cells, and delegates to provide the data and adjust the configuration. The class for the view is called **UICollectionView** and the following are some of its properties and methods.

allowsSelection—This property is a Boolean value that determines whether the selection of cells is allowed or not.

allowsMultipleSelection—This property is a Boolean value that determines whether multiple selection of cells is allowed or not.

backgroundView—This property sets or returns the view for the background of the cell. It is an optional value of type **UIView**.

collectionViewLayout—This property sets or returns the layout object in charge of setting the layout for the cells. It is an object of a subclass of the **UICollectionViewLayout** class.

numberOfSections—This property returns the number of sections available.

indexPathsForSelectedItems—This property returns an array of **IndexPath** structures with the indexes of the selected cells.

dequeueReusableCell(withReuseIdentifier: String, **for:** IndexPath)—This method returns a **UICollectionViewCell** object to represent a cell. The object is created from the prototype with the identifier defined by the **withReuseIdentifier** attribute.

dequeueReusableSupplementaryView(ofKind: String, **withReuseIdentifier:** String, **for:** IndexPath)—This method returns a `UICollectionReusableView` object to represent additional views like headers and footers. The object is created from the prototype view with the identifier defined by the **withReuseIdentifier** attribute. The **ofKind** attribute is a constant that represents the kind of views allowed by the layout object. The default object for the Collection Views include the constants `UICollectionElementKindSection-Header` and `UICollectionElementKindSectionFooter`.

reloadData()—This methods forces the Collection View to update the cells.

insertItems(at: [IndexPath])—This method inserts new cells in the positions indicated by the **at** attribute.

deleteItems(at: [IndexPath])—This method deletes the cells in the positions indicated by the **at** attribute.

selectItem(at: IndexPath?, **animated:** Bool, **scrollPosition:** ScrollPosition)—This method selects the cell at the position indicated by the **at** attribute. The **animated** attribute indicates if the process is going to be animated, and the **scrollPosition** attribute is a property of a structure called `ScrollPosition` included in the `UICollectionView` class that indicates how the Collection View is going to scroll to show the cell on the screen. The properties available are `top`, `bottom`, `left`, `right`, `centeredVertically`, and `centeredHorizontally`.

deselectItem(at: IndexPath, **animated:** Bool)—This method deselects the cell at the position indicated by the **at** attribute. The **animated** attribute indicates if the process is going to be animated.

scrollToItem(at: IndexPath, **at:** ScrollPosition, **animated:** Bool)—This method scrolls the Collection View to show on the screen the cell at the position indicated by the first **at** attribute. The second **at** attribute is a property of a structure called `ScrollPosition` included in the `UICollectionView` class that indicates how the Collection View is going to scroll. The properties available are `top, bottom, left, right, centeredVertically`, and `centeredHorizontally`. And the **animated** attribute is a Boolean value that indicates if the process is going to be animated

indexPath(for: UICollectionViewCell)—This method returns an `IndexPath` structure indicating the position of the cell referenced by the **for** attribute.

cellForItem(at: IndexPath)—This method returns the `UICollectionViewCell` object that represents the cell at the position indicated by the **at** attribute.

numberOfItems(inSection: Int)—This method returns an integer with the number of cells in the section specified by the **inSection** attribute.

Collection View Cells

Collection View's cells do not offer standard styles and therefore do not have predefined elements to display the data. They are empty cells that we have to customize as we did before for custom table cells. The cells are created from the `UICollectionViewCell` class and contain three empty views to manage their content: a view for the content, a view for the background, and a second background view that is shown when the cell is selected. The following are the properties to access these views.

contentView—This property returns the content view of the cell. All the elements added to customize the cell are incorporated as subviews of this view.

backgroundView—This property sets or returns the view for the background of the cell. It is an optional of type **UIView**.

selectedBackgroundView—This property sets or returns the view for the background when the cell is selected. It is an optional of type **UIView**.

Collection View Flow Layout

The big difference between Table Views and Collection Views is that the positions of the cells in a Collection View are not determined by the view, they are set by a layout object that works along with the Collection View to present the cells on the screen. This object is created from a subclass of the **UICollectionViewLayout** class. Although we can create our own subclass to provide any layout we want, Collection Views include by default a subclass called **UICollectionViewFlowLayout** that provides a very customizable grid-like layout that is usually more than enough for our projects. The layout is called *Flow*, and it includes the following properties for configuration.

scrollDirection—This property sets or returns the direction of the scroll. It is an enumeration called **ScrollDirection** included in the **UICollectionView** class. The values available are **vertical** and **horizontal** (with **vertical** set by default).

minimumInteritemSpacing—This property sets or returns a **CGFloat** value that determines the space between cells. In vertical scrolling, the value determines the space between cells in the same row, but in horizontal scrolling it determines the space between items in the same column.

minimumLineSpacing—This property sets or returns a **CGFloat** value that determines the space between cells. In vertical scrolling, the value determines the space between rows, but in horizontal scrolling it determines the space between columns.

sectionInset—This property sets or returns the margins for the sections. Its value is a structure of type **UIEdgeInsets** with the properties **top**, **bottom**, **left**, and **right**.

itemSize—This property sets or returns the size of the cells. It is a value of type **CGSize**.

estimatedItemSize—This property sets or returns the estimated size for the cells. It is a value of type **CGSize** and it used to improve performance. UIKit defines the constant **UICollectionViewFlowLayoutAutomaticSize** that we can assign to this property to let the system determine the estimated size based on the size of the cells currently available.

Collection View Protocols

As Table Views, Collection Views designate delegate objects to get the information they have to display and respond to the user. UIKit defines two protocols for Collection Views: **UICollectionViewDelegate** and **UICollectionViewDataSource**. The following are the most frequently implemented methods of the **UICollectionViewDelegate** protocol.

collectionView(UICollectionView, **didSelectItemAt:** IndexPath)—This method is called by the Collection View on its delegate when a cell is selected.

collectionView(UICollectionView, **didDeselectItemAt:** IndexPath)—This method is called by the Collection View on its delegate when a cell is deselected.

collectionView(UICollectionView, **willDisplay:** UICollectionViewCell, **forItemAt:** IndexPath)—This method is called by the Collection View on its delegate when a cell is going to be displayed. The **willDisplay** attribute is a reference to the object that represents the cell, and the **forItemAt** attribute indicates the cell's location.

collectionView(UICollectionView, **willDisplaySupplementaryView:** UICollectionReusableView, **forElementKind:** String, **at:** IndexPath**)**—This method is called by the Collection View on its delegate when a supplementary view is going to be displayed. The second attribute is a reference to the object that represents the view, the **forElementKind** attribute is a constant that determines the type of the view (`UICollectionElementKindSectionHeader` and `UICollectionElementKindSectionFooter` for the flow layout included by default), and the **at** attribute indicates the view's location.

The `UICollectionViewDataSource` protocol defines the following methods.

collectionView(UICollectionView, **numberOfItemsInSection:** Int**)**—This method is called by the Collection View on its delegate when it needs to know the number of cells in a section. It returns an integer with the number of cells available for the section indicated by the `numberOfItemsInSection` attribute.

numberOfSections(in: UICollectionView**)**—This method is called by the Collection View on its delegate when it needs to know the number of sections in the Collection View. It returns an integer with the number of sections.

collectionView(UICollectionView, **cellForItemAt:** IndexPath**)**—This method is called by the Collection View on its delegate when it needs the `UICollectionViewCell` object for a cell. The **cellForItemAt** attribute indicates the location of the cell.

collectionView(UICollectionView, **viewForSupplementaryElementOfKind:** String, **at:** IndexPath**)**—This method is called by the Collection View on its delegate when it needs the `UICollectionReusableView` object for a supplementary view. The second attribute is a constant that determines the type of view (`UICollectionElementKindSectionHeader` and `UICollectionElementKindSectionFooter` for the flow layout included by default), and the **at** attribute indicates the view's location.

Layout Protocol

The Flow layout can also designate a delegate to get specific values for individual cells. The methods are defined in the `UICollectionViewDelegateFlowLayout` protocol. The following are the most frequently used.

collectionView(UICollectionView, **layout:** UICollectionViewLayout, **sizeForItemAt:** IndexPath**)**—This method is called by the layout object to get the size of a cell. It must return a `CGSize` value with the size of the cell at the location indicated by the **sizeForItemAt** attribute.

collectionView(UICollectionView, **layout:** UICollectionViewLayout, **insetForSectionAt:** Int**)**—This method is called by the layout object to get the `UIEdgeInsets` structure with the inset values for the section (the margins). The **insetForSectionAt** attribute is an integer with the section's index.

collectionView(UICollectionView, **layout:** UICollectionViewLayout, **minimumLineSpacingForSectionAt:** Int**)**—This method is called by the layout object to get the `CGFloat` value that determines the minimum space between lines in a section. The **minimumLineSpacingForSectionAt** attribute is an integer with the section's index.

Collection Views

collectionView(UICollectionView, **layout:** UICollectionViewLayout, **minimumInteritemSpacingForSectionAt:** Int**)**—This method is called by the layout object to get the `CGFloat` value that determines the minimum space between cells in a section. The **minimumInteritemSpacingForSectionAt** attribute is an integer with the section's index.

Implementing Collection Views

Collection Views are like any other view; they may be created from code or added to the main view in the Storyboard from the option in the Object Library.

UICollectionView(frame: CGRect, **collectionViewLayout:** UICollectionViewLayout**)**—This initializer creates a `UICollectionView` object with the frame specified by the **frame** attribute and the layout object provided by the **collectionViewLayout** attribute. The object for the layout is created from a subclass of `UICollectionViewLayout`. We may specify our own layout object or assign the object by default (`UICollectionViewFlowLayout()`).

The Object Library includes the Collection View option to add a Collection View to the Storyboard.

Collection View - Displays data in a collection of cells.

Figure 15-2: Collection View option in the Object Library

Cells may also be created from code or added to the Storyboard from the option in the Object Library, but this is usually not necessary because Collection Views added to the Storyboard already include a prototype cell. Figure 15-3 shows a Collection View pinned to the edges of the main view with the cell by default (the little square at the top-left corner is the cell).

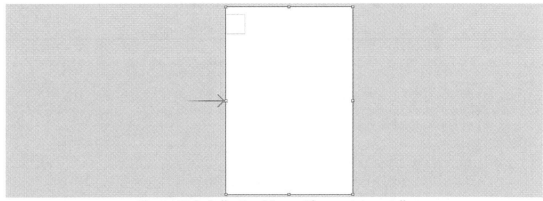

Figure 15-3: Collection View with a prototype cell

Collection Views do not include any standard cell, so we have to customize the prototype cell to be able to show content. The first step for customization is to give the cell the size we want. The size defined for the cell in the Storyboard is the size used by the Collection View to present the cell, unless we change it from the layout object. To define it, we can select the cell and drag the little squares around it to the position we want or specify the precise values from the Size Inspector panel. When we select the Collection View, the Size Inspector panel shows a list of options to define the size and aspects of several elements inside the view, including the header, the footer, and the cell. Figure 15-4 shows some of the options available. For this example, we have defined the size of the cell as 140 x 180 points.

Figure 15-4: Options to configure the Collection View

Once we set the size we want, we have to start adding elements to the cell. Figure 15-5 shows a cell with an Image View pinned to its margins.

Figure 15-5: Custom cell with an Image View

Because Collection View's cells are custom cells, we have to define our own subclass of **UICollectionViewCell** to manage their content. The following code defines a subclass called **BookCell** with an Outlet called **bookCover** to manage the cell of Figure 15-5.

```
import UIKit

class BookCell: UICollectionViewCell {
    @IBOutlet weak var bookCover: UIImageView!
}
```

Listing 15-1: Creating a subclass for a Collection View cell

As always, the model depends on the characteristics of our application. As an example, we are going to use a model that includes a list of books and their covers. We use an array called **items** for the names of the files and a dictionary called **itemsData** for the titles and authors.

```
struct ApplicationData {
    var items: [String]
    var itemsData: [String: [String]]
    init() {
        items = ["book1", "book2", "book3", "book4", "book5", "book6",
"book7", "book8", "book9", "book10", "book11", "book12"]
        itemsData = ["book1": ["Steve Jobs", "Walter Isaacson"], "book2":
["HTML5 for Masterminds", "J.D Gauchat"], "book3": ["The Road Ahead",
"Bill Gates"], "book4": ["The C Programming Language", "Brian W.
Kernighan"], "book5": ["Being Digital", "Nicholas Negroponte"], "book6":
["Only the Paranoid Survive", "Andrew S. Grove"], "book7": ["Accidental
Empires", "Robert X. Cringely"], "book8": ["Bobby Fischer Teaches Chess",
"Bobby Fischer"], "book9": ["New Guide to Science", "Isaac Asimov"],
"book10": ["Christine", "Stephen King"], "book11": ["IT", "Stephen
King"], "book12": ["Ending Aging", "Aubrey de Grey"]]
    }
}
var AppData = ApplicationData()
```

Listing 15-2: Creating the model for our Collection View

Collection Views

The view controller that manages the Collection View has to conform to at least the **UICollectionViewDataSource** protocol and implement two of its methods to report the number of cells to display and provide the **UICollectionViewCell** objects for every cell.

```
import UIKit

class ViewController: UIViewController, UICollectionViewDataSource {
   @IBOutlet weak var collectionItems: UICollectionView!

   override func viewDidLoad() {
      super.viewDidLoad()
      collectionItems.dataSource = self
      collectionItems.backgroundColor = UIColor.white
   }
   func collectionView(_ collectionView: UICollectionView,
numberOfItemsInSection section: Int) -> Int {
      return AppData.items.count
   }
   func collectionView(_ collectionView: UICollectionView, cellForItemAt
indexPath: IndexPath) -> UICollectionViewCell {
      let cell = collectionItems.dequeueReusableCell(withReuseIdentifier:
"myCell", for: indexPath) as! BookCell
      let file = AppData.items[indexPath.item]
      cell.bookCover.image = UIImage(named: file)
      return cell
   }
}
```

Listing 15-3: *Managing a Collection View*

The process to configure a Collection View is very similar to the one we used for tables. We have to implement the delegate methods to report the number of cells in the section (only one by default) and provide the cells. We also have to get the prototype cell calling the **dequeueReusableCell()** method with the identifier assigned to the cell from the Attributes Inspector panel ("myCell" in this example), cast it as our subclass (**BookCell** in this example), and then configure the elements in the cell. There is only one little detail that differs from tables. The **IndexPath** structure includes three properties: **section**, **row**, and **item**. We used the **section** and **row** properties before to identify the sections and each cell on a Table View, but Collection Views consider a cell to be an item, not an entire row, and therefore they use the **section** and **item** properties instead.

When we add a Collection View to the Storyboard, the system creates a **UICollectionViewFlowLayout** object and assigns it to the **collectionViewLayout** property of the Collection View's object. This layout object is configured by default to position the cells in a grid. The result is shown in Figure 15-6.

Figure 15-6: *Standard layout*

Do It Yourself: Create a new Single View Application project. Add a Collection View to the main view and pin it to the edges of the view (Figure 15-3). Connect the Collection View to the view controller with an Outlet called **collectionItems**. Select the Collection View and open the Size Inspector panel. Change the size of the cell to 140 x 180 (Figure 15-4). Select the cell and give it the identifier "myCell". Drag an Image View to the cell, pin it to its margins with Space constraints, and select its aspect mode as Aspect Fit. Create a file with a subclass of **UICollectionViewCell** called **BookCell** and assign it to the cell from the Identity Inspector panel. Connect the Image View to the **BookCell** class with an Outlet called **bookCover** (Listing 15-1). Create a Swift file for the model of Listing 15-2. Complete the **ViewController** class with the code of Listing 15-3. Download the covers from our website and add them to the Assets Catalog. Run the application. You should see something similar to Figure 15-6.

IMPORTANT: The same way it does for Table Views, the UIKit framework also includes a subclass of the **UIViewController** class to manage a full screen Collection View. The subclass is called **UICollectionViewController** and is represented in the Storyboard by a Scene created from an option in the Object Library called *Collection View Controller*.

Scroll Direction

The Flow layout (the layout object assigned by default to the Collection View) offers two directions for scrolling: Horizontal and Vertical. The Attributes Inspector panel includes an option called *Scroll Direction* to select the direction for the layout (Figure 15-7, number 1).

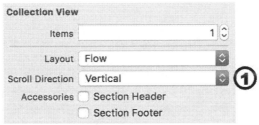

Figure 15-7: Flow layout options

The number of columns and rows generated by the layout always depends on the space available, the size of the cells, and the scrolling direction selected. For example, with a Vertical scroll, our example will only be able to fit one row of cells on small iPhones in landscape mode.

Figure 15-8: Horizontal scrolling in landscape mode

Collection Views

Selection

Collection View's cells show their selected background view when they are selected. The property containing this view is set to **nil** by default, so it is our responsibility to provide one. In the following example, we assign a new **UIView** object to the **selectedBackgroundView** property of each cell as soon as the cell is created.

```
import UIKit

class BookCell: UICollectionViewCell {
   @IBOutlet weak var bookCover: UIImageView!

   override func awakeFromNib() {
      super.awakeFromNib()

      selectedBackgroundView = UIView()
      selectedBackgroundView?.backgroundColor = UIColor(red: 0.9, green:
0.9, blue: 0.9, alpha: 1)
   }
}
```

Listing 15-4: *Adding the selected background view to the cell*

The **awakeFromNib()** method is called on the **UICollectionViewCell** subclass after the prototype cell is loaded from the Storyboard. This is a good place to prepare and configure the cell. In Listing 15-4 we assign a new **UIView** object to the cell's **selectedBackgroundView** property and give it a gray color. Notice that we do not need to declare the frame for the **UIView** object. The views added to background views are automatically expanded to occupy the space available.

Background views are positioned behind the content, so we have to make sure that the content leaves some room for the user to see them. For our example, we modified the Space constraints with a value of 8. Thus, when a cell is selected, the view is visible around the book cover, as shown in Figure 15-9.

Figure 15-9: *The book HTML5 for Masterminds is selected*

As well as Table Views, Collection Views call a method on the delegate to let our code know that a cell was selected. The method is called **collectionView(UICollectionView, didSelectItemAt:)**, but we do not need to implement it if we want to trigger a Segue. As mentioned in the previous chapter, if the Segue is created from the cell to the view, it is triggered when the cell is selected. Of course, to take advantage of this feature we have to create a full interface with all the necessary views and navigation tools. Figure 15-10 illustrates a possible interface for our example. The Collection View was embedded in a Navigation Controller and the prototype cell was connected to a detail view with a Show Segue.

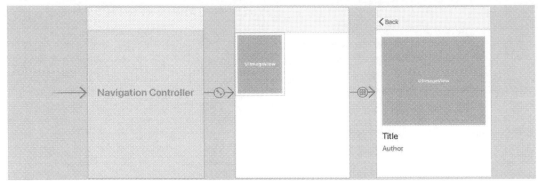

Figure 15-10: Collection View in a Navigation Controller

The view controller for the Collection View has to include the **prepare()** method to send the index of the selected cell to the detail view. The difference with Table Views is that the only method provided by Collection Views to get the path for the selected cell returns an array with all the cells selected. Because we are only working with a single selection, we have to retrieve the first element of this array and read its **item** property.

```
override func prepare(for segue: UIStoryboardSegue, sender: Any?) {
    if segue.identifier == "showDetails" {
        let controller = segue.destination as! DetailViewController
        if let paths = collectionItems.indexPathsForSelectedItems {
            let selectedCell = paths[0].item
            controller.selected = selectedCell
        }
    }
}
```

Listing 15-5: Sending the index of the selected cell to the detail view

The controller for the detail view receives the index of the selected cell and gets the information from the model to configure the elements on the screen. For this example, we called this view controller **DetailViewController** and defined three Outlets to show the cover, the title, and the author of the book on the screen.

```
import UIKit

class DetailViewController: UIViewController {
    @IBOutlet weak var bookCover: UIImageView!
    @IBOutlet weak var bookTitle: UILabel!
    @IBOutlet weak var bookAuthor: UILabel!
    var selected: Int!

    override func viewDidLoad() {
        super.viewDidLoad()
        let file = AppData.items[selected]
        bookCover.image = UIImage(named: file)
        if let data = AppData.itemsData[file] {
            bookTitle.text = data[0]
            bookAuthor.text = data[1]
        }
    }
}
```

Listing 15-6: Getting the values from the model and setting the detail view

Collection Views

When a cell is selected, the Segue is triggered and the view controller calls the **prepare()** method. This method gets the path of the selected cell and assigns its index to the **selected** property of the **DetailViewController** object. Using this index, the view controller gets the information from the model and shows it on the screen.

Figure 15-11: *Detail view for a Collection View*

 Do It Yourself: Embed the initial view of the previous example in a Navigation Controller. Add another Scene to represent the detail view. Connect the prototype cell to the detail view with a Show Segue (Figure 14-16). Assign the identifier "showDetails" to the Segue. Create a view controller called **DetailViewController** and assign it to the new Scene. Add an Image View and two labels to the detail view, as shown in Figure 15-10. Connect the elements to the Outlets shown in Listing 15-6. Complete the **DetailViewController** with the code of Listing 15-6. Add the **prepare()** method of Listing 15-5 to the **ViewController** class of Listing 15-3. Add the **awakeFromNib()** method of Listing 15-4 to the **BookCell** class. Run the application and select a book.

Again, we run into the problem that when we get back to the Collection View, the cell is still selected. As we did before, we can implement the **viewWillAppear()** method on the **ViewController** class and deselect the selected cell. Because the Collection View only provides a method that returns an array of cells, we have to iterate over the array to deselect each cell.

```
override func viewWillAppear(_ animated: Bool) {
    super.viewWillAppear(animated)
    if let paths = collectionItems.indexPathsForSelectedItems {
        for path in paths {
            collectionItems.deselectItem(at: path, animated: true)
        }
    }
}
```

Listing 15-7: *Deselecting cells*

 Do It Yourself: Add the method in Listing 15-7 to the **ViewController** class of Listing 15-3. Run the application, select a book, and go back to the Collection View. The book should be deselected.

Supplementary Views

Besides cells, Collection Views use other views to include additional content such as headers and footers. These views are called *Supplementary Views* and are managed by the layout object. The Flow layout includes two supplementary views, one for the header and another for the footer of every section. The options to add these views to the Collection View in the Storyboard are available in the Attributes Inspector panel (see Figure 15-7). Once any of the options is selected, the corresponding view is added to the Collection View. The views appear at the top and bottom of the prototype cell when the scroll direction is set to Vertical, and on the left and right when it is set to Horizontal.

Figure 15-12: Header and Footer in a vertical layout

Like cells, supplementary views added to the Storyboard are just prototypes. They are used as templates to create the headers and footers for every section. To set the size for these views, we have to select the Collection View and modify their values from the Size Inspector panel (Figure 15-4). The height defined in this panel is considered when the scroll direction is Vertical, and the width is considered when the scroll direction is Horizontal. The content of each view is defined as always. For our example, in the following interface, we added an Image View and a label to the header, and an Image View to the footer.

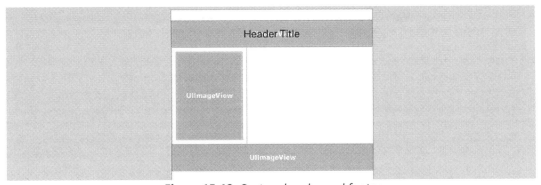

Figure 15-13: Custom header and footer

As well as cells, supplementary views are reusable. For this reason, they are not created from the **UIView** class but from a subclass called **UICollectionReusableView**. To connect the elements added to each view with our code, we have to create a subclass of the **UICollectionReusableView** class for every view, assign it to the view, and then create the Outlets. This is the same process we use for cells, but instead of the **UICollectionViewCell** class we use the **UICollectionReusableView** class as the superview. The following is the subclass we have created for the header of our example. It is called **HeaderView** and it contains an Outlet for the label called **headerTitle** and another for the Image View called **headerImage**.

```
import UIKit

class HeaderView: UICollectionReusableView {
    @IBOutlet weak var headerTitle: UILabel!
```

Collection Views

```
    @IBOutlet weak var headerImage: UIImageView!
}
```

Listing 15-8: Creating a subclass for the header view

The footer view also requires a subclass. We called this one **FooterView** and included an Outlet called **footerImage** for the Image View.

```
import UIKit

class FooterView: UICollectionReusableView {
    @IBOutlet weak var footerImage: UIImageView!
}
```

Listing 15-9: Creating a subclass for the footer view

When it is time to display the header or the footer of a section, the Collection View calls the **collectionView(UICollectionView, viewForSupplementaryElementOfKind:, at:)** method on its delegate. From this method, we have to get the instance of the supplementary view for the section, assign the values to its elements, and return it.

```
func collectionView(_ collectionView: UICollectionView,
viewForSupplementaryElementOfKind kind: String, at indexPath: IndexPath)
-> UICollectionReusableView {
    switch kind {
        case UICollectionView.elementKindSectionHeader:
            let headerView =
collectionItems.dequeueReusableSupplementaryView(ofKind:
UICollectionView.elementKindSectionHeader, withReuseIdentifier:
"myHeader", for: indexPath) as! HeaderView
            headerView.headerTitle.text = "My Books"
            headerView.headerImage.image = UIImage(named: "gradientTop")
            return headerView
        case UICollectionView.elementKindSectionFooter:
            let footerView =
collectionItems.dequeueReusableSupplementaryView(ofKind:
UICollectionView.elementKindSectionFooter, withReuseIdentifier:
"myFooter", for: indexPath) as! FooterView
            footerView.footerImage.image = UIImage(named: "gradientBottom")
            return footerView
        default:
            assert(false, "Error")
    }
}
```

Listing 15-10: Creating the supplementary views

The Collection View calls this method to get the view for the header and the footer, so the first step is to identify what kind of view is being requested. The Flow layout uses two type properties included in the **UICollectionView** class to identify each view. When the method is called, the value corresponding to the view is assigned to the **kind** parameter. Reading this parameter with a **switch** statement, we are able to know the kind of view we have to return. When the value of **kind** is equal to the value of the **elementKindSectionHeader** property, we create and return a header view, and when the value is equal to the value of the **elementKindSectionFooter** property, we create and return a footer view.

Because supplementary views are reusable, the instance is obtained from the **dequeueReusableSupplementaryView()** method. The method needs the identifier to create the instance from the prototype view in the Storyboard (for this example we called them "myHeader" and "myFooter", respectively), and also the constant for the **ofKind** attribute. The rest of the code accesses the elements in the views through the Outlets and assigns the values, as we did for cells before. The result is shown in Figure 15-14.

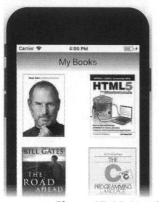 

Figure 15-14: Header and footer in the simulator

 Do It Yourself: To test supplementary views, start with the example of Figure 15-5 and the view controller of Listing 15-3. Download the images gradientTop.png and gradientBottom.png from our website and add them to the Assets Catalog. Select the Collection View and activate the options Section Header and Section Footer in the Attributes Inspector panel (Figure 15-7). The header and footer views should be automatically added to the Collection View, as shown in Figure 15-12. Add an Image View to each view and pin them to the sides. Add a label over the Image View in the header and pin it to the center of the view (Figure 15-13). Create two files with subclasses of the **UICollectionReusableView** class called **HeaderView** and **FooterView** and assign them to the supplementary views from the Identity Inspector panel. From the Attributes Inspector panel, assign the identifiers "myHeader" and "myFooter" to each view. Connect the elements of the views to Outlets, as shown in Listings 15-8 and 15-9. Add the method of Listing 15-10 to the view controller of Listing 15-3. Run the application. You should see something similar to Figure 15-14.

 The Basics: The **switch** statement must be exhaustive, which means that every option must be contemplated. If we cannot create a **case** for every option, we have to include a **default** statement. The problem in the example of Listing 15-10 is that the method has to return an object, no matter what. If there is no value to return, the execution of the application has to be interrupted. This is why in the **default** statement we call the **assert()** function with the value **false**. This function stops the execution of the application and prints a message in the console.

Sections

Collection Views may organize the information in sections. By default, a Collection View only has one section and all the items belong to the same section, but we may declare more from the **UICollectionViewDataSource** protocol's methods. The **numberOfSections()** method returns the number of sections available and reusable views can provide their titles, as we have seen in the previous example.

Collection Views cannot organize the information in sections, this structure must be provided by the data model. The following is our **ApplicationData** structure updated to present the data in sections.

```
struct ApplicationData {
   var categories: [String]
   var items: [[String]]
   var itemsData: [String: [String]]

   init() {
      categories = ["Fiction", "Non-Fiction", "Textbooks"]
      items = [["book10", "book11"], ["book1", "book3", "book5", "book6",
"book7", "book8", "book12"], ["book2", "book4", "book9"]]
      itemsData = ["book1": ["Steve Jobs", "Walter Isaacson"], "book2":
["HTML5 for Masterminds", "J.D Gauchat"], "book3": ["The Road Ahead",
"Bill Gates"], "book4": ["The C Programming Language", "Brian W.
Kernighan"], "book5": ["Being Digital", "Nicholas Negroponte"], "book6":
["Only the Paranoid Survive", "Andrew S. Grove"], "book7": ["Accidental
Empires", "Robert X. Cringely"], "book8": ["Bobby Fischer Teaches Chess",
"Bobby Fischer"], "book9": ["New Guide to Science", "Isaac Asimov"],
"book10": ["Christine", "Stephen King"], "book11": ["IT", "Stephen
King"], "book12": ["Ending Aging", "Aubrey de Grey"]]
   }
}
var AppData = ApplicationData()
```

Listing 15-11: Defining the model to present data in sections

The view controller requires only a few changes. We have to implement the **numberOfSections()** method to tell the view how many sections are available, and use the index of the section to return the information from the model.

```
import UIKit

class ViewController: UIViewController, UICollectionViewDataSource {
   @IBOutlet weak var collectionItems: UICollectionView!

   override func viewDidLoad() {
      super.viewDidLoad()
      collectionItems.dataSource = self
      collectionItems.backgroundColor = UIColor.white
   }
   func collectionView(_ collectionView: UICollectionView,
numberOfItemsInSection section: Int) -> Int {
      return AppData.items[section].count
   }
   func collectionView(_ collectionView: UICollectionView, cellForItemAt
indexPath: IndexPath) -> UICollectionViewCell {
      let cell = collectionItems.dequeueReusableCell(withReuseIdentifier:
"myCell", for: indexPath) as! BookCell
      let file = AppData.items[indexPath.section][indexPath.item]
      cell.bookCover.image = UIImage(named: file)
      return cell
   }
   func numberOfSections(in collectionView: UICollectionView) -> Int {
      return AppData.categories.count
   }
   func collectionView(_ collectionView: UICollectionView,
viewForSupplementaryElementOfKind kind: String, at indexPath: IndexPath)
-> UICollectionReusableView {
```

```
    switch kind {
        case UICollectionView.elementKindSectionHeader:
            let headerView =
collectionItems.dequeueReusableSupplementaryView(ofKind:
UICollectionView.elementKindSectionHeader, withReuseIdentifier:
"myHeader", for: indexPath) as! HeaderView
            headerView.headerTitle.text =
AppData.categories[indexPath.section]
            headerView.headerImage.image = UIImage(named: "gradientTop")
            return headerView
        case UICollectionView.elementKindSectionFooter:
            let footerView =
collectionItems.dequeueReusableSupplementaryView(ofKind:
UICollectionView.elementKindSectionFooter, withReuseIdentifier:
"myFooter", for: indexPath) as! FooterView
            footerView.footerImage.image = UIImage(named:
"gradientBottom")
            return footerView
        default:
            assert(false, "Error")
        }
    }
}
```

Listing 15-12: *Defining sections*

In the same way as in tables, the sequence of indexes for the items start from 0 in every section. The data has to observe this pattern, and this is why in the model of Listing 11 we use a multidimensional array to store the values. The first element of the **items** array is an array with the values for the cells of section 0, the second element is an array with the values for the cells of section 1, and so on. This provides a data structure that is easy to associate with the structure of the Collection View. For example, to return the number of items in a section from the **collectionView(UICollectionView, numberOfItemsInSection:)** method, all we have to do is count the elements in the array corresponding to the section (**AppData.items[section].count**). The same happens when we prepare the cell in the **collectionView(UICollectionView, cellForItemAt:)** method. The image is obtained from the **items** array using the values of the **section** and **item** properties as indexes.

For the titles of every section, we use a separate array called **categories**. Each element in this array corresponds to a section in the **items** array, and therefore we use it in the **numberOfSections()** method to count the sections available. The values of the **categories** array are also used to define the text for the label in the reusable view (**headerView.headerTitle.text = AppData.categories[indexPath.section]**). The result is shown in Figure 15.

Figure 15-15: *Sections with headers and footers*

Collection Views

Do It Yourself: Update the `ApplicationData` structure of the previous example with the code of Listing 11 and the `ViewController` class with the code of Listing 12. Run the application. You should see something similar to Figure 15.

Flow Layout

As we already mentioned, the Flow layout is the layout object assigned by default to the Collection View. The object comes preconfigured to create a grid of cells. The cells are positioned in sequential order from left to right or top to bottom, depending on the scrolling direction. If there is space left in the row or column, the layout object puts the space in between the cells. This is why the cells of our examples were always positioned close to the sides of the screen. We can modify this configuration assigning new values to the layout object. The `UICollectionViewFlowLayout` class offers properties to designate spaces in between the cells, between the lines, or around each section. For example, we can modify the `sectionInset` property to create a margin around the cells.

```
import UIKit

class ViewController: UIViewController, UICollectionViewDataSource {
   @IBOutlet weak var collectionItems: UICollectionView!

   override func viewDidLoad() {
      super.viewDidLoad()
      collectionItems.dataSource = self
      collectionItems.backgroundColor = UIColor.white

      let layout = collectionItems.collectionViewLayout as!
UICollectionViewFlowLayout
      layout.sectionInset = UIEdgeInsets(top: 25, left: 20, bottom: 25,
right: 20)
   }
   func collectionView(_ collectionView: UICollectionView,
numberOfItemsInSection section: Int) -> Int {
      return AppData.items.count
   }
   func collectionView(_ collectionView: UICollectionView, cellForItemAt
indexPath: IndexPath) -> UICollectionViewCell {
      let cell = collectionItems.dequeueReusableCell(withReuseIdentifier:
"myCell", for: indexPath) as! BookCell
      let file = AppData.items[indexPath.item]
      cell.bookCover.image = UIImage(named: file)
      return cell
   }
}
```

Listing 15-13: Configuring the Flow layout

The layout object is stored in the `collectionViewLayout` property of the Collection View. The property returns a generic object of type `UICollectionViewLayout` that we have to cast to our subclass (in this case `UICollectionViewFlowLayout`). In the code of Listing 15-13 we get the layout object and modify the value of its `sectionInset` property to generate margins of 25 points at the top and bottom and 20 points on the sides.

Figure 15-16: Margins around the cells in a section

By default, Flow layout organizes the cells considering the size set in the Storyboard. All the cells are displayed with the same size. In our example, the images are not all of the same size, but they are extended or contract to fit inside the Image View. If we want to give each cell the size of its image, we can conform to the **UICollectionViewDelegateFlowLayout** protocol and implement the **collectionView(UICollectionView, layout:, sizeForItemAt:)** method to return a specific size for every cell.

```
import UIKit

class ViewController: UIViewController, UICollectionViewDataSource,
UICollectionViewDelegateFlowLayout {
   @IBOutlet weak var collectionItems: UICollectionView!

   override func viewDidLoad() {
      super.viewDidLoad()
      collectionItems.dataSource = self
      collectionItems.backgroundColor = UIColor.white
      collectionItems.delegate = self

      let layout = collectionItems.collectionViewLayout as!
UICollectionViewFlowLayout
      layout.sectionInset = UIEdgeInsets(top: 25, left: 20, bottom: 25,
right: 20)
   }
   func collectionView(_ collectionView: UICollectionView,
numberOfItemsInSection section: Int) -> Int {
      return AppData.items.count
   }
   func collectionView(_ collectionView: UICollectionView, cellForItemAt
indexPath: IndexPath) -> UICollectionViewCell {
      let cell = collectionItems.dequeueReusableCell(withReuseIdentifier:
"myCell", for: indexPath) as! BookCell
      let file = AppData.items[indexPath.item]
      cell.bookCover.image = UIImage(named: file)
      return cell
   }
   func collectionView(_ collectionView: UICollectionView, layout
collectionViewLayout: UICollectionViewLayout, sizeForItemAt indexPath:
IndexPath) -> CGSize {
      var width: CGFloat = 140
      var height: CGFloat = 180
      let file = AppData.items[indexPath.item]
      if let image = UIImage(named: file) {
         width = image.size.width
         height = image.size.height
      }
```

Collection Views

```
        return CGSize(width: width, height: height)
    }
}
```

Listing 15-14: Declaring a specific size for each cell

The layout object calls the protocol methods on the delegate assigned to the Collection View's **delegate** property, so we have to designate our view controller as the delegate (**collectionItems.delegate = self**). The Flow layout calls the **collectionView(UICollectionView, layout:, sizeForItemAt:)** method every time it needs to know the size of a cell to calculate the layout. In this example, we decided to give the cell the size of the image it is going to display. We create a temporary **UIImage** object with the image file for the cell, get the value of its width and height from the **size** property, and return a **CGSize** structure with these values. Every cell in the Collection View will now have the size of its image.

Figure 15-17: Cells of different size

 Do It Yourself: Create a new Single View Application project. Add a Collection View and configure the cell as we did for the first example of this chapter. Add the book covers to the Assets Catalog and use the same model of Listing 15-2. Create the subclass for the cell and connect the elements with Outlets, as before. Complete the **ViewController** class with the code of Listing 15-12 and run the application. You should see something similar to Figure 15-17.

 IMPORTANT: Calculating the size of a cell every time it is going to be displayed is a resource-consuming process. In a real application, the images are stored in files or databases along with their metadata (size, name, etc.), and when the layout requires this information it retrieves it from the model. We will study how to permanently store information in Chapters 21 and 22.

Custom Layout

With the Flow layout, we can do things like modifying the margins of the sections from the **sectionInset** property (as we did in Listing 15-11), specifying the minimum space between cells from the **minimumInteritemSpacing** property, or declaring the size of each cell from the protocol methods, but the number of cells displayed in a row or column is always determined by the layout according to the space available (Figure 15-17). Flow layout gets the dimensions of the Collection View, subtracts the margins and the space between cells, and then positions the cells that fit in the remaining space. If, for example, we set the **minimumInteritemSpacing** property to a value too big to fit two cells in the same row, Flow layout will show only one cell and move the second cell to a new row. But as soon as we rotate the device and the space available becomes wider, the layout positions both cells back in the same row. The only way to make sure we have only the rows we expect, or the cells are organized the way we want, is by creating our own layout object.

A layout object is built from a subclass of the `UICollectionViewLayout` class. The class includes several properties and methods that we have to overwrite to provide the information required to organize the cells. Some of these properties and methods are optional, but there are a few that are required for the object to have enough information to calculate the layout.

collectionViewContentSize—This property is required to know the size of the Collection View's content. Collection Views are subclasses of Scroll Views and therefore they have a content area. The system needs to know how large the content area is to let the user scroll through it (see Chapter 11). The property must return a `CGSize` structure with the width and height of the area.

prepare()—This method is executed first by the Collection View to give the layout object the chance to perform some calculations and get the values it needs to construct the layout. When the number of cells in the Collection View is not significant, it is recommended to calculate their positions and sizes here as well.

layoutAttributesForItem(at: IndexPath)—This method is executed to get the attributes of every cell. The values must be returned as a `UICollectionViewLayoutAttributes` object. The **at** attribute indicates the location of the cell.

layoutAttributesForElements(in: CGRect)—This method is executed to get the attributes of all the cells located inside the rectangle determined by the **in** attribute. The method must detect which cells are inside the rectangle and return an array of `UICollectionViewLayoutAttributes` objects with the values of their attributes. The method is frequently used by the Collection View to get the attributes of the visible cells (the cells that are inside the rectangle of the screen).

shouldInvalidateLayout(forBoundsChange: CGRect)—This method returns a Boolean value that indicates whether or not the layout must be recalculated when the size of the Collection View changes (usually after the rotation of the device). The attribute is a `CGRect` structure with the values of the new internal frame.

The attributes for every cell are managed by objects of the `UICollectionView-LayoutAttributes` class. The class includes the following initializer.

UICollectionViewLayoutAttributes(forCellWith: IndexPath)—This initializer creates a `UICollectionViewLayoutAttributes` object for the cell in the location indicated by the **forCellWith** attribute.

The `UICollectionViewLayoutAttributes` class also includes the following properties to store and retrieve the values of the cell's attributes.

indexPath—This property sets or returns an `IndexPath` structure with the position of the cell the attributes belong to.

frame—This property sets or returns the frame of the cell. It is a value of type `CGRect`. Setting the value of this property also sets the values of the `size` and `center` properties.

bounds—This property sets or returns the bounds of the cell (the internal frame). It is a value of type `CGRect`. Setting the value of this property also sets the value of the `size` property.

center—This property sets or returns the coordinates for the center of the cell. It is a value of type `CGPoint`. Setting the value of this property changes the values in the `frame` property.

size—This property sets of returns the size of the cell. It is a `CGSize` structure. Setting the value of this property also sets the values for the size in the `frame` and `bounds` properties.

alpha—This property sets or returns the alpha value of the cell (transparency).

isHidden—This property sets or returns a Boolean value that indicates if the cell should be hidden. The value by default is `false`.

zIndex—This property sets or returns an integer that determines the order of the cells when they overlap. Cells with a higher value will appear on top of cells with a lower value.

transform—This property sets or returns a structure of type `CGAffineTransform` with values that determine different characteristics of the cell. The system works with two coordinate systems, one for the device and another to produce what the user sees. A transformation specifies how points in one coordinate system correlate to the points in the other. Modifying that correlation, we can perform operations on the object such as translation, scaling, or rotation (we will study `CGAffineTransform` in Chapter 24).

transform3D—This property sets or returns a structure of type `CATransform3D` with values that determine different characteristics of the cell. It works like the `transform` property introduced before, but it also processes values for the `z` axis, producing tridimensional effects (we will study `CATransform3D` in Chapter 24).

To create our custom layout class, we have to create a subclass of the `UICollectionViewLayout` class. These subclasses are created from the Cocoa Touch Class option, as we did before for other subclasses, but this time we have to select the `UICollectionViewLayout` class as the superclass (for our example, we called it `MyCustomLayout`).

Custom layout objects have to be assigned to the `collectionViewLayout` property of the Collection View, but the option is also available in the Attributes Inspector panel. We have to select Custom from the Layout option and insert the name of our subclass in the Class field.

Figure 15-18: Specifying a custom layout

The Collection View calls the methods in the layout object to know where to display the cells and the rest of the views. Therefore, the task of the layout object is to calculate the coordinates of every element according to the space available inside the Collection View and the layout we want to create. For our example, we are going to organize the cells always in two columns, independently of the space available, as shown in Figure 15-19.

Figure 15-19: Layout with only two columns

For a basic layout object, we need to overwrite at least five methods of the **UICollectionViewLayout** class. That includes the **prepare()** method to calculate the values for the layout, the **collectionViewContentSize()** method to return the size of the content area, the **shouldInvalidateLayout()** method to invalidate the layout when the device is rotated, and the **layoutAttributesForItem()** and **layoutAttributesForElements()** methods to return the attributes of the cells. The following is the subclass of the **UICollectionViewLayout** class we have developed to create the layout of Figure 15-19.

```
import UIKit
class MyCustomLayout: UICollectionViewLayout {
    let widthCell: CGFloat = 140
    let heightCell: CGFloat = 180
    let spaceCells: CGFloat = 10
    var listCells: [IndexPath: UICollectionViewLayoutAttributes] = [:]

    override func prepare() {
        let collection = collectionView!
        let bounds = collection.bounds
        let columnLeft = bounds.midX - widthCell
        let columnRight = bounds.midX
        let totalCells = collection.numberOfItems(inSection: 0)
        var posY: CGFloat = spaceCells
        for index in 0..<totalCells {
            let path = IndexPath(item: index, section: 0)
            let attributes = UICollectionViewLayoutAttributes(forCellWith:
path)
            if index % 2 == 0 {
                attributes.frame = CGRect(x: columnLeft, y: posY, width:
widthCell, height: heightCell)
            } else {
                attributes.frame = CGRect(x: columnRight, y: posY, width:
widthCell, height: heightCell)
                posY = posY + heightCell + spaceCells
            }
            listCells[path] = attributes
        }
    }
    override var collectionViewContentSize: CGSize {
        let collection = collectionView!
        let totalCells = collection.numberOfItems(inSection: 0)
        let totalColumn = ceil(CGFloat(totalCells) / 2)
        let width = collection.bounds.size.width
        let height = totalColumn * (heightCell + spaceCells)
        return CGSize(width: width, height: height)
    }
    override func layoutAttributesForItem(at indexPath: IndexPath) ->
UICollectionViewLayoutAttributes? {
        return listCells[indexPath]
    }
    override func layoutAttributesForElements(in rect: CGRect) ->
[UICollectionViewLayoutAttributes]? {
        var listAttributes: [UICollectionViewLayoutAttributes] = []
        for attributes in listCells.values {
            let cellRect = attributes.frame
            if cellRect.intersects(rect) {
                listAttributes.append(attributes)
            }
        }
    }
```

```
        return listAttributes
    }
    override func shouldInvalidateLayout(forBoundsChange newBounds:
CGRect) -> Bool {
        return true
    }
}
```

Listing 15-15: Creating a custom layout object

The first method called by the Collection View is **prepare()**. In this method, we have to calculate the values we need to later determine the position of the cells, such as the coordinates of the Collection View, margins, etc. Because the attributes of the cells are used by at least two other methods, it is recommended to also calculate those values in this method to improve performance. In the subclass of Listing 15-13, we adopt this approach. All the values to position the cells are calculated in the **prepare()** method and stored in a dictionary called **listCells**. Because in our layout the cells have always the same size and space in between, we declare those values in the **widthCell**, **heightCell**, and **spaceCells** properties. Their positions, on the other hand, are calculated according to their place on the list. The first cell is positioned at the top of the left column, the second cell on its right, and then the next cell is moved down to start a new row (Figure 15-19). We begin by getting the **CGRect** value corresponding to the bounds of the Collection View and read its **midX** property to get the **x** coordinate of the center of the view (see Chapter 4). Using this value, we calculate the horizontal position of the left and right columns. The vertical positions of every cell require more work. We first have to get the total amount of cells in the Collection View from the **numberOfItems()** method (we only consider one section), and then create a **for** loop with this value. Inside the loop, we need to create an **IndexPath** structure to represent the location of the cell and then use it to create the **UICollectionViewLayoutAttributes** object to hold its data. The vertical position depends on the row the cell is in, and the row depends on the number of cells we have already calculated. To determine where we are at any cycle of the loop, we get the remainder of the index divided by 2. If the result is equal to 0, it means the index is even and the cell belongs to the left column, otherwise the index is odd and therefore the cell belongs to the right column. Considering this result, we set the position of the cell to be in the left or right column, assign the values to the **frame** property, and finally store the **UICollectionViewLayoutAttributes** object in the **listCells** dictionary. Notice that when the cell is in the right column, we also calculate the vertical position for the next row (**posY = posY + heightCell + spaceCells**). After the loop is over, the dictionary contains a **UICollectionViewLayoutAttributes** object with the data for every cell.

The next member to overwrite is a computed property called **collection-ViewContentSize**. Its purpose is to return the size of the content area, so the system knows how long it has to scroll to let the user see all the cells. In our layout, the width of the content area is always the same as the Collection View (there is no horizontal scroll), but the height is calculated from the total number of cells in a column. To get this value, we first get the total number of cells from the **numberOfItems()** method, then divide it by two to get the cells in a single column, and finally calculate the height of the content area by multiplying the number of cells times their height and the space between them.

The Collection View calls two methods to get the attributes for the cells. The **layoutAttributesForItem()** method is called when the Collection View needs the attributes of a single cell, and the **layoutAttributesForElements()** method is called when the Collection View needs the attributes of all the cells inside a specific rectangle (usually called to get the attributes of the visible cells in the rectangle represented by the screen). The first method is simple, we just have to get the element of the **listCells** dictionary that corresponds to the cell's path (`listCells[indexPath]`), but the second method has to return an array of **UICollectionViewLayoutAttributes** objects corresponding to the cells inside the rectangle, so we have to read the values of every cell, compare their frames with the rectangle sent to the method, and add to the array the attributes of the cells that intersect. At first sight the task looks daunting, but the **intersects()** method provided by the **CGRect** structure makes it easy. This method compares the **CGRect** value of the structure with the **CGRect** value specify by its attribute and returns **true** if they intersect (see Chapter 4). All we have to do to know what attributes to return is to get the value of the **frame** property of each cell and compare it with the value of the **rect** attribute using this function. If they intersect, the **UICollectionViewLayoutAttributes** object is added to the array.

The last method in our subclass is **shouldInvalidateLayout()**. The purpose of this method is to indicate if we want the layout to be recalculated when the size of the Collection View changes. We return **true** to adapt the layout to every orientation.

 Do It Yourself: Create a new Single View Application project with the interface of Figure 15-5, the **UICollectionViewCell** subclass of Listing 15-1, the model of Listing 15-2, and the view controller of Listing 15-3. Add the book's covers to the Assets Catalog. Create a new file with a subclass of the **UICollectionViewLayout** class called **MyCustomLayout**, select the option Custom from the Attributes Inspector panel, and select the **MyCustomLayout** subclass (Figure 15-18). Complete this subclass with the code of Listing 15-13 and run the application. You should see something similar to Figure 15-19.

Real-Life Application

Custom layouts are usually not necessary in real life. The Flow layout provides enough flexibility to adapt the layout to the most common scenarios. For example, if we want to make sure that only one row is displayed at a time, independently of the space available on the screen, we can create a Collection View of the size of the cell. In the following example, we implement a Collection View with horizontal scroll and a specific height to always show only one column of items. To make it look more professional, we gave the interface a sense of depth using an Image View under a Visual Effect View (see Visual Effects in Chapter 8).

Figure 15-20: Collection View with a specific size

We have to start by creating a Single View Application project, add an Image View to the main view with the image we want to show in the background, and pin it to the sides with Space constraints (Figure 15-20, left). Next, we have to add a Visual Effect View over the Image View and also pin it to the sides of the main view with Space constraints (Figure 15-20, center). The Collection View has to be added over the Visual Effect View with Space constraints to the left and right sides, a Height constraint of 300 points, and a Vertical Alignment constraint to set its

Collection Views

position at the center of the screen (Figure 15-20, right). Finally, we have to select the Collection View and change the Scroll Direction option to Horizontal from the Attributes Inspector panel (Figure 15-7), and the size of the cell to 215 x 300 (Figure 15-4) from the Size Inspector panel.

For the content of the cell, we need an Image View that will show the cover of the book and two labels for the title and the author. To delimit the area, we can put the labels inside an empty view below the image, as shown in Figure 15-21. We have to add the view with a white background and pin it to the Image View on the top and to the cell's margins (Figure 15-21, center). The label at the top has to be pinned to the view's top, left, and right margins, and the label at the bottom with the label at the top and the view's left and right margins. The label at the top must be configured from the Attributes Inspector panel to have 2 lines to fit long titles.

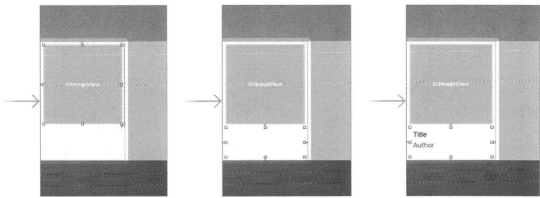

Figure 15-21: Configuring the prototype cell

To access the elements of the cell, we have to create a subclass of the **UICollectionViewCell** class called **BookCell**, assign it to the cell from the Identity Inspector panel, and connect the elements to the subclass with their corresponding Outlets.

```
import UIKit

class BookCell: UICollectionViewCell {
    @IBOutlet weak var bookCover: UIImageView!
    @IBOutlet weak var bookTitle: UILabel!
    @IBOutlet weak var bookAuthor: UILabel!
    @IBOutlet weak var titleView: UIView!

    override func awakeFromNib() {
        super.awakeFromNib()
        backgroundColor = UIColor(red: 0.7,green: 0.7,blue: 0.7,alpha: 0.3)
        titleView.backgroundColor = UIColor(red: 1.0, green: 1.0, blue:
1.0, alpha: 0.3)
    }
}
```

Listing 15-16: Modifying the cell's content and background

For this example, we want the cell and the white view containing the labels to be translucent. Translucency is usually achieved by modifying the alpha value of the element from the Attributes Inspector panel, but the problem is that this also affects the elements inside the view. The best way to make a container view translucent without affecting its content is to change the alpha value of the color. We can do this from the color picker opened by Interface Builder when we click on the color in the Attributes Inspector panel (the value is called Opacity), or by assigning a **UIColor** object with an alpha value different than 1.0 to the **backgroundColor** property of the elements. This time we have decided to do it from code. This is why the subclass of Listing 15-14 includes an Outlet for the white view and assigns **UIColor** objects to the **backgroundColor** properties of the cell and the view.

Now that the cell is ready, we have to create the view controller to manage the Collection View. The code is similar than previous examples, but we modified the Flow layout to improve the design, and also gave the Collection View a clear color so the background image can be seen through.

```
import UIKit

class ViewController: UIViewController, UICollectionViewDataSource {
   @IBOutlet weak var collectionItems: UICollectionView!

   override func viewDidLoad() {
      super.viewDidLoad()
      collectionItems.dataSource = self
      collectionItems.backgroundColor = UIColor.clear
      let layout = collectionItems.collectionViewLayout as!
UICollectionViewFlowLayout
      layout.sectionInset = UIEdgeInsets(top: 0, left: 40, bottom: 0,
right: 40)
      layout.minimumLineSpacing = 40
   }
   func collectionView(_ collectionView: UICollectionView,
numberOfItemsInSection section: Int) -> Int {
      return AppData.items.count
   }
   func collectionView(_ collectionView: UICollectionView, cellForItemAt
indexPath: IndexPath) -> UICollectionViewCell {
      let cell = collectionItems.dequeueReusableCell(withReuseIdentifier:
"myCell", for: indexPath) as! BookCell
      let file = AppData.items[indexPath.item]
      cell.bookCover.image = UIImage(named: file)
      if let data = AppData.itemsData[file] {
         cell.bookTitle.text = data[0]
         cell.bookAuthor.text = data[1]
      }
      return cell
   }
}
```

Listing 15-17: Modifying the design of the Collection View from the view controller

All that is left to do is to create the Swift file with the model of Listing 15-2 to provide the data. Remember to connect the Collection View to the **collectionItems** Outlet, assign the "myCell" identifier to the cell, and add to the Assets Catalog all the images with the covers and also the image for the Image View in the background.

Figure 15-22: One column Collection View

Collection Views

Chapter 16
Split View Controllers

16.1 Universal Container

The container view controllers studied so far are good for devices with small screens, such as iPhones and iPods, but the space available in devices like the iPads and iPhones Plus demand a more elaborated design. UIKit includes a subclass of **UIViewController** called **UISplitViewController** that can present two main views at a time, one called the Master view and another called the Detail view. The Master view is used to present the main interface, with controls that let the user select options and content, while the purpose of the Detail view is to show the selected content (similar to the custom detail views we have created in previous chapters).

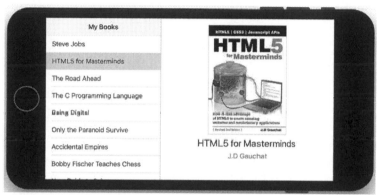

Figure 16-1: *Two main views presented by a Split View Controller*

The views are presented on the screen depending on the space available. On iPads and iPhones Plus in landscape mode, the Master and Detail views are shown together (Figure 16-1), but on the rest of the devices, and also on iPads and iPhones Plus in portrait mode, only one view is shown at a time. When only one view is displayed, the views replace one another. For example, if the Master view is embedded in a Navigation Controller (as it happens in the application of Figure 16-1), the Detail view is presented with a transition from right to left and a Back button is added to its Navigation Bar to let the user go back to the Master view, as shown in Figure 16-2.

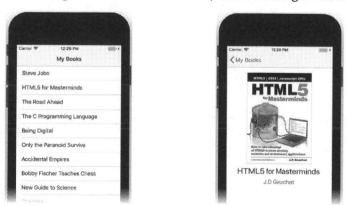

Figure 16-2: *Split View Controller in portrait mode*

Because of their capacity to adapt the interface to the space available, Split View Controllers are perfect to create universal applications that work on iPads, iPhones, and iPods. That is why Xcode offers a template called *Master-Detail App* that initializes the Storyboard with a Split View Controller and its Master and Detail views. Although this template includes everything we need to implement a Split View Controller, it also comes with preprogrammed code to produce a sample application that we usually have to erase to create our own. For this reason, it is better to start with a Single View Application project and then add the Split View Controller from the Object Library.

Split View Controller - A composite view controller that manages left and right view controllers.

Figure 16-3: Split View Controller option in the Object Library

The option adds to the Storyboard a Split View Controller with Master and Detail views, as shown in Figure 16-4.

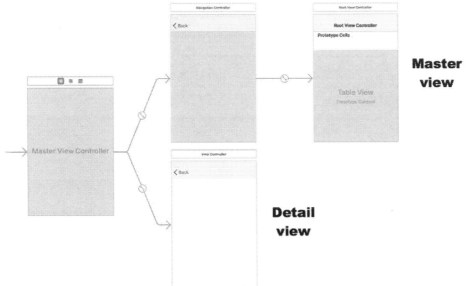

Figure 16-4: Split View Controller in the Storyboard

The Split View Controller is the view on the left, and the Master and Detail views are on the right. In this standard configuration, the Master view comes embedded in a Navigation Controller to provide tools for navigation. The Master and Detail views are connected to the Split View Controller with special Segues called *Master View Controller* and *Detail View Controller*.

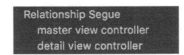

Figure 16-5: Segues for Split View Controllers

The Split View Controller offered by the Object Library already comes connected with a Master view and a Detail view, but we can delete these views and incorporate our own. After adding the views, all we have to do is to control-drag a line from the Split View Controller to the views and select the type of Segue according to their role in the interface (Figure 16-5).

Split View Controller

Split View Controllers automatically expand and collapse to adapt to the space available, but we can perform some adjustments and improve the interface from the properties and methods included in the **UISplitViewController** class. The following are the most frequently used.

viewControllers—This property sets or returns an array with references to the view controllers currently shown on the screen. In an expanded interface, the array contains two view controllers, the Master at index 0 and the Detail at index 1 (also called *primary* and *secondary*), but in a collapsed interface, the array contains only one view controller (by default, the Detail).

isCollapsed—This property returns a Boolean value that determines the state of the interface. The value `true` means the interface is collapsed (the Split View Controller is presenting only one view and it cannot be expanded). The value `false` means the interface is expanded (the Split View Controller is presenting or can present two views).

presentsWithGesture—This property sets or returns a Boolean value that determines whether or not a hidden view can be shown with a swipe gesture. Some configurations, like the iPad in portrait mode, present only one view and allow the user to make the other visible by swiping the finger. This property activates or deactivates the feature (`true` by default).

preferredPrimaryColumnWidthFraction—This property sets or returns a `CGFloat` value that determines the width of the primary view in relation to the secondary view. The value must be specified between 0.0 and 1.0. For example, a value of 0.5 gives the primary view a size of 50% the width of the space available.

primaryColumnWidth—This property returns a `CGFloat` value with the width of the primary view expressed in points.

minimumPrimaryColumnWidth—This property sets or returns a `CGFloat` value that determines the minimum width of the primary view in points (usually the Master view).

maximumPrimaryColumnWidth—This property sets of returns a `CGFloat` value that determines the maximum width of the primary view in points (usually the Master view).

preferredDisplayMode—This property sets of returns the preferred display mode. It is an enumeration called `DisplayMode` included in the `UISplitViewController` class. The values available are `automatic`, `primaryHidden`, `allVisible`, and `primaryOverlay`.

displayMode—This property returns the current display mode. It is an enumeration called `DisplayMode` included in the `UISplitViewController` class. The values available are `automatic`, `primaryHidden`, `allVisible`, and `primaryOverlay`.

displayModeButtonItem—This property returns a `UIBarButtonItem` object designed to create a button that lets the user change the Split View Controller's display mode.

Split View Controller Delegate

Split View Controllers can also designate a delegate to report changes in the views. The delegate must conform to the `UISplitViewControllerDelegate` protocol. The following are some of the methods defined in this protocol.

splitViewController(UISplitViewController, **willChangeTo:** DisplayMode**)**—This method is called by the Split View Controller to tell the delegate that the display mode is about to change. The **willChangeTo** attribute is an enumeration called `DisplayMode` included in the `UISplitViewController` class. The values available are `automatic`, `primaryHidden`, `allVisible`, and `primaryOverlay`.

splitViewController(UISplitViewController, **collapseSecondary:** UIView-Controller, **onto:** UIViewController**)**—This method is called by the Split View Controller on its delegate to know whether or not to incorporate the secondary view into the interface. The method must return `false` if we want the Split View Controller to try to incorporate the secondary view or `true` otherwise.

targetDisplayModeForAction(in: UISplitViewController)—This method is called by the Split View Controller on its delegate to know the display mode to apply after the user presses the bar button returned by the **displayModeButtonItem** property or swipes his finger over the secondary view. The value returned is an enumeration called **DisplayMode** included in the **UISplitViewController** class. The values available are **automatic**, **primaryHidden**, **allVisible**, and **primaryOverlay**.

Implementing Split View Controllers

An application based on a Split View Controller works like any other we have built so far. The elements for the interface are added to the views and view controllers are assigned to the Scenes to manage their content. For example, based on the views provided by a standard Split View Controller, we can create an application to manage a list of books. When a book is selected in the Master view, the Detail view shows its cover and title. Figure 16-6 illustrates the modifications we have to make on the Master and Detail views provided by the template to get a simple application like this.

Figure 16-6: *Master and Detail views*

Notice that only the Master view and the Detail view have been modified, the rest of the views in the Storyboard are containers and therefore do not have content of their own. In the Master view, we changed the title of the Navigation Bar and turned the custom cell provided by default to a Basic cell. The Detail view, on the other hand, was improved with new elements, including an Image View to present the cover of the selected book, and two labels for the title and the author.

Do It Yourself: Create a new Single View Application project. Erase the initial Scene and add a Split View Controller from the Object Library (Figure 16-3). Select the Split View Controller and activate the option Is Initial View Controller from the Attributes Inspector panel. Select the cell in the Master view, change its style to Basic, and give it the identifier "myCell". Double click on the Navigation Bar to change its title to "My Books". Add an Image View and two labels to the Detail view, as shown in Figure 16-6. Assign Space constraints to the elements to pin them to the sides of the view and with each other, and give the Image View a fixed size with a Height constraint (we used a value of 245). Because sometimes this view is going to be shown in big screens, you should adapt the size and position of its elements to different Size Classes, as we explained in Chapter 6.

The Master and Detail views work like any view studied before, the only difference is that they have a specific area assigned on the screen. If we connect another view to the Master view with a Show Segue, for example, the second view will replace the current view and become the Master view. If we use the normal type of Segues studied in Chapter 13, the views replace one another in the same area, but Split View Controllers include a special type of Segue to connect the Master view

Split View Controllers

with the Detail view called *Show Detail*. Every time a Segue of this type is triggered from the Master view, the view connected to this Segue is opened in the area of the Detail view. Figure 16-7 illustrates how we implement a Show Detail Segue in our example.

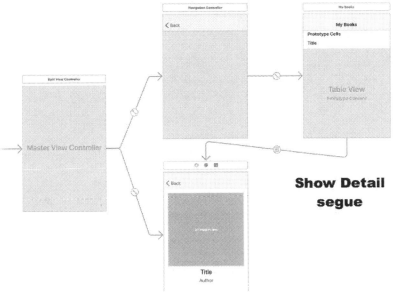

Figure 16-7: Show Detail Segue

The Show Detail Segue was connected from the cell in the Master view to the Detail view. Now every time the user selects a cell in the Master view, the Segue is triggered and a new Detail view is opened. Despite this new type of connection, the codes for the view controllers do not change significantly. The following is the code for the Master view of our example.

```
import UIKit

class MasterViewController: UITableViewController {
    override func tableView(_ tableView: UITableView, numberOfRowsInSection
section: Int) -> Int {
        return AppData.items.count
    }
    override func tableView(_ tableView: UITableView, cellForRowAt
indexPath: IndexPath) -> UITableViewCell {
        let cell = tableView.dequeueReusableCell(withIdentifier: "myCell",
for: indexPath)
        let file = AppData.items[indexPath.row]
        if let data = AppData.itemsData[file] {
            cell.textLabel?.text = data[0]
        }
        return cell
    }
    override func prepare(for segue: UIStoryboardSegue, sender: Any?) {
        if segue.identifier == "showDetail" {
            let controller = segue.destination as! DetailViewController
            let path = tableView.indexPathForSelectedRow
            controller.selected = path?.row
        }
    }
}
```

Listing 16-1: Controlling the Master view

Split View Controllers

The view created by Xcode for the Master view is a Table View Controller and therefore our view controller has to be a subclass of the **UITableViewController** class. In Listing 16-1, we call this subclass **MasterViewController**. In this class, we implement the required delegate methods to provide the data to the table, and the **prepare()** method to send the information of the selected cell to the Detail view when the Show Detail Segue is triggered (for this example, we identified the Segue with the string "showDetail" and used the same model and images implemented in the example of Chapter 15, Listing 15-2).

The view controller for the Detail view, on the other hand, is a subclass of the **UIViewController** class and it just has to provide the Outlets to access the elements in the main view and modify their values according to the information received through the **selected** property.

```
import UIKit

class DetailViewController: UIViewController {
   @IBOutlet weak var bookCover: UIImageView!
   @IBOutlet weak var bookTitle: UILabel!
   @IBOutlet weak var bookAuthor: UILabel!
   var selected: Int!

   override func viewDidLoad() {
      super.viewDidLoad()
      if selected != nil {
         let file = AppData.items[selected]
         bookCover.image = UIImage(named: file)
         if let data = AppData.itemsData[file] {
            bookTitle.text = data[0]
            bookAuthor.text = data[1]
         }
      }
   }
}
```

Listing 16-2: Controlling the Detail view

The codes for this application do not introduce anything new, but because the views are part of a Split View Controller and connected through a Show Detail Segue they now can be presented on the screen at the same time and work together to show the information requested by the user. The Split View Controller decides whether or not there is enough space on the screen to show both views or if it has to show one and include navigation tools to let the user access the other.

 Do It Yourself: Control-drag a line from the cell in the Master view to the Detail view and select the option Show Detail to create the Segue. Select the Segue and insert the identifier "showDetail" from the Attributes Inspector panel. Create a file with a subclass of **UITableViewController** called **MasterViewController** and assign it to the Master view. Create a file with a subclass of **UIViewController** called **DetailViewController** and assign it to the Detail view. Connect the elements in the Detail view with the Outlets in the **DetailViewController** class. Create a Swift file with the model of Listing 15-2 (you also have to add to the Assets Catalog the images with the books' covers used for the examples of Chapter 15). Run the application in the simulators for iPads and iPhones. Rotate the simulator to see how the Split View Controller responds.

In standard iPhones, the views are presented one at a time, similar to when the iPhones Plus are in portrait mode, but iPads exhibit a slightly different behaviour. They also present both views in landscape mode and one view in portrait mode, but instead of offering a Back button, they let the user swipe the finger to open the Master view as an overlay. The view shows up from the left of the screen and partially covers the Detail view, as shown in Figure 16-8.

Split View Controllers

Figure 16-8: `primaryOverlay` *mode in iPad*

The way views are presented is determined by modes defined by the Split View Controller. The mode used when the iPad is in portrait is called **primaryOverlay** (Figure 16-8, right). There is a total of four modes: **automatic** (the Split View Controller decides the appropriate mode), **primaryHidden** (the primary view is hidden), **allVisible** (both views are visible), and **primaryOverlay** (the primary view is displayed over the secondary view). If we do not want to let the Split View Controller decide how the views should be presented, we can modify the value of the **preferredDisplayMode** property. The Split View Controller considers this value and changes the mode when possible. For example, if instead of an overlay we want to show both views at the same time when the iPad is in portrait mode, we can assign the value **allVisible** to this property.

```
override func viewDidLoad() {
    super.viewDidLoad()
    splitViewController?.preferredDisplayMode = .allVisible
}
```

Listing 16-3: Changing the Split View Controller mode

Modifications to the configuration of the Split View Controller are usually performed in the Master view's view controller. View controllers offer the **splitViewController** property to access the Split View Controller they belong to. In the **viewDidLoad()** method of Listing 16-3, we use this property to get a reference to the Split View Controller and assign the value **allVisible** to its **preferredDisplayMode** property. Now, instead of the overlay used to access the Master view in an iPad in portrait, we will see the Master view along with the Detail view in both orientations.

 Do It Yourself: Add the **viewDidLoad()** method of Listing 16-3 to the **MasterViewController** class. Run the application in the iPad simulator and rotate the screen. You should always see both views on the screen.

If we want to change the mode only when the current mode is of a certain type, we can check the value of the **displayMode** property first. For example, in an iPad in portrait mode, the Master view is presented when the user swipes a finger over the Detail view. To hide the Master view, the user has to tap outside the view. If we want to close the Master view when a cell is selected, we have to implement the **tableView(UITableView, didSelectRowAt:)** method to change the mode to **primaryHidden**. This mode hides the Master view, but the problem is that we only want to do it when the Master view was presented as an overlay. The solution is to check the current mode and only change it if it is of type **primaryOverlay**.

```
override func tableView(_ tableView: UITableView, didSelectRowAt indexPath:
IndexPath) {
    let mode = splitViewController?.displayMode
```

Split View Controllers

```
    if mode == .primaryOverlay {
        splitViewController?.preferredDisplayMode = .primaryHidden
    }
}
override func viewWillTransition(to size: CGSize, with coordinator:
UIViewControllerTransitionCoordinator) {
    super.viewWillTransition(to: size, with: coordinator)
    splitViewController?.preferredDisplayMode = .automatic
}
```

Listing 16-4: Changing the mode from primaryOverlay *to* primaryHidden

The code of Listing 16-4 hides the Master view when a cell is selected and the view was presented as an overlay. This is fine when the app is in portrait mode, but when we go back to landscape mode, the display mode will still be **primaryHidden** and we won't be able to see the Master view. To let the Split View Controller decide again how it should show the views, we have to detect the rotation and set the display mode back to **automatic**. This is why in this example we have also implemented the **viewWillTransition()** method (see Chapter 6, Listing 6-9).

 Do It Yourself: Remove the **viewDidLoad()** method added in the previous example. Add the method of Listing 16-4 to the **MasterViewController** class. Run the application in an iPad simulator. In portrait mode, swipe your finger to show the Master view (Figure 16-8, right), and tap on a cell to select it. The Detail view should show the selected book and the Master view should be hidden.

 IMPORTANT: The mode set by the **preferredDisplayMode** property is only considered by the Split View Controller when the interface is expanded (both views are shown or have the possibility to be shown simultaneously on the screen). The value assigned to this property is a suggestion to the Split View Controller rather than an order. The Split View Controller takes the suggestion and accommodates the interface when possible.

16.2 Improving the Interface

Split View Controllers manage the views for us, but there are still many things we need to address. An important aspect of working with Split View Controllers is that in most cases the Detail view is shown on the screen before the user requests any information. This means that we have to prepare the Detail view to show something when no content is available. In previous examples, we just displayed the labels with the text defined in the Storyboard and an empty Image View, but this is not enough for a professional application. Fortunately, there are several alternatives we can adopt to improve the design.

Item by Default

The simplest option we can use to provide relevant information for the user in the Detail view when the app is launched is to search for any item in the model and show it as the item by default. For instance, the **viewDidLoad()** method of the **DetailViewController** class of our example could get and show the information of the first book in the **items** array if no book was selected yet.

```
import UIKit

class DetailViewController: UIViewController {
    @IBOutlet weak var bookCover: UIImageView!
    @IBOutlet weak var bookTitle: UILabel!
    @IBOutlet weak var bookAuthor: UILabel!
    var selected: Int!
```

```
override func viewDidLoad() {
   super.viewDidLoad()
   if selected == nil && !AppData.items.isEmpty {
      selected = 0
   }
   if selected != nil {
      let file = AppData.items[selected]
      bookCover.image = UIImage(named: file)
      if let data = AppData.itemsData[file] {
         bookTitle.text = data[0]
         bookAuthor.text = data[1]
      }
   }
}
```

Listing 16-5: Selecting the book by default

The code of Listing 16-5 compares the **selected** property to the value **nil** to know if a book was already selected and, if the **items** array is not empty, assigns the index 0 to the property. Now, the first book on the list will be shown in the Detail view until the user selects a different one.

 Do It Yourself: Replace the code in your **DetailViewController** class by the code of Listing 16-5 and run the application. The first screen you should see is the Detail view with the data of the book at index 0.

Detail View by Default

The previous solution does not solve all of our problems. If the **items** array is empty, we still have an empty Detail view. A better solution is to assign a view by default with a message that explains to the user what is going on and replace that view with another one when there is content to show. The easiest way to do it is to designate the view containing the message as the Detail view of our Split View Controller. This way, the view with the message will always be shown unless the user performs an action that replaces it with the Detail view that contains useful information.

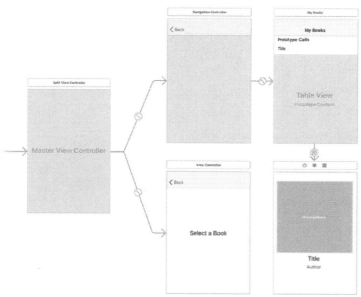

Figure 16-9: Split View Controller with a Detail view by default

Split View Controllers

The interface of Figure 16-9 designates a new Detail view for our Split View Controller, but the original Detail view is still connected to the Master view with a Show Detail Segue and it will be shown in the Detail view's area every time the user selects a cell.

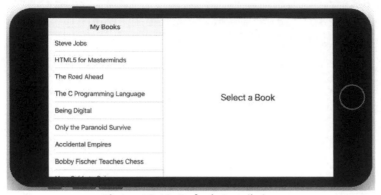

Figure 16-10: *Default Detail view*

 Do It Yourself: Delete the Detail View Controller Segue. Move the Detail view to the right and add in its place a new Scene from the Object Library (View Controller option). Add a label in the middle of the view with the message "Select a Book". Create a new Detail View Controller Segue from the Split View Controller to this view. Run the application. The initial screen should look like Figure 16-10.

Display Mode Button

At this point, the interface provides everything the user needs to navigate and access the information, but there are still issues we have to solve. First, when only the Detail view is visible, there are not enough clues for the user to know that there is another view available. And second, when the interface is expanded, there is no way for the user to show the Master view or remove it from the screen. The **UISplitViewController** class offers the **displayModeButtonItem** property to solve both problems. The property returns a bar button item called *Display Mode Button* that gives a hint to the users that there is more to see and lets them show or remove the views at will. The button returned by this property is a **UIBarButtonItem** object, so we have to embed the Detail view in a Navigation Controller to be able to incorporate it to the interface. Because in our example we have two Detail views, one to present the initial message and another to present the book's data, we have to repeat the process twice, embedding both views in their respective Navigation Controllers.

Figure 16-11: *Detail views embedded in Navigation Controllers*

Now that every Detail view has its Navigation Bar, we can add the bar button item to each one of them. The following example expands the **DetailViewController** class to add a Display Mode Button to the second Detail view and configure the bar.

```
import UIKit

class DetailViewController: UIViewController {
   @IBOutlet weak var bookCover: UIImageView!
   @IBOutlet weak var bookTitle: UILabel!
   @IBOutlet weak var bookAuthor: UILabel!
   var selected: Int!

   override func viewDidLoad() {
      super.viewDidLoad()
      let button = splitViewController?.displayModeButtonItem
      navigationItem.leftBarButtonItem = button
      navigationItem.leftItemsSupplementBackButton = true
      if selected != nil {
         let file = AppData.items[selected]
         bookCover.image = UIImage(named: file)
         if let data = AppData.itemsData[file] {
            bookTitle.text = data[0]
            bookAuthor.text = data[1]
         }
      }
   }
}
```

Listing 16-6: Adding a Display Mode Button to the Navigation Bar of the second Detail view

The code of Listing 16-6 stores the button returned by the **displayModeButtonItem** property in a constant and then assigns that constant to the **leftBarButtonItem** property of the bar's Navigation Item. This adds the button to the left side of the bar, which is a convenient place for a button that removes or shows the Master view, but because Navigation Bars hide the Back button when other buttons are present on the same side, we also have to modify the **leftItemsSupplementBackButton** property to tell the Navigation Bar to present both buttons at the same time (see Navigation Controllers in Chapter 13).

The previous code adds the button to the second Detail view, but we still have to add it to the initial Detail view (the one that is displayed when the app is launched). We have not created a view controller for this view yet, so we have to do it now. For this example, we called it **EmptyViewController**. The code to add the button is exactly the same implemented in the **DetailViewController** class.

```
import UIKit

class EmptyViewController: UIViewController {
   override func viewDidLoad() {
      super.viewDidLoad()
      let button = splitViewController?.displayModeButtonItem
      navigationItem.leftBarButtonItem = button
      navigationItem.leftItemsSupplementBackButton = true
   }
}
```

Listing 16-7: Adding a Display Mode Button to the Navigation Bar of the initial Detail view

There is one more thing we have to do for our example to work properly. Because the second Detail view is now embedded in a Navigation Controller, it is no longer the Segue's destination view controller, so we have to modify the **prepare()** method in the **MasterViewController** class to incorporate the new path. First, we have to get a reference to the Navigation Controller and then access the **DetailViewController** through its **topViewController** property (the **DetailViewController** object is now the top view controller of the Navigation Controller). If we do not perform this change, the **prepare()** method will try to modify the value of a property in the Navigation Controller that does not exist and the app will crash.

```
override func prepare(for segue: UIStoryboardSegue, sender: Any?) {
    if segue.identifier == "showDetail" {
        let navigation = segue.destination as! UINavigationController
        let controller = navigation.topViewController as!
DetailViewController
        let path = tableView.indexPathForSelectedRow
        controller.selected = path?.row
    }
}
```

Listing 16-8: Referencing the Detail view through the Navigation Controller

If both views are present on the screen, the button shows a double arrow (Figure 16-12, left). When the user taps on this arrow, the Master view is hidden, and the button turns into a single arrow pointing to the left (Figure 16-12, right).

Figure 16-12: Display Mode Button in action

 Do It Yourself: Embed the initial Detail view (the one with the message "Select a Book") in a Navigation Controller (Editor/Embed In/Navigation Controller). Do the same for the second Detail view (the view that presents the book's data). Copy the code of Listing 16-6 in the **DetailViewController** class. Create a new file with a subclass of the **UIViewController** class called **EmptyViewController** and assign it to the initial Detail view. Complete the subclass with the code of Listing 16-7. Replace the **prepare()** method of the **MasterViewController** class by the method of Listing 16-8. Run the application in an iPhone Plus simulator. Turn the simulator to landscape mode. Press the Display Mode Button. You should see something similar to Figure 16-12.

Implementing the Split View Controller Delegate

When the app is first launched, the Split View Controller decides how to display the views. If there is only space available for one view, by default it will show the Detail view. This means that, for example, when we launch the app for the first time in an iPhone in portrait mode, we will always see the Detail view until we press the Back button. The **UISplitViewControllerDelegate** protocol defines the **splitViewController(UISplitViewController, collapseSecondary:, onto:)** method to let us change this predefined behaviour. The method is called by the Split View Controller to know what we want to do with the secondary view (the Detail view) when there is a possibility to include it in the interface. Returning the value **false** from this method tells the Split View Controller to try to incorporate the secondary view, but if the value returned is **true**, the Split View Controller does nothing and the view is not shown on the screen.

Usually the view controller for the Master view is designated as the delegate of the Split View Controller. In the following example, we improve the **MasterViewController** class to include the protocol method and force the Split View Controller to show the Master view first.

```
import UIKit

class MasterViewController: UITableViewController,
UISplitViewControllerDelegate {
    override func viewDidLoad() {
        super.viewDidLoad()
        splitViewController?.delegate = self
    }
    override func tableView(_ tableView: UITableView, numberOfRowsInSection
section: Int) -> Int {
        return AppData.items.count
    }
    override func tableView(_ tableView: UITableView, cellForRowAt
indexPath: IndexPath) -> UITableViewCell {
        let cell = tableView.dequeueReusableCell(withIdentifier: "myCell",
for: indexPath)
        let file = AppData.items[indexPath.row]
        if let data = AppData.itemsData[file] {
            cell.textLabel?.text = data[0]
        }
        return cell
    }
    override func prepare(for segue: UIStoryboardSegue, sender: Any?) {
        if segue.identifier == "showDetail" {
            let navigation = segue.destination as! UINavigationController
            let controller = navigation.topViewController as!
DetailViewController
            let path = tableView.indexPathForSelectedRow
            controller.selected = path?.row
        }
    }
    func splitViewController(_ splitViewController: UISplitViewController,
collapseSecondary secondaryViewController: UIViewController, onto
primaryViewController: UIViewController) -> Bool {
        return true
    }
}
```

Listing 16-9: Showing the Master view instead of the Detail view when the app is launched

 Do It Yourself: Replace the code in the **MasterViewController** class by the code of Listing 16-9. Run the application in an iPhone in portrait mode. You should see the list of books instead of the "Select a Book" message you have seen so far.

16.3 Expanding the Interface

As we already mentioned, the interface can be expanded to include all the views we need. When the Master and Detail views are embedded in Navigation Controllers, the rest of the views can be connected with Show Segues, as we did before. For example, we can add a button below the book's cover in the detail view of our interface and connect it to a separate view to enlarge the cover.

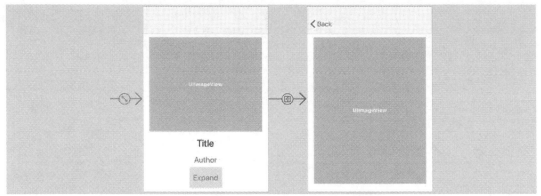

Figure 16-13: Expanding the interface

In Figure 16-13 we have incorporated the button below the book's data with the title "Expand" and connected it with a Show Segue to a view that includes an Image View inside. When this Segue is triggered, we have to pass the value of the **selected** property in the Detail view to the new view. For this purpose, the **DetailViewController** class has to implement the **prepare()** method.

```
override func prepare(for segue: UIStoryboardSegue, sender: Any?) {
    if segue.identifier == "showPicture" {
        let controller = segue.destination as! PictureViewController
        controller.selected = selected
    }
}
```

Listing 16-10: Sending the index of the selected book to the new Scene

The view controller for the new view has to include a property called **selected** to receive the index of the selected book sent by the Detail view and then update the Image View using this value. We called this view controller **PictureViewController**.

```
import UIKit

class PictureViewController: UIViewController {
    @IBOutlet weak var bookCover: UIImageView!
    var selected: Int!

    override func viewDidLoad() {
        super.viewDidLoad()
        if selected != nil {
            let file = AppData.items[selected]
            bookCover.image = UIImage(named: file)
        }
    }
}
```

Listing 16-11: Showing a maximized version of the book's cover

The code of Listing 16-11 declares the **selected** property to receive the index of the selected book and an Outlet to access the Image View. When the view is loaded, the **viewDidLoad()** method gets the information from the model, creates the image, and shows it on the screen. Figure 16-14 shows the application running in an iPhone 8 Plus. When the Expand button is pressed, the Detail view with the information of the book is replaced by another view that shows a bigger version of the cover and the Back button appears on the bar to return to the previous Detail view.

Split View Controllers

Figure 16-14: *Navigation in the Detail view's area*

 Do It Yourself: Add a button to the Detail view with the title "Expand". Add a Scene to the Storyboard. Connect the button with the new Scene using a Show Segue. Assign the identifier "showPicture" to the Segue. Add an Image View to the new view, as shown in Figure 16-13, right. Create a subclass of the `UIViewController` class called **PictureViewController** and assign it to the new Scene. Complete the class with the code of Listing 16-11 and connect the Image View to the **bookCover** Outlet. Add the method of Listing 16-10 to the **DetailViewController** class of Listing 16-6. Run the application, select a book, and press the Expand button. You should see something similar to Figure 16-14.

Modal Views

Besides adding views to the stack of a Navigation Controller, as we did in the previous example, we can expand the interface with modal views and popovers. We have already studied modal views in Chapter 13. They are normal views but connected with a Segue called *Present Modally*. In iPhones, these views are always opened full screen and with the transition set by the Segue, but in iPads and iPhones Plus in landscape mode they are presented with designs that take advantage of the larger screens. These designs are called *Presentation Styles*, and there are several available.

- **Full Screen** presents a view of the size of the screen over the current interface.
- **Current Context** presents a view in the place and of the size of the designated area.
- **Page Sheet** presents a view as a sheet that emerges from the bottom of the screen.
- **Form Sheet** presents a view as a sheet over the current interface and in the center of the screen.
- **Over Full Screen** presents a view over the interface and with the size of the screen (but without hiding the current views).
- **Over Current Context** presents a view in the place and with the size of the designated area (but without hiding the current view).

The presentation style is established by the Segue. The options are available from the Attributes Inspector panel when the Segue is selected. The panel includes the option to select the Presentation Style and also change the type of Segue. Figure 16-15 illustrates the different options available in this panel for Show Segues (left) and Present Modally Segues (right).

Figure 16-15: *Segue configuration*

If we turn the Show Segue in the interface of Figure 16-13 into a Present Modally Segue, we will see something similar to Figure 16-16 below. The Segue looks the same and it is still connecting the Expand button to the view, but now the view is not part of the Navigation Controller stack anymore, and therefore it does not include a Navigation Bar. Modal Segues open independent views that are used to present information not associated to the main interface and therefore they have to provide their own navigation tools. For our example, we added a Close button at the top to dismiss the view.

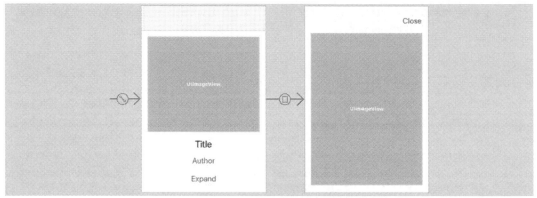

Figure 16-16: Interface with a Modal Segue

Depending on the presentation style selected and the device running the application, the view in Figure 16-16 will adopt different designs. For example, on a small iPhone, the view is always shown full screen with a transition determined by the Transition option, but on an iPad the view will be shown with the selected presentation style (in iPhones Plus in landscape mode, a presentation other than Full Screen always defaults to Page Sheet). Figure 16-17, next, illustrates what we see when we present the view with the Page Sheet mode on an iPad.

Figure 16-17: Page Sheet presentation style

 Do It Yourself: Select the Show Segue created for our interface in Figure 16-13. Change its type to Present Modally from the Attributes Inspector panel (Figure 16-15, right). Click on the Presentation option and select the presentation style Page Sheet. Add a button with the title Close to the view managed by the **PictureViewController** class. Set the constraints between the button and the Image View. If you pinned the elements to the margin of the main view, remember to set the vertical priority of the button higher than the Image View or otherwise the button will stretch vertically to occupy the space available. Run the application on the iPad simulator, select a book, and press the Expand button. You will see something similar to Figure 16-17.

Split View Controllers

When the view is presented as a Form Sheet or a Popover (as we will see later), we can specify its size from the Attributes Inspector panel. The option is called *Use Preferred Explicit Size*, and it appears at the bottom of the panel when the view is selected (Figure 16-18, number 1).

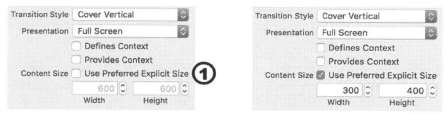

Figure 16-18: *Use Preferred Explicit Size option*

This is not the same option as the Simulated Size offered by the Size Inspector panel (Figure 11-11). The Simulated Size option determines the size of the view in the Storyboard, while the Use Preferred Explicit Size option sets the size the view is going to have when the application is running. We can set both options to the same values if we want to work on a view that matches what the user is going to see on the screen. Figure 16-19 shows the modal view from the previous example presented on an iPad as a Form Sheet and with an explicit size of 300 x 400.

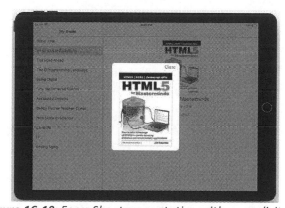

Figure 16-19: *Form Sheet presentation with an explicit size*

At this moment, the Close button does nothing, but its purpose is to provide the functionality to close the view. In Chapter 13, we studied how to do this with an Unwind Segue, but the **UIViewController** class also offers some properties and methods to present and dismiss views programmatically that simplify our work when we do not need to pass data from one view controller to another or when we need to create a view dynamically.

modalPresentationStyle—This property sets or returns the presentation style. When we present a view programmatically, we first have to set the presentation style with this property. It is an enumeration of type **UIModalPresentationStyle** with the values **fullScreen**, **pageSheet**, **formSheet**, **currentContext**, **overFullScreen**, **overCurrentContext**, **popover**, **none**, and **custom**.

modalTransitionStyle—This property sets or returns the transition style. When we present a view programmatically, we first have to set the transition style with this property. It is an enumeration of type **UIModalTransitionStyle** with the values **coverVertical**, **flipHorizontal**, **crossDissolve**, and **partialCurl**. Notice that some of these transitions are only available for the Full Screen presentation style.

present(UIViewController, **animated:** Bool, **completion:** Block**)**—This method presents a modal view. The first attribute is a reference to the view controller of the view we want to present, the **animated** attribute determines whether or not the process will be animated, and the **completion** attribute is an optional closure that is executed after the view is presented on the screen.

dismiss(animated: Bool, **completion:** Block?**)**—This method dismisses the view. The **animated** attribute is a Boolean value that determines whether or not the process will be animated, and the **completion** attribute is a closure that is executed after the view is closed.

To dismiss the view opened by the Modal Segue of Figure 16-16 we have to create an Action for the Close button that calls the **dismiss()** method. The following example implements the Action in the **PictureViewController** class.

```
import UIKit

class PictureViewController: UIViewController {
   @IBOutlet weak var bookCover: UIImageView!
   var selected: Int!

   override func viewDidLoad() {
      super.viewDidLoad()
      if selected != nil {
         let file = AppData.items[selected]
         bookCover.image = UIImage(named: file)
      }
   }
   @IBAction func closePicture(_ sender: UIButton) {
      dismiss(animated: true, completion: nil)
   }
}
```

***Listing 16-12:** Dismissing a modal view programmatically*

The view controller that presents the view is responsible for dismissing it, but we can call the **dismiss()** method from the presented view and the system will take care of asking the presenter to dismiss it. Listing 16-12 includes the **closePicture()** Action for the Close button. When the user taps on the button, the **dismiss()** method is executed and the view is closed.

 Do It Yourself: Update the **PictureViewController** class with the code of Listing 16-12. Connect the Close button added to the interface in Figure 16-16 to the **closePicture()** Action. Run the application in the iPad simulator, select a book, press the Expand button, and press the Close button to close the view.

Creating modal views in the Storyboard is easy, but there are times in which our application requires the creation of the views dynamically from code. There are at least three ways to do this. We can do it entirely from code, create separate files for the view and its view controller, or create an isolated view in the Storyboard and load it from the Storyboard's object. To demonstrate each alternative, we are going to open an additional view from a bar button in the Detail view called Help.

***Figure 16-20:** Help button*

Split View Controllers

The first alternative we are going to explore is creating the view and its view controller from code. This demands a lot of writing, but in some circumstances, it may be the only way to achieve our goal. For this purpose, we have to connect the Help button to an Action in the view controller that is going to present the view (**DetailViewController** in our example). Inside the Action, we have to create everything, from the view and the view controller object to the elements of the interface and their constraints. Our example creates a view with the message "Press Expand to maximize the cover" and a Close button to dismiss it.

```
import UIKit
class DetailViewController: UIViewController {
    @IBOutlet weak var bookCover: UIImageView!
    @IBOutlet weak var bookTitle: UILabel!
    @IBOutlet weak var bookAuthor: UILabel!
    var selected: Int!
    var controllerHelp: UIViewController!

    override func viewDidLoad() {
        super.viewDidLoad()
        let button = splitViewController?.displayModeButtonItem
        navigationItem.leftBarButtonItem = button
        navigationItem.leftItemsSupplementBackButton = true
        if selected != nil {
            let file = AppData.items[selected]
            bookCover.image = UIImage(named: file)
            if let data = AppData.itemsData[file] {
                bookTitle.text = data[0]
                bookAuthor.text = data[1]
            }
        }
    }
    override func prepare(for segue: UIStoryboardSegue, sender: Any?) {
        if segue.identifier == "showPicture" {
            let controller = segue.destination as! PictureViewController
            controller.selected = selected
        }
    }
    @IBAction func showHelp(_ sender: UIBarButtonItem) {
        let label = UILabel(frame: CGRect.zero)
        label.translatesAutoresizingMaskIntoConstraints = false
        label.text = "Press Expand to maximize the cover"
        label.textAlignment = .center
        label.numberOfLines = 2
        label.font = UIFont.systemFont(ofSize: 24)

        let closeButton = UIButton(type: .system)
        closeButton.translatesAutoresizingMaskIntoConstraints = false
        closeButton.setTitle("Close", for: .normal)
        closeButton.titleLabel?.font = UIFont.systemFont(ofSize: 20)
        closeButton.addTarget(self, action: #selector(closeHelp),
for: .touchUpInside)

        controllerHelp = UIViewController()
        controllerHelp.modalPresentationStyle = .pageSheet
        controllerHelp.view.backgroundColor = UIColor.white
        controllerHelp.view.addSubview(label)
        controllerHelp.view.addSubview(closeButton)

        let cView = controllerHelp.view!
        label.topAnchor.constraint(equalTo: cView.topAnchor, constant:
16).isActive = true
```

```
        label.leadingAnchor.constraint(equalTo: cView.leadingAnchor,
constant: 16).isActive = true
        label.trailingAnchor.constraint(equalTo: cView.trailingAnchor,
constant: -16).isActive = true

        closeButton.topAnchor.constraint(equalTo: label.bottomAnchor,
constant: 8).isActive = true
        closeButton.leadingAnchor.constraint(equalTo: cView.leadingAnchor,
constant: 16).isActive = true
        closeButton.trailingAnchor.constraint(equalTo: cView.trailingAnchor,
constant: -16).isActive = true

        present(controllerHelp, animated: true, completion: nil)
    }
    @objc func closeHelp() {
        controllerHelp.dismiss(animated: true, completion: nil)
    }
}
```

Listing 16-13: Creating a modal view from code

The code of Listing 16-13 adds a property and two methods to the view controller created before for the Detail view. The **controllerHelp** property stores a reference to the view controller we are going to create for the modal view, and the **showHelp()** and **closeHelp()** methods are the Actions for the Help and Close buttons, respectively. When the Help button in the Detail view is pressed, we perform a series of tasks to get our modal view ready. First, we create the **UILabel** and **UIButton** objects to represent the view's content. The objects are instantiated and then configured with the values we want. We also assign the target and action for the button with the **addTarget()** method to execute the **closeHelp()** method when the button is pressed (see **UIControl** in Chapter 4). Next, we create the **UIViewController** object to control the view. After this object is initialized, we set its presentation style as **pageSheet**, configure its view with a white background color, and add the label and the button as subviews. The last step to get the view ready is to set the element's constraints. We generate horizontal and vertical Space constraints for both elements, the label and the button, and finally present the view with the **present()** method. The result is illustrated in Figure 16-21.

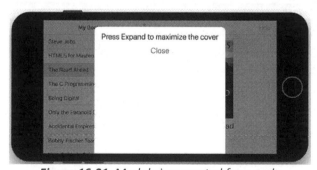

Figure 16-21: Modal view created from code

 Do It Yourself: Add a bar button item to the Navigation Bar of the Detail view called "Help". Update the **DetailViewController** class with the code of Listing 16-13. Run the application in the iPad simulator, select a book, and press the Help button. You should see the modal view emerge from the bottom.

Another alternative is to create a view controller with its own view and then load it from code. This greatly simplifies our work since we have a view in Interface Builder that we can edit the same way as we do with the views in the Storyboard. The file for the view controller is created as always; we go to the File menu at the top of the screen, select New/File and then click on the Cocoa Touch

Class icon, but in the window where we declare the name and the superclass for the view controller we have to activate the option called *Also create XIB file*. This option generates, along with the view controller's file, a file containing a single main view.

For our example, we called the class **HelpViewController**, therefore our project now has two more files: HelpViewController.swift and HelpViewController.xib. The HelpViewController.xib file works exactly like the Storyboard, but it is capable of managing only a single view. If we click on this file, the view is displayed in the Editor Area and we can begin adding elements to it. Figure 16-22 shows the view created for this example.

Figure 16-22: *View created with a XIB file*

Because both files were created at the same time, the view is already associated with its view controller, so we can connect the elements with Outlets and Actions right away. The following example adds an Action to the **HelpViewController** class to dismiss the view when the Close button is pressed.

```
import UIKit

class HelpViewController: UIViewController {
   @IBAction func closeHelp(_ sender: UIButton) {
      dismiss(animated: true, completion: nil)
   }
}
```

Listing 16-14: *Dismissing the view*

Now that we have created the view and prepare its view controller, we have to load it and present it from the Detail view. Because everything was done on Interface Builder, all the **DetailViewController** has to do is to create an instance of the **HelpViewController** class and present its view on the screen when the Help button is pressed.

```
import UIKit

class DetailViewController: UIViewController {
   @IBOutlet weak var bookCover: UIImageView!
   @IBOutlet weak var bookTitle: UILabel!
   @IBOutlet weak var bookAuthor: UILabel!
   var selected: Int!

   override func viewDidLoad() {
      super.viewDidLoad()
      let button = splitViewController?.displayModeButtonItem
      navigationItem.leftBarButtonItem = button
      navigationItem.leftItemsSupplementBackButton = true
```

```
        if selected != nil {
            let file = AppData.items[selected]
            bookCover.image = UIImage(named: file)
            if let data = AppData.itemsData[file] {
                bookTitle.text = data[0]
                bookAuthor.text = data[1]
            }
        }
    }
    override func prepare(for segue: UIStoryboardSegue, sender: Any?) {
        if segue.identifier == "showPicture" {
            let controller = segue.destination as! PictureViewController
            controller.selected = selected
        }
    }
    @IBAction func showHelp(_ sender: UIBarButtonItem) {
        let controllerHelp = HelpViewController()
        controllerHelp.modalPresentationStyle = .pageSheet
        present(controllerHelp, animated: true, completion: nil)
    }
}
```

Listing 16-15: Instantiating the view controller and presenting its view on the screen

 Do It Yourself: Go to the File menu at the top of the screen. Select the options New/File and click on Cocoa Touch Class. In the next window, insert the name **HelpViewController** for the class, select **UIViewController** for the superclass, and activate the option Also create XIB file. Your project now should have two more files: HelpViewController.swift and HelpViewController.xib. Click on the HelpViewController.xib file. You should see an empty view, like the one in Figure 16-22. Add a label, a button, and the necessary constraints. Connect the button to the **HelpViewController** class with an Action called **closeHelp()**. Complete the Action with the code of Listing 16-14. Replace the code in your **DetailViewController** class by the code of Listing 16-15. Test the application in the iPad simulator. It should create a modal view similar to Figure 16-21.

The last and final alternative we are going to explore involves the creation of the views in the Storyboard. This is not the same we have done so far, because these views are not going to be connected to any other view and therefore they are not part of the path set by the Storyboard.

As we explained in previous chapters, when the app is executed the Storyboard is loaded and processed. The objects representing the views and their content are created and connected with each other, but the system also creates an object that represents the Storyboard itself. This object is created from the **UIStoryboard** class and offers the following methods to access its content.

instantiateInitialViewController()—This method instantiates and returns the view controller of the initial view in the Storyboard.

instantiateViewController(withIdentifier: String)—This method instantiates and returns the view controller of the view in the Storyboard that was identified with the string specified by the **withIdentifier** attribute.

Single views are added to the Storyboard the same way we do with other views, but they are not connected to the rest of the views. Once we inserted the view, the process to generate its content and view controller are the same. For our example, we have added the view of Figure 16-23 to our interface with a view controller called **SingleViewController**.

Figure 16-23: Single view in the Storyboard

The view controller for this view only needs an Action for the Close button. We called it **SingleViewController**.

```
import UIKit

class SingleViewController: UIViewController {
   @IBAction func closeHelp(_ sender: UIButton) {
      dismiss(animated: true, completion: nil)
   }
}
```

Listing 16-16: Dismissing the single view

To be able to present this view from the Detail view, we have to assign an identifier for the view from the Identity Inspector panel. The option is called *Storyboard ID*. For our example, we called the view "helpView", as shown in Figure 16-24.

Figure 16-24: Option to assign an identifier to views

The **DetailViewController** class has to instantiate the view controller for this view with the **instantiateViewController()** method and present the view with the **present()** method.

```
import UIKit

class DetailViewController: UIViewController {
   @IBOutlet weak var bookCover: UIImageView!
   @IBOutlet weak var bookTitle: UILabel!
   @IBOutlet weak var bookAuthor: UILabel!
   var selected: Int!

   override func viewDidLoad() {
      super.viewDidLoad()
      let button = splitViewController?.displayModeButtonItem
      navigationItem.leftBarButtonItem = button
      navigationItem.leftItemsSupplementBackButton = true
      if selected != nil {
         let file = AppData.items[selected]
         bookCover.image = UIImage(named: file)
```

```
        if let data = AppData.itemsData[file] {
            bookTitle.text = data[0]
            bookAuthor.text = data[1]
        }
    }
}
override func prepare(for segue: UIStoryboardSegue, sender: Any?) {
    if segue.identifier == "showPicture" {
        let controller = segue.destination as! PictureViewController
        controller.selected = selected
    }
}
@IBAction func showHelp(_ sender: UIBarButtonItem) {
    if let story = storyboard {
        let controllerHelp =
story.instantiateViewController(withIdentifier: "helpView") as!
SingleViewController
        controllerHelp.modalPresentationStyle = .pageSheet
        present(controllerHelp, animated: true, completion: nil)
    }
}
}
```

Listing 16-17: Instantiating the view from the Storyboard

To provide access to the **UIStoryboard** object, the **UIViewController** class offers the **storyboard** property. In Listing 16-17, we read this property and execute the **instantiateViewController()** method to create an instance of the **SingleViewController** class. The instance is stored in the **controllerHelp** constant and its view is presented on the screen as we did before.

 Do It Yourself: Add a new Scene to the Storyboard (the View Controller option). Add a label and a button to the view with their respective constraints (Figure 16-23). Create a new **UIViewController** subclass called **SingleViewController**. Select the Scene, open the Identity Inspector panel, and assign the subclass to the Scene and the string "helpView" to the Storyboard ID option (Figure 16-24). Connect the Close button to the **SingleViewController** class with an Action called **closeHelp()** and complete the class with the code of Listing 16-16. Replace the code in your **DetailViewController** class by the code of Listing 16-17. Run the application again. It should create a modal view similar to Figure 16-21.

Presentation Controller

UIKit defines a class called **UIPresentationController** to manage the presentations of modal views, including popovers. When a modal view is created and presented by any of the techniques we have just introduced, an object of the **UIPresentationController** class is automatically created to manage the presentation. The object is assigned to a property of the view controller that is being presented called **presentationController**. From this property, we can access the object and read its current configuration. The following are its most frequently used properties.

presentingViewController—This property returns a reference to the view controller that initiated the presentation.

presentedViewController—This property returns a reference to the view controller that is being presented.

containerView—This property returns a reference to the view in which the presentation occurs.

Split View Controllers

presentationStyle—This property returns the presentation style used to present the view. It is an enumeration of type `UIModalPresentationStyle` with the values `fullScreen`, `pageSheet`, `formSheet`, `currentContext`, `overFullScreen`, `overCurrentContext`, `popover`, `none`, and `custom`.

adaptivePresentationStyle—This property returns the presentation style used when the horizontal Size Class becomes compact.

We can also designate a delegate for the `UIPresentationController` object to change its configuration according to the current state of the interface. The delegate must conform to the `UIAdaptivePresentationControllerDelegate` protocol and implement its methods.

adaptivePresentationStyle(for: UIPresentationController)—This method is called on the delegate to know the presentation style to use when the horizontal Size Class becomes compact.

presentationController(UIPresentationController,
viewControllerForAdaptivePresentationStyle: UIModalPresentationStyle)—This method is called on the delegate to get the view controller to present for the style determined by the second attribute. The method is used to assign a different view to each presentation style.

The `UIPresentationController` object has two presentation styles, one for the normal state and one for the adaptive state. The adaptive state is currently considered to be the state in which the horizontal Size Class is compact. This is the state we will find in small iPhones, the iPod Touch, or when the app is opened in an iPad in multitasking mode. When a modal view is presented in these conditions, the presentation style is automatically changed to `fullScreen`, but we can specify the style we want implementing the protocol methods. The advantage of these methods is that they are called not only to know the presentation style to use in the adaptive state but also to get the view controller we want to present, and therefore we can designate a completely different view controller for each state. The following example adds another view to our interface to present as the modal view when we are in an adaptive state.

Figure 16-25: *Two views for the same modal view*

The view on the left is the same view we introduced in Figure 16-23, and the view on the right is the new view we will open in the adaptive state (when the horizontal Size Class is compact). What we did for this view is to assign a Clear Color to its background and add a Visual Effect View on top of it so on iPads the modal view will have a solid white background but on iPhones it will be translucent and blurry. To control this new view, we have created a class called `iPhoneViewController`, the only purpose of which is to close the view when the Close button is pressed.

```
import UIKit

class iPhoneViewController: UIViewController {
    @IBAction func closeHelp(_ sender: UIButton) {
        dismiss(animated: true, completion: nil)
    }
}
```

Listing 16-18: Dismissing the adaptive view

We now have the two views we are going to present when the Help button is pressed, so all that is left to do is to implement the protocol methods in the **DetailViewController** class to load the second view every time the horizontal class is Compact.

```
import UIKit

class DetailViewController: UIViewController,
UIAdaptivePresentationControllerDelegate {
    @IBOutlet weak var bookCover: UIImageView!
    @IBOutlet weak var bookTitle: UILabel!
    @IBOutlet weak var bookAuthor: UILabel!
    var selected: Int!

    override func viewDidLoad() {
        super.viewDidLoad()
        let button = splitViewController?.displayModeButtonItem
        navigationItem.leftBarButtonItem = button
        navigationItem.leftItemsSupplementBackButton = true
        if selected != nil {
            let file = AppData.items[selected]
            bookCover.image = UIImage(named: file)
            if let data = AppData.itemsData[file] {
                bookTitle.text = data[0]
                bookAuthor.text = data[1]
            }
        }
    }
    override func prepare(for segue: UIStoryboardSegue, sender: Any?) {
        if segue.identifier == "showPicture" {
            let controller = segue.destination as! PictureViewController
            controller.selected = selected
        }
    }
    @IBAction func showHelp(_ sender: UIBarButtonItem) {
        if let story = storyboard {
            let controllerHelp =
story.instantiateViewController(withIdentifier: "helpView") as!
SingleViewController
            controllerHelp.modalPresentationStyle = .formSheet
            let presentation = controllerHelp.presentationController
            presentation?.delegate = self
            present(controllerHelp, animated: true, completion: nil)
        }
    }
    func adaptivePresentationStyle(for controller: UIPresentationController)
-> UIModalPresentationStyle {
        return .overFullScreen
    }
```

Split View Controllers

```
      func presentationController(_ controller: UIPresentationController,
viewControllerForAdaptivePresentationStyle style: UIModalPresentationStyle)
-> UIViewController? {
      var controller: iPhoneViewController!
      if style == .overFullScreen {
          if let story = storyboard {
              controller = story.instantiateViewController(withIdentifier:
"iPhoneView") as? iPhoneViewController
          }
      }
      return controller
   }
}
```

Listing 16-19: Showing an alternative modal view

As always, the first thing we have to do is to conform to the protocol and declare the object as the delegate. Although we have done this dozens of times before, in this opportunity the object we want our class to be delegate of is the **UIPresentationController** object of the view controller that is being presented, so we have to get a reference to this object from the **presentationController** property first and then modify its **delegate** property. In our example, we have to access this property from the instance created by the **showHelp()** method. We get the reference first, store it in the **presentation** constant, and then assign **self** to its **delegate** property. With the delegate set, we can now implement its methods.

By default, the presentation style set for the adaptive state is **fullScreen**. This is why in previous examples the modal views were opened full screen in iPhones. Usually, this behaviour is the right one for our app, but this time we have created an alternative view with a transparent background to let the user see a blurry image of the Detail view in the back, so we need to change the presentation style for the adaptive state to **overFullScreen**. When the view is in this state, the **UIPresentationController** object calls the **adaptivePresentationStyle()** method to know what presentation style to use, so we have to return the **overFullScreen** value from this method and the presentation is set to the style we want.

At this point, the presentation style is different for an iPad than an iPhone, but the view shown on the screen is always the same. To specify a different view for the adaptive state we have to implement the **presentationController(UIPresentationController, viewController-ForAdaptivePresentationStyle:)** method. This method is called by the **UIPresentationController** object on its delegate to know which view it has to present in every style, so this is our chance to instantiate the view controller of the second view we just added to the interface in Figure 16-25 and return it when the style is **overFullScreen** (we have identified this view in the Storyboard with the string "iPhoneView"). The result is shown in Figure 16-26, below. If we open the view on an iPad or an iPhone Plus in landscape mode, the first view is presented on the screen, but if we do the same on an iPhone or an iPod in portrait mode, the view with the translucent background is presented instead.

Figure 16-26: Alternative views for different devices

Do It Yourself: Add a new Scene to the Storyboard. Select its main view, go to the Attributes Inspector panel, and assign the Clear color as its background color. Add a Visual Effect View and pin it to the edges. Also add a button and a label to reproduce the interface of Figure 16-25, right. Create a new **UIViewController** subclass called **iPhoneViewController**. Select the Scene, open the Identity Inspector panel, assign the subclass to the Scene, and give it the identifier "iPhoneView". Connect the Close button to an Action called **closeHelp()** and complete the class with the code of Listing 16-18. Update the **DetailViewController** class with the code of Listing 16-19. Run the application in the iPad and iPhone simulators to see how the modal views are presented.

 IMPORTANT: The delegate methods are only called when the original presentation style is **formSheet**, **popover**, or **custom**. This is the reason why we assigned the presentation style **formSheet** to the original view instead of the **pageSheet** used in previous examples.

Popover Presentation Controller

The **UIPresentationController** object has a presentation style to present the modal views as popovers, but when we select this style, the presentation object is not created from the **UIPresentationController** class but form one of its subclasses called **UIPopoverPresentationController**. This is because the system needs more information to present a popover, such as its margins or the anchor point that determines its position. The following are some of the properties added by the subclass to configure the popover.

popoverLayoutMargins—This property sets or returns the margins that define the maximum portion of the screen designated for the popover. It is a value of type **UIEdgeInsets**.

permittedArrowDirections—This property sets or returns a value that determines the position of the popover's arrow. Every popover contains a little arrow that points to the element that triggered the presentation. This property is used to set the position of that arrow before the popover is presented. It is a structure of type **UIPopoverArrowDirection** with the properties **up**, **down**, **left**, **right**, **any**, and **unknown**.

arrowDirection—This property returns the direction of the arrow. It is a structure of type **UIPopoverArrowDirection** with the properties **up**, **down**, **left**, **right**, **any**, and **unknown**.

sourceView—This property sets or returns the view to which the popover is anchored. It is an optional value of type **UIView**.

sourceRect—This property sets or returns the rectangle of the view to which the popover is anchored. The rectangle is considered to be inside the view assigned to the **sourceView** property. This property is of type **CGRect**.

barButtonItem—This property sets or returns the bar button item to which the popover is anchored. It is an optional value of type **UIBarButtonItem**.

The **UIPopoverPresentationController** object can also work with a delegate to report the state of the popover. The delegate must conform to the **UIPopoverPresentation-ControllerDelegate** protocol, which defines the following methods.

prepareForPopoverPresentation(UIPopoverPresentationController**)**—This method is called to notify the delegate that the popover is about to be presented on the screen.

popoverPresentationControllerShouldDismissPopover(UIPopoverPresentationC ontroller**)**—This method is called to know if the popover should be dismissed or not.

popoverPresentationControllerDidDismissPopover(UIPopoverPresentationCont roller**)**—This method is called to notify the delegate that the popover was dismissed.

popoverPresentationController(UIPopoverPresentationController, **willRepositionPopoverTo:** CGRect, **in:** UIView**)**—This method is called to notify the delegate that the popover is going to be repositioned to the rectangle and view determined by the attributes.

The steps to add a popover to the Storyboard are the same as for modal views, with the exception that we have to use a specific Segue called *Present As Popover*. Figure 16-27 shows a small view connected to a button in our Detail view with this type of Segue. For this example, we have added a button called Total Books and created a view with an explicit size of 300 x 100.

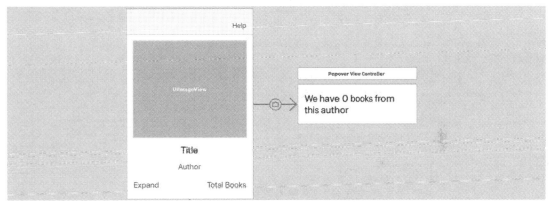

Figure 16-27: Popover in the Storyboard

A Present As Popover Segue assigns values by default to the **UIPopover-PresentationController** object, but we can modify some of them from the Attributes Inspector panel.

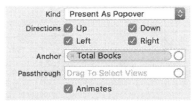

Figure 16-28: Popover configuration

The most important option is Directions. These values indicate where the arrow that points to the element that triggered the presentation is going to be located. For example, if we position the arrow at the top (Up), the view is going to be positioned below the element. By default, the Segue activates all the values to let the system decide the most appropriate, but we can suggest a specific position by activating only the ones we want.

The popover of our example shows a message with the number of books that belong to a particular author, so we have to pass the index of the selected book from the Detail view to the popover and then perform a search in the model from the popover's view controller to get the total of books available. The first step is to modify the **prepare()** method of the **DetailViewController** class to send the index of the book when the popover's Segue is triggered. The Segue was identified with the "showPopover" string (notice that we are still working over the same example introduced in this chapter, so the code for the "showPicture" Segue is still available).

```
override func prepare(for segue: UIStoryboardSegue, sender: Any?) {
    if segue.identifier == "showPicture" {
        let controller = segue.destination as! PictureViewController
        controller.selected = selected
    } else if segue.identifier == "showPopover" {
        let controller = segue.destination as! PopoverViewController
        controller.selected = selected
    }
}
```

Listing 16-20: Preparing the popover

Next, we have to create a new view controller for the popover and assign it to the Scene. This view controller has to perform the search to count the books available from the selected author and show it on the screen. We called it **PopoverViewController**.

```
import UIKit

class PopoverViewController: UIViewController {
    @IBOutlet weak var messageLabel: UILabel!
    var selected: Int!
    override func viewDidLoad() {
        super.viewDidLoad()
        var author = ""
        if selected != nil {
            let file = AppData.items[selected]
            if let data = AppData.itemsData[file] {
                author = data[1]
            }
            let search = AppData.itemsData.filter({ (item) in
                let data = item.1
                if data[1] == author {
                    return true
                }
                return false
            })
            let total = search.count
            messageLabel.text = "We have \(total) books from this author"
        }
    }
}
```

Listing 16-21: Counting books

The code of Listing 16-21 gets the name of the selected author first and then calls the **filter()** method to search for the name inside the **itemsData** dictionary of our model (see Listing 15-2). The **filter()** method returns an array with the items that match the name of the author, so we count the elements in the array and assign a string containing this value to the **messageLabel** label. In an iPad, we will see something similar to Figure 16-29.

Figure 16-29: Popover

Split View Controllers

Do It Yourself: Add a button with the title Total Books next to the Expand button in the Detail view. Add a new Scene to the Storyboard. Add a label to the view, as shown in Figure 16-27. Connect the button to the view with a Present As Popover Segue. Give the Segue the identifier "showPopover". Select the new Scene and modify its explicit size from the Attributes Inspector panel (Figure 16-20). You can also modify the size in the Storyboard from the Size Inspector panel (Figure 11-11). Create a subclass of **UIViewController** called **PopoverViewController** and assign it to the new Scene. Complete the subclass with the code of Listing 16-21. Connect the label to the **messageLabel** Outlet. Replace the **prepare()** method in the **DetailViewController** class of Listing 16-19 by the method of Listing 16-20. Run the application in the iPad simulator, select a book, and press the Total Books button. You should see something similar to Figure 16-29.

If we leave the Segue with the configuration by default, the system decides where to position the arrow and the view for us. In this case, it decided that it was better to present the view on the left side of the Total Books button, but in this place the view covers the title and the author. To move the view below the button and keep the labels visible, we have to deactivate the directions Left, Right, and Down from the Attributes Inspector panel and let only the Up option activated.

> We have 2 books from this author

Figure 16-30: Popover with an Up arrow

This forces the system to show the view where we want, but there is still a problem, the view now covers the button. This occurs because the anchor point is always at the coordinates 0, 0 of the button's frame, independently of the direction of the arrow. To modify the anchor point, we have to assign a new **CGRect** value to the **sourceRect** property of the **UIPopoverPresentationController** object. The following are the modifications we have to introduce to the **prepare()** method of the **DetailViewController** to set the anchor at the bottom of the Total Books button.

```
override func prepare(for segue: UIStoryboardSegue, sender: Any?) {
    if segue.identifier == "showPicture" {
        let controller = segue.destination as! PictureViewController
        controller.selected = selected
    } else if segue.identifier == "showPopover" {
        let controller = segue.destination as! PopoverViewController
        controller.selected = selected
        let presentation = controller.presentationController as!
UIPopoverPresentationController
        let frame = presentation.sourceView?.bounds
        presentation.sourceRect = frame!
    }
}
```

Listing 16-22: Moving the anchor point

The **presentationController** property returns a **UIPresentationController** object that we have to cast as **UIPopoverPresentationController** to have access to the properties of this class. The properties we need are **sourceView** and **sourceRect**. The **sourceView** property gives us access to the **UIView** object to which the popover is anchored, and the **sourceRect** property is the rectangle inside that view to which the popover's arrow points to. Therefore, to displace the arrow and the view we have to assign a new **CGRect** value to the **sourceRect** property. In the **prepare()** method of Listing 16-22, we get the internal frame of the view from its **bounds** property and assign it to the **sourceRect** property. This sets the rectangle as the size of the view and therefore the arrow points to the bottom and the center of the button, positioning the view below. The result is shown in Figure 16-31.

Figure 16-31: *Position of popover set from code*

 Do It Yourself: Select the Segue that connects the Total Books button with the popover view, go to the Attributes Inspector panel and deactivate the directions Left, Right, and Down. Replace the **prepare()** method in the **DetailViewController** class by the method of Listing 16-22. Run the application in the iPad simulator, select a book, and then press the Total Books button. You should see something similar to Figure 16-31.

This works fine on iPads. The view is presented as a popover and it can be dismissed tapping anywhere else on the screen. But in a compact horizontal Size Class, the popover is shown full screen and there is no way to dismiss it. To solve this problem, we can implement the protocol methods we used before for modal views. One alternative is to return the **none** value from the **adaptivePresentationStyle()** method. This tells the **UIPresentationController** object that we want the view to be presented with its original presentation style, so the view always looks like a popover, no matter the Size Class.

Because we have already declared the **DetailViewController** as the delegate of the view opened by the Help button (see Figure 16-25 and Listing 16-19), we are going to designate the **PopoverViewController** as the delegate this time. But there is a catch. The **UIPopoverPresentationController** controller includes its own **delegate** property but for objects that conform to the **UIPopoverPresentationControllerDelegate** protocol and the protocol we want to conform to is **UIAdaptivePresentationControllerDelegate**, so we have to assign the object to the **delegate** property of the **UIPresentationController** object (the object without casting). The following is an update of the **prepare()** method that designates this delegate.

```
override func prepare(for segue: UIStoryboardSegue, sender: Any?) {
   if segue.identifier == "showPicture" {
      let controller = segue.destination as! PictureViewController
      controller.selected = selected
   } else if segue.identifier == "showPopover" {
      let controller = segue.destination as! PopoverViewController
      controller.selected = selected
      let presentation = controller.presentationController as!
UIPopoverPresentationController
      let frame = presentation.sourceView?.bounds
      presentation.sourceRect = frame!
```

Split View Controllers

```
        controller.presentationController?.delegate = controller
    }
}
```

Listing 16-23: Assigning the delegate

At the end of the method of Listing 16-23 we get a reference to the **UIPresentationController** object assigned to the **UIPopoverViewController** object and declare its delegate to be the same **UIPopoverViewController** object. Now, we have to conform to the **UIAdaptivePresentationControllerDelegate** protocol from the **PopoverViewController** class and implement the delegate method.

```
import UIKit

class PopoverViewController: UIViewController,
UIAdaptivePresentationControllerDelegate {
    @IBOutlet weak var messageLabel: UILabel!
    var selected: Int!

    override func viewDidLoad() {
        super.viewDidLoad()
        var author = ""
        if selected != nil {
            let file = AppData.items[selected]
            if let data = AppData.itemsData[file] {
                author = data[1]
            }
            let search = AppData.itemsData.filter({ (item) in
                let data = item.1
                if data[1] == author {
                    return true
                }
                return false
            })
            let total = search.count
            messageLabel.text = "We have \(total) books from this author"
        }
    }
    func adaptivePresentationStyle(for controller: UIPresentationController)
-> UIModalPresentationStyle {
        return .none
    }
}
```

Listing 16-24: Implementing the protocol's methods

The new **PopoverViewController** is practically the same as before, we just conform to the protocol and return the value **none** from the **adaptivePresentationStyle()** method. From now on, every time the popover is about to be presented in a compact horizontal Size Class, the **UIPopoverPresentationController** object receives the **none** value and therefore does not adapt the presentation style (the popover is not shown full screen). Figure 16-32 shows what the popover looks like on an iPhone in portrait.

Figure 16-32: Popover on an iPhone in portrait mode

Do It Yourself: Replace the **prepare()** method in the **DetailViewController** class by the method of Listing 16-23. Update the **PopoverViewController** class with the code of Listing 16-24. Run the application in the iPhone simulator, select a book, and press the Total Books button to open the popover.

That was a simple solution, but popovers do not look good in devices with small screens. The best alternative is to present a different view for every style, as we did before for modal views. For example, we can add a new single view to the Storyboard with a Close button and the same message as the popover and then open this view when the presentation style is **fullScreen**.

Figure 16-33: Alternative view for the popover

The view controller for this view shares the same code with the **PopoverViewController** class, but it also has to include an Action for the Close button to dismiss the view. We called it **SinglePopoverViewController**.

```
import UIKit

class SinglePopoverViewController: UIViewController {
   @IBOutlet weak var messageLabel: UILabel!
   var selected: Int!

   override func viewDidLoad() {
      super.viewDidLoad()
      var author = ""
```

Split View Controllers

```
        if selected != nil {
            let file = AppData.items[selected]
            if let data = AppData.itemsData[file] {
                author = data[1]
            }
            let search = AppData.itemsData.filter({ (item) in
                let data = item.1
                if data[1] == author {
                    return true
                }
                return false
            })
            let total = search.count
            messageLabel.text = "We have \(total) books from this author"
        }
    }
    @IBAction func closePopover(_ sender: UIButton) {
        dismiss(animated: true, completion: nil)
    }
}
```

Listing 16-25: Controlling the alternative view

To present this view when the popover is shown full screen, we have to implement the **presentationController(UIPresentationController, viewControllerForAdaptivePresentationStyle:)** method in the delegate (the **PopoverViewController** class).

```
func presentationController(_ controller: UIPresentationController,
viewControllerForAdaptivePresentationStyle style: UIModalPresentationStyle)
-> UIViewController? {
    var controller: SinglePopoverViewController!
    if style == .fullScreen || style == .formSheet {
        if let story = storyboard {
            controller = story.instantiateViewController(withIdentifier:
"singlePopover") as? SinglePopoverViewController
            controller.selected = selected
        }
    }
    return controller
}
```

Listing 16-26: Presenting the alternative view

Notice that we cannot implement this method along with the method of Listing 16-24. When the **UIPresentationController** object receives the value **none** from the previous method, it considers that as an order not to adapt the presentation style and therefore never calls the method of Listing 16-26. Also, besides the **fullScreen** style we have to check for the **formSheet** style. This is because iPhones Plus in landscape mode adapt the presentation style to **formSheet** instead of **fullScreen**.

Do It Yourself: Add a new Scene to the Storyboard. Include a button and a label, as shown in Figure 16-33. Create a subclass of **UIViewController** with the name **SinglePopoverViewController** and assign it to the Scene. Give to the Scene the identifier "singlePopover" (Figure 16-24). Complete the subclass with the code of Listing 16-25. Connect the label to the Outlet and the Close button to the Action.

Erase the `adaptivePresentationStyle()` method from the `PopoverViewController` class and add the method of Listing 16-26. Run the application in the iPhone simulator. Open the popover in portrait mode. You should see the view of Figure 16-33 full screen instead of a popover.

Split View Controllers

17.1 Alert Views

Alert views are predefined modal views that can display messages and receive input form the user. Their purpose is to deliver to the user important information that requires immediate attention. For example, an Alert View may be used to ask confirmation from the user before deleting a file or data from the model. They may include a title, message, Text Fields, and buttons, and be presented full screen or as popovers in some devices. UIKit includes a subclass of the **UIViewController** class called **UIAlertController** to define these views, but there is no option to add them to the Storyboard, they have to be created from code using the following initializer.

UIAlertController(title: String?, **message:** String?, **preferredStyle:** Style)—This initializer creates a **UIAlertController** object configured with the values assigned to the attributes. The **title** attribute is a text shown at the top of the view, the **message** attribute is a message shown below the title, and the **preferredStyle** attribute is an enumeration called **Style** included in the **UIAlertController** class. The values available are **alert** and **actionSheet**, to indicate the type of view we want to create (Alert or Action Sheet).

The class also includes properties and methods to add and configure the view's elements.

title—This property sets or returns the title.

message—This property sets or returns the message

actions—This property returns an array with references to the actions (buttons) in the view.

textFields—This property returns an array with references to the Text Fields in the view.

addAction(UIAlertAction)—This method adds a new action to the view. Actions are objects that create buttons for the view with specific configurations and purposes.

addTextField(configurationHandler: Block)—This method adds a Text Field to the view. The attribute is a closure that provides the configuration for the Text Field.

Alert Views present buttons along with the text to receive input from the user. The buttons are created from the **UIAlertAction** class. The class includes the following initializer and properties.

UIAlertAction(title: String?, **style:** Style, **handler:** Block)—This initializer creates a **UIAlertAction** object configured with the values assigned to the attributes. The **title** attribute is the title for the button. The **style** attribute defines the purpose of the button. The possible values are **default** (for a generic type of button), **cancel** (for a button that cancels the request), and **destructive** (for a button that performs a destructive task, such as deleting a file). The **handler** attribute is a closure that is executed when the button is pressed.

title—This property returns a string with the title of the button.

style—This property returns the type of the button. It is an enumeration called **Style** included in the **UIAlertAction** class. The values available are **default**, **cancel**, and **destructive**.

isEnabled—This property sets or returns a Boolean value that determines whether the button is enabled or not.

There are two types of Alert Views available: Alert and Action Sheet. Alert Views of type Alert are presented in the center of the screen, like the Form Sheet modal views studied in Chapter 16, while those of type Action Sheet are anchored to the bottom of the screen in small devices or presented as popovers in devices with bigger screens. They may both include messages and buttons, but only the Alert types are capable of including Text Fields.

Alerts

Alert Views of type Alert are usually presented to report to the user that a specific task has been completed or something has gone wrong. For example, we may show an Alert View of type Alert to report an error when the user tries to save the value of an empty Text Field. The following interface includes a Text Field and a button to let the user insert a name. If the user presses the button before inserting any text, the code shows an Alert View reminding the user that a name must be inserted.

Figure 17-1: Interface to test Alert Views

The view controller for this view has to check whether the Text Field contains text or not and show the alert if it is empty.

```
import UIKit

class ViewController: UIViewController {
    @IBOutlet weak var nameText: UITextField!

    @IBAction func saveName(_ sender: UIButton) {
        var text = nameText.text!
        text = text.trimmingCharacters(in: .whitespaces)
        if text == "" {
            showAlert()
        } else {
            print("Value stored: \(text)")
            nameText.text = ""
        }
    }
    func showAlert() {
        let alert = UIAlertController(title: "Error", message: "Insert your
name in the field", preferredStyle: .alert)
        let action = UIAlertAction(title: "OK", style: .default, handler:
nil)
        alert.addAction(action)
        present(alert, animated: true, completion: nil)
    }
}
```

Listing 17-1: Presenting an Alert View

Alert Views

The view controller of Listing 17-1 includes an Outlet for the Text Field called **nameText** and an Action for the button called **saveName**. When the user presses the button, the Action checks the value of the field's **text** property. If the value is empty, it calls the **showAlert()** method to present an Alert View, otherwise it prints a message on the console and clears the field.

Our **showAlert()** method is responsible for showing the Alert View. The first step is to create the view controller for the Alert View with the **UIAlertController()** initializer. From this initializer we define the view's title and the message, and also its type (Alert in this case). Next, we have to create and add to the view a **UIAlertAction** object for every button we want to include. The initializer for this class also lets us define the information required, like the button's title, its purpose, and a closure that is going to be executed when the button is pressed. For this example, we need only one button of type Default. We are not going to perform any task when the button is pressed so we declared the handler as **nil**. The action is added to the Alert View with the **addAction()** method and then the view is presented on the screen with the **present()** method, as we did for other modal views in Chapter 16. If we run the application and press the Save button before inserting any text in the field, an Alert View is opened to remind us that we have to insert our name, as shown in Figure 17-2.

Figure 17-2: *Alert View of type Alert with a single button*

 Do It Yourself: Create a new Single View Application project. Add a label, a Text Field and a button to the main view. Connect the Text Field to the view controller with an Outlet called **nameText** and the button to an Action called **saveName()**. Complete the **ViewController** class with the code of Listing 17-1. Run the application and press the button. You should see something similar to Figure 17-2.

The Alert View can only be dismissed pressing one of its buttons. If we want to perform another task other than dismissing the view when the button is pressed, we have to provide a closure for the **handler** attribute of the **UIAlertAction** initializer. For example, the following code changes the background color of the Text Field after the OK button is pressed.

```
func showAlert() {
    let alert = UIAlertController(title: "Error", message: "Insert the
name in the field", preferredStyle: .alert)
    let action = UIAlertAction(title: "OK", style: .default, handler: {
(action) in
        self.nameText.backgroundColor = UIColor(red: 255.0/255.0, green:
230.0/255.0, blue: 230.0/255.0, alpha: 1.0)
    })
```

```
    alert.addAction(action)
    present(alert, animated: true, completion: nil)
}
```

Listing 17-2: Changing the background color of the Text Field when the button is pressed

The closure receives a reference to the **UIAlertAction** object, so we have to include an attribute for the closure to capture this reference and then declare the statements after the **in** instruction. In this example, we change the background color of the Text Field to red.

 IMPORTANT: Properties inside a closure must always be referenced from **self**. This is a requirement of Swift to remind us that referencing a property of the class from inside the closure could create a strong reference cycle (see Chapter 3). For more information on how to avoid strong reference cycles from closures, visit our website and follow the links for this chapter.

We can add more buttons to the Alert View. The following example asks the user if the application should store the empty fields anyways and offers a Cancel button to cancel the operation.

```
func showAlert() {
    let alert = UIAlertController(title: "The field is empty", message:
"Are you sure do you want to store an empty string?", preferredStyle:
.alert)
    let action = UIAlertAction(title: "Yes", style: .default, handler: {
(action) in
        print("Value stored")
    })
    alert.addAction(action)
    let cancel = UIAlertAction(title: "Cancel", style: .cancel, handler:
nil)
    alert.addAction(cancel)
    present(alert, animated: true, completion: nil)
}
```

Listing 17-3: Adding a Cancel button

The **UIAlertController** object places the buttons inside the view in the order they were created in the code. We may add all the buttons we need, except for buttons of type Cancel, of which only one is permitted per view.

Because we did not include a closure for the **handler** attribute of the Cancel button, the function of the button is just to dismiss the view, but all buttons can perform additional tasks, including this one.

 Do It Yourself: Replace the **showAlert()** method of Listing 17-1 by the methods of Listings 17-2 and 17-3 to try each example.

Alert Views of type Alert may also include Text Fields. Text Fields are usually added to an Alert View to create sign-up or log-in forms. For instance, we can create an interface with an initial view that lets the user log in, and a second view that is opened if the values inserted by the user coincide with the data we have in our model. The interface of Figure 17-3 includes a welcoming window with a button called Log In to open an Alert View to insert an email and a password.

Alert Views

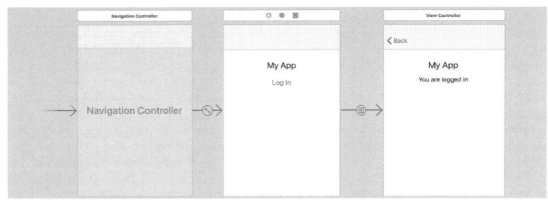

Figure 17-3: Interface to log in

Text Fields are added directly to the Alert View with the **addTextField()** method. In our example we need two, one for the email and another for the password. The view controller of the initial view has to include an Action for the Log In button to create the Alert View with the Text Fields.

```
import UIKit

class ViewController: UIViewController {
    @IBAction func loginUser(_ sender: UIButton) {
        let alert = UIAlertController(title: "Insert Email and Password",
message: nil, preferredStyle: .alert)

        let cancel = UIAlertAction(title: "Cancel", style: .cancel,
handler: nil)
        alert.addAction(cancel)

        let action = UIAlertAction(title: "Login", style: .default,
handler: { (action) in
            if let fields = alert.textFields {
                let email = fields[0].text
                let password = fields[1].text

                if email == "test@yahoo.com" && password == "12345" {
                    self.performSegue(withIdentifier: "showMainScreen",
sender: self)
                }
            }
        })
        alert.addAction(action)

        alert.addTextField(configurationHandler: { (textField) in
            textField.placeholder = "Email"
        })
        alert.addTextField(configurationHandler: { (textField) in
            textField.placeholder = "Password"
            textField.isSecureTextEntry = true
        })
        present(alert, animated: true, completion: nil)
    }
}
```

Listing 17-4: Creating and processing a login form

The **addTextField()** method includes an attribute to provide a closure where we can configure the Text Field. For the email, we only need to set a placeholder, but the Text Field for the password has to be declared as secure with the **isSecureTextEntry** property so the password is not shown on the screen (see Chapter 7).

The Alert View includes two buttons: Cancel and Login. When the user presses the Login button, we have to compare the values inserted in the fields with the data we have in our model (usually a database in the device or in a server). To access the Text Fields from inside the closure for the Login button, we read the **textFields** property of the Alert View. This property contains an array with references to the Text Fields in the view. The indexes of the array follow the order of the Text Fields in the code (the first one is at index 0, the next one at index 1, and so on). For this example, we keep it simple and compare the values of each Text Field with hard-coded strings. If the values coincide, we trigger the Segue to open the second view where the user can begin working with our app (the Segue is a Show Segue identified with the string "showMainScreen").

Figure 17-4: *Logging in*

 Do It Yourself: Create a new Single View Application project. Embed the initial Scene in a Navigation Controller. Add a button with the title Log In to the initial view. Add a second Scene to the Storyboard. Add a label with the text "You are logged in" to the second view. Connect the first view to the second view with a Show Segue. Give the Segue the identifier "showMainScreen". Connect the Log In button with an Action called **loginUser()**. Complete the Action with the code of Listing 17-4. Run the application and press the Log In button. Insert the email "test@yahoo.com" and the password "12345". Press the Login button. You should see something similar to Figure 17-4.

Action Sheets

Alert Views of type Action Sheet are usually presented when our application needs the user to decide and there is more than one option available. As shown in the following example, the creation of an Action Sheet is similar to Alert Views, but we have to use the **actionSheet** style for the initializer. The example assumes that the interface contains a button connected to an Action called **openSheet()**.

```
import UIKit

class ViewController: UIViewController {
    @IBAction func openSheet(_ sender: UIButton) {
        let alert = UIAlertController(title: "Emails", message: "What do
you want to do with the message?", preferredStyle: .actionSheet)
```

Alert Views

```
        let action1 = UIAlertAction(title: "Move to Inbox", style:
.default, handler: nil)
        alert.addAction(action1)
        let action2 = UIAlertAction(title: "Delete", style: .destructive,
handler: nil)
        alert.addAction(action2)
        let cancel = UIAlertAction(title: "Cancel", style: .cancel,
handler: nil)
        alert.addAction(cancel)

        present(alert, animated: true, completion: nil)
    }
}
```

Listing 17-5: *Creating an Action Sheet*

The code of Listing 17-5 creates an Alert View of type Action Sheet when the user presses the button in the interface. This Action Sheet contains a total of three buttons: a **default** button called Move to Inbox, a **destructive** button called Delete, and a **cancel** button called Cancel. We didn't include any handler for the buttons, so their only purpose is to dismiss the view, but the example illustrates how an Action Sheet is created and how the buttons are organized inside the view. No matter the position of the buttons in the code, the **cancel** button is always displayed at the end, in a separate box, and the **destructive** button is highlighted in color red.

Figure 17-5: *Action Sheet*

 Do It Yourself: Create a new Single View Application project. Add a button called Open Sheet to the initial view. Connect the button to the **ViewController** with an Action called **openSheet()**. Complete the Action with the code of Listing 17-5. Run the application in an iPhone simulator and press the button. You should see something similar to Figure 17-5.

As we already mentioned, Action Sheets are presented as modal views at the bottom of the screen in small devices, but as popovers in iPads. The problem is that the system cannot display a popover without the necessary information. If we execute the previous application on an iPad, we get an error and the application crashes. To make sure that the code works in every device, we have to change the configuration of the presentation. For this purpose, the **UIAlertController** object includes the **popoverPresentationController** property with a reference to the **UIPopoverPresentationController** object that is in charge of the presentation when the presentation style is **popover**. The values we need to provide to this object are the view to which the Action Sheet is anchored, the rectangle inside the view the popover's arrow points to, and the directions the arrow can take.

```
import UIKit

class ViewController: UIViewController {
    @IBOutlet weak var sheetButton: UIButton!

    @IBAction func openSheet(_ sender: UIButton) {
        let alert = UIAlertController(title: "Emails", message: "What do
you want to do with the message?", preferredStyle: .actionSheet)
        if let popover = alert.popoverPresentationController {
            popover.sourceView = sheetButton
            popover.sourceRect = sheetButton.bounds
            popover.permittedArrowDirections = [.up]
        }
        let action1 = UIAlertAction(title: "Move to Inbox", style:
.default, handler: nil)
        alert.addAction(action1)
        let cancel = UIAlertAction(title: "Cancel", style: .cancel,
handler: nil)
        alert.addAction(cancel)
        let action2 = UIAlertAction(title: "Delete", style: .destructive,
handler: nil)
        alert.addAction(action2)
        present(alert, animated: true, completion: nil)
    }
}
```

Listing 17-6: Presenting the Action Sheet as a popover in iPads

The view controller of Listing 17-6 adds the configuration for the popover to the previous example. We decided to anchor the popover to the button that opens the view, so we created an Outlet to reference the button called **sheetButton** and then assigned that reference to the **sourceView** property of the **UIPopoverPresentationController** object. This anchors the popover to the button, but we still have to determine to which part of the button's view the arrow is going to point to. Assigning the internal frame of the button's view to the **sourceRect** property we make sure that the arrow always points to one of the sides of the button and the button is not covered by the view (see Listing 16-22). Finally, we set the **permittedArrowDirections** property with only the value **up**, so the view is positioned below the button, as shown in Figure 17-6.

Figure 17-6: Action Sheet on the iPad

The Action Sheet not only adapts its presentation to the space available but also its design. If we run the example of Listing 17-6 in an iPad, the Cancel button is automatically removed because the user can dismiss the popover by tapping anywhere else on the screen.

Alert Views

18.1 Operations

iOS can separate pieces of code and execute them in simultaneous operations. Operations are objects used to wrap a set of statements that perform a task. These operations can then be put in a queue and executed in order, one after another, according to a level of priority assigned by the system or explicitly by the application. The advantage of this process is that the operations can be performed concurrently, which means they can take advantage of the hardware capacity to execute multiple instructions at the same time. For example, we may have a code that downloads a big file from the Internet and another code that shows the progress on the screen. In cases like this, we cannot wait for one code to be over to execute the other; we need the two pieces of code to work at the same time. Using operations, we can wrap the code to download the file in one operation and the code that shows a progress bar in another, and then make them work simultaneously.

 IMPORTANT: This chapter introduces basic concepts of operations and concurrency. As we will see later, simultaneous operations are usually required to keep the interface responsive when the application access complex frameworks that perform time-consuming operations. We will see a few practical examples in further chapters.

Block Operations

Foundation includes the **Operation** class to create operation objects. The class provides all the necessary functionality to configure an operation, but we must create a subclass to include the statements the operation is required to perform. To simplify the process, the framework defines a standard subclass of **Operation** called **BlockOperation**. This subclass can create an operation from the statements provided by a closure. The following is its initializer.

BlockOperation(block: Block)—This initializer creates an operation with the statements specified by the closure assigned to the **block** attribute.

Because the **BlockOperation** class is a subclass of **Operation**, it has access to its properties and methods. The following are the most useful.

completionBlock—This property sets a closure with the statements we want to execute after the operation is completed.

queuePriority—This property sets the operation's priority. It is an enumeration called **QueuePriority** included in the **Operation** class. The values available are **veryLow, low, normal, high**, and **veryHigh**.

cancel()—This method asks the system to cancel the operation.

The operations have to be added to a queue to be scheduled for execution. For this purpose, Foundation includes the **OperationQueue** class. Once an instance of this class is created, we can use the following methods to manage the operations in the queue.

addOperation(Operation**)**—This method adds the operation specified by the operation attribute to the queue. The attribute is an object created from an `Operation` subclass.

addOperations([Operation], **waitUntilFinished:** Bool**)**—This method adds the operations specified by the first attribute to the queue. The **waitUntilFinished** attribute determines whether the thread will be blocked until the operations are finished or not.

addOperation(Block**)**—This method creates an `Operation` object from the statements provided by the attribute and adds it to the queue. The attribute is a closure with the statements we want to include in the operation.

cancelAllOperations()—This method cancels all the operations in the queue.

By default, iOS places the application's code in a single queue called *Main Queue*. If we want some code to be executed in a different queue, we have to create an operation and add it to a new queue.

```
import UIKit
class ViewController: UIViewController {
    override func viewDidLoad() {
        super.viewDidLoad()
        let operation = BlockOperation(block: {
            var total: Double = 1
            for f in 1..<100 {
                total = log(total + Double(f))
            }
            print("Total: \(total)")
        })
        let queue = OperationQueue()
        queue.addOperation(operation)
        print("Printed in the Main Queue")
    }
}
```

Listing 18-1: Adding operations to a queue

The operation is created by the `BlockOperation()` initializer. This initializer takes a closure with the statements we want to execute (in this case, a loop to calculate the logarithm of a sequence of values) and creates the operation. With the operation ready, we initialize a new `OperationQueue` object to represent the queue and add the operation to it.

When the code of Listing 18-1 is executed, the system creates the operation, adds it to a new queue, and runs it as soon as it can. At this point, the system is running two codes at the same time, the code in the main queue and the code in the new queue we have just created. As a result, we will see the message "Printed in the Main Queue" on the console first, and then the message produced by the operation, because the operation takes more time to complete.

This code guarantees that the code in the main queue is executed, no matter how much time the statements in the operation take to finish the process. If we hadn't created the operation and added it to a new queue, the system would have had to wait until the execution of the loop was over to execute the last statement and print the message on the console.

 Do It Yourself: Create a new Single View Application project. Update the `ViewController` class of the initial view with the code of Listing 18-1 and run the application. The Xcode's console should print the message "Printed in the Main Queue" first and then another message with the result of the operation.

Operation Queues

Main Queue

Some frameworks, like UIKit, can only work in the main queue. If we try to access the elements of the interface from a different queue, the application will produce unexpected results. The **OperationQueue** class offers the following type property to get a reference to the main queue when we need to add operations to it.

main—This type property returns a reference to the **OperationQueue** object representing the main queue.

Code inside a closure may sometimes be executed in a different queue. Every time we have to execute code inside an operation or a block of code, we have to consider whether that code can be executed in any queue or it only works properly in the main queue. If the code is required to be executed in the main queue, we have to insert it in an operation, get a reference to the main queue from the **main** property, and add the operation to it, as in the following example.

```
import UIKit

class ViewController: UIViewController {
    @IBOutlet weak var totalLabel: UILabel!

    override func viewDidLoad() {
        super.viewDidLoad()
        let operation = BlockOperation(block: {
            var total: Double = 1
            for f in 1..<100 {
                total = log(total + Double(f))
            }
            let main = OperationQueue.main
            main.addOperation({
                self.totalLabel.text = "Total: \(total)"
            })
        })
        let queue = OperationQueue()
        queue.addOperation(operation)
        print("Printed in the Main Queue")
    }
}
```

Listing 18-2: Adding operations to the main queue

In Listing 18-2, instead of printing a message to the console we update a label with the result produced by the loop. The elements of the interface can only be modified from the main queue, so we get a reference to this queue and then update the label from inside an operation added with the **addOperation()** method. This method creates a new operation on the fly with the code inside the block and adds it to the queue, simplifying the process. At the end, we get a similar result to the previous application; the loop is executed along with the rest of the code, but when it is over, the operation that updates the label is executed, showing the result on the screen.

 Do It Yourself: Add a label to the initial view and connect it to the view controller with an Outlet called **totalLabel**. Update the **ViewController** class with the code of Listing 18-2. Run the application. You should see the result produced by the loop on the screen.

Dependencies

The operations are performed asynchronously and therefore the order in which they are executed is not determined by the Operation Queue but rather by the system. Some operations are executed simultaneously and others in an order different than the one established by the queue. If our code requires the operations to be executed in a specific order, we have to declare dependencies between them. A dependency makes an operation dependent on the execution of another. For instance, if we have an operation One and add a dependency to operation Two, the operation One won't be executed until the operation Two's execution is over. The **Operation** class includes two methods to add and remove dependencies.

addDependency(Operation**)**—This method adds a dependency to the operation. The attribute is a reference to the operation to which the original operation depends on.

removeDependency(Operation**)**—This method removes a dependency. The attribute is a reference to the operation to which the original operation depends on.

The following example illustrates how to add a dependency between two operations.

```
import UIKit

class ViewController: UIViewController {
    override func viewDidLoad() {
        super.viewDidLoad()

        let firstoperation = BlockOperation(block: {
           print("First Operation Executed")
        })
        let secondoperation = BlockOperation(block: {
           print("Second Operation Executed")
        })
        firstoperation.addDependency(secondoperation)

        let queue = OperationQueue()
        queue.addOperations([firstoperation, secondoperation],
waitUntilFinished: false)
    }
}
```

Listing 18-3: *Adding a dependency*

The process is simple, we just have to define the operations and then call the **addDependency()** method on the operation we want to make dependent on another. In Listing 18-3, we create two operations called **firstoperation** and **secondoperation** and then make the **firstoperation** dependent on the **secondoperation**. Because of this, the **firstoperation** is only executed after the execution of the **secondoperation** is over.

 Do It Yourself: Replace the code in your **ViewController** class by the code of Listing 18-3. Erase the label added in the previous example if necessary. Run the application. You should see the message "Second Operation Executed" on the console before the message "First Operation Executed".

Operation Queues

18.2 Grand Central Dispatch

Apple has been developing frameworks since the introduction of its first personal computer. Over time, some of these frameworks were replaced and others improved, creating a huge SDK with some of the frameworks performing similar tasks but at a different technical level. This means that for some tasks we can select the framework we want to work with depending on the level of customization our app needs. Among these duplicated frameworks are two dedicated to performing operations. These are the Foundation's Operations studied before and a system called Grand Central Dispatch (GCD). GCD is a framework programmed in the C language that works like Operations in Foundation but at a lower level, offering a deeper access to the system.

Although Foundation's Operations are sufficient for most of the scenarios we may find in a professional application, a few old frameworks programmed in Objective-C require the use of GCD to perform concurrent tasks and therefore both systems remain useful. For this reason, Apple decided to introduce an additional framework called *Dispatch* to make GCD easier to implement.

Dispatch Framework

The Dispatch framework includes an extensive list of classes to provide access to all the original features of GCD, but with a friendly API. To schedule an operation, all we need to do is to create an instance of the **DispatchQueue** class. The following is the class initializer.

DispatchQueue(label: String)—This initializer creates a queue identified with the value specified by the **label** attribute.

Once the **DispatchQueue** instance is created, we have to call its methods to add a task to the queue. The class includes two methods to dispatch tasks synchronously (the operation must finish before others are initiated) or asynchronously (multiple operations are executed simultaneously).

async(execute: Block)—This method asynchronously executes the statements in the closure specified by the **execute** attribute.

sync(execute: Block)—This method synchronously executes the statements in the closure specified by the **execute** attribute.

The Dispatch framework is just another way to perform multiple tasks simultaneously. The following example repeats the code we used before with Operations, but this time the task is performed with a **DispatchQueue** object.

```
import UIKit

class ViewController: UIViewController {
   override func viewDidLoad() {
      super.viewDidLoad()
      let queue = DispatchQueue(label: "myqueue")
      queue.async(execute: {
         var total: Double = 1
         for f in 1..<100 {
            total = log(total + Double(f))
         }
```

```
        print("Total: \(total)")
     })
     print("Printed in the Main Queue")
   }
}
```

Listing 18-4: Dispatching tasks with GCD

The **DispatchQueue** class also offers a type property to access the main queue.

main—This type property returns the **DispatchQueue** object referencing the main queue.

As we did before, the following example updates a previous code to perform a task in the main queue inside an asynchronous operation.

```
import UIKit

class ViewController: UIViewController {
   @IBOutlet weak var totalLabel: UILabel!

   override func viewDidLoad() {
      super.viewDidLoad()
      let queue = DispatchQueue(label: "myqueue")
      queue.async(execute: {
         var total: Double = 1
         for f in 1..<100 {
            total = log(total + Double(f))
         }
         let main = DispatchQueue.main
         main.sync(execute: {
            self.totalLabel.text = "Total: \(total)"
         })
      })
      print("Printed in the Main Queue")
   }
}
```

Listing 18-5: Working on the main queue with GCD

When the code of Listing 18-5 is executed, it creates a queue with a closure to calculate the logarithm of a series of values. When the operation is over, the task gets a reference to the main queue and performs a second task to update a label on the interface with the result. This last operation is performed synchronously since we are already inside an asynchronous operation.

 Do It Yourself: These examples work exactly the same way as the examples introduced for Foundation's Operations. As well as the example of Listing 18-2, the example of Listing 18-5 requires the interface to include a label connected to an Outlet called **totalLabel**.

Dispatch Group

Like Operations, the tasks we assign to a queue are not performed in order. They can be executed simultaneously or in an order different than the one established by the queue. To control the situation, the Dispatch framework offers the **DispatchGroup** class that we can use to track the completion of multiple operations. With an object of this class, we can indicate when a task begins and finishes and then execute a closure when they are all over. The class includes the following methods for this purpose.

enter()—This method indicates that a task has enter the group of tasks to be monitored.

leave()—This method indicates that a task in the group has finished.

notify(queue: DispatchQueue, **execute:** Block)—This method executes a closure when all the tasks in the group are over. The **queue** attribute determines the queue in which the closure will be processed, and the **execute** attribute is the closure to be executed.

The following example adds two tasks to a queue called "myqueue", but unlike previous examples, we include each one of them in a dispatch group and print a message when all the tasks are over.

```
import UIKit

class ViewController: UIViewController {
    override func viewDidLoad() {
        super.viewDidLoad()

        let group = DispatchGroup()
        let queue = DispatchQueue(label: "myqueue")

        group.enter()
        queue.async(execute: {
            print("First Task Executed")
            group.leave()
        })
        group.enter()
        queue.async(execute: {
            print("Second Task Executed")
            group.leave()
        })
        group.notify(queue: .main, execute: {
            print("The tasks are over")
        })
    }
}
```

Listing 18-6: Adding tasks to a Dispatch Group

A dispatch group is created from an instance of the **DispatchGroup** class and the tasks are added to the group with the **enter()** and **leave()** methods. In the example of Listing 18-6, we create the **DispatchGroup** object and then add two tasks to the queue. Before adding each task, we call the **enter()** method, and after the task is over we call the **leave()** method to communicate the situation to the group. At the end, we call the **notify()** method to print a message when the execution of all the tasks is over.

 The Basics: The **DispatchGroup** class was defined in the Dispatch framework, but you can also create dispatch groups for operations.

Operation Queues

19.1 Notification Center

Besides the techniques we have seen so far to transfer data between different parts of an application, such as sending values from one view controller to another or providing a common model from which every view controller can get the information it needs, we can also send notifications to report changes across the application. Foundation includes the **NotificationCenter** class from which the system creates an object that serves as a Notification Center for the whole application. We can send notifications (messages) to this object and then listen to those notifications from anywhere in the code. The class includes the following property to get a reference to this object.

> **default**—This type property returns the **NotificationCenter** object assigned by default to the application.

The Notification Center is like a bulletin board; we can post a notification from anywhere in the code and then read it from other objects. The readers are called *observers*. Observers are just objects we add to the Notification Center to tell it who wants to know when a particular notification arrives. For example, our model may post a notification every time some of its values change, and we can set an observer in one of our view controllers to listen to that particular notification. When a value in the model changes, the model posts a notification, the Notification Center looks for observers of that notification, and finally calls a method in the view controller to let it know that a notification arrived. The **NotificationCenter** class includes the following methods to post notifications and also add and remove observers.

> **post(name:** Name, **object:** Any?, **userInfo:** Dictionary)—This method posts a notification to the Notification Center. The **name** attribute determines the name of the notification, the **object** attribute is a reference to the object that sent the notification, and the **userInfo** attribute is a dictionary with the information we want to pass to the observer.

> **addObserver(**Any, **selector:** Selector, **name:** Name?, **object:** Any?)—This method adds an observer for a specific notification to the Notification Center. The first attribute is a reference to the object that is going to listen to the notification, the **selector** attribute is a reference to the method that is going to be executed when the notification is received, the **name** attribute determines the name of the notification we want to listen to, and the **object** attribute is a reference to the object that is sending the notification.

> **removeObserver(**Any, **name:** Name?, **object:** Any?)—This method removes an observer from the Notification Center. The attributes are the same provided to the **addObserver()** method when the observer was created.

Notifications are created from the **Notification** class. The **post()** method automatically creates a **Notification** object to represent the notification we want to post, but we can also do it ourselves from the class initializer.

> **Notification(name:** Name, **object:** Any?, **userInfo:** Dictionary)—This initializer creates a **Notification** object with the information defined by the attributes. The **name** attribute determines the name of the notification, the **object** attribute is a reference to the object that is sending the notification, and the **userInfo** attribute is a dictionary with the information we want to pass to the observer.

The class includes the following properties to read the values of the notification.

name—This property returns the name of the notification.

object—This property returns a reference to the object that posted the notification.

userInfo—This property returns the dictionary attached to the notification.

The name of the notification is created from a structure included in the **Notification** class called **Name**. The structure provides the following initializer to define new names.

Name(String**)**—This initializer creates a structure that represents the notification's name. The attribute is a string with the name we want to assign to the notification.

Notifications are used for multiple purposes. We can post a notification after a long process is over to tell a view controller that it is time to update the interface, we can communicate view controllers in a large interface with each other, or we can keep a view controller up to date posting notifications from the model. The following example includes a model that posts a notification every time a new value is inserted. For didactic purposes, we are going to use a simple interface that includes just enough views to show the number of values available and insert new ones.

Figure 19-1: *Interface to test notifications*

The model has to store the value inserted by the user in the Text Field and then post a notification, so the initial view can update its interface.

```
import Foundation

struct ApplicationData {
   var names: [String]

   mutating func addNewName(newName: String) {
      names.append(newName)

      let center = NotificationCenter.default
      let name = Notification.Name("Update Data")
      center.post(name: name, object: nil, userInfo: nil)
   }
}
var AppData = ApplicationData(names: [])
```

Listing 19-1: *Sending notifications from the model*

The **ApplicationData** structure created for this example contains only one property called **names**, but we have also included a method called **addNewName()** to assign new values to it. After adding the new value to the **names** array, the method gets a reference to the **NotificationCenter** object assigned to our app and posts a notification we called "Update Data" to report the action.

The view controller for the initial view has to add itself as an observer of this notification and update its interface every time the notification is received.

Notifications

```
import UIKit
class ViewController: UIViewController {
    @IBOutlet weak var counter: UILabel!

    override func viewDidLoad() {
        super.viewDidLoad()
        let center = NotificationCenter.default
        let name = Notification.Name("Update Data")
        center.addObserver(self, selector:
#selector(updateCounter(notification:)), name: name, object: nil)
    }
    @objc func updateCounter(notification: Notification) {
        let main = OperationQueue.main
        main.addOperation({
            let current = AppData.names
            self.counter.text = String(current.count)
        })
    }
}
```

Listing 19-2: Adding an observer

Observers are usually added as soon as the object is loaded and after the initialization is over. This is to avoid conflicts between the values managed by the object and those produced when the notification is received. Again, we have to get a reference to the **NotificationCenter** object assigned to our app first and then add the view controller as the observer of the "Update Data" notification posted by the model. The first attribute for the **addObserver()** method is the reference to the observer (in this case the **ViewController** object), and the second attribute is a selector referencing the method we are going to execute when the notification is received. The method, which we called **updateCounter()**, gets the amount of elements in the **names** property and updates the label with this value (Notice that observers are sometimes executed from a different thread, so we have to access the main thread to avoid conflict).

The values in the model are added from the second view. The view controller for this view has to take the value inserted in the Text Field and call the **addNewName()** method to add it to the model.

```
import UIKit
class SecondViewController: UIViewController {
    @IBOutlet weak var name: UITextField!

    @IBAction func saveName(_ sender: UIButton) {
        if let value = name.text {
            AppData.addNewName(newName: value)
        }
        name.text = ""
    }
}
```

Listing 19-3: Adding new values to the model

When we insert a new name into the Text Field and press the Save button, the **saveName()** method adds the value to the model by calling the model's **addNewName()** method. After this, the model receives the value, stores it in the **names** array, and posts the "Update Data" notification. The Notification Center informs the **ViewController** object that an "Update Data" notification has arrived and the object executes the **updateCounter()** method (see Listing 19-2). This method counts the values in the **names** array and shows the result on the screen.

Notifications

Do It Yourself: Create a new Single View Application project. Embed the initial Scene in a Navigation Controller. Add a second Scene to the Storyboard. Add two labels and a button to the initial view, and a label, a Text Field, and a button to the second view, as shown in Figure 19-1. Connect the button in the initial view to the second view with a Show Segue. Create a subclass of **UIViewController** called **SecondViewController** and assign it to the second Scene. Complete the **ViewController** class with the code of Listing 19-2, and the **SecondViewController** class with the code of Listing 19-3. Connect the elements to their respective Outlets and Actions. Run the application, press the button to go to the second view, and insert a few names. Move back to the initial view. The view should show the total number of names already inserted.

The **addObserver()** method sends to the action a reference to the **Notification** object that represents the notification. In the example of Listing 19-2, we included the **notification** attribute in the **updateCounter()** method to receive this value. From this reference, we can read the notification's properties. The most useful is **userInfo**, because it allows us to send information from one object to another. The values that can be included in this dictionary are called Property List values, which are the values allowed in a plist file. This includes the classes and structures **NSNumber**, **NSString**, **NSDate**, **NSArray**, **NSDictionary**, **NSData**, and also their equivalents in Swift. There are multiple applications for this property. Considering our previous example, we may include a string to describe the value that was updated in the model.

```
import Foundation

struct ApplicationData {
    var names: [String]

    mutating func addNewName(newName: String) {
        names.append(newName)
        let center = NotificationCenter.default
        let name = Notification.Name("Update Data")
        let info = ["type": "New Name"]
        center.post(name: name, object: nil, userInfo: info)
    }
}
var AppData = ApplicationData(names: [])
```

Listing 19-4: Including information in the notification

The code of Listing 19-4 declares a dictionary with the key "type" and the value "New Name" and assigns it to the **userInfo** attribute of the **post()** method. In the **ViewController** class, we can check this value and decide whether or not to update the label.

```
import UIKit

class ViewController: UIViewController {
    @IBOutlet weak var counter: UILabel!

    override func viewDidLoad() {
        super.viewDidLoad()
        let center = NotificationCenter.default
        let name = Notification.Name("Update Data")
        center.addObserver(self, selector:
#selector(updateCounter(notification:)), name: name, object: nil)
    }
```

Notifications

```
@objc func updateCounter(notification: Notification) {
    let main = OperationQueue.main
    main.addOperation({
        if let info = notification.userInfo {
            let type = info["type"] as? String
            if type == "New Name" {
                let current = AppData.names
                self.counter.text = String(current.count)
            }
        }
    })
}
```

Listing 19-5: Reading the value received by the observer

The values from the dictionary are returned as values of type **Any**, so we have to cast them to the right type. The example of Listing 19-5 reads the value of the "type" key, cast it as a **String**, and then compares it with the string "New Name". If the values match, we modify the label.

 Do It Yourself: Update the **ApplicationData** structure with the code of Listing 19-4 and the **ViewController** class with the code of Listing 19-5. Run the application. It should work like before. Change the string "New Name" in the view controller by a different string. Now the label is not updated anymore.

If we do not want the object to respond to new notifications or the application does not need it anymore, we have to remove the observer from the Notification Center. The **NotificationCenter** class provides the **removeObserver()** method for this purpose. For example, we can remove the observer in the **ViewController** class of our example after the first notification arrives, so the label is only updated once.

```
import UIKit

class ViewController: UIViewController {
    @IBOutlet weak var counter: UILabel!
    override func viewDidLoad() {
        super.viewDidLoad()
        let center = NotificationCenter.default
        let name = Notification.Name("Update Data")
        center.addObserver(self, selector:
#selector(updateCounter(notification:)), name: name, object: nil)
    }
    @objc func updateCounter(notification: NSNotification) {
        let main = OperationQueue.main
        main.addOperation({
            if let info = notification.userInfo {
                let type = info["type"] as? String
                if type == "New Name" {
                    let current = AppData.names
                    self.counter.text = String(current.count)
                }
            }
            let center = NotificationCenter.default
            let name = Notification.Name("Update Data")
            center.removeObserver(self, name: name, object: nil)
        })
    }
}
```

Listing 19-6: Removing the observer

Notifications

System Notifications

Besides the notifications our app posts, the system also posts notifications to the Notification Center all the time to report changes in the interface or in other objects running the application. At this time, there are hundreds of notifications for the iOS system, including those defined in some of the classes we already studied. They work exactly like the custom notifications we studied before but are preprogramed in the classes, so the only thing we have to do is to add the observers for the notifications we want to receive. We will probably never use most of the notifications available, but some are very useful. For example, the `UIWindow` class defines a few notifications to manage the keyboard. The following are the properties that we have to read to get the names of the notifications related to the keyboard.

keyboardWillShowNotification—This notification is posted before the keyboard is shown.

keyboardDidShowNotification—This notification is posted after the keyboard was shown.

keyboardWillHideNotification—This notification is posted before the keyboard is hidden.

keyboardDidHideNotification—This notification is posted after the keyboard was hidden.

keyboardWillChangeFrameNotification—This notification is posted before the keyboard's frame changes (due to a device rotation).

keyboardDidChangeFrameNotification—This notification is posted after the keyboard's frame changes (due to a device rotation).

These notifications not only report the state of the keyboard, but they also provide the values of the keyboard's frame through the `userInfo` property, so we can calculate the space available to reposition the elements in the interface. The values in the `userInfo` dictionary are identified by strings stored in additional `UIWindow` properties. The most frequently used properties are `keyboardFrameBeginUserInfoKey` (returns a value with the frame occupied by the keyboard when closed) and `keyboardFrameEndUserInfoKey` (returns a value with the frame occupied by the keyboard when opened).

The main view of the following example contains a button and a Text View. When the user tries to edit the text, the keyboard appears, and the Text View adapts its size to the remaining space, but when the button is pressed, the keyboard is closed, and the Text View goes back to its original size.

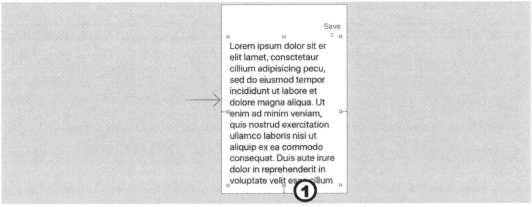

Figure 19-2: Interface to test keyboard notifications

Notifications

There are different ways to change the size of an element and rearrange the interface. In this example, we are going to adapt the size of the Text View by modifying the Space constraint that pins the bottom edge of the Text View to the bottom of the main view (Figure 19-2, number 1). Extending this constraint, we change the size of the Text View to make it fit in the space left by the keyboard.

```
import UIKit

class ViewController: UIViewController {
    @IBOutlet weak var heightBottom: NSLayoutConstraint!
    @IBOutlet weak var mainText: UITextView!
    var constraintHeight: CGFloat!

    override func viewDidLoad() {
        super.viewDidLoad()
        constraintHeight = heightBottom.constant

        let center = NotificationCenter.default
        center.addObserver(self, selector:
#selector(openKeyboard(notification:)), name:
UIWindow.keyboardWillShowNotification, object: nil)
        center.addObserver(self, selector:
#selector(closeKeyboard(notification:)), name:
UIWindow.keyboardWillHideNotification, object: nil)
    }
    @objc func openKeyboard(notification: Notification) {
        if let info = notification.userInfo {
            let value = info[UIWindow.keyboardFrameEndUserInfoKey] as!
NSValue
            let frame = value.cgRectValue
            let newHeight = frame.size.height + constraintHeight
            heightBottom.constant = newHeight
        }
    }
    @objc func closeKeyboard(notification: Notification) {
        heightBottom.constant = constraintHeight
    }
    @IBAction func saveText(_ sender: UIButton) {
        mainText.resignFirstResponder()
    }
}
```

Listing 19-7: Observing keyboard's notifications

In the **ViewController** class of Listing 19-7, we have connected the constraint at the bottom of the Text View to an Outlet called **heightBottom** and defined a property called **constraintHeight** to store the height of the constraint when the keyboard is closed. The **viewDidLoad()** method reads the current height of the constraint, assigns it to the **contraintHeight** property, and then adds two observers to the Notification Center for the **keyboardWillShowNotification** and **keyboardWillHideNotification** notifications. When the keyboard is opened or closed, the **UIWindow** object posts these notifications and the observers execute the **openKeyboard()** and **closeKeyboard()** methods, respectively. The **openKeyboard()** method reads the **userInfo** property, gets the frame of the keyboard with the **keyboardFrameEndUserInfoKey** key, and calculates the new size of the constraint by adding the height of the keyboard to the normal height of the constraint (the one defined in the Storyboard).

Notice that the value returned by the **keyboardFrameEndUserInfoKey** key is of type **NSValue**. This is a basic class in Foundation that can store values of different types, including all the structures from the Core Graphics framework. The only problem is that the class was designed to store objects, not structures, so it provides some properties that return the structure we want. The following are the most frequently used.

cgRectValue—This property returns a `CGRect` value.

cgSizeValue—This property returns a `CGSize` value.

cgPointValue—This property returns a `CGPoint` value.

cgVectorValue—This property returns a `CGVector` value.

 Do It Yourself: Create a new Single View Application project. Add a Save button and a Text View to the initial view. Pin both elements with Space constraints to the sides of the main view and between each other (remember to assign a high vertical priority to the button). Connect the Text View to the `ViewController` class with an Outlet called `mainText` and the Space constraint at the bottom of the Text View with an Outlet called `heightBottom` (Figure 19-2, number 1). Connect the Save button to an Action called `saveText` and complete the `ViewController` class with the code of Listing 19-7. Run the application and tap on the Text View. The keyboard should emerge, and the Text View should adapt to the remaining space.

There are also useful notifications available for some of the classes we have already studied and others we will learn about in further chapters. For example, the `UITextView` class includes notifications like `textDidChangeNotification` to let the observer know that the content of the Text View changed. The following is a simple `ViewController` class we can use to test this notification with the interface of Figure 19-2. Every time the user changes the text, the Text View posts the `textDidChangeNotification` notification and the observer in the view controller responds printing a message on the console.

```
import UIKit

class ViewController: UIViewController {
    @IBOutlet weak var mainText: UITextView!

    override func viewDidLoad() {
        super.viewDidLoad()

        let center = NotificationCenter.default
        center.addObserver(self, selector:
#selector(reportChange(notification:)), name:
UITextView.textDidChangeNotification, object: nil)
    }
    @objc func reportChange(notification: Notification) {
        print("The Text View was modified")
    }
}
```

Listing 19-8: Responding to a Text View notification

Another useful notification is called **didChangeNotification**, defined in a structure called **UIContentSizeCategory**. This notification is posted every time the user changes the size of the Dynamic Font types from the Settings app. We introduced Dynamic Font types in Chapter 4. They can be created from code with the **preferredFont()** method of the **UIFont** class (see Listing 4-55) or selected from the Attributes Inspector panel. There are different types available, such as Body, Headline, and more. When we select one of these types, the system adapts the

Notifications

size of the font to the size selected by the user from the Settings app (Settings/General/Accessibility/Large Text). The problem is that the views that were already loaded are not automatically updated. To make sure that all the important text in our interface is updated to the current size selected by the user, we have to listen to the **didChangeNotification** notification and perform the update ourselves.

```
import UIKit

class ViewController: UIViewController {
    @IBOutlet weak var mainText: UITextView!

    override func viewDidLoad() {
        super.viewDidLoad()

        let center = NotificationCenter.default
        center.addObserver(self, selector:
#selector(fontChanged(notification:)), name:
UIContentSizeCategory.didChangeNotification, object: nil)
    }
    @objc func fontChanged(notification: Notification) {
        mainText.font = UIFont.preferredFont(forTextStyle: .body)
    }
}
```

Listing 19-9: Responding to font size changes from the Settings app

When the system detects a change in the size of the fonts performed from the Settings app, it posts the **didChangeNotification** notification to communicate that the content size is different. In the example of Listing 19-9, we have implemented the **fontChanged()** method to respond to this notification. In this method, we update the **font** property of the Text View with a new **UIFont** object defined with the same style we assigned to the element in Interface Builder (Body). This forces the system to update the interface and show the text inside the Text View with the current size.

 Do It Yourself: Update the view controller of Listing 19-7 with the example you want to try. Remember to delete the Action for the button and the Outlet for the constraint in the Storyboard if you are not using them anymore. To test the **didChangeNotification** notification, assign the font style Body to the Text View from the Attributes Inspector panel, run the application, click the Home button to take the simulator to the home screen, and change the size of the font from the Settings app (Settings/General/Accessibility/Large Text). Click the Home button again and open the app. You should see the text in the Text View with the new font size selected from Settings.

There is at least one more notification worth mentioning called orientation-DidChangeNotification, defined in the **UIDevice** class. This notification is posted to the Notification Center by the system when the orientation of the device changes, but it requires the accelerometer to be enabled for the information to be accurate. As we mentioned in Chapter 4, the UIDevice class offers two methods for this purpose. Every time we want to know the current orientation of the device, we have to call the beginGenerating-DeviceOrientationNotifications() method first to make sure that we are getting accurate information, and when our app does not require updates anymore, we have to call the endGeneratingDeviceOrientationNotifications() method to tell the system that it can turn off the accelerometer. In the following example, we apply these methods to know the orientation every time the device is rotated and print it on the console.

```
import UIKit

class ViewController: UIViewController {
    var device = UIDevice.current

    override func viewWillAppear(_ animated: Bool) {
        device.beginGeneratingDeviceOrientationNotifications()

        let center = NotificationCenter.default
        center.addObserver(self, selector:
#selector(changeOrientation(notification:)), name:
UIDevice.orientationDidChangeNotification, object: nil)
    }
    override func viewDidDisappear(_ animated: Bool) {
        device.endGeneratingDeviceOrientationNotifications()
    }
    @objc func changeOrientation(notification: Notification) {
        let orientation = device.orientation
        switch orientation {
            case .portrait, .portraitUpsideDown:
                print("Portrait")
            case .landscapeLeft, .landscapeRight:
                print("Landscape")
            default:
                print("Undefined")
        }
    }
}
```

Listing 19-10: Detecting the current orientation

Because we want to detect every rotation while the view is active, we ask the system to enable the accelerometer in the `viewWillAppear()` method and add an observer for the `orientationDidChangeNotification` notification right after. Every time the system detects a rotation, it posts a notification and the observer executes the `changeOrientation()` method. In this method, we get the current orientation from the `orientation` property of the `UIDevice` object and print it on the console (see `UIDevice` in Chapter 4).

Notice that we also called the `endGeneratingDeviceOrientationNotifications()` method in the `viewDidDisappear()` method. This is not necessary in our application because we only have one view, but in a more complex interface it is good to tell the system that we no longer require updates on the state of the device. The system stops posting notifications and powers down the accelerometer if no other part of the application is using it.

 Do It Yourself: To try this last example, erase the button and the Text View from the Scene and update the `ViewController` class with the code of Listing 19-10. Run the application and rotate the simulator. You should see the orientation printed on the console every time it changes.

19.2 User Notifications

A different type of notification is the User Notification. These are notifications shown to the user by the system when the app has an event to report, such as the completion of a task or real-life events that user wants to be reminded of.

There are three different types of User Notifications: alert, badge, and sound. A badge-type notification displays a badge with a number over the app's icon, a sound-type notification plays a sound, and an alert-type notification may be displayed as a banner, an Alert View, or a message on the lock screen, depending on the current state of the device and the configuration set by the user. They can be scheduled all at once or independently. For instance, we can schedule a notification that displays an alert and plays a sound, another that displays an alert and shows a badge, or another that just plays a sound to warn the user that something happened (e.g., an alarm clock).

 IMPORTANT: User Notifications are divided in Local Notifications and Remote Notifications (also known as Push Notifications). Local Notifications are notifications generated by the application running on the device, while Remote Notifications are generated by remote servers and received by the system through the network. In this chapter, we are going to study Local Notifications. We will see an example of how to handle Remote Notifications in Chapter 23. For more information, visit our website and follow the links for this chapter.

User Notifications Framework

User Notifications are created and managed by classes of the User Notifications framework. The framework includes multiple classes to control every step of the process. The most important is the **UNUserNotificationCenter** class, which creates a Notification Center to schedule and manage user notifications. This is similar to the Notification Center studied before but specific for User Notifications. The system creates a **UNUserNotificationCenter** object to serve as the Notification Center for the application that we can retrieve with the following type method.

current()—This type method returns a reference to the **UNUserNotificationCenter** object assigned to the app.

From the **UNUserNotificationCenter** object, we can manage the notifications and also ask the user for permission to show them. For this purpose, the class includes the following methods.

requestAuthorization(options: UNAuthorizationOptions, **completionHandler:** Block)—This method asks the user for authorization to show notifications. The **options** attribute is a set of properties that determine the type of notifications we want to show. The properties available are **badge**, **sound**, **alert**, **carPlay**, **criticalAlert**, and **provisional**. The **completionHandler** attribute is a closure that is executed after the response from the user is received. The closure includes two parameters, a Boolean value that determines if the permission was granted and an **NSError** value to report errors.

getNotificationSettings(completionHandler: Block)—This method gets the current configuration set on the device to deliver notifications and sends the values to the closure specified by the **completionHandler** attribute. The closure receives an object of type **UNNotificationSettings** that contains properties to report the current settings. The most useful property is **authorizationStatus**, which returns an enumeration value that reflects the current status of the authorization (the user may change the status of the authorization anytime from the Settings app). The possible values are **denied**, **authorized**, **notDetermined**, and **provisional**.

add(UNNotificationRequest, **withCompletionHandler:** Block)—This method schedules a new notification in the Notification Center. The first attribute is an object with the request for the notification, and the **withCompletionHandler** attribute is a closure that is executed when the process is over. The closure receives a parameter of type **NSError** to report errors.

removePendingNotificationRequests(withIdentifiers: [String])—This method removes the pending notifications with the identifiers specified by the attribute.

setNotificationCategories(Set)—This method configures the Notification Center to work with the types of notifications and actions we want to support. The settings are established by a set of objects of the `UNNotificationCategory` class called *Categories*.

 The Basics: The `NSError` value produced by some of these methods is an object that encapsulates information about the error. The `NSError` class offers the `userInfo` property that contains a dictionary with information about the error and also what caused it. The value is an optional, so if you don't need to access all this information, you can just compare it against `nil` to see whether there is an error or not and proceed accordingly. We will learn how to work with errors and read their values in further chapters.

The framework includes the `UNMutableNotificationContent` class to store the content of a notification. The following are the most frequently used properties included in this class.

title—This property sets or returns the notification's title.

subtitle—This property sets or returns the notification's subtitle.

body—This property sets or returns the notification's message or description.

badge—This property sets or returns a number to show over the app's icon.

sound—This property sets or returns the sound we want to play when the notification is delivered to the user. It is an object of type `UNNotificationSound`.

threadIdentifier—This property sets or returns a string used to identify each group of notifications. If no identifier is provided, the system groups the notifications by app.

summaryArgument—This property sets or returns the string that is added by the notificaiton to the category's summary.

summaryArgumentCount—This property sets or returns the number of items the notification adds to the category's summary.

userInfo—This property sets or returns a dictionary with the custom information we want to associate to the notification.

categoryIdentifier—This property sets or returns the identifier of the Category we want to use to configure the notification. Categories are objects that establish the type of notification and the actions allowed.

attachments—This property sets or returns an array of `UNNotificationAttachment` objects with the information about the media files we want to show with the notification.

Some of these properties define the information the notification is going to show to the user. Most of them, like the `title` and `body`, work with strings, except for the `badge` property, which takes a number, and the `sound` property which takes an object of the `UNNotificationSound` class. This class includes the following initializer and property to get the object.

UNNotificationSound(named: UNNotificationSoundName)—This initializer creates a `UNNotificationSound` object with the sound in the file specified by the **named** attribute.

default—This type property returns a `UNNotificationSound` object with the sound defined in the system by default.

The names of the sounds are defined by a structure of type `UNNotificationSoundName`. The structure includes the following initializer.

Notifications

UNNotificationSoundName(rawValue: String)—This initializer creates a `UNNotificationSoundName` object with the name of the file that contains the sound we want to play with the notification.

User Notifications are posted to the User Notification Center and then presented by the system when a certain condition is met. These conditions are established by objects called *Triggers*. There are three types of triggers available for Local Notifications (the notifications posted by the app): Time Interval, (the notification is delivered after a certain period of time), Calendar (the notification is delivered on a specific date), and Location (the notification is delivered in a specific location). The framework defines three classes to create these triggers: `UNTimeIntervalNotificationTrigger`, `UNCalendarNotificationTrigger`, and `UNLocationNotificationTrigger`. The following are their initializers.

UNTimeIntervalNotificationTrigger(timeInterval: TimeInterval, **repeats:** Bool)—This initializer creates a Time Interval trigger that will deliver the notification after the period of time determined by the **timeInterval** attribute (in seconds). The **repeats** attribute determines if the notification will be delivered once or infinite times.

UNCalendarNotificationTrigger(dateMatching: DateComponents, **repeats:** Bool)—This initializer creates a Calendar trigger that delivers the notification at the date determined by the **dateMatching** attribute. The **repeats** attribute determines if the notification will be delivered once or infinite times.

UNLocationNotificationTrigger(region: CLRegion, **repeats:** Bool)—This initializer creates a Location trigger that delivers the notification when the device is inside a region in the real world determined by the **region** attribute (this value must be specified as an instance of a subclass of the `CLRegion` class called `CLCircularRegion`). The **repeats** attribute determines if the notification will be delivered once or infinite times.

To deliver a notification, we must create a request that contains a notification, an identifier, and a trigger. For this purpose, the framework defines the `UNNotificationRequest` class.

UNNotificationRequest(identifier: String, **content:** UNNotificationContent, **trigger:** UNNotificationTrigger?)—This initializer creates a request to deliver the notification specified by the **content** attribute and at the time or place specified by the **trigger** attribute. The **identifier** attribute is a string that we can use later to manage or remove the request.

The first step we have to take to be able to deliver notifications in our application is to request authorization to the user with the `requestAuthorization()` method. The following example shows a possible implementation in the app's delegate.

```
import UIKit
import UserNotifications

@UIApplicationMain
class AppDelegate: UIResponder, UIApplicationDelegate {
   var window: UIWindow?

   func application(_ application: UIApplication,
didFinishLaunchingWithOptions launchOptions:
[UIApplication.LaunchOptionsKey : Any]? = nil) -> Bool {
      let notificationcenter = UNUserNotificationCenter.current()
      notificationcenter.requestAuthorization(options: [.alert, .sound],
completionHandler: { (granted, error) in
```

```
        if granted && error == nil {
            print("Permission Granted")
        }
    })
    return true
  }
}
```

Listing 19-11: Asking permission to the user

To be able to work with the classes included in the User Notifications framework, we have to import the framework with the **import** instruction. In Listing 19-11, we import the framework and then call the **current()** method of the **UNUserNotificationCenter** class to get a reference to the User Notification Center created for our app. Once we get this object, we call its **requestAuthorization()** method to ask the user permission to deliver notifications of type alert and sound (**[.alert, .sound]**). When this code is executed for the first time, the system shows an Alert View with two buttons for the user to decide what to do, as shown in Figure 19-3.

Figure 19-3: Authorization to deliver notifications

In this example, we use the completion block of the **requestAuthorization()** method to print a message on the console when permission is granted and no errors are found, but we can use this closure to update information in our app.

If permission is granted, we can start posting notifications. The interface bellow was designed for this purpose. We included a Text Field to introduce the message that the notification is going to show and a button to schedule the notification.

Figure 19-4: Interface to schedule notifications

When the Save Notification button is pressed, we have to get the text inserted in the Text Field and use it to configure a new notification. The following example delivers a notification 30 seconds after it was created.

```
import UIKit
import UserNotifications
class ViewController: UIViewController {
    var notificationcenter: UNUserNotificationCenter!
    @IBOutlet weak var messageField: UITextField!

    override func viewDidLoad() {
        notificationcenter = UNUserNotificationCenter.current()
    }
    @IBAction func saveNotification(_ sender: UIButton) {
        notificationcenter.getNotificationSettings(completionHandler: {
(settings) in
```

Notifications

```
            if settings.authorizationStatus == .authorized {
                let main = OperationQueue.main
                main.addOperation({
                    self.sendNotification()
                })
            }
        })
    }
    func sendNotification() {
        let content = UNMutableNotificationContent()
        content.title = "Reminder"
        content.body = self.messageField.text!
        content.sound = UNNotificationSound(named:
UNNotificationSoundName(rawValue: "alarm.mp3"))
        let trigger = UNTimeIntervalNotificationTrigger(timeInterval: 30,
repeats: false)
        let id = "reminder-\(UUID())"
        let request = UNNotificationRequest(identifier: id, content:
content, trigger: trigger)
        notificationcenter.add(request, withCompletionHandler: { (error) in
            let main = OperationQueue.main
            main.addOperation({
                self.messageField.text = ""
            })
        })
    }
}
```

Listing 19-12: Scheduling a notification

Before scheduling a notification, the code of Listing 19-12 checks whether the app was authorized to do it. When the user presses the Save Notification button, the **saveNotification()** method executes the **getNotificationSettings()** method to get the current status. If the status is equal to **authorized**, we call the **sendNotification()** method to create the notification.

The process to schedule a notification is simple. We have to create an instance of the **UNMutableNotificationContent** class with the values we want the notification to show to the user, create a trigger (in this case we use a Time Interval trigger), create an instance of the **UNNotificationRequest** class with these values to request the delivery of the notification, and finally add the request to the User Notification Center with the **add()** method. Notice that the request identifier must be unique. To assign a unique value to each request, we created a string with the word "reminder" followed by a random value generated by the **UUID()** function. The **UUID()** function is provided by the Foundation framework and its purpose is to create random values that never repeat.

 Do It Yourself: Create a new Single View Application project. Update the **AppDelegate** class with the code of Listing 19-11. Add a label, a Text Field and a button to the initial view, as in the interface of Figure 19-4. Connect the Text Field to the **ViewController** class with an Outlet called **messageField** and the button with an Action called **saveNotification()**. Complete the **ViewController** class with the code of Listing 19-12. Download the alarm.mp3 file from our website and drag it to your project. The first time you run the application the system will ask you to allow the app to deliver notifications. Press the Allow button. Insert a text in the field and press the Save Notification button. Press the Home button to close the app. After a few seconds, you should see the notification popping up on the screen.

Asking the user for permission can be a bit disruptive for some applications. If we consider that, based on the characteristics of our app, the user's acceptance to receive notifications may be implicit, we can post provisional notifications. These are quiet notifications that only show in the Notification Center (they are not displayed in the Locked or Home screens) and include buttons for the user to decide whether to keep them or turn them off. To get our app to post provisional notifications, all we have to do is to add the **provisional** option to the **requestAuthorization()** method, as shown next.

```
func application(_ application: UIApplication,
didFinishLaunchingWithOptions launchOptions:
[UIApplication.LaunchOptionsKey : Any]? = nil) -> Bool {
    let notificationcenter = UNUserNotificationCenter.current()
    notificationcenter.requestAuthorization(options: [.alert, .sound,
.provisional], completionHandler: { (granted, error) in
        if granted && error == nil {
            print("Permission Granted")
        }
    })
    return true
}
```

Listing 19-13: Scheduling provisional notifications

If we use provisional notification, the user is not prompted for authorization, the app is automatically authorized to post notifications, but the status is set as **provisional** instead of **authorized**, so we have to consider this condition when we check the status in our view controller.

```
@IBAction func saveNotification(_ sender: UIButton) {
    notificationcenter.getNotificationSettings(completionHandler: {
(settings) in
        let status = settings.authorizationStatus
        if status == .authorized || status == .provisional {
            let main = OperationQueue.main
            main.addOperation({
                self.sendNotification()
            })
        }
    })
}
```

Listing 19-14: Checking the status of provisional authorization

Because provisional notifications are only shown on the Notification Center, the user has to open the Notification Center and then decide whether to keep them or turn them off.

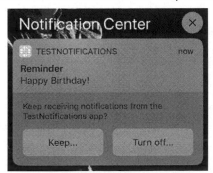

Figure 19-5: Provisional notifications in the Notification Center

Notifications

Do It Yourself: Update the `AppDelegate` class with the code of Listing 19-13 and the `ViewController` class with the code of Listing 19-14. Uninstall the app and run it again from Xcode. Post a notification. Go to the Home screen and drag your finger from the top to open the Notification Center. You should see the provisional notification, as shown in Figure 19-5.

The system automatically groups notifications together by app. For instance, if our application sends multiple notifications to the Notification Center, they will all be grouped together and only the last one will be shown to the user.

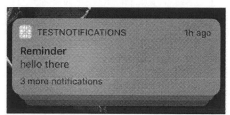

Figure 19-6: Notifications grouped by app

This is the automatic behavior. If notifications from multiple apps accumulate in the Notification Center, the system groups them by app. But we can separate them in custom groups by assigning a value to the **threadIdentifier** property of the **UNMutableNotificationContent** object. All the notifications with the same identifier will be grouped together. The following example separates notifications in two groups called Group One and Group Two.

```
func sendNotification() {
    var groupid = "Group One"
    if count >= 2 {
        groupid = "Group Two"
    }
    count += 1

    let content = UNMutableNotificationContent()
    content.title = "Reminder"
    content.body = self.messageField.text!
    content.threadIdentifier = groupid

    let trigger = UNTimeIntervalNotificationTrigger(timeInterval: 30,
repeats: false)

    let id = "reminder-\(UUID())"
    let request = UNNotificationRequest(identifier: id, content: content,
trigger: trigger)
    notificationcenter.add(request, withCompletionHandler: { (error) in
        let main = OperationQueue.main
        main.addOperation({
            self.messageField.text = ""
        })
    })
}
```

Listing 19-15: Organizing notifications into groups

For didactic purposes, we defined the groups based on the number of notifications posted by the app. The first three notifications scheduled by the application go into the Group One group and the rest are assigned to the Group Two group. As a result, if we schedule more than three notifications, they will be separated into two groups.

Figure 19-7: *Notifications in two groups*

Do It Yourself: Update the `ViewController` class with the method of Listing 19-15. The example assumes that you have added a property to the class called `count` with an initial value of 0. Run the application and schedule more than three notifications. Lock the device. You should see the notifications grouped by the value of their identifier, as shown in Figure 19-7 (If you post Provisional notifications, you will have to press the Keep button in the Notification Center to be able to see the groups in the lock screen).

If the user is working with the app when a notification is delivered, the notification is not displayed on the screen, but we can assign a delegate to the User Notification Center to change this behaviour. For this purpose, the framework defines the `UNUserNotification-CenterDelegate` protocol. This protocol allows us to do two things: we can decide whether to show the notification or not when the app is running, and we can also respond to the user.

userNotificationCenter(UNUserNotificationCenter, **willPresent:** UNNotification, **withCompletionHandler:** Block)—This method is called by the User Notification Center on the delegate when the application is active and a notification has to be delivered. The **withCompletionHandler** attribute is a closure that we have to execute to tell the system what to do with the notification. The closure receives an attribute of type `UNNotificationPresentationOptions` to define what type of notification to show. The possible values are `badge`, `sound`, and `alert`.

userNotificationCenter(UNUserNotificationCenter, **didReceive:** UNNotificationResponse, **withCompletionHandler:** Block)—This method is called by the User Notification Center when the user performs an action. The **didReceive** attribute is an object with information about the notification, and the **withCompletionHandler** attribute is a closure we must execute after we finish processing the user response.

When a notification is triggered and the app is being executed, the User Notification Center calls the `userNotificationCenter(UNUserNotificationCenter, willPresent:, withCompletionHandler:)` method on its delegate to ask the application what to do. In this method, we can perform any task we need and then execute the closure received by the method to specify what we want the system to do with the notification. If we do not want to show the notification, we have to execute the closure with no parameters, otherwise we have to provide a value that determines the type of notification we want to show.

We can declare any of our view controllers as the User Notification Center's delegate, but because we have to assign the delegate when the app is launched, it is recommendable to conform to the protocol in the view controller in charge of the initial view. Once we make our view controller conform to the `UNUserNotificationCenterDelegate` protocol, we can implement the delegate method to show notifications while the app is running. The following is the method we must implement in the `ViewController` class to show alert notifications.

Notifications

```
func userNotificationCenter(_ center: UNUserNotificationCenter,
willPresent notification: UNNotification, withCompletionHandler
completionHandler: @escaping (UNNotificationPresentationOptions) -> Void){
   completionHandler([.alert])
}
```

Listing 19-16: Showing notifications when the app is being used

Because the delegate must be determined when the app is launched, we have to assign our view controller as the delegate in the **AppDelegate** class. The **UIWindow** class offers a property called **rootViewController** to reference the view controller that controls the initial view (the view that is marked with the single arrow in the Storyboard). The following are the modifications we have to introduce to the **AppDelegate** class to assign our **ViewController** class as the User Notification Center's delegate.

```
import UIKit
import UserNotifications

@UIApplicationMain
class AppDelegate: UIResponder, UIApplicationDelegate {
   var window: UIWindow?

   func application(_ application: UIApplication,
didFinishLaunchingWithOptions launchOptions:
[UIApplication.LaunchOptionsKey : Any]? = nil) -> Bool {
      let notificationcenter = UNUserNotificationCenter.current()
      notificationcenter.requestAuthorization(options: [.alert, .sound],
completionHandler: { (granted, error) in
         if granted && error == nil {
            let main = OperationQueue.main
            main.addOperation({
               notificationcenter.delegate =
self.window?.rootViewController as! ViewController
            })
         }
      })
      return true
   }
}
```

Listing 19-17: Assigning the ViewController *class as the delegate*

The example of Listing 19-17 defines our **ViewController** class as the User Notification Center's delegate. To get a reference to the **ViewController** class, we read the **rootViewController** property of the **window** property. This property returns a generic **UIViewController** class that we have to cast to our view controller's type (**as! ViewController**) before assigning it to the **delegate** property.

Notice that the **rootViewController** property must be accessed from the main thread and the closure for the completion handler is not guaranteed to be executed in this thread, so we had to create a new Operation Queue before reading this property.

 Do It Yourself: Make the **ViewController** class conform to the **UNUserNotificationCenterDelegate** protocol and add the method of Listing 19-16 to it. Update your **AppDelegate** class with the code of Listing 19-17. Run the application, insert a message, and press the Save Notification button. Wait for 30 seconds to see the notification on the screen.

Notifications can show custom actions in the form of buttons and input fields that the user can use to provide feedback without having to open our app. The actions are defined by two classes: **UNNotificationAction** and **UNTextInputNotificationAction**. The following are their initializers.

UNNotificationAction(identifier: String, **title:** String, **options:** UNNotificationActionOptions**)**—This initializer creates an action represented by a custom button. The **identifier** attribute is a string that we can use to identify the action, the **title** attribute is the text shown on the button, and the **options** attribute is a set of properties that determine how the action should be performed. The properties available are **authenticationRequired** (the user is required to unlock the device), **destructive** (the button is highlighted), and **foreground** (the app is opened to perform the action).

UNTextInputNotificationAction(identifier: String, **title:** String, **options:** UNNotificationActionOptions, **textInputButtonTitle:** String, **textInputPlaceholder:** String**)**—This initializer creates an action represented by a custom button that when pressed prompts the system to display an input field. Despite the attributes included by a normal action, these types of actions also include the **textInputButtonTitle** and **textInputPlaceholder** attributes to define the button and the placeholder for the input field.

After the actions we want to include in the notification are defined, we have to create a category to group them together. The framework offers the **UNNotificationCategory** class to create a category. The following is the class' initializer.

UNNotificationCategory(identifier: String, **actions:** [UNNotificationAction], **intentIdentifiers:** [String], **options:** UNNotificationCategoryOptions**)**—This initializer creates a category with the actions specified by the **actions** attribute. The **identifier** attribute is a string that allows us to identify the category, the **intentIdentifiers** is an array of strings used to guide Siri to produce a better response, and the **options** attribute is a property that determines how the notifications associated to this category are going to be handled. The properties available are **customDismissAction** (processes the dismiss action) and **allowInCarPlay** (allows car play to show notifications).

When an action is performed, the User Notification Center calls the **userNotificationCenter(UNUserNotificationCenter, didReceive:, withCompletionHandler:)** method on its delegate with information about the action and the notification. The following example adds an action to the notification scheduled in previous examples and implements this method to process the response.

```
import UIKit
import UserNotifications

class ViewController: UIViewController, UNUserNotificationCenterDelegate{
   var notificationcenter: UNUserNotificationCenter!
   @IBOutlet weak var messageField: UITextField!

   override func viewDidLoad() {
      notificationcenter = UNUserNotificationCenter.current()
   }
   @IBAction func saveNotification(_ sender: UIButton) {
      notificationcenter.getNotificationSettings(completionHandler: {
(settings) in
         if settings.authorizationStatus == .authorized {
            let main = OperationQueue.main
            main.addOperation({
```

Notifications

```
                self.sendNotification()
            })
        }
    })
}
func sendNotification() {
    let actionDelete = UNNotificationAction(identifier: "deleteButton",
title: "Delete", options: .destructive)
    let category = UNNotificationCategory(identifier: "listActions",
actions: [actionDelete], intentIdentifiers: [], options: [])
    notificationcenter.setNotificationCategories([category])
    let content = UNMutableNotificationContent()
    content.title = "Reminder"
    content.body = messageField.text!
    content.categoryIdentifier = "listActions"

    let trigger = UNTimeIntervalNotificationTrigger(timeInterval: 30,
repeats: false)
    let id = "reminder-\(UUID())"
    let request = UNNotificationRequest(identifier: id, content:
content, trigger: trigger)
    notificationcenter.add(request, withCompletionHandler: { (error) in
        let main = OperationQueue.main
        main.addOperation({
            self.messageField.text = ""
        })
    })
}
func userNotificationCenter(_ center: UNUserNotificationCenter,
didReceive response: UNNotificationResponse, withCompletionHandler
completionHandler: @escaping () -> Void) {
    let identifier = response.actionIdentifier
    if identifier == "deleteButton" {
        print("Delete Message")
    }
    completionHandler()
}
}
```

Listing 19-18: Adding and processing actions for notifications

The view controller of Listing 19-18 creates a destructive action with the title Delete and includes it in a category called "listActions". Categories have to be added to the User Notification Center first with the **setNotificationCategories()** method and then assigned to the notification's property **categoryIdentifier** to configure the notification. In devices with 3D Touch enabled, actions are displayed when the user presses over the notification, otherwise they are displayed when the user drags the notification down or selects the option View to see it.

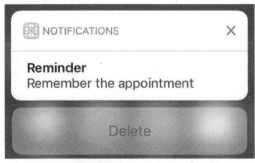

Figure 19-8: Actions in a notification

When the user performs an action (presses the button), the User Notification Center calls the delegate method to let the application perform the task. For this purpose, the center sends a **UNNotificationResponse** object with the information about the action and the notification. The class includes the following properties to read the values.

actionIdentifier—This property sets or returns a string with the action's identifier.

notification—This property sets or returns a **UNNotification** object representing the notification. The object includes the **date** property to get the date the notification was delivered and the **request** property with a reference to the **UNNotificationRequest** object used to schedule the notification, which in turn offers the **content** property to access the values of the notification.

In the example of Listing 19-18, we read the **actionIdentifier** property and compare it with the string "deleteButton" to confirm that the user pressed the Delete button. In this example, we just print a message on the console, but we can perform more complex tasks, such as modifying a value in the model or deleting a record in a database, as we will see in further chapters. This example implements a simple action for the notification that shows a button when the notification is expanded, but we can also include a button that shows an input field, so the user can provide feedback right from the screen where the notification is shown. The following are the changes we have to introduce to the previous example to add an action of this type.

```
func sendNotification() {
   let actionDelete = UNNotificationAction(identifier: "deleteButton",
title: "Delete", options: .destructive)
   let actionInput = UNTextInputNotificationAction(identifier:
"inputField", title: "Message", options: [])

   let category = UNNotificationCategory(identifier: "listActions",
actions: [actionDelete, actionInput], intentIdentifiers: [], options: [])
   notificationcenter.setNotificationCategories([category])

   let content = UNMutableNotificationContent()
   content.title = "Reminder"
   content.body = messageField.text!
   content.categoryIdentifier = "listActions"

   let trigger = UNTimeIntervalNotificationTrigger(timeInterval: 30,
repeats: false)
   let id = "reminder-\(UUID())"
   let request = UNNotificationRequest(identifier: id, content: content,
trigger: trigger)
   notificationcenter.add(request, withCompletionHandler: { (error) in
      let main = OperationQueue.main
      main.addOperation({
         self.messageField.text = ""
      })
   })
}
func userNotificationCenter(_ center: UNUserNotificationCenter,
didReceive response: UNNotificationResponse, withCompletionHandler
completionHandler: @escaping () -> Void) {
   let identifier = response.actionIdentifier
   if identifier == "deleteButton" {
     print("Delete Message")
   } else if identifier == "inputField" {
     print("Send: \((response as!
UNTextInputNotificationResponse).userText)")
   }
```

```
completionHandler()
}
```

Listing 19-19: Processing an input action

The text inserted by the user in the text field is sent to the delegate method in the response object. The framework offers a special class to represent this response called **UNTextInput-NotificationResponse**. To access the value inserted by the user, we have to cast the response object to this class and then read its **userText** property, as we did in Listing 19-19.

 Do It Yourself: Update your **ViewController** class with the code of Listing 19-19 and run the application. Insert a message to schedule a notification. Go to the home screen and wait until the notification is displayed. Expand the notification to see the actions. Click the Message button. You should see an input field over the keyboard. Insert a value and press the Send button. You should see a message on the console with the text you have just inserted.

19.3 Key/Value Observing

KVO (Key/Value Observing) is a system we can use to perform a task when the value of a property is modified. This is similar to what the **didSet()** method does for the properties of our own structures and classes (see Property Observers in Chapter 3), with the difference that some predefined classes provided by Apple come ready to work with this system and therefore we can monitor the values of their properties as we do with our own from anywhere in the code.

There are several situations in which KVO can be useful. For example, we may have a property that reflects the status of an operation and Is required by other parts of the application to know when the process is over. The problem is that we do not know when that is going to happen and which are going to be the objects that have to be notified when a change occurs. Constantly checking the property from every object to see if its value has changed is not practical. KVO allows us to add observers in every object that will keep an eye on the property. Every time the property is modified, the system notifies these observers, so the objects can perform the task they need, such as updating the interface or initiating another operation.

KVC

For the KVO system to be able to monitor the values of a property, the object in which the property was defined must comply with the **NSKeyValueCoding** protocol. This protocol defines another system called KVC (Key/Value Coding) that allows us to access properties using their names as keys. Instead of using dot notation to access the values of a property, we call methods defined in this protocol with a string that identifies the property we want to modify. The following are the most frequently used.

setValue(Any?, forKeyPath: String)—This method assigns a value to the property specified by the **forKeyPath** attribute. The first attribute is the value we want to assign to the property and the **forKeyPath** attribute is a string with the name of the property.

value(forKey: String)—This method retrieves the value of the property identified by the **forKey** attribute. The attribute is a string with the name of the property.

Some of the frameworks provided by Apple define classes that are ready to work with KVC, but we can define our own. An easy way to make our custom classes KVC compliant is to declare them as subclasses of the **NSObject** class. This is the class from which the rest of the Objective-C classes are created, and it already includes an implementation of the protocol. For example, the following code defines a subclass of **NSObject** called **MyControl** (KVC is a system developed in Objective-C and therefore the properties must be preceded by the @objc prefix).

```
import Foundation
class MyControl: NSObject {
   @objc var round = false
}
```

Listing 19-20: Defining a custom class to work with KVC

Because the **MyControl** class is a subclass of **NSObject**, we can call the **NSKeyValueCoding** protocol methods on instances of this class to set or retrieve the value of the **round** property. In the following example, we present a **ViewController** class that creates an instance of **MyControl** and modifies the value of the **round** property every time the user changes the value of a Stepper. The example assumes that the initial view contains an interface with a Stepper and a label, as the one introduced in Figure 5-31.

```
import UIKit
class ViewController: UIViewController {
   @IBOutlet weak var counterLabel: UILabel!
   var control: MyControl!

   override func viewDidLoad() {
      super.viewDidLoad()
      control = MyControl()
   }
   @IBAction func updateValue(_ sender: UIStepper) {
      let current = Int(sender.value)
      if current % 10 == 0 {
         control.setValue(true, forKey: "round")
      } else {
         control.setValue(false, forKey: "round")
      }
      counterLabel.text = String(current)
   }
}
```

Listing 19-21: Modifying property values using KVC

The **ViewController** class of Listing 19-21 creates an instance of the **MyControl** class and then implements an Action for the Stepper to change the value of its **round** property every time the value of the Stepper is modified. The Action gets the Stepper's current value and then sets the value of the **round** property to **true** or **false** depending on whether the current value is multiple of 10 or not.

KVO

When properties are set using the **setValue()** method instead of the = sign, they automatically become KVO compliant and therefore notifications are posted to report when their values change. As the notifications studied at the beginning of this chapter, these notifications can be read from any object that has registered an observer for them. Foundation includes the **NSKeyValueObserving** protocol, which the view controller classes conform to by default, to define methods to add and remove observers. The following are the most frequently used.

addObserver(NSObject, **forKeyPath:** String, **options:** NSKeyValue-ObservingOptions, **context:** UnsafeMutablePointer?**)**—This method adds an observer to the object. The first attribute is the object that responds to the notification, the

forKeyPath attribute is a string with the name or the path to the property, the **options** attribute is a Set with enumeration values that determine the values that are going to be sent to the method that responds to the notification (possible values are **new, old, initial,** and **prior**), and the **context** attribute is a generic value that identifies the observer (used when a class and its subclasses observe the same property).

removeObserver(NSObject, **forKeyPath:** String, **context:** UnsafeMutable-Pointer?**)**—This method removes an observer. The attributes are the same values specified in the **addObserver()** method when the observer was added.

With Key/Value Observing, an object can observe the property of another object. When the value of the property changes, the method that responds to the notification is executed. This is not a custom method but a predefined method called **observeValue()**. Every observer added to an object calls this same method, as shown in the following example.

```
import UIKit

class ViewController: UIViewController {
    @IBOutlet weak var counterLabel: UILabel!
    var control: MyControl!

    override func viewDidLoad() {
        super.viewDidLoad()
        control = MyControl()
        control.addObserver(self, forKeyPath: "round", options: [],
context: nil)
    }
    @IBAction func updateValue(_ sender: UIStepper) {
        let current = Int(sender.value)
        if current % 10 == 0 {
            control.setValue(true, forKey: "round")
        } else {
            control.setValue(false, forKey: "round")
        }
        counterLabel.text = String(current)
    }
    override func observeValue(forKeyPath keyPath: String?, of object:
Any?, change: [NSKeyValueChangeKey : Any]?, context:
UnsafeMutableRawPointer?) {
        if keyPath == "round" {
            if control.round {
                counterLabel.textColor = UIColor.red
            } else {
                counterLabel.textColor = UIColor.black
            }
        }
    }
}
```

Listing 19-22: Observing the value of a property

In Listing 19-22, we update the **ViewController** class of the previous example to add an observer to monitor the value of the **round** property. When the user modifies the value of the Stepper, the **updateValue()** method is called and the value of the **round** property is modified with the **setValue()** method. This prompts the property to post a notification to report the change. The observer added to the **ViewController** class receives this notification and executes the **observeValue()** method. In this method, we check if the name or path of the property matches the name or path of the property we want to read and then perform the task according to its value. In this example, if the value of **round** is **true**, we change the color of the label to red, and if it is **false** we change it back to black.

 Do It Yourself: Create a new Single View Application project. Add a Stepper and a label to the main view. Connect the Stepper with an Action called **updateValue()** and the label with an Outlet called **counterLabel**. Create a new Swift file called **MyControl** and copy the code of Listing 19-20 inside. Complete the **ViewController** class with the code of Listing 19-22 and run the application. Press the Stepper to change the value. The **counterLabel** label should turn red every time the value is a multiple of 10.

Setting the value of the property with the **setValue()** method makes the property post a notification, but this means that every time we want the changes in a property to be noticed by the observers we have to perform those changes calling the **setValue()** method. If we want every change to be reported, including those performed with traditional methods like the = sign, we have to make the property compliant with KVO by implementing some of the methods provided by the **NSKeyValueObserving** protocol. The simplest way to do this is by calling the following protocol methods from the property's **didSet()** and **willSet()** methods.

willChangeValue(forKey: String)—This method informs the class that the value of the property is about to change. The **forKey** attribute is a string with the property's name or path.

didChangeValue(forKey: String)—This method informs the class that the value of the property was changed. The **forKey** attribute is a string with the property's name or path.

The following example implements these two methods to make the **round** property report the changes before and after they happen.

```
import Foundation

class MyControl: NSObject {
   @objc var round = false {
      didSet {
         self.didChangeValue(forKey: "round")
      }
      willSet {
         self.willChangeValue(forKey: "round")
      }
   }
}
```
Listing 19-23: Reporting changes to the class

Now, we can assign new values to the **round** property as we always do and also get a notification. The following example shows the new action for the Stepper.

```
@IBAction func updateValue(_ sender: UIStepper) {
   let current = Int(sender.value)
   if current % 10 == 0 {
      control.round = true
   } else {
      control.round = false
   }
   counterLabel.text = String(current)
}
```
Listing 19-24: Working with a KVO compliant property

Notifications

20.1 Errors

Simple frameworks and classes usually work as expected. If we call a method from one of those classes, it completes its task without failure. If the method does fail, it usually returns a neutral value like 0 or `nil` to indicate that there was a problem. But this is not always enough. More complex frameworks cannot guarantee success and may encounter multiple problems while trying to fulfill their purpose. For this reason, Swift introduces a systematic process to report and handle errors called *Error Handling*.

Throwing Errors

When a method reports an error, it is said that it *throws* the error. Several frameworks provided by Apple are already programmed to throw errors, as we will see in further chapters, but we can also do it from our own structures and classes. To throw an error, we have to use the `throw` and `throws` keywords. The `throw` keyword is used to throw the error and the `throws` keyword is specified in the method's declaration to indicate to the rest of the code that the method can throw errors.

Because a method can throw multiple errors, we also have to indicate the type of error found with values of an enumeration type. This is a custom enumeration that conforms to the `Error` protocol. For instance, let's consider the following example.

```
struct Stock {
   var totalLamps = 5
   mutating func sold(amount: Int) {
      totalLamps = totalLamps - amount
   }
}
var mystock = Stock()

mystock.sold(amount: 8)
print("Lamps in stock: \(mystock.totalLamps)")   // "Lamps in stock: -3"
```

Listing 20-1: Producing an error inside a method

The code of Listing 20-1 defines a structure called `Stock` that manages the stock of lamps available at the store. The class includes the `totalLamps` property to store the number of lamps we still have available and the `sold()` method to process the lamps sold. The method updates the stock by subtracting the number of lamps we have sold from the value of the `totalLamps` property. If the number of lamps sold is less than the number of lamps in stock, everything is fine, but when we sell more lamps than we have, as in this example, there is clearly a problem we have to report.

To throw an error, we have to declare the types of errors available for the method, declare the method as a throwing method adding the `throws` keyword in the declaration (between the attributes and the returning data types), detect the error, and throw it with the `throw` keyword.

```
enum Errors: Error {
   case OutOfStock
}
struct Stock {
   var totalLamps = 5
   mutating func sold(amount: Int) throws {
      if amount > totalLamps {
         throw Errors.OutOfStock
      } else {
         totalLamps = totalLamps - amount
      }
   }
}
var mystock = Stock()
```

Listing 20-2: Throwing errors

In Listing 20-2, we declare an enumeration called **Errors** that conforms to the **Error** protocol and includes a case called **OutOfStock**. Declaring **sold()** as a throwing method with the **throws** keyword, we can now throw the **OutOfStock** error every time we try to sell more lamps than we have. If the lamps sold are more than the number of lamps in stock, the method throws the error, otherwise the stock is updated.

Handling Errors

Now that we have a method that can throw errors, we have to handle the errors when the method is executed. Swift includes the **try** keyword and the **do catch** statements for this purpose. The **do catch** statements create two blocks of code. If the statements inside the **do** block return an error, the statements in the **catch** block are executed. To execute a method that throws errors, we have to declare these statements and call the method inside the **do** statement with the **try** keyword in front of it, as shown in the following example.

```
enum Errors: Error {
   case OutOfStock
}
struct Stock {
   var totalLamps = 5
   mutating func sold(amount: Int) throws {
      if amount > totalLamps {
         throw Errors.OutOfStock
      } else {
         totalLamps = totalLamps - amount
      }
   }
}
var mystock = Stock()

do {
   try mystock.sold(amount: 8)
} catch Errors.OutOfStock {
   print("We do not have enough lamps")
}
```

Listing 20-3: Handling errors

Error Handling

The code of Listing 20-3 expands the previous example to handle the error thrown by the **sold()** method. Because of the addition of the **try** keyword, the system tries to execute the **sold()** method in the **mystock** structure and check for errors. If the method returns the **OutOfStock** error, the statements inside the **catch** block are executed. This pattern allows us to respond every time there is an error and report it to the user or correct the situation without having to crash the app or produce unexpected results.

 Do It Yourself: Create a new Playground file. Copy the code of Listing 20-3 inside the file. You should see the message "We do not have enough lamps" printed on the console. Replace the number 8 with the number 3. Now the message should disappear because there are enough lamps in stock.

 The Basics: You can add as many errors as you need to the **Errors** enumeration. The errors can be checked later with multiple **catch** statements in sequence. Also, you may add all the statements you need to the **do** block. The statements before **try** are always executed, while the statements after **try** are only executed if no error is found.

If we do not care about the error returned, we can force the **try** keyword to return an optional with the syntax **try?**. If the method throws an error, the instruction returns **nil**, and therefore we can avoid the use of the **do catch** statements.

```
enum Errors: Error {
    case OutOfStock
}
struct Stock {
    var totalLamps = 5
    mutating func sold(amount: Int) throws {
        if amount > totalLamps {
            throw Errors.OutOfStock
        } else {
            totalLamps = totalLamps - amount
        }
    }
}
var mystock = Stock()
try? mystock.sold(amount: 8)   // nil
```

Listing 20-4: Catching errors with try?

The instruction at the end of Listing 20-4 returns the value **nil** if the method throws an error, or an optional with the value returned by the method if everything goes right.

Sometimes we know beforehand that a throwing method is not going to throw an error and therefore we want to avoid writing unnecessary code. In cases like this, we can use the syntax **try!**. For instance, the following code checks if there are enough lamps before calling the **sold()** method, so we know that the instruction will never throw the **OutOfStock** error.

```
enum Errors: Error {
    case OutOfStock
}
struct Stock {
    var totalLamps = 5
```

```
    mutating func sold(amount: Int) throws {
        if amount > totalLamps {
            throw Errors.OutOfStock
        } else {
            totalLamps = totalLamps - amount
        }
    }
}
var mystock = Stock()

if mystock.totalLamps > 3 {
    try! mystock.sold(amount: 3)
}
print("Lamps in stock: \(mystock.totalLamps)")
```

Listing 20-5: Ignoring the errors

 IMPORTANT: As well as with optionals, if the method throws an error and we declare the **try** keyword with an exclamation mark, the app crashes, so we have to be sure that the method is not going to throw an error before creating instructions with **try!**.

Error Handling

Chapter 21
Storage

21.1 User Preferences

Up to this point, all the data was stored in arrays and dictionaries created in the model and the values were hard-coded, which means they are always the same every time the app is launched. If we add a new value to the model, it is only preserved for the time the app is running, but as soon as the app is closed, we lose that value, and everything is back to the initial state. The data stored this way is called *temporary data* and it is useful when our app requires values that never change or when a long process generates partial results that we have to access later to complete a task. Temporary data is always necessary for our apps, but users require persistent sources of information that they can modify at will and preserve for as long as they want. Apple includes several systems to store persistent data. They are all based on files, but can take several forms, from simple text to databases (indexed data).

The simplest system available in iOS is called *Users Defaults*. This system was designed to store user preferences, which may include values set by the user to determine how our app should work and also values set by the app itself to restore a previous state. These values are stored in a database managed by the system and therefore they continue to exist after the app is closed and as long as the user or the app decides to keep them.

User Defaults

The Foundation framework defines a class called **UserDefaults** to manage the preferences of our application. Only one **UserDefaults** object is assigned per application, so we can reference this object anywhere in the code and always process the same values. The class offers the following type property to get a reference to the object created for the app.

standard—This type property returns a reference to the app's **UserDefaults** object.

The values are assigned to the **UserDefaults** object with an associated key that we can use to retrieve them later, similar to how dictionaries work. The types of values we can work with are restricted to Property List values (**NSNumber**, **NSString**, **NSDate**, **NSArray**, **NSDictionary**, **NSData**, and their equivalents in Swift), but we can also work with other types of values, including custom objects, by converting them into **NSData** objects, as we will see in further chapters. The **UserDefaults** class includes the following methods to store, retrieve, and delete values of any of these types.

set(Any?, forKey: String)—This method stores the value specified by the first attribute with the key specified by the **forKey** attribute. If the value already exists, it is updated.

object(forKey: String)—This method retrieves the value associated with the key specified by the **forKey** attribute. If the value does not exist, it returns **nil**. The attribute is the same string used to store the value.

removeObject(forKey: String)—This method removes the value associated with the key specified by the **forKey** attribute. The attribute is the same string used to store the value.

Because the methods above process values of any type, they return them as objects of type **Any**. This means that we have to cast the values to the right type before to use them. To simplify our work, the class includes methods to retrieve the values for specific types.

bool(forKey: String)—This method retrieves a value of type `Bool`. If there is no value set for the key, the method returns the value `false`.

float(forKey: String)—This method retrieves a value of type `Float`. If there is no value set for the key, the method returns the value 0.0.

integer(forKey: String)—This method retrieves a value of type `Int`. If there is no value set for the key, the method returns the value 0.

double(forKey: String)—This method retrieves a value of type `Double`. If there is no value set for the key, the method returns the value 0.0.

string(forKey: String)—This method retrieves a value of type `String`.

array(forKey: String)—This method retrieves an array.

dictionary(forKey: String)—This method retrieves a dictionary.

data(forKey: String)—This method retrieves a value of type `Data`.

url(forKey: String)—This method retrieves a value of type `URL`.

The User Defaults system can store any amount of data we want, but it is recommendable to use it to store simple strings and values. Its main purpose is to serve as a storage system for the app's settings. For example, we may have an app that plays videos and we want to let the user set the volume by default. Using the User Defaults system, we can store this value and set the volume back to its last state every time the app is executed. The interface of Figure 21-1 includes a Stepper and a label to illustrate how the process works.

Figure 21-1: Interface to store settings

The view controller for this view has to update the value of the label when the view is shown on the screen and store it in the User Defaults system every time the user sets a new one.

```
import UIKit
class ViewController: UIViewController {
    @IBOutlet weak var counter: UIStepper!
    @IBOutlet weak var counterLabel: UILabel!
    var defaultValues: UserDefaults!

    override func viewDidLoad() {
        super.viewDidLoad()
        defaultValues = UserDefaults.standard
        if let number = defaultValues.object(forKey: "counter") as? Double{
            counter.value = number
            counterLabel.text = String(number)
        }
    }
    @IBAction func incrementValue(_ sender: UIStepper) {
        let current = counter.value
        defaultValues.set(current, forKey: "counter")
        counterLabel.text = String(current)
    }
}
```

Listing 21-1: Storing values in the User Defaults system

Storage

The way we store the value is simple. We have to get a reference to the **UserDefaults** object of our application and then call any of the methods provided by the object to this effect. In Listing 21-1, we declare a property called **defaultValues** to store the reference to the object and use the **object()** and **set()** methods to read and store a value with the key "counter". The **object()** method returns an optional of type **AnyObject**, so we have to unwrap the value using an **if** statement and cast it to the real type (in this case a **Double**). If there is already a value stored with the key "counter", we assign it to the **value** property of the Stepper to start counting from that number and also to the label to show it on the screen.

The Stepper is connected to an Action called **incrementValue()**. When the user presses the buttons of the Stepper, this method gets the current value, stores it in the User Defaults system with the key "counter", and updates the label. In consequence, the label always reflects the current value, even after the app was closed.

Do It Yourself: Create a new Single View Application project. Add a Stepper and a label to the main view. Connect the Stepper to the view controller with an Outlet called **counter** and the label with an Outlet called **counterLabel**. Connect the Stepper with an Action called **incrementValue()**. Complete the **ViewController** class with the code of Listing 21-1 and run the application. Press the buttons of the Stepper to change the value on the label. Stop the execution of the app from the Stop button in Xcode. Run the application again. The value of the label should be the last one selected.

As we mentioned, we can also store values generated by the app. For example, we may add a value to User Settings to keep track of the time the user has spent without using the app. The following code updates the last view controller to store this value. The code reads the value when the main view is loaded, compares it with the current date, and prints the difference on the console. At the end, we update the value with the current date for the next cycle.

```
import UIKit

class ViewController: UIViewController {
    @IBOutlet weak var counter: UIStepper!
    @IBOutlet weak var counterLabel: UILabel!
    var defaultValues: UserDefaults!

    override func viewDidLoad() {
        super.viewDidLoad()
        defaultValues = UserDefaults.standard
        if let number = defaultValues.object(forKey:"counter") as? Double {
            counter.value = number
            counterLabel.text = String(number)
        }
        if let lastDate = defaultValues.object(forKey:"lastDate") as? Date{
            let calendar = Calendar.current
            let components = calendar.dateComponents([.year, .month, .day,
.hour, .minute, .second], from: lastDate, to: Date())
            print("You haven't use this app in \(components.year!) years,
\(components.month!) months, \(components.day!) days, \(components.hour!)
hours, \(components.minute!) minutes, \(components.second!) seconds")
        }
        defaultValues.set(Date(), forKey: "lastDate")
    }
    @IBAction func incrementValue(_ sender: UIStepper) {
        let current = counter.value
        defaultValues.set(current, forKey: "counter")
```

```
        counterLabel.text = String(current)
    }
}
```

Listing 21-2: Storing app values

The interface introduced in Figure 21-1 was designed for didactic purposes, but views presenting the app's settings are usually set apart from the main interface. Depending on the design of our app, they may be presented modally to denote its dissociation with the main interface or as part of the navigation stack of a Navigation Controller. The following example implements this last strategy to illustrate how the settings view is usually implemented in professional applications.

Figure 21-2 introduces the new interface. We have embedded the initial view in a Navigation Controller, added a Text View and a bar button called Settings to the main view, and a Table View Controller with a static table containing two sections and three cells to present the controls users can manipulate to set their preferences. The cell in the first section contains a Segmented Control with three buttons to set the color of the text: Dark, Medium, and Light, and the cells in the second section contain Switches to set whether the Text View is going to be editable and have auto-correction activated or not.

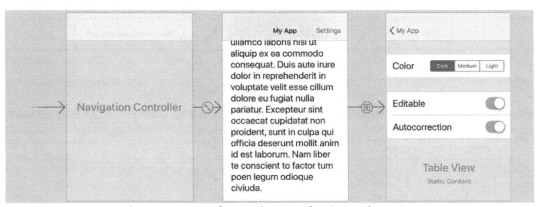

Figure 21-2: Interface with a view for the app's settings

The view controller for the initial view has to read the values and update the Text View.

```swift
import UIKit

class ViewController: UIViewController {
    @IBOutlet weak var textEditor: UITextView!

    override func viewWillAppear(_ animated: Bool) {
        super.viewWillAppear(animated)

        let defaultValues = UserDefaults.standard
        if let color = defaultValues.object(forKey: "color") as? Int {
            let colorList = [UIColor.black, UIColor.gray, UIColor.lightGray]
            textEditor.textColor = colorList[color]
        }
        if let editable = defaultValues.object(forKey:"editable") as? Bool {
            textEditor.isEditable = editable
        }
        if let correction = defaultValues.object(forKey: "correction") as?
Bool {
            if correction {
                textEditor.spellCheckingType = .yes
```

Storage

```
        } else {
            textEditor.spellCheckingType = .no
        }
    }
}
```

Listing 21-3: Configuring the Text View according to the values set by the user

For this example, we use three values with the keys "color", "editable", and "correction" to store the current settings. If the values were already set, which means that the user changed them at some point in the past, we configure the Text View with those values, otherwise the application uses the values assigned in the Storyboard. For example, the color for the text in the Text View is set as black by default in the Storyboard, but if there is a value stored with the key "color" we use it to get the right color from an array (black, gray, or light gray).

In the view controller for the settings view, we have to read the values to update the elements as well, but we also have to get the user's input and store the new values for future reference.

```
import UIKit

class SettingsViewController: UITableViewController {
    @IBOutlet weak var controlColors: UISegmentedControl!
    @IBOutlet weak var controlEditable: UISwitch!
    @IBOutlet weak var controlCorrection: UISwitch!
    var defaultValues: UserDefaults!

    override func viewDidLoad() {
        super.viewDidLoad()

        defaultValues = UserDefaults.standard
        if let color = defaultValues.object(forKey: "color") as? Int {
            controlColors.selectedSegmentIndex = color
        }
        if let editable = defaultValues.object(forKey:"editable") as? Bool{
            controlEditable.isOn = editable
        }
        if let correction = defaultValues.object(forKey: "correction") as?
Bool {
            controlCorrection.isOn = correction
        }
    }
    @IBAction func saveColor(_ sender: UISegmentedControl) {
        let current = controlColors.selectedSegmentIndex
        defaultValues.set(current, forKey: "color")
    }
    @IBAction func saveEditable(_ sender: UISwitch) {
        let current = controlEditable.isOn
        defaultValues.set(current, forKey: "editable")
    }
    @IBAction func saveCorrection(_ sender: UISwitch) {
        let current = controlCorrection.isOn
        defaultValues.set(current, forKey: "correction")
    }
}
```

Listing 21-4: Saving the settings

The settings view contains a Segmented Control with the buttons Dark, Medium, and Light, and two Switches to set the edition and auto correction features of the Text View. These elements were connected to Outlets that we use in the **viewDidLoad()** method to update their states according to the values already selected, and also to Actions that update the settings every time the values of the elements are changed by the user (the Value Changed event is fired). In consequence, every time the user opens the settings view, the state of the elements is modified according to the values stored in User Settings, and as soon as the user modifies the position of a Switch or taps a button on the Segmented Control, the new value is stored in this system.

 Do It Yourself: Create a new Single View Application project. Embed the initial view in a Navigation Controller. Add a bar button called Settings and a Text View to the main view. Add a Table View Controller to the Storyboard. Connect the Settings button to the table with a Show Segue. Select the table, go to the Attributes Inspector panel, and change the Content option to Static Cells, the value of Sections to 2, and the Style to Grouped. Select the header of each section and erase their titles. Leave only one cell for the first section and two for the second section and change their heights to 60 (Figure 14-10). Add labels, a Segmented Control with the buttons Dark, Medium, and Light, and also switches to the interface as shown in Figure 21-2. Create a subclass of the **UITableViewController** class called **SettingsViewController** and assign it to the second Scene. Complete the **ViewController** class and the **SettingsViewController** class with the codes of Listings 21-3 and 21-4. Connect the elements to their respective Outlets and Actions. Run the application and set new values. Wait a few seconds for the system to store the values in User Defaults. Stop the application and run it again. The Text View should be always configured according to the values you set before.

So far, we have used a generic method to retrieve the values, but the methods for specific types provided by the **UserDefault** class may simplify our code in some circumstances. The following example updates the **ViewController** class of Listing 21-3 to read the values with the methods according to their type.

```
import UIKit

class ViewController: UIViewController {
    @IBOutlet weak var textEditor: UITextView!

    override func viewWillAppear(_ animated: Bool) {
        super.viewWillAppear(animated)

        let defaultValues = UserDefaults.standard
        let color = defaultValues.integer(forKey: "color")
        let colorList = [UIColor.black, UIColor.gray, UIColor.lightGray]
        textEditor.textColor = colorList[color]
        textEditor.isEditable = defaultValues.bool(forKey: "editable")

        let correction = defaultValues.bool(forKey: "correction")
        if correction {
            textEditor.spellCheckingType = .yes
        } else {
            textEditor.spellCheckingType = .no
        }
    }
}
```

Listing 21-5: Reading values with specific methods

Storage

The code is simplified because we no longer have to unwrap the values, but there is a problem. Some of these methods return values by default. For example, the **integer()** method in Listing 21-5 will return the value 0 if no value was stored before for the "color" key. In the case of the color, we actually want the value by default to be 0, so the text is displayed in color black the first time the user runs the application, but the value by default for Booleans is **false**, which means that the features we set for the Text View will be deactivated by default. The solution is to provide our own default values. The **UserDefaults** class includes the **register()** method to set these values. The method receives a dictionary of type **[String: Any]** with the keys and values we want to set by default and stores them in the User Defaults system. Because the values may be modified from anywhere in our app, it is good practice to set the values by default when the app is launched.

```
import UIKit

@UIApplicationMain
class AppDelegate: UIResponder, UIApplicationDelegate {
   var window: UIWindow?
   func application(_ application: UIApplication,
didFinishLaunchingWithOptions launchOptions:
[UIApplication.LaunchOptionsKey : Any]? = nil) -> Bool {
      let list: [String : Any] = ["color": 0, "editable": true,
"correction": false]
      let defaultValues = UserDefaults.standard
      defaultValues.register(defaults: list)
      return true
   }
}
```

Listing 21-6: Setting values by default

 Do It Yourself: Replace the code in your **ViewController** class by the code of Listing 21-5. Update the **AppDelegate** class with the code of Listing 21-6. Open the simulator, press the Home button, and delete the application to clean the User Default system (the simulator works exactly like a real device, you have to keep pressing the mouse button on the icon of the app you want to delete and click on the X button to remove it). Run the application again. The settings should be set according to the values specified in the **list** dictionary.

 IMPORTANT: iOS allows you to include the settings for your app in the Settings app on your device. To add your app to the list of applications in Settings, you have to create a Settings Bundle. The option is available in the Resource window. The topic is beyond the scope of this book. For more information, visit our website and follow the links for this chapter.

21.2 Files

iOS, as any other operative system, allows users to create and access files, but the iOS file system is like no other. The system restricts applications to their own space and a handful of directories to ensure that they do not interfere with each other. This means that we can only access the files and directories that belong to our app.

Several frameworks and classes use files to store data in a variety of formats. For this reason, Foundation defines a class called **FileManager** that has the sole purpose of managing files and directories. One object of this class is assigned to the app and from it we can create, delete, copy, and move files and directories in the storage space reserved for our app. The class offers the following type property to get a reference to this object.

default—This type property returns a reference to the app's `FileManager` object.

File Manager

The `FileManager` class offers multiple properties and methods to manage files and directories. The following are the most frequently used.

urls(for: SearchPathDirectory, **in:** SearchPathDomainMask**)**—This method returns an array with the location of a directory. The **for** attribute is an enumeration with values that represent common system directories, such as Documents, and the **in** attribute is another enumeration with values that determine the domain in which the files are located.

createDirectory(at: URL, **withIntermediateDirectories:** Bool, **attributes:** Dictionary?**)**—This method creates a new directory. The **at** attribute specifies the location of the directory, including its name, the **withIntermediateDirectories** attribute indicates whether or not intermediate directories will also be created, and the **attributes** attribute is a dictionary with values that determine the directory's attributes (e.g., ownership). The value `nil` sets the attributes by default, which are usually enough for iOS applications.

createFile(atPath: String, **contents:** Data?, **attributes:** Dictionary?**)**—This method creates a file. The **atPath** attribute specifies the location of the file, including its name and extension, the **contents** attribute represents the content of the file, and the **attributes** attribute is a dictionary with values that determine the file's attributes (e.g., ownership). The value `nil` sets the attributes by default, which are usually enough for iOS applications.

contents(atPath: String**)**—This method returns the content of the file at the path specified by the **atPath** attribute. The value returned is an optional of type `Data`.

contentsOfDirectory(atPath: String**)**—This method returns an array with the paths of the files and directories inside the directory indicated by the **atPath** attribute.

copyItem(atPath: String, **toPath:** String**)**—This method copies the file or directory at the path specified by the **at** attribute to the path specified by the **to** attribute.

moveItem(atPath: String, **toPath:** String**)**—This method moves the file or directory at the path specified by the **at** attribute to the path specified by the **to** attribute.

removeItem(atPath: String**)**—This method removes the file or directory at the path indicated by the **atPath** attribute.

fileExists(atPath: String**)**—This method returns a Boolean value that determines whether the file or the directory at the path specified by the **atPath** attribute exists or not.

attributesOfItem(atPath: String**)**—This method returns a dictionary with the attributes of the file or directory at the location indicated by the **atPath** attribute. The `FileManager` class includes constants to define the attributes, including `creationDate`, `modificationDate`, `size`, and `type`, among others.

URLs and Paths

As in any other operative system, files in iOS are organized in directories. There is a basic directory called *root* that can contain files and also other directories. These directories in turn can contain other files and directories, creating a tree-like structure. For example, we may have a directory inside the root directory called *Pictures* and another directory inside Pictures called *Travels* and inside Travels a file called *hawaii.png* with an image of Hawaii. To access the picture, we have to move inside the root directory, then inside the Pictures directory, and then inside the

Travels directory. To reproduce this route in code, iOS adopts a conventional syntax that separates each part of the route with a forward slash (/), starting with a single slash to indicate the root directory. Using this syntax, the previous route would look like this /Pictures/Travels/Hawaii.png. This is called *path*, and it is used to access any file in the system.

Paths are a simple way to access files but are not enough for the system to identify the location of a file in the storage system. This is because in practice files are usually not stored in a single storage space, but in several units or even in remote servers. Following a long path to find a file also takes time and consumes resources. For these reasons, locations are always identified by URLs (Uniform Resource Locator). URLs are the most efficient way to identify the location of a resource (usually a file) in local or remote systems. They are just strings, like paths, but provide more information to the system and follow a convention that systems can take advantage of to manage and access files in a more efficient way. Foundation defines a structure to work with URLs called **URL**. The following are some of the initializers, properties and methods provided by this structure to work with files.

URL(fileURLWithPath: String)—This initializer returns a **URL** object referencing a local file or directory. The **fileURLWithPath** attribute is a string with the file's path.

URL(fileURLWithPath: String, relativeTo: URL)—This initializer returns a **URL** object referencing a local file or directory. The **fileURLWithPath** attribute is a string with the file's path, and the **relativeTo** attribute is a **URL** object referencing the base URL.

path—This property returns the path of a URL. It is a conditional of type **String**.

pathComponents—This property returns an array of **String** values that represent the components of a path extracted from a URL (the strings between forward slashes).

lastPathComponent—This property returns a string with the last component of a path extracted from a URL. It is usually used to get the file's name and extension.

pathExtension—This property returns a string with the extension of the path extracted from a URL. It is usually used to get the file's extension.

appendingPathComponent(String)—This method returns a new **URL** structure with the URL of the original object plus the component specified by the attribute.

 IMPORTANT: The **FileManager** class includes methods to work with both paths and URLs. For example, there are two versions of the **createDirectory()** method, one to create the directory from a path and another from a URL. The methods that work with paths take care of converting the path into a URL and are usually easier to implement, but you can use any method you need. For a complete list, visit our website and follow the links for this chapter.

Files and Directories

When the application is installed on the device, iOS creates a group of standard directories that we can use. The most useful are the Documents directory, where we can store the user's files, and the Application Support directory, for files that our app needs to create during run time that are not directly generated by the user. The location of these directories is not guaranteed, so we always have to ask iOS for the current URL that points to the directory or file we want to access. To get the location of common directories like Documents, the **FileManager** class includes the **urls()** method. The method requires two attributes. The first attribute is an enumeration with values that represent different directories. There are several values available for the iOS and OSX operative systems, including **documentDirectory** to reference the Documents directory and

applicationSupportDirectory to reference the Application Support directory. The second attribute is another enumeration with values that indicate the domain where the directory is located. The system organizes directories and files in separate domains depending on their intended usage. The domain where our app's files are stored is the User Domain, identified with the constant **userDomainMask**. In consequence, to get the URL of any of the directories generated for our app and start creating files to store the user's data, we have to get a reference to the **FileManager** object and then call the **urls()** method with the values that represent the location we want to use.

Files can be managed from anywhere in the code, but it is a common practice to prepare the files our app requires from the app's delegate object, so they are ready when needed. The following example shows how to obtain the Documents directory's URL.

```
import UIKit

@UIApplicationMain
class AppDelegate: UIResponder, UIApplicationDelegate {
    var window: UIWindow?

    func application(_ application: UIApplication,
didFinishLaunchingWithOptions launchOptions:
[UIApplication.LaunchOptionsKey : Any]? = nil) -> Bool {
        let manager = FileManager.default
        let documents = manager.urls(for: .documentDirectory, in:
.userDomainMask)
        let docURL = documents.first!
        print(docURL)
        return true
    }
}
```

Listing 21-7: Getting the Documents directory's URL

The **urls()** method returns an array of optional **URL** structures with all the possible locations of the directory. In the case of the Documents directory, the right value is the first item of the array, so in Listing 21-7 we get this value from the **first** property, unwrap it, assign it to the **docURL** constant, and print it on the console.

Now that we have the URL, we can start adding other directories and files inside the Documents directory. The **FileManager** class includes the **createFile()** method to create new files. The method requires three values: the path where the file is going to be created (including the file's name and extension), a value with the content, and the file's attributes. The content and the attributes are optional. If we declare these values as **nil**, the file is created empty and with attributes by default, as in the following example.

```
import UIKit

@UIApplicationMain
class AppDelegate: UIResponder, UIApplicationDelegate {
    var window: UIWindow?

    func application(_ application: UIApplication,
didFinishLaunchingWithOptions launchOptions:
[UIApplication.LaunchOptionsKey : Any]? = nil) -> Bool {
        let manager = FileManager.default
        let documents = manager.urls(for: .documentDirectory, in:
.userDomainMask)
        let docURL = documents.first!
```

```
    let newFileURL = docURL.appendingPathComponent("mytext.txt")
    let path = newFileURL.path
    manager.createFile(atPath: path, contents: nil, attributes: nil)
    return true
  }
}
```

Listing 21-8: Creating a file inside Documents

The path must represent the whole route to the file, including its name and extension. The **URL** class includes the **appendingPathComponent()** method to extend a URL. The method adds a string to the end of the URL and takes care of including the necessary forward slashes to ensure its validity. In Listing 21-8, we use it to get the URL for the new file. After this, we obtain its path from the **path** property and finally call the **createFile()** method to create the file (if the file already exists, the method does nothing). At the end, the Documents directory of this application will contain an empty file called mytext.txt.

The same way we created a file, we can create a directory. The method to create a directory is called **createDirectory()**. Again, the method takes three values: the path of the new directory (including its name), a Boolean value that indicates if we want to create all the directories included in the path that does not exist (in case the path includes directories we have not created yet), and the directory's attributes. This method throws an error if it cannot complete the task, so we have to handle the error with the **try** keyword.

```
import UIKit

@UIApplicationMain
class AppDelegate: UIResponder, UIApplicationDelegate {
  var window: UIWindow?

  func application(_ application: UIApplication,
didFinishLaunchingWithOptions launchOptions:
[UIApplication.LaunchOptionsKey : Any]? = nil) -> Bool {
    let manager = FileManager.default
    let documents = manager.urls(for: .documentDirectory, in:
.userDomainMask)
    let docURL = documents.first!

    let newDirectoryURL = docURL.appendingPathComponent("myfiles")
    let path = newDirectoryURL.path
    do {
      try manager.createDirectory(atPath: path,
withIntermediateDirectories: false, attributes: nil)
    } catch {
      print("The directory already exists")
    }
    return true
  }
}
```

Listing 21-9: Creating a directory inside Documents

The **FileManager** class also offers methods to list the content of a directory. We can use the **contentsOfDirectory()** method to get an array of strings with the names of the files and directories in a specific path. In the following example, we create another method inside the **AppDelegate** class to list files and directories. The method receives the URL we want to search and then creates a **for in** loop to print the items found.

```
import UIKit

@UIApplicationMain
class AppDelegate: UIResponder, UIApplicationDelegate {
    var window: UIWindow?

    func application(_ application: UIApplication,
didFinishLaunchingWithOptions launchOptions:
[UIApplication.LaunchOptionsKey : Any]? = nil) -> Bool {
        let manager = FileManager.default
        let documents = manager.urls(for: .documentDirectory, in:
.userDomainMask)
        let docURL = documents.first!
        listItems(directory: docURL)
        return true
    }
    func listItems(directory: URL) {
        let manager = FileManager.default
        if let list = try? manager.contentsOfDirectory(atPath:
directory.path) {
            if list.isEmpty {
                print("The directory is empty")
            } else {
                for item in list {
                    print(item)
                }
            }
        }
    }
}
```

Listing 21-10: Listing the content of a directory

In the **application(UIApplication, didFinishLaunchingWithOptions:)** method we get the Documents directory's URL and then call the **listItems()** method to list the files and directories inside Documents. The **listItems()** method has to get its own reference of the **FileManager** object and then use it to call the **contentsOfDirectory()** method to get the list of items. Notice that this method throws, so we use the **try?** keyword to handle the errors.

 Do It Yourself: Create a new Single View Application project. Update the **AppDelegate** class with the code of Listing 21-8 and run the application to create the mytext.txt file. Update the **AppDelegate** class again with the code of Listing 21-9 and run the application to create the myfiles directory. Update the **AppDelegate** class one more time with the code of Listing 21-10 and run the application. You should see the file and directory's names on the console.

In the example of Listing 21-8, we have created a file inside the Documents directory, but we can also create files inside the directories our app generates. For example, we can create a new file inside the myfiles directory created in Listing 21-9.

```
import UIKit

@UIApplicationMain
class AppDelegate: UIResponder, UIApplicationDelegate {
    var window: UIWindow?
    func application(_ application: UIApplication,
didFinishLaunchingWithOptions launchOptions:
[UIApplication.LaunchOptionsKey : Any]? = nil) -> Bool {
```

```
        let manager = FileManager.default
        let documents = manager.urls(for: .documentDirectory, in:
.userDomainMask)
        let docURL = documents.first!

        let newFileURL =
docURL.appendingPathComponent("myfiles/anotherfile.txt")
        let path = newFileURL.path
        let created = manager.createFile(atPath: path, contents: nil,
attributes: nil)
        if !created {
            print("We couldn't create the file")
        }
        return true
    }
}
```

Listing 21-11: Creating files in a custom directory

The code of Listing 21-11 adds the necessary components to the Documents directory's URL and then creates the file as we did before. In this example, we add the components all at once, separating each component with a forward slash, but we could have called the **appendingPathComponent()** method for every component and add them one by one.

We can also move a file or directory from one location to another. All we have to do is to provide the paths for the origin and destination and then call the **moveItem()** method. For example, we can move the mytext.txt file to the myfiles directory created before.

```
import UIKit

@UIApplicationMain
class AppDelegate: UIResponder, UIApplicationDelegate {
    var window: UIWindow?

    func application(_ application: UIApplication,
didFinishLaunchingWithOptions launchOptions:
[UIApplication.LaunchOptionsKey : Any]? = nil) -> Bool {
        let manager = FileManager.default
        let documents = manager.urls(for: .documentDirectory, in:
.userDomainMask)
        let docURL = documents.first!

        let originURL = docURL.appendingPathComponent("mytext.txt")
        let destinationURL =
docURL.appendingPathComponent("myfiles/mytext.txt")
        let originPath = originURL.path
        let destinationPath = destinationURL.path
        do {
            try manager.moveItem(atPath: originPath, toPath:
destinationPath)
        } catch {
            print("File was not moved")
        }
        return true
    }
}
```

Listing 21-12: Moving files

The same way we move, we can also copy. The following example copies the anotherfile.txt file created inside the myfiles in Listing 21-11 into the Documents directory.

```
import UIKit

@UIApplicationMain
class AppDelegate: UIResponder, UIApplicationDelegate {
   var window: UIWindow?
   func application(_ application: UIApplication,
didFinishLaunchingWithOptions launchOptions:
[UIApplication.LaunchOptionsKey : Any]? = nil) -> Bool {
      let manager = FileManager.default
      let documents = manager.urls(for: .documentDirectory, in:
.userDomainMask)
      let docURL = documents.first!

      let originURL =
docURL.appendingPathComponent("myfiles/anotherfile.txt")
      let destinationURL =
docURL.appendingPathComponent("anotherfile.txt")
      let originPath = originURL.path
      let destinationPath = destinationURL.path
      do {
         try manager.copyItem(atPath: originPath, toPath:
destinationPath)
      } catch {
         print("File was not copied")
      }
      return true
   }
}
```

Listing 21-13: Copying files

Removing files or directories also does not take too much work. We have to get the path to the file and call the **removeItem()** method.

```
import UIKit

@UIApplicationMain
class AppDelegate: UIResponder, UIApplicationDelegate {
   var window: UIWindow?

   func application(_ application: UIApplication,
didFinishLaunchingWithOptions launchOptions:
[UIApplication.LaunchOptionsKey : Any]? = nil) -> Bool {
      let manager = FileManager.default
      let documents = manager.urls(for: .documentDirectory, in:
.userDomainMask)
      let docURL = documents.first!

      let fileURL = docURL.appendingPathComponent("anotherfile.txt")
      let path = fileURL.path
      do {
         try manager.removeItem(atPath: path)
      } catch {
         print("File was not removed")
      }
      return true
   }
}
```

Listing 21-14: Removing files

Storage

Do It Yourself: Update the `AppDelegate` class with the codes of Listings 21-11, 21-12, 21-13, and 21-14, and run the application every time. Incorporate the `listItems()` method of Listing 21-10 to the class so you can see the files being created and moved.

Files Attributes

Some applications need to know more than the name of the file. The `FileManager` class offers the `attributesOfItem()` method to get file attributes, such as the date of creation or the size. The method returns a dictionary with predefined keys to identify each value. There are several constants available we can use as keys. The most common are `creationDate` (the date the file was created), `modificationDate` (last time it was modified), `size`, and `type`. The following code gets the attributes of the mytext.txt file created in previous examples.

```
import UIKit

@UIApplicationMain
class AppDelegate: UIResponder, UIApplicationDelegate {
    var window: UIWindow?

    func application(_ application: UIApplication,
didFinishLaunchingWithOptions launchOptions:
[UIApplication.LaunchOptionsKey : Any]? = nil) -> Bool {
        let manager = FileManager.default
        let documents = manager.urls(for: .documentDirectory, in:
.userDomainMask)
        let docURL = documents.first!

        let fileURL = docURL.appendingPathComponent("myfiles/mytext.txt")
        let filePath = fileURL.path
        if let attributes = try? manager.attributesOfItem(atPath: filePath) {
            let type = attributes[.type] as! FileAttributeType
            let size = attributes[.size] as! Int
            let date = attributes[.creationDate] as! Date
            if type != FileAttributeType.typeDirectory {
                print("Name: \(fileURL.lastPathComponent)")
                print("Size: \(size)")
                print("Created: \(date)")
            }
        }
        return true
    }
}
```

Listing 21-15: Reading file's attributes

The attributes are returned as **Any** values, so we have to cast them to their corresponding types. Most of the values are of data types we already know, such as **Int** or **Date**, but the **type** key returns a property of a structure called **FileAttributeType** that represent the resource's type. There are properties available to represent different types of resources. The most frequently used are **typeRegular** to represent files and **typeDirectory** to represent directories. If we want to know if the resource is a file, we can compare the value returned by the **type** key with the **typeDirectory** property, as we did in the example of Listing 21-15. If they are different, it means that the resource is a file and we can process its attributes.

Files Content

Storage systems, like hard drives and flash memories, store information the only way a computer knows, as a series of ones and zeros. Therefore, the information we want to store in files has to be converted into a stream of bytes that can be later turned back into the original data. Foundation offers the **Data** structure for this purpose. The structure provides properties and methods to process raw data, but we usually have to rely on properties and methods of other structures and classes to create the instances. We have already introduced the **pngData()** and **jpegData()** methods of the **UIImage** class to convert images into **Data** structures, but other common data types also offer these kinds of methods. For example, the **String** structure includes a method that turns a string into data an also an initializer that can get back the string from a **Data** structure.

String(data: Data, **encoding:** Encoding**)**—This initializer creates a **String** value with the text in the **Data** structure provided by the **data** attribute. The **encoding** attribute is a value provided by properties of a structure called **Encoding** included in the **String** structure that determine the type of encoding used to generate the string. The encoding usually depends on the language the text was written in (e.g., **utf8** and **ascii**).

data(using: Encoding, **allowLossyConversion:** Bool**)**—This method returns a **Data** structure containing the string in the original **String** value. The **using** attribute is a value provided by properties of the **Encoding** structure that determine the type of encoding used to generate the string. The encoding usually depends on the language the text was written in. The most frequently used are **utf8** and **ascii**. The **allowLossyConversion** attribute determines the precision of the conversion.

The structures and classes capable of processing **Data** structures and files also provide specific methods to write and read a file. For example, the **String** structure includes the following method to turn a string into data and store it in a file, all at once.

write(to: URL, **atomically:** Bool, **encoding:** Encoding**)**—This method converts a string into a **Data** structure and stores it in the file located at the URL specified by the **to** attribute. The **atomically** attribute determines if we want the data to be stored in an auxiliary file first to ensure that the original file is not corrupted (the value **true** is recommended). The **encoding** attribute is a value provided by properties of the **Encoding** structure that determine the type of encoding used to generate the string (e.g., **utf8** and **ascii**).

With methods like this, we can store the information generated by the user and always keep the file updated. For example, we can get input from the user through a Text View and preserve in a file everything the user writes.

Figure 21-3: Interface to generate file content

The view controller for the view of Figure 21-3 has to perform two tasks: write the text inside the Text View into a file every time the user changes the content and read the content back from the file every time the user loads the application to show the Text View as it was the last time.

```swift
import UIKit

class ViewController: UIViewController, UITextViewDelegate {
    @IBOutlet weak var diaryText: UITextView!
    var fileURL: URL!

    override func viewDidLoad() {
        super.viewDidLoad()
        diaryText.delegate = self
        let manager = FileManager.default
        let documents = manager.urls(for: .documentDirectory, in:
.userDomainMask)
        let docURL = documents.first!
        fileURL = docURL.appendingPathComponent("userdata.txt")
        let filePath = fileURL.path
        if manager.fileExists(atPath: filePath) {
            if let content = manager.contents(atPath: filePath) {
                diaryText.text = String(data: content, encoding: .utf8)
            }
        } else {
            manager.createFile(atPath: filePath, contents: nil, attributes:
nil)
        }
    }
    func textViewDidChange(_ textView: UITextView) {
        let text = diaryText.text!
        do {
            try text.write(to: fileURL, atomically: true, encoding: .utf8)
        } catch {
            print("Error")
        }
    }
}
```

Listing 21-16: Managing the file's content

The first thing we do in the **ViewController** class of Listing 21-16 is to call the **fileExists()** method to check if the file where we are going to store the data already exists. If the file exists, we read its content with the **contents()** method, convert the data into a string with the **String** initializer, and assign the string to the Text View. This way, the user always sees the last text stored in the file as soon as the app is launched. If the file does not exist, however, we create it with the **createFile()** method and an empty content (**nil**). To keep the file updated with the text inserted by the user in the Text View, we declare the **ViewController** class as the delegate of the Text View and implement the **textViewDidChange()** method (see Chapter 7). This method is called by the Text View every time its content changes. Inside the method we read the current text and call its **write()** method to store it in the file. Now, everything the user writes in the Text View is persistently preserved and always available.

 Do It Yourself: Create a new Single View Application project. Add a label and a Text View to the initial view to get the interface of Figure 21-3. Connect the Text View to the **ViewController** class with an Outlet called **diaryText**. Complete the **ViewController** class with the code of Listing 21-16. Run the application and insert a text in the Text View. Stop the application from Xcode and run it again. You should see the same text inserted before on the screen.

Bundle

In previous examples, we have worked with files created at run time, but sometimes we need to get access to files added to our project during development. This could be simple text files or even complex databases. But the app's files, code, and resources are not just stored in a single directory; they are encapsulated in a bundle. Bundles are directories assigned exclusively to each application. They create a hierarchical structure to organize all the app's files and resources. For this reason, to get access to the files in our project, we have to access the content of our app's bundle.

To create and manage bundles, Foundation includes the **Bundle** class. The class offers properties and methods to work with bundles and get their location, including a type property that returns a reference to the bundle created by default for our app.

main—This type property returns a reference to the app's bundle.

bundleURL—This property returns a **URL** structure with the bundle's URL.

bundlePath—This property returns a string with the bundle's path.

Because we are not able to determine the location of our app's files and resources during development, every time we want to access these files from code we have to get their URLs from the **Bundle** object. The class provides the following methods for this purpose.

url(forResource: String?, **withExtension:** String?)—This method returns a **URL** structure with the URL of a file or directory inside the bundle. The first attribute specifies the name of the file or directory we are looking for, and the **withExtension** attribute specifies its extension (set as **nil** for resources that do not have an extension).

path(forResource: String?, **ofType:** String?)—This method returns the path of a file or directory inside the bundle. The first attribute specifies the name of the file or directory we are looking for, and the **ofType** attribute specifies its extension (set as **nil** for resources that do not have an extension).

We frequently have to use the **Bundle** object in professional applications to access files that are required for some services, like databases, for example, but we can also take advantage of this object to load files with initial data to populate the model when the app is launched for the first time or to restore an initial state. The following example loads a text file called quote.txt from the bundle as soon as the application is launched. The file must be added to the project during development by dragging it from Finder to the Navigator Area.

```
import UIKit

@UIApplicationMain
class AppDelegate: UIResponder, UIApplicationDelegate {
   var window: UIWindow?

   func application(_ application: UIApplication,
didFinishLaunchingWithOptions launchOptions:
[UIApplication.LaunchOptionsKey : Any]? = nil) -> Bool {
      let bundle = Bundle.main
      let filePath = bundle.path(forResource: "quote", ofType: "txt")

      let manager = FileManager.default
      if let data = manager.contents(atPath: filePath!) {
         let message = String(data: data, encoding: .utf8)
         print(message!)
      }
```

```
        return true
    }
}
```

Listing 21-17: Loading a project's file

The code of Listing 21-17 gets a reference to the app's bundle and then finds the path for the quote.txt file with the **path()** method. After we get the path, we can read the file as we did before. In this example, we print the string on the console, but this information is usually stored in the model or assigned to other objects that require it.

 Do It Yourself: Create a new Single View Application project and update its **AppDelegate** class with the code of Listing 21-17. Create a text file with a text editor, write some text in it, save it with the name quote.txt, and add it to your project (Figures 8-3 and 8-4). Run the application. You should see the text inside the file printed on the console.

 IMPORTANT: Getting files from the bundle is necessary for non-conventional resources. Conventional resources, like images, provide their own mechanisms to load files, as we have seen in Chapter 8.

21.3 Archiving

The methods we have just studied to store data in files are enough for simple models but present some limitations. We can only work with single values and with classes that already provide a way to turn their content into data. Professional applications rely on more elaborated models that include collection of values and also custom objects. To give us more flexibility, Foundation offers the **NSCoder** class. This class can encode and decode values to **Data** structures for storage purposes in a process called *Archiving* (**NSCoder** is also used for data distribution but archiving is its most important feature).

Archiving with **NSCoder** is a very powerful tool. An **NSCoder** object not only encodes an object but also the objects it is connected to, preserving the connections and the hierarchy. For example, we may have two objects with properties that reference the other object. Object 1 references Object 2 and Object 2 references Object 1. The structure built by the objects and their connections is called *Object Graph*. If we only store Object 1, we will have to recreate Object 2 and reconstruct the references, but storing the complete Object Graph we do not have to worry about it. Both objects are encoded, stored, and then decoded and connected again when we need them.

Encoding and Decoding

The **NSCoder** class provides all the methods necessary to encode and decode the values of an object, but all the work is done by instances of two **NSCoder** subclasses called **NSKeyedArchiver** and **NSKeyedUnarchiver**. The **NSKeyedArchiver** class calls the **encode()** method on the objects to encode their values and stores the data in a **Data** structure or a file. The **NSKeyedUnarchiver** class, on the other hand, initializes the objects with the protocol's initializer and returns the original values.

The **NSKeyedArchiver** class offers the following type method to encode an Object Graph and store it in a **Data** structure.

archivedData(withRootObject: Any, **requiringSecureCoding:** Bool)—This type method encodes the Object Graph of the object specified by the **withRootObject** attribute and stores it in a **Data** structure. The **requiringSecureCoding** attribute is a Boolean value that determines whether the data will be secured or not.

The **NSKeyedUnarchiver** class offers the following type method to decode an Object Graph from a **Data** structure.

unarchivedObject(ofClass: Class, **from:** Data)—This type method decodes the data specified by the **from** attribute and returns the original Object Graph. The **ofClass** attribute determines the data type of the decoded object.

unarchivedObject(ofClasses: [AnyClass], **from:** Data)—This type method decodes the data specified by the **from** attribute and returns the original Object Graph. The **ofClasses** attribute determines the data types of the decoded object.

We can take different approaches to encode and decode values. Implementing the methods of the **NSKeyedArchiver** and **NSKeyedUnarchiver** classes, we can generate **Data** structures for processing, or we can just store and retrieve the data from a file. In the following example, we encode and decode a string to a **Data** structure and use **FileManager** methods to create and read the file.

```
import UIKit
class ViewController: UIViewController {
    override func viewDidLoad() {
        super.viewDidLoad()

        let manager = FileManager.default
        let documents = manager.urls(for: .documentDirectory, in:
.userDomainMask)
        let docURL = documents.first!

        let fileURL = docURL.appendingPathComponent("quotes.dat")
        let filePath = fileURL.path
        if manager.fileExists(atPath: filePath) {
            if let content = manager.contents(atPath: filePath) {
                if let result = try?
NSKeyedUnarchiver.unarchivedObject(ofClass: NSString.self, from: content)
as String? {
                    if let message = result {
                        print(message)
                    }
                }
            }
        } else {
            let quote = "Fiction is the truth inside the lie"
            if let fileData = try?
NSKeyedArchiver.archivedData(withRootObject: quote,
requiringSecureCoding: false) {
                manager.createFile(atPath: filePath, contents: fileData,
attributes: nil)
            }
        }
    }
}
```

Listing 21-18: Encoding and decoding data

Listing 21-18 presents a view controller with a simple example. A single string is encoded and stored in a file called quotes.dat. As we did in previous examples, we first check if the file exists with the **fileExists()** method and then proceed according to the result. If the file does not exist, we convert the string in the **quote** constant to a **Data** value with the **archivedData()**

method and then create a file with this data as its content, but if the file already exists, we read its content with the **contents()** method and decode the data with the **unarchivedObject()** method to get back the string. Notice that the methods can throw errors, so we have to check the values returned with the **try** keyword.

The **unarchivedObject()** method can only work with data types that conform to a protocol called **NSCoding**. That is the reason why we had to specify the **NSString** class as the value of the **ofClass** attribute and convert it at the end to a **String** structure with the **as** operator (the **NSString** class conforms to the **NSCoding** protocol but the **String** structure doesn't). Specifying the class alone is not enough, we have to use the **self** keyword to tell the compiler that we are referencing the data type.

 Do It Yourself: Create a new Single View Application project. Update the **ViewController** class with the code of Listing 21-18. Run the application. The first time, the file is created, and no message is printed on the console. Stop and run the application again. Now you should see the quote on the console.

The methods of the **NSKeyedArchiver** and **NSKeyedUnarchiver** classes work with values of the types included in a Property List. A Property List is a data classification created to provide a convenient way to store data. The problem is that it only includes specific types of data (**NSNumber**, **NSString**, **NSDate**, **NSArray**, **NSDictionary**, **NSData**, and their equivalents in Swift). In the previous example, we had to use an **NSString** value, but if we want to provide our own data types, we have to convert them to Property List values. Foundation offers two classes for this purpose, **PropertyListEncoder** and **PropertyListDecoder**, which include the following methods to encode and decode values.

encode(Value**)**—This method of the **PropertyListEncoder** class encodes a value into a Property List value.

decode(Type, **from:** Data**)**—This method of the **PropertyListDecoder** class decodes a Property List value into a value of the type specified by the first attribute. The **from** attribute is a **Data** structure with the data to be decoded.

Another requirement for custom structures is that they implement the initializers and methods defined in the **NSCoding** protocol for the system to be able to encode and decode the data. Fortunately, the Swift Standard Library defines a protocol called **Codable** that turns a structure into an encodable and decodable data type. All we have to do, is to get our structure to conform to the protocol and the compiler takes care of adding all the methods required to encode and decode its values. The following example creates a structure to store information about books.

```
struct Book: Codable {
   var title: String
   var author: String
   var edition: Int
}
```

Listing 21-19: Encoding and decoding a custom class

Once our custom structure is ready, we can start creating instances and archiving them. The next example follows the process established before. When the main view is loaded, we check if the file already exists and read it or create a new one accordingly. To archive and unarchive the data, we use the same methods as in the previous example, but this time we encode or decode the values into a Property List.

```
import UIKit

class ViewController: UIViewController {
    override func viewDidLoad() {
        super.viewDidLoad()

        let manager = FileManager.default
        let documents = manager.urls(for: .documentDirectory, in:
.userDomainMask)
        let docURL = documents.first!

        let fileURL = docURL.appendingPathComponent("userdata.dat")
        let filePath = fileURL.path
        if manager.fileExists(atPath: filePath) {
            if let content = manager.contents(atPath: filePath) {
                if let result = try?
NSKeyedUnarchiver.unarchivedObject(ofClass: NSData.self, from: content)
as Data? {
                    if let data = result {
                        let decoder = PropertyListDecoder()
                        if let books = try? decoder.decode([Book].self, from:
data) {
                            for book in books {
                                print("\(book.title) - \(book.author) -
\(book.edition)")
                            }
                        }
                    }
                }
            }
        } else {
            let book1 = Book(title: "IT", author: "Stephen King", edition:
2)
            let book2 = Book(title: "Pet Sematary", author: "Stephen King",
edition: 1)
            let book3 = Book(title: "The Shining", author: "Stephen King",
edition: 1)
            let list = [book1, book2, book3]

            let encoder = PropertyListEncoder()
            if let data = try? encoder.encode(list) {
                if let fileData = try?
NSKeyedArchiver.archivedData(withRootObject: data, requiringSecureCoding:
false) {
                    manager.createFile(atPath: filePath, contents: fileData,
attributes: nil)
                }
            }
        }
    }
}
```

Listing 21-20: Encoding and decoding arrays of custom objects

In this example, we store an array of three `Book` structures. First, we convert the array into a Property List value with the `encode()` method of the `PropertyListEncoder` class, then we archive the data, and finally we store it in a file called userdata.dat. To get the information back from the file, we decode the data with the `decode()` method of the `PropertyListDecoder` class.

Do It Yourself: Create a new Single View Application project. Create a new Swift file for the structure of Listing 21-20. Update the `ViewController` class with the code of Listing 21-21. As it happened with the previous example, the first time we run the application, the file is created and nothing is printed on the console, but if you run the application again, the view controller decodes the content of the file created before and prints the values of every `Book` object on the console.

Real-Life Application

The possibility to encode and decode collections of objects, standard or custom, allows us to store the entire model of our app in files using archiving. In the following example, we are going to build a small application to insert names in the model and list them in a table. The names are going to be managed by a model that archives all the values and stores them in a file for future reference, so every time the app is launched, the values in the model are recovered from the file.

Figure 21-4, next, shows the interface required for this example. We have to create a new Single View Application project, delete the initial Scene, add a Table View Controller to the Storyboard, and embed it in a Navigation Controller. The Navigation Controller has to be declared as the initial view controller from the Attributes Inspector panel, and we also have to add a second Scene to let the user insert new names and update current values.

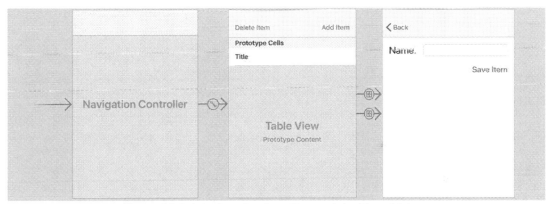

Figure 21-4: Interface to store the model with archiving

We have to configure the cell with the Basic style and give it the identifier "myCell". The Table View Controller also needs two bar buttons, one to edit the table and another to open the second view to add new values. We called these buttons Delete Item and Add Item (Figure 21-4, center). In the second view, we have to include a Text Field to allow the user to insert a name and a button to save it (Figure 21-4, right).

The second view is going to be opened two times: when the user wants to add a new name and when the user wants to update an existing one. To manage these situations, we have to connect two Show Segues to the second Scene, one from the Add Item button and another from the cell. After the Segues are created, the interface will look like Figure 21-4. To identify which Segue was triggered, we have to select the Segue that connects the cell to the second Scene and give it the identifier "editItem".

The interface is ready; now it is time to create the model. For this example, we only need one property to store the list of names, but we want to store the data on file every time it is modified, so we decided to expand previous versions and create a more professional model that privatizes its properties and only let the rest of the code access the data from its methods.

```
import Foundation

struct ApplicationData {
    private let manager = FileManager.default
    private var items: [String]
    private var filePath: String!

    init() {
        items = []
        let documents = manager.urls(for: .documentDirectory, in:
.userDomainMask)
        let docURL = documents.first!
        let fileURL = docURL.appendingPathComponent("items.dat")
        filePath = fileURL.path
        if manager.fileExists(atPath: filePath) {
            if let content = manager.contents(atPath: filePath) {
                if let result = try?
NSKeyedUnarchiver.unarchivedObject(ofClass: NSArray.self, from: content){
                    if let list = result as? [String] {
                        items = list
                    }
                }
            }
        } else {
            archiveItems()
        }
    }
    func getItem(atIndex: Int) -> String {
        return items[atIndex]
    }
    func getTotal() -> Int {
        return items.count
    }
    mutating func addNewItem(name: String) {
        items.append(name)
        archiveItems()
    }
    mutating func removeItem(index: Int) {
        items.remove(at: index)
        archiveItems()
    }
    mutating func updateItem(index: Int, name: String) {
        items[index] = name
        archiveItems()
    }
    func archiveItems() {
        if let fileData = try? NSKeyedArchiver.archivedData(withRootObject:
items, requiringSecureCoding: false) {
            manager.createFile(atPath: filePath, contents: fileData,
attributes: nil)
        }
    }
}
var AppData = ApplicationData()
```

Listing 21-21: Archiving the model's data

When the model is initialized, we have to get the path to the file we are going to use to store the data. This is the same process we have followed in previous examples, but the difference this time is that we have to store the data in the file again every time it changes. For this purpose, we have created three methods: **addNewItem()**, **removeItem()**, and **updateItem()**. The **addNewItem()** method takes the new name inserted by the user and adds it to the **items** array. The **removeItem()** method performs a similar task, but instead of adding a new name, it removes the item at the index specified by the **index** attribute. Finally, the **updateItem()** method replaces the current value of the item at the index specified by the **index** attribute with the new value specified by the **name** attribute. After performing their tasks, the three methods execute an additional method called **archiveItems()** to archive the array and store it.

 IMPORTANT: Notice that we have initialized the file with an empty array (**items = []**). This is not only allowed but also required because the methods provided by the **NSKeyedArchiver** and **NSKeyedUnarchiver** classes cannot work with empty data.

Because the **items** property was declared as **private**, it will not be accessible from other structures and classes, so we have to create methods to let other objects read its values. This is why we have also added the **getItem()** and **getTotal()** methods to the **ApplicationData** structure. The **getItem()** method returns the value of the item at the index specified by the **atIndex** attribute, and the **getTotal()** method returns an integer with the number of elements in the array.

With the model ready, it is time to show the names in the Table View and let the user edit the values. Because we erased the initial Scene and replaced it with a Table View Controller, we have to create a new file with a subclass of **UITableViewController** to work as the view controller of the table. We have called this subclass **ItemsViewController**.

```
import UIKit

class ItemsViewController: UITableViewController {
    override func viewWillAppear(_ animated: Bool) {
        super.viewWillAppear(animated)
        tableView.reloadData()
    }
    override func tableView(_ tableView: UITableView,
numberOfRowsInSection section: Int) -> Int {
        return AppData.getTotal()
    }
    override func tableView(_ tableView: UITableView, cellForRowAt
indexPath: IndexPath) -> UITableViewCell {
        let cell = tableView.dequeueReusableCell(withIdentifier: "myCell",
for: indexPath)
        cell.textLabel?.text = AppData.getItem(atIndex: indexPath.row)
        return cell
    }
    override func tableView(_ tableView: UITableView, commit editingStyle:
UITableViewCell.EditingStyle, forRowAt indexPath: IndexPath) {
        if editingStyle == .delete {
            AppData.removeItem(index: indexPath.row)
            tableView.deleteRows(at: [indexPath], with: .automatic)
        }
    }
    @IBAction func editItems(_ sender: UIBarButtonItem) {
        if tableView.isEditing {
            tableView.setEditing(false, animated: true)
        } else {
            tableView.setEditing(true, animated: true)
        }
    }
}
```

```
override func prepare(for segue: UIStoryboardSegue, sender: Any?) {
    if segue.identifier == "editItem" {
        let controller = segue.destination as! EditItemViewController
        if let indexPath = tableView.indexPathForSelectedRow {
            controller.index = indexPath.row
            controller.name = AppData.getItem(atIndex: indexPath.row)
            tableView.deselectRow(at: indexPath, animated: true)
        }
    }
}
}
```

Listing 21-22: Displaying the model's data

Nothing has changed in the code of Listing 21-22 from previous examples of Table View Controllers (see Chapter 14). The model is in charge of archiving the data, so the only thing the view controller has to do is to call the model's methods to get the values it has to show inside the cells. Besides the protocol methods necessary for the Table View, we have also implemented an Action for the Delete Items button called **editItems()** to activate and deactivate the table's edition, and the **prepare()** method to send the index of the selected row to the second view.

For the second view, we need a subclass of **UIViewController**. We called it **EditItemViewController**.

```
import UIKit
class EditItemViewController: UIViewController {
    @IBOutlet weak var nameText: UITextField!
    var index: Int!
    var name: String!

    override func viewDidLoad() {
        super.viewDidLoad()
        if name != nil {
            nameText.text = name
        }
    }
    @IBAction func saveItem(_ sender: UIButton) {
        if index != nil && name != nil {
            let text = nameText.text!
            AppData.updateItem(index: index, name: text)
        } else {
            let text = nameText.text!
            AppData.addNewItem(name: text)
        }
        navigationController?.popViewController(animated: true)
    }
}
```

Listing 21-23: Adding and updating the model's values

This view controller has to contemplate two scenarios: users can open the view by selecting a cell to edit its value and also by pressing the Add Item button in the Navigation Bar to add a new name. We determine the situation by checking the content of the **index** and **name** properties. If their values are not **nil**, it means that the user selected a cell, so we assign the value of the **name** property to the Text Field and call the **updateItem()** method when the Save Item button is pressed to update the value. If the values of **index** and **name** are **nil**, it means that the user pressed the Add Item button to add a new name, so we call the **addNewItem()** method instead.

Storage

Chapter 22
Core Data

22.1 Custom Object Graph

With archiving, we can store not only objects but also their connections. As we mentioned in Chapter 21, this structure of objects and the connections between them is called *Object Graph*. Archiving is a good tool to store an Object Graph on file but presents some limitations. The Object Graph we can store is difficult to expand and usually inflexible. The entire graph has to be stored in the file again after the smallest change, and it is hard to control the connections between objects and determine exactly which objects are going to be stored. The solution is called *Core Data*. Core Data is an Object Graph manager that defines and manages its own objects and connections. We can establish the composition of those objects and how they are going to relate to each other, and also store as many objects as we need. The system takes care of encoding and decoding the objects, preserving consistency, and storing the Object Graph on file in an efficient way.

Data Model

The structure of the Core Data's Object Graph is defined with a data model. This has nothing to do with the data model of the MVC pattern created in previous chapters, a Core Data model is a definition of the type of objects the graph is going to contain (called *Entities*) and their connections (called *Relationships*).

A model can be created from code, but Xcode offers a practical editor that we can use to define the structure of the graph. The model is stored in a file and then the file is compiled and included in the Core Data system created for our app. Xcode offers a template to create this file.

Figure 22-1: Option to create a Core Data model in the iOS panel

The file may be created with any name we want but it has to have the extension xcdatamodel. Once created, it is included in our project along with the rest of the files. Clicking on it reveals the Xcode editor, illustrated in Figure 22-2, next.

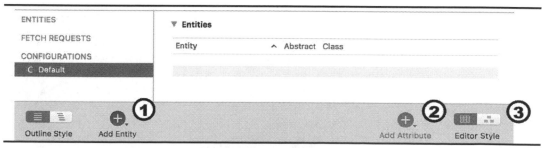

Figure 22-2: Model editor

The model contains three main components: Entities, Attributes, and Relationships. Entities are the descriptions of what the objects are going to contain, Attributes are the descriptions of the objects' properties, and Relationships are the connections we will be allowed to establish between objects. The first step is to add Entities to the model. Entities are created from the Add Entity button at the bottom of the editor (Figure 22-2, number 1). When we press this button, Xcode creates an entity with the generic name "Entity".

Figure 22-3: *New Entities*

We can change the name of the newly created entity by double-clicking the name (Figure 22-3, number 1) or editing the field in the Data Model Inspector panel (Figure 22-3, number 2).

An entity defines the composition of objects that are going to be part of the Object Graph, so the next step is to declare the type of values those objects are going to manage. For this purpose, entities include Attributes. To add an attribute, we have to select the entity and press the + button under the Attributes area (Figure 22-3, number 3) or press the Add Attribute button at the bottom of the editor (Figure 22-2, number 2). The attribute is added with the generic name "attribute" and the data type Undefined. Again, we can change the name of the attribute by double-clicking on it or editing the Name field in the Data Model Inspector panel. For our example, we called the entity *Books* and the first attribute *title* (Figure 22-4, number 1).

Figure 22-4: *New Attributes*

 IMPORTANT: The name of entities has to start with an upper-case letter and the names of attributes and relationships have to start with a lower-case letter.

Every attribute has to be associated with a data type for the objects to know what kind of values they can manage (Figure 22-4, number 2). Clicking on the attribute's type, we can open a menu to select the right data type. The most frequently used are Integer 16, Integer 32, Integer 64, Decimal, Double, Float, String, Boolean, Date, Binary Data, and Transformable. The Integer 16, 32, or 64 options are for `Int16`, `Int32`, and `Int64` values, Decimal is for `NSDecimalNumber` values, Double and Float are for `Double` and `Float` values, String is for `String` values, Boolean is for `Bool` values, Date is for `Date` values, Binary Data is for `Data` values, and Transformable is for predefined and custom objects that include their own `NSCoder` methods to encode and decode the data, like the structures we have created in Chapter 21. The Binary Data and the Transformable options are frequently used to store images, but Transformable is more convenient because it takes care of archiving the `UIImage` object and turns it into a `Data` value, while with the Binary Data option we have to do it ourselves.

Core Data was designed for Objective-C and therefore it works with objects and not primitive values or structures. All the numbers, including integers, floating-point, and Boolean values, are stored as `NSNumber` values, so we must convert them to objects of this class for processing.

An entity may contain as many attributes as our objects need. For example, we may add a few more attributes to complement the book's information.

Figure 22-5: Multiple Attributes

We could have also included another attribute for the author's name, but this is when we have to start thinking about the structure of the Object Graph and how we need the information to be stored. If we include a String type attribute for the author's name inside the Books entity, every time the user inserts a new book it will have to type the name of the author. This is error prone, time consuming, and when several books of the same author are available, it is impossible to make sure that all of them share the same exact name (one book could have the author's middle name and others just the first one, for example). Without the certainty of having the exact same name, we can never incorporate features in our app such as ordering the books by author or getting the list of books written by a particular author. Things get worse when, along with the name, we also decide to store other information about the author, like his or her date of birth. A proper organization of this information demands the creation of separate objects and therefore we have to create new entities to represent them. Additional entities are added to the model the same way we did with the first one. Figure 22-6, next, shows our example with a new entity called *Authors* containing an attribute called *name*.

Figure 22-6: Multiple Entities

Entities are blueprints for objects, similar to what a class is, so we use them to define the characteristics of the objects we want to store. For instance, when we want to store a new book in our example, we create a new object based on the Books entity. That object will have four properties corresponding to the values of its title, year, cover, and thumbnail. The same happens when we want to store the information of an author. We create a new object based on the Authors entity and assign the name of the author to its name property. At the end, we will have two objects in the storage space, one for the book and another for the author. But if we want to retrieve these objects later, we need a way to know what Books object is related to what Authors object. We have to connect these objects, so when we look for the Books object we can also get the corresponding Authors object representing its author, otherwise we will not be able to show the name of the author along with the information of the book. To create this connection, the Core Data model includes Relationships.

Relationships are like properties in an object containing references to another object. They could have a reference to one object or a set of objects. For example, in the Books entity, we can create a relationship that contains a reference to only one object of the Authors entity, because there could only be one author per book (for this example we are assuming that our app is storing books written only by one author). On the contrary, in the Authors entity, we need to establish a relationship that contains references to multiple Books objects, because an author may have written several books, not just one. Core Data calls these relationships according to the number of objects they may reference. The names are To-One and To-Many and they are created pressing the + button in the Relationships area below the Attributes area. Figure 22-7 shows a relationship called *author* we have created for the Books entity of our example (we called it *author* because it is going to be used to retrieve the author of the book).

Figure 22-7: Relationship for the Books entity

A relationship only needs two values: its name (the name of the property) and the destination (the type of objects it is referencing), but it requires some parameters to be set. We have to tell the model if the relationship is going to be optional, define its type (To-One or To-Many), and determine what should happen to the destination object if the source object is deleted (the Delete Rule). All these options are available in the Data Model Inspector panel when the relationship is selected, as shown in Figure 22-8.

Figure 22-8: Relationship settings

By default, the relationship is set as Optional, which means that the source may be connected to a destination object or not (a book can have an author or not), the Type of the relationship is set to To-One (a book can only have one author), and the Delete Rule is set to Nullify. The following are all the values available for this rule.

- **Deny:** If there is at least one object at the destination, the source is not deleted (if there is an Authors object assigned to the Books object, the book is not deleted).
- **Nullify:** The connection between objects are removed, but the objects at the destination are not deleted (if a Books object is deleted, the Authors object associated with that book loses the connection but is not deleted).
- **Cascade:** The objects at the destination are deleted when the source is deleted (the Authors object is deleted if one of its books is deleted).
- **No Action:** The objects at the destination are not deleted or modified (the connections are preserved, even when the source object does not exist anymore).

To find the right rule for a relationship, we have to think in terms of the information we are manipulating. Is it right to delete the author if one of its books is deleted? In our case, the answer is simple. An author can have more than one book, so we cannot delete the author when we delete a book because there could be other books that are connected to that same author.

Core Data

Therefore, the Nullify rule set by default is the right one for this relationship. But this could change when we create the opposite relationship, connecting the Authors entity to the Books entity. We need this second relationship to search for books that belong to an author. Figure 22-9 shows a relationship called *books* that we have created for the Authors entity.

▼ **Relationships**

Entity	Relationship ▲	Destination	Inverse
Authors	◎ books	Books	◇ No Inverse ◇

＋　－

Figure 22-9: Relationship for the Authors entity

 IMPORTANT: Relationships must always be bidirectional. If we set a relationship from entity A to entity B, we have to set the opposite relationship from entity B to A. Core Data offers another type of relationship called *Fetched Properties* to connect entities in only one direction. You can add a Fetched Property from the area below the Relationships area in the model's editor.

The new relationship added in Figure 22-9 is in the Authors entity, so every Authors object will have a property called **book** that we can use to retrieve the Books objects the author was connected to. Because one author can have many books, the setting of this relationship is going to differ from the previous one. Now we have to set the Type of the relationship as To-Many (to many books) and modify the Delete Rule according to how we want our application to respond when an author is deleted. If we don't want to keep books that do not have an author assigned, we should select the Cascade option, so when an author is deleted all of his or her books are deleted too. But if we don't mind having books with no author, then the option should be Nullify.

 The Basics: The Delete Rules are a way to ensure that the objects remaining in the Object Graph are those that our application and the user need. We can always set the rule as Nullify and take care of deleting all the objects ourselves.

There is a third value for the relationship called *Inverse*. Once we set the relationships on both sides, it is highly recommended to set this value. It just tells the model what the name of the opposite relationship is. Core Data needs this to ensure the consistency of the Object Graph. Figure 22-10 shows the final setup for both relationships.

Relationship for the Books entity

Entity	Relationship ▲	Destination	Inverse
Books	◎ author	Authors	◇ books ◇

Relationship for the Authors entity

Entity	Relationship ▲	Destination	Inverse
Authors	Ⓜ books	Books	◇ author ◇

Figure 22-10: Inverse Relationships

Two relationships are simple to follow, but multiple relationships connecting several entities together can turn the model into an indecipherable mess. To help us identify every component of the model, Xcode offers an additional visualization style that displays the entities as boxes and the relationships as arrows connecting the boxes. The option, called *Editor Style*, is at the bottom of the screen (Figure 22-2, number 3). Figure 22-11, next, shows what our model looks like when we switch to this style (Notice that the To-Many relationship is represented by double arrows).

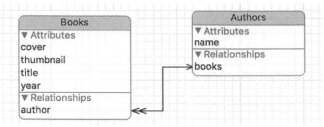

Figure 22-11: Graphic Style

 Do It Yourself: Create a new Single View Application project. Open the File menu at the top of the screen, go to New and select the File... option to create a new file. Move to the Core Data section and select the option Data Model from the iOS panel (Figure 22-1). Save the file with the name "books". Click on the file to open the editor (Figure 22-2). Press the Add Entity button to create two new entities with the names Authors and Books. Create the attributes for these entities as illustrated in Figures 22-6 and 22-7. Create the relationships for every entity as shown in Figure 22-10. Set the books relationship as To-Many and keep the rest of the values by default. Click on the Editor Style button to see a graphic representation of the model (Figure 22-11).

Core Data Stack

The creation of the model is just the first step in the definition of the Core Data system. Once we have all the entities along with their attributes and relationships set up, we have to initialize Core Data for our application. Core Data is created from a group of objects that manage all the processes, from the organization of the Object Graph to the storage of the graph on file. There is an object that manages the model, an object that stores the data on file, and an object that intermediates between this persistent store and our own code. The scheme is called *stack*. Figure 22-12 illustrates a common Core Data stack.

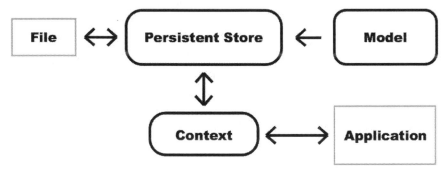

Figure 22-12: Core Data stack

The code in our application interacts with the Context to manage the objects it needs to access and their values, the Context asks the Persistent Store to read or add new objects to the graph, and the Persistent Store processes the Object Graph and save it in a file.

The Core Data framework offers classes to create objects that represent every part of the stack. The **NSManagedObjectModel** class manages the model, the **NSPersistentStore** class manages a persistent store, the **NSPersistentStoreCoordinator** class is used to manage all the persistent stores available (a Core Data stack may have multiple persistent stores), and the **NSManagedObjectContext** creates and manages the context that intermediates between our app and the store. Although we can instantiate these objects and create the stack ourselves, the framework offers the **NSPersistentContainer** class that takes care of everything for us. The class includes the following initializer and also properties to access each object of the stack.

Core Data

NSPersistentContainer(name: String**)**—This initializer creates an **NSPersistent-Container** object that defines a Core Data stack. The **name** attribute is a string representing the name of the container. This value must match the name of the Core Data model (the file's name, without the extension).

managedObjectModel—This property sets or returns an **NSManagedObjectModel** object that represents the Core Data model.

persistentStoreCoordinator—This property sets or returns the **NSPersistentStoreCoordinator** object that manages all the Persistent Stores available.

viewContext—This property sets or returns the **NSManagedObjectContext** object in charge of the stack's context that we have to use to access and modify the Object Graph.

To create the Core Data stack from our app, we have to initialize a new **NSPersistentContainer** object and then load the persistent stores (one by default). Because the stores may take time to load, the class offers a specific method for this purpose.

loadPersistentStores(completionHandler: Block**)**—This method loads the persistent stores and executes a closure when the process is over. The closure receives two attributes, an **NSPersistentStoreDescription** object with the configuration of the stack, and an optional **NSError** value to report errors.

All the communication between our app and the data in the Persistent Store is done through the context. The context is created by the container from the **NSManagedObjectContext** class. This class includes properties and methods to manage the context and the objects in the Persistent Store. The following are the most frequently used.

hasChanges—This property returns a Boolean value that indicates if the context has changes that have to be saved to the Persistent Store.

save()—This method saves the changes in the context to the Persistent Store.

reset()—This method resets the context to a basic state. All the objects and modification our app introduced to the context are ignored.

delete(NSManagedObject**)**—This method deletes an object from the Persistent Store.

count(for: NSFetchRequest**)**—This method returns the number of objects found in the Persistent Store for the request. The **for** attribute is an object that allow us to configure a request.

Because every view controller needs to access the container to get a reference to the context to read or store objects in the Persistent Store, we have to create an instance of the **NSPersistentContainer** class in a place that is accessible for the rest of the code. Apple recommends doing it in the app's delegate, because this way we make sure that everything is created as soon as the app is launched and accessible everywhere in the code. The following example initializes the stack and stores a reference to the container in a property.

```
import UIKit
import CoreData

@UIApplicationMain
class AppDelegate: UIResponder, UIApplicationDelegate {
    var window: UIWindow?
    var container: NSPersistentContainer!
    var context: NSManagedObjectContext!
```

```
    func application(_ application: UIApplication,
didFinishLaunchingWithOptions launchOptions:
[UIApplication.LaunchOptionsKey : Any]? = nil) -> Bool {
        container = NSPersistentContainer(name: "books")
        container.loadPersistentStores(completionHandler: {
(storeDescription, error) in
            if error == nil {
                self.context = self.container.viewContext
            } else {
                print("Error")
            }
        })
        return true
    }
}
```

Listing 22-1: Initializing the Core Data stack in the app's delegate

The name we use in the **NSPersistentContainer** initializer must be the same name we used to create the file for the model. The code of Listing 22-1 assumes that we have called our model "books" and initializes the **NSPersistentContainer** object with that name. The object creates the stack but does not load the Persistent Stores, so we have to do it ourselves by calling the **loadPersistentStores()** method. After completion, the method executes a closure. In this closure, we check for errors and assign the **NSManagedObjectContext** object created by the container to a property called **context**. This way, we get two properties in the app's delegate with references to the container and the context that we can use from anywhere in the code to access the Core Data stack.

The property with the reference to the **NSManagedObjectContext** object is the one we use in our app's view controllers to add, fetch, and remove objects from the store. We have studied how to access the app's delegate properties before (see Chapter 5, Listings 5-1 and 5-2). The following code illustrates a possible implementation that uses an additional property to have a convenient reference we can use from other methods inside the class.

```
import UIKit
import CoreData

class ViewController: UIViewController {
    var context: NSManagedObjectContext!

    override func viewDidLoad() {
        super.viewDidLoad()
        let app = UIApplication.shared
        let appDelegate = app.delegate as! AppDelegate
        context = appDelegate.context
    }
}
```

Listing 22-2: Accessing the context from a view controller

 Do It Yourself: Update the **AppDelegate** class of the project created before for the model with the code of Listing 22-1. Replace the value of the **name** attribute in the **NSPersistentContainer** initializer by the name of your model's file. At this moment, the app doesn't do anything other than creating the stack.

Core Data

IMPORTANT: When the app is launched for the first time, the Core Data stack creates a Persistent Store based on the current model. If you later modify the model, adding new entities or deleting attributes, for example, the app will crash. To test the app with a new model, you have to uninstall it first to erase the old Persistent Store. If you already shipped your app to the App Store or do not want to lose the information inserted for testing, you have to migrate from the old model to the new one. We will study migration later in this chapter.

Managed Object

Core Data does not store our custom objects; it defines a class called **NSManagedObject** to provide the basic functionality for the objects stored in the Persistent Store. The class includes the following initializer and methods to create and manage the instances.

init(context: NSManagedObjectContext)—This initializer creates a new instance of the **NSManagedObject** class and adds it to the context specified by the **context** attribute.

fetchRequest()—This type method generates a fetch request for an entity. A fetch request is a request we use to fetch objects of a particular entity from the Persistent Store.

Every time we want to store information in the database, we have to create an **NSManagedObject** object, associate that object to an Entity, and store the data the entity allows. For example, if we create an object associated to the Books entity, we are only allowed to store five values that corresponds to the Entity's attributes (title, year, cover, thumbnail, and author). To simplify our work, the system lets us define subclasses of this class that correspond to the entitles of our model (Instead of creating instances of the **NSManagedObject** class, we create instances of the **Books** or **Authors** classes). Because this is a common task for any developer, Xcode does it automatically for us. All we have to do is associate each Entity with a subclass from the Data Model Inspector panel. The option is available in a section called *Class*, as shown in Figure 22-13.

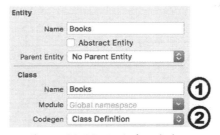

Figure 22-13: Entity's subclass

To tell Xcode to create the subclasses for us, we have to select the entities one by one, select the Class Definition value for the Codegen option (number 2), and make sure that the name of the subclass is specified in the Name field (number 1). Once the options are set, the classes are automatically created. For example, when we set these options for the entities incorporated to our model before, Xcode creates a subclass of **NSManagedObject** called **Books** with the properties **title**, **year**, **cover**, **thumbnail**, and **author**, and a second subclass called **Authors** with the properties **name** and **books**. From now on, all we have to do to store a book in the Persistent Store is to create an instance of the **Books** class.

 Do It Yourself: Click on the Core Data model file to open the model. Select the Books and the Authors entity, open the Data Model Inspector panel, and make sure that the value of the Codegen option is set to Class Definition and the name of the class is assigned to the Name field, as shown in Figure 22-13.

The Basics: The subclasses of the **NSManagedObject** class created to represent each entity in our model are not visible in Xcode. They are created internally and automatically modified every time entities or attributes are added or removed from the model. If you decide not to use these subclasses, you can select the value Manual/None from the Codegen option and work directly with **NSManagedObject** objects or define your own subclasses.

Managing Objects

As we mentioned before, all the interaction between our code and the Persistent Store is done through the context. When we want to access the objects already stored, add new ones, remove them or modify any of their values, we have to do it in the context and then move those changes from the context to the Persistent Store. To illustrate how this process works, we are going to create a simple example similar to the one we used before for Archiving in Chapter 21.

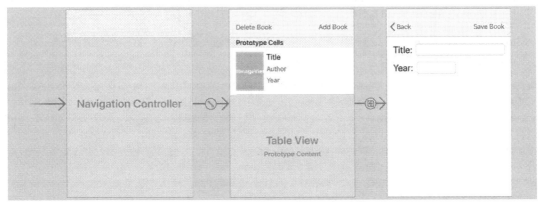

Figure 22-14: *Interface to list and add books*

The Navigation Bar in the Table View Controller includes two bar buttons: Delete Book to delete books and Add Book to add new ones. The Add Book button is connected to the second view with a Show Segue. This view includes two Text Fields to let the user insert the title and year of a new book and a bar button called Save Book to save it. To show the values in the table, we have designed a custom cell with four elements: an image view for the cover of the book and three labels for the title, author, and year. The following is the **UITableViewCell** subclass we need for this cell.

```
import UIKit

class BooksCell: UITableViewCell {
    @IBOutlet weak var bookCover: UIImageView!
    @IBOutlet weak var bookTitle: UILabel!
    @IBOutlet weak var bookAuthor: UILabel!
    @IBOutlet weak var bookYear: UILabel!
}
```

Listing 22-3: *Creating the Outlets for the elements in the prototype cell*

Do It Yourself: Delete the initial view of the project you have created for this chapter. Add a Table View Controller to the Storyboard and embed it in a Navigation Controller. Add two bar buttons to the Navigation Bar called Delete Book and Add Book. Add a new Scene. Connect the Add Book button to this Scene with a Show Segue. Add a Navigation Item to the Navigation Bar of the second view and a bar button called Save Book. Add two labels and two Text

Core Data

Fields to the second view, as illustrated in Figure 22-14. Select the prototype cell in the Table View, assign the value 100 to its height from the Size Inspector panel, and give it the identifier "booksCell" from the Attributes Inspector panel. Add to the cell an image view with Width and Height constraints of 60 and 80, respectively, and the labels "Title", "Author", and "Year". Create a **UITableViewCell** subclass called **BooksCell** and assign it to the cell. Complete the class with the code of Listing 22-3. Connect the elements in the cell to their respective Outlets.

The purpose of this application is to show the list of objects already stored in the Persistent Store and create new ones. The initial view is going to list all the books available in the Persistent Store and the second view is going to create new objects with the values provided by the user. To create a new object, we have to use the **NSManagedObject** initializer from our subclass (**Books**) and then assign the values to the object's properties. The process is introduced next in the **EditBookViewController** class we have created to control the second view.

```
import UIKit
import CoreData

class EditBookViewController: UIViewController {
    @IBOutlet weak var bookTitle: UITextField!
    @IBOutlet weak var bookYear: UITextField!
    var context: NSManagedObjectContext!

    override func viewDidLoad() {
        super.viewDidLoad()
        bookTitle.becomeFirstResponder()
        let app = UIApplication.shared
        let appDelegate = app.delegate as! AppDelegate
        context = appDelegate.context
    }
    @IBAction func saveBook(_ sender: UIBarButtonItem) {
        let year = Int32(bookYear.text!)
        let title = bookTitle.text!.trimmingCharacters(in: .whitespaces)
        if title != "" && year != nil {
            let newBook = Books(context: context)
            newBook.title = title
            newBook.year = year!
            newBook.cover = UIImage(named: "nocover")
            newBook.thumbnail = UIImage(named: "nothumbnail")
            newBook.author = nil
            do {
                try context.save()
            } catch {
                print("Error")
            }
            navigationController?.popViewController(animated: true)
        }
    }
}
```

Listing 22-4: Adding new objects to the Persistent Store

As illustrated in the example of Listing 22-2, the first thing we need to do in any view controller that wants to access Core Data is to get a reference to the context from the app's delegate and assign it to a property. In the example of Listing 22-4, we call that property **context**. When the user presses the Save Book button, the **saveBook()** method gets the values form the Text Fields and uses the reference to the context to create and store a new object into the Persistent Store. The process begins with the creation of the new object with the **Books()** initializer. This not only creates a new object of type **Books** but it also adds it to the context. The next step is to assign the values we want to store to the properties of this object. We assign the value of the first Text Field to the **title** property, the value of the second Text Field to the **year** property (casted as an **Int32** type), the images nocover.png and nothumbnail.png to the **cover** and **thumbnail** properties, respectively (the images are available on our website), and the **nil** value to the **author** property (we still don't have an **Authors** object to associate with this book).

The **Books()** initializer inserts the new object into the context, but this change is not permanent. If we close the app after the values are assigned to the properties, the object is lost. To persist the changes, we have to save the context with the **save()** method. This method takes the information in the context and modifies the Persistent Store with it, so everything is stored on file.

 Do It Yourself: Create a subclass of the **UIViewController** class called **EditBookViewController** and assign it to the second Scene. Connect the first Text Field with an Outlet called **bookTitle** and the second Text Field with an Outlet called **bookYear**. Connect the Save Book button in the Navigation Bar with an Action called **saveBook()**. Complete the class with the code of Listing 22-4.

 IMPORTANT: Because the **save()** method can throw errors, we call it inside a **do catch** statement. In this example, we just print a message if something goes wrong, but you should consider warning users with an Alert View and keeping the information safe to give them the chance to try again.

The process to get the objects back from the Persistent Store is the opposite. Instead of moving the changes in the context to the Persistent Store, we have to get the objects from the Persistent Store and move them into the context. Once the objects are in the context, we can read their properties, modify their values, or delete them. Core Data includes the **NSFetchRequest** class to request objects from the store. The class includes the following properties for configuration.

predicate—This property sets or returns the predicate used to filter the objects fetched by the request. It is a value of type **NSPredicate**, a Foundation class used to establish logical conditions that describe objects in the Persistent Store.

sortDescriptors—This property sets or returns an array of sort descriptors that determine how the objects obtained by the request should be ordered. It is an array of values of type **NSSortDescriptor**, a Foundation class used to sort the objects according to the value of a property in ascending or descending order.

fetchLimit—This property sets or returns the maximum number of objects that the request should return. It takes a value of type **Int**.

resultType—This property sets or returns a value that determines the type of data returned by the request. The framework offers the **NSFetchRequestResultType** structure with properties to define its value. The properties available are **managedObjectResultType** (it returns values of type **NSManagedObject**), **managedObjectIDResultType** (it returns the identification values of the **NSManagedObject** objects instead of the objects themselves), **dictionaryResultType** (it returns a dictionary with the values of the properties), and **countResultType** (it returns an integer value with the total of objects found).

propertiesToFetch—This property sets or returns an array of values that determine the properties we want to get (by default, all the properties of the **NSManagedObject** objects are returned). The properties of an entity (attributes) are represented by objects of the **NSPropertyDescription** class, or subclasses of it.

propertiesToGroupBy—This property sets or returns an array of **NSPropertyDescription** objects that determine the properties that are going to be used to group the **NSManagedObject** objects together. When objects are grouped together, only one value is returned per group, so this is usually used with operations performed over the values, such as counting the number of books with the same title (the property only works when the **resultType** property is set to **dictionaryResultType**).

Every time we want to read objects from the Persistent Store we have to create an **NSFetchRequest** object to determine what type of objects we want. Because the request has to be associated to an entity, the subclasses of the **NSManagedObject** class representing our entities include the **fetchRequest()** method. This method returns an **NSFetchRequest** object already associated to the entity. Once the request object is ready, we have to fetch the objects with the **fetch()** method provided by the context. The following is the view controller for the Table View of our example. The code performs a request, stores the objects in an array, and then shows their values in the table.

```swift
import UIKit
import CoreData

class BooksViewController: UITableViewController {
    var context: NSManagedObjectContext!
    var listOfBooks: [Books] = []

    override func viewDidLoad() {
        super.viewDidLoad()
        tableView.rowHeight = 100
        let app = UIApplication.shared
        let appDelegate = app.delegate as! AppDelegate
        context = appDelegate.context
    }
    override func viewWillAppear(_ animated: Bool) {
        super.viewWillAppear(animated)
        let request: NSFetchRequest<Books> = Books.fetchRequest()
        do {
            listOfBooks = try context.fetch(request)
        } catch {
            print("Error")
        }
        tableView.reloadData()
    }
    override func tableView(_ tableView: UITableView,
numberOfRowsInSection section: Int) -> Int {
        return listOfBooks.count
    }
    override func tableView(_ tableView: UITableView, cellForRowAt
indexPath: IndexPath) -> UITableViewCell {
        let cell = tableView.dequeueReusableCell(withIdentifier:
"booksCell", for: indexPath) as! BooksCell
        let book = listOfBooks[indexPath.row]
        cell.bookTitle.text = book.title
        cell.bookCover.image = book.thumbnail as? UIImage
        cell.bookYear.text = "Year: \(book.year)"
```

```
        let author = book.author
        if author != nil {
           cell.bookAuthor.text = author!.name
        } else {
           cell.bookAuthor.text = "Not Defined"
        }
        return cell
    }
}
```

Listing 22-5: Fetching values from the Persistent Store

There are different places from where we can perform a request, depending on the requirements of our application. In this example, we do it from the `viewWillAppear()` method, so the objects are retrieved and the table is updated every time the user opens the view. To make a request, we first have to get the `NSFetchRequest` object by calling the `fetchRequest()` method on the subclass that corresponds to the objects we want to read (in this case we want to get books, so we call it on the `Books` class). The next step is to fetch the objects with the context's `fetch()` method. This method returns an array of objects that we can assign to a property to be able to access the values from other methods in the class. In this example, we called that property `listOfBooks`.

 IMPORTANT: The `NSFetchRequest` class is generic. We have studied how to create generic functions in Chapter 3, but you can also create generic structures and classes. When a generic class is initialized, we have to specify the data type that the instance is going to use between angle brackets (`NSFetchRequest<Books>`). This is why you can also initialize generic arrays, sets and dictionaries with the data type between angle brackets, as we mentioned in Chapter 2 (`var myarray = Array<Int>()`).

Once we get the objects in an array, the rest of the process is similar to any other example we have seen before. We have to get the `Books` object that corresponds to the cell from the `listOfBooks` property and then assign the values of its properties to the elements of the cell. In the case of the `author` property, because we are allowing the user to store books without an author, we compare it to `nil` and then show the name of the author or a message indicating that the author was not defined. The result is illustrated in Figure 22-15.

Figure 22-15: Adding books to a Persistent Store

 Do It Yourself: Create a `UITableViewController` subclass called `BooksViewController` and assign it to the Table View Controller. Complete the class with the code of Listing 22-5. Download the images nocover.png and nothumbnail.png from our website and add them to the Assets Catalog. Run the application. The first screen will show an empty Table View (Figure 22-15, left). Press the Add Book button and insert the values of a book (Figure 22-15, center). At the end, the table should look like the right picture of Figure 22-15.

Core Data

The **Authors** objects are generated and stored exactly the same way as the **Books** objects. This demands our application to provide new views where the user can select and add new objects. For our example, we have decided to expand our interface with another Table View Controller to list the authors available and another single view to insert more. To provide access to these new views, we have added a button called Select Author to the **EditBookViewController**'s view, along with a label to show the name of the author.

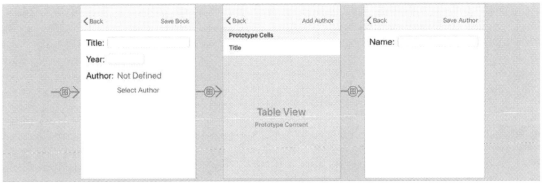

Figure 22-16: Interface to list and add authors

When the user presses the Add Book button in the initial view (Figure 22-14, center), the next view now shows three input options, a Text Field to insert the title of the book, a Text Field to insert the year, and the Select Author button to select the author (Figure 22-16, left). This button is connected with a Show Segue to a Table View Controller that lists all the authors available (Figure 22-16, center). In addition, this Table View Controller includes a bar button called Add Author to open a view that includes a Text Field to insert the name of a new author (Figure 22-16, right).

 Do It Yourself: Add two labels and a button called Select Author to the **EditBookViewController**'s view (Figure 22-16, left). Add a Table View Controller to the Storyboard and connect the Select Author button to this view with a Show Segue (Figure 22-16, center). Select the cell in the new Table View and change its style to Basic and its identifier to "authorsCell". Add a bar button to this view called Add Author. Add a new Scene to the Storyboard and connect the Add Author button to this view with a Show Segue (Figure 22-16, right). Add a label, an input field, and a bar button called Save Author to the last view. Your interface should look like the combination of Figures 22-15 and 22-17.

Every time an author is selected or created, we have to get its **Authors** object and send it back to the **EditBookViewController** class to assign it to the book. As we have already seen, there are different ways to do it, but for this example we are going to use Unwind Segues (see Chapter 13, Figure 13-19). We need two Unwind Segues, one that is triggered when the user selects an author from the Table View Controller, and another that is triggered when the user inserts a new author. When the Unwind Segues are triggered, we have to get the **Authors** object that represents the author and update the view with the value of its **name** property. To receive and process this information, we have to modify the **EditBookViewController** class to include the Action for the Unwind Segues and properties to store and manage the **Authors** object.

```
import UIKit
import CoreData
```

```
class EditBookViewController: UIViewController {
    @IBOutlet weak var bookTitle: UITextField!
    @IBOutlet weak var bookYear: UITextField!
    @IBOutlet weak var authorName: UILabel!
    var context: NSManagedObjectContext!
    var selectedAuthor: Authors!

    override func viewDidLoad() {
        super.viewDidLoad()
        bookTitle.becomeFirstResponder()
        let app = UIApplication.shared
        let appDelegate = app.delegate as! AppDelegate
        context = appDelegate.context
    }
    @IBAction func saveBook(_ sender: UIBarButtonItem) {
        let year = Int32(bookYear.text!)
        let title = bookTitle.text!.trimmingCharacters(in: .whitespaces)
        if title != "" && year != nil {
            let newBook = Books(context: context)
            newBook.title = title
            newBook.year = year!
            newBook.cover = UIImage(named: "nocover")
            newBook.thumbnail = UIImage(named: "nothumbnail")
            newBook.author = selectedAuthor

            do {
                try context.save()
            } catch {
                print("Error")
            }
            navigationController?.popViewController(animated: true)
        }
    }
    @IBAction func backAuthor(_ segue: UIStoryboardSegue) {
        if segue.identifier == "backFromList" {
            let controller = segue.source as! AuthorsViewController
            selectedAuthor = controller.selectedAuthor
            authorName.text = selectedAuthor.name
        } else if segue.identifier == "backFromNew" {
            let controller = segue.source as! EditAuthorViewController
            selectedAuthor = controller.selectedAuthor
            authorName.text = selectedAuthor.name
        }
    }
}
```

Listing 22-6: Adding an author to the book

The view controller of Listing 22-6 manages the view that lets the user insert new books. When the user selects or inserts a new author, the **backAuthor()** method is executed (due to the Unwind Segues we will create later), and the code gets the **Authors** object that represents the author, assigns it to the **selectedAuthor** property to let other methods have access to it, and updates the label on the screen with the value of its **name** property (this process is done twice, one for each Unwind Segue).

The process to list and create new **Authors** objects is exactly the same we used for books. The following is the view controller for the Table View Controller added to the interface in Figure 22-16. We called it **AuthorsViewController**.

Core Data

```
import UIKit
import CoreData

class AuthorsViewController: UITableViewController {
    var context: NSManagedObjectContext!
    var listOfAuthors: [Authors] = []
    var selectedAuthor: Authors!

    override func viewDidLoad() {
        super.viewDidLoad()
        let app = UIApplication.shared
        let appDelegate = app.delegate as! AppDelegate
        context = appDelegate.context
    }
    override func viewWillAppear(_ animated: Bool) {
        super.viewWillAppear(animated)
        let request: NSFetchRequest<Authors> = Authors.fetchRequest()
        do {
            listOfAuthors = try context.fetch(request)
        } catch {
            print("Error")
        }
        tableView.reloadData()
    }
    override func tableView(_ tableView: UITableView,
numberOfRowsInSection section: Int) -> Int {
        return listOfAuthors.count
    }
    override func tableView(_ tableView: UITableView, cellForRowAt
indexPath: IndexPath) -> UITableViewCell {
        let cell = tableView.dequeueReusableCell(withIdentifier:
"authorsCell", for: indexPath)
        let author = listOfAuthors[indexPath.row]
        cell.textLabel?.text = author.name
        return cell
    }
    override func tableView(_ tableView: UITableView, didSelectRowAt
indexPath: IndexPath) {
        selectedAuthor = listOfAuthors[indexPath.row]
        performSegue(withIdentifier: "backFromList", sender: self)
    }
}
```

Listing 22-7: Listing authors

Other than changing the name for the array (**listOfAuthors**), the rest of the code, including the fetch request, is exactly the same we used to list books. This time we implement a cell with a Basic style, so all we have to do to show the authors in the Table View is to get the value of their **name** property and assign it to the label in the cell.

This code also implements the protocol method **tableView(UITableView, didSelectRowAt:)** to assign the selected author to the **selectedAuthor** property and trigger the Unwind Segue (the example assumes that we have created an Unwind Segue from the Table View Controller to the **backAuthor()** Action and have identified the Segue with the string "backFromList". Unwind Segues are explained in Chapter 13, Figures 13-16 and 13-19).

The view controller to add new authors is also very similar to the one we used to add new books. We have to take the text inserted by the user in the Text Field, create the new **Authors** object to represent the author, save the context, and finally trigger the Unwind Segue to move back to the **EditBookViewController**'s view (again, the example assumes that we have created an Unwind Segue from this Scene to the **backAuthor()** Action identified with the string "backFromNew"). We called this view controller **EditAuthorViewController**.

```
import UIKit
import CoreData

class EditAuthorViewController: UIViewController {
   @IBOutlet weak var authorName: UITextField!
   var context: NSManagedObjectContext!
   var selectedAuthor: Authors!

   override func viewDidLoad() {
      super.viewDidLoad()
      authorName.becomeFirstResponder()
      let app = UIApplication.shared
      let appDelegate = app.delegate as! AppDelegate
      context = appDelegate.context
   }
   @IBAction func saveAuthor(_ sender: UIBarButtonItem) {
      let name = authorName.text!.trimmingCharacters(in: .whitespaces)
      if name != "" {
         selectedAuthor = Authors(context: context)
         selectedAuthor.name = name
         do {
            try context.save()
            performSegue(withIdentifier: "backFromNew", sender: self)
         } catch {
            print("Error")
         }
      }
   }
}
```

Listing 22-8: Inserting new authors

With these additions, our basic app is complete. Now authors can be assigned to new books. When we pressed the Select Author button, the app opens a Table View with all the authors available (Figure 22-17, center). If there are no authors yet or the one we want is not on the list, we can press the Add Author button and insert a new one (Figure 22-17, right). Every time we select an author from the list or insert a new one, the app goes back to the view with the book's information and shows the name of the selected author on the screen (Figure 22-17, left). The **Authors** object that represents the author is assigned to the book's **author** property and therefore the name of the author is now shown on the list of books.

Figure 22-17: Assigning an author to a book

Core Data

Do It Yourself: Update the `EditBookViewController` class with the code of Listing 22-6. Connect the label that is going to show the name of the author to the Outlet `authorName`. Create a `UITableViewController` subclass called `AuthorsViewController` and assign it to the new Table View Controller (Figure 22-16, center). Complete the class with the code of Listing 22-7. Create an Unwind Segue to the `backAuthor()` method for this view with the identifier "backFromList" (see Figure 13-19). Create a `UIViewController` subclass called `EditAuthorViewController` and assign it to the last Scene (Figure 22-16, right). Connect the Text Field in this view with an Outlet called `authorName` and complete the `EditAuthorViewController` class with the code of Listing 22-8. Create an Unwind Segue to the `backAuthor()` method for this view with the identifier "backFromNew" (see Figure 13-19). Run the application and press the Add New Book button. Press the Select Author button and insert the name of an author. Save the book. You should see a list of books with their respective authors.

Images

Storing images in a database, as we did in these examples, is convenient but not always appropriate. Storing large amounts of data in a persistent store can affect the system's performance and slow down essential processes like searching for values or migrating the model. One alternative is to store the image on disk and only keep its URL in the database, but this is a complex process. The application has to select a unique name for the file, determine its URL, and then store it. When it is time to read it back, it has to get the URL, read the file, and recreate the `UIImage` object from it. This process gets even more complex when the images has to be shared between devices, as we will see in the next chapter. Fortunately, Core Data can perform this process for us. All we have to do is to store the image as Binary Data instead of Transformable and select the option Allow External Storage, available in the Data Model inspector panel inside the Utilities Area, as shown in Figure 22-18.

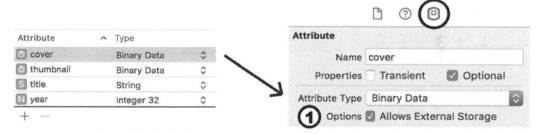

Figure 22-18: Option to store images outside the Persistent Store

As mentioned before, to store the images as Binary Data, we have to convert the images to raw data ourselves. For this purpose, we can use the methods provided by the `UIImage` class. For instance, the `pngData()` method returns the `Data` structure required to store the image in the persistent store. The following example shows the modifications we have to introduce to the `saveBook()` method in our `EditBookViewController` class to work with Binary Data instead of Transformable.

```
@IBAction func saveBook(_ sender: UIBarButtonItem) {
   let year = Int32(bookYear.text!)
   let title = bookTitle.text!.trimmingCharacters(in: .whitespaces)
   if title != "" && year != nil {
      let newBook = Books(context: context)
      newBook.title = title
      newBook.year = year!
```

```
    let nocover = UIImage(named: "nocover")
    let nothumbnail = UIImage(named: "nothumbnail")
    newBook.cover = nocover?.pngData()
    newBook.thumbnail = nothumbnail?.pngData()
    newBook.author = selectedAuthor

    do {
        try context.save()
    } catch {
        print("Error")
    }
    navigationController?.popViewController(animated: true)
    }
}
```

Listing 22-9: Converting images into raw data

To perform the opposite process, convert the data back into an image, we have to recreate the **UIImage** object from the value stored in the persistent store using the **UIImage(data:)** initializer. The following code shows the modifications we have to introduce to our **BooksViewController** class.

```
override func tableView(_ tableView: UITableView, cellForRowAt indexPath: IndexPath) -> UITableViewCell {
    let cell = tableView.dequeueReusableCell(withIdentifier: "booksCell", for: indexPath) as! BooksCell

    let book = listOfBooks[indexPath.row]
    cell.bookTitle.text = book.title
    if book.thumbnail != nil {
        cell.bookCover.image = UIImage(data: book.thumbnail!)
    }
    cell.bookYear.text = "Year: \(book.year)"

    let author = book.author
    if author != nil {
        cell.bookAuthor.text = author!.name
    } else {
        cell.bookAuthor.text = "Not Defined"
    }
    return cell
}
```

Listing 22-10: Getting back the images from data

In the code of Listing 22-10, we check whether the **thumbnail** property contains an image and then recreate the **UIImage** object from its value. The initializer used in this example doesn't include the attribute for the scale because we consider all the images in this application to be of a scale of 1, but that may change in other circumstances.

 Do It Yourself: Select the Book entity in your Core Data Model. Change the type of the cover and thumbnail attributes to Binary Data. Click on each attribute and select the option Allows External Storage from the Data Model Inspector panel (Figure 22-18). Update the **EditBookViewController** and **BooksViewController** classes with the codes of Listings 22-9 and 22-10. The application should work as it did before, but now the images are automatically stored on disk instead of the database.

Core Data

Counting Objects

The **NSManagedObjectContext** class includes the **count()** method to count the number of objects in a request. The method returns an integer with the number of objects we would get if we call the **fetch()** method with the same request. The method does not fetch the objects, so we can call it without being afraid of consuming too much memory. For example, we can use it in the **EditBookViewController** class to get the number of authors already available.

```
override func viewDidLoad() {
   super.viewDidLoad()

   bookTitle.becomeFirstResponder()
   let app = UIApplication.shared
   let appDelegate = app.delegate as! AppDelegate
   context = appDelegate.context

   let request: NSFetchRequest<Authors> = Authors.fetchRequest()
   if let total = try? context.count(for: request) {
      print("Total Authors: (\(total))")
   }
}
```

Listing 22-11: Counting the authors available

 Do It Yourself: Replace the **viewDidLoad()** method of Listing 22-6 by the method of Listing 22-11. In this example, we just print the result on the console, but you could add a new label to the view managed by the **EditBookViewController** class and show the value to the user.

If what we want is to get the number of objects associated to a To-Many relationship, we just have to count the number of items returned by the property that represents the relationship. For example, we can count the number of books of every author and show it along with the name.

```
override func tableView(_ tableView: UITableView, cellForRowAt indexPath:
IndexPath) -> UITableViewCell {
   let cell = tableView.dequeueReusableCell(withIdentifier:
"authorsCell", for: indexPath)
   let author = listOfAuthors[indexPath.row]
   let name = author.name

   var total = 0
   if let totalBooks = author.books {
      total = totalBooks.count
   }
   cell.textLabel?.text = "\(name!) (\(total))"
   return cell
}
```

Listing 22-12: Counting the books of each author

The method of Listing 22-12 replaces the same method in the **AuthorsViewController** class of Listing 22-7. Instead of assigning just the name of the author to the cell's label, we get the books associated with each author, assign it to the **totalBooks** constant, and then create a string with the name plus the number of books available from that author.

Predicates

The requests performed in previous examples are getting all the objects associated to a particular entity and the values of all their properties. The Core Data framework defines a class called **NSPredicate** to set filters that allow us to fetch only the objects that comply to certain rules. For example, we could get only the books that were published in the year 1983. The class defines the following initializer to create a predicate with all the conditions we need.

NSPredicate(format: String, **argumentArray:** [Any]?**)**—This initializer creates a **NSPredicate** object with the conditions set by the **format** attribute. The **argumentArray** attribute is an optional array of values that replace placeholders in the string assigned to the **format** attribute. The **argumentArray** attribute may be ignored or replaced by a list of values separated by commas.

To filter values in a request, we have to create the **NSPredicate** object and assign it to the request's **predicate** property. The following example assigns an **NSPredicate** object to the **predicate** property of the request in the **BooksViewController** class to search for the books that has the value 1983 assigned to their **year** property.

```
override func viewWillAppear(_ animated: Bool) {
   super.viewWillAppear(animated)

   let request: NSFetchRequest<Books> = Books.fetchRequest()
   request.predicate = NSPredicate(format: "year = 1983")
   do {
      listOfBooks = try context.fetch(request)
   } catch {
      print("Error")
   }
   tableView.reloadData()
}
```

Listing 22-13: Filtering books by year

If we are trying to search for a value in a relationship, we can concatenate the properties with dot notation in a construction called *key path*. For example, the following request searches for books written by Stephen King.

```
override func viewWillAppear(_ animated: Bool) {
   super.viewWillAppear(animated)

   let request: NSFetchRequest<Books> = Books.fetchRequest()
   request.predicate = NSPredicate(format: "author.name = 'Stephen
King'")
   do {
      listOfBooks = try context.fetch(request)
   } catch {
      print("Error")
   }
   tableView.reloadData()
}
```

Listing 22-14: Filtering books by author

The name of the author was inserted inside the string using single quotes, but we do not always know beforehand what value we have to search for. To incorporate the value of a variable inside the formatted string, we can use placeholders. Placing the characters %@ inside the string, for example, indicates to the initializer that the value in the **arguments** attribute goes in that place.

```
override func viewWillAppear(_ animated: Bool) {
    super.viewWillAppear(animated)
    let search = "Stephen King"
    let request: NSFetchRequest<Books> = Books.fetchRequest()
    request.predicate = NSPredicate(format: "author.name = %@", search)
    do {
        listOfBooks = try context.fetch(request)
    } catch {
        print("Error")
    }
    tableView.reloadData()
}
```

Listing 22-15: Creating filters with placeholders

We may include all the placeholders and arguments we need. The placeholders are replaced by the arguments one by one, in consecutive order, as with formatted strings (see **String** Structures in Chapter 3). For example, we can search for books of a particular author and year (notice that since the value of the **year** property is an integer we have to use the %d placeholder).

```
override func viewWillAppear(_ animated: Bool) {
    super.viewWillAppear(animated)
    let search = "Stephen King"
    let year = 1983
    let request: NSFetchRequest<Books> = Books.fetchRequest()
    request.predicate = NSPredicate(format: "author.name = %@ && year =
%d", search, year)
    do {
        listOfBooks = try context.fetch(request)
    } catch {
        print("Error")
    }
    tableView.reloadData()
}
```

Listing 22-16: Creating filters with multiple values

 Do It Yourself: Replace the **viewWillAppear()** method in the **BooksViewController** class of Listing 22-5 by any of the methods presented above to see how predicates work. Add books with different authors and years to test the filters.

 IMPORTANT: The placeholder %@ is replaced by the value specified in the attributes between quotes. If you need to add the value to the predicate without the quotes, you have to use the placeholder %K instead (usually called *Dynamic Key*). We will see an example in Chapter 23.

Predicates use comparison and logical operators similar to those offered by Swift. For example, we can compare values with the operators =, !=, >, <, >= and <=, and also concatenate conditions with the characters **&&** (or the word **AND**), **||** (or the word **OR**) and **!** (or the word **NOT**). Predicates also include keywords for a more precise search. The following are the most frequently used.

BEGINSWITH—The condition determined by this keyword is true when the expression on the left begins with the expression on the right.

CONTAINS—The condition determined by this keyword is true when the expression on the left contains the expression on the right.

ENDSWITH—The condition determined by this keyword is true when the expression on the left ends with the expression on the right.

LIKE—The condition determined by this keyword is true when the expression on the left is equal to the expression on the right.

IN—The condition determined by this keyword is true when the expression on the left is equal to any of the values included in the expression on the right. The values are provided as an array between parentheses.

These keywords may be accompanied by the characters **c** or **d** between square brackets to specify a case and diacritic insensitive search. For example, we may search for authors with a name beginning with the word "stephen", without considering upper- or lower-case letters.

```
override func viewWillAppear(_ animated: Bool) {
   super.viewWillAppear(animated)

   let search = "stephen"
   let request: NSFetchRequest<Books> = Books.fetchRequest()
   request.predicate = NSPredicate(format: "author.name BEGINSWITH[c]
%@", search)
   do {
      listOfBooks = try context.fetch(request)
   } catch {
      print("Error")
   }
   tableView.reloadData()
}
```

Listing 22-17: Filtering values with predicate keywords

 IMPORTANT: The list of keywords and options to create conditions for predicates is extensive. The topic is beyond the scope of this book. For more information, visit our website and follow the links for this chapter.

 The Basics: Diacritics are the small marks used in certain languages to change the pronunciation of a letter, like the visible stress over Spanish vowels. When we specify the character **d** between square brackets, the search ignores these marks and looks for the letter in its basic form. The **c** and **d** characters are usually implemented together, as in **[cd]**.

A practical application of predicates is to check for duplicates. The inclusion of duplicated values is something that every application must be prepared to prevent. For example, if in the application we have created so far, we insert an author that already exists, two Authors objects with the same name are stored in the Persistent Store. To avoid this situation, we can use a request with a predicate that searches for authors of the same name before creating a new object. The following example modifies the **saveAuthor()** method of the **EditAuthorViewController** class to avoid duplicates.

```
@IBAction func saveAuthor(_ sender: UIBarButtonItem) {
    let name = authorName.text!.trimmingCharacters(in: .whitespaces)
    if name != "" {
        let request: NSFetchRequest<Authors> = Authors.fetchRequest()
        request.predicate = NSPredicate(format: "name = %@", name)
        if let total = try? context.count(for: request) {
            if total == 0 {
                selectedAuthor = Authors(context: context)
                selectedAuthor.name = name
                do {
                    try context.save()
                    performSegue(withIdentifier: "backFromNew", sender: self)
                } catch {
                    print("Error")
                }
            }
        }
    }
}
```

Listing 22-18: Checking for duplicates

The method of Listing 22-18 creates a request for the Authors entity and uses the value inserted in the Text Field by the user to create a predicate. The predicate searches for objects with the name equal to the value of the **name** constant. Using this request, we call the **count()** method in the context to get the total amount of objects that match the conditions in the predicate. If the value returned is 0, we know that there are no authors in the Persistent Store with that name and we can create and add the new **Authors** object.

 Do It Yourself: Replace the **saveAuthor()** method in the **EditAuthor-ViewController** class of Listing 22-9 by the method of Listing 22-18. Run the application and try to insert an author that already exists. Use the same filter in the **EditBookViewController** class to avoid duplicates when inserting new books. You can create a predicate that checks for books with the same title and author (the placeholder characters %@ can take any kind of values and objects, including **NSManagedObject** objects).

Sort Descriptors

Objects returned from a request are usually in the order they were created, but this is not guaranteed. To sort the objects in a specific order, Core Data lets us associate the request with an object of type **NSSortDescriptor**. From this class, we can create objects that specify an order according to the values of a property. The sorting criteria is determined by methods provided by the values themselves. For example, data types like **Date** implement only the **compare()** methods to compare their values, but the **NSString** class implements other methods that allow us to do things like order strings without differentiating between lower- and upper-case letters (see **NSString** in Chapter 4). By default, an **NSSortDescriptor** object uses the **compare()** method to compare any type of value, but we can specify others from the initializers.

NSSortDescriptor(key: String?, **ascending:** Bool)—This initializer creates an **NSSortDescriptor** object that orders the objects according to the value of the property specified by the **key** attribute. The **key** attribute is a string with the name of the property, and the **ascending** attribute determines if the objects will be sort in ascending or descending order. The object created by this initializer sorts the values with the **compare()** method.

NSSortDescriptor(key: String?, **ascending:** Bool, **selector:** Selector?)—This initializer creates an **NSSortDescriptor** object that orders the objects according to the value of the property specified by the **key** attribute. The **key** attribute is a string with the name of the property, the **ascending** attribute determines if the objects will be sorted in ascending or descending order, and the **selector** attribute is the comparison method that determines the sorting criteria.

The **FetchRequest** class includes the **sortDescriptors** property to define the order of a request. All we have to do to order the objects is to create at least one **NSSortDescriptor** object and assign it to this property. The following example sorts the **Books** objects by title in ascending order.

```
override func viewWillAppear(_ animated: Bool) {
   super.viewWillAppear(animated)

   let request: NSFetchRequest<Books> = Books.fetchRequest()
   let sort = NSSortDescriptor(key: "title", ascending: true)
   request.sortDescriptors = [sort]
   do {
      listOfBooks = try context.fetch(request)
   } catch {
      print("Error")
   }
   tableView.reloadData()
}
```

Listing 22-19: Sorting the books by title

The **sortDescriptors** property takes an array of **NSSortDescriptor** objects, so we can specify different conditions to sort the list. The final order is established according to the location of the **NSSortDescriptor** objects in the array. For example, we can sort the books by author first and then by year.

```
override func viewWillAppear(_ animated: Bool) {
   super.viewWillAppear(animated)

   let request: NSFetchRequest<Books> = Books.fetchRequest()
   let sort1 = NSSortDescriptor(key: "author.name", ascending: true)
   let sort2 = NSSortDescriptor(key: "year", ascending: true)
   request.sortDescriptors = [sort1, sort2]
   do {
      listOfBooks = try context.fetch(request)
   } catch {
      print("Error")
   }
   tableView.reloadData()
}
```

Listing 22-20: Sorting books by author and year

When we compare string values, we can use other comparison methods than **compare()**. The method must be assigned to the **selector** attribute of the **NSSortDescriptor** initializer. The most frequently used method is **caseInsensitiveCompare()** because it compares values without differentiating between lowercase and uppercase letters. The following example implements this method to sort the books by title.

Core Data

```
override func viewWillAppear(_ animated: Bool) {
   super.viewWillAppear(animated)
   let request: NSFetchRequest<Books> = Books.fetchRequest()
   let sort = NSSortDescriptor(key: "title", ascending: true, selector:
#selector(NSString.caseInsensitiveCompare(_:)))
   request.sortDescriptors = [sort]
   do {
      listOfBooks = try context.fetch(request)
   } catch {
      print("Error")
   }
   tableView.reloadData()
}
```

Listing 22-21: Sorting by title without differentiating between lowercase and uppercase letters

 Do It Yourself: Replace the **viewWillAppear()** method in the **BooksView-Controller** class of Listing 22-5 by any of the methods presented above to see how sort descriptors work.

Delete Objects

In the initial interface presented in Figure 22-14, we included a bar button called Delete Book to activate the table's edition mode, but we have not seen how to delete **NSManagedObject** objects yet. The **NSManagedObjectContext** class offers the **delete()** method for this purpose. The method takes a reference to the **NSManagedObject** object we want to delete and removes it from the context. As always, the change is only performed in the context, so we have to save it, or the object will not be deleted from the Persistent Store.

The following are the two methods we have to incorporate to the **BooksViewController** class of Listing 22-5 to activate the table's edition mode and delete the **Books** object from the Persistent Store when the user presses the Delete button.

```
@IBAction func editBooks(_ sender: UIBarButtonItem) {
   if tableView.isEditing {
      tableView.setEditing(false, animated: true)
   } else {
      tableView.setEditing(true, animated: true)
   }
}
override func tableView(_ tableView: UITableView, commit editingStyle:
UITableViewCell.EditingStyle, forRowAt indexPath: IndexPath) {
   if editingStyle == .delete {
      let book = listOfBooks[indexPath.row]
      context.delete(book)
      do {
         try context.save()
         listOfBooks.remove(at: indexPath.row)
         tableView.deleteRows(at: [indexPath], with: .automatic)
         tableView.setEditing(false, animated: true)
      } catch {
         print("Error")
      }
   }
}
```

Listing 22-22: Deleting a book

The first method is the Action we have to associate to the Delete Books button. As always, this method activates or deactivates the table's edition mode depending on its current state. When the mode is activated and the user presses the Delete button in one of the rows, the table calls the **tableView(UITableView, commit:, forRowAt:)** method on its delegate to perform the action. This method has to check if the style of the action is **delete** and then erase the object from the context, remove it from the array, and save the context, in that order. In the code of Listing 22-22, we get the **Books** object from the **listOfBooks** array corresponding to the row selected by the user and then call the **delete()** method to remove it from the context. The context is saved and, if no error is found, the object is removed from the **listOfBooks** array and the row is deleted from the table.

 Do It Yourself: Add the methods of Listing 22-22 to the **BooksView-Controller** class of Listing 22-5. Connect the Delete Book button on the Navigation Bar to the **editBooks()** method. Run the application, press the Delete Book button and remove a book. Stop and run the application again to check that the book was removed from the Persistent Store.

 IMPORTANT: If we need to delete several objects in the same action, we have to call the **save()** method at the end to improve performance. This also applies to other operations with the context.

22.2 Fetched Results Controller

Working with arrays to store the results returned by a request is not recommended most of the time. Tables are capable of managing thousands of items and putting all those items in an array consumes too much memory. The solution is to get from the Persistent Store only the objects the table needs at a particular moment, but this is error prone and demands our code to keep track of the elements already loaded and request only those that we do not have. Programming an application to do this work efficiently is difficult. For this reason, Core Data offers the **NSFetchedResultsController** class. This class provides highly optimized code that intermediates between the table and the Persistent Store; taking care of fetching the objects the table needs and updating the list of objects available when some are modified, added, or removed. To create the controller, the class provides the following initializer.

NSFetchedResultsController(fetchRequest: NSFetchRequest, **managed-ObjectContext:** NSManagedObjectContext, **sectionNameKeyPath:** String?, **cacheName:** String?)—This initializer creates an **NSFetchedResultsController** object that fetches **NSManagedObject** objects from the Persistent Store according to the request specified by the **fetchRequest** attribute. The **fetchRequest** attribute is an **NSFetchRequest** object with the request we want the controller to use to get the objects, the **managedObjectContext** attribute is a reference to the Core Data context, the **sectionNameKeyPath** attribute identifies the name of the property used to create the table's sections, and the **cacheName** attribute defines the name of the file the controller uses to cache the objects returned by the request.

When we work with an **NSFetchedResultsController** object, we have to ask this object for any information we need about the request (the objects returned, their values, etc.). The class offers the following properties and methods to access its values.

fetchRequest—This property returns a reference to the **NSFetchRequest** object that defines the request used by the controller.

fetchedObjects—This property returns an array with the **NSManagedObjects** currently fetched by the controller.

sections—This property returns an array of objects with information about every section of the table. The objects implement the properties defined in the `NSFetched-ResultsSectionInfo` protocol to provide this information.

sectionIndexTitles—This property returns an array of strings with the titles for the index of every section.

performFetch()—This method executes the fetch request set for the controller. The controller does not return any value until this method is called.

object(at: IndexPath)—This method returns the `NSManagedObject` object at the index path specified by the **at** attribute.

indexPath(forObject: ResultType)—This method returns the index path of the `NSManagedObject` object specified by the **forObject** attribute. The value returned is an `IndexPath` structure.

After the `NSFetchedResultsController` object is initialized, we have to call its `performFetch()` method to execute the request. The results produced by the request are stored in a temporal container and automatically updated by the `NSFetchedResultsController` object every time a modification is introduced to the context (an object is modified, deleted, moved, or new objects are added). Because of the close relationship between this controller and the Table View, it is important to make sure that all the changes are immediately reflected on the table. Core Data simplifies this task with the addition of the `NSFetchedResultsControllerDelegate` protocol. The protocol defines methods that are called every time a change occurred in the objects managed by the `NSFetchedResultsController` object, and therefore we can use them to update the table.

controllerWillChangeContent(NSFetchedResultsController)—This method is called on the delegate when the controller is going to start processing changes.

controller(NSFetchedResultsController, **didChange:** AnyObject, **at:** IndexPath?, **for:** NSFetchedResultsChangeType, **newIndexPath:** IndexPath?)— This method is called on the delegate when an object managed by the controller changed. The **didChange** attribute is a reference to the `NSManagedObject` object that changed, the **at** and **newIndexPath** attributes are `IndexPath` structures that represent the old and the new index path of the object, and the **for** attribute is an enumeration that indicates the type of change. The possible values are `insert`, `delete`, `move`, and `update`.

controller(NSFetchedResultsController, **didChange:** NSFetchedResultsSection-Info, **atSectionIndex:** Int, **for:** NSFetchedResultsChangeType)—This method is called on the delegate when a section changed. The **didChange** attribute is an object that conforms to the `NSFetchedResultsSectionInfo` protocol to provide information about the section, the **atSectionIndex** attribute is an integer with the index of the section, and the **for** attribute is an enumeration that indicates the type of change. The possible values are `insert`, `delete`, `move`, and `update`.

controllerDidChangeContent(NSFetchedResultsController)—This method is called on the delegate when the controller finished processing changes.

controller(NSFetchedResultsController, **sectionIndexTitleForSectionName:** String)—This method is called on the delegate to get the title for the index of a section. The **sectionIndexTitleForSectionName** attribute defines the name of the section. If the method is not implemented, the controller returns the capitalized first letter of the section's name.

A Table View associated with an **NSFetchedResultsController** object works exactly like any other table; with the exception that now the information is provided by the object instead of an array. In the following example, we modify the **BooksViewController** class introduced in Listing 22-5 to fetch books using an **NSFetchedReusltsController** object.

```
import UIKit
import CoreData

class BooksViewController: UITableViewController,
NSFetchedResultsControllerDelegate {
    var context: NSManagedObjectContext!
    var fetchedController: NSFetchedResultsController<Books>!

    override func viewDidLoad() {
        super.viewDidLoad()

        tableView.rowHeight = 100
        let app = UIApplication.shared
        let appDelegate = app.delegate as! AppDelegate
        context = appDelegate.context

        let request: NSFetchRequest<Books> = Books.fetchRequest()
        let sort = NSSortDescriptor(key: "title", ascending: true,
selector: #selector(NSString.caseInsensitiveCompare(_:)))
        request.sortDescriptors = [sort]
        fetchedController = NSFetchedResultsController(fetchRequest:
request, managedObjectContext: context, sectionNameKeyPath: nil,
cacheName: nil)
        fetchedController.delegate = self
        do {
            try fetchedController.performFetch()
        } catch {
            print("Error")
        }
    }
    override func tableView(_ tableView: UITableView,
numberOfRowsInSection section: Int) -> Int {
        if let sections = fetchedController.sections {
            let sectionInfo = sections[section]
            return sectionInfo.numberOfObjects
        }
        return 0
    }
    override func tableView(_ tableView: UITableView, cellForRowAt
indexPath: IndexPath) -> UITableViewCell {
        let cell = tableView.dequeueReusableCell(withIdentifier:
"booksCell", for: indexPath) as! BooksCell
        updateCell(cell: cell, path: indexPath)
        return cell
    }
    func updateCell(cell: BooksCell, path: IndexPath) {
        let book = fetchedController.object(at: path)
        cell.bookTitle.text = book.title
        if book.thumbnail != nil {
            cell.bookCover.image = UIImage(data: book.thumbnail!)
        }
        let year = book.year
        cell.bookYear.text = "Year: \(year)"
        let authorName = book.author?.name
```

```
        if authorName != nil {
          cell.bookAuthor.text = authorName
        } else {
          cell.bookAuthor.text = "Not Defined"
        }
      }
   }
}
```

Listing 22-23: Fetching objects with an NSFetchedResultsController *object*

The first thing we need to do as soon as the view is loaded is to initialize the **NSFetchedResultsController** object and call its **performFetch()** method to execute the request. The request must include a sort descriptor for the controller to know the order in which the **Books** objects are going to be offered to the table, so in Listing 22-23 we create the **NSFetchRequest** object for the Books entity and assign to it a sort descriptor that orders the books by title. Besides the request, the **NSFetchedResultsController** initializer requires three more values: a reference to the context, the name of the property that is going to be used to create the sections for the table, and the name of the file used to cache the information for better performance. In this example, we are not going to use the last two parameters, so we declared them as **nil**.

The next step is to tell the table how many rows it has to create per section from the **tableView(UITableView,   numberOfRowsInSection:)**   method.   The **NSFetchedResultsController** class was designed to work with sections and defines objects that implement properties of the **NSFetchedResultsSectionInfo** protocol to provide information for every section, including the number of objects they contain. The properties defined by this protocol are the following.

numberOfObjects—This property returns an integer with the number of objects designated to the section.

objects—This property returns an array with references to the objects in the section.

name—This property returns the name of the section.

indexTitle—This property returns the index's title for the section (by default, the index's title is the capitalized first letter of the name of the section).

In the **tableView(UITableView, numberOfRowsInSection:)** method of Listing 22-23 we read the **sections** property of the **NSFetchedResultsController** object to get the array of objects that represent the sections, get the object corresponding to the current section, and return the value of its **numberOfObjects** property to tell the table how many objects are in the section.

The last step to configure the table is to get the values of every cell. For this example, we configured the cell in a separate method called **updateCell()** because, as we will see later, other protocol methods may need to update the values of the cell and we want to avoid duplicating code. To access the **Books** objects returned by the request and get the values for the cells, the **NSFetchedResultsController** object offers the **object()** method. Using the cell's index path as the method's attribute, we get back the **Books** object corresponding to the cell and read its values as we did in previous examples.

 IMPORTANT: Like the **NSFetchRequest** class, the **NSFetchedResults-Controller** class is also a generic class and therefore we have to declare the types of values our instance is going to work with after the name and between angle brackets.

Do It Yourself: Replace the `BooksViewController` class in your project with the class of Listing 22-23 (this example does not include the Action for the Delete Book button, so you should delete the connection before executing the app). Run the application. The Table View Controller should list the books as it did before.

At this point, the view controller can show the books available, but if we introduce new books or try to delete them, the application will not work as before or will even return an error because the information managed by the `NSFetchedResultsController` object does not match the information contained by the table. To keep the Table View updated, we have to modify it from the delegate's methods to match the values managed by the Fetched Results Controller. In the example of Listing 22-23, we have already conformed to the `NSFetchedResultsControllerDelegate` protocol and declare the view controller as the delegate of the `NSFetchedResultsController` object, so all that is left is to add the protocol methods to the class.

```
func controller(_ controller:
NSFetchedResultsController<NSFetchRequestResult>, didChange anObject:
Any, at indexPath: IndexPath?, for type: NSFetchedResultsChangeType,
newIndexPath: IndexPath?) {
   switch type {
      case .delete:
         if let path = indexPath {
            tableView.deleteRows(at: [path], with: .fade)
         }
      case .insert:
         if let path = newIndexPath {
            tableView.insertRows(at: [path], with: .fade)
         }
      case .update:
         if let path = indexPath {
            let cell = tableView.cellForRow(at: path) as! BooksCell
            updateCell(cell: cell, path: path)
         }
      default:
         break
   }
}
```

Listing 22-24: Updating the table

Because our table just has one section so far, the only protocol method required to keep it updated is `controller(NSFetchedResultsController, didChange:, at:, for:, newIndexPath:)`. This method receives a value of type `NSFetchedResultsChangeType` that we can use to know the type of change performed and update the table accordingly. In this example, we check if an object has been deleted (`delete`), added (`insert`), or modified (`update`) with a `switch` statement. If an object was deleted, we delete its row, if it was inserted, we insert a new row (notice that we have to use the value of the `newIndexPath` attribute this time), and if the object was updated, we get a reference to its cell and call the `updateCell()` method to update its values.

Do It Yourself: Add the method of Listing 22-24 to the `BooksView-Controller` class of Listing 22-23. Run the application and add a new book. The Table View should update its rows to show the new object.

Core Data

If we perform multiple changes at the same time, we must tell the table to update all of its rows at the end by calling the **beginUpdates()** method when the process starts and the **endUpdates()** method when it is over. The **NSFetchedResultsControllerDelegate** protocol defines the methods **controllerWillChangeContent()** and **controllerDid-ChangeContent()** for this purpose.

```
func controllerWillChangeContent(_ controller:
NSFetchedResultsController<NSFetchRequestResult>) {
   tableView.beginUpdates()
}
func controllerDidChangeContent(_ controller:
NSFetchedResultsController<NSFetchRequestResult>) {
   tableView.endUpdates()
}
```

Listing 22-25: Updating the table all at once

 IMPORTANT: The **BooksViewController** class we have implemented with these examples does not include the methods necessary to activate the table's edition mode and delete books, like those introduced in Listing 22-22. You can incorporate those methods to your class, just remember to remove the call to the Table View's **deleteRows()** method, because now the table is updated from the **NSFetchedResultsControllerDelegate** protocol methods.

Sections

As we mentioned before, the **NSFetchedResultsController** object was designed to work with sections. It can take a property of an **NSManagedObject** object and generate sections with its values. For example, we can create one section for every author's name. The **NSFetchedResultsController** object divides the information in sections, with every section containing the books of a particular author, and automatically assigns the name of the author to the section's title. All we have to do is to declare the property we want to use as the value of the **sectionNameKeyPath** attribute of the object's initializer, as shown in the following example.

```
override func viewDidLoad() {
   super.viewDidLoad()

   tableView.rowHeight = 100
   let app = UIApplication.shared
   let appDelegate = app.delegate as! AppDelegate
   context = appDelegate.context

   let request: NSFetchRequest<Books> = Books.fetchRequest()
   let sort1 = NSSortDescriptor(key: "author.name", ascending: true,
selector: #selector(NSString.caseInsensitiveCompare(_:)))
   let sort2 = NSSortDescriptor(key: "title", ascending: true, selector:
#selector(NSString.caseInsensitiveCompare(_:)))
   request.sortDescriptors = [sort1, sort2]
   fetchedController = NSFetchedResultsController(fetchRequest: request,
managedObjectContext: context, sectionNameKeyPath: "author.name",
cacheName: nil)
   fetchedController.delegate = self
   do {
      try fetchedController.performFetch()
   } catch {
```

```
        print("Error")
    }
}
```

Listing 22-26: Organizing the Books *objects in sections*

The value of the **sectionNameKeyPath** attribute only determines the property we want to use to separate the objects in sections (**author.name** in this case), but we also have to sort the objects to coincide with this configuration. We can assign to the request as many sort descriptors as we want, but the first one has to order the objects by the value of the same property we used to generate the sections. In the example of Listing 22-26, we sort the sections by the value of the **name** property of the **author** relationship first and then add another **NSSortDescriptor** object to sort the objects inside each section by the value of the **title** property.

Of course, this is not enough to get the table to present the information in sections. We also have to implement the necessary protocol methods, including the **UITableViewDataSource** protocol methods to let the table know the number of sections available and their titles, and an additional **NSFetchedResultsControllerDelegate** protocol method to update the sections.

```
override func numberOfSections(in tableView: UITableView) -> Int {
    if let sections = fetchedController.sections {
        return sections.count
    }
    return 1
}
override func tableView(_ tableView: UITableView, titleForHeaderInSection
section: Int) -> String? {
    if let sections = fetchedController.sections {
        let sectionInfo = sections[section]
        return sectionInfo.name
    }
    return nil
}
func controller(_ controller:
NSFetchedResultsController<NSFetchRequestResult>, didChange sectionInfo:
NSFetchedResultsSectionInfo, atSectionIndex sectionIndex: Int, for type:
NSFetchedResultsChangeType) {
    switch type {
        case .insert:
            let index = IndexSet(integer: sectionIndex)
            tableView.insertSections(index, with: .fade)
        case .delete:
            let index = IndexSet(integer: sectionIndex)
            tableView.deleteSections(index, with: .fade)
        default:
            break
    }
}
```

Listing 22-27: Implementing the necessary protocol methods to work with sections

To return the number of sections available, we just count the values in the **sections** property of the **NSFetchedResultsController** object. For the name of the section, we need to get the object that represents the section and return its **name** property. Finally, to update the sections in the table after every change, we execute the Table View's **insertSections()** and **deleteSections()** methods to insert or remove a section depending on the type of change reported by the **NSFetchedResultsController** object.

Core Data

Sections are identified with an **IndexSet** structure. This structure can store a single integer or a range of integers that represent indexes (in this case, the indexes of the sections). The Table View's methods require these values to recognize the section to be affected. That is why, in Listing 22-27, we create these objects before modifying the section.

With the inclusion of these methods, now the table can present sections organized according to the name of the authors and ordered by title. The result is shown in Figure 22-18.

Figure 22-19: Organizing the books in sections

 Do It Yourself: Replace the **viewDidLoad()** method of the **BooksViewController** class of Listing 22-23 with the method of Listing 22-26. Add the methods in Listing 22-27 to the class. Select the Table View in the Storyboard and change the style to Grouped from the Attributes Inspector panel. Run the application. You should see something similar to Figure 22-19.

If we want to incorporate an index for the sections, as we did in the examples of Chapter 14 (Listing 14-7), we have to implement the method **sectionIndexTitles()** of the **UITableViewDataSource** protocol and return the array we get from the **sectionIndexTitles** property, as in the following example (the property returns an array with the initial letters of the sections' names capitalized).

```
override func sectionIndexTitles(for tableView: UITableView) -> [String]? {
    return fetchedController.sectionIndexTitles
}
```

Listing 22-28: Generating an index

Search

The process to let users search for values in a Table View associated with an **NSFetchedResultsController** object does not differ from a normal Table View. We have to define a Search Controller, conform to the **UISearchResultsUpdating** and **UISearchBarDelegate** protocols, and implement their methods (see Chapter 14, Listing 14-29). In the **updateSearchResults(for:)** method, we have to modify the predicate of the request assigned to the **NSFetchedResultsController** object to search for the value inserted by the user, and we also have to implement the **searchBarCancelButtonClicked()** to assign an empty predicate to clear the controller and list all the books available again when the Cancel button is pressed. The following example presents the protocol methods necessary for our **BooksViewController** class to search for books with titles that match the search.

```
import UIKit
import CoreData

class BooksViewController: UITableViewController,
NSFetchedResultsControllerDelegate, UISearchResultsUpdating,
UISearchBarDelegate {
    var context: NSManagedObjectContext!
```

```swift
    var fetchedController: NSFetchedResultsController<Books>!
    var searchController: UISearchController!

    override func viewDidLoad() {
        super.viewDidLoad()
        tableView.rowHeight = 100
        let app = UIApplication.shared
        let appDelegate = app.delegate as! AppDelegate
        context = appDelegate.context
        searchController = UISearchController(searchResultsController: nil)
        searchController.searchResultsUpdater = self
        searchController.obscuresBackgroundDuringPresentation = false
        searchController.searchBar.delegate = self
        navigationItem.searchController = searchController
        let request: NSFetchRequest<Books> = Books.fetchRequest()
        let sort = NSSortDescriptor(key: "title", ascending: true,
selector: #selector(NSString.caseInsensitiveCompare(_:)))
        request.sortDescriptors = [sort]
        fetchedController = NSFetchedResultsController(fetchRequest:
request, managedObjectContext: context, sectionNameKeyPath: nil,
cacheName: nil)
        fetchedController.delegate = self
        do {
            try fetchedController.performFetch()
        } catch {
            print("Error")
        }
    }
    override func tableView(_ tableView: UITableView,
numberOfRowsInSection section: Int) -> Int {
        if let sections = fetchedController.sections {
            let sectionInfo = sections[section]
            return sectionInfo.numberOfObjects
        }
        return 0
    }
    override func tableView(_ tableView: UITableView, cellForRowAt
indexPath: IndexPath) -> UITableViewCell {
        let cell = tableView.dequeueReusableCell(withIdentifier:
"booksCell", for: indexPath) as! BooksCell
        updateCell(cell: cell, path: indexPath)
        return cell
    }
    func updateCell(cell: BooksCell, path: IndexPath) {
        let book = fetchedController.object(at: path)
        cell.bookTitle.text = book.title
        if book.thumbnail != nil {
            cell.bookCover.image = UIImage(data: book.thumbnail!)
        }
        let year = book.year
        cell.bookYear.text = "Year: \(year)"
        let authorName = book.author?.name
        if authorName != nil {
            cell.bookAuthor.text = authorName
        } else {
            cell.bookAuthor.text = "Not Defined"
        }
    }
    func controller(_ controller:
NSFetchedResultsController<NSFetchRequestResult>, didChange anObject:
Any, at indexPath: IndexPath?, for type: NSFetchedResultsChangeType,
newIndexPath: IndexPath?) {
```

```
            switch type {
                case .delete:
                    if let path = indexPath {
                        tableView.deleteRows(at: [path], with: .fade)
                    }
                case .insert:
                    if let path = newIndexPath {
                        tableView.insertRows(at: [path], with: .fade)
                    }
                case .update:
                    if let path = indexPath {
                        let cell = tableView.cellForRow(at: path) as! BooksCell
                        updateCell(cell: cell, path: path)
                    }
                default:
                    break
            }
        }
        func updateSearchResults(for searchController: UISearchController) {
            if let text = searchController.searchBar.text {
                let search = text.trimmingCharacters(in: .whitespaces)
                if !search.isEmpty {
                    let request = fetchedController.fetchRequest
                    request.predicate = NSPredicate(format: "title
CONTAINS[cd] %@", search)
                    do {
                        try fetchedController.performFetch()
                    } catch {
                        print("Error")
                    }
                    tableView.reloadData()
                }
            }
        }
        func searchBarCancelButtonClicked(_ searchBar: UISearchBar) {
            let request = fetchedController.fetchRequest
            request.predicate = nil
            do {
                try fetchedController.performFetch()
            } catch {
                print("Error")
            }
            tableView.reloadData()
        }
    }
```

Listing 22-29: Searching books

To perform a search, we do not have to replace the request or create a new **NSFetchedResultsController** object, all we have to do is to assign a new predicate to the request with the conditions we need and call the **performFetch()** method to execute the request again. In Listing 22-29, we modify the predicate every time the text in the search bar changes and assign the original predicate back when the search is cancelled (in this case there was no original predicate, so we declare it as **nil**).

 Do It Yourself: Update the **BooksViewController** class with the code of Listing 22-29. Run the application and scroll down the table to uncover the search bar. The rows and sections should appear or disappear according to the term you insert in the bar.

22.3 Migration

The Persistent Container creates the Persistent Stores based on the Core Data model defined for the application. All the examples in this chapter work on the Core Data model introduced at the beginning. We did not perform any modification to the entities or their attributes. But if we had introduced a change, no matter how insignificant, the app would have crashed, because the new model would not have matched the one used to create the Persistent Store. If we want to update the model, adding or modifying entities, attributes, or relationships, we have to generate a new version of the model. This is a process called *migration*, and it involves the creation of a new model based on the old one.

The option to add the new version of the model is available in the Editor menu at the top of the screen when the model is selected. If we click on the Add Model Version option, a pop-up window asks for the name we want to assign to the new model and the model it is based on, as shown in Figure 22-20.

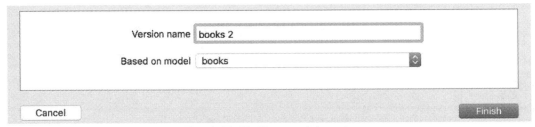

Figure 22-20: New model version

After we click on Finish, the new version is created and added to the models available in the Navigator Area. We can click on the arrow at the left side of the xcdatamodel file to see the list.

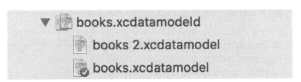

Figure 22-21: Model versions available

There is a green badge indicating the current active model. To start using the new version, we have to select it from the File Inspector panel in the Utilities Area. The option is called Model Version, as shown in Figure 22-22.

Figure 22-22: Selecting model version

Once we select the new version from this panel, the green badge is assigned to it in the Navigator Area. Now, when the xcdatamodel file is selected, the new model is shown in the Editor Area. All the modifications must be introduced in the new version; the old version is only preserved as reference. Once the app is executed, the system automatically migrates the Persistent Store to the new model.

Chapter 23
iCloud

23.1 Data in the Cloud

These days, users own more than one device. If we create an application that works on multiple devices, we have to provide a way for the users to share their data, otherwise they will have to insert the same information on every device they own. But the only way to do it effectively is through a server. The data from one device has to be stored in a server and then retrieved from other devices. Setting up a server to run this kind of system is complicated and costly. To provide a standard solution that every developer can easily implement without any prior investment, Apple created a system called *iCloud*. iCloud allows applications to synchronize data across devices using Apple servers. It provides three basic services: Key-Value Storage, to store single values, Document Storage, to store files, and CloudKit Storage, to store structured data in public and private databases.

Enabling iCloud

The iCloud service must be enabled for each application we create. We have to create entitlements to authorize our app to use the service and also a container in iCloud where our app's data will be stored. Fortunately, Xcode can set up everything for us by just turning on a switch. The option is available in the Capabilities panel inside the app's settings window (Figure 5-3, number 6). When we open this panel, we see all the external services provided by Apple, including iCloud at the top of the list, as shown in Figure 23-1, below.

 IMPORTANT: iCloud services are only available for developers that are members of the Apple Developer Program. At the time of this writing, the membership costs $99 US Dollars per year. You also have to register your account with Xcode, as we explained in Chapter 5 (see Figures 5-7 and 5-8).

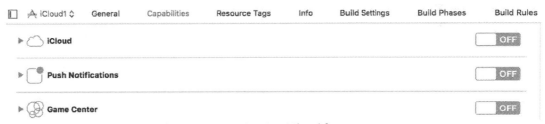

Figure 23-1: Activating iCloud for our app

After we turn on the switch, the iCloud option is expanded to show the services available. We have to select the services we want to activate for our app and Xcode takes care of creating the entitlements and the container if necessary. Figure 23-2 shows the panel with the Key-Value storage service activated.

▼ iCloud   **ON**

Services: ☑ Key-value storage
           ☐ iCloud Documents
           ☐ CloudKit

Figure 23-2: Activating iCloud services

Do It Yourself: Create a new Single View Application project. Click on the app's settings option at the top of the Navigator Area (Figure 5-3, number 6) and open the Capabilities panel (Figure 23-1). Turn on the iCloud switch and check the option Key-value storage. This iCloud service is now available in your application.

Testing Devices

The best way to test an iCloud application is running the app in two different devices, but Apple has made iCloud services available in the simulator as well. Thanks to this feature, we can synchronize data between a device and the simulator to test our app.

For the devices and the simulators to be able to access iCloud services, we have to register our iCloud account in the Settings app. We have to go to the Home screen, access the Settings app, tap on the option Sign in to your iPhone/iPad (Figure 23-3, center), and sign in to Apple's services with our Apple ID (Figure 23-3, right). The process has to be repeated for every device or simulator we want to use.

Figure 23-3: iCloud account in the simulator

23.2 Key-Value Storage

The Key-Value storage system is the `UserDefaults` system for iCloud. It works exactly like the User Defaults system studied in Chapter 21, and even shares some of its methods to assign and retrieve values, but all the data is stored in iCloud servers instead of the device's storage space. We can use it to store the app's preferences or current state, or any other value that we need to be set automatically in every device.

Foundation defines the `NSUbiquitousKeyValueStore` class to provide access to this system. The class includes the following methods to store and retrieve values.

set(Value, **forKey:** String)—This method stores the value specified by the first attribute with the key specified by the **forKey** attribute. The class provides versions of this method for every data type we are allowed to store in the system, such as `String`, `Bool`, `Data`, `Double`, `Int64`, dictionaries, arrays, and also the Property List values we have studied before (`NSNumber`, `NSString`, `NSDate`, `NSArray`, `NSDictionary`, `NSData`, and their equivalents in Swift).

bool(**forKey:** String)—This method retrieves a value of type `Bool`.

double(**forKey:** String)—This method retrieves a value of type `Double`.

longLong(**forKey:** String)—This method retrieves a value of type `Int64`.

string(**forKey:** String)—This method retrieves a value of type `String`.

array(forKey: String)—This method retrieves an array.

dictionary(forKey: String)—This method retrieves a dictionary.

data(forKey: String)—This method retrieves a value of type **Data**.

object(forKey: String)—This method retrieves an object.

To store or access a value, we have to initialize an **NSUbiquitousKeyValueStore** object and then call its methods. The object takes care of establishing the connection with iCloud and downloading or uploading the values. As we already mentioned, the system is used to storing discrete values that represent the user's preferences or the app's status. For example, we may have a Stepper that lets the user set a limit to the number of items the application can manage.

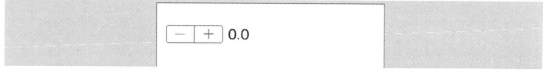

Figure 23-4: Interface to test Key-Value storage

If the user decides to set the limit to 5 in one device, the same limit should be established when the application is executed on a different device. To achieve this, we have to read the value from iCloud when the view is loaded and store it back when the user sets a new one. The following is the view controller necessary for this application.

```
import UIKit

class ViewController: UIViewController {
    @IBOutlet weak var stepper: UIStepper!
    @IBOutlet weak var counter: UILabel!
    var kvStorage: NSUbiquitousKeyValueStore!

    override func viewDidLoad() {
        super.viewDidLoad()
        kvStorage = NSUbiquitousKeyValueStore()
        let control = kvStorage.double(forKey: "control")
        stepper.value = control
        counter.text = String(control)
    }
    @IBAction func changeValue(_ sender: UIStepper) {
        let current = stepper.value
        counter.text = String(current)
        kvStorage.set(current, forKey: "control")
        kvStorage.synchronize()
    }
}
```

Listing 23-1: Storing settings in iCloud

The example of Listing 23-1 creates the **NSUbiquitousKeyValueStore** object as soon as the view is loaded and reads a value of type **Double** identified with the key "control" from iCloud. Like it happens with some of the methods included in the **UserDefaults** class, the **double()** method used in this example returns 0 if the value is not found, so the first time the application is executed, the value assigned to the label will be 0. To update the value, we have created an Action for the Stepper called **changeValue()**. In this method, we get the current Stepper's value, assign it to the label to reflect the change on the screen, and then store the value in iCloud with the "control" key using the **set()** method. If the user opens the application in a different device, the process starts again by reading the value associated with the "control" key from iCloud, but this time instead of returning 0 it will find the last number stored by the `set()` method.

Notice that we have to execute a method called **synchronize()** after storing a new value. This is a method provided by the **NSUbiquitousKeyValueStore** class to force the system to send the new value to iCloud right away. It is not always necessary, only when we want to make sure that the value is there as soon as possible.

 Do It Yourself: Create a new Single View Application project. Add a Stepper and a label to the initial view, as illustrated in Figure 23-4. Connect the Stepper to the **ViewController** class with an Outlet called **stepper** and the label with an Outlet called **counter**. Connect the Stepper with an Action called **changeValue()** and complete the **ViewController** class with the code of Listing 23-1. Run the application in a simulator. Press the Stepper's button to change the value to 5. Stop the application and run it again. The label should contain the value 5 this time. If you run the app on a device or a different simulator, you should see the value 5 again on the screen (remember to activate the same iCloud account in any of the simulators or devices you try).

The previous example stores in iCloud a value associated with the key "control", and every time the app is executed the value is retrieved from iCloud servers and shown on the screen. The problem is that at this moment the application does not know when the value is modified from another device. If we launch the app on an iPhone, set the value to 5, and then launch it again on an iPad, we will see the value 5 on the iPad's screen, but modifying the value thereafter will not produce any effect on the other device. To report the changes, Foundation defines a notification for the **NSUbiquitousKeyValueStore** class called **didChangeExternallyNotification**. This notification is posted to the Notification Center when the system detects a change in the values on the Key-Value storage.

```
import UIKit

class ViewController: UIViewController {
    @IBOutlet weak var stepper: UIStepper!
    @IBOutlet weak var counter: UILabel!
    var kvStorage: NSUbiquitousKeyValueStore!

    override func viewDidLoad() {
        super.viewDidLoad()

        kvStorage = NSUbiquitousKeyValueStore()
        let control = kvStorage.double(forKey: "control")
        stepper.value = control
        counter.text = String(control)

        let center = NotificationCenter.default
        center.addObserver(self, selector:
#selector(valueReceived(notification:)), name:
NSUbiquitousKeyValueStore.didChangeExternallyNotification, object:
kvStorage)
    }
    @IBAction func changeValue(_ sender: UIStepper) {
        let current = stepper.value
        counter.text = String(current)
        kvStorage.set(current, forKey: "control")
        kvStorage.synchronize()
    }
}
```

```
@objc func valueReceived(notification: NSNotification) {
    let control = kvStorage.double(forKey: "control")
    stepper.value = control
    counter.text = String(control)
}
}
```

Listing 23-2: Updating the interface when a new value is received

The notification is registered in the **viewDidLoad()** method, so every device that is running the application will get a notification when the value is modified from another device. When a notification is posted, the observer executes the **valueReceived()** method. In this method, we read the new value and update the interface. Now, we can have the application running simultaneously on different devices and the user will see the value automatically changing on the screen when it is modified from another device.

 Do It Yourself: Update the **ViewController** class of your project with the code of Listing 23-2. Run the application simultaneously in a simulator and a device. Modify the value on the simulator and check the device to see how the label changes.

 IMPORTANT: The simulator does not update the information automatically. Most of the time, you have to force the update. If you modify the value on your device and do not see it changing on the simulator, open the Debug menu at the top of the screen and select the option Trigger iCloud Sync. This will synchronize the application with iCloud and update the values right away.

23.3 iCloud Documents

The Key-Value storage system was developed to store simple values. The purpose is to allow users to set preferences or configuration parameters across devices. Although very useful, it presents some limitations, especially on the amount of data we can store (currently no more than 1 megabyte). If what we need is to store large amounts of data, we can activate the iCloud Documents option in the Capabilities panel and upload files instead (see Figure 23-2).

We already studied how to create and read files in Chapter 21, but iCloud presents some challenges that the **FileManager** class cannot overcome. The most important is coordination. Because of the unreliability of network connections, at any moment iCloud may find different versions of the same file. Modifications that were introduced to the file from one device may not have reached iCloud and therefore may later be in conflict with updates introduced from another device. The application has to decide which version of the file to preserve or what data is more valuable when the file is edited from two different devices at the same time. These issues are not easy to solve and can turn development into a nightmare. Considering all the problems a developer has to face, Apple introduced a class called **UIDocument**, designed specifically to manage files for iCloud. The class includes capabilities to coordinate and synchronize files of any size, and also presents features that simplify the manipulation of documents in iOS devices, like progression reports, automatic thumbnail generation, undo manager, and others.

Like other UIKit classes, the **UIDocument** class was not designed to be implemented directly in our code; it is more like an interface between the app's data and the files we use to store it. To take advantage of this class, we have to create a subclass and overwrite some of its methods. Once we have the subclass, we can create the object with the following initializer.

init(fileURL: URL)—This initializer creates a new **UIDocument** object. The **fileURL** attribute is a **URL** structure with the location of the file in iCloud.

The following are the methods we need to overwrite in the subclass of **UIDocument** to provide the data for the file and to retrieve it later.

contents(forType: String**)**—This method is called when the **UIDocument** object needs to store the content of the document on file. The method must return an object with the document's data (usually a **Data** structure). The **forType** attribute identifies the type of the file (by default, it is determined from the file's extension).

load(fromContents: Any, **ofType:** String?**)**—This method is called when the **UIDocument** object loads the content of the document from the file. The **fromContents** attribute is an object with the content of the file (usually a **Data** structure that is internally turned into an **NSData** object), and the **ofType** attribute is a string that identifies the type of the file (by default, it is determined from the file's extension).

The **UIDocument** class also offers methods to manage the file, including the following to open and save it.

open(completionHandler: Block**)**—This method asks the **UIDocument** object to open the file and load its content. The **completionHandler** attribute is a closure with the statements to execute after the process is over.

save(to: URL, **for:** SaveOperation, **completionHandler:** Block**)**—This method asks the **UIDocument** object to save the content of the document on file. The **for** attribute is an enumeration called **SaveOperation** included in the **UIDocument** class that indicates the type of operation to perform. The values available are **forCreating** (to save the file for the first time) and **forOverwriting** (to overwrite the file's current version). The **completionHandler** attribute is a closure with the statements to execute after the process is over.

Accessing the files is also complicated in iCloud. We cannot just get a list of files with methods like **contentsOfDirectory()** from the **FileManager** class because there could be some files that have not been downloaded yet to the device. What we can do instead is to get the information pertaining to the files. This data is called *metadata*, and refers to all the information associated with a particular file, such as its name, the date it was created, etc. To get the metadata, Foundation defines the **NSMetadataQuery** class. This class provides the properties and methods necessary to retrieve the information and also keep watching for updates.

predicate—This property sets or returns the predicate for the query. It is an optional of type **NSPredicate**.

sortDescriptors—This property sets or returns the sort descriptors for the query. It is an array of **NSSortDescriptor** objects.

searchScopes—This property sets or returns a value that indicates the scope of the query. It is an array with constants that represent a predefined scope. The constants available for iOS are **NSMetadataQueryUbiquitousDocumentsScope** (searches all files in the Documents directory of the iCloud's container) and **NSMetadataQueryUbiquitous-DataScope** (searches files that are not in the Documents directory of the iCloud's container).

results—This property returns an array with the query's results. By default, the array contains **NSMetadataItem** objects with the metadata of every file found.

resultCount—This property returns an **Int** with the number of results produced by the query.

result(at: Int**)**—This method returns the **NSMetadataItem** object from the query's results array at the index specified by the **at** attribute.

start()—This method initiates the query.

stop()—This method stops the query.

enableUpdates()—This method enables query updates.

disableUpdates()—This method disables query updates.

The `NSMetadataQuery` class also includes some notifications to report when new data is available. The following are the most frequently used.

NSMetadataQueryDidUpdate—This notification is posted when the results of the query change.

NSMetadataQueryDidFinishGathering—This notification is posted when the query finishes getting all the information.

The results of a query are communicated through the `results` property in the form of an array of `NSMetadataItem` objects. This is a simple class created to contain the attributes of a file. The class provides the following method to retrieve the values.

value(forAttribute: String)—This method returns the value of the file's attribute determined by the **forAtttribute** attribute. The `NSMetadataItem` class defines a list of constants to represent the attributes. The constants available are `NSMetadata-ItemFSNameKey` (file's name), `NSMetadataItemDisplayNameKey` (document's name), `NSMetadataItemURLKey` (file's URL), `NSMetadataItemPathKey` (file's path), `NSMetadataItemFSSizeKey` (file's size), `NSMetadataItemFSCreationDateKey` (date of creation), and `NSMetadataItemFSContentChangeDateKey` (date the file was modified).

The interface for an application capable of processing documents has to include a way to select the document the user wants to see and the tools to edit its content. For the following example, we will work with only one document to keep it simple. The initial view includes a button connected to a second view containing a Text View to edit the document's content.

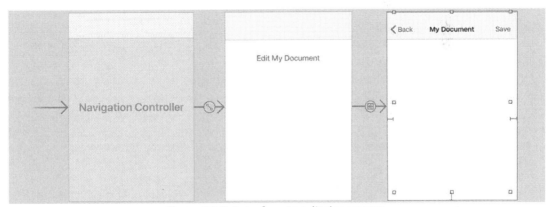

Figure 23-5: Interface to edit documents

 Do It Yourself: Create a new Single View Application project. Embed the initial view in a Navigation Controller. Add the Edit My Document button to the initial view. Add a second Scene to the Storyboard. Connect the button with a Show Segue to the second Scene. Add a Navigation Item and then a bar button with the title Save to the Navigation Bar of the second view. Add a Text View to the second view and pin it to the edges of the view. Click on the first item in the Navigator Area to open the app's Settings. Select the Capabilities panel, turn the iCloud switch on, and enable Key-value storage and iCloud documents.

The first step is to create the **UIDocument** subclass that is going to be in charge of managing our documents (in this example only one). As always, it is recommended to create a separate file for the subclass. We just have to follow the steps to create a Cocoa Touch Class file, as we did for other UIKit subclasses before, and select the **UIDocument** class as the superclass. For this example, we called it **MyDocument**.

```
import UIKit

class MyDocument: UIDocument {
    var fileContent: String = ""

    override func contents(forType typeName: String) throws -> Any {
        var data = Data()
        if let fileData = try? NSKeyedArchiver.archivedData(withRootObject:
fileContent, requiringSecureCoding: false) {
            data = fileData
        }
        return data
    }
    override func load(fromContents contents: Any, ofType typeName:
String?) throws {
        if let text = contents as? Data {
            if !text.isEmpty {
                if let result = try?
NSKeyedUnarchiver.unarchivedObject(ofClass: NSString.self, from: text) as
String? {
                    if let message = result {
                        fileContent = message
                    }
                }
            }
        }
    }
}
```

Listing 23-3: Creating the document

When the **UIDocument** object is asked to store or load the data in file, it calls its **contents()** and **load()** methods, respectively. In these methods, we have to prepare the application's data to be stored or extracted from the content of the file. For this purpose, we use the methods provided by the **NSKeyedArchiver** and **NSKeyedUnarchiver** classes (see Chapter 21). The document of our example contains only a string, so we turn the string into a **Data** structure to provide the content for the file in the **contents()** method and get the string back when the file is loaded in the **load()** method. Notice that the **unarchivedObject()** method cannot work with empty values, so we first check if the **Data** structure is empty.

The next step is to create the view controller to manage the document. In this example, we work with only one file, so all the logic is managed by the second view (all the functionality for the initial view at this time is provided by the Segue connected to the button). We call the view controller for the second view **EditionViewController**. In this class, we have to check the files available, get the one we are interested in, and create the **MyDocument** object to represent it. The following example introduces the properties and the initial statements for this class.

```
import UIKit

class EditionViewController: UIViewController {
    @IBOutlet weak var mycontent: UITextView!
    var document: MyDocument!
```

```
   var iCloudURL: URL!
   var metaData: NSMetadataQuery!

   override func viewDidLoad() {
      super.viewDidLoad()
      let center = NotificationCenter.default
      center.addObserver(self, selector:
#selector(metadataReceived(notification:)), name:
NSNotification.Name.NSMetadataQueryDidFinishGathering, object: nil)

      metaData = NSMetadataQuery()
      metaData.searchScopes = [NSMetadataQueryUbiquitousDocumentsScope]
      metaData.start()
   }
}
```

Listing 23-4: Editing the document

Because of the logic of our application, we need a property to store the reference to the **MyDocument** object we are going to use to access the file, a property to store the file's URL in iCloud, and a property to reference the **NSMetadataQuery** object that will let us search for the files available. In Listing 23-4, we call these properties **document**, **iCloudURL**, and **metaData**.

The first thing we have to do is to check whether the file exists or not and get its metadata. In Listing 23-4, we initialize the **NSMetadataQuery** object as soon as the view is loaded and start the process with the **start()** method. The query was configured to look into the ICloud's Documents directory because this is the recommended directory for our files.

Once the query begins, the results are reported by the **NSMetadataQuery** object through notifications. Because these notifications can be posted right after the process begins, we have to register the observers before the **start()** method is called. The only notification we care about in our example is the **NSMetadataQueryDidFinishGathering**, posted when the process of gathering data is over. In the method assigned to this notification, we have to create the **MyDocument** object and connect it to the file (an existing one or a new one if no file was found). The following is the implementation of the **metadataReceived()** method assigned to the observer in our example.

```
@objc func metadataReceived(notification: NSNotification) {
   metaData.stop()
   let center = NotificationCenter.default
   center.removeObserver(self, name:
NSNotification.Name.NSMetadataQueryDidFinishGathering, object: nil)

   if metaData.resultCount > 0 {
      let file = metaData.result(at: 0) as! NSMetadataItem
      let fileURL = file.value(forAttribute: NSMetadataItemURLKey) as! URL
      document = MyDocument(fileURL: fileURL)
      document.open(completionHandler: { (success) in
         if success {
            self.mycontent.text = self.document.fileContent
            self.iCloudURL = fileURL
         }
      })
   } else {
      let manager = FileManager.default
      if let fileURL = manager.url(forUbiquityContainerIdentifier: nil) {
         iCloudURL =
fileURL.appendingPathComponent("Documents/myfile.dat")
         document = MyDocument(fileURL: iCloudURL)
```

```
        document.save(to: iCloudURL, for: .forCreating,
completionHandler: nil)
        }
    }
}
```

Listing 23-5: Processing query results

The **NSMetadataQuery** object generates a live process. It keeps querying iCloud for new information until we tell it to make a pause or stop. In our example, we just want to know if our file exists, so we stop the query all together with the **stop()** method. Because we are not going to listen for more data, it does not make sense to keep observing the **NSMetadataQuery** notification, so we remove the observer as well. The next step is to load the file if it already exists or create a new one. For better performance, it is recommended to read the **resultCount** property of the query instead of counting the elements of the **results** array. If this property returns a value greater than 0, we get the first element with the **result()** method (we are only working with one file), get its URL with the **value()** method, and use it to create the **MyDocument** object. This tells the **MyDocument** object what is the URL of its file, but we still have to call the **open()** method to open it. This method asks the instance of **MyDocument** to load the content of the file. The instance then executes its **load()** method and assigns the content to its **fileContent** property. In the completion handler, we assign the value of this property to the Text View and the text is shown on the screen.

On the other hand, if the file does not exist, we have to generate the URL and create a new one. In this case, we take advantage of a method provided by the **FileManager** class to get iCloud locations called **url(forUbiquityContainerIdentifier:)**. This method returns the URL of the location of our app's iCloud container. Because an app can have several containers, the method takes an attribute to specify the container's identifier (declared as **nil** to use the container by default). The URL returned by this method is the root directory, so we have to add the Documents directory and the file's name to create the file. With the final URL, we create a **MyDocument** object and call its **save()** method to create the file. Internally, the **MyDocument** instance calls its **contents()** method to get the content and then it creates the file.

The codes added so far to the **EditionViewController** class load or create a file and show its content on the screen, but we still have to store the changes when the document is saved. The following is the Action method for the Save button. In this method, we get the text from the Text View, assign it to the **fileContent** property of the **MyDocument** object, and then call its **save()** method to save it on file. The operation assigned to the method is **forOverwriting** because at this point we already know that there is a file available and we just need to update its content.

```
@IBAction func saveDocument(_ sender: UIBarButtonItem) {
    document.fileContent = mycontent.text
    document.save(to: iCloudURL, for: .forOverwriting, completionHandler:
nil)
    navigationController?.popViewController(animated: true)
}
```

Listing 23-6: Saving the document

 Do It Yourself: Create a new file with a subclass of **UIDocument** called **MyDocument** and complete the class with the code of Listing 23-3. Create a subclass of **UIViewController** called **EditionViewController** and assign it to the second view. Connect the Text View with an Outlet called **mycontent**. Complete the class with the code of Listing 23-4 and the method of Listing 23-5.

Connect the Save button with an action called `saveDocument()` and complete the method with the code of Listing 23-6. Run the application in the simulator. Press the Edit My Document button, insert some text in the Text View and press the Save button. Run the app on a device and press the Edit My Document button again. You should see on the screen the text inserted before in the simulator. Remember that the simulator takes time to upload and download changes from iCloud, so you have to select Trigger iCloud Sync from the Debug menu to force the synchronization.

In the previous example, we searched for every file in the iCloud's container, but we can make the query more selective using predicates. For example, if we want to make sure that the query returns the file myfile.dat used in our application, we can assign an **NSPredicate** object to the **NSMetadataQuery** object, as shown in the following example.

```
override func viewDidLoad() {
   super.viewDidLoad()
   let center = NotificationCenter.default
   center.addObserver(self, selector:
#selector(metadataReceived(notification:)), name:
NSNotification.Name.NSMetadataQueryDidFinishGathering, object: nil)

   metaData = NSMetadataQuery()
   metaData.predicate = NSPredicate(format: "%K == %@",
NSMetadataItemFSNameKey, "myfile.dat")
   metaData.searchScopes = [NSMetadataQueryUbiquitousDocumentsScope]
   metaData.start()
}
```

Listing 23-7: Filtering the query

The format of the predicate for a query requires comparing the value of a file's attribute with the string we are looking for. The attribute is represented by the constants defined in the **NSMetadataItem** class (described above). In Listing 23-7, we use the **NSMetadataItemFSNameKey** constant to filter the files by name (the value of the constant has to be introduced to the string with the %K placeholder to avoid the quotes). The query now returns only files with the name myfile.dat.

 Do It Yourself: Update the `viewDidLoad()` method of the **EditionViewController** class with the code of Listing 23-7. Run the application. The Text View should show the content of the myfile.dat file again.

Multiple Documents

The initial view of our previous example offers a single button to open a document and show the content on the screen, however, most applications allow the user to create and manage all the documents they need. As we mentioned before, an **NSMetadataQuery** object generates a live query. The query keeps looking for documents until we tell it to stop, and this is how we work with multiple documents in iCloud. We have to create a query and keep it running to update the list of documents available in case one is created or removed from another device.

Multiple documents conform a list of items, and the best way to present this type of information is with a table or a collection view. To illustrate how the process works, we replaced the initial Scene or our example with a Table View Controller, as shown next.

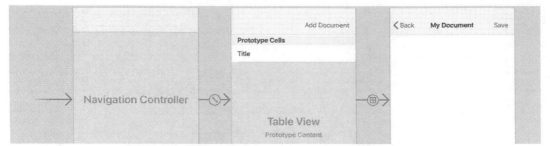

Figure 23-6: Interface to work with multiple documents

 Do It Yourself: Delete the initial Scene of the interface introduced in Figure 23-5. Add a Table View Controller in its place. Connect the Navigation Controller to the Table View Controller with a Root View Controller Segue. Connect the cell to the second Scene with a Show Segue and give the segue the identifier "showDocument". Add a bar button to the Table View Controller with the title Add Document. Select the cell, change its style to Basic and give it the identifier "documentCell".

The Table View Controller includes a bar button to add new documents and a Basic cell to display the name of the documents. The view controller for this view has to create a query to get the documents available and then show their names on the table. We called this class **DocumentsViewController**. The following code defines the properties we need to manage the data and it also configures the query.

```
import UIKit

class DocumentsViewController: UITableViewController {
    var documentsList: [String] = []
    var metaData: NSMetadataQuery!

    override func viewDidLoad() {
        super.viewDidLoad()
        let center = NotificationCenter.default
        center.addObserver(self, selector:
#selector(updateList(notification:)), name:
NSNotification.Name.NSMetadataQueryDidFinishGathering, object: nil)
        center.addObserver(self, selector:
#selector(updateList(notification:)), name:
NSNotification.Name.NSMetadataQueryDidUpdate, object: nil)

        metaData = NSMetadataQuery()
        metaData.searchScopes = [NSMetadataQueryUbiquitousDocumentsScope]
        metaData.start()
    }
}
```

Listing 23-8: Initiating the query

Because we are not only getting the list of documents available but also monitoring iCloud for changes, the view controller for this view has to register observers for two notifications: the **NSMetadataQueryDidFinishGathering** to know when the process of gathering the initial data is over, and the **NSMetadataQueryDidUpdate** to know when there are updates available. In Listing 23-8, we register these observers and assign them the **updateList()** method. The method is in charge of getting the results returned by the query, updating the values, and refreshing the table.

iCloud

```
@objc func updateList(notification: NSNotification) {
   metaData.disableUpdates()
   for item in metaData.results as! [NSMetadataItem] {
      let name = item.value(forAttribute: NSMetadataItemFSNameKey) as!
String
      if documentsList.index(of: name) == nil {
         documentsList.append(name)
      }
   }
   documentsList.sort(by: { (value1, value2) in value1 < value2 })

   tableView.reloadData()
   metaData.enableUpdates()
}
```

Listing 23-9: Keeping the table updated

Every time the query gets information, it posts notifications to let our code know what happened. To avoid conflicts with the data we are processing and the new data received, we have to pause the query until the process is over. This is done by the **disableUpdates()** and **enableUpdates()** methods of the **NSMetadataQuery** class. In the method of Listing 23-9, we call these methods at the beginning and the end to be sure that the **updateList()** method is not executed again until we get the new information and refresh the table.

Usually, an application like this gets the values it needs from the results returned by the query and stores them in a place the rest of the class can read, such as a property, a model, or a more complex storage system like Core Data. For this example, we defined a single property called **documentsList** to contain an array with the names of the documents. Because the **updateList()** method is called when the query finishes gathering the data and also when it finds changes, we have to check for duplicates before introducing a new name into this array. The code in Listing 23-9 creates a loop to go through every new value, gets the attribute for the name, and checks if it already exists with the **index()** method. Comparing the value returned by this method to **nil**, we can be sure that there will not be any duplicates on the list. After the list is updated, the table is refreshed.

The Table View methods required to show this information are simple, we just have to get the values from the **documentsList** and create the cells.

```
override func tableView(_ tableView: UITableView, numberOfRowsInSection
section: Int) -> Int {
   return documentsList.count
}
override func tableView(_ tableView: UITableView, cellForRowAt indexPath:
IndexPath) -> UITableViewCell {
   let cell = tableView.dequeueReusableCell(withIdentifier:
"documentCell", for: indexPath)
   cell.textLabel?.text = documentsList[indexPath.row]
   return cell
}
```

Listing 23-10: Populating the table

We have connected the prototype cell on the table to the second view with a Show Segue. This is so every time the user selects a cell, the content of the document is shown on the screen. For this to work, we need to implement the **prepare()** method to tell the second view which document was selected. The following example assigns the document's name to a property in the **EditionViewController** class called **selected** (we will define this property later).

```
override func prepare(for segue: UIStoryboardSegue, sender: Any?){
    if segue.identifier == "showDocument" {
        let controller = segue.destination as! EditionViewController
        if let path = tableView.indexPathForSelectedRow {
            controller.selected = documentsList[path.row]
        }
    }
}
```

Listing 23-11: Sending the name of the selected document to the second view

The **DocumentsViewController** class is not complete until we include the code necessary for the user to create new documents. To simplify this example, we decided to create an Alert View with a Text Field to insert the name of the new document. The following example defines the Action for the Add Document button and a method called **saveFile()** to create the new document and store it in iCloud.

```
@IBAction func addDocument(_ sender: UIBarButtonItem) {
    let alert = UIAlertController(title: "New File", message: nil,
preferredStyle: .alert)
    let cancel = UIAlertAction(title: "Cancel", style: .cancel, handler:
nil)
    alert.addAction(cancel)
    let action = UIAlertAction(title: "Create", style: .default, handler:
{ (action) in
        if let fields = alert.textFields {
            let file = fields[0].text
            self.saveFile(name: file!)
        }
    })
    alert.addAction(action)
    alert.addTextField(configurationHandler: { (textField) in
        textField.placeholder = "Insert name and extension"
    })
    present(alert, animated: true, completion: nil)
}
func saveFile(name: String) {
    if documentsList.index(of: name) == nil {
        let manager = FileManager.default
        if let fileURL = manager.url(forUbiquityContainerIdentifier: nil) {
            let iCloudURL =
fileURL.appendingPathComponent("Documents/\(name)")
            let document = MyDocument(fileURL: iCloudURL)
            document.save(to: iCloudURL, for: .forCreating,
completionHandler: nil)
        }
    }
}
```

Listing 23-12: Creating new documents

The code of Listing 23-12 creates an Alert View with a Text Field and a button with the title Create. When this button is pressed, the value of the Text Field is assigned to a constant and sent to the **saveFile()** method. This method takes the new name, checks if it already exists in the **documentsList** array, and if it cannot find it, it creates the new document.

Do It Yourself: Create a subclass of `UITableViewController` called `DocumentsViewController` and assign it to the Table View Controller added as the initial view. Update the class with the code of Listing 23-8. Add the methods of Listings 23-9, 23-10, 23-11 and 23-12 to the class, and connect the Add Document button to the `addDocument()` Action.

In the `EditionViewController` class we do not have to create a new document anymore, we just have to read the selected document, show it on the screen, and save the changes introduced by the user.

```
import UIKit

class EditionViewController: UIViewController {
    @IBOutlet weak var mycontent: UITextView!
    var document: MyDocument!
    var iCloudURL: URL!
    var metaData: NSMetadataQuery!
    var selected: String!

    override func viewDidLoad() {
        super.viewDidLoad()

        let center = NotificationCenter.default
        center.addObserver(self, selector:
#selector(metadataReceived(notification:)), name:
NSNotification.Name.NSMetadataQueryDidFinishGathering, object: nil)
        metaData = NSMetadataQuery()
        metaData.predicate = NSPredicate(format: "%K == %@",
NSMetadataItemFSNameKey, selected)
        metaData.searchScopes = [NSMetadataQueryUbiquitousDocumentsScope]
        metaData.start()
    }
    @objc func metadataReceived(notification: NSNotification) {
        metaData.stop()
        let center = NotificationCenter.default
        center.removeObserver(self, name:
NSNotification.Name.NSMetadataQueryDidFinishGathering, object: nil)
        if metaData.resultCount > 0 {
            let file = metaData.result(at: 0) as! NSMetadataItem
            let fileURL = file.value(forAttribute: NSMetadataItemURLKey) as!
URL
            document = MyDocument(fileURL: fileURL)
            document.open(completionHandler: { (success: Bool) in
                if success {
                    self.mycontent.text = self.document.fileContent
                    self.iCloudURL = fileURL
                }
            })
        }
    }
    @IBAction func saveDocument(_ sender: UIBarButtonItem) {
        document.fileContent = mycontent.text
        document.save(to: iCloudURL, for: .forOverwriting,
completionHandler: nil)
        navigationController?.popViewController(animated: true)
    }
}
```

Listing 23-13: Reading and modifying a document

The query for this view controller now contains a predicate to search the selected document, but the rest of the code is the same as before. The only difference is that now instead of working with a unique file, we can process every file on the list.

 Do It Yourself: Update the `EditionViewController` class with the code of Listing 23-13. Run the application in the simulator. Press the Add Document button. Insert the name and extension of the document you want to create, and press Create. After a moment, the new document should be added to the table. Run the application on a device. The document you just created in the simulator should appear on the device's screen. Add another document in the simulator and select the Trigger iCloud Sync option in the Debug menu to make sure the simulator is synchronized with iCloud. The document you just added should appear on the device's screen after a few seconds. Select a document in the simulator, insert some text, and press the Save button. After a moment, the document should contain the same text on the device.

 IMPORTANT: In these examples, we have stored only a single string in the documents, but we can archive all the values we want, including custom classes, as we did in the examples of Chapter 21. When working with documents that manage content of several files, like text files and image files, instead of encoding all together in one file it is recommended to use a file wrapper for better performance. The wrapper is created with objects of the `NSFileWrapper` class. If the content of the document is created with a wrapper, iCloud is able to download and upload only the files inside the wrapper that present changes, reducing bandwidth usage. For more information, visit our website and follow the links for this chapter.

23.4 CloudKit

CloudKit is a database system in iCloud. Using this system, we can store structured data online with different levels of accessibility. The system offers three types of databases to determine who has access to the information.

- **Private Database** to store data that is accessible only to the user.
- **Public Database** to store data that is accessible to every user running the app.
- **Shared Database** to store data the user wants to share with other users.

As we did with the rest of the iCloud services, the first step to use CloudKit is to activate it from the Capabilities panel (see Figure 23-2). Because CloudKit uses Remote Notifications to report changes in the databases, when we activate CloudKit, Xcode automatically activates an additional service called *Push Notifications*, as shown in Figure 23-7.

Figure 23-7: *Activating Push Notifications*

Remote Notifications are similar to the Local Notifications introduced in Chapter 19, but instead of being posted by the app they are sent from a server to inform our app or the user that something changed or needs attention. The Remote Notifications posted by CloudKit are sent from Apple servers when something changes in the databases. Because this may happen not only when the user is working with the app but also when the app is in the background, to get these notifications, we have to activate two additional services from the Background Modes section called *Background Fetch* and *Remote Notifications*.

Modes: ☐ Audio, AirPlay, and Picture in Picture
        ☐ Location updates
        ☑ Background fetch
        ☑ Remote notifications

Figure 23-8: *Activating background notifications*

Container

When CloudKit is activated from the Capabilities panel, Xcode creates entitlements to authorize the app to use the service and a container for the app's databases. The container is like a space in Apple's servers designated to our app. The CloudKit framework provides a class called `CKContainer` to access the container and the databases it contains. Because an app may have more than one container, the class includes an initializer to get a reference to a specific container and also a type method to get a reference to the container by default.

CKContainer(identifier: String)—This initializer creates the `CKContainer` object that references the container identified with the string specified by the **identifier** attribute.

default()—This type method returns the `CKContainer` object that references the container by default.

Container objects provide the following properties to get access to each database.

privateCloudDatabase—This property returns a `CKDatabase` object with a reference to the user's Private database.

publicCloudDatabase—This property returns a `CKDatabase` object with a reference to the app's Public database.

sharedCloudDatabase—This property returns a `CKDatabase` object with a reference to the user's Shared database.

CloudKit databases have specific purposes and functionalities. The Private database is used when we want the user to be able to share private information among his or her own devices (only the user can access the information stored in this database), and the Public and Shared databases are used to share information between users (the information stored in the Public database is accessible to all the users running our app and the information stored in the Shared database is accessible to the users the user decides to share the data with).

The data is stored in the database as records and records are stored in zones. The Private and Public databases include a default zone, but the Private and Shared databases also work with custom zones (called Shared Zones in a Shared database), as illustrated in Figure 23-9.

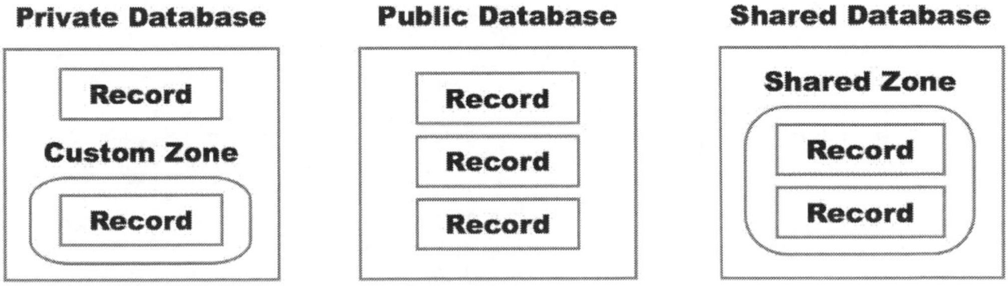

Private Database	Public Database	Shared Database
Record	**Record**	**Shared Zone**
Custom Zone	**Record**	**Record**
Record	**Record**	**Record**

Figure 23-9: *Databases configuration*

Records

Once we have decided which database we are going to use, we have to generate records to store the user's data. Records are objects that store information as key/value pairs, similar to dictionaries. These objects are classified by types to determine the characteristics of the record. For example, if we want to store records that contain information about books, we can use the type "Books", and if later we want to store records with information about authors, we can use the type "Authors" (a type is analog to the Entities in Core Data). The framework provides the **CKRecord** class to create and manage records. The class includes the following initializer.

CKRecord(recordType: String, **recordID:** CKRecord.ID**)**—This initializer creates a **CKRecord** object of the type and with the ID specified by the attributes. The **recordType** attribute is a custom identifier for the type, and the **recordID** attribute is the record's identifier.

Records are identified with an ID that includes a name and a reference to the zone the record belongs to (if a custom ID is not specified, the record is stored with an ID generated by CloudKit). To create and access the ID and its values, the **CKRecord** class defines the **ID** class with the following initializers and properties.

CKRecord.ID(recordName: String**)**—This initializer creates an **CKRecord.ID** object to identify a record. The **recordName** attribute is the name we want to give to the record (it must be unique).

CKRecord.ID(recordName: String, **zoneID:** CKRecordZone.ID**)**—This initializer creates an **CKRecord.ID** object to identify a record stored with the name and in the zone specified by the attributes. The **recordName** attribute is the name we want to give to the record, and the **zoneID** attribute is the identifier of the custom zone where we want to store the record.

recordName—This property returns a string with the name of the record.

zoneID—This property returns a **CKRecordZone.ID** object with the ID of the zone the record belongs to.

The **CKRecord** class offers properties to set or get the record's ID and other attributes. The following are the most frequently used.

recordID—This property returns the **CKRecord.ID** object that identifies the record.

recordType—This property returns a string that determines the record's type.

recordChangeTag—This property returns a string with the tag assigned to the record (each record is assigned a tag by the server).

creationDate—This property returns a **Date** value with the date in which the record was created.

modificationDate—This property returns a **Date** value that indicates the last time the record was modified.

Because the values of a record are stored as key/value pairs, we can use square brackets to read and modify them (as dictionaries), but the class also includes the following methods.

setObject(Value?, **forKey:** String**)**—This method sets or updates a value in the record. The fist attribute is the value we want to store, and the **forKey** attribute is the key we want to use to identify the value. The value must be of any of the following types: **NSString**, **NSNumber**, **NSData**, **NSDate**, **NSArray**, **CLLocation**, **CKAsset**, and **Reference**.

object(forKey: String)—This method returns the value associated with the key specified by the **forKey** attribute. The value is returned as a generic `CKRecordValue` type that we have to cast to the right data type.

Zones

As illustrated in Figure 23-9, the Public database can only store records in a default zone, but the Private and Shared databases can include custom zones. In the case of the Private database, the custom zones are optional (although they are required for synchronization, as we will see later). Zones are like divisions inside a database to separate records that are not directly related. For example, we may have an app that stores locations, like the names of cities and countries, but also lets the user store a list of Christmas gifts. In cases like this, we can create a zone to store the records that include information about cities and countries and another zone to store the records that include information about the gifts. The CloudKit framework provides the `CKRecordZone` class to represent the zones. The class includes an initializer to create new custom zones and a type method to get a reference to the zone by default.

CKRecordZone(zoneName: String)—This initializer creates a `CKRecordZone` object to represent a zone with the name specified by the **zoneName** attribute.

default()—This type method returns the `CKRecordZone` object that represents the zone by default in the database.

Query

When we want to access data stored in CloudKit, we have to download the records from the database and read their values. Records may be fetched from a database one by one using their ID or in a batch using a query. To define a query, the framework provides the `CKQuery` class. The class includes the following initializer and properties.

CKQuery(recordType: String, **predicate:** NSPredicate)—This initializer creates a `CKQuery` object to fetch multiple records from a database. The **recordType** attribute specifies the type of records we want to fetch, and the **predicate** attribute determines the matching criteria we want to use to select the records.

recordType—This property sets or returns a string that determines the type of records we want to fetch.

predicate—This property sets or returns an `NSPredicate` object that defines the matching criteria for the query.

sortDescriptors—This property sets or returns an array of `NSSortDescriptor` objects that determine the order of the records returned by the query.

Operations

CloudKit is an online service and therefore any task may take time to process. For this reason, the CloudKit framework uses asynchronous operations to access the information on the servers. An operation has to be created for every process we want to perform in a database, including storing, reading, and organizing records. These are the same operations we have studied in Chapter 18, but they are created from subclasses of a base class called `CKDatabaseOperation`. Once the operation is defined, it must be added to the `CKDatabase` object that represents the database we want to modify. The `CKDatabase` class offers the following method for this purpose.

add(CKDatabaseOperation**)**—This method executes the operation specified by the attribute on the database. The attribute is an object of a subclass of the **CKDatabaseOperation** class.

Although we can create single operations and assign them to the database, as we will see later, the **CKDatabase** class also offers convenient methods to generate and execute the most common. The following are the methods available to process records.

fetch(withRecordID: CKRecord.ID, **completionHandler:** Block**)**—This method fetches the record with the ID specified by the **withRecordID** attribute. The **completionHandler** attribute is a closure that is executed when the process is over. The closure receives two values, a **CKRecord** object representing the record fetched, and a **CKError** object to report errors.

save(CKRecord, **completionHandler:** Block**)**—This method stores a record in the database (if the record already exists, it updates its values). The first attribute is a reference to the record we want to store, and the **completionHandler** attribute is a closure that is executed when the process is over. The closure receives two values, a reference to the **CKRecord** object we tried to save, and a **CKError** object to report errors.

delete(withRecordID: CKRecord.ID, **completionHandler:** Block**)**—This method deletes from the database the record with the ID specified by the **withRecordID** attribute. The **completionHandler** attribute is a closure that is executed when the process is over. The closure receives two values, a **CKRecord.ID** object with the ID of the record we tried to delete, and a **CKError** object to report errors.

The following are the methods provided by the **CKDatabase** class to process zones.

fetch(withRecordZoneID: CKRecordZone.ID, **completionHandler:** Block**)**—This method fetches the zone with the ID specified by the **withRecordZoneID** attribute. The **completionHandler** attribute is a closure that is executed when the process is over. The closure receives two values, a **CKRecordZone** object representing the zone that was fetched, and a **CKError** object to report errors.

fetchAllRecordZones(completionHandler: Block**)**—This method fetches all the zones available in the database. The **completionHandler** attribute is a closure that is executed when the process is over. The closure receives two values, an array with **CKRecordZone** objects representing the zones that were fetched, and a **CKError** object to report errors.

save(CKRecordZone, **completionHandler:** Block**)**—This method creates a zone in the database. The first attribute is the object representing the zone we want to create, and the **completionHandler** attribute is a closure that is executed when the process is over. The closure receives two values, a reference to the **CKRecordZone** object we tried to save, and a **CKError** object to report errors.

delete(withRecordZoneID: CKRecordZone.ID, **completionHandler:** Block**)**—This method deletes from the database the zone with the ID specified by the **withRecordZoneID** attribute. The **completionHandler** attribute is a closure that is executed when the process is over. The closure receives two values, a **CKRecordZone.ID** object with the ID of the zone we tried to delete, and a **CKError** object to report errors.

To perform a query, the **CKDatabase** class includes the following method.

perform(CKQuery, **inZoneWith:** CKRecordZone.ID?, **completionHandler:** Block)—This method performs the query specified by the first attribute in the zone specified by the `inZoneWith` attribute. The **completionHandler** attribute is a closure that is executed when the process is over. The closure receives two values, an array of **CKRecord** objects representing the records that were fetched, and a **CKError** object to report errors.

References

Records of different types are usually related. For example, along with records of type Countries we may have records of type Cities to store information about the cities of each country. To create these relationships, records may include references. References are objects that store information about a connection between one record and another. They are created from the **Reference** class defined inside the **CKRecord** class. The following are its initializers.

CKRecord.Reference(recordID: CKRecord.ID, **action:** CKRecord_Reference_Action)—This initializer creates a **Reference** object pointing to the record identified with the ID specified by the `recordID` attribute. The **action** attribute is an enumeration that determines what the database should do with the record when the record that is referencing is deleted. The possible values are **none** (nothing is done) and **deleteSelf** (when the record referenced by the reference is deleted, the record with the reference is deleted as well).

CKRecord.Reference(record: CKRecord, **action:** CKRecord_Reference_Action)—This initializer creates a **Reference** object pointing to the record specified by the **record** attribute. The **action** attribute is an enumeration that determines what the database should do with the record when the record that is referencing is deleted. The possible values are **none** (nothing is done) and **deleteSelf** (when the record referenced by the reference is deleted, the record with the reference is deleted as well).

References in CloudKit are called *Back References* because they are supposed to be assigned to the record that is the children of another record. Following our example, the reference should be assigned to the city and not the country, as illustrated next.

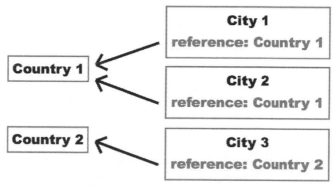

Figure 23-10: Back references

CloudKit Dashboard

CloudKit creates a model of our app's database on its servers as the records are added to the database. For example, if our app stores records of type "Books", the first time a record is created CloudKit adds the type "Books" to the list of record types available for our app and creates fields to represent each of the record's values. This way, the system establishes the database's structure from the data we store during development, saving us the trouble of configuring the database beforehand (we do not have to create a model as we do with Core

Data). But there are some configuration parameters that the system cannot determine by itself and we have to set up ourselves. For this purpose and to help us develop a CloudKit application, Apple provides the CloudKit dashboard. This is an online control panel available at https://icloud.developer.apple.com/dashboard/ that we can use to manage the CloudKit databases, add, update, or remove records, and configure the system.

The first thing we see when we access the dashboard is information about the developer team and a list of buttons representing all the containers created by our apps. Figure 23-11, below, shows the initial screen with a button to access the container created for the app we are going to use in this chapter to test CloudKit.

Figure 23-11: CloudKit dashboard

When we click on the button that represents the container we want to work with, the dashboard displays two menus, one to access the Development environment and another to access the Production environment. The Development environment is where our records and all the configuration of our CloudKit database is stored during development. Here, we can configure the database, create zones, records, record types, and subscriptions for testing, and also assign indexes to perform searches. Once the app is ready for distribution, we deploy the database to production and the database's structure defined in Development is copied to the Production environment.

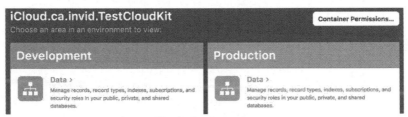

Figure 23-12: Environments menu

The most important section in the Development environment is accessible from the Data option. After we select this option, the window shows a list of panels from which we can modify each database, zones, and records created by our app.

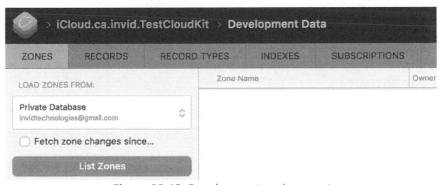

Figure 23-13: Development environment

iCloud

All the elements of the database are created automatically every time the app performs an operation in CloudKit, including the record types and indexes, but we can modify every aspect of the structure from these panels, as we will see next.

Implementing CloudKit

To illustrate how to work with CloudKit databases, we are going to create a simple application that lets the user save a list of locations. The initial interface presents two views inside a Navigation Controller. The views include a bar button to insert the name of a country or a city and a Table View to list the names already stored in the database.

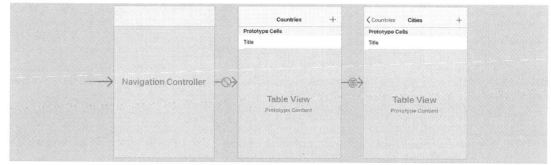

Figure 23-14: *Interface to work with CloudKit*

 Do It Yourself: Create a new Single View Application project. Activate CloudKit from the Capabilities panel and the options from the Background Modes section, as shown in Figures 23-2 and 23-8. Erase the initial Scene and add two Table View Controllers embedded in a Navigation Controller (Figure 23-14). Add a bar button of type Add to the Navigation Bar of each Scene. Select the cells and declare their types as Basic and their identifiers as "countriesCell" and "citiesCell", respectively. Create a Segue from the cell of the first view to the second view and assign the identifier "showCities" to it. Assign the title Countries to the first Scene and the title Cities to the second Scene (add the Navigation Item if necessary).

 IMPORTANT: CloudKit is a low-level framework, which means that we have to take care of every step of the process, from preparing the records, to define each operation, process the information received, and check for errors. This means that our codes are going to be extensive. We recommend that you read the descriptions in this chapter once, then study the codes in your Xcode project, and return to the text when you need help understanding any of the processes involved.

There are several ways to implement CloudKit. It all depends on the characteristics of our application and how it is organized. For the examples of this chapter, we have decided to keep it simple and manage all the CloudKit tasks from a single global object. As we did before, we called this class **ApplicationData**.

```
import UIKit
import CloudKit

class ApplicationData {
    var database: CKDatabase!
    var selectedCountry: CKRecord.ID!
    var listCountries: [CKRecord] = []
    var listCities: [CKRecord] = []
```

```
    init() {
        let container = CKContainer.default()
        database = container.privateCloudDatabase
    }
    func insertCountry(name: String) {
        let text = name.trimmingCharacters(in: .whitespaces)
        if text != "" {
            let id = CKRecord.ID(recordName: "idcountry-\(UUID())")
            let record = CKRecord(recordType: "Countries", recordID: id)
            record.setObject(text as NSString, forKey: "name")

            database.save(record, completionHandler: {(recordSaved, error) in
                if error != nil {
                    print("Error: record not saved")
                } else {
                    self.listCountries.append(record)
                    self.updateInterface()
                }
            })
        }
    }
    func insertCity(name: String) {
        let text = name.trimmingCharacters(in: .whitespaces)
        if text != "" {
            let id = CKRecord.ID(recordName: "idcity-\(UUID())")
            let record = CKRecord(recordType: "Cities", recordID: id)
            record.setObject(text as NSString, forKey: "name")
            let reference = CKRecord.Reference(recordID: selectedCountry,
action: .deleteSelf)
            record.setObject(reference, forKey: "country")

            database.save(record, completionHandler: {(recordSaved, error) in
                if error != nil {
                    print("Error: record not saved")
                } else {
                    self.listCities.append(record)
                    self.updateInterface()
                }
            })
        }
    }
    func readCountries() {
        let predicate = NSPredicate(format: "TRUEPREDICATE")
        let query = CKQuery(recordType: "Countries", predicate: predicate)
        database.perform(query, inZoneWith: nil, completionHandler: {
(records, error) in
            if error != nil {
                print("Error: records not found")
            } else if let list = records {
                self.listCountries = []
                for record in list {
                    self.listCountries.append(record)
                }
                self.updateInterface()
            }
        })
    }
    func readCities() {
        if selectedCountry != nil {
            let predicate = NSPredicate(format: "country = %@",
selectedCountry)
```

```
        let query = CKQuery(recordType: "Cities", predicate: predicate)
        database.perform(query, inZoneWith: nil, completionHandler: {
(records, error) in
            if error != nil {
                print("Error: records not found")
            } else if let list = records {
                self.listCities = []
                for record in list {
                    self.listCities.append(record)
                }
                self.updateInterface()
            }
        })
    }
}
    func updateInterface() {
        let main = OperationQueue.main
        main.addOperation({
            let center = NotificationCenter.default
            let name = Notification.Name("Update Interface")
            center.post(name: name, object: nil, userInfo: nil)
        })
    }
}
var AppData = ApplicationData()
```

Listing 23-14: Creating the model

The first thing the class of Listing 23-14 does is to define the properties required to store the data locally. The **listCountries** property is an array with the list of the countries already inserted in the database, the **listCities** property is another array with the list of the cities available for a specific country, and the **selectedCountry** property is going to be used as a reference to know which country has been selected by the user at any given moment.

Another property included in the class is **database**. This property stores a reference to the CloudKit's database, so we can have access to it from anywhere in the code. The property is initialized in the **init()** method with a reference to the Private Database (we use the private database because we only want the user to be able to share the data between his own devices).

After the initialization, we define two methods: **insertCountry()** and **insertCity()**. These methods are going to be called from the view controllers when the user inserts a new country or city. Their task is to create the records and upload them to CloudKit. The process begins by defining a record ID, which is a unique value that identifies each record. For the countries, we use the string "idcountry" followed by a random value generated by the **UUID()** function (see Chapter 19). After we have the ID, we create the **CKRecord** object of type Countries, add a property called name with the value received by the method, and finally save it in CloudKit servers with the **save()** method of the **CKDatabase** object. This method generates an operation that communicates with the servers asynchronously and reports back the result to the closure assigned to the **completionHandler** attribute when the process is over. The closure receives two values, the first value is a reference to the record we tried to save, and the second value contains the errors produced by the operation. If there are no errors (the **error** parameter is equal to **nil**), we add the record to the **listCountries** property and then call the **updateInterface()** method to tell the views that they have to update the tables.

The method to add a city is the same, with the exceptions that we had to define the type of records as Cities and add an extra attribute to the record with a reference to the country the city belongs to. For this purpose, we create a **Reference** object with the record ID stored in the **selectedCountry** property, and an action of type **deleteSelf**, so when the record of the country is deleted, this record is deleted as well.

Next are the methods we are going to call from the view controllers to get the countries and cities already stored in the database. In the **readCountries()** method, we define a predicate with the TRUEPREDICATE keyword and a query for records of type Countries. The type asks the server to only look for countries, and the TRUEPREDICATE keyword determines that the predicate will always return the value **true**, so we get back all the records available. If the query doesn't return any errors, we add the list of records received to the **listCountries** array and then call the **updateInterface()** method to tell the views that new information is available.

The **readCities()** method is very similar, except that this time we are getting the list of cities that belong to the country selected by the user (the view that shows the cities only opens when the user taps on a cell to select a country). The rest of the code is the same. We get the records that represent the cities, store them in the **listCities** array, and call the **updateInterface()** method to ask the views to update the tables.

All the methods mentioned above call the **updateInterface()** method when the process is over. The purpose of this method is to tell the rest of the application that new information is available and should be shown to the user. In this example, we achieve it by posting a notification. The **updateInterface()** method posts a notification called "Update Interface" that the view controllers can observe to update the Table Views (see Notification Center in Chapter 19). For instance, the following is the view controller for the view that shows the countries. The first task we perform when the view is loaded is to register an observer for this notification, so when the notification is received, the observer calls a method to update the table. We called this view controller **CountriesViewController**.

```
import UIKit
import CloudKit

class CountriesViewController: UITableViewController {
   override func viewDidLoad() {
      super.viewDidLoad()
      let center = NotificationCenter.default
      let name = Notification.Name("Update Interface")
      center.addObserver(self, selector:
#selector(updateInterface(notification:)), name: name, object: nil)
      AppData.readCountries()
   }
   @objc func updateInterface(notification: Notification) {
      tableView.reloadData()
   }
   override func tableView(_ tableView: UITableView,
numberOfRowsInSection section: Int) -> Int {
      return AppData.listCountries.count
   }
   override func tableView(_ tableView: UITableView, cellForRowAt
indexPath: IndexPath) -> UITableViewCell {
      let cell = tableView.dequeueReusableCell(withIdentifier:
"countriesCell", for: indexPath)
      let record = AppData.listCountries[indexPath.row]
      if let name = record["name"] as? String {
         cell.textLabel?.text = name
      }
      return cell
   }
   @IBAction func addCountry(_ sender: UIBarButtonItem) {
      let alert = UIAlertController(title: "Insert Country", message:
nil, preferredStyle: .alert)
      let cancel = UIAlertAction(title: "Cancel", style: .cancel,
handler: nil)
      alert.addAction(cancel)
```

```
            let action = UIAlertAction(title: "Save", style: .default, handler:
{ (action) in
            if let fields = alert.textFields {
                let name = fields[0].text!
                AppData.insertCountry(name: name)
            }
        })
        alert.addAction(action)
        alert.addTextField(configurationHandler: nil)
        present(alert, animated: true, completion: nil)
    }
    override func prepare(for segue: UIStoryboardSegue, sender: Any?) {
        if segue.identifier == "showCities" {
            if let indexPath = self.tableView.indexPathForSelectedRow {
                let record = AppData.listCountries[indexPath.row]
                AppData.selectedCountry = record.recordID
            }
        }
    }
}
```

Listing 23-15: Reading and storing countries in the Private database

The view controller begins by defining an observer for the "Update Interface" notification. If a notification is received, the **updateInterface()** method is called, and the Table View is updated. The observer updates the table to show the values currently available, but we also have to read and show these values when the view is loaded. This is done by calling the **readCountries()** method defined in our model. The method performs a query on the database to get all the countries available and posts a notification when it is over (this is why we register the observer for the notification before calling the method).

To let the user add a new country, we defined an Action for the bar button called **addCountry()**. When the user presses the button, we create an Alert View with a Text Field inside. After the user inserts a name and presses the Save button, we call the **insertCountry()** method in the model with this value to add the record to the database.

The view controller also includes all the methods of the **UITableViewDataSource** protocol necessary to read the values in the **listCountries** array and show them on the screen, and the **prepare()** method as well to prepare the information when a country is selected. If the user taps on a cell, this method assigns the record ID of that country to the **selectedCountry** property in the model before opening the second Scene, so the view controller of this Scene can show the list of cities that belong to that country. We called this view controller **CitiesViewController**.

```
import UIKit
import CloudKit

class CitiesViewController: UITableViewController {
    override func viewDidLoad() {
        super.viewDidLoad()
        let center = NotificationCenter.default
        let name = Notification.Name("Update Interface")
        center.addObserver(self, selector:
#selector(updateInterface(notification:)), name: name, object: nil)
        AppData.readCities()
    }
    @objc func updateInterface(notification: Notification) {
        tableView.reloadData()
    }
```

```
    override func tableView(_ tableView: UITableView,
numberOfRowsInSection section: Int) -> Int {
        return AppData.listCities.count
    }
    override func tableView(_ tableView: UITableView, cellForRowAt
indexPath: IndexPath) -> UITableViewCell {
        let cell = tableView.dequeueReusableCell(withIdentifier:
"citiesCell", for: indexPath)
        let record = AppData.listCities[indexPath.row]
        if let name = record["name"] as? String {
            cell.textLabel?.text = name
        }
        return cell
    }
    @IBAction func addCity(_ sender: UIBarButtonItem) {
        let alert = UIAlertController(title: "Insert City", message: nil,
preferredStyle: .alert)
        let cancel = UIAlertAction(title: "Cancel", style: .cancel,
handler: nil)
        alert.addAction(cancel)
        let action = UIAlertAction(title: "Save", style: .default, handler:
{ (action) in
            if let fields = alert.textFields {
                let name = fields[0].text!
                AppData.insertCity(name: name)
            }
        })
        alert.addAction(action)
        alert.addTextField(configurationHandler: nil)
        present(alert, animated: true, completion: nil)
    }
}
```

Listing 23-16: *Storing cities in the Private database*

This view controller is similar to the previous one, except this time we are working with records of type Cities instead of Countries. After registering the observer for the "Update Interface" notification, we call the **readCities()** method in the model. Because we already stored the record ID of the country selected by the user in the **selectedCountry** property, the method will only get the cities that belong to that country, and therefore those will be the only cities displayed on the table.

 Do It Yourself: Create a Swift file called ApplicationData.swift for the code of Listing 23-14. Create a subclass of **UITableViewController**, call it **CountriesViewController**, assign it to the initial Scene, and complete it with the code of Listing 23-15. Connect the bar button of this Scene with the Action **addCountry()**. Create another subclass of **UITableView-Controller**, call it **CitiesViewController**, assign it to the second Scene, and complete it with the code of Listing 23-16. Connect the bar button of this Scene with the Action **addCity()**. Run the application in your device and press the bar button to insert a country. If you run the application on the simulator, remember to log in to your account from the Settings app to activate iCloud and to select the option Trigger iCloud Sync from the Debug menu to get the information uploaded to the Apple servers.

The application is ready. When the user inserts a new value, the code creates a record and uploads it to CloudKit's servers. But if we stop and run the application again, we won't see any countries on the screen and we will get the message "Error: records not found" on the console.

This is because we haven't defined the required index. CloudKit automatically creates indexes for every value we include in the records, except for the record's ID. If we go to the CloudKit dashboard, click on the container for our app, select the option Data from the Development environment menu, select the Indexes panel, and click on the record type Countries, we will see the indexes assigned to the fields, as shown in Figure 23-15.

ZONES	RECORDS	RECORD TYPES	INDEXES	SUBSCRIPTIONS	SUBSCRIPTION

SHOW INDEXES FOR TYPE:	Fields		Index Type	
Countries 3 indexes	name	Single Field	QUERYABLE	✕
Users 0 indexes	name	Single Field	SEARCHABLE	✕
	name	Single Field	SORTABLE	✕

Figure 23-15: *Indexes*

There are three types of indexes: Queryable (it can be included in a query), Searchable (it can be searched), and Sortable (it can be sorted). In our example, we only have one custom field for the countries called *name*. Because the system does not know the type of indexes our app is going to need for this field, it automatically adds all of them, but only for this field. When we query the database in the `readCountries()` method of the `ApplicationData` class, we do not specify any field in the predicate and therefore the system fetches the records from their identifier, which is described in the database as recordName. For this reason, to get the countries, we have to add a Queryable index to the recordName field for the Countries record type. The panel includes a button called Add Index at the bottom of the list for this purpose. When we click this button, a new line is added to the list with fields to select the field's name and the type of index we want to assign to it.

name	Single Field	QUERYABLE	✕
name	Single Field	SEARCHABLE	✕
name	Single Field	SORTABLE	✕
recordName ⬦	Single Field	QUERYABLE ⬦	✕

Figure 23-16: *New Index*

Once we select the field recordName and the index Queryable, we can press the Save Record Type button at the bottom-right corner of the window to save the changes. Now, if we run the application again from Xcode, the records added to the database are shown on the table.

 Do It Yourself: Stop the application if you haven't done it yet. Go to the CloudKit dashboard, click on the container for your app, select the option Data from the Development environment menu, select the Indexes panel, click on the record type Countries, click on the Add Index button, and add the index for the recordName field, as shown in Figure 23-16. Press the Save Record Type button to save the changes and run the application again. You should see on the screen the countries you have inserted before.

Assets

Records may also include files, and the files may contain anything from pictures to sound or even videos. To add a file to a record, we have to create an asset with the **CKAsset** class. The class includes the following initializer.

CKAsset(fileURL: URL)—This initializer creates a **CKAsset** object with the content of the file in the location determined by the **fileURL** attribute.

The assets are added to a record with a key, as any other value. For our example, we are going to store a picture in the record of every city and add a view to show the picture when the city is selected.

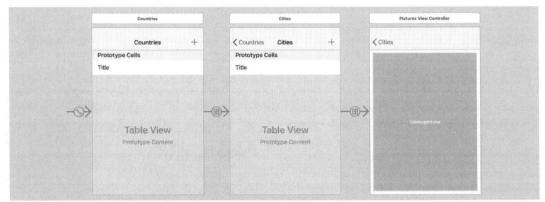

Figure 23-17: Interface to store and show assets

 Do It Yourself: Add a new Scene to the Storyboard. Connect the cell of the second view to the new Scene with a Show Segue and give the Segue the identifier "showPicture". Add an Image View to the new Scene and pin it to the margins of the safe area, as shown in Figure 23-17.

The following are the changes we have to introduce to the **insertCity()** method of the **ApplicationData** class to get the URL of the image and assign the asset to the record.

```
func insertCity(name: String) {
    let text = name.trimmingCharacters(in: .whitespaces)
    if text != "" {
        let id = CKRecord.ID(recordName: "idcity-\(UUID())")
        let record = CKRecord(recordType: "Cities", recordID: id)
        record.setObject(text as NSString, forKey: "name")
        let reference = CKRecord.Reference(recordID: selectedCountry,
action: .deleteSelf)
        record.setObject(reference, forKey: "country")

        let bundle = Bundle.main
        if let fileURL = bundle.url(forResource: "Toronto", withExtension:
"jpg") {
            let asset = CKAsset(fileURL: fileURL)
            record.setObject(asset, forKey: "picture")
        }
        database.save(record, completionHandler: { (recordSaved, error) in
            if error != nil {
                print("Error: record not saved")
            } else {
                self.listCities.append(record)
```

```
            self.updateInterface()
        }
    })
  }
}
```

In the new **insertCity()** method introduced in Listing 23-17, we get the URL of an image included in the project called Toronto.jpg, create a **CKAsset** object with it, and assign the object to the record of every city with the key "picture" (see how to access the bundle in Chapter 21). Now, besides the name, a file with this image will be stored for every city inserted by the user. To get the asset back, we have to implement the **prepare()** method in the **CitiesViewController** class to pass the record ID of the selected city to the view controller in charge of showing the image to the user.

```
override func prepare(for segue: UIStoryboardSegue, sender: Any?) {
    if segue.identifier == "showPicture" {
        if let indexPath = self.tableView.indexPathForSelectedRow {
            let controller = segue.destination as! PicturesViewController
            controller.selectedCity = AppData.listCities[indexPath.row]
        }
    }
}
```

Listing 23-18: Passing the selected city to the view controller

Because the values stored in the **listCities** array are references to the records of every city, to show the image on the screen we just have to read the asset from the record, create an image with it, and assign it to the Image View. All this process is done by the view controller of the Scene added in Figure 23-17. We call this view controller **PicturesViewController**.

```
import UIKit
import CloudKit

class PicturesViewController: UIViewController {
    @IBOutlet weak var cityPicture: UIImageView!
    var selectedCity: CKRecord!

    override func viewDidLoad() {
        if selectedCity != nil {
            if let asset = selectedCity["picture"] as? CKAsset {
                self.cityPicture.image = UIImage(contentsOfFile:
asset.fileURL.path)
            }
        }
    }
}
```

Listing 23-19: Reading assets

How to read the asset stored in the record depends on the type of content managed by the asset. In this example, we have to use the asset's path to create a **UIImage** object and then assign the image object to the **UIImageView** on the interface. As a result, every time the user selects a city, the asset is turned into an image and shown on the screen.

In this example, we load always the same image from the bundle. We will study how to get images from the Photo Library and take photos from the camera in Chapter 26.

Do It Yourself: Update the `ApplicationData` class with the method of Listing 23-17, and the `CitiesViewController` class with the method of Listing 23-18. Download the Toronto.jpg picture from our website and add the file to your project. Create a subclass of the `UIViewController` class called `PicturesViewController` and assign it to the last Scene. Complete the class with the code of Listing 23-19. Connect the Image View with the Outlet called `cityPicture`. Run the application, select a country and add a new city. Select the city. You should see the Toronto.jpg image on the screen.

 IMPORTANT: Uploading and downloading images takes time. Therefore, it is better to keep a local cache, so the users don't have to wait for the images to download every time they want to see them. We will learn how to store the information locally later in this chapter.

Subscriptions

The previous example fetches the records available and shows them on the screen every time the view is loaded. This means that records added to the database from another device will not be visible until the view is loaded again. This is not the behaviour expected by the user. When working with applications that store information online, users expects the information to be updated as soon as it becomes available. To provide this feature, CloudKit uses subscriptions. Subscriptions are queries stored by our application in the CloudKit servers. When a change occurs in the database, the query detects the modification and triggers the delivery of a Remote Notification from the iCloud servers to the copy of the app that registered the subscription.

Database subscriptions are created from the `CKDatabaseSubscription` class (a subclass of a more generic class called `CKSubscription`). The class includes the following initializer and property to create and configure the subscription.

CKDatabaseSubscription(subscriptionID: String)—This initializer creates a `CKDatabaseSubscription` object that represents a subscription with the ID specified by the **subscriptionID** attribute.

notificationInfo—This property is a value of type `NotificationInfo`, a class included in the `CKSubscription` class, that contains a configuration of the Remote Notification the server is going to send to the application when the subscription detects changes in the database.

As always, a subscription must be added to CloudKit servers with an operation, but the `CKDatabase` class also offers convenient methods to create these operations.

save(CKSubscription, **completionHandler:** Block)—This method stores in the servers the subscription specified by the first attribute. The **completionHandler** attribute is a closure that is executed when the process is over. The closure receives two values, a `CKSubscription` object representing the subscription we tried to save, and a `CKError` object to report errors.

delete(withSubscriptionID: String, **completionHandler:** Block)—This method removes from the server the subscription with the ID specified by the **withSubscriptionID** attribute. The **completionHandler** attribute is a closure that is executed when the process is over. The closure receives two values, a string with the subscription ID that we tried to delete and a `CKError` object to report errors.

After our app registers a subscription in the servers, we have to listen to Remote Notifications and download the changes. The first step our application has to take to be able to receive these notifications is to register with the iCloud servers. The **UIApplication** class offers the following method for this purpose.

registerForRemoteNotifications()—This method registers the app in the iCloud servers to receive Remote Notifications. A token is generated to identify each copy of our app, so the notifications are delivered to the right user.

To report to our application that a Remote Notification was received, the **UIApplication** object calls a method in the app's delegate. The following is the method defined by the **UIApplicationDelegate** class for this purpose.

application(UIApplication, **didReceiveRemoteNotification:** Dictionary, **fetch-CompletionHandler:** Block**)**—This method is called by the application on its delegate when a Remote Notification is received. The **didReceiveRemoteNotification** attribute is a dictionary with information about the notification, and the **fetchCompletionHandler** attribute is a closure that we have to execute after all the custom tasks are performed. The closure must be called with a value that describes the result of the operation. For this purpose, UIKit offers the **UIBackgroundFetchResult** enumeration with the values **newData** (new data was downloaded), **noData** (no data was downloaded), and **failed** (the app failed to download the data).

Setting up a subscription on CloudKit servers is easy, but because subscriptions report the changes through Remote Notifications, there are several steps we have to take to prepare our application. We will begin with the changes we have to introduce in the **AppDelegate** class of our example. Here, we need to call the **registerForRemoteNotifications()** method of the **UIApplication** object as soon as the application is launched to tell the system that we want to register the application to receive Remote Notifications from iCloud servers (the Apple Push Notification service). If the registration is successful, the system calls the delegate method every time a notification is received, so we have to implement this method as well.

```
import UIKit
import CloudKit

@UIApplicationMain
class AppDelegate: UIResponder, UIApplicationDelegate {
    var window: UIWindow?

    func application(_ application: UIApplication,
didFinishLaunchingWithOptions launchOptions:
[UIApplication.LaunchOptionsKey: Any]?) -> Bool {
        let userSettings = UserDefaults.standard
        let values = ["subscriptionSaved": false, "zoneCreated": false]
        userSettings.register(defaults: values)

        application.registerForRemoteNotifications()
        AppData.configureDatabase(executeClosure: {})
        return true
    }
    func application(_ application: UIApplication,
didReceiveRemoteNotification userInfo: [AnyHashable : Any],
fetchCompletionHandler completionHandler: @escaping
(UIBackgroundFetchResult) -> Void) {
        let notification = CKNotification(fromRemoteNotificationDictionary:
userInfo) as? CKDatabaseNotification
        if notification != nil {
            AppData.checkUpdates(finishClosure: { (result) in
                let mainQueue = OperationQueue.main
```

```
            mainQueue.addOperation({
                completionHandler(result)
            })
        })
    }
  }
}
```

Listing 23-20: Processing Remote Notifications

Subscriptions only report changes in customs zones. If we want to receive notifications, besides creating the subscription we also have to create a record zone and store all our records in it. Hence, the first thing we do is to store two Boolean values in the User Defaults database called "subscriptionSaved" and "zoneCreated". These values will be used later to know whether or not we have already created the subscription and the custom zone.

Next, we call the **registerForRemoteNotifications()** method on the **UIApplication** object to register the application with iCloud servers and a method called **configureDatabase()** that we are going to define later in our **ApplicationData** class to create the subscription and the custom zone for the first time.

The **registerForRemoteNotifications()** method prepares the application to receive notifications, but the notifications are processed by the delegate method. The first thing we have to do in this method is to check whether the notification received is a notification sent by a CloudKit server. For this purpose, the CloudKit framework includes the **CKNotification** class with properties we can use to process the dictionary and read its values. The class includes the following initializer.

CKNotification(fromRemoteNotificationDictionary: Dictionary)—This initializer creates a **CKNotification** object from the information included in the notification (the value of the **userInfo** parameter in the delegate method).

Because CloudKit servers can send other types of notifications, after we get the **CKNotification** object with this initializer, we check whether the notification received is of type **CKDatabaseNotification** with the **as?** operator. In case of success, we proceed to download the new data from the application.

Before going to the process of downloading the new information from CloudKit servers, we have to consider that the system requires us to report the result of the operation. Notifications may be received when the application is closed or in the background. If this happens, the system launches our application and puts it in the background to allow it to contact the servers and process the information. But because this process consumes resources, the system needs to know when the operation is over and therefore it requires us to report it by calling the closure received by the **completionHandler** parameter with a value of the **UIBackgroundFetchResult** enumeration that determines what happened (**newData** if we downloaded new data, **noData** if there was nothing to download, and **failed** if the process failed). By calling the closure, we tell the system that the process is over, but because the operations are performed asynchronously, we can't do it until they are finished. That is why, in the example of Listing 23-20, we send a closure to the method we use to download the new information which sole purpose is to execute the **completionHandler** closure with the value returned by the operations.

All the code we need to prepare our application is ready. Now we have to implement the methods that are going to contact the CloudKit servers and process the information. In the application's delegate, we call two methods of our **ApplicationData** class: the **configureDatabase()** method to create the subscription and the zone, and the **checkUpdates()** method to download and process the information. The following is our implementation of the **configureDatabase()** method.

```
func configureDatabase(executeClosure: @escaping () -> Void) {
    let userSettings = UserDefaults.standard
    if !userSettings.bool(forKey: "subscriptionSaved") {
        let newSubscription = CKDatabaseSubscription(subscriptionID:
"updatesDatabase")
        let info = CKSubscription.NotificationInfo()
        info.shouldSendContentAvailable = true
        newSubscription.notificationInfo = info

        database.save(newSubscription, completionHandler: { (subscription,
error) in
            if error != nil {
                print("Error Creating Subscription")
            } else {
                userSettings.set(true, forKey: "subscriptionSaved")
            }
        })
    }
    if !userSettings.bool(forKey: "zoneCreated") {
        let newZone = CKRecordZone(zoneName: "listPlaces")
        database.save(newZone, completionHandler: { (zone, error) in
            if error != nil {
                print("Error Creating Zone")
            } else {
                userSettings.set(true, forKey: "zoneCreated")
                executeClosure()
            }
        })
    } else {
        executeClosure()
    }
}
```

Listing 23-21: Configuring the database

When it comes to organizing our code, we have to consider that every process executed in CloudKit servers has to be performed through asynchronous operations. This means that we have to consider the order in which the operations are executed. For some operations, the order doesn't matter, but for others it is crucial. For instance, we cannot store records in a zone before the zone is created. As we have seen in Chapter 18, we can use Dependencies or even Dispatch Groups to control the order in which operations are performed, but we can also use closures to execute code only after an operation is over, and this is the approach we take in the examples of this chapter. The procedure is as follows. Every time we call the **configureDatabase()** method to create the subscription and the zone, we send a closure to the method with the code we want to be executed once the operation is over. This way, we make sure that the operations are over before doing anything else.

 The Basics: There are two types of closures, escaping and non-escaping. An escaping closure lives outside the function in which it is declared, and a non-escaping closure is destroyed (removed from memory) when the execution of the function is over. By default, all closures are non-escaping, this is why in the **configureDatabase()** method of Listing 23-21 we use the **@escaping** keyword to declare the closure as escaping and being able to execute it outside the method.

The first thing we do in the `configureDatabase()` method is to check the subscriptionSaved value in the User Defaults to know if the subscription was already created. If not, we use the **CKDatabaseSubscription** initializer to create the subscription and then define the **notificationInfo** property to configure the notifications that are going to be sent by the server. For this purpose, the framework defines the **CKNotificationInfo** class. This class includes multiple properties to configure Remote Notifications for CloudKit, but database subscriptions only require us to set the **shouldSendContentAvailable** property to **true**. Next, the subscription is saved on the server with the **save()** method of the **CKDatabase** object and the subscriptionSaved value is changed to **true** if the operation is successful.

The next step is to create the custom zone. Again, we check the Boolean value stored in User Defaults to know if the zone was already created, and if not, we create a zone called listPlaces to store our records. In this case, if the operation is successful, besides assigning the value **true** to the zoneCreated value, we also have to call the closure. This is because we don't care whether the subscription was saved or not, but we have to be sure that the zone was created before trying to store any records. Notice that the closure is also called if the zone was already created to make sure that its code is always executed.

And finally, we have to create the **checkUpdates()** method to download and process the changes in the database. As we already mentioned, this method has to receive a closure to be able to report to the system the result of the operation, but we also have to consider that there could have being an error when we tried to create the subscription and the zone, so we have to call the **configureDatabase()** method again just in case.

```
func checkUpdates(finishClosure: @escaping (UIBackgroundFetchResult) ->
Void) {
    configureDatabase(executeClosure: {
    let mainQueue = OperationQueue.main
        mainQueue.addOperation({
            self.downloadUpdates(finishClosure: finishClosure)
        })
    })
}
```

Listing 23-22: Initiating the process to get the updates from the server

The **checkUpdates()** method receives the closure we have to execute to report the result of the operation and then calls the **configureDatabase()** method to make sure that the database is configured properly. The value we send to this method is another closure that contains the code we want to execute after we make sure that the zone was created.

To simplify the code, we moved the statements to an additional method called **downloadUpdates()**, so after we confirm that the zone was created, we call this method with a reference to the closure received by the **configureDatabase()** method.

 The Basics: Passing closures from one function to another is a way to control the order in which the code is executed when we use asynchronous operations. We chose this programming pattern for the examples in this chapter because it simplifies the code, but as we mentioned before you can use Dependencies or Dispatch Groups. For more information, see Chapter 18.

Before implementing the **downloadUpdates()** method and process the changes in the database, we have to study the operations provided by the CloudKit framework for this purpose. The operation to fetch the list of changes available in the database is created from a subclass of the **CKDatabaseOperation** class called **CKFetchDatabaseChangesOperation**. This class includes the following initializer:

CKFetchDatabaseChangesOperation(previousServerChangeToken: CKServer-ChangeToken?)—This initializer creates a `CKFetchDatabaseChangesOperation` object to fetch changes from a database. The attribute is a token that determines which changes were already fetched. If we specify a token, only the changes that occurred after the token was created are fetched.

The class also includes properties to define completion handlers for every step of the process.

recordZoneWithIDChangedBlock—This property sets a closure that is executed to report which zones present changes. The closure receives a value of type `CKRecordZone.ID` with the ID of the zone that changed.

changeTokenUpdatedBlock—This property sets a closure that is executed to report the last database token. The closure receives an object of type `CKServerChangeToken` with the current token that we can store to send to subsequent operations.

fetchDatabaseChangesCompletionBlock—This property sets a closure that is executed when the operation is over. The closure receives three values, a `CKServerChangeToken` object with the last token, a Boolean value that indicates if there are more changes available, and a `CKError` value to report errors.

After completion of this operation, we have to perform another operation to download the changes. For this purpose, the framework includes the `CKFetchRecordZoneChangesOperation` class with the following initializer.

CKFetchRecordZoneChangesOperation(recordZoneIDs: [CKRecordZone.ID], **configurationsByRecordZoneID:** Dictionary)—This initializer creates a `CKFetchRecordZoneChangesOperation` object to download changes from a database. The **recordZoneIDs** attribute is an array with the IDs of all the zones that present changes, and the **configurationsByRecordZoneID** attribute is a dictionary with configuration values for each zone. The dictionary takes `CKRecordZone.ID` objects as keys and options determined by an object of the `ZoneConfiguration` class included in the `CKFetchRecordZoneChangesOperation` class. The class includes three properties to define the options: **desiredKeys** (array of strings with the keys we want to retrieve), **previousServerChangeToken** (`CKServerChangeToken` object with the current token), and **resultsLimit** (integer that determines the maximum number of records to retrieve).

The `CKFetchRecordZoneChangesOperation` class also includes properties to define completion handlers for every step of the process.

recordChangedBlock—This property sets a closure that is executed when a new or updated record is downloaded. The closure receives a `CKRecord` object representing the record that changed.

recordWithIDWasDeletedBlock—This property sets a closure that is executed when the operation finds a deleted record. The closure receives two values, a `CKRecord.ID` object with the ID of the record that was deleted, and a string with the record's type.

recordZoneChangeTokensUpdatedBlock—This property sets a closure that is executed when the change token for the zone is updated. The closure receives three values, a `CKRecordZone.ID` with the ID of the zone associated to the token, a `CKServerChangeToken` object with the current token, and a `Data` structure with the last token sent by the app to the server.

recordZoneFetchCompletionBlock—This property sets a closure that is executed when the operation finishes downloading the changes of a zone. The closure receives five values, a `CKRecordZone.ID` with the zone's ID, a `CKServerChangeToken` object with the current token, a `Data` structure with the last token sent by the app to the server, a Boolean value that indicates if there are more changes available, and a `CKError` value to report errors.

fetchRecordZoneChangesCompletionBlock—This property sets a closure that is executed after the operation is over. The closure receives a `CKError` value to report errors.

CloudKit servers use tokens to know which changes were already sent to every copy of the app, so the information is not downloaded twice from the same device. If a device stores or modifies a record, the server generates a new token, so next time a device accesses the servers only the changes introduced after the last token will be downloaded, as shown in Figure 23-18.

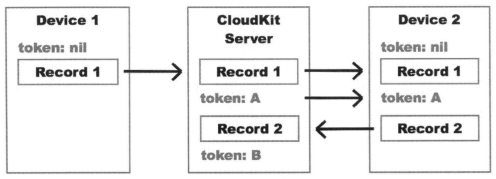

Figure 23-18: *Tokens*

In the process depicted in Figure 23-18, the app in Device 1 stores a new record in the server (Record 1). To reflect the changes, the server generates a new token (A). When the app in Device 2 connects to the server, the server detects that this device does not have the latest token, so it returns Record 1 and the current token (A) to set the state of the information in this device. If later the user decides to create a new record from Device 2 (Record 2), a new token will be created (B). The next time Device 1 connects with the server, it will find that its token is different than the server's token, so it will download the modifications inserted after its token (in this case, every change on the server, including Record 1).

Tokens are great because they allow us to only get the latest changes, but this process is not automatic, we are responsible of storing the current tokens and preserve the state for our app. The server creates a token for the database and a token for each of the custom zones. For our example, we need two tokens, one to keep track of the changes in the database and another for the custom zone created by the `configureDatabase()` method. To work with these values, we are going to use two properties `changeToken` for the database token and `fetchChangeToken` for the token of our custom zone, and we are going to store them permanently in User Settings for future reference. All this process is performed by the `downloadUpdates()` method, as shown next.

```
func downloadUpdates(finishClosure: @escaping (UIBackgroundFetchResult) -
> Void) {
    var changeToken: CKServerChangeToken!
    var changeZoneToken: CKServerChangeToken!

    let userSettings = UserDefaults.standard
    if let data = userSettings.value(forKey: "changeToken") as? Data {
```

```
            if let token = try? NSKeyedUnarchiver.unarchivedObject(ofClass:
CKServerChangeToken.self, from: data) {
                changeToken = token
            }
        }
        if let data = userSettings.value(forKey: "changeZoneToken") as? Data {
            if let token = try? NSKeyedUnarchiver.unarchivedObject(ofClass:
CKServerChangeToken.self, from: data) {
                changeZoneToken = token
            }
        }
    }
    var zonesIDs: [CKRecordZone.ID] = []
    let operation =
CKFetchDatabaseChangesOperation(previousServerChangeToken: changeToken)
    operation.recordZoneWithIDChangedBlock = { (zoneID) in
        zonesIDs.append(zoneID)
    }
    operation.changeTokenUpdatedBlock = { (token) in
        changeToken = token
    }
    operation.fetchDatabaseChangesCompletionBlock = {(token, more, error) in
        if error != nil {
            finishClosure(UIBackgroundFetchResult.failed)
        } else if !zonesIDs.isEmpty {
            changeToken = token
            let configuration =
CKFetchRecordZoneChangesOperation.ZoneConfiguration()
            configuration.previousServerChangeToken = changeZoneToken
            let fetchOperation =
CKFetchRecordZoneChangesOperation(recordZoneIDs: zonesIDs,
configurationsByRecordZoneID: [zonesIDs[0]: configuration])
            fetchOperation.recordChangedBlock = { (record) in
                if record.recordType == "Countries" {
                    let index = self.listCountries.firstIndex(where: {(item) in
                        return item.recordID == record.recordID
                    })
                    if index != nil {
                        self.listCountries[index!] = record
                    } else {
                        self.listCountries.append(record)
                    }
                } else if record.recordType == "Cities" {
                    if let country = record["country"] as? CKRecord.Reference{
                        if country.recordID == self.selectedCountry {
                            let index = self.listCities.firstIndex(where:
{(item) in
                                return item.recordID == record.recordID
                            })
                            if index != nil {
                                self.listCities[index!] = record
                            } else {
                                self.listCities.append(record)
                            }
                        }
                    }
                }
            }
            fetchOperation.recordWithIDWasDeletedBlock = { (recordID,
recordType) in
                if recordType == "Countries" {
                    let index = self.listCountries.firstIndex(where: {(item) in
```

```
                return item.recordID == recordID
            })
            if index != nil {
                self.listCountries.remove(at: index!)
            }
        } else if recordType == "Cities" {
            let index = self.listCities.firstIndex(where: { (item) in
                return item.recordID == recordID
            })
            if index != nil {
                self.listCities.remove(at: index!)
            }
        }
    }
}
fetchOperation.recordZoneChangeTokensUpdatedBlock = { (zoneID,
token, data) in
    changeZoneToken = token
}
fetchOperation.recordZoneFetchCompletionBlock = { (zoneID,
token, data, more, error) in
    if error != nil {
        print("Error")
    } else {
        changeZoneToken = token
    }
}
fetchOperation.fetchRecordZoneChangesCompletionBlock = {(error) in
    if error != nil {
        finishClosure(UIBackgroundFetchResult.failed)
    } else {
        if changeToken != nil {
            if let data = try?
NSKeyedArchiver.archivedData(withRootObject: changeToken,
requiringSecureCoding: false) {
                userSettings.set(data, forKey: "changeToken")
            }
        }
        if changeZoneToken != nil {
            if let data = try?
NSKeyedArchiver.archivedData(withRootObject: changeZoneToken,
requiringSecureCoding: false) {
                userSettings.set(data, forKey: "changeZoneToken")
            }
        }
        self.updateInterface()
        finishClosure(UIBackgroundFetchResult.newData)
    }
}
self.database.add(fetchOperation)
    } else {
        finishClosure(UIBackgroundFetchResult.noData)
    }
    }
    database.add(operation)
}
```

Listing 23-23: *Getting the updates from the server*

This is a very long method that we need to study piece by piece. As mentioned before, we start by defining the properties we are going to use to store the tokens (one for the database and another for the custom zone). Next, we check if there are tokens already stored in the User Defaults database. Because the tokens are instances of the `CKServerChangeToken` class, we can't store their values directly in User Defaults, we first have to convert them into `Data` structures. This is why, when we read the values in the User defaults, we cast them as `Data` with the `as?` operator and then unarchive them with the `unarchivedObject()` method of the `NSKeyedUnarchiver` class (see Chapter 19).The first time we do this, there won't be any values stored in User Defaults and therefore the values of the properties will be `nil` and all the changes will be downloaded from the database.

Next, we configure the operations necessary to get the updates from the server. We have to perform two operations on the database, one to download the list of changes available and another to download the actual changes and show them to the user. The operations are performed and then the results are reported to the closures assigned to their properties.

The first operation we need to perform is the `CKFetchDatabaseChangesOperation` operation. Its initializer requires the previous database token to get only the changes that are not available on the device, so we pass the value of the `changeToken` property. Next, we define the closures for each of its properties. This operation includes three properties, one to report the zones that changed, one to report the creation of a new database token, and another to report the conclusion of the operation. The first property defined in our example is `recordZoneWithIDChangedBlock`. The closure assigned to this property is executed every time the system finds a zone whose content has changed. In this closure, we add the zone ID to an array to keep a reference of each zone that changed. Something similar happens with the closure assigned next to the `changeTokenUpdatedBlock` property. This closure is executed every time the system decides to perform the operation again to download the changes in separate processes. To make sure that we only receive the changes that we did not process yet, we use this closure to update the `changeToken` property with the current token. The last property we have defined for this operation is `fetchDatabaseChangesCompletionBlock`. The closure assigned to this property is executed to let the app know that the operation is over, and this is the signal that indicates that we have all the information we need to begin downloading the changes with the second operation. This last closure receives three values: the latest database token, a Boolean value that indicates whether there are more changes available (by default, the system takes care of fetching all the changes, so we don't need to consider this value), and a `CKError` structure to report errors. If there are errors (`error != nil`), we execute the `finishClosure` closure with the value `failed` and the operation is over. If there are no errors, we check if the `zoneIDs` array contains any zone ID. If it is empty, it means that there are no changes available and therefore we execute the `finishClosure` closure with the value `noData` (see the `else` at the end of the method), but if the array is not empty, we configure the `CKFetchRecordZoneChangesOperation` operation to get the changes.

The `CKFetchRecordZoneChangesOperation` operation is performed over the zones that changed, so we have to initialize it with the array of zone IDs generated by the previous operation. The initializer also requires a dictionary with the zone IDs as keys and `ZoneConfiguration` objects that include the previous token for each zone as values. Because in this example we only work with one zone, we read the first element of the `zonesIDs` array to get the ID of our custom zone and provide a `ZoneConfiguration` object with the current token stored in the `changeZoneToken` property.

This operation works like the previous one. The changes are fetched, and the results are reported to the closures assigned to its properties. The first property declared in Listing 23-23 is `recordChangedBlock`. This closure is called every time a new or updated record is received. Here, we check if the record is of type Countries or Cities and store it in the corresponding array. When the record is of type Countries, we use the `firstIndex()` method to look for duplicates. If the record already exists in the array, we update its values, otherwise, we add the record to the list. With the Cities we do something similar, except this time we first check whether the record contains a reference to a country and only update or add the record to the array if the reference corresponds to the country currently selected by the user (the **listCities** array only contains the cities of the selected country).

The closure of the **recordWithIDWasDeletedBlock** property defined next is executed every time the app receives the ID of a deleted record (a record that was deleted from the CloudKit database). In this case, we do the same as before but instead of updating or adding the record we remove it from the list with the **remove()** method.

The closures of the next two properties, **recordZoneChangeTokensUpdatedBlock** and **recordZoneFetchCompletionBlock**, are executed when the process completes a cycle, either because the system decides to download the data in multiple processes or the operation finished fetching the changes in a zone. Depending on the characteristics of our application, we may need to perform some tasks in these closures, but in our example, we just have to store the current token in the **fetchChangeToken** property so the next time the operation is performed we only get the changes we have not downloaded yet.

Finally, the closure assigned to the **fetchRecordZoneChangesCompletionBlock** property is executed to report that the operation is over. The closure receives a value to report errors. If there is an error (**error != nil**), we call the **finishClosure** closure with the value **failed**, to tell the system that the operation failed, but if no error is found, we permanently store the current tokens in the User Defaults database, call the **updateInterface()** method to post the notification and update the interface, and finally call the **finishClosure** closure with the value **newData**, to tell the system that new data has been downloaded. Notice that to store the tokens we have to turn them into **Data** structures and encode them with the **archivedData()** method of the **NSKeyedArchiver** class, as we mentioned before.

Lastly, after the definition of each operation and their properties, we call the **add()** method of the **CKDatabase** object to add them to the database.

There is one more change we have to introduce to our **ApplicationData** class for subscriptions to work. So far, we have stored the records in the zone by default, but as we already mentioned, subscriptions require the records to be stored in a custom zone. The following are the changes we have to introduce to the **insertCountry()** and **insertCity()** methods to store the records inside the listPlaces zone created before.

```
func insertCountry(name: String) {
    configureDatabase(executeClosure: {
        let mainQueue = OperationQueue.main
        mainQueue.addOperation({
            let text = name.trimmingCharacters(in: .whitespaces)
            if text != "" {
                let zone = CKRecordZone(zoneName: "listPlaces")
                let id = CKRecord.ID(recordName: "idcountry-\(UUID())",
zoneID: zone.zoneID)
                let record = CKRecord(recordType: "Countries", recordID: id)
                record.setObject(text as NSString, forKey: "name")
                self.database.save(record, completionHandler: { (recordSaved,
error) in
                    if error != nil {
                        print("Error: record not saved")
                    } else {
                        self.listCountries.append(record)
                        self.updateInterface()
                    }
                })
            }
        })
    })
}
```

```
func insertCity(name: String) {
    configureDatabase(executeClosure: {
        let mainQueue = OperationQueue.main
        mainQueue.addOperation({
            let text = name.trimmingCharacters(in: .whitespaces)
            if text != "" {
                let zone = CKRecordZone(zoneName: "listPlaces")
                let id = CKRecord.ID(recordName: "idcity-\(UUID())", zoneID:
zone.zoneID)
                let record = CKRecord(recordType: "Cities", recordID: id)
                record.setObject(text as NSString, forKey: "name")
                let reference = CKRecord.Reference(recordID:
self.selectedCountry, action: .deleteSelf)
                record.setObject(reference, forKey: "country")

                let bundle = Bundle.main
                if let fileURL = bundle.url(forResource: "Toronto",
withExtension: "jpg") {
                    let asset = CKAsset(fileURL: fileURL)
                    record.setObject(asset, forKey: "picture")
                }
                self.database.save(record, completionHandler: { (recordSaved,
error) in
                    if error != nil {
                        print("Error: record not saved")
                    } else {
                        self.listCities.append(record)
                        self.updateInterface()
                    }
                })
            }
        })
    })
}
```

Listing 23-24: *Storing the records in a custom zone*

All we have to do to store a record in a custom zone is to create the **CKRecordZone** object and assign its ID to the record ID by including it in the initializer of the **CKRecord.ID** object.

Notice that the code for both methods was inserted in operations and the operations were included in the closure sent as the value of the **configureDatabase()** method. We call this method again, so every time a record is inserted, we check that the subscription and the zone were already added to the database. The **configureDatabase()** method checks that the database is configured properly and then calls the closure to execute the code.

 Do It Yourself: Update the **AppDelegate** class with the code of Listing 23-20. Add the methods of Listings 23-21, 23-22, and 23-23 to the **ApplicationData** class. Update the **insertCountry()** and **insertCity()** methods of the **ApplicationData** class with the code of Listing 23-24. Run the application in two different devices and insert a new country. You should see the country appear on the screen of the second device.

 IMPORTANT: Remote Notifications can only be tested on a real device (they do not work on the simulator). If you only have one device, you can test your applications with the CloudKit dashboard. Open the Records panel, click on the Create New Record button, and insert the value for the title of the new record in the panel on the right. Press the Save button to save it. The new record should appear on the screen of your device.

Batch Operations

Although the methods provided by the **CKDatabase** class are very convenient and easy to implement, they only perform one request at a time. The problem is that CloudKit servers have a limit on the number of operations we can perform per second (currently 40 requests per second are allowed), so if our application relies heavily on CloudKit, at one point some of the requests may be rejected if we send them one by one. The solution is to create operations that allow us to perform multiple requests at once. The framework defines three subclasses of the **CKDatabaseOperation** class for this purpose. The **CKModifySubscriptionsOperation** class creates an operation to add or modify subscriptions, the **CKModifyRecordZones-Operation** class is used to add or modify record zones, and the **CKModifyRecordsOperation** class is for adding and modifying records. The following are their initializers.

CKModifySubscriptionsOperation(subscriptionsToSave: [CKSubscription], **subscriptionIDsToDelete:** [CKSubscription.ID])—This initializer returns an operation that adds or modifies one or more subscriptions. The **subscriptionsToSave** attribute is an array with the subscriptions we want to add or modify, and the **subscriptionIDsToDelete** is an array with the IDs of the subscriptions we want to delete from the server.

CKModifyRecordZonesOperation(recordZonesToSave: [CKRecordZone], **recordZoneIDsToDelete:** [CKRecordZone.ID])—This initializer returns an operation that adds or modifies one or more record zones. The **recordZonesToSave** attribute is an array with the record zones we want to add or modify, and the **recordZoneIDsToDelete** is an array with the IDs of the record zones we want to delete from the server.

CKModifyRecordsOperation(recordsToSave: [CKRecord], **recordIDsToDelete:** [CKRecord.ID])—This operation adds or modifies one or more records. The **recordsToSave** attribute is an array with the records we want to add or modify, and the **recordIDsToDelete** attribute is an array with the IDs of the records we want to delete from the server.

The operations must be initialized first and then added to the database with the **add()** method of the **CKDatabase** class, as we did before in the example of Listing 23-23. Each initializer offers the options to modify elements and remove them. If we only need to perform one task, the other can be declared as **nil**. We will see some examples next.

Local Cache

Loading the information from CloudKit every time the app is launched is not practical or even reliable. The device may get disconnected, the servers may not be always available, or the response may take too long to arrive. For these reasons, Subscriptions are usually implemented to keep data updated in a local storage. The application stores the information in a persistent local storage, like a Core Data persistent store, and uses CloudKit to share that data with other devices and keep them synchronized. Using Cloudkit in this manner, we can create an application that automatically uploads and downloads the data to the servers, so we always present the same information to the user no matter where the app is running.

The following example illustrates how to work with subscriptions using Core Data to store the information locally. The purpose of the app is to store a list of locations, as we did in previous examples, so we are going to use the same interface of Figure 23-14.

The Core Data model for this example requires a total of three Entities: Countries to store the countries, Cities to store the cities, and another one we called CKDelete to store the ID's of the objects deleted by the user. The following are the attributes for each Entity.

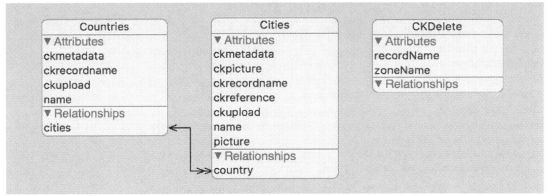

Figure 23-19: Core Data Model

There are probably hundreds of ways of organizing our code to coordinate a local storage with a CloudKit database. For this example, we have decided to keep it simple and store all the information of the CloudKit records in each Core Data object. The Countries entity includes the name attribute to store the name of the country and then three attributes to work with CloudKit. The ckmetadata attribute is a Binary Data value we are going to use to store the record's metadata, the ckrecordname attribute is a String value to store the record's name, and the ckupload attribute is a Boolean value we use to indicate whether the record was modified and it has to be uploaded to the CloudKit server or not. We did something similar for the Cities entity, but in this case, we also added a Boolean attribute called ckpicture to indicate whether the picture assigned to the city also has to be uploaded (this is to avoid uploading the same picture over and over again).

 Do It Yourself: For this example, we are going to use the same project created for Subscriptions. Add a Core Data Model file to the project and call it "places". Select the file and add three entities called Countries, Cities, and CKDelete, as shown in Figure 23-19. Select the entity Country and add the attributes ckmetadata (Binary Data), ckrecordname (String), ckupload (Boolean), name (String), and a To-Many relationship called cities (Cities). Select this relationship and change the Delete Rule from Nullify to Cascade to erase all the cities when a country is deleted. For the Cities entity, add the attributes ckmetadata (Binary Data), ckpicture (Boolean), ckrecordname (String), ckreference (String), ckupload (Boolean), name (String), picture (Binary Data), and a To-One relationship called country (Countries). Select the picture attribute and mark the option Allow External Storage from the Data Model inspector panel. Finally, add two attributes of type String to the CKDelete entity called recordName and zoneName.

To illustrate how to delete a record, we have decided to add a bar button called Edit to the Countries and Cities views that we are going to use to active the table's edition mode.

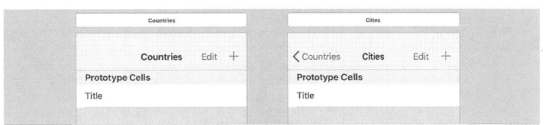

Figure 23-20: Edit buttons

Once the Core Data model and the interface are ready, we have to update the code. The first step is to modify the **AppDelegate** class to initialize the Core Data persistent store.

```
import UIKit
import CloudKit
import CoreData

@UIApplicationMain
class AppDelegate: UIResponder, UIApplicationDelegate {
    var window: UIWindow?
    var container: NSPersistentContainer!
    var context: NSManagedObjectContext!

    func application(_ application: UIApplication,
didFinishLaunchingWithOptions launchOptions:
[UIApplication.LaunchOptionsKey: Any]?) -> Bool {
        let userSettings = UserDefaults.standard
        let values = ["subscriptionSaved": false, "zoneCreated": false]
        userSettings.register(defaults: values)

        container = NSPersistentContainer(name: "places")
        container.loadPersistentStores(completionHandler: {
(storeDescription, error) in
            if error != nil {
                print("Error")
            } else {
                self.context = self.container.viewContext
            }
        })
        application.registerForRemoteNotifications()
        AppData.checkUpdates(finishClosure: {(result) in return})
        return true
    }
    func application(_ application: UIApplication,
didReceiveRemoteNotification userInfo: [AnyHashable : Any],
fetchCompletionHandler completionHandler: @escaping
(UIBackgroundFetchResult) -> Void) {
        let notification = CKNotification(fromRemoteNotificationDictionary:
userInfo) as? CKDatabaseNotification
        if notification != nil {
            AppData.checkUpdates(finishClosure: { (result) in
                let mainQueue = OperationQueue.main
                mainQueue.addOperation({
                    completionHandler(result)
                })
            })
        }
    }
}
```

Listing 23-25: Preparing Core Data and CloudKit

When the app is executed for the first time, we have to consider that there might be data already available in CloudKit servers, and therefore, after creating the persistent store, we also have to check for change in the servers with the **checkUpdates()** method to seed the persistent store with all the information the user inserted from other devices. We have introduced this method before. It is in charge of downloading updates from the server when a notification is received, and it has to report to the system the result of the operation, but because this time we don't have to report anything, we just call it with an empty closure (a closure that doesn't perform any process and returns nothing).

Although we are calling the same methods in our model, because we are working with Core Data their implementations change. Let's begin with the initialization of the class and basic elements.

```
import UIKit
import CloudKit
import CoreData

class ApplicationData {
    var context: NSManagedObjectContext!
    var database: CKDatabase!
    init() {
        let app = UIApplication.shared
        let appDelegate = app.delegate as! AppDelegate
        context = appDelegate.context

        let container = CKContainer.default()
        database = container.privateCloudDatabase
    }
    func checkUpdates(finishClosure: @escaping (UIBackgroundFetchResult) -
> Void) {
        configureDatabase(executeClosure: {
            self.downloadUpdates(finishClosure: finishClosure)
        })
    }
    func configureDatabase(executeClosure: @escaping () -> Void) {
        let userSettings = UserDefaults.standard
        if !userSettings.bool(forKey: "subscriptionSaved") {
            let newSubscription - CKDatabaseSubscription(subscriptionID:
"updatesDatabase")
            let info = CKSubscription.NotificationInfo()
            info.shouldSendContentAvailable = true
            newSubscription.notificationInfo = info

            database.save(newSubscription, completionHandler: {
(subscription, error) in
                if error != nil {
                    print("Error Creating Subscription")
                } else {
                    userSettings.set(true, forKey: "subscriptionSaved")
                }
            })
        }
        if !userSettings.bool(forKey: "zoneCreated") {
            let newZone = CKRecordZone(zoneName: "listPlaces")
            database.save(newZone, completionHandler: { (zone, error) in
                if error != nil {
                    print("Error Creating Zone")
                } else {
                    userSettings.set(true, forKey: "zoneCreated")
                    executeClosure()
                }
            })
        } else {
            executeClosure()
        }
    }
}
var AppData = ApplicationData()
```

Listing 23-26: Initializing the model

iCloud

In this example, we are going to work with the same CloudKit database than before, and therefore the **checkUpdates()** and the **configureDatabase()** methods are the same. The only modification so far is a reference to the Core Data context that we had to add to the **ApplicationData** class, so the rest of the code will be able to access and modify the persistent store. As always, when the application calls the **checkUpdates()** method to check for updates, the method calls the **configureDatabase()** method first to make sure that the subscription and the custom zone were created, and then executes the **downloadUpdates()** method to look for changes in CloudKit servers. Because now we are storing those changes in the persistent store, this method has to be modified.

```
func downloadUpdates(finishClosure: @escaping (UIBackgroundFetchResult) -
> Void) {
    var listRecordsUpdated: [CKRecord] = []
    var listRecordsDeleted: [String: String] = [:]
    var changeToken: CKServerChangeToken!
    var changeZoneToken: CKServerChangeToken!

    let userSettings = UserDefaults.standard
    if let data = userSettings.value(forKey: "changeToken") as? Data {
        if let token = try? NSKeyedUnarchiver.unarchivedObject(ofClass:
CKServerChangeToken.self, from: data) {
            changeToken = token
        }
    }
    if let data = userSettings.value(forKey: "changeZoneToken") as? Data {
        if let token = try? NSKeyedUnarchiver.unarchivedObject(ofClass:
CKServerChangeToken.self, from: data) {
            changeZoneToken = token
        }
    }
    var zonesIDs: [CKRecordZone.ID] = []
    let operation =
CKFetchDatabaseChangesOperation(previousServerChangeToken: changeToken)
    operation.recordZoneWithIDChangedBlock = { (zoneID) in
        zonesIDs.append(zoneID)
    }
    operation.changeTokenUpdatedBlock = { (token) in
        changeToken = token
    }
    operation.fetchDatabaseChangesCompletionBlock = {(token, more, error) in
        if error != nil {
            finishClosure(UIBackgroundFetchResult.failed)
        } else if !zonesIDs.isEmpty {
            changeToken = token
            let configuration =
CKFetchRecordZoneChangesOperation.ZoneConfiguration()
            configuration.previousServerChangeToken = changeZoneToken
            let fetchOperation =
CKFetchRecordZoneChangesOperation(recordZoneIDs: zonesIDs,
configurationsByRecordZoneID: [zonesIDs[0]: configuration])
            fetchOperation.recordChangedBlock = { (record) in
                listRecordsUpdated.append(record)
            }
            fetchOperation.recordWithIDWasDeletedBlock = { (recordID,
recordType) in
                listRecordsDeleted[recordID.recordName] = recordType
            }
            fetchOperation.recordZoneChangeTokensUpdatedBlock = { (zoneID,
token, data) in
```

```
                changeZoneToken = token
        }
        fetchOperation.recordZoneFetchCompletionBlock = { (zoneID,
token, data, more, error) in
            if error != nil {
                print("Error")
            } else {
                changeZoneToken = token
                self.updateLocalRecords(listRecordsUpdated:
listRecordsUpdated)
                self.deleteLocalRecords(listRecordsDeleted:
listRecordsDeleted)
                listRecordsUpdated.removeAll()
                listRecordsDeleted.removeAll()
            }
        }
        fetchOperation.fetchRecordZoneChangesCompletionBlock = {(error) in
            if error != nil {
                print("Error")
                finishClosure(UIBackgroundFetchResult.failed)
            } else {
                if changeToken != nil {
                    if let data = try?
NSKeyedArchiver.archivedData(withRootObject: changeToken,
requiringSecureCoding: false) {
                        userSettings.set(data, forKey: "changeToken")
                    }
                }
                if changeZoneToken != nil {
                    if let data = try?
NSKeyedArchiver.archivedData(withRootObject: changeZoneToken,
requiringSecureCoding: false) {
                        userSettings.set(data, forKey: "changeZoneToken")
                    }
                }
                self.updateLocalReferences()
                finishClosure(UIBackgroundFetchResult.newData)
            }
        }
        self.database.add(fetchOperation)
    } else {
        finishClosure(UIBackgroundFetchResult.noData)
    }
    }
    database.add(operation)
}
```

Listing 23-27: Downloading changes

This time the operations store the records that were updated in an array called **listRecordsUpdated** and the record IDs of the records that were deleted in a dictionary called **listRecordsDeleted**. When the fetching of the record zone is finished, we call the methods **updateLocalRecords()** and **deleteLocalRecords()** with these values to perform the corresponding changes in the persistent store.

Storing the records in the persistent store is easy, we have to look for an object with the same record name and update its values if it exists, or create a new one if it doesn't. The problem is that CloudKit adds additional information to the record, like the date it was created, the date it was modified, and also a tag that we can use to determine whether the information of the record we are trying to save is up-to-date. This tag is like the tokens we use to determine the state of the database. When the user stores a new record from one device, CloudKit adds a tag to it. If the user tries to upload the same record again or from another device, the server will reject the operation because it will detect that the tag of the record the user is trying to save is older than the tag of the record in the database. This is how the server prevents the user from overwriting records that were updated before from other devices, as illustrated below.

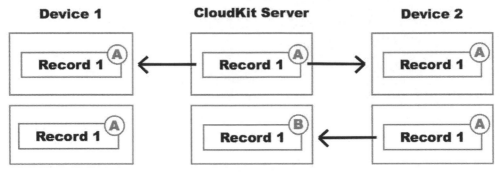

Figure 23-21: Record's tag

In this example, the user downloads a record from two devices. This record was assigned the tag A. So far, all the records have the same tag, but when the user modifies the record in Device 2 and uploads it to the server, the database assigns a new tag to this record (the server assigns a new tag to each record every time they are modified). Now the record on the server has the tag B. If the user modifies the record form Device 1 and tries to upload it to the server, the operation will fail because the database will detect that the record the user is trying to upload has an older tag than the record on the server. This is great because it prevents us from uploading an older record to the server and loosing data (the values assigned to the record from Device 2 won't be lost). The problem is that for this process to work, we have to store the record's tag in the persistent store along with the rest of the record's data. This is why we have added an attribute to the Countries and Cities entities called **ckmetadata**. This is a Binary Data attribute that we will use to store all the record's metadata, including its tag. And this is the first thing we have to do every time we want to store a record in the persistent store. The following is our implementation of the **updateLocalRecords()** method, called by the **CKFetchRecordZoneChangesOperation** operation to store the records in Core Data.

```
func updateLocalRecords(listRecordsUpdated: [CKRecord]) {
   for record in listRecordsUpdated {
      let coder = NSKeyedArchiver(requiringSecureCoding: true)
      record.encodeSystemFields(with: coder)
      let recordMetadata = coder.encodedData
      let recordType = record.recordType
      let recordName = record.recordID.recordName
      if recordType == "Countries" {
         let request: NSFetchRequest<Countries> =
Countries.fetchRequest()
         request.predicate = NSPredicate(format: "ckrecordname = %@",
recordName)
         do {
            var country: Countries!
            let result = try context.fetch(request)
            if result.isEmpty {
               country = Countries(context: context)
               country.ckrecordname = recordName
            } else {
               country = result[0]
            }
```

```
                    country.ckmetadata = recordMetadata
                    country.ckupload = false
                    country.name = record["name"] as? String
                } catch {
                    print("Error Fetching")
                }
            } else if recordType == "Cities" {
                let request: NSFetchRequest<Cities> = Cities.fetchRequest()
                request.predicate = NSPredicate(format: "ckrecordname = %@",
recordName)
                do {
                    var city: Cities!
                    let result = try context.fetch(request)
                    if result.isEmpty {
                        city = Cities(context: context)
                        city.ckrecordname = recordName
                    } else {
                        city = result[0]
                    }
                    city.ckmetadata = recordMetadata
                    city.ckupload = false
                    city.ckpicture = false
                    city.name = record["name"] as? String
                    if let reference = record["country"] as? CKRecord.Reference {
                        city.ckreference = reference.recordID.recordName
                    }
                    if let asset = record["picture"] as? CKAsset {
                        let picture = UIImage(contentsOfFile: asset.fileURL.path)
                        city.picture = picture?.pngData()
                    }
                } catch {
                    print("Error Fetching")
                }
            }
        }
    }
    if context.hasChanges {
        do {
            try context.save()
        } catch {
            print("Error Saving Context")
        }
    }
}
```

Listing 23-28: Updating records

The **updateLocalRecords()** method is called after all the records are downloaded from CloudKit. Here, we have to read each record, extract the information, and store it in the persistent store. In the example of Listing 23-28, we first get the record's metadata. Because this is a collection of values, the framework offers a convenient method for this purpose called **encodeSystemFields()**. This method takes an **NSKeyedArchiver** object to encode all the values at once and produces a **Data** structure we can get from the object's **encodedData** property. With this **Data** structure containing the record's metadata, the record's type, and its identifier (record's name), we have all the information we need to insert the record in the persistent store.

The process to store records of type Countries is slightly different than the process to store records of type Cities, so we check first whether the type is Countries or Cities and proceed accordingly. The first thing we do is to create a predicate to look for a record with the same record name (this is not the name of the country or city but the name of the record we defined with the **UUID()** function when the record was created for the first time). If the record is not found (**result** is empty), we create a new **Countries** object and assign the record name to its **ckrecordname** property, otherwise, we get the record from Core Data and update its attributes. With the cities, we follow the same procedure, but at the end we store the record name of the country the city belongs to (stored in the **Reference** object identified with the string "country") and get the picture from the **CKAsset**.

If records were deleted in CloudKit, we get a list of their IDs. The process to delete these records is very similar, we have to find the records of the same type and with the same name in the persistent store and then use the **delete()** method to delete them.

```
func deleteLocalRecords(listRecordsDeleted: [String: String]) {
   for (recordName, recordType) in listRecordsDeleted {
      if recordType == "Countries" {
         let request: NSFetchRequest<Countries> =
Countries.fetchRequest()
         request.predicate = NSPredicate(format: "ckrecordname = %@",
recordName)
         do {
            let result = try context.fetch(request)
            if !result.isEmpty {
               let country = result[0]
               context.delete(country)
            }
         } catch {
            print("Error Fetching")
         }
      } else if recordType == "Cities" {
         let request: NSFetchRequest<Cities> = Cities.fetchRequest()
         request.predicate = NSPredicate(format: "ckrecordname = %@",
recordName)
         do {
            let result = try context.fetch(request)
            if !result.isEmpty {
               let city = result[0]
               context.delete(city)
            }
         } catch {
            print("Error Fetching")
         }
      }
   }
   if context.hasChanges {
      do {
         try context.save()
      } catch {
         print("Error Saving Context")
      }
   }
}
```

Listing 23-29: Deleting records

The process is not over. Besides storing and deleting the records, we have to define their relationships. Storing the record name we get from the **Reference** object into the **ckreference** attribute of the **Cities** object is not enough to link a city with its country in the persistent store. Core Data uses relationships for this purpose, so the next step is to read all the

Cities objects that have a value stored in the **ckreference** attribute and connect them with their **Countries** object through their **country** attribute. We assigned this task to a separate method called **updateLocalReferences()** that is executed when the operation to fetch the records is over (see the closure assigned to the **fetchRecordZoneChangesCompletionBlock** property in Listing 23-27).

```
func updateLocalReferences() {
    let requestCities: NSFetchRequest<Cities> = Cities.fetchRequest()
    requestCities.predicate = NSPredicate(format: "ckreference != nil")
    do {
        let listCities = try context.fetch(requestCities)
        for city in listCities {
            let requestCountries: NSFetchRequest<Countries> =
Countries.fetchRequest()
            requestCountries.predicate = NSPredicate(format: "ckrecordname =
%@", city.ckreference!)
            do {
                let listCountries = try context.fetch(requestCountries)
                if !listCountries.isEmpty {
                    city.country = listCountries[0]
                    city.ckreference = nil
                }
            } catch {
                print("Error Fetching")
            }
        }
    } catch {
        print("Error Fetching")
    }
    if context.hasChanges {
        do {
            try context.save()
        } catch {
            print("Error Saving Context")
        }
    }
}
```

Listing 23-30: Assigning references

We use the value of the **ckreference** attribute in the **Cities** objects to determine whether the reference was already created in Core Data or not. If the value is different than **nil**, we search for a country with that record name and if we find it, we assign it to the **country** property of the **Cities** object, thus defining the relationship and connecting the city with its country.

The code to download the updates is over. Now we have to define the methods to upload the records the user creates and delete those that the user removes. As we mentioned before, uploading the records one by one is not appropriate when working with a local storage. We have to anticipate problems in the connection or the operation that will prevent some records from being uploaded to the server. This is why we decided to mark each object in the persistent store with a Boolean value stored in the **ckupload** attribute. If the attribute is **true**, we know that the record was not uploaded yet and therefore we can include it on the list. This way, if a process failed before, we do it again until all the records are uploaded to the CloudKit database. The following is the method we are going to use to perform this operation.

```
func uploadRecords() {
    let listRecordsToUpload = getRecordsToUpload()
    if !listRecordsToUpload.isEmpty {
        configureDatabase(executeClosure: {
            let operation = CKModifyRecordsOperation(recordsToSave:
listRecordsToUpload, recordIDsToDelete: nil)
            operation.modifyRecordsCompletionBlock = { (records, recordsID,
error) in
                if error != nil {
                    print("Error uploading records")
                } else {
                    self.clearCoreDataRecords()
                }
            }
            self.database.add(operation)
        })
    }
}
```

Listing 23-31: Uploading multiple records

The method begins by getting the list of records to upload from another method called **getRecordsToUpload()**. With this list, it creates a **CKModifyRecordsOperation** operation (see Batch Operations introduced earlier). Notice that we call the **configureDatabase()** method first, as we did before, to make sure the database is properly configured. When the operation is over, it calls the closure assigned to the **modifyRecordsCompletionBlock** property. In this closure, if no error is found, we execute another method called **clearCoreDataRecords()** that we are going to use to set the values of the **ckupload** attribute of each record in the persistent store back to **false**, so they are not uploaded again.

The following is the **getRecordsToUpload()** method we use to get all the records in the persistent store that has to be uploaded. The method looks for the **Countries** and **Cities** objects with the **ckupload** attribute equal to **true**, adds them to an array, and returns it.

```
func getRecordsToUpload() -> [CKRecord] {
    var list: [CKRecord] = []
    let requestCountries: NSFetchRequest<Countries> =
Countries.fetchRequest()
    requestCountries.predicate = NSPredicate(format: "ckupload = true")
    do {
        let result = try context.fetch(requestCountries)
        for item in result {
            var recordtemp: CKRecord!
            if let coder = try? NSKeyedUnarchiver(forReadingFrom:
item.ckmetadata!) {
                coder.requiresSecureCoding = true
                recordtemp = CKRecord(coder: coder)
                coder.finishDecoding()
            }
            if let record = recordtemp {
                record.setObject(item.name! as NSString, forKey: "name")
                list.append(record)
            }
        }
    } catch {
        print("Error Fetching")
    }
```

```
    let requestCities: NSFetchRequest<Cities> = Cities.fetchRequest()
    requestCities.predicate = NSPredicate(format: "ckupload = true")
    do {
        let result = try context.fetch(requestCities)
        for item in result {
            var recordtemp: CKRecord!
            if let coder = try? NSKeyedUnarchiver(forReadingFrom:
item.ckmetadata!) {
                coder.requiresSecureCoding = true
                recordtemp = CKRecord(coder: coder)
                coder.finishDecoding()
            }
            if let record = recordtemp {
                record.setObject(item.name! as NSString, forKey: "name")

                if item.ckpicture && item.picture != nil {
                    var url = URL(fileURLWithPath: NSTemporaryDirectory())
                    url = url.appendingPathComponent("tempfile.png")
                    do {
                        let pngImage = item.picture!
                        try pngImage.write(to: url, options: .atomic)
                        let asset = CKAsset(fileURL: url)
                        record.setObject(asset, forKey: "picture")
                    } catch {
                        print("Image not stored")
                    }
                }
                if let country = item.country {
                    let zone = CKRecordZone(zoneName: "listPlaces")
                    let id = CKRecord.ID(recordName: country.ckrecordname!,
zoneID: zone.zoneID)
                    let reference = CKRecord.Reference(recordID: id, action:
.deleteSelf)
                    record.setObject(reference, forKey: "country")
                }
                list.append(record)
            }
        }
    } catch {
        print("Error Fetching")
    }
    return list
}
```

Listing 23-32: *Getting the list of records to upload*

We can't send Core Data objects to CloudKit, we first have to convert them to **CKRecord** objects. The problem is that if we just create a new **CKRecord** object every time the user modifies an existing record in the persistent store, the database won't be able to match the records and will add a new record instead of modifying the old one. This is another reason why we included the **ckmetadata** attribute in every **Countries** and **Cities** object with the metadata of the record. To allow the server to match the record we are sending with those already stored in the database, we have to include the values contained in this metadata, and this is the first thing we do with each record in Listing 23-32. The metadata is unarchived with an **NSKeyedUnarchiver** object and we get a **CKRecord** object in return. The **NSKeyedUnarchiver(forReadingFrom:)** initializer creates an object to unarchive the data and the **CKRecord(coder:)** initializer returns a **CKRecord** object with these values. All that is left to do is to assign to this **CKRecord** object the rest of the values that were modified by the user (e.g., the name of the country), and finally add the record to the array.

Adding the values for the cities in our example presents a little complication. Now, to add the picture, we have to create a **CKAsset** object from the Binary Data stored in the **picture** attribute of the **Cities** object. A way to do it is to create a temporary file with this data and then create the **CKAsset** object from the URL of this file. iOS includes a directory called *temp* that every app can use to store temporary files. If the files are not erased, they are erased later by the system. To get the URL of this directory, Foundation includes the **NSTemporaryDirectory()** function. Once we get the URL, we can add the name of the file to the path with the **appendingPathComponent()** we introduced in Chapter 21. To store the data in the file, the **Data** structure includes the **write()** method with two attributes, the **to** attribute defines the URL of the file where the data is going to be stored and the **options** attribute specifies how the process will take place. This last attribute includes multiple options provided by the **NSData.WritingOptions** structure. The most common are **atomic** (an auxiliary file is created first to prevent data corruption), and **withoutOverwriting** (to avoid overwriting an existing file).

When the operation finish uploading all the records, we have to change the values of the **ckupload** attribute of each object to **false**, so they are not uploaded again. The following is our implementation of the **clearCoreDataRecords()**. Notice that for the **Cities** objects, we also have to change the value of the **ckpicture** attribute to indicate that the pictures were also uploaded

```
func clearCoreDataRecords() {
   let requestCountries: NSFetchRequest<Countries> =
Countries.fetchRequest()
   requestCountries.predicate = NSPredicate(format: "ckupload = true")
   do {
      let result = try context.fetch(requestCountries)
      for item in result {
         item.ckupload = false
      }
   } catch {
      print("Error Fetching")
   }
   let requestCities: NSFetchRequest<Cities> = Cities.fetchRequest()
   requestCities.predicate = NSPredicate(format: "ckupload = true")
   do {
      let result = try context.fetch(requestCities)
      for item in result {
         item.ckupload = false
         item.ckpicture = false
      }
   } catch {
      print("Error Fetching")
   }
   if context.hasChanges {
      do {
         try context.save()
      } catch {
         print("Error Saving Context")
      }
   }
}
```

Listing 23-33: Cleaning up the objects in the persistent store

There is only one additional task we have to perform in our model, and this is to erase the records in CloudKit that correspond to the objects removed by the user from the persistent store. In the interface of Figure 23-20, we included an Edit button in each view to allow the user to remove records. The procedure we decided to follow for this example is to create an object of type **CKDelete** with the record name of each of the **Countries** and **Cities** objects deleted by the user and then remove them from the persistent store. This way, to reflect the changes in the CloudKit database, we just have to call a method in our model to erase the records that match the record names stored in the **CKDelete** entity. We called this method **removeRecords()**.

```
func removeRecords() {
   var listRecordsToDelete: [CKRecord.ID] = []

   let request: NSFetchRequest<CKDelete> = CKDelete.fetchRequest()
   do {
      let result = try context.fetch(request)
      for item in result {
         let zone = CKRecordZone(zoneName: item.zoneName!)
         let id = CKRecord.ID(recordName: item.recordName!, zoneID:
zone.zoneID)
         listRecordsToDelete.append(id)
      }
   } catch {
      print("Error fetching record IDs")
   }
   if !listRecordsToDelete.isEmpty {
      let operation = CKModifyRecordsOperation(recordsToSave: nil,
recordIDsToDelete: listRecordsToDelete)
      operation.modifyRecordsCompletionBlock = { (records, recordsID,
error) in
         if error != nil {
            print("Error deleting records")
         } else {
            let request: NSFetchRequest<CKDelete> =
CKDelete.fetchRequest()
            do {
               let result = try self.context.fetch(request)
               for item in result {
                  self.context.delete(item)
               }
               try self.context.save()
            } catch {
               print("Error deleting")
            }
         }
      }
      database.add(operation)
   }
}
```

Listing 23-34: Removing records from CloudKit

In the example of Listing 23-34, we use the same batch operation we used before to upload records, but instead of assigning the array to the **recordsToSave** attribute we do it to the **recordIDsToDelete** attribute. This erases all the records in the array. If the operation is successful, we erase the **CKDelete** objects from the persistent store, so the application won't try to delete these records again.

Do It Yourself: Add a bar button to each view and change their names to Edit (see Figure 23-20). Update your `AppDelegate` class with the code of Listing 23-26. Replace the code in the ApplicationData.swift file with the code of Listing 23-26. Add to this class the methods of Listings 23-27, 23-28, 23-29, 23-30, 23-31, 23-32, 23-33, and 23-34. These codes and projects are available on our website.

This may seem like a lot of code for a CloudKit application, but it is just part of it. We still have to prepare our view controllers to work with Code Data and process CloudKit records. The following is our new `CountriesViewController` class.

```swift
import UIKit
import CloudKit
import CoreData

class CountriesViewController: UITableViewController,
NSFetchedResultsControllerDelegate {
    var context: NSManagedObjectContext!
    var fetchedController: NSFetchedResultsController<Countries>!

    override func viewDidLoad() {
        super.viewDidLoad()
        let app = UIApplication.shared
        let appDelegate = app.delegate as! AppDelegate
        context = appDelegate.context

        let request: NSFetchRequest<Countries> = Countries.fetchRequest()
        let sort = NSSortDescriptor(key: "name", ascending: true)
        request.sortDescriptors = [sort]
        fetchedController = NSFetchedResultsController(fetchRequest:
request, managedObjectContext: context, sectionNameKeyPath: nil,
cacheName: nil)
        fetchedController.delegate = self
        do {
            try fetchedController.performFetch()
        } catch {
            print("Error")
        }
    }
    override func tableView(_ tableView: UITableView,
numberOfRowsInSection section: Int) -> Int {
        if let sections = fetchedController.sections {
            let sectionInfo = sections[section]
            return sectionInfo.numberOfObjects
        }
        return 0
    }
    override func tableView(_ tableView: UITableView, cellForRowAt
indexPath: IndexPath) -> UITableViewCell {
        let cell = tableView.dequeueReusableCell(withIdentifier:
"countriesCell", for: indexPath)
        let country = fetchedController.object(at: indexPath)
        cell.textLabel?.text = country.name
        return cell
    }
    func controller(_ controller:
NSFetchedResultsController<NSFetchRequestResult>, didChange anObject:
Any, at indexPath: IndexPath?, for type: NSFetchedResultsChangeType,
newIndexPath: IndexPath?) {
```

```
        switch type {
            case .delete:
                if let path = indexPath {
                    tableView.deleteRows(at: [path], with: .fade)
                }
            case .insert:
                if let path = newIndexPath {
                    tableView.insertRows(at: [path], with: .fade)
                }
            case .update:
                if let path = indexPath {
                    let cell = tableView.cellForRow(at: path)
                    let country = fetchedController.object(at: path)
                    cell?.textLabel?.text = country.name
                }
            default:
                break
        }
    }
    func controllerWillChangeContent(_ controller:
NSFetchedResultsController<NSFetchRequestResult>) {
        tableView.beginUpdates()
    }
    func controllerDidChangeContent(_ controller:
NSFetchedResultsController<NSFetchRequestResult>) {
        tableView.endUpdates()
    }
    @IBAction func addCountry(_ sender: UIBarButtonItem) {
        let alert = UIAlertController(title: "Insert Country", message:
nil, preferredStyle: .alert)
        let cancel = UIAlertAction(title: "Cancel", style: .cancel,
handler: nil)
        alert.addAction(cancel)
        let action = UIAlertAction(title: "Save", style: .default, handler:
{ (action) in
            if let fields = alert.textFields {
                let name = fields[0].text!
                let text = name.trimmingCharacters(in: .whitespaces)
                if !text.isEmpty {
                    let newCountry = Countries(context: self.context)
                    newCountry.name = name
                    newCountry.ckupload = true
                    let recordName = "idcountry-\(UUID())"
                    let zone = CKRecordZone(zoneName: "listPlaces")
                    let id = CKRecord.ID(recordName: recordName, zoneID:
zone.zoneID)
                    let record = CKRecord(recordType:"Countries", recordID:id)
                    let coder = NSKeyedArchiver(requiringSecureCoding: true)
                    record.encodeSystemFields(with: coder)
                    let metadata = coder.encodedData
                    newCountry.ckmetadata = metadata
                    newCountry.ckrecordname = recordName
                    do {
                        try self.context.save()
                        AppData.uploadRecords()
                    } catch {
                        print("Error")
                    }
                }
            }
        }
    })
```

```
        alert.addAction(action)
        alert.addTextField(configurationHandler: nil)
        present(alert, animated: true, completion: nil)
    }
    override func prepare(for segue: UIStoryboardSegue, sender: Any?) {
        if segue.identifier == "showCities" {
            let controller = segue.destination as! CitiesViewController
            if let indexPath = tableView.indexPathForSelectedRow {
                let country = fetchedController.object(at: indexPath)
                controller.selectedCountry = country
            }
        }
    }
    @IBAction func editCountries(_ sender: UIBarButtonItem) {
        if tableView.isEditing {
            tableView.setEditing(false, animated: true)
        } else {
            tableView.setEditing(true, animated: true)
        }
    }
    override func tableView(_ tableView: UITableView, commit editingStyle:
UITableViewCell.EditingStyle, forRowAt indexPath: IndexPath) {
        if editingStyle == .delete {
            let country = fetchedController.object(at: indexPath)
            let newItem = CKDelete(context: context)
            newItem.zoneName = "listPlaces"
            newItem.recordName = country.ckrecordname
            context.delete(country)

            do {
                try context.save()
                AppData.removeRecords()
            } catch {
                print("Error")
            }
            tableView.setEditing(false, animated: true)
        }
    }
}
```

Listing 23-35: Processing and listing countries

As we did several times before, the view controller defines an
NSFetchedResultsController object to get the objects from the persistent store and feed
the table view, but now, when we store a new object we also have to get all the data we are
going to need to upload that object to the CloudKit server, and this includes the record's
metadata. This is why, every time the user inserts a new country, we have to create a temporary
CKRecord object and encode its metadata with an **NSKeyedArchiver** object. After this, we
have all the information we need to call the **uploadRecords()** method to upload the record.

The process to delete a record is simpler. When the user presses the Edit button to edit the
table, selects a row, and taps on the Delete button, we add a **CKDelete** object to the persistent
store with the information about the record we have to delete from CloudKit, and then delete
the **Countries** object from Core Data (the cities that belong to that country are automatically
erased by the persistent store and CloudKit because we defined the relationships in Core Data as
Cascade and the references in CloudKit as **deleteSelf**).

The **CitiesViewController** is very similar, but instead of getting all the countries in the
persistent store, we just read and show the cities that belong to the country selected by the user.

```swift
import UIKit
import CloudKit
import CoreData

class CitiesViewController: UITableViewController,
NSFetchedResultsControllerDelegate {
    var context: NSManagedObjectContext!
    var fetchedController: NSFetchedResultsController<Cities>!
    var selectedCountry: Countries!

    override func viewDidLoad() {
        super.viewDidLoad()
        let app = UIApplication.shared
        let appDelegate = app.delegate as! AppDelegate
        context = appDelegate.context
        if selectedCountry != nil {
            let request: NSFetchRequest<Cities> = Cities.fetchRequest()
            request.predicate = NSPredicate(format: "country = %@",
selectedCountry)
            let sort = NSSortDescriptor(key: "name", ascending: true)
            request.sortDescriptors = [sort]
            fetchedController = NSFetchedResultsController(fetchRequest:
request, managedObjectContext: context, sectionNameKeyPath: nil,
cacheName: nil)
            fetchedController.delegate = self
            do {
                try fetchedController.performFetch()
            } catch {
                print("Error")
            }
        }
    }
    override func tableView(_ tableView: UITableView,
numberOfRowsInSection section: Int) -> Int {
        if let sections = fetchedController.sections {
            let sectionInfo = sections[section]
            return sectionInfo.numberOfObjects
        }
        return 0
    }
    override func tableView(_ tableView: UITableView, cellForRowAt
indexPath: IndexPath) -> UITableViewCell {
        let cell = tableView.dequeueReusableCell(withIdentifier:
"citiesCell", for: indexPath)
        let city = fetchedController.object(at: indexPath)
        cell.textLabel?.text = city.name
        return cell
    }
    func controller(_ controller:
NSFetchedResultsController<NSFetchRequestResult>, didChange anObject:
Any, at indexPath: IndexPath?, for type: NSFetchedResultsChangeType,
newIndexPath: IndexPath?) {
        switch type {
            case .delete:
                if let path = indexPath {
                    tableView.deleteRows(at: [path], with: .fade)
                }
            case .insert:
                if let path = newIndexPath {
                    tableView.insertRows(at: [path], with: .fade)
                }
```

```
            case .update:
                if let path = indexPath {
                    let cell = tableView.cellForRow(at: path)
                    let city = fetchedController.object(at: path)
                    cell?.textLabel?.text = city.name
                }
            default:
                break
            }
        }
    func controllerWillChangeContent(_ controller:
NSFetchedResultsController<NSFetchRequestResult>) {
        tableView.beginUpdates()
    }
    func controllerDidChangeContent(_ controller:
NSFetchedResultsController<NSFetchRequestResult>) {
        tableView.endUpdates()
    }
    @IBAction func addCity(_ sender: UIBarButtonItem) {
        let alert = UIAlertController(title: "Insert City", message: nil,
preferredStyle: .alert)
        let cancel = UIAlertAction(title: "Cancel", style: .cancel,
handler: nil)
        alert.addAction(cancel)
        let action = UIAlertAction(title: "Save", style: .default, handler:
{ (action) in
            if let fields = alert.textFields {
                let name = fields[0].text!
                let text = name.trimmingCharacters(in: .whitespaces)
                if !text.isEmpty {
                    let newCity = Cities(context: self.context)
                    newCity.name = name
                    newCity.country = self.selectedCountry
                    newCity.ckupload = true
                    newCity.ckpicture = true
                    newCity.ckreference = self.selectedCountry.ckrecordname
                    if let picture = UIImage(named: "Toronto.jpg") {
                        newCity.picture = picture.pngData()
                    }
                    let recordName = "idcity-\(UUID())"
                    let zone = CKRecordZone(zoneName: "listPlaces")
                    let id = CKRecord.ID(recordName: recordName, zoneID:
zone.zoneID)
                    let record = CKRecord(recordType: "Cities", recordID: id)
                    let coder = NSKeyedArchiver(requiringSecureCoding: true)
                    record.encodeSystemFields(with: coder)
                    let metadata = coder.encodedData

                    newCity.ckmetadata = metadata
                    newCity.ckrecordname = recordName
                    do {
                        try self.context.save()
                        AppData.uploadRecords()
                    } catch {
                        print("Error")
                    }
                }
            }
        })
        alert.addAction(action)
        alert.addTextField(configurationHandler: nil)
```

```
                present(alert, animated: true, completion: nil)
        }
        override func prepare(for segue: UIStoryboardSegue, sender: Any?) {
            if segue.identifier == "showPicture" {
                let controller = segue.destination as! PicturesViewController
                if let indexPath = tableView.indexPathForSelectedRow {
                    let city = fetchedController.object(at: indexPath)
                    controller.selectedCity = city
                }
            }
        }
        @IBAction func editCities(_ sender: UIBarButtonItem) {
            if tableView.isEditing {
                tableView.setEditing(false, animated: true)
            } else {
                tableView.setEditing(true, animated: true)
            }
        }
        override func tableView(_ tableView: UITableView, commit editingStyle:
    UITableViewCell.EditingStyle, forRowAt indexPath: IndexPath) {
            if editingStyle == UITableViewCell.EditingStyle.delete {
                let city = fetchedController.object(at: indexPath)
                let newItem = CKDelete(context: context)
                newItem.zoneName = "listPlaces"
                newItem.recordName = city.ckrecordname
                context.delete(city)
                do {
                    try context.save()
                    AppData.removeRecords()
                } catch {
                    print("Error")
                }
                tableView.setEditing(false, animated: true)
            }
        }
    }
}
```

Listing 23-36: Processing and listing cities

And finally, because we are working with **NSManagedObject** objects instead of **CKRecord** objects, we have to update the **PicturesViewController** class to read the **picture** attribute of the selected city and show the image on the screen.

```
import UIKit
import CloudKit

class PicturesViewController: UIViewController {
    @IBOutlet weak var cityPicture: UIImageView!
    var selectedCity: Cities!

    override func viewDidLoad() {
        if selectedCity != nil {
            if let picture = selectedCity.picture {
                cityPicture.image = UIImage(data: picture)
            }
        }
    }
}
```

Listing 23-37: Showing the picture of the selected city

Do It Yourself: Replace the code in your `CountriesViewController` class with the code of Listing 23-35, the code in your `CitiesViewController` class with the code of Listing 23-36, and the code in your `PicturesViewController` class with the code of Listing 23-37. Connect the Edit button in the Countries view with the `editCountries()` Action and the Edit button in the Cities view with the `editCities()` Action. Run the application on a device. If you previously stored records in CloudKit servers, you should see them on the screen. Open the application on a second device and press the Edit button. Erase a record. You should see the record disappear from both devices.

Errors

As complete as our application may look, it is barely finished. Without a process to respond to errors, the application we have created so far is useless. One single error in the connection or a rejected operation and the data in the user's devices may become inconsistent or corrupted.

Checking for errors is an essential part of CloudKit. The service is highly dependable on the network connection and how reliable it is. If the device is disconnected or the connection is not good enough, the operations may not be performed or may be lost. CloudKit does not provide a standard solution for these situations, it just returns an error and expects our application to solve the problem.

The most common error is related to the user's iCloud account. Every user must have an iCloud account to access CloudKit servers. If an iCloud account was not set up on the device or has restrictions due to Parental Control or Device Management, the app will not be able to connect to the servers. The `CKContainer` class offers the following method to check the status of the user's account.

accountStatus(completionHandler: Block)—This method attempts to access the user's iCloud account and calls the closure specified by the **completionHandler** attribute with a value that determines the current status. The closure receives two values, a `CKAccountStatus` enumeration to report the current status and a `CKError` value to report errors. The enumeration includes the values `couldNotDetermine`, `available`, `restricted`, and `noAccount`.

If the status of the iCloud account changes later, the system posts a notification that we can observe from our application to perform updates.

CKAccountChanged—This notification is posted by the system when the status of the user's iCloud account registered on the device changes.

When and where we check the status of the iCloud account depends on our application. We could do it every time the code tries to access the CloudKit servers, or every time we get an error from an operation indicating that no iCloud account was found, but probably the best way to do it is to set a value in User Defaults at launch and check that value every time an operation is performed, as shown next.

```
func application(_ application: UIApplication,
didFinishLaunchingWithOptions launchOptions:
[UIApplication.LaunchOptionsKey: Any]?) -> Bool {
    let userSettings = UserDefaults.standard
    let values = ["subscriptionSaved": false, "zoneCreated": false,
"iCloudAvailable": false]
```

```
    userSettings.register(defaults: values)

    container = NSPersistentContainer(name: "places")
    container.loadPersistentStores(completionHandler: { (storeDescription,
error) in
        if error != nil {
            print("Error")
        } else {
            self.context = self.container.viewContext
        }
    })
    application.registerForRemoteNotifications()

    let containerCloudKit = CKContainer.default()
    containerCloudKit.accountStatus(completionHandler: {(status, error) in
        if status == CKAccountStatus.available {
            let mainQueue = OperationQueue.main
            mainQueue.addOperation({
                userSettings.set(true, forKey: "iCloudAvailable")
                AppData.checkUpdates(finishClosure: {(result) in return})
            })
        } else {
            print("Error")
        }
    })
    return true
}
```

Listing 23-38: Checking the status of the iCloud account

In the example of Listing 23-38, we modify the **application(UIApplication, didFinishLaunchingWithOptions:)** method of our **AppDelegate** class to check the status of the iCloud account. If an account is available, we update the iCloudAvailable value in User Defaults and then call the **checkUpdates()** method in our model to initialize the database with the records already stored in the servers. Now, every time we want to perform an operation on the servers, we can check the value of the iCloudAvailable key to know whether an iCloud account is available. To keep this value up-to-date, we can listen to the **CKAccountChanged** notification or change it when an error is received from an operation, as we will see later.

 Do It Yourself: Update the **AppDelegate** class with the method of Listing 23-38. Uninstall the application in your device and run it again. You shouldn't see any changes unless you deactivate your iCloud account.

Every single operation reports the errors that happened in the process, if any. The values are sent to the closures as objects that conform to the **Error** protocol. In CloudKit, the errors are of type **CKError**, so we have to cast the value received to this type and then read its properties. The following is the property that returns the error code.

code—This property returns a value that identifies the error found. The property is of type **Code**, an enumeration inside the **CKError** structure with values that correspond to each type of error produced by CloudKit. The list of values available is extensive. The most frequently used are **partialFailure**, **networkUnavailable**, **networkFailure**, **serviceUnavailable**, **unknownItem**, **operationCancelled**, **changeTokenExpired**, **quotaExceeded**, **zoneNotFound**, and **limitExceeded**.

How to respond to an error, how to organize the code, or even whether to respond or not, depends on the error and the characteristics of our application, but because the errors don't change from one operation to another, it is usually better to check for errors and produce the appropriate response from a single method. For instance, if the user is not logged into iCloud, any operation will return the **notAuthenticated** error. In these circumstances, we can check whether the error is of type **notAuthenticated** and proceed to change the value of the iCloudAvailable key in User Defaults to **false** to indicate that no iCloud account is available, as shown in the following example.

```
func processErrors(error: CKError) {
    switch error.code {
        case .notAuthenticated:
            let userSettings = UserDefaults.standard
            userSettings.set(false, forKey: "iCloudAvailable")
        default:
            print("ERROR: \(error.code)")
            break
    }
}
```

Listing 23-39: Responding to errors

Once we have implemented the method to respond to errors, we must call it from every CloudKit operation. For instance, the following are the modifications we have to introduce to the closure for the **recordZoneFetchCompletionBlock** of the **CKFetchRecordZoneChangesOperation** operation to process the errors received when the operation finishes fetching the records of a zone (see Listing 23-38).

```
fetchOperation.recordZoneFetchCompletionBlock = { (zoneID, token, data,
more, error) in
    if let ckerror = error as? CKError {
        self.processErrors(error: ckerror)
    } else {
        changeZoneToken = token
        self.updateLocalRecords(listRecordsUpdated: listRecordsUpdated)
        self.deleteLocalRecords(listRecordsDeleted: listRecordsDeleted)
        listRecordsUpdated.removeAll()
        listRecordsDeleted.removeAll()
    }
}
```

Listing 23-40: Calling a method to process errors

If there is an error and we can cast it as a **CKError** object, the **processErrors()** method is executed. This method receives the error, checks whether it corresponds to any of the types of errors we want to respond to, and produce the response.

Some errors require us to perform the operations again. In cases like this, we could initialize a timer to call the methods in charge of those operations after a certain period of time. For example, the **changeTokenExpired** error tells us that the tokens we are using are not valid anymore, which means that we have to clean the tokens stored in User Defaults and call our **checkUpdates()** method again. The following is our implementation of the **processErrors()** method to respond to this error.

```
func processErrors(error: CKError) {
    switch error.code {
        case .notAuthenticated:
            let userSettings = UserDefaults.standard
            userSettings.set(false, forKey: "iCloudAvailable")
        case .changeTokenExpired:
            let userSettings = UserDefaults.standard
            userSettings.removeObject(forKey: "changeToken")
            userSettings.removeObject(forKey: "changeZoneToken")
            Timer.scheduledTimer(timeInterval: 30, target: self, selector:
#selector(checkUpdates), userInfo: nil, repeats: false)
        default:
            print("ERROR: \(error.code)")
            break
    }
}
```

Listing 23-41: Responding to the changeTokenExpired *error*

If the **CKError** object received by the method contains a **changeTokenExpired** error, the **processErrors()** method removes the changeToken and changeZoneToken values from User Defaults, so the next time we access the server all the updates available will be fetched. The response also creates a **Timer** object to execute the **checkUpdates()** method again after 30 seconds.

Most **CKError** objects contain single errors that usually demand us to execute the operations again or warn the user that there is a problem, like the **quotaExceeded** error that is returned when there is no more storage space in the user's iCloud account. But there is an error called **partialFailure** that determines that some of the records were updated and some failed, either because the data was corrupt, or a new version of the record was detected on the server. This error returns an **NSDictionary** object containing a list of record IDs and the errors produced when the server tried to modify them. For instance, if in the application we developed previously, we let the user update the name of a country or a city, when we try to send that record, the server may detect that the tag in the metadata of the record we are trying to upload is older than the tag of the record already stored in the server. As we have seen in Figure 23-21, this occurs because every time we upload a record to the server, the database assigns a new tag to it. If later we try to upload the same record from the same or a different device, the tags won't match, and the server will reject it. In cases like this, we have to get the current tag and assign it to the object in our local storage before attempting to upload that record again. Because this is a common error, each item in the dictionary returned by the **partialFailure** error contains a copy of the record that produced the error, so we can get the new metadata from this object, update the object in our local storage, and try to upload it again.

```
func processErrors(error: CKError) {
    switch error.code {
        case .notAuthenticated:
            let userSettings = UserDefaults.standard
            userSettings.set(false, forKey: "iCloudAvailable")
        case .changeTokenExpired:
            let userSettings = UserDefaults.standard
            userSettings.removeObject(forKey: "changeToken")
            userSettings.removeObject(forKey: "changeZoneToken")
            Timer.scheduledTimer(timeInterval: 30, target: self, selector:
#selector(checkUpdates), userInfo: nil, repeats: false)
```

```
        case .partialFailure:
            if let listErrors = error.userInfo[CKPartialErrorsByItemIDKey]
as? NSDictionary {
                var listFailedRecords: [CKRecord] = []
                for (_, error) in listErrors {
                    if let recordError = error as? CKError {
                        if let record =
recordError.userInfo[CKRecordChangedErrorServerRecordKey] as? CKRecord {
                            listFailedRecords.append(record)
                        }
                    }
                }
                self.uploadFailedRecords(failedRecords: listFailedRecords)
            }
        default:
            print("ERROR: \(error.code)")
            break
    }
}
func uploadFailedRecords(failedRecords: [CKRecord]) {
    for record in failedRecords {
        let coder = NSKeyedArchiver(requiringSecureCoding: true)
        record.encodeSystemFields(with: coder)
        let recordMetadata = coder.encodedData
        let recordType = record.recordType
        let recordName = record.recordID.recordName

        if recordType == "Countries" {
            let request: NSFetchRequest<Countries> =
Countries.fetchRequest()
            request.predicate = NSPredicate(format: "ckrecordname = %@",
recordName)
            do {
                let result = try context.fetch(request)
                if !result.isEmpty {
                    let item = result[0]
                    item.ckmetadata = recordMetadata
                }
            } catch {
                print("Error Fetching Record")
            }
        } else if recordType == "Cities" {
            let request: NSFetchRequest<Cities> = Cities.fetchRequest()
            request.predicate = NSPredicate(format: "ckrecordname = %@",
recordName)
            do {
                let result = try context.fetch(request)
                if !result.isEmpty {
                    let item = result[0]
                    item.ckmetadata = recordMetadata
                }
            } catch {
                print("Error Fetching Record")
            }
        }
    }
    if context.hasChanges {
        do {
            try context.save()
            uploadRecords()
```

```
      } catch {
         print("Error Saving Context")
      }
   }
}
```

Listing 23-42: Uploading records that failed

The way errors provide additional information is through a dictionary assigned to their **userInfo** property (an **NSDictionary** object). To get the records that failed, we have to read the value in this dictionary with the key **CKPartialErrorsByItemIDKey**. In turn, this key returns another **NSDictionary** object with a list of the record IDs of the records that failed and the corresponding error each operation returned.

The process of uploading a record may failed for different reasons. If we want to get the records that failed because of a tag mismatch, we have to read the **CKRecordChangedErrorServerRecordKey** key of the **userInfo** dictionary of each error. The key returns a **CKRecord** object with the record found on the server, so we can get the new tag from this record, update the object in the local storage with it, and try to upload it again. In the example of Listing 23-42, we follow this process to create a list of the records that failed and then call a method to update the Core Data objects and upload the records again.

The **uploadFailedRecords()** method processes the failed records one by one. First, it gets the metadata from the record received from the server (the metadata includes the record's tag) and then updates the **ckmetadata** attribute of the corresponding object in the persistent store with this value. When all the objects in the persistent store are updated, we call the **uploadRecords()** method to upload everything again.

Now, every time we try to upload a record which tag is older than the tag of the record on the server, the local object is updated and uploaded again. In our example, we just update the local tag and upload the records again. This process completely replaces the values of the records on the server. For example, if the user updates the name of a country from Device 1 and then does the same from Device 2, the name inserted from Device 1 will be lost. Depending on the characteristics of our application, we might need to proceed in a different manner or warn the user about the situation.

Do It Yourself: If you want to try these examples, remember to call the **processErrors()** method from every operation, as we did in the example of Listing 23-40. Also, consider that calling the same method after an error was received may cause an infinite loop if for some reason the same error is returned by the server over and over again. In our example, we call the **uploadRecords()** method from the **uploadFailedRecords()** method to simplify the code, but you should consider to check if the method was already called by a previous operation or implement another method to process errors.

IMPORTANT: As we already mentioned, how to handle errors depends on the error itself and the characteristics of your application, but you cannot ignore them, you always have to perform a task that solves the problem or tells the user what to do or otherwise your app sooner or later will become useless. To learn more about the errors returned by CloudKit operations, you can read the descriptions of all the values included in the **CKError.Code** enumeration. The link is available on our website.

Deploy to Production

Once our app is ready and the definition of the database's structure in CloudKit is complete, we have to deploy it to production. The button to start the process is at the bottom of the Development environment's menu, as shown in Figure 23-22.

Figure 23-22: Development environment buttons

The Deploy to Production button opens a popup window where we can see the features that are going to be transferred to the Production environment. This includes record types and indexes, but it does not include records. If we agree, we have to press the Deploy Changes button to finish the process, and our database in CloudKit will be ready for distribution.

 IMPORTANT: The Production environment is used by apps that were submitted to iTunes or built for testing. To learn how to publish your app, read Chapter 30. For more information on how to build your app for testing, visit our website and follow the links for this chapter.

Chapter 24
Graphics

24.1 Core Graphics

All the views we have used so far are created from subclasses of the **UIView** class that include additional code to draw content on the screen. For instance, a label is a view that can draw text, a button is a view that can draw its title, and a Slider is a view that can draw the horizontal bar and the indicator the user moves to set a new value. All those graphics are created by predefined code included in the subclasses. We can provide some values for configuration, like the color for the text or the shape of the box around a Text Field, for example, but if we want to show custom graphics, we have to define our own **UIView** subclasses and create the code to draw the graphics ourselves. For this purpose, Apple offers the Core Graphics framework.

We have introduced Core Graphics in Chapter 4. This is an old framework programmed in the C language and developed to provide a two-dimensional drawing engine for Apple systems. In Chapter 4, we presented its data types, like **CGFloat** and **CGRect**, but the framework also includes a powerful drawing API for the creation of graphics known as Quartz 2D.

Destination

Quartz 2D can generate graphics for multiple destinations including printers, PDF files, or windows, but the most common use in iOS is to create the graphics for custom **UIView** subclasses. The **UIView** subclass is created in a separate file and then assigned to the view in the Storyboard where the graphics are going to be shown. Figure 24-1 shows the initial Scene of a Single View Application project with a view inside associated with a custom **UIView** subclass called **DrawingView**.

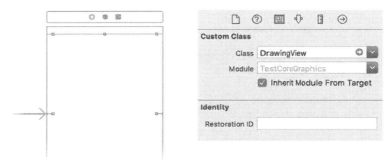

Figure 24-1: View associated with a subclass

The **UIView** class includes a method called **draw()** that is executed every time the system needs to draw the view's content on the screen. Overwriting this method in a **UIView** subclass, we can create our own graphics for the view. The following example shows this method in the **DrawingView** subclass we have created for the view of Figure 24-1.

```
import UIKit

class DrawingView: UIView {
   override func draw(_ rect: CGRect) {
   }
}
```

Listing 24-1: Defining a UIView subclass

Do It Yourself: Create a new Single View Application project. Add an empty view from the Object Library to the initial Scene (Figure 5-38). Create a new file with a subclass of **UIView** called **DrawingView** and assign it to the view from the Identity Inspector panel, as shown in Figure 24-1.

 The Basics: The **draw()** method receives a **CGRect** value that represents the portion of the view that needs updating. Sometimes this value may be equal to the view's boundaries, but that is not always the case. If you need to know the size of the view to calculate the coordinates for the graphics, you can get the width and height from the view's **bounds** property (e.g., **self.bounds.size.height**).

Context

Because Quartz 2D can draw on multiple destinations, the first thing we have to do to create our own graphics is to define the context in which the graphics are going to be drawn. The context is an object of type **CGContext** that contains the drawing parameters and all the information required to draw the graphics. Contexts may be created from the class' initializers, but they are also defined automatically by some of the classes included in UIKit. For example, **UIView** objects create their own context before calling the **draw()** method. The UIKit framework offers the following functions to get a reference to the current context or set our own.

UIGraphicsGetCurrentContext()—This function gets a reference to the current graphic context.

UIGraphicsPushContext(CGContext)—This function sets a new context as the current context. The contexts are added to a stack. The current context is considered to be the last context added to the stack.

UIGraphicsPopContext()—This function removes the current context from the stack.

Paths

The graphics in Quartz 2D are defined as paths. We have to create a path first and then send it to the context to be drawn. The **CGContext** class offers the following methods to set the beginning and the ending of a path.

beginPath()—This method indicates the beginning of a path.

closePath()—This method closes the current path. If the path is not a closed path, the function adds a line between the end of the path and the beginning to close it.

The path is created as a combination of straight lines and curves. The strokes move from one point to another in the view's coordinates, as if following the movement of a pen. The **CGContext** class offers a set of methods to define the position of the pen and generate the path; the following are the most frequently used.

move(to: CGPoint)—This method moves the pen to the coordinates indicated by the **to** attribute.

addLine(to: CGPoint)—This method adds a straight line to the path that goes from the pen's current position to the coordinates indicated by the **to** attribute.

addLines(between: [CGPoint])—This method adds multiple lines to the path. The **between** attribute is an array with the coordinates for the lines (the lines are added in sequence).

Graphics

addArc(center: CGPoint, **radius:** CGFloat, **startAngle:** CGFloat, **endAngle:** CGFloat, **clockwise:** Bool)—This method adds an arc to the path. The **center** attribute specifies the coordinates of the center of the circle formed by the arc, the **radius** attribute is the length of the circle's radius, the **startAngle** attribute is the angle in which the arc starts (expressed in radians), the **endAngle** attribute is the angle in which the arc ends (expressed in radians), and the **clockwise** attribute specifies the orientation in which the arc is calculated (`true` for clockwise and `false` for counterclockwise).

addArc(tangent1End: CGPoint, **tangent2End:** CGPoint, **radius:** CGFloat)—This method adds an arc to the path using tangent points. The **tangent1End** attribute defines the coordinates of the end of the first tangent line, the **tangent2End** attribute defines the coordinates of the end of the second tangent line, and the **radius** attribute is the length of the circle's radius.

addRect(CGRect)—This method adds the rectangle defined by the attribute to the path.

addEllipse(in: CGRect)—This method adds an ellipse to the path. The **in** attribute determines the area of the ellipse. If the rectangle is a square, the ellipse will be a circle.

addQuadCurve(to: CGPoint, **control:** CGPoint)—This method adds a quadratic Bézier curve to the path with one control point. The `to` attribute defines the coordinates of the ending point, and the `control` attribute defines the coordinates of the control point.

addCurve(to: CGPoint, **control1:** CGPoint, **control2:** CGPoint)—This method adds a cubic Bézier curve to the path with two control points. The `to` attribute defines the coordinates of the ending point, the `control1` attribute defines the coordinates of the first control point, and the `control2` attribute defines the second control point.

A path defines the line to trace, but it does not draw anything. To draw the path in the context, and therefore show it on the view, the `CGContext` class offers two methods.

strokePath()—This method draws a line that follows the current path.

fillPath(using: CGPathFillRule)—This method paints the area within the current path. The **using** attribute is an enumeration that establishes how the area to be painted will be determined. The values available are `evenOdd` and `winding` (default).

To create a path, we have to call the methods in order, following the line of the pen. The following example gets a reference to the current context and creates a path with the shape of a triangle.

```
import UIKit

class DrawingView: UIView {
    override func draw(_ rect: CGRect) {
        if let context = UIGraphicsGetCurrentContext() {
            context.beginPath()
            context.move(to: CGPoint(x: 10, y: 150))
            context.addLine(to: CGPoint(x: 100, y: 150))
            context.addLine(to: CGPoint(x: 10, y: 250))
            context.closePath()
            context.strokePath()
        }
    }
}
```

Listing 24-2: Drawing a triangle

By default, the pen's initial position is at the coordinates 0, 0 (top-left corner of the view). If we want our graphic to start from a different position, we have to call the **move()** method. In Listing 24-2, we indicate the beginning of the path with the **beginPath()** method and then move the pen to the coordinates 10, 150 before adding the first line. The lines and curves added to the path are generated from the current position of the pen to the coordinates indicated by the method (every line or curve starts from the point the previous one ended). For instance, after setting the initial point in our example, we create a line from that point to the point 100, 150. The next line starts at 100, 150 and ends at 10, 250. Figure 24-2 shows the path created by this example.

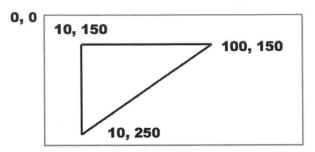

Figure 24-2: *Representation of a path*

Notice that in our example we only created two lines. The line that goes from the point 10, 250 to the point 10, 150 is created by the **closePath()** method to close the path. If we want to create an open path, we can ignore this method.

Our code calls the **strokePath()** method to draw the path in the context and generate an empty figure, but we can call the **fillPath()** method instead if we want the figure to be solid.

Do It Yourself: Update the **DrawingView** class with the code of Listing 24-2 and run the application. You should see a shape similar to Figure 24-2 on the screen. Use the same project to test the following examples.

Combining different methods, we can create complex paths. The following path creates a graphic with two lines and an arc.

```
import UIKit

class DrawingView: UIView {
    override func draw(_ rect: CGRect) {
        if let context = UIGraphicsGetCurrentContext() {
            context.beginPath()
            context.move(to: CGPoint(x: 10, y: 150))
            context.addLine(to: CGPoint(x: 100, y: 150))

            let startAngle = CGFloat(270 * Float.pi / 180)
            let endAngle = CGFloat(90 * Float.pi / 180)
            context.addArc(center: CGPoint(x: 100, y: 170), radius: 20,
startAngle: startAngle, endAngle: endAngle, clockwise: false)
            context.addLine(to: CGPoint(x: 10, y: 190))

            context.strokePath()
        }
    }
}
```

Listing 24-3: *Complex paths*

Graphics

The angle for arcs and ellipses has to be expressed in radians. Radian is the standard unit to measure angles, but we can easily convert degrees into radians with the formula **degrees * PI / 180**, where **degrees** is the value of the angle in degrees and **PI** is the value of PI (see Chapter 4). Because arcs are calculated based on the coordinates of the center of the circle and its radius, we have to consider these two values to connect the arc with the previous stroke. If the initial coordinates of the arc do not coincide with the current position of the pen, a line is created between these two points to connect the path. Figure 24-3 illustrates the path we get with the example of Listing 24-3 and what we will see if we move up the center of the circle by 10 points.

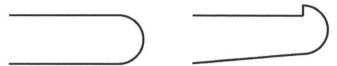

Figure 24-3: Path combining lines and arcs

The **addRect()** and **addEllipse()** methods allow us to add rectangles and circles to the path. The methods add the figures to the current path, but they move the pen to the position indicated by the rectangle, so it can be considered as an independent shape.

```
import UIKit

class DrawingView: UIView {
    override func draw(_ rect: CGRect) {
        if let context = UIGraphicsGetCurrentContext() {
            context.beginPath()
            context.move(to: CGPoint(x: 10, y: 150))
            context.addLine(to: CGPoint(x: 100, y: 150))

            let frame = CGRect(x: 100, y: 140, width: 20, height: 20)
            context.addEllipse(in: frame)
            context.strokePath()
        }
    }
}
```

Listing 24-4: Adding circles to the path

In this case, no line is generated between the current position of the pen and the circle if they are not connected. Figure 24-4 illustrates the path we get with the example of Listing 24-4 and what we will see if we move the area of the circle 10 points to the right.

Figure 24-4: Paths with straight lines and circles

Every time we want to create a shape we have to initialize a path, add all the strokes necessary for the shape, and draw the path in the context. Because simple geometric shapes like rectangles and circles are very common, the **CGContext** class offers a group of methods that draw directly into the context, significantly reducing the amount of code we have to write.

stroke(CGRect)—This method draws an empty rectangle in the context.

fill(CGRect)—This method draws a solid rectangle in the context.

clear(CGRect)—This method clears a rectangular area in the context.

strokeEllipse(in: CGRect)—This method draws an empty ellipse in the context. The attribute determines the position and size of the area occupied by the ellipse.

fillEllipse(in: CGRect)—This method draws a solid ellipse in the context. The attribute determines the position and size of the area occupied by the ellipse.

These methods create their own path and draw it into the context all at once. The following example draws a few circles inside a rectangle to simulate the face of a robot. Notice that when we use these methods we do not have to open and close the path anymore.

```
import UIKit

class DrawingView: UIView {
    override func draw(_ rect: CGRect) {
        if let context = UIGraphicsGetCurrentContext() {
            var frame = CGRect(x: 10, y: 150, width: 100, height: 100)
            context.stroke(frame)
            frame = CGRect(x: 25, y: 170, width: 20, height: 20)
            context.fillEllipse(in: frame)
            frame = CGRect(x: 75, y: 170, width: 20, height: 20)
            context.fillEllipse(in: frame)
            frame = CGRect(x: 40, y: 200, width: 40, height: 40)
            context.strokeEllipse(in: frame)
        }
    }
}
```

Listing 24-5: Drawing basic shapes

Figure 24-5: Shapes drawn directly into the context

Colors

Core Graphics is programmed in the C Language and therefore it does not work with high-level classes like **UIColor**. The framework defines its own class to generate colors called **CGColor**. As well as **UIColor**, the **CGColor** class can work with colors of different types, including CMYK and RGB. The **UIColor** class includes the following property to get a **CGColor** object.

cgColor—This property returns a **CGColor** object from the values of the **UIColor** object.

By default, the color assigned to the path is black, but we can assign a different color before the path is drawn in the context using the following methods provided by the **CGContext** class.

setStrokeColor(CGColor)—This method defines the color for the stroke of the path.

setFillColor(CGColor)—This method defines the color for the interior of the path.

Only one color per path can be defined (one for the stroke and another for the filling). If we want our graphic to have more than one color, we have to create different paths and change the color before the paths are drawn. The following example shows how to define a color for a path.

Graphics

```
import UIKit

class DrawingView: UIView {
    override func draw(_ rect: CGRect) {
        if let context = UIGraphicsGetCurrentContext() {
            let color = UIColor(red: 1.0, green: 0.2, blue: 0.2, alpha: 1.0)
            context.setStrokeColor(color.cgColor)

            context.beginPath()
            context.move(to: CGPoint(x: 10, y: 10))
            context.addLine(to: CGPoint(x: 100, y: 100))
            context.strokePath()
        }
    }
}
```

Listing 24-6: Changing the color of the path

Configuration

The **CGContext** class also includes methods to configure the lines before drawing the path in the context. The following are the most frequently used.

setLineWidth(CGFloat**)**—This method defines the line's width.

setLineDash(phase: CGFloat, lengths: [CGFloat])—This method defines the line as a dashed line. The **phase** attribute determines where the line begins, and the **lengths** attribute is an array with values that specify the lengths of the segments.

setLineCap(CGLineCap**)**—This method sets the style for the ending of the lines. The attribute is an enumeration with the values **butt** (squared end), **round** (round end), and **square** (squared end extended half the width of the line).

setLineJoin(CGLineJoin**)**—This method sets the style of the joints of two connected lines. The attribute is an enumeration with the values **miter** (joins the lines with a sharp end), **round** (joins the lines with a rounded end), and **bevel** (joins the lines with a square end).

setMiterLimit(CGFloat**)**—This method sets the limit of the lines when the joint is set as **miter**. The attribute is a value that determines how long the joint will extend.

setBlendMode(CGBlendMode**)**—This method sets the blend mode used when paths overlap. The attribute is an enumeration with the values **normal**, **multiply**, **screen**, **overlay**, **darken**, **lighten**, **colorDodge**, **colorBurn**, **softLight**, **hardLight**, **difference**, **exclusion**, **hue**, **saturation**, **color**, **luminosity**, **clear**, **copy**, **sourceIn**, **sourceOut**, **sourceAtop**, **destinationOver**, **destinationIn**, **destinationOut**, **destinationAtop**, **xor**, **plusDarker**, and **plusLighter**.

The following example creates a path with two lines configured as dashed lines with a width of 10 points and round endings.

```
import UIKit

class DrawingView: UIView {
    override func draw(_ rect: CGRect) {
        if let context = UIGraphicsGetCurrentContext() {
            context.setLineWidth(10)
            context.setLineCap(.round)
```

```
        context.setLineJoin(.round)
        context.setLineDash(phase: 0, lengths: [15])

        context.beginPath()
        context.move(to: CGPoint(x: 20, y: 80))
        context.addLine(to: CGPoint(x: 70, y: 10))
        context.addLine(to: CGPoint(x: 120, y: 80))
        context.strokePath()
      }
    }
}
```

Listing 24-7: Configuring the lines

Figure 24-6: Dashed lines with round endings

Saving the State

Changes in the configuration are performed in the context and affect all the paths drawn after the changes were made. Sometimes we need to configure the context only for one path, but we do not want the rest of the paths to be affected. If the change we have performed is simple, like when we modify the width of the line, we can call the same function again to restore the previous value, but when going back to a previous state is not that simple, we have to save and restore the context's state using the following methods provided by the **CGContext** class.

saveGState()—This method saves the current state of the context.

restoreGState()—This method restores the previous state of the context.

The state must be saved before any change is introduced and restored after the path is drawn in the context. For example, we can change the width of the lines to 10 points for the first path and then restore the state to use the value by default for the remaining paths in the graphic.

```
import UIKit

class DrawingView: UIView {
    override func draw(_ rect: CGRect) {
        if let context = UIGraphicsGetCurrentContext() {
            context.saveGState()
            context.setLineWidth(10)
            context.beginPath()
            context.move(to: CGPoint(x: 20, y: 20))
            context.addLine(to: CGPoint(x: 20, y: 100))
            context.strokePath()
            context.restoreGState()
            context.strokeEllipse(in: CGRect(x: 40, y: 60, width: 40,
height: 40))
        }
    }
}
```

Listing 24-8: Saving and restoring the state of the context

Graphics

Figure 24-7: Paths drawn in different states

Clipping

The context creates a mask that delimits the space available for the graphics to the boundaries of the drawing surface (in our example, this is the view's frame). We can create our own mask to determine which parts of the area can be drawn and which not with the following method of the **CGContext** class.

clip(using: CGPathFillRule)—This method creates a mask from the current path. The **using** attribute is an enumeration that establishes how the area to be clipped will be determined. The values available are **evenOdd** and **winding** (default).

The mask is created from a path, so we have to define the path first and then call the **clip()** method later. The following example creates a circular mask and then draws a path with multiple straight lines. Only the part of the lines that are inside the mask are drawn.

```
import UIKit

class DrawingView: UIView {
    override func draw(_ rect: CGRect) {
        if let context = UIGraphicsGetCurrentContext() {
            context.addEllipse(in:CGRect(x:50, y:50, width:100, height:100))
            context.clip()

            context.beginPath()
            let list = stride(from: 10, to: 150, by: 10)
            for pos in list {
                context.move(to: CGPoint(x: 50, y: pos))
                context.addLine(to: CGPoint(x: 150, y: pos))
            }
            context.strokePath()
        }
    }
}
```

Listing 24-9: Delimiting the drawing area

Figure 24-8: Mask

Gradients

Quartz 2D also allows us to fill the paths with gradients. There are two types of gradients: linear and radial. The linear gradient is composed of lines of color distributed along an axis, while a radial gradient is composed of circles of different color that extend along an axis. Core Graphics defines the **CGGradient** class to represent gradients. The class includes the following initializer.

CGGradient(colorsSpace: CGColorSpace?, **colors:** [CGColor], **locations:** [CGFloat]?**)**—This initializer creates a `CGGradient` object with a gradient configured according to the values specified by the attributes. The **colorsSpace** attribute is a `CGColorSpace` object that defines the type of colors we want to use to present the colors, the **colors** attribute is an array with the colors we want to include in the gradient, and the **locations** attribute is an array with values between 0.0 and 1.0 that represent the locations along the axis in which the gradient turns from one color to another.

After the gradient is created, we have to draw it in the context. The `CGContext` class offers the following methods for this purpose.

drawLinearGradient(CGGradient, **start:** CGPoint, **end:** CGPoint, **options:** CGGradientDrawingOptions**)**—This method adds a linear gradient to the context. The first attribute is a reference to the `CGGradient` value we want to use, the **start** and **end** attributes indicate the starting and ending point of the gradient, and the **options** attribute indicates whether the gradient will extend beyond the starting location or after the ending location. The framework offers the `CGGradientDrawingOptions` structure with the properties `drawsBeforeStartLocation` and `drawsAfterEndLocation` to specify this value.

drawRadialGradient(CGGradient, **startCenter:** CGPoint, **startRadius:** CGFloat, **endCenter:** CGPoint, **endRadius:** CGFloat, **options:** CGGradientDrawingOptions**)**—This method adds a radial gradient to the context. Radial gradients are created from one circle to another. The first attribute is a reference to the `CGGradient` value we want to use, the **startCenter** and **endCenter** attributes determine the positions of the center of the circles, the **startRadius** and **endRadius** attributes determine the radius of the circles, and the **options** attribute indicates whether the gradient will extend beyond the starting location or after the ending location. The framework offers the `CGGradientDrawingOptions` structure with the properties `drawsBeforeStartLocation` and `drawsAfterEndLocation` to specify this value.

Colors are presented on the screen according to a color model or color space. When we create a `CGColor` object from a `UIColor` value, the system uses generic color spaces, but to create a gradient we have to specify the color space ourselves. To create and represent a color space, the framework includes the `CGColorSpace` class and the following global functions.

CGColorSpaceCreateDeviceCMYK()—This function creates a color space based on the CMYK color model. This model uses the basic colors cyan, magenta, yellow, and black to create all the colors in the spectrum.

CGColorSpaceCreateDeviceGray()—This function creates a color space composed of a scale of grays.

CGColorSpaceCreateDeviceRGB()—This function creates a color space based on the RGB model. This model uses the basic colors red, green, and blue to create all the colors in the spectrum.

Gradients are applied to the context. If we want to paint a path with a gradient, we have to create a mask with that path to delimit the area of the gradient. The following example creates a rectangular path to use as a mask and then adds a linear gradient to the context from the color white to black.

Graphics

```
import UIKit

class DrawingView: UIView {
    override func draw(_ rect: CGRect) {
        if let context = UIGraphicsGetCurrentContext() {
            context.beginPath()
            context.addRect(CGRect(x: 10, y: 10, width: 100, height: 100))
            context.clip()

            let space = CGColorSpaceCreateDeviceRGB()
            let color1 = UIColor.white
            let color2 = UIColor.black
            let colors = [color1.cgColor, color2.cgColor] as CFArray
            let locations: [CGFloat] = [0.0, 0.9]
            let gradient = CGGradient(colorsSpace: space, colors: colors,
locations: locations)

            let startPoint = CGPoint(x: 10, y: 10)
            let endPoint = CGPoint(x: 110, y: 110)
            context.drawLinearGradient(gradient!, start: startPoint, end:
endPoint, options: .drawsBeforeStartLocation)
        }
    }
}
```

Listing 24-10: *Creating a linear gradient*

There are two steps involved in the creation of a gradient. We have to initialize the **CGGradient** object first and then add the gradient to the context with the function corresponding to the gradient we want to generate (linear or radial). The **CGGradient** initializer requires a few values to configure the gradient. The first value is the color space we want to use to define the colors of the gradient. In Listing 24-10, we used the most common model called RGB. The second value is an array with the list of colors that are going to participate in the gradient. The colors are added to the gradient in the order they are declared in this array (notice that the **drawLinearGradient()** method takes an array of type **CFArray**, so we have to cast the array of colors to this type). The last value is another array containing values between 0.0 and 1.0 indicating the position in which every color will start. In our example, we decided to create a gradient from white to black, starting with white (0.0) and positioning the color black close to the end (0.9). Once the gradient is defined, we add it to the context as a linear gradient with the **drawLinearGradient()** method. Because linear gradients are composed of straight lines perpendicular to an axis, we have to provide the points in which the axis starts and ends. In this example, we define those points to be the corners of the rectangular area we want to paint, so the gradient is distributed homogeneously throughout that area.

Figure 24-9: *Linear gradient*

Shadows

Another good effect we can achieve with Quartz 2D is shadows. Shadows are declared as part of the context's configuration. Once the shadow is set, every path drawn afterwards will include it. The **CGContext** class provides the following methods to set a shadow.

setShadow(offset: CGSize, **blur:** CGFloat)—This method configures the shadow for the context with the color by default. The **offset** attribute determines the horizontal and vertical offset of the shadow in relation to the path, and the **blur** attribute specifies the amount of blur.

setShadow(offset: CGSize, **blur:** CGFloat, **color:** CGColor?)—This method configures the shadow for the context with a specific color. The **offset** attribute determines the horizontal and vertical offset of the shadow in relation to the path, the **blur** attribute specifies the amount of blur, and the **color** attribute determines the color of the shadow.

```
import UIKit

class DrawingView: UIView {
    override func draw(_ rect: CGRect) {
        if let context = UIGraphicsGetCurrentContext() {
            context.setLineWidth(10)
            context.setShadow(offset: CGSize(width: 5, height: 5), blur: 5)
            context.strokeEllipse(in: CGRect(x: 10, y: 10, width: 100,
height: 100))
        }
    }
}
```

Listing 24-11: Generating shadows

Figure 24-10: Shadows

Transformations

As we mentioned in Chapter 4, Apple devices work with two coordinate systems, one expressed in pixels that represent the native resolution of each device and another expressed in points that provide a standard resolution for all devices. Quartz 2D is responsible of transforming the graphics from one coordinate system to another. The process is performed using a transformation matrix that calculates the positions of every pixel. This transformation matrix (identified with the letters CTM for Current Transformation Matrix) may be modified to change the aspect of the graphics without changing the graphics themselves. By modifying the CTM, we can introduce multiple changes to the graphics. The most common operations are translation, scaling, and rotation. The **CGContext** class offers the following methods to achieve these effects.

translateBy(x: CGFloat, **y:** CGFloat)—This method changes the origin of the coordinates system. The **x** and **y** attributes determine the new position of the origin.

rotate(by: CGFloat)—This method rotates the coordinate system. The **by** attribute is a value with the angle of rotation in radians.

scaleBy(x: CGFloat, **y:** CGFloat)—This method changes the scale of the coordinate system. The **x** and **y** attributes determine the scaling factor (1.0 keeps the current scale and negative values invert the coordinate system).

The transformations are performed in the context, affecting all the paths drawn afterwards. For example, if we translate the origin of the coordinate system to a new position, from that moment on the position of the paths in the context will be determined according to this new origin. The following example creates a rectangle and an ellipse, both with the same size and positioned at the coordinates 5, 5, but because the origin is changed to the point 100, 50, they are drawn close to the center.

```
import UIKit

class DrawingView: UIView {
    override func draw(_ rect: CGRect) {
        if let context = UIGraphicsGetCurrentContext() {
            context.translateBy(x: 100, y: 50)
            let frame = CGRect(x: 5, y: 5, width: 50, height: 20)
            context.stroke(frame)
            context.strokeEllipse(in: frame)
        }
    }
}
```

Listing 24-12: Translating the coordinate system's origin

Figure 24-11 below shows how translation affects the paths. The picture on the left shows the paths drawn without translation, and the picture on the right shows the paths drawn after the origin is displaced 100 points to the right.

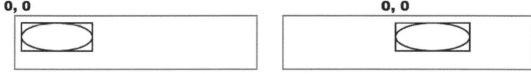

Figure 24-11: Translation

Establishing the origin of the coordinate system is useful in many circumstances but especially when we need to rotate the graphics. The rotation is performed around the origin, so if we want to rotate a path around its center we have to move the origin to the center of the path before performing the rotation.

```
import UIKit

class DrawingView: UIView {
    override func draw(_ rect: CGRect) {
        if let context = UIGraphicsGetCurrentContext() {
            let degrees = CGFloat(90 * Float.pi / 180)
            context.translateBy(x: 100, y: 100)
            context.rotate(by: degrees)
            let frame = CGRect(x: -25, y: -10, width: 50, height: 20)

            context.stroke(frame)
        }
    }
}
```

Listing 24-13: Applying two transformations to rotate a shape

0, 0　　　　　　　　　　　　　　　　**0, 0**

Figure 24-12: Rotation

The transformations are accumulative. For instance, if we rotate the context 45 degrees, and then apply another rotation of 45 degrees, the final rotation of the context will be 90 degrees. The following example takes advantage of this feature to draw multiple rectangles in the context, each with a different rotation.

```
import UIKit

class DrawingView: UIView {
    override func draw(_ rect: CGRect) {
        if let context = UIGraphicsGetCurrentContext() {
            context.translateBy(x: 100, y: 100)

            let list = stride(from: 0, to: 360, by: 45)
            for pos in list {
                let degrees = CGFloat(Float(pos) * Float.pi / 180)
                context.rotate(by: degrees)
                let frame = CGRect(x: 0, y: 0, width: 50, height: 20)
                context.stroke(frame)
            }
        }
    }
}
```

Listing 24-14: *Applying successive transformations*

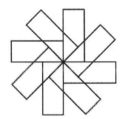

Figure 24-13: *Multiple rotations*

We can also change the scale of the context with the **scaleBy()** method. For example, if we want to duplicate the size of the paths drawn in the context, we can call this method with the values 2.0 for the horizontal scale and 2.0 for the vertical scale. But modifying the scale is not only about resizing the graphics; we can also achieve cool effects. For example, we can compress or expand paths by declaring different values for the horizontal and vertical scales, or we can create a mirror image by declaring a negative value. The following example implements this trick to invert the coordinate system and draw an inverted triangle on the other side of the screen.

```
import UIKit

class DrawingView: UIView {
    override func draw(_ rect: CGRect) {
        if let context = UIGraphicsGetCurrentContext() {
            drawTriangle(context: context)
            context.translateBy(x: self.bounds.size.width, y: 0)
            context.scaleBy(x: -1.0, y: 1.0)
```

Graphics

```
         drawTriangle(context: context)
      }
   }
   func drawTriangle(context: CGContext) {
      context.beginPath()
      context.move(to: CGPoint(x: 10, y: 10))
      context.addLine(to: CGPoint(x: 60, y: 60))
      context.addLine(to: CGPoint(x: 10, y: 110))
      context.addLine(to: CGPoint(x: 10, y: 10))
      context.strokePath()
   }
}
```

Listing 24-15: Inverting the context

The axis used to create the mirror is determined by the origin. If we create a horizontal mirror, the negative values are now on the right side of the horizontal origin and the positive values are on the left. If we want the paths with positive coordinates to appear on the screen, we have to translate the context, as we do in Listing 24-15. This code creates a method called **drawTriangle()** to draw a triangle on the left side of the context. The first time the method is called, the context is in its state by default, but the second time, the method is called after the context was transformed and therefore the new triangle is inverted and drawn on the right side of the view.

Figure 24-14: Mirror context

Besides modifying the current transformation matrix, we can also create a new one. Core Graphics defines the **CGAffineTransform** structure to store a transformation matrix. The structure includes the following initializers.

CGAffineTransform(translationX: CGFloat, **y:** CGFloat)—This initializer creates a matrix that translates the coordinate system. The **translationX** and **y** attributes determine the new positions of the origin.

CGAffineTransform(rotationAngle: CGFloat)—This initializer creates a matrix that rotates the coordinate system. The attribute is a value with the rotation angle in radians.

CGAffineTransform(scaleX: CGFloat, **y:** CGFloat)—This initializer returns a matrix that scales the coordinate system. The **scaleX** and **y** attributes determine the scaling factor (1.0 keeps the current scale and negative values invert the coordinate system).

A **CGAffineTransform** transformation matrix is usually applied by methods that require their own matrix, as we will see later, but we can also apply it directly to the context using a method provided by the **CGContext** class called **concatenate()**. The method takes a **CGAffineTransform** value and concatenates this matrix with the CTM.

```
import UIKit

class DrawingView: UIView {
   override func draw(_ rect: CGRect) {
      if let context = UIGraphicsGetCurrentContext() {
         context.translateBy(x: 100, y: 100)
```

Graphics 687 | P a g e

```
        let degrees = CGFloat(45 * Float.pi / 180)
        let matrix = CGAffineTransform(rotationAngle: degrees)
        context.concatenate(matrix)
        context.stroke(CGRect(x: -25, y: -10, width: 50, height: 20))
    }
  }
}
```

Listing 24-16: Concatenating matrices

Figure 24-15: Rotation with an Affine Transformation matrix

Text

There are different ways to draw text, but Apple recommends using Core Text. Core Text is the low-level framework Apple systems use to draw text on the screen. Several high-level elements like **UILabel**, for example, use this framework to generate their content. Core text can style and configure lines and entire paragraphs of text, but it is usually implemented along with Core Graphics to draw labels in the context. The framework defines a data type called **CTLine** to store a line of text and the following functions to create the line and draw it in the context.

CTLineDraw(CTLine, CGContext**)**—This function draws a line in the context. The first attribute is an object that contains the line of text we want to draw.

CTLineCreateWithAttributedString(CFAttributedString**)**—This function returns a **CTLine** value that represents a line of text. The attribute is the attributed string we want to assign to the line.

CTLineCreateTruncatedLine(CTLine,   Double,   CTLineTruncationType, CTLine?**)**—This function returns a **CTLine** value with a truncated line created from an existing line of text. The first attribute is an object that contains the line of text we want to truncate, the second attribute determines where the line is truncated, the third attribute is an enumeration that indicates where the truncation should be performed (the possible values are **start**, **end**, and **middle**), and the fourth attribute is an optional value that determines the characters added where the truncation took place (**nil** cuts the line off).

CTLineCreateJustifiedLine(CTLine, CGFloat, Double**)**—This function returns a **CTLine** value with a justified line created from an existing line of text. The first attribute is an object with the line of text we want to justify, the second attribute is a value around 1.0 that determines the degree of justification performed (values below 1.0 determine partial justification and values over 1.0 determine full justification), and the third attribute determines the width to which the line has to be justified.

Core Graphics and Core Text use a coordinate system that is a mirror of the coordinate system implemented by UIKit. When we work with Core Graphics and **UIView** objects, the view takes care of inverting the coordinate system to show the graphics in the right position on the screen, but it does not do that for text generated by Core Text. For this reason, before drawing any text in the context we have to apply the necessary transformations to invert and position the text. The **CGContext** class offers two practical properties to set the text's position and its own transformation matrix, so we do not have to deal with changing the transformation matrix of the entire context.

Graphics

textPosition—This property sets or returns the position of the text in the context. The vertical position is determined from the text baseline. It is of type `CGPoint`.

textMatrix—This property sets or returns the transformation matrix for the text. It is of type `CGAffineTransform`.

The line of text is created from an attributed string, so the first thing we need to do is to create an `NSMutableAttributedString` object. With the attributed text ready, we can call the Core Text functions to draw it in the context.

```
import UIKit

class DrawingView: UIView {
    override func draw(_ rect: CGRect) {
        if let context = UIGraphicsGetCurrentContext() {
            let font = UIFont(name: "BradleyHandITCTT-Bold", size: 30)
            let attributes = [NSAttributedString.Key.font: font!]
            let string = NSMutableAttributedString(string: "Hello",
attributes: attributes)

            let line = CTLineCreateWithAttributedString(string)
            context.textMatrix = CGAffineTransform(scaleX: 1.0, y: -1.0)
            context.textPosition = CGPoint(x: 10, y: 150)
            CTLineDraw(line, context)
        }
    }
}
```

Listing 24-17: Drawing text in the context

Images

Core Graphics defines its own data type to work with images called **CGImage**. The **CGImage** class provides a low-level representation of images that is used by other high-level frameworks like UIKit to process images. Most applications use **CGImage** objects to modify images stored in **UIImage** objects and this is why the **UIImage** class offers an initializer to create a **UIImage** object from a **CGImage** value and a property to get a **CGImage** value from a **UIImage** object.

UIImage(cgImage: CGImage, scale: CGFloat, orientation: Orientation)—This initializer creates a **UIImage** object with the image of a **CGImage** object. The **cgImage** attribute is the image we want to transform, the **scale** attribute determines the scale of the image, and the **orientation** attribute is an enumeration called **Orientation** included in the **UIImage** class that indicates the orientation of the image. The values available are **up**, **down**, **left**, **right**, **upMirrored**, **downMirrored**, **leftMirrored**, and **rightMirrored**.

cgImage—This property returns a **CGImage** object with the image in the **UIImage** object.

The **CGImage** class includes multiple properties and methods to process the image. The following are the most frequently used.

width—This property sets or returns the image's width. It is of type **Int**.

height— This property sets or returns the image's height. It is of type **Int**.

cropping(to: CGRect)—This method returns a **CGImage** object with an image extracted from the original image. The **to** attribute indicates the rectangle of the original image we want to use to create the new one.

To draw a `CGImage` object in the context, the `CGContext` class offers the following method.

draw(CGImage, **in:** CGRect, **byTiling:** Bool**)**—This method draws an image in the context. The first attribute is the image we want to draw, the **in** attribute determines the location and size of the area in which the image will be drawn (the image is scaled to fit this area), and the **byTiling** attribute is a Boolean value that determines if the image is going to be drawn multiple times to cover the context's area.

The `UIImage` class also offers methods to draw an image onto the context without having to turn it first into a `CGImage` object. The following are the most frequently used.

draw(at: CGPoint**)**—This method draws the image at the location specified by the **at** attribute.

draw(in: CGRect**)**—This method draws the image inside the rectangle determined by the **in** attribute.

The difference between `CGImage` and `UIImage` objects is that `UIImage` was designed to work along with other UIKit elements and therefore it considers aspects of the image like the scale and orientation, while `CGImage` just stores an array of pixels. Therefore, depending on what we need for our app, we may work with one or another. The following example creates a `UIImage` object as we always do, reads its `cgImage` property, and use its value to draw the image in the context.

```
import UIKit

class DrawingView: UIView {
    override func draw(_ rect: CGRect) {
        if let context = UIGraphicsGetCurrentContext() {
            if let image = UIImage(named: "husky") {
                let imageData = image.cgImage
                let width = image.size.width
                let height = image.size.height
                context.draw(imageData!, in: CGRect(x: 0, y: 50, width:
width, height: height))
            }
        }
    }
}
```

Listing 24-18: Drawing an image in the context

Drawing `CGImage` values into the context, as we did in Listing 24-18, presents the same problem we had when working with Core Text. The coordinate system used with `CGImage` values is not the same as the one used by UIKit, and therefore the image is inverted. Unlike Core Text, the `CGImage` data type does not provide its own matrix function so we have to transform the image ourselves. One solution is to translate and scale the entire context, as shown next.

```
import UIKit

class DrawingView: UIView {
    override func draw(_ rect: CGRect) {
        if let context = UIGraphicsGetCurrentContext() {
            if let image = UIImage(named: "husky") {
                let imageData = image.cgImage
                let width = image.size.width
                let height = image.size.height
```

Graphics

```
            let posX: CGFloat = 0
            let posY: CGFloat = 50

            context.translateBy(x: 0, y: height + (posY * 2))
            context.scaleBy(x: 1.0, y: -1.0)
            context.draw(imageData!, in: CGRect(x: posX, y: posY, width:
width, height: height))
         }
      }
   }
}
```

Listing 24-19: Inverting the image

The coordinates of UIKit establish the origin at the top-left corner of the context, however the origin in Core Graphics is at the bottom-left corner. The positive coordinates are also inverted. In UIKit, they are incremented from top to bottom, and in Core Graphics, they are incremented from bottom to top. This means that the image drawn by the **draw()** method is inverted. To get it to the right position, we not only have to mirror the context but also calculate new coordinates. The easiest way to do it is to move the origin to the point below the image that represents the origin in UIKit coordinates and only then mirror the context. For this, we need to know the position of the image before it is drawn in the context and that is why in Listing 24-19 we use the **posX** and **posY** constants to store the values.

The example of Listing 24-19 accomplishes what we need, the image is drawn at the right position and with the right orientation, but the final code is too long and error prone. The **UIImage** class offers its own **draw()** methods that highly simplify this task. The methods draw the image contained in the **UIImage** object directly into the current context using the UIKit coordinate system.

```
import UIKit

class DrawingView: UIView {
    override func draw(_ rect: CGRect) {
        if let image = UIImage(named: "husky") {
            let width = image.size.width
            let height = image.size.height
            image.draw(in: CGRect(x: 0, y: 50, width: width, height:
height))
        }
    }
}
```

Listing 24-20: Drawing a UIImage object directly into the context

The **draw()** method used in Listing 24-20 draws the image directly into the context, so unless we want to draw other graphics besides the image, a reference to the current context is not required.

 Do It Yourself: Download the husky.png image from our website and add it to the Assets Catalog. Update the **DrawingView** class in your project with the codes of Listings 24-18, 24-19, and 24-20 to test each example.

Drawing Cycle

Views are not drawn just once; the system actually calls the **draw()** method in each view every time it determines that the interface needs an update. We do not have control over this process but we can indicate to the system that the view's content has changed by calling a method provided by the **UIView** class called **setNeedsDisplay()**. There may be an infinite number of situations in which we need to update the view. For instance, our application may draw a clock and need to update the graphics every second, or the graphics may respond to the user and the view has to be updated every time an action is performed. The following example follows this last approach. We draw a circle in the context when the user taps on the view. For this, we need to add a gesture recognizer to the view and create the method to respond to that gesture. The following are the modifications we have to make in the **ViewController** class of our application to prepare the view.

```
import UIKit

class ViewController: UIViewController {
   @IBOutlet weak var surface: DrawingView!

   override func viewDidLoad() {
      super.viewDidLoad()
      let gesture = UITapGestureRecognizer(target: surface, action:
#selector(surface.addCircle(sender:)))
      surface.addGestureRecognizer(gesture)
   }
}
```

Listing 24-21: Responding to the tap gesture

In Listing 24-21, we have added an Outlet called **surface** to connect the view in the interface of Figure 24-1 to the **ViewController** class. When the main view is loaded, this reference is used to add a Tap Gesture to the view. The gesture recognizer defines the view as the target and the **addCircle()** method as the method that responds to the gesture. This method is called on the view and therefore it is defined in the **DrawingView** class, but the method does not perform any drawing. The only time we have access to a drawing context is when the **draw()** method is executed. The context is created by the view before this method is called and it is destroyed when the execution of the method is over. Therefore, the response to the user is indirect. When the **addCircle()** method is called, we have to calculate the position of the graphics and then ask the system to update the view by calling the **setNeedsDisplay()** method. The system considers our request and executes the **draw()** method as soon as it can to draw the graphics.

The following **DrawingView** class draws a circle at the position the user touched the screen. The location is processed by the **addCircle()** method and stored in a property called **position**, so when the **draw()** method is executed, we can read the current value of **position** and draw the circle in the context.

```
import UIKit

class DrawingView: UIView {
   var position: CGPoint!
   override func draw(_ rect: CGRect) {
      if let context = UIGraphicsGetCurrentContext() {
         if position != nil {
            let radius: CGFloat = 20
            let frame = CGRect(x: position.x - radius, y: position.y -
radius, width: radius * 2, height: radius * 2)
            context.fillEllipse(in: frame)
         }
      }
   }
```

Graphics

```
@objc func addCircle(sender: UITapGestureRecognizer) {
    let location = sender.location(in: self)
    position = CGPoint(x: location.x, y: location.y)
    self.setNeedsDisplay()
  }
}
```

Listing 24-22: Drawing circles at the location determined by the tap gesture

Every time the **draw()** method is called, the view has to perform all the drawings again, not only those that are being added. The system clears the context and expects the view to provide all the graphics again. In our example, we only store the coordinates of the last touch, so only one circle is drawn at a time.

 Do It Yourself: Update the **ViewController** class with the code of Listing 24-21. Update the **DrawingView** class with the code of Listing 24-22. Run the application and tap on the screen. Every time you tap, the system should erase the previous circle and draw a new one where your finger is.

 IMPORTANT: A view creates its own coordinate system, with the origin at its top-left corner (position 0, 0). When the view does not occupy the entire screen, the coordinates of the view and the screen do not match. For example, if the view is positioned at the screen's coordinates 20, 20, anything drawn at the top-left corner of the view will be 20 points from the side of the screen, but it will be positioned at the view's coordinates 0, 0 (not 20, 20). If we need to transform the coordinates from one view to another, we can use the methods **convert(CGPoint, to: UIView?)** and **convert(CGPoint, from: UIView?)**. These methods are provided by the **UIView** class and can transform the coordinates of one view to the coordinates of another.

Image Context

The context used by a **UIView** object is intended to display the graphics within a view, but we can also create an image context to draw the graphics into an image and then store the image, process it, or show it to the user when necessary. The UIKit framework includes the **UIGraphicsImageRenderer** class to create and manage a renderer that works with image contexts. The class includes initializers to create the renderer and methods to render the image. The following are the most frequently used.

UIGraphicsImageRenderer(size: CGSize)—This initializer creates a renderer to manage an image of the size determined by the **size** attribute.

UIGraphicsImageRenderer(size: CGSize, **format:** UIGraphicsImageRendererFormat)—This initializer creates a renderer to manage an image with a size and a format determined by its attributes. The **size** attribute determines the image's size, and the **format** attribute defines the characteristics of the renderer. To specify the values, the class includes the properties **opaque (Bool)**, **prefersExtendedRange (Bool)**, and **scale (CGFloat)**.

image(actions: Block)—This method generates the image context and sends it to the closure assigned to the **actions** attribute. The value received by the closure is an object of type **UIGraphicsRendererContext** with the renderer's image context that we can use to create the image.

An image context is represented by an object of the **UIGraphicsImageRendererContext** class (a subclass of **UIGraphicsRendererContext**). This object offers the following properties.

cgContext—This property returns a **CGContext** object representing the drawing context.

currentImage—This property returns a **UIImage** object with the image in the context.

Because the purpose of an image context is to create an image, if we want to show the result on the screen, instead of a **UIView** object we should use a **UIImageView** object. The following example assumes that we have added a **UIImageView** to the initial view and connected it to an Outlet in the **ViewController** class called **imageDraw**. The code creates an image context of the size of the Image View and then draws a circle on it.

```
import UIKit

class ViewController: UIViewController {
    @IBOutlet weak var imageDraw: UIImageView!

    override func viewDidLoad() {
        super.viewDidLoad()
        view.setNeedsLayout()
        view.layoutIfNeeded()
        let width = imageDraw.bounds.size.width
        let height = imageDraw.bounds.size.height
        let imageSize = CGSize(width: width, height: height)

        let render = UIGraphicsImageRenderer(size: imageSize)
        render.image(actions: { (renderContext) in
            let context = renderContext.cgContext
            let frame = CGRect(x: 10, y: 10, width: width - 20, height:
height - 20)
            context.strokeEllipse(in: frame)
            imageDraw.image = renderContext.currentImage
        })
    }
}
```

Listing 24-23: Creating a new image

The first thing we do in the code of Listing 24-23 is to get the current width and height of the Image View to define the size of the renderer. After the renderer is created, we call its **image()** method to get the image context. Inside the closure, we get the drawing context from the **cgContext** property to be able to draw a circle. After the drawing is over, we get the image in the context from the **currentImage** property and assign it to the Image View to show it on the screen.

Do It Yourself: Create a new Single View Application project. Add an Image View to the initial view and pin it to the sides of the main view. Connect the Image View to the **ViewController** class with an Outlet called **imageDraw**. Complete the class with the code of Listing 24-23 and run the application. You should see an ellipse covering the entire area occupied by the Image View.

The Basics: The **UIGraphicsImageRenderer** initializer implemented in Listing 24-23 creates a renderer to process an image of the size determined by its attribute and with the scale of the device. If we want to work with a different scale, we have to create an object of the **UIGraphicsImage-RendererFormat** class, assign the scale we want to work with to the object's **scale** property, and assign this object to the initializer's **format** attribute.

Graphics

24.2 Core Animation

Core Animation is the framework in charge of rendering and animating the visual elements of an application. The drawing of the user interface and also basic transitions, like those generated by a Segue, are produced by code from this framework. Several high-level frameworks use the capacity of Core Animation to render the content they produce, but we can also implement this framework to modify the elements ourselves and create custom animations.

Layers

Core Animation uses a system of layers to manage the graphics. When a view draws its content, the graphics are stored in a layer that can be processed by the graphics hardware and presented on the screen. These layers store a bitmap (a series of values that represent every pixel of the image) and also the information associated with it, like the position of the image, its size, etc. This process is very efficient and allows the system to produce smooth transitions and animations by just modifying the values associated with the layers involved.

Layers are created from a class provided by Core Animation called **CALayer**. The class includes the following properties to modify the layer's configuration.

position—This property sets or returns a **CGPoint** value with the layer's coordinates.

frame—This property sets or returns a **CGRect** that determines the layer's origin and size.

bounds—This property sets or returns a **CGRect** value that determines the layer's origin and size in its own coordinate space.

anchorPoint—This property sets or returns a **CGPoint** value that determines the layer's anchor point. The coordinates are values between 0.0 and 1.0, with 0, 0 being the top-left corner of the layer. Any transformation applied to the layer occurs around the anchor point. The values by default are 0.5, 0.5, which positions the anchor point at the center of the layer.

cornerRadius—This property sets or returns a **CGFloat** value that determines the radius used to draw the corners of the layer.

opacity—This property sets or returns a **Float** value that determines the layer's opacity. The possible values are from 0.0 (transparent) to 1.0 (opaque).

isHidden—This property sets or returns a Boolean value that determines whether the layer is visible or not.

borderWidth—This property sets or returns a **CGFloat** value that determines the width of the layer's border. By default, this value is set to 0.0 (no border).

borderColor—This property sets or returns a **CGColor** value that determines the color of the layer's border.

backgroundColor—This property sets or returns a **CGColor** value that determines the layer's background color.

shadowColor—This property sets or returns a **CGColor** value that determines the color of the layer's shadow.

shadowOffset—This property sets or returns a **CGSize** value that determines the shadow's offset.

shadowRadius—This property sets or returns a **CGFloat** value that determines the blur radius of the shadow.

shadowOpacity—This property sets or returns a **Float** value that determines the shadow's opacity. The possible values are between 0.0 (transparent) and 1.0 (opaque).

In iOS, a layer is automatically assigned to each view. The **UIView** class includes the **layer** property to get a reference to the layer that belongs to the view. From this reference, we can modify any property of the layer, as shown in the following example.

```
import UIKit

class ViewController: UIViewController {
    @IBOutlet weak var animationView: UIView!

    override func viewDidLoad() {
        super.viewDidLoad()
        let layer = animationView.layer
        layer.borderColor = UIColor.black.cgColor
        layer.borderWidth = 5
        layer.cornerRadius = 10
    }
}
```

Listing 24-24: Modifying the layer

This example assumes that we have added a view to the initial view of a Single View Application project and the view is connected to the **ViewController** class with an Outlet called **animationView**. In the **viewDidLoad()** method, we assign new values to the layer's properties to generate a black border of 5 points wide and round corners. The result is shown in Figure 24-16 (for this example, we have created a small view pinned to the center of the screen containing a label with the text "The Layer").

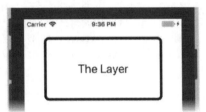

Figure 24-16: Custom layer

 Do It Yourself: Create a new Single View Application project. Add a small view and pin it with constraints to the center and top of the main view. Add a label to the view with the text "The Layer". Connect the view to the **ViewController** class with an Outlet called **animationView**. Complete the **ViewController** class with the code of Listing 24-24. Run the application. You should see something similar to Figure 24-16.

Layers can also contain sublayers. These are instances of the **CALayer** class added to the layer with a method provided by the class called **addSublayer()**. The following example adds a small layer with a round shape at the top-left corner of the layer.

```
import UIKit

class ViewController: UIViewController {
    @IBOutlet weak var animationView: UIView!

    override func viewDidLoad() {
        super.viewDidLoad()
        let layer = animationView.layer
        layer.borderColor = UIColor.black.cgColor
        layer.borderWidth = 5
        layer.cornerRadius = 10
```

Graphics

```
        let sublayer = CALayer()
        sublayer.frame = CGRect(x: 10, y: 10, width: 30, height: 30)
        sublayer.backgroundColor = UIColor.black.cgColor
        sublayer.cornerRadius = 15
        layer.addSublayer(sublayer)
    }
}
```

Listing 24-25: Adding a sublayer

Figure 24-17: Sublayer

3D Transformations

Another attribute managed by a **CALayer** object is the layer's transformation matrix. As we explained before, a transformation matrix specifies what points in one coordinate system correspond to the points in another coordinate system, but unlike the **CGAffineTransform** transformation matrix we used before in this chapter, layers work with the **CATransform3D** matrix, allowing us to transform the graphics in a tridimensional space.

The **CALayer** class includes a property called **transform** to specify the **CATransform3D** matrix for the layer. The framework offers multiple global functions to define a **CATransform3D** matrix. The following are the most frequently used.

CATransform3DTranslate(CATransform3D, CGFloat, CGFloat, CGFloat**)**—This function returns a transformation matrix of type **CATransform3D** that translates the layer in a tridimensional space. The first attribute is the matrix from which the new matrix is calculated, and the rest of the attributes determine the coordinates of the translation (**x**, **y**, and **z**).

CATransform3DScale(CATransform3D, CGFloat, CGFloat, CGFloat**)**—This function returns a transformation matrix of type **CATransform3D** that scales the layer in a tridimensional space. The first attribute is the matrix from which the new matrix is calculated, and the rest of the attributes determine the new scale of each axis (**x**, **y**, and **z**).

CATransform3DRotate(CATransform3D, CGFloat, CGFloat, CGFloat, CGFloat**)**—This function returns a transformation matrix of type **CATransform3D** that rotates the layer in a tridimensional space. The first attribute is the matrix from which the new matrix is calculated, the second attribute is the rotation angle in radians, and the rest of the attributes determine the axis in which the rotation is going to take place (**x**, **y**, and **z**). The value 0.0 cancels the rotation for that axis and values greater than 0 activate the rotation (the values frequently used are 0.0 and 1.0).

These functions calculate the new matrix from another matrix. When we are applying changes to a layer for the first time, we can use the identity transform matrix. This is a neutral value that represents the matrix of a layer in its initial state. The **CALayer** class includes the **CATransform3DIdentity** constant to return the identity transform matrix defined by Core Animation.

```
import UIKit

class ViewController: UIViewController {
    @IBOutlet weak var animationView: UIView!

    override func viewDidLoad() {
        super.viewDidLoad()
        let layer = animationView.layer
        layer.borderColor = UIColor.black.cgColor
        layer.borderWidth = 5
        layer.cornerRadius = 10
        let degrees = CGFloat(10 * Float.pi / 180)
        var matrix = CATransform3DIdentity
        matrix = CATransform3DRotate(matrix, degrees, 0, 0, 1)
        layer.transform = matrix
    }
}
```

Listing 24-26: *Transforming a layer*

3D transformations operate on the three axes. If we do something like rotating the layer, we have to specify around which axis the rotation will be performed. In the example of Listing 24-26, we decided to rotate the layer clockwise 10 degrees on its **z** axis (the axis that determines depth and is defined by the line between the user and the screen). The result is shown in figure 24-18.

Figure 24-18: *Layer transformed with a rotation matrix*

The layer may be rotated around any of the three axes, **x**, **y**, and **z**. When the layer is rotated around the **z** axis, as we did in the example of Listing 24-26, it just turns clockwise around the axis the amount of degrees we specified, but when the rotation is around the **x** or **y** axes, the transformation makes one side of the layer move to the back and the other side to the front. The problem is that in real life, the side that moves to the back looks smaller than the side that moves to the front. This effect is called *perspective*, but it is not included in the matrix produced by the methods provided by Core Animation. To add perspective to the transformation, we have to define the values of the matrix ourselves.

A tridimensional matrix is composed of values placed in a grid of 4 columns and 4 rows. These values are represented by indexes according to their position in the matrix. The value at the top-left corner of the grid is identified with the index 1-1, the value on its right is identified with the index 1-2, and so on. To provide access to these values, the **CATransform3D** structure defines a series of properties, the names of which start with the letter **m** and end with the index numbers (e.g., **m11**, **m12**, etc.). To provide perspective to the rotation, we have to modify the value at the position 3-4, which is represented by the **m34** property.

```
import UIKit

class ViewController: UIViewController {
    @IBOutlet weak var animationView: UIView!

    override func viewDidLoad() {
        super.viewDidLoad()
```

Graphics

```
        let layer = animationView.layer
        layer.borderColor = UIColor.black.cgColor
        layer.borderWidth = 5
        layer.cornerRadius = 10
        let degrees = CGFloat(45 * Float.pi / 180)

        var matrix = CATransform3DIdentity
        matrix.m34 = 1 / -500.0
        matrix = CATransform3DRotate(matrix, degrees, 0, 1, 0)
        layer.transform = matrix
    }
}
```

Listing 24-27: Adding perspective to the layer

The value assigned to the **m34** property affects the skew factor of the transformation, altering the perspective. The further this value gets to 0 the deepest is the illusion of perspective. The formula to obtain the value divides 1 by the negative of the distance in the **z** axis. The distance could be determined by the size of the layer, but it always depends on the effect we want to achieve. In Listing 24-27 we use the value -500.0 that is usually considered as the value by default in most transformations. The result is shown next.

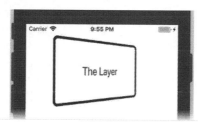

Figure 24-19: Layer with perspective

View Animations

The most important feature of Core Animation is, of course, the capacity to animate layers. The framework provides a specific class to perform animations called **CABasicAnimation**, but because of the close relationship between layers and the views they belong to, Apple developers decided to simplify our work including a class in the UIKit framework called **UIViewPropertyAnimator** to create and configure animations. The class takes care of creating everything, we just have to set a few configuration parameters and indicate the values we want to change during the animation. The following are its most frequently used initializers.

UIViewPropertyAnimator(duration: TimeInterval, **curve:** AnimationCurve, **animations:** Block)—This initializer creates a **UIViewPropertyAnimator** object to produce an animation with a predefined timing curve. The **duration** attribute is the time in seconds the animation is going to last, the **curve** attribute is an enumeration called **AnimationCurve** included in the **UIView** class that determines the variations in time during the animation. The values available are **easeInOut**, **easeIn**, **easeOut**, and **linear**. And the **animations** attribute is a closure where we specify the properties and values that are going to change during the animation.

UIViewPropertyAnimator(duration: TimeInterval, **timingParameters:** UITimingCurveProvider)—This initializer creates a **UIViewPropertyAnimator** object to produce an animation with a custom timing curve. The **duration** attribute is the time in seconds the animation is going to last, and the **timingParameters** attribute is an object that conforms to the **UITimingCurveProvider** protocol to define the variations in time during the animation.

The **UIViewPropertyAnimator** class offers the following properties and methods to configure the animations.

duration—This property sets or returns a **TimeInterval** value that determines the duration of the animation.

timingParameters—This property sets or returns the timing curve used to perform the animation. It is an object that conforms to the **UITimingCurveProvider** protocol.

isInterruptible—This property sets or returns a Boolean value that determines if the animation can be paused or stopped.

isUserInteractionEnabled—This property sets or returns a Boolean value that determines if the views being animated can receive touch events.

pausesOnCompletion—This property sets or returns a Boolean value that determines whether the animation is going to remain in the active state when it is over.

delay—This type property sets or returns a **TimeInterval** value that determines the time in seconds the animator will wait to start the animation.

addAnimations(Block**)**—This method adds a new animation block to the animator. The attribute is a closure with the properties and values we want to change during the animation. The animations added with this method are performed alongside the rest of the animations assigned to the animator.

addAnimations(Block, **delayFactor:** CGFloat**)**—This method adds a new animation block to the animator. The first attribute is a closure with the properties and values we want to change during the animation, and the **delayFactor** attribute determines the time in seconds the animator will wait to start the animation. The animations added with this method are performed alongside the rest of the animations assigned to the animator.

addCompletion(Block**)**—This method assigns a completion handler to the animator. The attribute is the closure we want to execute after the animations are over. The closure receives a value of type **UIViewAnimatingPosition** that determines where the animation ended. This is an enumeration with the values **end**, **start**, and **current**.

continueAnimation(withTimingParameters: UITimingCurveProvider?, **durationFactor:** CGFloat**)**—This method changes the timing parameters for a paused animation. The **withTimingParameters** attribute defines the new timing curve, and the **durationFactor** defines the new delay.

A **UIViewPropertyAnimator** conforms to the **UIViewAnimating** protocol. This protocol defines a series of properties and methods we can use to control animations.

fractionComplete—This property sets or returns the animation's completion percentage.

isReversed—This property sets or returns a Boolean value that determines if the animation is running in reverse.

state—This property returns a value that determines the current state of the animation. It is an enumeration of type **UIViewAnimatingState** with the values **inactive**, **active**, and **stopped**.

isRunning—This property returns a Boolean value that determines whether the animation is running or not.

startAnimation()—This method starts the animation.

pauseAnimation()—This method pauses the animation.

stopAnimation(Bool**)**—This method stops the animation. The attribute indicates whether the animator will be deactivated, or it will stay active for further actions.

Animations begin from the current state and move to the state specified by the statements inside the **animations** closure. The following example initializes a **UIViewPropertyAnimator** object to animate a change in the transformation matrix of the view used in our previous examples. The animation starts from the current matrix and ends with the matrix defined by the **CATransform3DTranslate()** function, displacing the view vertically from the top to the center of the screen.

```
import UIKit

class ViewController: UIViewController {
    @IBOutlet weak var animationView: UIView!

    override func viewDidLoad() {
        super.viewDidLoad()
        let layer = animationView.layer
        layer.borderColor = UIColor.black.cgColor
        layer.borderWidth = 5
        layer.cornerRadius = 10
        let gesture = UITapGestureRecognizer(target: self, action:
#selector(animateView(sender:)))
        view.addGestureRecognizer(gesture)
    }
    @objc func animateView(sender: UITapGestureRecognizer) {
        let layer = animationView.layer
        var matrix = CATransform3DIdentity
        matrix = CATransform3DTranslate(matrix, 0.0, 200.0, 0.0)
        let animator = UIViewPropertyAnimator(duration: 2.0, curve:
.linear, animations: {
            layer.transform = matrix
        })
        animator.startAnimation()
    }
}
```

Listing 24-28: Animating a view with `UIViewPropertyAnimator`

The code of Listing 24-28 modifies the view's layer to include a border with round corners as we did before, but at the end it adds a gesture recognizer to execute a method when the user taps on the view. The method, called **animateView()**, generates a new matrix to translate the view's layer to a new position, but instead of assigning the matrix right away we do it inside the **animations** block of a **UIViewPropertyAnimator** object, so the values change gradually from the original position to the last position determined by the matrix, animating the view.

 Do It Yourself: In this example, we are using the same view introduced before, so all you have to do is to update the **ViewController** class of your project with the code of Listing 24-28. Run the application and tap on the view. The view should be displaced to the center of the screen in a smooth transition.

The initializer we have implemented in Listing 24-28 uses a standard timing curve called **linear**. Timing curves are virtual paths, usually defined by Bézier curves, that determine how the animation will progress over time. For example, the standard timing curve **easeInOut** causes the animation to begin slowly, then to accelerate in the middle, and finally to slow down again towards the end. This and the rest of the values in the **UIViewAnimationCurve** enumeration (**easeInOut, easeIn, easeOut,** and **linear**) represent the most common timing curves, but we can define our own custom timing curves with the classes **UICubicTimingParameters** and **UISpringTimingParameters**. These classes allow us to include custom parameters to define the timing curve followed by the animation exactly the way we need. For example, with the `UICubicTimingParameters` class, we can specify the two points required for the creation of a Cubic Bézier curve. The following is the class' initializer.

UICubicTimingParameters(controlPoint1: CGPoint, **controlPoint2:** CGPoint)— This initializer creates a timing curve from the points specified by the attributes.

On the other hand, the `UISpringTimingParameters` class allows us to create more complex timing curves that produce an effect that imitates a spring. The class includes the following initializers.

UISpringTimingParameters(dampingRatio: CGFloat)—This initializer creates a timing curve that produces a bouncing effect. The **dampingRatio** attribute determines the amount of oscillation (values close to 0 increase oscillation).

UISpringTimingParameters(dampingRatio: CGFloat, **initialVelocity:** CGVector)—This initializer creates a timing curve that produces a bouncing effect. The **dampingRatio** attribute determines the amount of oscillation (values close to 0 increase oscillation), and the **initialVelocity** attribute is a vector that specifies the animation's initial velocity.

UISpringTimingParameters(mass: CGFloat, **stiffness:** CGFloat, **damping:** CGFloat, **initialVelocity:** CGVector)—This initializer creates a timing curve that produces a bouncing effect. The **mass** attribute determines the virtual mass we want to assign to the view, the **stiffness** determines the stiffness of the virtual spring, the **damping** attribute determines the amount of oscillation (values close to 0 increase oscillation), and the **initialVelocity** attribute is a vector that specifies the animation's initial velocity.

To assign a custom timing curve to an animator, we have to create the `UIViewPropertyAnimator` object with the initializer that includes the `timingParameters` attribute. When we use this initializer, we have to add the animation block with the `addAnimations()` method, as in the following example.

```
@objc func animateView(sender: UITapGestureRecognizer) {
    let layer = animationView.layer
    var matrix = CATransform3DIdentity
    matrix = CATransform3DTranslate(matrix, 0.0, 200.0, 0.0)

    let timing = UISpringTimingParameters(dampingRatio: 0.3,
initialVelocity: CGVector(dx: 10.0, dy: 0.0))
    let animator = UIViewPropertyAnimator(duration: 2.0, timingParameters:
timing)
    animator.addAnimations({
        layer.transform = matrix
    })
    animator.startAnimation()
}
```

Listing 24-29: *Setting a custom timing curve*

The code of Listing 24-29 updates the `animateView()` method of our previous example. In this example, we have created a `UISpringTimingParameters` timing curve with a damping ratio and an initial velocity that will make our view bounce several times before it reaches its final position. Notice that we have declared only the **dx** value of the velocity vector because the **dy** value is usually not considered by the animator.

25.1 Video

Almost every mobile device is capable of playing videos these days, and Apple devices are no exception. Due to the importance of video, Apple provides a framework designed specifically to work with video and audio called *AV Foundation*. The framework defines several classes to create the structure necessary to play media. There is a class in charge of the asset (video or audio), a class in charge of providing the media to the player, a class in charge of playing the media, and a class in charge of displaying the media on the screen. Figure 25-1 illustrates this structure.

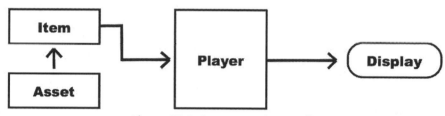

Figure 25-1: System to play media

Assets

The information of the media we want to play is called *asset*. An asset is composed of one or more tracks of media, including video, audio, subtitles, etc. The AV Foundation framework defines a class called **AVAsset** to load an asset and a subclass called **AVURLAsset** to create an asset object from the contents of a URL. This last subclass includes the following initializer.

AVURLAsset(url: URL)—This initializer creates an **AVURLAsset** object with the media in the location indicated by the **url** attribute. The attribute is a **URL** structure with the location of a local or remote resource.

Player Item

An asset contains static information and cannot manage its state when it is being played. To control the asset, the framework defines the **AVPlayerItem** class. With this class, we can reference an asset and manage its timeline. The class includes multiple initializers. The following is the most frequently used.

AVPlayerItem(asset: AVAsset)—This initializer creates an **AVPlayerItem** object to represent the asset defined by the **asset** attribute.

The **AVPlayerItem** class also includes properties and methods to control the state of the asset. The following are the most frequently used.

status—This property returns a value that indicates the status of the player item. It is an enumeration called **Status** included in the **AVPlayerItem** class. The values available are **unknown**, **readyToPlay**, and **failed**.

duration—This property returns a value that indicates the duration of the player item. It is a structure of type **CMTime**.

currentTime()—This method returns a **CMTime** value with the current time of the player.

seek(to: CMTime, **completionHandler:** Block)—This method moves the playback cursor to the time specified by the **to** attribute. The **completionHandler** attribute is a closure to be executed after the process is over. The closure receives a Boolean value that determines whether the seek operation is finished or not.

Player

The **AVPlayerItem** object manages the information necessary for playback but it does not play the media; this is done by an instance of the **AVPlayer** class. The class provides the following initializer to create the player.

AVPlayer(playerItem: AVPlayerItem?)—This initializer creates an **AVPlayer** object to play the media represented by the **playerItem** attribute.

The **AVPlayer** class also includes properties and methods to control the playback.

volume—This property sets or returns a value that determines the player's volume. It is a value of type **Float** between 0.0 and 1.0.

isMuted—This property is a Boolean value that determines whether the player's audio is muted or not.

rate—This property sets or returns a **Float** value that determines the rate at which the media is being played. A value of 0.0 pauses the video and 1.0 sets the normal rate.

play()—This method begins playback.

pause()—This method pauses playback.

addPeriodicTimeObserver(forInterval: CMTime, **queue:** DispatchQueue?, **using:** Block)—This method adds an observer that executes a closure repeatedly every certain period of time. The **forInterval** attribute determines the time between executions, the **queue** attribute is the queue in which the closure should be executed (the main queue is recommended), and the **using** attribute is the closure we want to execute. The closure receives a value of type **CMTime** with the time at which the closure was called.

Player Layer

The last object required by the structure is the one in charge of displaying the media on the screen. This is a subclass of the **CALayer** class called **AVPlayerLayer** that provides the code necessary to draw the media's frames. The class includes the following initializer and property to create and configure the layer.

AVPlayerLayer(player: AVPlayer?)—This initializer creates an **AVPlayerLayer** object associated with the player specified by the **player** attribute.

videoGravity—This property defines how the video adjusts its size to the preview layer's size. The framework defines the following constants to assign to this property: **AVLayerVideoGravityResizeAspect**, **AVLayerVideoGravityResizeAspectFill**, and **AVLayerVideoGravityResize**.

Time

Because the precision of floating-point values is not appropriate for media playback, the framework adopts, among other things, the **CMTime** structure defined in an old framework called Core Media. The structure contains multiple values to represent time as a fraction. The most important are **value** and **timescale**, which represent the numerator and denominator, respectively. To determine the time, we have to specify at least these two values. For example, if we want to create a **CMTime** structure to represent 0.5 seconds, we may declare 1 as the numerator and 2 as the denominator (1 divided by 2 is equal to 0.5). The class includes initializers and type properties to create these values. The following are the most frequently used.

CMTime(value: CMTimeValue, **timescale:** CMTimeScale)—This initializer creates a **CMTime** structure with the values specified by the **value** and **timescale** attributes. The attributes are integers of type **Int64** and **Int32**, respectively.

CMTime(seconds: Double, **preferredTimescale:** CMTimeScale)—This initializer creates a **CMTime** structure from a floating-point value representing the seconds and a timescale. The **seconds** attribute determines the seconds we want to assign to the structure, and the **preferredTimescale** attribute determines the scale we want to use. A value of 1 preserves the value in seconds assigned to the first attribute.

zero—This type property returns a **CMTime** structure with a value of 0.

The **CMTime** structure also includes multiple properties to set and retrieve the values. The following are the most frequently used.

seconds—This property returns the time of a **CMTime** structure in seconds. It is of type **Double**.

value—This property returns the value of a **CMTime** structure.

timescale—This property returns the time scale of a **CMTime** structure.

Video Player

The process to create a player is straightforward. We have to load the asset (**AVURLAsset**), create the item to manage the asset (**AVPlayerItem**), add the item to the player (**AVPlayer**), and associate the player to a layer to display the media on the screen (**AVPlayerLayer**). But playing the media requires an additional step. The media does not become immediately available after it is loaded and therefore we cannot play it right away, we have to wait until its state is ready. The state is reported by the **status** property of the **AVPlayerItem** object, so we have to use KVO to add an observer for this property to start playing the media only after the property returns the value **readyToPlay**.

The following code demonstrates how to build a video player. The example assumes that we have added a file called trailer.mp4 to the project and have an interface with a single view.

```
import UIKit
import AVFoundation

class ViewController: UIViewController {
    @IBOutlet weak var videoView: UIView!
    var playerItem: AVPlayerItem!
    var player: AVPlayer!
    var playerLayer: AVPlayerLayer!

    override func viewDidLoad() {
        super.viewDidLoad()
        let bundle = Bundle.main
        let videoURL = bundle.url(forResource: "trailer", withExtension:
"mp4")
```

```
        let asset = AVURLAsset(url: videoURL!)
        playerItem = AVPlayerItem(asset: asset)
        playerItem.addObserver(self, forKeyPath: "status", options: [],
context: nil)

        player = AVPlayer(playerItem: playerItem)
        playerLayer = AVPlayerLayer(player: player)

        playerLayer.frame = view.bounds
        let layer = videoView.layer
        layer.addSublayer(playerLayer)
    }
    override func observeValue(forKeyPath keyPath: String?, of object:
Any?, change: [NSKeyValueChangeKey : Any]?, context:
UnsafeMutableRawPointer?) {
        if keyPath == "status" {
            if playerItem.status == .readyToPlay {
                playerItem.removeObserver(self, forKeyPath: "status")
                player.play()
            }
        }
    }
    override func viewWillTransition(to size: CGSize, with coordinator:
UIViewControllerTransitionCoordinator) {
        super.viewWillTransition(to: size, with: coordinator)
        playerLayer.frame.size = size
    }
}
```

Listing 25-1: *Building a video player*

In Listing 25-1, we load the video from the bundle and create the player structure as soon as the view is loaded. The player is associated with an **AVPlayerLayer** layer and the layer is added as a sublayer of the view where we want to show the video, but the video does not start until the value of the **status** property is **readyToPlay** (see Key/Value Observing in Chapter 19).

The size of the layer for the player is defined according to the size of the view (**playerLayer.frame = view.bounds**). Because this value is not determined by constraints, we have to update it ourselves when the device is rotated. This is why at the end of the view controller we added the **viewWillTransition()** method. Before rotating the interface, the system calls this method to report the new size that the view is going to adopt. By changing the layer's size to this value, we effectively adapt the video to any orientation.

 Do It Yourself: Create a new Single View Application project. Add an empty view to the initial view and pin it to the sides with Space constraints. Connect the view to the **ViewController** class with an Outlet called **videoView**. Complete the class with the code of Listing 25-1. Download the file trailer.mp4 from our website and add it to your project (remember to mark the option Add to Target). Run the application. The video should start playing as soon as the application is launched.

The previous example plays the video, but it does not provide any tools for the user to control the process. The **AVPlayer** class includes methods to play, pause, and check the state of the media, but we are responsible for creating the interface. Figure 25-2, next, introduces an interface with the view to show the video and an additional view on top of it with two controls, a button and a Progress View, to let the user play and pause the video and see its progression.

Figure 25-2: *Controllers for a custom video player*

How we control the process and respond to the interface depends on the requirements of our application. For this example, we have decided to define two properties to keep track of the state of the media, **ready** and **playing**. The **ready** property will be **true** when the media is ready to be played and the **playing** property will be **true** while the media is being played.

```
import UIKit
import AVFoundation

class ViewController: UIViewController {
   @IBOutlet weak var videoView: UIView!
   @IBOutlet weak var playButton: UIButton!
   @IBOutlet weak var progressBar: UIProgressView!
   var playerItem: AVPlayerItem!
   var player: AVPlayer!
   var playerLayer: AVPlayerLayer!
   var ready = false
   var playing = false

   override func viewDidLoad() {
      super.viewDidLoad()
      playButton.isEnabled = false
      let bundle = Bundle.main
      let videoURL = bundle.url(forResource: "trailer", withExtension:
"mp4")
      let asset = AVAsset(url: videoURL!)
      playerItem = AVPlayerItem(asset: asset)
      playerItem.addObserver(self, forKeyPath: "status", options: [],
context: nil)
      player = AVPlayer(playerItem: playerItem)
      playerLayer = AVPlayerLayer(player: player)
      playerLayer.frame = view.bounds
      let layer = videoView.layer
      layer.addSublayer(playerLayer)
   }
}
```

Listing 25-2: *Preparing the video player*

In Listing 25-2, we add a few more Outlets to the **ViewController** class to reference the elements of the interface and disable the Play button until the video is ready to play, but the code to prepare the player remains the same. The difference is in how the video is played, because this time we have to wait until the user presses the Play button. This change is reflected in the **observeValue()** method. Instead of playing the video when the value of the **status** property changes to **readyToPlay**, we assign the value **true** to the **ready** property to let the rest of the code know that the video is ready. But this is not all the method has to do. We also have to register an observer to keep the progress bar updated while the video is being played. Normal observers are not fast enough, so the AV Foundation framework offers the `addPeriodicTimeObserver()` method to create an observer that will provide a more accurate response. The method requires a `CMTime` value to determine the frequency in which the code will be executed, a reference to the main queue (see Chapter 18), and a closure with the code we want to execute every time the observer is triggered.

```
override func observeValue(forKeyPath keyPath: String?, of object: Any?,
change: [NSKeyValueChangeKey : Any]?, context:UnsafeMutableRawPointer?) {
    if keyPath == "status" {
        if playerItem.status == .readyToPlay {
            ready = true
            playButton.isEnabled = true
            playerItem.removeObserver(self, forKeyPath: "status")

            let mainQueue = DispatchQueue.main
            let interval = CMTime(value: 1, timescale: 2)
            player.addPeriodicTimeObserver(forInterval: interval, queue:
mainQueue, using: { (time) in
                let duration = self.playerItem.duration
                let position = time.seconds / duration.seconds
                self.progressBar.progress = Float(position)
            })
        }
    }
}
```

Listing 25-3: Updating the progress bar

In Listing 25-3, we create a `CMTime` value to represent a time of 0.5 seconds, and then use it in the call of the `addPeriodicTimeObserver()` method to register the observer. After this, the closure provided to the observer will be executed every 0.5 seconds during playback. In this closure, we get the current time and the duration of the video in seconds and calculate the right position of the progress bar by turning seconds into a value between 0.0 and 1.0 (the minimum and maximum values of a Progress View by default).

The player and the progress bar are ready, so the only thing left is to add the Action for the Play button. This is a simple method that executes the player's `play()` or `pause()` methods depending on the value of the `playing` property.

```
@IBAction func playVideo(_ sender: UIButton) {
    if ready {
        if playing {
            player.pause()
            playing = false
            playButton.setTitle("Play", for: .normal)
        } else {
            player.play()
            playing = true
            playButton.setTitle("Pause", for: .normal)
        }
    }
}
```

Listing 25-4: Playing and pausing the video

Media

Figure 25-3: Custom video player
© Copyright 2008, Blender Foundation / www.bigbuckbunny.org

Do It Yourself: Add a view with a height of 45 points and pin it to the bottom and the sides of the main view to represent the control bar for the video player (you can momentarily uninstall the video view to facilitate this process). Change the color of the bar to gray. Click on the color, select the Custom option to open the Color Picker, and give it an opacity of 50%. Position the small view on top of the video view using the Document Outline panel, and include a button called Play and a Progress View inside (Figure 25-2). Select the Progress View and assign the value 0 to it from the Attributes Inspector panel. Connect the button, and the Progress View with Outlets called **playButton** and **progressBar**. Connect the Play button with an Action called **playVideo()**. Update the **ViewController** class with the codes of Listings 25-2, 25-3, and 25-4. Remember to add the **viewWillTransition()** method of Listing 25-1 to adapt the layer to any orientation. Run the application and press Play.

IMPORTANT: You cannot only play videos from files added to the project (local) but also from the web (remote). All you need to do is to create a **URL** structure with the web URL pointing to the file you want to play and use it as the source for the asset. There is a restriction though. You can only play remote files that are stored in secure servers (only URLs starting with https://). In Chapter 27, we will learn how to create **URL** structures to access remote documents and how to configure the application to be able to work with unsecure URLs.

The observer added by the **addPeriodicTimeObserver()** method is not the only observer we can have for our player. The **AVPlayerItem** class defines several notifications to report events that happened during playback. For example, we can add an observer to the **AVPlayerItemDidPlayToEndTime** notification to know when the video finishes playing.

```
let center = NotificationCenter.default
center.addObserver(self, selector: #selector(videoEnded(notification:)),
name: NSNotification.Name.AVPlayerItemDidPlayToEndTime, object:
playerItem)
```

Listing 25-5: Adding an observer to detect the end of the video

The method that responds to the notification has to move the playback cursor back to the beginning and prepare the interface to let the user play the video again.

```
@objc func videoEnded(notification: NSNotification) {
    playerItem.seek(to: CMTime.zero, completionHandler: {(finished) in
        if finished {
            let main = OperationQueue.main
            main.addOperation {
                self.playing = false
```

```
              self.playButton.setTitle("Play", for: .normal)
            }
         }
      })
}
```

Listing 25-6: Restarting the video

 Do It Yourself: Add the code of Listing 25-5 to the **viewDidLoad()** method and the **videoEnded()** method of Listing 25-6 to the **ViewController** class. Run the application, play the video, and wait until it is over. Press the Play button to play it again.

If we want to play multiple videos in sequence, we could use this notification to assign a new asset to the **AVPlayer** object, but the framework offers a subclass of the **AVPlayer** class called **AVQueuePlayer** designed specifically for this purpose. The class creates a playlist from an array of **AVPlayerItem** objects. The following are the class' initializer and some of its methods.

AVQueuePlayer(items: [AVPlayerItem]**)**—This initializer creates a play list with the items specified by the **items** attribute.

advanceToNextItem()—This method advances the playback to the next item on the list.

insert(AVPlayerItem, **after:** AVPlayerItem?**)**—This method inserts a new item on the list.

remove(AVPlayerItem**)**—This method removes an item from the list.

An **AVQueuePlayer** object replaces the **AVPlayer** object used to represent the media. All we have to do to play a sequence of videos is to create the **AVPlayerItem** objects to load each video and create an **AVQueuePlayer** object to replace the **AVPlayer** object we have used so far. The following example introduces the necessary modifications to the **ViewController** class of Listing 25-2 to play two videos called videobeaches.mp4 and videotrees.mp4.

```
import UIKit
import AVFoundation
class ViewController: UIViewController {
    @IBOutlet weak var videoView: UIView!
    @IBOutlet weak var playButton: UIButton!
    @IBOutlet weak var progressBar: UIProgressView!
    var playerItem: AVPlayerItem!
    var player: AVQueuePlayer!
    var playerLayer: AVPlayerLayer!
    var ready = false
    var playing = false

    override func viewDidLoad() {
        super.viewDidLoad()
        playButton.isEnabled = false
        let bundle = Bundle.main
        var videoURL = bundle.url(forResource: "videobeaches",
withExtension: "mp4")
        var asset = AVAsset(url: videoURL!)
        playerItem = AVPlayerItem(asset: asset)
        playerItem.addObserver(self, forKeyPath: "status", options: [],
context: nil)

        videoURL = bundle.url(forResource: "videotrees", withExtension:
"mp4")
```

Media

```
    asset = AVAsset(url: videoURL!)
    let playerItem2 = AVPlayerItem(asset: asset)
    player = AVQueuePlayer(items: [playerItem, playerItem2])

    playerLayer = AVPlayerLayer(player: player)
    playerLayer.frame = view.bounds
    let layer = videoView.layer
    layer.addSublayer(playerLayer)
    }
}
```

Listing 25-7: Playing a list of videos

 Do It Yourself: Update the code in the **ViewController** class of Listing 25-2 with the code of Listing 25-7. Download the videos videobeaches.mp4 and videotrees.mp4 from our website and add them to your project. Remember to include the methods of Listing 25-3 and 25-4, and also the **viewWillTransition()** method of Listing 25-1. Run the application. The videos should be played one after another.

AVKit Framework

The video player created in the previous example shows how much code we have to write to provide all the tools a modern player demands, and we still have not added a gesture recognizer to detect a tap in the progress bar and move the playback cursor to the position selected by the user, labels to show the current time and duration, buttons to jump to the next video, or buttons to cancel the operation. There is a lot we can add to our player, but this work is usually not necessary. Since most applications provide a similar interface, Apple decided to design a small framework called *AVKit*, which offers all the classes we need to create a standard video player. The most important is the **AVPlayerViewController** class. This class creates an entire new view controller to show a view player with all the controls necessary for the user to manage the media. All the controller needs is an **AVPlayer** object to know what to play. The following example shows how to create, configure, and open an **AVPlayerViewController** controller.

```
import UIKit
import AVFoundation
import AVKit

class ViewController: UIViewController {
    @IBAction func playVideo(_ sender: UIButton) {
        let bundle = Bundle.main
        let videoURL = bundle.url(forResource: "trailer", withExtension:
"mp4")
        let player = AVPlayer(url: videoURL!)
        let controller = AVPlayerViewController()
        controller.player = player
        present(controller, animated: true, completion: {
            player.play()
        })
    }
}
```

Listing 25-8: Using a standard video player

This example assumes that we have a button in the initial view connected to an Action in the **ViewController** class called **playVideo()**. When the button is pressed, the method creates the **AVPlayer** object from a URL, initializes the **AVPlayerViewController** controller, assigns the player object to the controller's **player** property, and presents the controller on the screen. In this example we use the completion handler of the **present()** method to play the video as soon as the view is loaded, but we can let the user decide.

***Figure 25-4:** AVKit video player*
© Copyright 2008, Blender Foundation / www.bigbuckbunny.org

 Do It Yourself: Create a new Single View Application project. Add a button called Play Video to the initial view. Connect the button to an Action called **playVideo()**. Complete the **ViewController** class with the code of Listing 25-8. Download the trailer.mp4 file from our website and add it to your project. Run the application and press the button. A new view is shown on the screen with a standard video player. Press the X button in the view to remove it.

25.2 Audio

Although the **AVPlayer** class can play video and audio, the AV Foundation framework defines specific classes for audio alone. The class we need to instantiate to create an audio player is called **AVAudioPlayer**. The following are some of its initializers, properties, and methods.

AVAudioPlayer(contentsOf: URL)—This initializer creates an **AVAudioPlayer** object with an audio player configured to play the media in the location specified by the attribute.

volume—This property sets or returns a **Float** value between 0.0 and 1.0 to set the volume.

duration—This property returns the duration of the audio in seconds. It is a value of type **TimeInterval**.

currentTime—This property sets or returns the position of the playback cursor in seconds. It is a value of type **TimeInterval**.

numberOfLoops—This property sets or returns an integer that determines the number of times the audio player is going to play the audio.

isPlaying—This property is a Boolean value that indicates whether the audio is currently being played or not.

play()—This method plays the audio assigned to the audio player.

play(atTime: TimeInterval)—This method moves the playback cursor to the time indicated by the **atTime** attribute. The attribute is a value of type **TimeInterval**.

pause()—This method pauses the audio player.

stop()—This method stops the audio player.

prepareToPlay()—This method preloads the audio and connects the audio player to the hardware to minimize the lag when the audio starts playing.

Media

When playing audio, we do not need to check for the state of the media, we can play it right away, but it is recommended to get the media ready as soon as the view is loaded and execute the **prepareToPlay()** method to avoid any delay. The following example loads an mp3 file from the bundle called beach.mp3 and provide all the controls for the user to be able to play, stop, and pause the player.

```
import UIKit
import AVFoundation

class ViewController: UIViewController {
    var audioPlayer: AVAudioPlayer!

    override func viewDidLoad() {
        super.viewDidLoad()
        let bundle = Bundle.main
        let audioURL = bundle.url(forResource: "beach", withExtension:
"mp3")
        audioPlayer = try? AVAudioPlayer(contentsOf: audioURL!)
        if audioPlayer != nil {
            audioPlayer.prepareToPlay()
        }
    }
    @IBAction func playAudio(_ sender: UIButton) {
        if let player = audioPlaycr {
            player.play()
        }
    }
    @IBAction func stopAudio(_ sender: UIButton) {
        if let player = audioPlayer {
            player.stop()
            player.currentTime = 0
        }
    }
    @IBAction func pauseAudio(_ sender: UIButton) {
        if let player = audioPlayer {
            player.pause()
        }
    }
}
```

Listing 25-9: Playing audio

The example of Listing 25-9 assumes that we have created an interface with three buttons to play, stop, and pause the player, and they are connected to the Actions **playAudio()**, **stopAudio()**, and **pauseAudio()**, respectively. The code creates the **AVAudioPlayer** object and prepares the media to be played. Notice that the **stop()** method does not rewind the media and we have to do it ourselves modifying the **currentTime** property. The difference between **stop()** and **pause()** is that the first one resets the player and frees the hardware.

 Do It Yourself: Create a new Single View Application project. Add three buttons called Play, Stop, and Pause to the initial view. Connect the buttons to Actions called **playAudio()**, **stopAudio()**, and **pauseAudio()**. Complete the **ViewController** class with the code of Listing 25-9. Download the beach.mp3 file from our website and add it to your project. Run the application and press Play.

Audio Player Delegate

AV Foundation defines the **AVAudioPlayerDelegate** protocol to report changes in the state of the audio player. The protocol includes the following methods.

audioPlayerDidFinishPlaying(AVAudioPlayer, **successfully:** Bool)—This method is called on the delegate when the audio has finished playing.

audioPlayerDecodeErrorDidOccur(AVAudioPlayer, **error:** Error?)—This method is called on the delegate when an error occurs while processing the audio.

The **AVAudioPlayer** class includes the **delegate** property to assign a delegate to the audio player. The **ViewController** class in the following example conforms to the protocol and implements the **audioPlayerDidFinishPlaying()** method to modify the interface when the audio is over. The example assumes that we only have one button to stop and play the audio. Every time the button is pressed, we check the **playing** property to know the state of the player and respond accordingly.

```
import UIKit
import AVFoundation

class ViewController: UIViewController, AVAudioPlayerDelegate {
    @IBOutlet weak var playButton: UIButton!
    var audioPlayer: AVAudioPlayer!

    override func viewDidLoad() {
        super.viewDidLoad()
        let bundle = Bundle.main
        let audioURL = bundle.url(forResource: "beach", withExtension:
"mp3")
        audioPlayer = try? AVAudioPlayer(contentsOf: audioURL!)
        if audioPlayer != nil {
            audioPlayer.delegate = self
            audioPlayer.prepareToPlay()
        }
    }
    func audioPlayerDidFinishPlaying(_ player: AVAudioPlayer, successfully
flag: Bool) {
        playButton.setTitle("Play", for: .normal)
    }
    @IBAction func playAudio(_ sender: UIButton) {
        if let player = audioPlayer {
            if player.isPlaying {
                playButton.setTitle("Play", for: .normal)
                player.stop()
                player.currentTime = 0
            } else {
                playButton.setTitle("Stop", for: .normal)
                player.play()
            }
        }
    }
}
```

Listing 25-10: Detecting when the audio has finished playing

Do It Yourself: Erase the buttons in the previous interface and empty the **ViewController** class. Add a single button to the initial view with the title Play. Connect the button to the **ViewController** class with an Outlet called **playButton** and an Action called **playAudio()**. Complete the **ViewControler** class with the code of Listing 25-10 and run the application. The title of the Play button should change to Stop every time you press it and when the audio finishes playing.

Recording

AV Foundation also offers the possibility to record audio. The class to create an audio recorder is called **AVAudioRecorder**. The following is its initializer.

AVAudioRecorder(url: URL, **settings:** Dictionary)—This initializer creates an audio recorder object. The **url** attribute is a **URL** structure with the location of the file where the audio will be stored, and the **settings** attribute is a dictionary with the settings for the recording session. The framework defines multiple keys for configuration. The most frequently used are **AVFormatIDKey** (audio format), **AVEncoderAudioQualityKey** (audio quality), **AVEncoderBitRateKey** (audio bit rate), **AVSampleRateKey** (sample rate in hertz), and **AVNumberOfChannelsKey** (number of audio channels).

The **AVAudioRecorder** class includes the following properties and methods to configure and manage the recording.

currentTime—This property returns the time in seconds since the beginning of the recording. It is a value of type **TimeInterval**.

isRecording—This property returns a Boolean value that indicates if the recorder is recording.

prepareToRecord()—This method creates the audio file and prepares the system for recording.

record()—This method begins or resumes recording.

record(atTime: TimeInterval)—This method begins recording at the time specified by the **atTime** attribute.

record(forDuration: TimeInterval)—This method begins recording and ends at the time specified by the **forDuration** attribute (in seconds).

record(atTime: TimeInterval, **forDuration:** TimeInterval)—This method begins recording at the time specified by the **atTime** attribute and ends at the time specified by the **forDuration** attribute (in seconds).

stop()—This method stops the recording.

pause()—This method pauses the recording. To continue recording, we have to call the **record()** method again.

As well as the **AVAudioPlayer** class, the **AVAudioRecorder** class can designate a delegate to report the state of the process. The delegate must conform to the **AVAudioRecorderDelegate** protocol and implement its methods.

audioRecorderDidFinishRecording(AVAudioRecorder, **successfully:** Bool)— This method is called on the delegate when the recording is over.

audioRecorderEncodeErrorDidOccur(AVAudioRecorder, **error:** Error?)—This method is called on the delegate when an error occurs.

The system creates an audio session that connects the application to the hardware and is shared by every app installed on the device. By default, this session is not configured to work with the microphone. To record sounds, we have to get a reference to the audio session and change its configuration. The session is created from an object of the **AVAudioSession** class, which includes the following type method to get the reference.

sharedInstance()—This type method returns a reference to the shared audio session.

The following are the methods provided by the **AVAudioSession** class to configure the audio session and ask for permission to use the microphone.

recordPermission—This property returns the current permission status. It is an enumeration called **RecordPermission** included in the **AVAudioSession** class. The values available are **undetermined**, **denied** and **granted**.

setCategory(Category, **mode:** Mode, **options:** CategoryOptions**)**—This method sets the session's category. The first attribute is a property of the **Category** structure included in the **AVAudioSession** class that determines how the audio is going to be used. The properties available are **ambient**, **audioProcessing**, **multiRoute**, **playAndRecord**, **playback**, **record** and **soloAmbient**. The **mode** attribute determines how the audio is going to be processed. It is a property of the **Mode** structure included in the **AVAudioSession** class. The properties available are **default**, **gameChat**, **measurement**, **moviePlayback**, **spokenAudio**, **videoChat**, **videoRecording**, **voiceChat** and **voicePrompt**. And the **options** attribute is a property of the **CategoryOptions** structure included in the **AVAudioSession** class. The properties available are **mixWithOthers**, **duckOthers**, **interruptSpokenAudioAndMixWithOthers**, **allowBluetooth**, **allowBluetoothA2DP**, **allowAirPlay** and **defaultToSpeaker**.

requestRecordPermission(Block**)**—This method asks the user's permission to use the microphone. The attribute is a closure that is executed after the user accepts or declines the request (permission is requested only once). The closure receives a Boolean value to indicate if the user granted permission or not.

setActive(Bool**)**—This method activates or deactivates the audio session.

Every time we initiate a session to record audio, the system automatically asks the user for authorization to use the microphone, so we do not need to request permission from code unless we want to do it before the session is created. Although this process is automatic, we have to set a variable in the app's configuration file to specify the message we want to show to the user.

Every project offers a file called info.plist to configure some aspects of the application. This is a Property List file that orders the information in a hierarchy. The values are identified with keys and may contain other values inside, like dictionaries inside dictionaries. When we select this file from the Navigator Area, Xcode shows an editor in the Editor Area with the current values.

Key		Type	Value
▼ Information Property List	⊕	Dictionary	(14 items)
Localization native development region		String	en
Executable file	⌃	String	$(EXECUTABLE_NAME)
Bundle identifier	⌃	String	$(PRODUCT_BUNDLE_IDENTIFIER)
InfoDictionary version	⌃	String	6.0
Bundle name	⌃	String	$(PRODUCT_NAME)
Bundle OS Type code	⌃	String	APPL
Bundle versions string, short	⌃	String	1.0
Bundle version		String	1

***Figure 25-5:** Content of the info.plist file*

If we move the mouse over an item, the editor shows a + button to add another item to the item's hierarchy. For example, to add a new option to the main list, we have to click on the + button of the root item called "Information Property List" (circled in Figure 25-5). When we click this button, the editor shows a list of possible options to choose from. The option we have to select to specify the text we want to show when the user is requested authorization to use the microphone is called "Privacy - Microphone Usage Description". After this option is selected, we have to write the text we want to show as the option's value, as illustrated by Figure 25-6.

Key		Type	Value
▼ Information Property List		Dictionary	(15 items)
Privacy - Microphone Usage Description	◇	String	We need the microphone to record audio

Figure 25-6: Microphone Usage Description option

With the app's configured to work with the microphone, we are ready to write the code. As always, we have to set up the system first and then record or play the audio in response to feedback from the user. To prepare the audio recorder, we have to create a URL pointing to the file in which the recording is going to be stored, configure the audio session to work with the microphone, create the **AVAudioRecorder** object with the settings we want, and call the **prepareToRecord()** method to get it ready to start recording.

```
import UIKit
import AVFoundation

class ViewController: UIViewController, AVAudioPlayerDelegate {
    @IBOutlet weak var recordButton: UIButton!
    @IBOutlet weak var playButton: UIButton!
    var audioRecorder: AVAudioRecorder!
    var audioPlayer: AVAudioPlayer!

    override func viewDidLoad() {
        super.viewDidLoad()
        playButton.isEnabled = false
        let manager = FileManager.default
        let documents = manager.urls(for: .documentDirectory, in:
.userDomainMask)
        let docURL = documents.first!
        let audioURL = docURL.appendingPathComponent("myaudio.caf")

        let audioSession = AVAudioSession.sharedInstance()
        do {
            try
audioSession.setCategory(AVAudioSession.Category.playAndRecord, mode:
.default, options: .defaultToSpeaker)
            let recordSettings: [String: Any] = [AVEncoderAudioQualityKey:
AVAudioQuality.medium.rawValue, AVEncoderBitRateKey: 16, AVSampleRateKey:
44100.0, AVNumberOfChannelsKey: 2]
            audioRecorder = try AVAudioRecorder(url: audioURL, settings:
recordSettings)
            if audioRecorder != nil {
                audioRecorder.prepareToRecord()
            }
        } catch {
            print("Error")
        }
    }
}
```

Listing 25-11: Setting up the recorder

In Listing 25-11 we call the audio file *myaudio.caf*. The caf extension is short for Core Audio Format, an audio container designed to contain audio in different formats, such as AAC, MP3, etc. Once the file's URL is created, we set the category for the audio session as **playAndRecord** to be able to record and also play the recording later, and then establish the settings for the recorder. The settings include values for different aspects of the audio, including the level of quality, which is defined with an enumeration of type **AVAudioQuality** that includes the values **min**, **low**, **medium**, **high**, and **max** (the method requires the raw value for this parameter).

The **prepareToRecord()** method prepares the recorder, but does not begin recording. This is done by the **record()** method that we call when the user or our application decides it is time to do it. For this purpose, our example includes two Actions to let the user decide whether to begin recording or play the audio already recorded.

```
@IBAction func recordAudio(_ sender: UIButton) {
   if audioRecorder != nil {
      if audioRecorder.isRecording {
         audioRecorder.stop()
         playButton.isEnabled = true
         recordButton.setTitle("Record", for: .normal)
      } else {
         audioRecorder.record()
         playButton.isEnabled = false
         recordButton.setTitle("Stop", for: .normal)
      }
   }
}
@IBAction func playAudio(_ sender: UIButton) {
   if let player = audioPlayer {
      if player.isPlaying {
         playButton.setTitle("Play", for: .normal)
         recordButton.isEnabled = true
         player.stop()
         player.currentTime = 0
      } else {
         startPlayer()
      }
   } else {
      startPlayer()
   }
}
func startPlayer() {
   if let audioURL = audioRecorder?.url {
      audioPlayer = try? AVAudioPlayer(contentsOf: audioURL)
      if audioPlayer != nil {
         playButton.setTitle("Stop", for: .normal)
         recordButton.isEnabled = false
         audioPlayer.delegate = self
         audioPlayer.play()
      }
   }
}
func audioPlayerDidFinishPlaying(_ player: AVAudioPlayer, successfully
flag: Bool) {
   playButton.setTitle("Play", for: .normal)
   recordButton.isEnabled = true
}
```

Listing 25-12: Recording and playing the audio recorded

The procedure is similar to the one we used before. Every time a button is pressed, we check the current condition of the recorder or the player and execute the methods to begin or stop the recording or playback. Notice that for the recorder we check the condition with the **recording** property and for the player we use the **playing** property, as we did in previous examples.

 Do It Yourself: Create a new Single View Application project. Add two buttons called Record and Play to the initial view. Connect the buttons to the **ViewController** class with Outlets called **recordButton** and **playButton** and Actions called **recordAudio()** and **playAudio()**, respectively. Complete the **ViewController** class with the codes of Listings 25-11 and 25-12. Add the "Privacy - Microphone Usage Description" option to the info.plist file, as explained above. Run the application and press Record. Say something and press Stop. Now press the Play button to listen to the recording.

25.3 Media

Besides playing video and audio files incorporated to our application, we can also access and play the media already on the device. There is a framework we can use for this purpose called Media Player. This framework provides access to the media added to the device from iTunes, including songs, audio podcasts, audio books, etc. The framework offers two alternatives to let the user select what to play: we can use a predefined controller or generate a media query to access the media from code.

Media Controller

Media Player defines the **MPMediaPickerController** class to create a view controller with a predefined interface to select media items. The class includes the following initializer.

MPMediaPickerController(mediaTypes: MPMediaType)—This initializer creates a media controller configured for the media type specified by the attribute. The attribute is an enumeration that defines the type of media we want to retrieve. The possible values are **music**, **podcast**, **audioBook**, **anyAudio**, **movie**, **tvShow**, **videoPodcast**, **musicVideo**, **videoITunesU**, **anyVideo**, and **any**.

The **MPMediaPickerController** class works with a delegate to inform our view controller the decisions made by the user. The framework defines the **MPMediaPickerController-Delegate** protocol for this delegate with the following methods.

mediaPicker(MPMediaPickerController, **didPickMediaItems:** MPMediaItem-Collection)—This method is called on the delegate when the user selects a media item. The **didPickMediaItems** attribute is an object that contains a list of **MPMediaItem** objects that represent each of the selected items.

mediaPickerDidCancel(MPMediaPickerController)—This method is called on the delegate when the user presses the Cancel button to close the controller.

When the user selects an item, the controller returns an object of type **MPMediaItemCollection** that contains a collection of **MPMediaItem** objects. To retrieve the items, the **MPMediaItemCollection** class offers the following properties.

items—This property returns an array with the **MPMediaItem** objects in the collection.

count—This property returns an integer with the number of items in the collection.

The items returned are objects of type **MPMediaItem**. This class includes a series of properties to retrieve the item's attributes. The following are the most frequently used.

assetURL—This property returns a **URL** structure with the item's URL.

mediaType—This property returns an enumeration of type **MPMediaType** that represents the type of media. The values included in the enumeration are **music**, **podcast**, **audioBook**, **anyAudio**, **movie**, **tvShow**, **videoPodcast**, **musicVideo**, **videoITunesU**, **anyVideo**, and **any**.

title—This property returns a string with the item's title.

albumTitle—This property returns a string with the title of the album the item belongs to.

artist—This property returns a string with the name of the artist associated to the item.

playbackDuration—This property returns a **TimeInterval** value with the item's duration.

artwork—This property returns an **MPMediaItemArtwork** object with the image associated to the item.

releaseDate—This property returns a **Date** structure with the date the item was released.

The **MPMediaPickerController** controller also requires authorization from the user to access the device's media library. The process is automatic, as soon as we present the controller to the user the system shows an Alert View asking for permission, but we have to provide the text for the message in the info.plist file, as we did before to access the microphone (Figure 25-5). The key we have to insert in the plist file is called "Privacy - Media Library Usage Description"

In our view controller, we have to initialize the **MPMediaPickerController** object, present it on the screen like we did with other presentation view controllers before, and implement the methods of the **MPMediaPickerControllerDelegate** protocol to get the media item selected by the user.

```
import UIKit
import MediaPlayer

class ViewController: UIViewController, MPMediaPickerControllerDelegate {
    @IBOutlet weak var playButton: UIButton!
    @IBOutlet weak var titleLabel: UILabel!
    var audioPlayer: AVAudioPlayer!

    @IBAction func selectSong(_ sender: UIButton) {
        let controller = MPMediaPickerController(mediaTypes: .music)
        controller.delegate = self
        present(controller, animated: true, completion: nil)
    }
    func mediaPicker(_ mediaPicker: MPMediaPickerController,
didPickMediaItems mediaItemCollection: MPMediaItemCollection) {
        let item = mediaItemCollection.items[0]
        let mediaURL = item.assetURL
        audioPlayer = try? AVAudioPlayer(contentsOf: mediaURL!)
        if audioPlayer != nil {
            titleLabel.text = item.title
            audioPlayer.prepareToPlay()
            playButton.setTitle("Play", for: .normal)
        }
        dismiss(animated: true, completion: nil)
    }
```

```
func mediaPickerDidCancel(_ mediaPicker: MPMediaPickerController) {
    dismiss(animated: true, completion: nil)
}
@IBAction func playSong(_ sender: UIButton) {
    if let player = audioPlayer {
        if player.isPlaying {
            playButton.setTitle("Play", for: .normal)
            player.stop()
            player.currentTime = 0
        } else {
            playButton.setTitle("Stop", for: .normal)
            player.play()
        }
    }
}
}
```

Listing 25-13: Playing songs stored in the device

The example of Listing 25-13 assumes that we have an interface with two buttons called Select Song and Play to select a song and play it, and a label to show the name of the song to the user. When the Select Song button is pressed, the **selectSong()** method is executed. In this method, we create the **MPMediaPickerController** controller to retrieve Music items, declare the **ViewController** object as its delegate, and present it on the screen with the **present()** method. The view includes all the tools necessary for the user to perform a selection. Once the user selects an item, the **mediaPicker()** method is executed and we can read the item's properties from the **mediaItemCollection** attribute. In our example, we get the first item in the collection (we only work with one item this time) and read its **assetURL** property to get the URL pointing to the item. With this URL, we create the **AVAudioPlayer** object we need to play the audio. In this method, we also read the **title** property and assign its value to the label on the interface to show the song's title on the screen. At the end, the view controller is dismissed, taking the user back to the initial view where the Play button is ready to play the song (the Action for this button is the same we used in the example of Listing 25-10 to play an audio file).

 Do It Yourself: Create a new Single View Application project. Add two buttons to the initial view called Select Song and Play. Add a label with the message "No Song Selected". Connect the Play button with an Outlet called **playButton** and an Action called **playSong()**. Connect the label with an Outlet called **titleLabel** and the Select Song button with an Action called **selectSong()**. Complete the **ViewController** class with the code of Listing 25-13. Open the info.plist file and add the option "Privacy - Media Library Usage Description" with the message you want to display to the user. Run the application on your device. When you press the Select Song button, a view with an interface to select a song from the media library will open. Select a song and then press the Play button to play it.

Query Media

The media controller is an easy way to provide access to the user's media on the device, but we can also create our custom picker or search for specific media items using a query. The class that provides this functionality is **MPMediaQuery**. We can create a generic query to retrieve all the media items available, use a predicate to filter the items, or execute type methods to get a query configured to return a specific type of media. The following are the initializer and some of the type methods available in this class.

MPMediaQuery(filterPredicates: Set?**)**—This initializer creates an `MPMediaQuery` object with the predicates determined by the attribute. The **filterPredicates** attribute is a set of `MPMediaPropertyPredicate` objects. We can also declare the attribute as `nil` and assign the predicate later with the object's `addFilterPredicate()` method.

albums()—This type method creates a `MPMediaQuery` object that returns music items sorted by album.

artists()—This type method creates a `MPMediaQuery` object that returns music items sorted by the name of the artist.

songs()—This type method creates a `MPMediaQuery` object that returns music items sorted by the title of the songs.

playlists()—This type method creates a `MPMediaQuery` object that returns library items sorted by the title of the playlist they belong to.

podcasts()—This type method creates a `MPMediaQuery` object that returns podcast items sorted by title.

audiobooks()—This type method creates a `MPMediaQuery` object that returns audio books items sorted by title.

The `MPMediaQuery` class offers properties to configure the query and return the items.

items—This property returns an array with the media items retrieved by the query. The items are objects of type `MPMediaItem`.

groupingType—This property determines how the media items are going to be grouped to create collections. It is an enumeration of type `MPMediaGrouping` with the values `title` (value by default), `album`, `artist`, `albumArtist`, `composer`, `genre`, `playlist`, and `podcastTitle`.

collections—This property returns an array of `MPMediaItemCollection` objects that contain a list of `MPMediaItem` objects that represent the items in the collection.

Query predicates are defined with an object of the `MPMediaPropertyPredicate` class. The class includes the following initializer.

MPMediaPropertyPredicate(value: Any?, **forProperty:** String**)**—This initializer creates an `MPMediaPropertyPredicate` object with a predicate that matches the property defined by the **forProperty** attribute, and with the value specified by the **value** attribute. The **value** attribute is the value we want the property of the media to have, and the **forProperty** attribute is one of the properties of the `MPMediaItem` object. The most frequently used are `MPMediaItemPropertyAssetURL`, `MPMediaItemPropertyMediaType`, `MPMediaItemPropertyTitle`, `MPMediaItemPropertyAlbumTitle`, `MPMediaItemPropertyArtist`, `MPMediaItemPropertyPlaybackDuration`, `MPMediaItemPropertyArtwork`, and `MPMediaItemPropertyReleaseDate`.

With media queries, we can get a list of media items of certain type and present them on the screen for the user to choose from. The following example searches for a song with the title "Road of Resistance" and lets the user play it or prints an error message on the console if it cannot find it.

```swift
import UIKit
import MediaPlayer

class ViewController: UIViewController {
    @IBOutlet weak var playButton: UIButton!
    var audioPlayer: AVAudioPlayer!

    override func viewDidLoad() {
        super.viewDidLoad()

        let predicate = MPMediaPropertyPredicate(value: "Road of
Resistance", forProperty: MPMediaItemPropertyTitle)
        let mediaItems = MPMediaQuery(filterPredicates: [predicate])
        if let items = mediaItems.items {
            if !items.isEmpty {
                let song = items[0]
                let songURL = song.assetURL
                audioPlayer = try? AVAudioPlayer(contentsOf: songURL!)
                if audioPlayer != nil {
                    audioPlayer.prepareToPlay()
                }
            } else {
                print("Song not found")
            }
        }
    }
    @IBAction func playSong(_ sender: UIButton) {
        if let player = audioPlayer {
            if player.isPlaying {
                playButton.setTitle("Play", for: .normal)
                player.stop()
                player.currentTime = 0
            } else {
                playButton.setTitle("Stop", for: .normal)
                audioPlayer.play()
            }
        }
    }
}
```

Listing 25-14: Searching for a song

After creating the **MPMediaQuery** object, all we need to do is to read its **items** property to get a list of the media items retrieved by the query. In Listing 25-14, we check if there are items available in the **items** property, get the first item, and create an **AVAudioPlayer** object with its URL. The example assumes that we have a Play button connected to an Action called **playSong()**. When the button is pressed, the song returned by the query is played.

 Do It Yourself: Create a new Single View Application project. Add a button called Play to the initial view and connect it to the **ViewController** class with an Outlet called **playButton** and an Action called **playSong()**. Complete the **ViewController** class with the code of Listing 25-14. Replace the name of the song in the predicate with the name of a song you have in your device (or buy the album Metal Resistance, by Babymetal). Add the option "Privacy - Media Library Usage Description" to the info.plist file, as explained before, and run the application.

Media

Chapter 26
Pictures and Videos

26.1 Image Picker Controller

Taking and storing pictures are the most common uses of mobile devices, and this is why no device is sold without a camera anymore. Because of how normal it is for an application to access the camera and manage pictures, UIKit offers a controller with built-in functionality to provide all the tools necessary for the user to take pictures and videos or select them from storage. The class to create this controller is called **UIImagePickerController**. The following are the properties included in this class for configuration.

sourceType—This property sets or returns a value that determines the type of source we want to use to get the pictures. It is an enumeration called **SourceType** included in the **UIImagePickerController** class. The values available are **camera** (for the camera), **photoLibrary** (for all the photos available on the device), and **savedPhotosAlbum** (for the photos taken by the camera).

mediaTypes—This property sets or returns a value that determines the type of media we want to work with. It takes an array of strings with the values that represent every media we want to use. The most common values are public.image for pictures and public.movie for movies (these values can be represented by the constants **kUTTypeImage** and **kUTTypeMovie**).

cameraCaptureMode—This property sets or returns a value that determines the capture mode used by the camera. It is an enumeration called **CameraCaptureMode** included in the **UIImagePickerController** class. The values available are **photo** and **video**.

cameraFlashMode—This property sets or returns a value that determines the flash mode used by the camera. It is an enumeration called **CameraFlashMode** included in the **UIImagePickerController** class. The values available are **on**, **off**, and **auto**.

allowsEditing—This property sets or returns a Boolean value that determines if the user is allowed to edit the image.

videoQuality—This property sets or returns a value that determines the quality of the recorded video. It is an enumeration called **QualityType** included in the **UIImagePickerController** class. The values available are **typeHigh**, **typeMedium**, **typeLow**, **type640x480**, **typeIFrame960x540**, and **typeIFrame1280x720**.

The **UIImagePickerController** class also offers the following type methods to detect the source available (Camera or Photo Library) and the type of media the sources can manage.

isSourceTypeAvailable(SourceType**)**—This type method returns a Boolean value that indicates if the source specified by the attribute is supported by the device. The attribute is an enumeration called **SourceType** included in the **UIImagePickerController** class. the values available are **camera** (for the camera), **photoLibrary** (for all the photos available on the device), and **savedPhotosAlbum** (for the photos taken by the camera).

availableMediaTypes(for: SourceType**)**—This type method returns an array with strings that represent the media types available for the source specified by the attribute. The attribute is an enumeration called **SourceType** included in the **UIImagePicker-**

Controller class. The values available are **camera** (for the camera), **photoLibrary** (for all the photos available on the device), and **savedPhotosAlbum** (for the photos taken by the camera).

isCameraDeviceAvailable(CameraDevice**)**—This type method returns a Boolean value that indicates if the camera specified by the attribute is available on the device. The attribute is an enumeration called **CameraDevice** included in the **UIImagePickerController** class. The values available are **rear** and **front**.

The **UIImagePickerController** class creates a new view where the user can take pictures or select old ones from storage (depending on how we have configured the controller). After the image is created or selected, the view controller has to be dismissed and the selected image processed. The way our code gets access to this image and is able to know when to dismiss the view controller is through a delegate that conforms to the **UIImagePickerControllerDelegate** protocol. We have to declare the view controller that opens the **UIImagePickerController** controller as its delegate and implement the following methods.

imagePickerController(UIImagePickerController, **didFinishPickingMediaWith-Info:** Dictionary**)**—This method is called on the delegate when the user finishes taking or selecting the image or video. The second attribute contains a dictionary with the information about the media. The values in the dictionary are identified with properties of the **InfoKey** structure included in the **UIImagePickerController** class. The properties available are **cropRect**, **editedImage**, **imageURL**, **livePhoto**, **mediaMetadata**, **mediaType**, **mediaURL**, **originalImage**, and **phAsset**.

imagePickerControllerDidCancel(UIImagePickerController**)**—This method is called on the delegate when the user cancels the process.

Camera

As we did for the media picker in the previous chapter, we have to include an action that the user can perform to open the controller. For this example, we have decided to create a simple interface with an Image View to show the image taken or selected, and a button called Get Picture to open the controller.

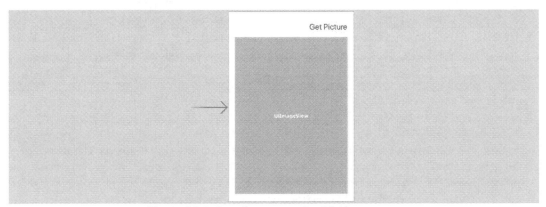

Figure 26-1: Interface to work with the camera

The view controller that is going to be the delegate of the **UIImagePickerController** controller is required to conform to two protocols: **UINavigationControllerDelegate** and

Pictures and Videos

UIImagePickerControllerDelegate. The following example includes an Action for the Get Picture button that creates, configures, and presents a **UIImagePickerController** controller to take pictures from the camera. The class also implements the methods defined in the **UIImagePickerControllerDelegate** protocol to process the media received from the controller.

```
import UIKit

class ViewController: UIViewController, UINavigationControllerDelegate,
UIImagePickerControllerDelegate {
    @IBOutlet weak var pictureView: UIImageView!

    @IBAction func takePicture(_ sender: UIButton) {
        let mediaPicker = UIImagePickerController()
        mediaPicker.delegate = self
        let sourceAvailable =
UIImagePickerController.isSourceTypeAvailable(.camera)

        if sourceAvailable {
            mediaPicker.sourceType = .camera
            mediaPicker.mediaTypes = ["public.image"]
            mediaPicker.allowsEditing = false
            mediaPicker.cameraCaptureMode = .photo
            present(mediaPicker, animated: true, completion: nil)
        } else {
            print("The media is not available")
        }
    }
    func imagePickerController(_ picker: UIImagePickerController,
didFinishPickingMediaWithInfo info: [UIImagePickerController.InfoKey :
Any]) {
        let picture = info[.originalImage] as! UIImage
        pictureView.image = picture
        dismiss(animated: true, completion: nil)
    }
    func imagePickerControllerDidCancel(_ picker: UIImagePickerController)
{
        dismiss(animated: true, completion: nil)
    }
}
```

Listing 26-1: Taking a picture

When the button is pressed, the **takePicture()** method creates an instance of the **UIImagePickerController** class and assigns the **ViewController** object as its delegate. Next, it checks if the camera is available and presents the controller in case of success or shows a message on the console otherwise. Before calling the **present()** method to show the view on the screen, the code configures the controller. The **sourceType** property is assigned the value **camera** to tell the controller that we are going to get the picture from the camera, the **mediaTypes** property is assigned an array with the value public.image to set images as the media we want to retrieve, the **allowEditing** property is set as **false** to not let the user edit the image, and the **cameraCaptureMode** is assigned the value **photo** to only let the user take pictures. The interface created by the controller is shown in Figure 26-2 (right).

Figure 26-2: Camera's interface

 IMPORTANT: To access the camera, you have to ask authorization to the user. The process is automatic, but you have to add the "Privacy - Camera Usage Description" option to the info.plist file with the text you want to show to the user when permission is requested, as explained in the previous chapter (see Figure 25-5).

The camera's interface includes buttons to control the camera and take the picture. After the user takes the picture, a new set of buttons is shown to let the user select the picture or take another one. If the user decides to use the current picture, the controller calls the `imagePickerController()` method on its delegate to report the action. This method receives a parameter called `info` that we can read to get the media returned by the controller and process it (stores it in a file, Core Data, or show it on the screen). In our example, we read the value of the `originalImage` key to get a `UIImage` object that represents the image taken by the user and assign this object to the Image View to show the picture on the screen.

 Do It Yourself: Create a new Single View Application project. Add an Image View and a button to the initial view, as shown in Figure 26-1. Connect the Image View to the `ViewController` class with an Outlet called `pictureView` and the button with an Action called `takePicture()`. Complete the `ViewController` class with the code of Listing 26-1. Add the "Privacy - Camera Usage Description" option to the info.plist file with the text you want to show to the user. Run the application and press the button. Take a picture and press the button to use it. You should see the photo on the screen.

Photo Library

Except for the value of the `sourceType` property, the rest of the configuration values used in the previous example are the ones defined by default, so if all we want to do is to let the user take a picture, we do not need to declare anything else. The same goes for the Photo Library. If we want to let the user select a picture from the list of images available on the device, we just have to indicate the new source changing the value of the `sourceType` property, as shown in the following example.

```
import UIKit

class ViewController: UIViewController, UINavigationControllerDelegate,
UIImagePickerControllerDelegate {
    @IBOutlet weak var pictureView: UIImageView!

    @IBAction func takePicture(_ sender: UIButton) {
        let mediaPicker = UIImagePickerController()
```

Pictures and Videos

```
        mediaPicker.delegate = self
        mediaPicker.sourceType = .savedPhotosAlbum
        present(mediaPicker, animated: true, completion: nil)
    }
    func imagePickerController(_ picker: UIImagePickerController,
didFinishPickingMediaWithInfo info: [UIImagePickerController.InfoKey :
Any]) {
        let picture = info[.originalImage] as! UIImage
        pictureView.image = picture
        dismiss(animated: true, completion: nil)
    }
    func imagePickerControllerDidCancel(_ picker:UIImagePickerController){
        dismiss(animated: true, completion: nil)
    }
}
```

Listing 26-2: *Selecting a picture*

There are two values we can assign to the **sourceType** property to load photos: **photoLibrary** and **savedPhotosAlbum**. The **photoLibrary** option shows all the photos organized in a list of albums, and the **savedPhotosAlbum** option gives priority to the photos in the camera roll. In Listing 26-2 we choose this last option. With this simple change, instead of showing a view with an interface to operate the camera, the system now opens a view with a list of the pictures available. When the user selects a picture, the **imagePickerController()** method is called on the controller's delegate and the picture is shown on the screen.

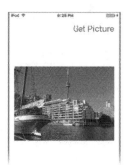

Figure 26-3: *Photo Library's interface*

The Photo Library may contain images and also videos. We can define the type of media we want the controller to display assigning a new value to the **mediaTypes** property and then read the value associated to the **mediaType** key to select the media we want.

```
import UIKit

class ViewController: UIViewController, UINavigationControllerDelegate,
UIImagePickerControllerDelegate {
    @IBOutlet weak var pictureView: UIImageView!

    @IBAction func takePicture(_ sender: UIButton) {
        let mediaPicker = UIImagePickerController()
        mediaPicker.delegate = self
        mediaPicker.sourceType = .savedPhotosAlbum
        mediaPicker.mediaTypes = ["public.image", "public.movie"]
        present(mediaPicker, animated: true, completion: nil)
    }
```

```
    func imagePickerController(_ picker: UIImagePickerController,
didFinishPickingMediaWithInfo info: [UIImagePickerController.InfoKey :
Any]) {
        let media = info[.mediaType] as! String
        if media == "public.image" {
            let picture = info[.originalImage] as! UIImage
            pictureView.image = picture
        }
        dismiss(animated: true, completion: nil)
    }
    func imagePickerControllerDidCancel(_ picker: UIImagePickerController)
{
        dismiss(animated: true, completion: nil)
    }
}
```

Listing 26-3: *Selecting images or videos*

Adapting the Controller

By default, the view managed by the **UIImagePickerController** controller is presented full screen, but we can take advantage of the bigger screens offered by iPads and show the view with a different format, such as a popover. All we have to do is to configure the presentation style of the view controller and set the required parameters. The following example shows the view in a popover.

```
import UIKit

class ViewController: UIViewController, UINavigationControllerDelegate,
UIImagePickerControllerDelegate {
    @IBOutlet weak var pictureView: UIImageView!
    @IBOutlet weak var pictureButton: UIButton!

    @IBAction func takePicture(_ sender: UIButton) {
        let mediaPicker = UIImagePickerController()
        mediaPicker.delegate = self
        mediaPicker.sourceType = .savedPhotosAlbum

        mediaPicker.modalPresentationStyle = .popover
        if let popover = mediaPicker.popoverPresentationController {
            popover.sourceView = pictureButton
            popover.sourceRect = pictureButton.bounds
            popover.permittedArrowDirections = [.up]
        }
        present(mediaPicker, animated: true, completion: nil)
    }
    func imagePickerController(_ picker: UIImagePickerController,
didFinishPickingMediaWithInfo info: [UIImagePickerController.InfoKey :
Any]) {
        let picture = info[.originalImage] as! UIImage
        pictureView.image = picture
        dismiss(animated: true, completion: nil)
    }
    func imagePickerControllerDidCancel(_ picker:UIImagePickerController){
        dismiss(animated: true, completion: nil)
    }
}
```

Listing 26-4: *Showing the view in a popover*

Pictures and Videos

In this example, we anchor the popover to the Get Picture button, so the view is going to show up below the button, close to where the user's finger is at the moment. If we open the view in a device with a small screen, the system shows it full screen, but if we do it on an iPad, the system creates a popover presentation controller and assigns it to the **popoverPresentationController** property. Reading this property, we know how the controller is going to be shown and are able to set the values for the presentation, as we did for Action Sheets in Chapter 17, Listing 17-6.

 Do It Yourself: Connect the Get Picture button to the **ViewController** class with an Outlet called **pictureButton**. Update the **ViewController** class with the code of Listing 26-4. Run the application on an iPad and press the Get Picture button. The view should be opened in a popover.

Storing Pictures

In the previous examples, we show the picture on the screen, but we can store it in a file or in Core Data. An alternative, sometimes useful when working with the camera, is to store the picture in the device's Photo Library to make it accessible from other applications. The UIKit framework offers two functions to store images and videos.

UIImageWriteToSavedPhotosAlbum(UIImage, Any?, Selector?, Unsafe-MutableRawPointer?**)**—This function adds the image specified by the first attribute to the camera roll. The second attribute is a reference to the object that contains the method we want to execute when the process is over, the third attribute is a selector that represents that method, and the last attribute is an object with additional data to pass to the method.

UISaveVideoAtPathToSavedPhotosAlbum(String, Any?, Selector?, Unsafe-MutableRawPointer?**)**—This function adds the video at the path indicated by the first attribute to the camera roll. The second attribute is a reference to the object that contains the method we want to execute when the process is over, the third attribute is a selector that represents that method, and the last attribute is an object with additional data for the method.

These functions store the picture or video taken by the camera in the Photo Library and then call a method to report the result of the operation. We can declare the target object and the selector as **nil** if we don't want to know what happened or define a method in our view controller to handle the response. This method can have any name we want, but it is required to have a specific definition that includes three attributes. For images, the attributes are **(image: UIImage, didFinishSavingWithError error: NSError?, contextInfo: UnsafeRawPointer)** and for videos the attributes are **(video: String, didFinishSavingWithError error: NSError?, contextInfo: UnsafeRawPointer)**. In the following example, we show the picture taken with the camera on the screen, store it in the Photo Library, and open an Alert View in case of success to inform to the user that the picture is available with the rest of the photos.

```
import UIKit

class ViewController: UIViewController, UINavigationControllerDelegate,
UIImagePickerControllerDelegate {
   @IBOutlet weak var pictureView: UIImageView!

   @IBAction func takePicture(_ sender: UIButton) {
      let mediaPicker = UIImagePickerController()
      mediaPicker.delegate = self
```

```
        let sourceAvailable =
UIImagePickerController.isSourceTypeAvailable(.camera)
        if sourceAvailable {
            mediaPicker.sourceType = .camera
            present(mediaPicker, animated: true, completion: nil)
        } else {
            print("The media is not available")
        }
    }
    func imagePickerController(_ picker: UIImagePickerController,
didFinishPickingMediaWithInfo info: [UIImagePickerController.InfoKey :
Any]) {
        let picture = info[.originalImage] as! UIImage
        pictureView.image = picture
        UIImageWriteToSavedPhotosAlbum(picture, self,
#selector(confirmImage(image:didFinishSavingWithError:contextInfo:)),
nil)
        dismiss(animated: true, completion: nil)
    }
    func imagePickerControllerDidCancel(_ picker:UIImagePickerController){
        dismiss(animated: true, completion: nil)
    }
    @objc func confirmImage(image: UIImage, didFinishSavingWithError
error: NSError?, contextInfo: UnsafeRawPointer) {
        if error == nil {
            let alert = UIAlertController(title: "Picture Saved", message:
"The picture was added to your photos", preferredStyle: .alert)
            let action = UIAlertAction(title: "OK", style: .default,
handler: nil)
            alert.addAction(action)
            present(alert, animated: true, completion: nil)
        } else {
            print("Error")
        }
    }
}
```

Listing 26-5: Storing pictures in the Photo Library

When we get media from the Photo Library, the system takes care of the security aspects for us, but when we try to store new pictures or videos in the device, we have to configure the app to ask the user's authorization. As always, this is done from the info.plist file. In this case, we have to add the option "Privacy - Photo Library Additions Usage Description" with the message we want to show to the user when authorization is requested. In our example, because the image we are going to store in the Photo Library is taken from the camera, we also have to add the option "Privacy - Camera Usage Description".

 Do It Yourself: Update the **ViewController** class with the code of Listing 26-5. If you erase the Outlet for the button created in Listing 26-4, remember to delete it also from the button in the Storyboard (see Figure 5-26). Add the options "Privacy - Photo Library Additions Usage Description" and "Privacy - Camera Usage Description" to the info.plist file to get access to the Photo Library and the Camera. Run the application and take a picture. You should see an Alert View with the message "Picture Saved" and the picture should be available in your device's Photo Library.

Pictures and Videos

Modifying Pictures

Due to the limited capacity of mobile devices, we cannot work with multiple images in their original size at the same time. Pictures have to be immediately stored and, in some cases, reduced in size for future use. A common practice is to store the original picture along with a thumbnail to use as preview. The following example creates a thumbnail of the picture taken by the camera.

```
import UIKit

class ViewController: UIViewController, UINavigationControllerDelegate,
UIImagePickerControllerDelegate {
   @IBOutlet weak var pictureView: UIImageView!

   @IBAction func takePicture(_ sender: UIButton) {
      let mediaPicker = UIImagePickerController()
      mediaPicker.delegate = self
      let sourceAvailable =
UIImagePickerController.isSourceTypeAvailable(.camera)
      if sourceAvailable {
         mediaPicker.sourceType = .camera
         present(mediaPicker, animated: true, completion: nil)
      } else {
         print("The media is not available")
      }
   }
   func imagePickerController(_ picker: UIImagePickerController,
didFinishPickingMediaWithInfo info: [UIImagePickerController.InfoKey :
Any]) {
      let picture = info[.originalImage] as! UIImage
      let scale = UIScreen.main.scale
      let maximum: CGFloat = 80
      var width = picture.size.width / scale
      var height = picture.size.height / scale

      if width > height {
         height = height * maximum / width
         width = maximum
      } else {
         width = width * maximum / height
         height = maximum
      }
      let render = UIGraphicsImageRenderer(size: CGSize(width: width,
height: height))
      render.image(actions: { (renderContext) in
         let context = renderContext.cgContext
         UIGraphicsPushContext(context)
         picture.draw(in: CGRect(x: 0, y: 0, width: width, height:
height))
         pictureView.image = renderContext.currentImage
      })
      dismiss(animated: true, completion: nil)
   }
   func imagePickerControllerDidCancel(_ picker:UIImagePickerController){
      dismiss(animated: true, completion: nil)
   }
}
```

Listing 26-6: Creating a thumbnail

The code of Listing 26-6 takes the picture returned by the camera, calculates the width and height considering a maximum size of 80 points, and creates a new image with this information. Notice that the **UIImage** returned by the **originalImage** key is defined in pixels, so we have to calculate its size in points dividing the width and height by the scale of the device. Because we are using the **draw()** method of the **UIImage** class to draw the image, we turn the graphic context into the current context by adding it to the stack with the **UIGraphicsPushContext()** function (see Chapter 24). After the current context is set, we draw the image and then retrieve the result with the **currentImage** property to show it on the screen.

 Do It Yourself: Update the **ViewController** class with the code of Listing 26-6. Set the Content Mode for the Image View as Top Left, so you can see the thumbnail in its original size. Remember to set a higher Content Hugging Priority for the button so it does not expand to cover the space left by the image.

26.2 Custom Controllers

The **UIImagePickerController** controller is built from classes defined in two frameworks: AV Foundation and Photos. The AV Foundation framework provides the codes necessary to process media and control input devices, like the camera and the microphone, and the Photos framework provides access to the user's photos in the device. We can use the classes in these frameworks directly to build our own controller and customize the process and the interface.

Camera

Creating our own controller to access the camera and retrieve information from that device demands the manipulation and coordination of several systems. We need to configure the input from at least two devices, the camera and the microphone, process the data received from this input, show a preview to the user, and also generate the output in the form of an image, live photo, video, or audio. Figure 26-4 illustrates all the elements involved.

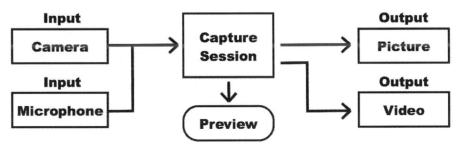

Figure 26-4: System to capture media

The first thing we need to do to build this structure is to determine the input devices. The AV Foundation framework defines the **AVCaptureDevice** class for this purpose. An instance of this class can represent any type of input device, including cameras and microphones. The following are the type methods included in the class to access and manage a device.

default(for: AVMediaType)—This type method returns an **AVCaptureDevice** object that represents the default capture device for the media specified by the attribute. The **for** attribute is a structure of type **AVMediaType** with properties to define the type of media. The properties available to work with the cameras and microphones are **video** and **audio**.

devices(for: AVMediaType)—This type method returns an array of **AVCaptureDevice** objects that represent the devices of the type specified by the attribute. The **for** attribute is a structure of type `AVMediaType` with properties to define the type of media. The properties available to work with the cameras and microphones are `video` and `audio`.

requestAccess(for: AVMediaType, **completionHandler:** Block)—This type method asks permission to the user to access the device. The **for** attribute is a structure of type `AVMediaType` with properties to define the type of media. The properties available to work with the cameras and microphones are `video` and `audio`. The **completionHandler** attribute is a closure with the statements we want to execute after the request is completed.

authorizationStatus(for: AVMediaType)—This type method returns a value that determines the status of the authorization to use the device. The **for** attribute is a structure of type `AVMediaType` with properties to define the type of media. The properties available to work with the cameras and microphones are `video` and `audio`. The method returns an enumeration of type `AVAuthorizationStatus` with the values `notDetermined`, `restricted`, `denied`, and `authorized`.

An instance of the `AVCaptureDevice` class represents a capture device. To define this device as an input device, we have to create an object that controls the ports and connections of the input. The framework defines the `AVCaptureDeviceInput` class for this purpose. The class includes the following initializer to create the input object for the device.

AVCaptureDeviceInput(device: AVCaptureDevice)—This initializer creates an input for the device specified by the **device** attribute.

As well as inputs, we also have to define outputs to process the data captured by the device. The framework defines subclasses of a base class called `AVCaptureOutput` to describe the outputs. There are several subclasses available, such as `AVCaptureVideoDataOutput` to process the frames of a video, and `AVCaptureAudioDataOutput` to get the audio, but the most frequently used is the `AVCapturePhotoOutput` to capture a single video frame (take a picture). This class works with a delegate that conforms to the `AVCapturePhotoCaptureDelegate` protocol, which among other methods defines the following to return an image.

photoOutput(AVCapturePhotoOutput, **didFinishProcessingPhoto:** AVCapturePhoto, **error:** Error?)—This method is called on the delegate after the image is captured. The **didFinishProcessingPhoto** attribute is a container with information about the image, and the **error** attribute is used to report errors.

To control the flow of data from input to output, the framework defines the `AVCaptureSession` class. From an instance of this class, we can control the inputs and outputs and also when the process begins and ends by calling the following methods.

addInput(AVCaptureInput)—This method adds an input to the capture session. The attribute represents the input device we want to add.

addOutput(AVCaptureOutput)—This method adds an output to the capture session. The attribute represents the output we want to generate from the capture session.

startRunning()—This method starts the capture session.

stopRunning()—This method stops the capture session.

The framework also defines the `AVCaptureVideoPreviewLayer` class with the specific purpose of showing a preview to the user. This is a subclass of `CALayer` that creates a sublayer with predefined code to display the video captured by the input device. The class includes the following initializer and properties to create and manage the preview layer.

AVCaptureVideoPreviewLayer(session: AVCaptureSession)—This initializer creates an **AVCaptureVideoPreviewLayer** object with a preview layer connected to the capture session defined by the **session** attribute.

videoGravity—This property defines how the video adjusts its size to the size of the preview layer. It is an enumeration of type **AVLayerVideoGravity** with the values **resizeAspect**, **resizeAspectFill**, and **resize**.

connection—This property returns an object of type **AVCaptureConnection** that defines the connection between the capture session and the preview layer.

The input, output, and preview layers are connected to the capture session by objects of the **AVCaptureConnection** class. The class manages the information of the connection, including ports and data. The following are its most frequently used properties.

videoOrientation—This property sets or returns the orientation of the video. It is an enumeration of type **AVCaptureVideoOrientation** with the values **portrait**, **portraitUpsideDown**, **landscapeRight**, and **landscapeLeft**.

isVideoOrientationSupported—This property returns a Boolean value that determines whether or not it is allowed to set the video's orientation.

Because we are not presenting the view generated by the **UIImagePickerController** class anymore, we have to create our own. Figure 26-5, below, shows the interface we have created for this example. The initial view was embedded in a Navigation Controller and an additional view was included to manage the camera. The initial view includes an Image View to show the picture taken, and a bar button called Get Picture to open the second view. The second view has an empty view to which we can add the preview layer, and a narrow view at the bottom added over the preview view with an image button to let the user take a picture.

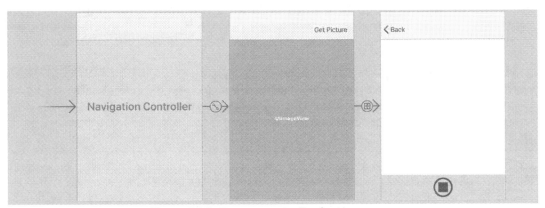

Figure 26-5: Custom controller for the camera

 Do It Yourself: Create a new Single View Application project. Embed the initial Scene in a Navigation Controller. Add an Image View and a bar button with the title Get Picture to the initial view (Figure 26-5, center). Add a new Scene to the Storyboard. Connect the Get Picture button to the second Scene with a Show Segue. Add a view to the second view with a gray background and a Height constraint of 64 points. Click on the background color of this view and select the option Custom to open the color picker. Set an Opacity value of 50% to make it translucent. Pin this view to the bottom of the main view and add a button at the center (Figure 26-5, right). Download the images camerabutton.png and camerabuttondown.png from our website and assign them to the button for the Default and Highlighted state. Add another empty view for the preview layer and pin it to the edges of the main view to adopt the size of the screen (highlighted in Figure 26-5, right). Move this view to the back from the Document Outline panel or from the Editor menu to position it below the toolbar. The final interface should look like Figure 26-5.

The view controller for the initial view is simple, we just have to get the picture from the second view and show it on the screen. For this example, we have decided to create an Action that we are going to connect to an Unwind Segue to get the image from the second view and assign it to the Image View (the image will be stored in a property called **picture**).

```
import UIKit

class ViewController: UIViewController {
    @IBOutlet weak var pictureView: UIImageView!

    @IBAction func goBack(_ segue: UIStoryboardSegue) {
        let controller = segue.source as! CameraViewController
        pictureView.image = controller.picture
    }
}
```

***Listing 26-7:** Showing on the screen the picture taken by the camera*

For the second view, we have created a subclass of **UIViewController** called **CameraViewController**. In this view controller, we have to follow a series of steps to activate the camera, let the user take a picture, and process the image. But before to even access the camera we have to ask the user's permission. This is done automatically when we use a **UIImagePickerController** controller, but we have to do it ourselves in a custom controller using the type methods provided by the **AVCaptureDevice** class.

```
import UIKit
import AVFoundation

class CameraViewController: UIViewController,
AVCapturePhotoCaptureDelegate {
    @IBOutlet weak var cameraView: UIView!

    var captureSession: AVCaptureSession!
    var stillImage: AVCapturePhotoOutput!
    var previewLayer: AVCaptureVideoPreviewLayer!
    var picture: UIImage!
    var imageOrientation: UIImage.Orientation!

    override func viewDidLoad() {
        super.viewDidLoad()
        let device = UIDevice.current
        device.beginGeneratingDeviceOrientationNotifications()

        let status = AVCaptureDevice.authorizationStatus(for: .video)
        if status == .authorized {
            prepareCamera()
        } else if status == .notDetermined {
            AVCaptureDevice.requestAccess(for: .video, completionHandler: {
(granted: Bool) in
                OperationQueue.main.addOperation({
                    if granted {
                        self.prepareCamera()
                    } else {
```

```
            self.notAuthorized()
        }
      })
    })
  } else {
    notAuthorized()
  }
}
}
```

Listing 26-8: Asking permission to use the camera

The **authorizationStatus()** method returns an **AVAuthorizationStatus** value to inform the current status of the authorization. If the value is **authorized**, it means that we have been previously authorized and we can use the camera, but if the value is **notDetermined**, we have to call the **requestAccess()** method to ask permission. This method includes a closure as the second parameter that is executed after the user responds to the request. The closure includes an attribute of type **Bool** to report the user's decision (We have to add the "Privacy - Camera Usage Description" option to the info.plist file with the text we want to show to the user when permission to use the camera is requested, as we did before for the **UIImagePickerController** class).

We use two methods to respond to each situation. The **prepareCamera()** method is executed every time the code detects that we are authorized to use the camera, and the **notAuthorized()** method is executed otherwise. In the following implementation of the latter, we show and Alert View to inform the situation to the user.

```
func notAuthorized() {
   let alert = UIAlertController(title: "No Camera", message: "This app
is not authorized to use the camera", preferredStyle: .alert)
   let action = UIAlertAction(title: "OK", style: .default, handler: nil)
   alert.addAction(action)
   present(alert, animated: true, completion: nil)
}
```

Listing 26-9: Informing the user that the camera is not available

The **prepareCamera()** method is where we begin to build the network of objects introduced in Figure 26-4. This method gets a reference to the current capture device for video and creates the inputs and outputs we need to capture a still image (to take a picture).

```
func prepareCamera() {
   captureSession = AVCaptureSession()
   if let device = AVCaptureDevice.default(for: AVMediaType.video) {
      if let input = (try? AVCaptureDeviceInput(device: device)) {
         captureSession.addInput(input)
         stillImage = AVCapturePhotoOutput()
         captureSession.addOutput(stillImage)
         showCamera()
      } else {
         notAuthorized()
      }
   } else {
      notAuthorized()
   }
}
```

Listing 26-10: Initializing the camera

Pictures and Videos

We can create and add to the session all the inputs and outputs we need, in any possible order, but because the **AVCaptureDeviceInput()** initializer throws an error, we use it first. This initializer creates an object that manages the input for the capture device. If the initializer is successful, we add it to the capture session with the **addInput()** method and then create the output. For this example we have decided to use the session to capture a still image, so we use the **AVCapturePhotoOutput** class to create the output and add it to the session with the **addOutput()** method.

After adding the inputs and outputs to the capture session, the **prepareCamera()** method executes an additional method called **showCamera()** to generate the preview layer and show the video generated by the camera on the screen. In this method, we have to create the layer and set its size and orientation.

```
func showCamera() {
    view.setNeedsLayout()
    view.layoutIfNeeded()
    let width - cameraView.bounds.size.width
    let height = cameraView.bounds.size.height

    previewLayer = AVCaptureVideoPreviewLayer(session: captureSession)
    previewLayer.videoGravity = .resizeAspectFill
    previewLayer.frame = CGRect(x: 0, y: 0, width: width, height: height)

    let videoOrientation = getCurrentOrientation()
    let connection = previewLayer.connection
    connection?.videoOrientation = videoOrientation

    let layer = cameraView.layer
    layer.addSublayer(previewLayer)
    captureSession.startRunning()
}
```

Listing 26-11: Showing the video from the camera on the screen

The **AVCaptureVideoPreviewLayer()** initializer creates a layer that we have to adjust to the size of its view and add as a sublayer of the current view's layer. But setting the position and size of the layer does not determine how its content is going to be shown. The video coming from the camera could have a different size and orientation. How the video is going to adjust to the size of the layer is determined by the value of the layer's **videoGravity** property, but the orientation is set from the connection established between the capture session and the preview layer. This is why, after setting the value of the **videoGravity** property and the layer's frame, we get a reference to the connection from the layer's **connection** property. By modifying the **videoOrientation** property of the connection, we can adjust the orientation according to the device's orientation and finally add the sublayer to the view's layer with the **addSublayer()** method. When the sublayer is ready, the capture session can be initiated with the **startRunning()** method.

To determine the orientation, we implemented a method called **getCurrentOrientation()**. We need to know the device's orientation to be able to define the orientation of the preview layer, so the video is shown in the view with the right orientation, and also to define the orientation of the image taken by the camera. For these reasons, our method returns the **AVCaptureVideoOrientation** value we need to set the orientation of the preview layer, and also stores a **UIImage.Orientation** value in the **imageOrientation** property to later set the orientation of the image.

```
func getCurrentOrientation() -> AVCaptureVideoOrientation {
    var orientation: AVCaptureVideoOrientation = .portrait
    let device = UIDevice.current
    switch device.orientation {
        case .portrait:
            orientation = .portrait
            imageOrientation = .right
        case .landscapeRight:
            orientation = .landscapeLeft
            imageOrientation = .down
        case .landscapeLeft:
            orientation = .landscapeRight
            imageOrientation = .up
        default:
            break
    }
    return orientation
}
```

Listing 26-12: Detecting the device's orientation

 IMPORTANT: The camera always encodes the image in its native orientation, which is landscape-right. In consequence, when the device is in portrait mode, we have to set the orientation of the image to right, when it is in landscape-left mode, we have to set the image's orientation to down, and when it is in landscape-right mode, we have to set it to up. Also, the landscape orientation of the video is the opposite of the device. When the device is in the landscape-right orientation, the video orientation is landscape-left, and vice versa.

At this point, the video is playing on the screen and the system is ready to perform a capture. To allow the user to take a picture, we have to connect the button added at the bottom of the view (Figure 26-5, right) to an Action in the **CameraViewController** class. The process to capture an image is initiated by the output object. The **AVCapturePhotoOutput** class we use to capture a still image offers the following method for this purpose.

capturePhoto(with: AVCapturePhotoSettings, **delegate:** AVCapturePhoto-CaptureDelegate)—This method initiates a photo capture with the settings specified by the **with** attribute. The **delegate** attribute is a reference to the object that implements the methods of the **AVCapturePhotoCaptureDelegate** protocol to receive the data generated by the output.

The type of photo captured by the output is determined by an **AVCapturePhotoSettings** object. The class includes multiple initializers. The following are the most frequently used.

AVCapturePhotoSettings()—This initializer creates an **AVCapturePhotoSettings** object with the format by default.

AVCapturePhotoSettings(format: Dictionary)—This initializer creates a **AVCapturePhotoSettings** object with the format specified by the **format** attribute. The attribute is a dictionary with keys and values to set the characteristics of the image. Some of the keys available are **kCVPixelBufferPixelFormatTypeKey** (uncompressed format), **AVVideoCodecKey** (compressed format), **AVVideoQualityKey** (compression quality).

The following are the properties available in this class to configure the image and the preview.

Pictures and Videos

previewPhotoFormat—This property set or returns a dictionary with keys and values that determine the characteristics of the preview image. The keys available are `kCVPixelBufferPixelFormatTypeKey` (uncompressed format), `kCVPixelBuffer-WidthKey` (maximum width) and `kCVPixelBufferHeightKey` (maximum height).

flashMode—This property sets or returns the flash mode used when the image is captured. It is an enumeration of type `FlashMode` with the values **on**, **off**, and **auto**.

isAutoStillImageStabilizationEnabled—This property is a Boolean value that determines if automatic image stabilization is enabled or not.

isHighResolutionPhotoEnabled—This property is a Boolean value that determines if the image is going to be taken in high resolution.

To capture an image, we have to define the settings with an `AVCapturePhotoSettings` object, call the `capturePhoto()` method of the `AVCapturePhotoOutput` object, and define the delegate method that is going to receive the image returned. The following example implements the delegate method and an Action to initiate the process when the user presses the button.

```
@IBAction func takePicture(_ sender: UIButton) {
    let settings = AVCapturePhotoSettings()
    stillImage.capturePhoto(with: settings, delegate: self)
}
func photoOutput(_ output: AVCapturePhotoOutput, didFinishProcessingPhoto
photo: AVCapturePhoto, error: Error?) {
    let scale = UIScreen.main.scale
    if let imageData = photo.fileDataRepresentation() {
        picture = UIImage(data: imageData, scale: scale)
        picture = UIImage(cgImage: picture.cgImage!, scale: scale,
orientation: imageOrientation)
        performSegue(withIdentifier: "goBackSegue", sender: self)
    }
}
```

Listing 26-13: Taking a picture

When the user presses the button to take the picture, the `takePicture()` method calls the `capturePhoto()` method to ask the output object to capture an image. After the image is captured, this object sends the result to the delegate method. The value received by the method is an object of type `AVCapturePhoto`, which is a container with information about the image. The class includes two convenient methods to get the data representing the image.

fileDataRepresentation()—This method returns a data representation of the image that we can use to create a `UIImage` object.

cgImageRepresentation()—This method returns the image as a `CGImage` object.

In our example, we have implemented the `fileDataRepresentation()` method to create a `UIImage` object. Immediately after we get this object, we create another `UIImage` object with this image to be able to set its orientation with the value we stored before in the `imageOrientation` property. This sets the orientation of the image according to the orientation of the device when the picture was taken, so the image is always displayed correctly.

After the image is processed, we trigger the Unwind Segue identified with the string "goBackSegue" to take the user back to the initial view. This is the Unwind Segue we have created for the `goBack()` Action included in the `ViewController` class of Listing 26-7 (see

Figure 13-19 to learn how to create the Unwind Segue and Figure 13-16 to learn how to change its name).

The controller for the camera is ready, but there is one more method we need to add to the `CameraViewController` class to adapt the preview layer to the orientation of the device. As we have done before for other projects in this book, we can implement the `viewWillTransition()` method to get the new main view's size and adjust the preview layer according to the orientation.

```
override func viewWillTransition(to size: CGSize, with coordinator:
UIViewControllerTransitionCoordinator) {
   super.viewWillTransition(to: size, with: coordinator)
   if previewLayer != nil {
      previewLayer.frame.size = size

      let videoOrientation = getCurrentOrientation()
      let connection = previewLayer.connection
      connection?.videoOrientation = videoOrientation
   }
}
```

Listing 26-14: Rotating the preview layer

 Do It Yourself: Update the `ViewController` class with the code of Listing 26-7. Create a subclass of `UIViewController` called `CameraViewController` and assign it to the second view. Connect the view for the preview layer with an Outlet called `cameraView`. Complete the class with the code of Listing 26-8. Add the methods of Listings 26-9, 26-10, 26-11, and 26-12 to this class. Connect the button in the second view to an Action called `takePicture()` and complete the method with the code of Listing 26-13. Complete the `CameraViewController` class with the method of Listing 26-14. Create an Unwind Segue in this Scene connected to the `goBack()` method of the `ViewController` class and give it the identifier "goBackSegue". Remember to add the option "Privacy - Camera Usage Description" to the info.plist file. Run the application and take a picture.

Photos

The same way we can create a custom controller for the cameras we can do it for the Photo Library. Apple provides a specific framework called Photos to access the photos and videos stored in the device. The framework defines the `PHAsset` class to create objects that represent the images and videos we retrieve from the library. The following are the properties included in the class to return the asset's attributes.

playbackStyle—This property returns a value that determines the type of the media. It is an enumeration of type `PlaybackStyle` with the values `image`, `imageAnimated`, `livePhoto`, `unsupported`, `video`, and `videoLooping`.

pixelWidth—This property returns an integer with the width of the photo or video.

pixelHeight—This property returns an integer with the height of the photo or video.

creationDate—This property returns a `Date` value with the media's date of creation.

modificationDate—This property returns a `Date` value with the date the last time the media was modified.

duration—This property returns a value of type `TimeInterval` that determines the duration of the video.

isFavorite—This property returns a Boolean value that determines whether or not the asset is marked as favourite.

The class also defines its own methods to retrieve the assets.

fetchAssets(with: PHFetchOptions?**)**—This type method retrieves all the assets available in the Photo library. The **with** attribute is an object with properties called `predicate` and `sortDescriptors` to define a predicate and sort descriptors to filter and order the results.

fetchAssets(with: PHAssetMediaType, **options:** PHFetchOptions?**)**—This type method retrieves assets from the Photo library of the type specified by the **with** attribute. The **with** attribute is an enumeration with the values `unknown`, `image`, `video`, and `audio`, and the **options** attribute is an object with properties called `predicate` and `sortDescriptors` to define a predicate and sort descriptors to filter and order the results.

A `PHAsset` object only includes information related to the media but not the media itself. To get the photo or the video represented by the asset, we have to load it using a manager. The framework offers the `PHImageManager` class to create and use a manager. The system automatically creates a manager and assigns it to the Photo library. The following are some of the methods provided by the class to get a reference to the default manager and load the assets.

default()—This method returns a reference to the `PHImageManager` object that represents the manager assigned to the app by default.

requestImage(for: PHAsset, **targetSize:** CGSize, **contentMode:** PHImage-ContentMode, **options:** PHImageRequestOptions?, **resultHandler:** Block**)**—This method requests the image of the `PHAsset` object specified by the **for** attribute. The **targetSize** attribute determines the size we want to give to the image (usually used to create thumbnails), the **contentMode** attribute is an enumeration with the values `aspectFit` and `aspectFill` that determines how the photo is going to adapt to the size of the image returned, the **options** attribute specifies the image attributes (usually declared as `nil`), and the **resultHandler** attribute is a closure that is executed when the image is loaded. The closure receives two attributes with the image and a dictionary containing the status of the request.

requestImageData(for: PHAsset, **options:** PHImageRequestOptions?, **resultHandler:** Block**)**—This method requests the image of the `PHAsset` object specified by the **for** attribute in its full size. The **options** attribute specifies the image attributes (usually declared as `nil`), and the **resultHandler** attribute is a closure that is executed when the image is loaded. The closure receives four attributes: a `Data` structure with the image data, a string with the image UTI (the image identifier), a `UIImage.Orientation` value with the image's orientation, and a dictionary containing the status of the request.

requestPlayerItem(forVideo: PHAsset, **options:** PHVideoRequestOptions?, **resultHandler:** Block**)**—This method requests a representation of the video for playback. The **forVideo** attribute is a `PHAsset` object with the video we want to play, the **options** attribute specifies the video attributes (usually declared as `nil`), and the **resultHandler** attribute is a closure that is executed when the video is ready to be played. The closure receives two attributes, an `AVPlayerItem` object we can use to play the video and a dictionary containing the status of the request.

As an example, we are going to adapt the previous project to include a Collection View Controller to present photos from the Photo library instead of the video from the camera.

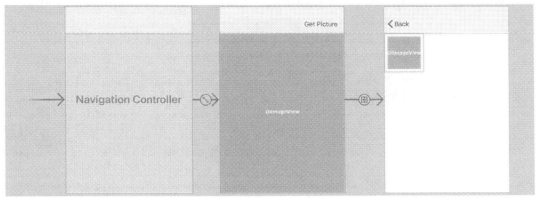

Figure 26-6: Custom controller for photos

The initial view and its view controller are the same, but the second view is now a Collection View Controller with a cell containing an Image View to present each photo.

 Do It Yourself: Remove the second Scene in the previous project and delete the CameraViewController.swift file. Add a Collection View Controller to the Storyboard. Connect the Get Picture button to this Scene with a Show Segue. Create the Unwind Segue for the second view, connect it to the **goBack()** Action introduced in Listing 26-7, and give it the identifier "goBackSegue". Create a file with a subclass of **UICollectionViewController** called **PhotosViewController** and assign it to the Collection View Controller. Add an Image View to the cell and give the cell a size of 100 x 100 points (see Figure 15-4). Create a subclass of **UICollectionViewCell** called **PhotosCell** and assign it to the cell. Connect the Image View in the cell to the **PhotosCell** class with an Outlet called **imagePhoto**. Give the cell the identifier "photosCell". Replace the name of the class **CameraViewController** by **PhotosViewController** inside the **ViewController** class.

When accessing the Photo Library in this manner, we have to ask the user's authorization. The system asks for permission automatically as soon as we try to fetch some assets, but in case we want to control the process, the framework defines the **PHPhotoLibrary** class, which includes the following methods for this purpose.

authorizationStatus()—This type method returns a value that determines the status of the authorization to access the Photo library. It returns an enumeration of type **PHAuthorizationStatus** with the values **notDetermined**, **restricted**, **denied**, and **authorized**.

requestAuthorization(Block**)**—This type method requests to the user access to the Photo Library. The attribute is a closure to be executed after the request is completed.

Besides these methods, we also have to define an option in the info.plist file called "Privacy - Photo Library Usage Description" with the message we want to show to the user when permission is requested.

The following example shows the whole process. The code asks for authorization and calls different methods according to the user's response.

Pictures and Videos

```
import UIKit
import Photos

class PhotosViewController: UICollectionViewController {
    var photosList: PHFetchResult<PHAsset>!
    var picture: UIImage!

    override func viewDidLoad() {
        super.viewDidLoad()
        let status = PHPhotoLibrary.authorizationStatus()
        if status == PHAuthorizationStatus.authorized {
            loadPhotos()
        } else if status == PHAuthorizationStatus.notDetermined {
            PHPhotoLibrary.requestAuthorization({ (status) in
                OperationQueue.main.addOperation({
                    if status == PHAuthorizationStatus.authorized {
                        self.loadPhotos()
                        self.collectionView?.reloadData()
                    } else {
                        self.notAuthorized()
                    }
                })
            })
        } else {
            notAuthorized()
        }
    }
    func notAuthorized() {
        let alert = UIAlertController(title: "No Photos", message: "This
app is not authorized to access the photos", preferredStyle: .alert)
        let action = UIAlertAction(title: "OK", style: .default, handler:
nil)
        alert.addAction(action)
        present(alert, animated: true, completion: nil)
    }
}
```

Listing 26-15: Asking permission to access the photos

The procedure is very similar to the one we used before to get authorization for the camera, although this time we have to implement the methods provided by the Photos framework. If the user gives permission, we call the **loadPhotos()** method to get a list of the photos available. In this method, we only have to get the list of **PHAsset** objects available and assign it to a property we called **photosList**, so the Collection View methods have access to them.

```
func loadPhotos() {
    photosList = PHAsset.fetchAssets(with: .image, options: nil)
}
```

Listing 26-16: Getting the list of photos available

 The Basics: The **photosList** property is of type **PHFetchResult**. This is a class defined to store an array of assets or collections of assets. It works like an array, but it is a generic type, which means that we have to declare the type we are going to store in the property between angle brackets, as we did in Listing 26-15 (**PHFetchResult<PHAsset>**).

Now that we have the list of photos, we can use it to create the Collection View's cells. The following are the protocol methods we need to implement in the **PhotosViewController** class to show the pictures on the screen and let the user select one.

```
override func collectionView(_ collectionView: UICollectionView,
numberOfItemsInSection section: Int) -> Int {
    if photosList != nil {
        return photosList.count
    }
    return 0
}
override func collectionView(_ collectionView: UICollectionView,
cellForItemAt indexPath: IndexPath) -> UICollectionViewCell {
    let cell = collectionView.dequeueReusableCell(withReuseIdentifier:
"photosCell", for: indexPath) as! PhotosCell
    let asset = photosList[indexPath.item]
    let manager = PHImageManager.default()
    manager.requestImage(for: asset, targetSize: CGSize(width: 100,
height: 100), contentMode: .aspectFit, options: nil, resultHandler: {
(image, info) in
        cell.imagePhoto.image = image
    })
    return cell
}
override func collectionView(_ collectionView: UICollectionView,
didSelectItemAt indexPath: IndexPath) {
    let asset = photosList[indexPath.item]
    let manager = PHImageManager.default()
    manager.requestImageData(for: asset, options: nil, resultHandler: {
(data, dataUTI, orientation, info) in
        if data != nil {
            let scale = UIScreen.main.scale
            self.picture = UIImage(data: data!, scale: scale)
            self.performSegue(withIdentifier: "goBackSegue", sender: self)
        }
    })
}
```

Listing 26-17: Showing the photos in the Collection View

As we already mentioned, to get the image associated with an asset object we have to load it using a manager. In Listing 26-17, we use this manager first to get a thumbnail of the image for each cell and then again to get the image in its original size when a cell is selected. The method we use to create the thumbnail is called **requestImage()**. This method produces a **UIImage** object with an image of the size specified by its **targetSize** attribute that can be assigned to the cell's Image View. The second method is called **requestImageData()**. This method produces a **Data** structure with the data for the entire image that can be used to create the **UIImage** object necessary for the initial view to present the photo to the user.

In this example, we use the same process implemented before to provide the image to the initial view. The original image is assigned to the **picture** property and then the Unwind Segue is triggered to move back to the initial view and show the photo on the screen.

 Do It Yourself: Update the **PhotosViewController** class with the code of Listing 26-15. Add the methods of Listings 26-16 and 26-17 to the class. Make sure that the option "Privacy - Photo Library Usage Description" is included in the info.plist file and run the application. Press the Get Picture button. You should see a list of photos. Tap on a photo to select it.

Pictures and Videos

The `fetchAssets()` method used in Listing 26-16 to retrieve the list of photos available in the Photo Library receives an attribute that we can use to filter and order the results. This attribute is an object of a class called **PHFetchOptions** that includes the **predicate** and **sortDescriptors** properties to provide an **NSPredicate** object and an array of **NSSortDescriptor** objects to filter and order the results, as we did in Chapter 22 for Core Data requests. The following example orders the photos by date (the names of the keys for the sort descriptor corresponds to the name of the properties defined in the **PHAsset** class).

```
func loadPhotos() {
    let options = PHFetchOptions()
    let sort = NSSortDescriptor(key: "creationDate", ascending: false)
    options.sortDescriptors = [sort]
    photosList = PHAsset.fetchAssets(with: .image, options: options)
}
```

Listing 26-18: Sorting the photos

Do It Yourself: Replace the **loadPhotos()** method of the **PhotosViewController** class by the method of Listing 26-18. Run the application. The photos should be ordered according to the date they were created.

Videos

The same way we get the photos from the Photo Library we can get the videos. There is only one change we have to perform in the previous example to get a list of videos instead of photos. The **fetchAssets()** type method used in the **loadPhotos()** method to fetch the assets in the Photo Library contains an attribute to specify the media. Changing this attribute to **video**, we get a list of the videos available on the device.

```
func loadPhotos() {
    let options = PHFetchOptions()
    let sort = NSSortDescriptor(key: "creationDate", ascending: false)
    options.sortDescriptors = [sort]
    photosList = PHAsset.fetchAssets(with: .video, options: options)
}
```

Listing 26-19: Fetching videos

This time, the asset selected by the user has to be processed with the manager's **requestPlayerItem()** method. This method gets the video from the asset and creates an **AVPlayerItem** object that we can use to play the video. In the following example, we create an **AVPlayer** object with the player item received by the closure and present it on the screen with an **AVPlayerViewController** controller (see Chapter 25).

```
override func collectionView(_ collectionView: UICollectionView,
didSelectItemAt indexPath: IndexPath) {
    let asset = photosList[indexPath.item]
    let manager = PHImageManager.default()
    manager.requestPlayerItem(forVideo: asset, options: nil,
resultHandler: { (playerItem, info) in
        if let item = playerItem {
            OperationQueue.main.addOperation({
                let player = AVPlayer(playerItem: item)
                let controller = AVPlayerViewController()
```

```
            controller.player = player
            self.present(controller, animated: true, completion: {
                player.play()
            })
        })
    }
    })
}
```

Listing 26-20: Playing videos

 Do It Yourself: Update the `loadPhotos()` method in the `PhotosView-Controller` class with the code of Listing 26-19 and the `collectionView(UICollectionView, didSelectItemAt:)` method with the code of Listing 26-20. Import the AVKit framework to be able to work with the `AVPlayerViewController` class (`import AVKit`). Run the application and select a video to play it.

26.3 Core Image

Core Image is a small but very powerful framework to process images. The framework is used along with other frameworks to apply filters to images and edit pictures. Although its main function is to apply filters, it can also be used to detect faces, remove red eyes, change balance, tone curve, etc.

The framework defines its own class to represent images called `CIImage`. A `CIImage` object can be created from different sources, such as `UIImage` objects, image files, and image data. The following are some of its initializers.

CIImage(cgImage: CGImage)—This initializer creates a `CIImage` object from the `CGImage` object specified by the attribute.

CIImage(image: UIImage)—This initializer creates a `CIImage` object from the `UIImage` object specified by the attribute.

CIImage(contentsOf: URL)—This initializer creates a `CIImage` object with the image in the URL specified by the attribute.

CIImage(data: Data)—This initializer creates a `CIImage` object with the data specified by the attribute.

To render the image, Core Image uses a context. The class is called `CIContext` and provides multiple initializers and type methods to create the context and get the image from it. The following are the most frequently used.

CIContext(options: Dictionary?)—This initializer creates a `CIContext` object with the configuration specified by the **options** attribute. The attribute is a dictionary containing the options and values for configuration. The dictionary's keys are defined by properties of the `CIContextOption` structure. The properties available are `cacheIntermediates`, `highQualityDownsample`, `outputColorSpace`, `outputPremultiplied`, `priority-RequestLow`, `useSoftwareRenderer`, `workingColorSpace`, and `workingFormat`.

createCGImage(CIImage, **from:** CGRect)—This method returns a `CGImage` object created from the image and size specified by the attributes. The first attribute is the `CIImage` object with the image we want to transform and the **from** attribute determines the size of the image.

As we mentioned, the main function of the framework is to apply filters to an image. This process is performed by an instance of the `CIFilter` class. The class includes several initializers to create a filter. The following is the most frequently used.

CIFilter(name: String)—This initializer creates a `CIFilter` object containing the type of filter defined by the **name** attribute. The attribute is a string with the name of the filter we want to apply (e.g., CIGaussianBlur, CISepiaTone, CIGlassDistortion, CIComicEffect).

The characteristics of the filter are configured through parameters set and retrieved by the `setValue()` and `value()` methods. The framework defines keys for the parameters of each filter, including two parameters common to every filter that are used to set the input image and to retrieve the output image. To apply a filter, we have to get a `CIImage` object representing the image, create the filter, set its parameters, and get the image back from the context.

```
import UIKit

class ViewController: UIViewController {
    @IBOutlet weak var pictureView: UIImageView!
    var picture: UIImage!
    override func viewDidLoad() {
        super.viewDidLoad()
        picture = UIImage(named: "husky")
        pictureView.image = picture
    }
    @IBAction func applyFilter(_ sender: UIButton) {
        let context = CIContext(options: nil)
        let image = CIImage(image: picture)
        if let filter = CIFilter(name: "CIComicEffect") {
            filter.setValue(image, forKey: "inputImage")
            if let result = filter.value(forKey:"outputImage") as? CIImage {
                let frame = result.extent
                let resultImage = context.createCGImage(result, from: frame)
                let newImage = UIImage(cgImage: resultImage!)
                pictureView.image = newImage
            }
        }
    }
}
```

Listing 26-21: Applying a filter

This example assumes that we have an interface with a button and an Image View and have included the husky.png image in the Assets Catalog. When the button is pressed, the `applyFilter()` method creates a `CIContext` object with the configuration by default, a `CIImage` object from the picture we want to modify, and finally a filter of type CIComicEffect. Every filter includes two basic parameters: the inputImage parameter to set the input image and the outputImage parameter to get the output image. In Listing 26-21, we assigned the `CIImage` object as the filter's input and then obtained the filtered image with the outputImage key.

The `value()` method returns a `CIImage` object, but we can retrieve the image as a `CGImage` object from the context by calling its `createCGImage()` method. The method requires a reference to the `CIImage` object and also a `CGRect` value that determines its size. To get the size, we read a property provided by the `CIImage` class called **extent**. This property returns a `CGRect` value with the image's size, which is exactly what we need. Finally, the `CGImage` object is used to create a `UIImage` object that we assign to the Image View to show it on the screen.

In Listing 26-21, we first assign the original image to the Image View and then apply the filter when the user presses the button. The result is shown in Figure 26-7.

Pictures and Videos

Figure 26-7: Image before and after a filter is applied

 IMPORTANT: There is an extensive list of predefined filters available and each filter in turn defines its own unique parameters. For a complete list, visit our website and follow the links for this chapter.

The CIComicEffect filter does not have any additional parameters, but other filters require the definition of one or more parameters to work properly. For example, a filter called CISepiaTone that turns the colors in the image into shades of brown have a parameter called inputIntensity to define its intensity.

```
@IBAction func applyFilter(_ sender: UIButton) {
   let context = CIContext(options: nil)
   let image = CIImage(image: picture)
   if let filter = CIFilter(name: "CISepiaTone") {
      filter.setValue(image, forKey: "inputImage")
      filter.setValue(0.8, forKey: "inputIntensity")
      if let result = filter.value(forKey: "outputImage") as? CIImage {
         let frame = result.extent
         let resultImage = context.createCGImage(result, from: frame)
         let newImage = UIImage(cgImage: resultImage!)
         pictureView.image = newImage
      }
   }
}
```

Listing 26-22: Defining the filter's parameters

 Do It Yourself: Create a new Single View Application project. Download the husky.png image from our website and add it to the project. Add a button called Apply Filter and an Image View to the initial view. Connect the Image View to the **ViewController** class with an Outlet called **pictureView** and the button with an Action called **applyFilter()**. Complete the **ViewController** class with the code of Listing 26-21. Run the application and press the Apply Filter button. You should see the image changing as illustrated in Figure 26-7. Replace the **applyFilter()** method by the method of Listing 26-22 and run the application again to test the CISepiaTone filter.

 IMPORTANT: Core Image is a simple framework but provides multiple alternatives to process images and videos. Besides the **CIFilter** class, the framework includes very powerful classes like **CIDetector** to identify features such as faces or barcodes, or the **CIFilterGenerator** class to create our own filters. The topic is beyond the scope of this book. For more information, visit our website and follow the links for this chapter.

27.1 Links

The most important aspect of the web is the ease with which we can access documents with a simple link. A link is a text or an image associated with a URL that indicates the location of a document. When the user clicks the link, the document is opened. Links were designed for the web, but we can add them to our applications and let the system decide where to open the document. If the link contains a web address, the system opens the default browser and asks it to load the document.

Web addresses are created from **URL** structures. We have used these types of structures before to determine the location of files, but we can also use them to access remote documents. The class includes the following initializer to create a URL.

URL(string: String)—This initializer creates a **URL** structure with the URL specified by the **string** attribute.

URL(string: String, **relativeTo:** URL?)—This initializer creates a **URL** structure with the URL specified by the attributes. The URL is created by adding the value of the **string** attribute to the value of the **relativeTo** attribute. For example, if the value of the **string** attribute is the string "http://www.formasterminds.com" and the value of the **relativeTo** attribute is the string "index.php", the **URL** structure will contain the URL "http://www.formasterminds.com/index.php".

URL(dataRepresentation: Data, **relativeTo:** URL?, **isAbsolute:** Bool)—This initializer creates a **URL** structure with the URL specified by the attributes. The URL is created by adding the value of the **dataRepresentation** attribute to the value of the **relativeTo** attribute. The **isAbsolute** attribute is a Boolean value that determines if the URL is absolute or not (it includes all the information required to access the resource).

The **URL** structure is just a container for the location of the document we want to open, but the document is opened from methods of the **UIApplication** class. We have to access the **UIApplication** object created for our app and use the following methods to process the URL.

open(URL, **options:** Dictionary, **completionHandler:** Block)—This method opens the URL specified by the first attribute. The **options** attribute is a dictionary with predefined keys and values to configure the operation (standard options are declared with an empty dictionary), and the **completionHandler** attribute is the closure to be executed when the process is over. The closure receives a Boolean value that determines whether the document was opened or not.

canOpenURL(URL)—This method analyzes the URL specified by the attribute and returns a Boolean value that determines if the URL can be opened by an application installed on the device.

The following example opens the website www.formasterminds.com when a button in the initial view is pressed. The code stores a string with the URL in a constant, creates the **URL** structure from this value, and finally calls the **open()** method to open the URL. The system reads the URL, detects that it is a web address and opens the browser to load the website.

```
import UIKit

class ViewController: UIViewController {
    @IBAction func openWeb(_ sender: UIButton) {
        let web = "http://www.formasterminds.com"
        if let webURL = URL(string: web) {
            let app = UIApplication.shared
            app.open(webURL, options: [:], completionHandler: { (success) in
                if success {
                    print("Successful")
                }
            })
        }
    }
}
```

Listing 27-1: Opening a website

 Do It Yourself: Create a Single View Application project. Add a button to the initial view and connect it to the **ViewController** class with an Action called **openWeb()**. Complete the **ViewController** class with the code of Listing 27-1. Run the application and press the button. The system should open the browser and load the website.

In this example, we have defined the URL in code, but sometimes the URL is provided by the user or taken from another document. In cases like this, the URL may contain characters that are not allowed and can cause the location to be impossible to identify. To make sure that the URL is valid, we have to turn unsafe characters into percent-encoding characters. These are characters represented by the % sign followed by a hexadecimal number. Fortunately, there are methods that can easily correct unsafe characters in a string for us. We have studied a method like this provided by the **String** structure in Chapter 21. The **data(using: Encoding, allowLossyConversion: Bool)** method turns a string into a **Data** structure using a type of encoding that corrects the characters for us.

```
import UIKit

class ViewController: UIViewController {
    @IBAction func openWeb(_ sender: UIButton) {
        let web = "http://www.formasterminds.com"
        let dataURL = web.data(using: String.Encoding.utf8,
allowLossyConversion: false)
        let webURL = URL(dataRepresentation: dataURL!, relativeTo: nil,
isAbsolute: true)
        let app = UIApplication.shared
        app.open(webURL!, options: [:], completionHandler: { (success) in
            if success {
                print("Successful")
            }
        })
    }
}
```

Listing 27-2: Encoding URLs

The **utf8** format used in Listing 27-2 works with ASCII characters and therefore it is suitable for the creation of URLs. The method returns a **Data** structure containing the URL, so we have to use the appropriate **URL** initializer for this type of value. Once the **URL** structure is created, the process to open the URL is the same.

27.2 Safari View Controller

Links provide access to the web from our app, but they open the document in an external application. Considering how important it is for our application to capture the user's attention, Apple includes a framework called SafariServices. This framework allows us to incorporate the Safari browser into our app to offer a better experience to our users. The framework includes the **SFSafariViewController** class to create a view controller that incorporates its own view to display web pages and tools for navigation. The following are its initializers.

SFSafariViewController(url: URL**)**—This initializer creates a new Safari view controller that automatically loads the website indicated by the **url** attribute.

SFSafariViewController(url: URL, **configuration:** Configuration**)**—This initializer creates a new Safari view controller with the configuration specified by the **configuration** attribute that automatically loads the website indicated by the **url** attribute. The **configuration** attribute is a property of an object of the **Configuration** class included in the **SFSafariViewController** class. The properties available are **entersReaderIfAvailable** and **barCollapsingEnabled**.

To include a Safari view controller in our app, we have to create the controller with one of the initializers and present it as a modal view with the **present()** method. The following example creates a Safari View Controller to load the website www.formasterminds.com. The code assumes that we have included a button in the main view connected to an Action called **openWeb()**, as we did for the previous example.

```
import UIKit
import SafariServices

class ViewController: UIViewController {
    @IBAction func openWeb(_ sender: UIButton) {
        let url = URL(string: "http://www.formasterminds.com")
        let controller = SFSafariViewController(url: url!)
        present(controller, animated: true, completion: nil)
    }
}
```

Listing 27-3: Loading a website with a Safari view controller

 Do It Yourself: Update the **ViewController** class of previous examples with the code of Listing 27-3. Run the application and press the button. The system should open a modal view with a browser and the tools required for navigation.

The **SFSafariViewController** class also offers the following properties for configuration.

dismissButtonStyle—This property sets or returns a value that determines the type of button the view controller is going to show to dismiss the view. It is an enumeration of type **DismissButtonStyle** with the values **done** (default), **close**, and **cancel**.

preferredBarTintColor—This property sets or returns a **UIColor** value that determines the color of the bars.

preferredControlTintColor—This property sets or returns a **UIColor** value that determines the color of the controls.

The following example takes advantage of these properties to match the colors of the browser with the colors of the www.formasterminds.com website.

```
import UIKit
import SafariServices

class ViewController: UIViewController {
   @IBAction func openWeb(_ sender: UIButton) {
      let url = URL(string: "http://www.formasterminds.com")

      let controller = SFSafariViewController(url: url!)
      controller.dismissButtonStyle = .close
      controller.preferredBarTintColor = UIColor(red: 81/255, green:
91/255, blue: 119/255, alpha: 1.0)
      controller.preferredControlTintColor = UIColor.white
      present(controller, animated: true, completion: nil)
   }
}
```

Listing 27-4: Configuring the view

The code of Listing 27-4 also modifies the `dismissButtonStyle` property to change the type of button shown by the browser to close the view from Done to Close. The result is illustrated in Figure 27-1.

Figure 27-1: Custom Safari view controller

When the user scrolls the page, the controller collapses the bars to make more room for the content. This makes difficult for the user to dismiss the view or use its tools. If we think that is more appropriate for our app to always keep the bars at their original size, we can initialize the controller with a configuration object and assign the value false to the `barCollapsingEnabled` property. The `Configuration` class is defined inside the `SFSafariViewController` class and provides a simple initializer with no parameters. Once the object is created, we can configure its properties, and finally assign it to the Safari View Controller from the controller's initializer, as shown in the following example.

```
import UIKit
import SafariServices

class ViewController: UIViewController {
   @IBAction func openWeb(_ sender: UIButton) {
      let url = URL(string: "http://www.formasterminds.com")

      let config = SFSafariViewController.Configuration()
      config.barCollapsingEnabled = false
      let controller = SFSafariViewController(url: url!, configuration:
config)
```

Web

```
        present(controller, animated: true, completion: nil)
   }
}
```

Listing 27-5: Preserving the size of the bars

 Do It Yourself: Update the `ViewController` class with the code of Listing 27-5. Run the application and scroll the page. The bars should stay at the same size and the buttons should be always visible.

The framework also defines the `SFSafariViewControllerDelegate` protocol, so we can assign a delegate to the Safari View Controller to control the process. The following are some of the methods defined by this protocol.

safariViewController(SFSafariViewController, **didCompleteInitialLoad:** Bool)— This method is called by the controller when the initial website finish loading.

safariViewControllerDidFinish(SFSafariViewController)—This method is called by the controller when the view is dismissed (the user pressed the Done button).

The Safari View Controller includes the `delegate` property to define its delegate. The following example assigns the `ViewController` class as the delegate and implements the `safariViewControllerDidFinish()` method to deactivate the button on the interface when the user dismisses the view (the user is only able to open the view once).

```
import UIKit
import SafariServices

class ViewController: UIViewController, SFSafariViewControllerDelegate {
   @IBOutlet weak var openButton: UIButton!

   @IBAction func openWeb(_ sender: UIButton) {
      let url = URL(string: "http://www.formasterminds.com")
      let controller = SFSafariViewController(url: url!)
      controller.delegate = self
      present(controller, animated: true, completion: nil)
   }
   func safariViewControllerDidFinish(_ controller:
SFSafariViewController){
      openButton.isEnabled = false
   }
}
```

Listing 27-6: Assigning a delegate to the Safari view controller

27.3 WebKit Framework

Including a Safari web browser in our interface is a good way to keep the users inside our app, but in some cases this option is not customizable enough. To provide more alternatives, Apple offers the WebKit framework. With this framework we can display web content within a view. The class provided for this purpose is a subclass of `UIView` called `WKWebView`. The following is its initializer.

WKWebView(frame: CGRect, **configuration:** WKWebViewConfiguration)—This initializer creates a `WKWebView` with the size determined by the **frame** attribute and the configuration set by the **configuration** attribute.

The Object Library also includes an option to add a WebKit View to the Storyboard.

WebKit View - Displays embedded web content and enables content navigation.

Figure 27-2: Web View option in the Object Library

The **WKWebView** class provides the following properties and methods to load and manage the content.

title—This property returns a string with the current page's title.

url—This property returns a URL structure with the current page's URL.

customUserAgent—This property sets or returns a string with the name of the user agent (`nil` by default).

isLoading—This property returns a Boolean value that determines if the view is in the process of loading a URL or not.

canGoBack—This property returns a Boolean value that determines if the view can navigate to the previews page.

canGoForward—This property returns a Boolean value that determines if the view can navigate to the next page.

estimatedProgress—This property returns a value of type `Double` between 0.0 and 1.0 that determines the fraction of the content that has been already loaded.

load(URLRequest**)**—This method loads the content of a URL. The attribute is an object with the request for the URL we want to open.

goBack()—This method navigates to the previous web page on the list.

goForward()—This method navigates to the next web page on the list.

go(to: WKBackForwardListItem**)**—This method navigates to the web page indicated by the attribute. The **to** attribute is an object that represents a web page in a navigation list.

reload()—This method reloads the current page (it refreshes the web page).

stopLoading()—This method stops the loading of the content.

URLs are addresses that indicate the location of a file, but they also establish the kind of protocol we are going to use to set the connection with that location. The UIKit framework offers the **URLRequest** structure to manage this information. The structure includes the following initializers.

URLRequest(url: URL, **cachePolicy:** CachePolicy, **timeoutInterval:** Time-Interval**)**—This initializer creates a **URLRequest** structure for the URL and protocol specified by the **url** attribute (the information of the protocol is taken from the URL itself). The **cachePolicy** attribute is an enumeration that determines how the request will work with the cache. The possible values are: **useProtocolCachePolicy** (default), **reloadIgnoringLocalCacheData**, **reloadIgnoringLocalAndRemoteCacheData**, **returnCacheDataElseLoad**, **returnCacheDataDontLoad**, and **reloadRevalidatingCacheData**. The **timeoutInterval** attribute is the maximum time allowed to the system to process the request (60.0 by default).

URLRequest(url: URL)—This initializer creates a `URLRequest` structure for the URL and protocol specified by the **url** attribute (the rest of the parameters required by the request are defined with values by default).

A WebKit View can report the state of the content through a delegate. For this purpose, the framework defines the `WKNavigationDelegate` protocol. The following are some of its methods.

webView(WKWebView, **decidePolicyFor:** WKNavigationAction, **decision-Handler:** Block)—This method is called on the delegate to determine if the view should process a request. The **decidePolicyFor** attribute is an object with information about the request, and the **decisionHandler** attribute is a closure that we have to execute to report our decision. The closure takes a value of type `WKNavigationActionPolicy`, an enumeration with the properties `cancel` and `allow`.

webView(WKWebView, **didStartProvisionalNavigation:** WKNavigation!)—This method is called on the delegate when the view begins loading new content.

webView(WKWebView, **didFinish:** WKNavigation!)—This method is called on the delegate when the view finishes loading the content.

webView(WKWebView, **didFailProvisionalNavigation:** WKNavigation!, **with-Error:** Error)—This method is called on the delegate when an error occurs loading the content.

webView(WKWebView, **didReceiveServerRedirectForProvisionalNavigation:** WKNavigation!)—This method is called on the delegate when the server redirects the navigator to a different destination.

The process to load a website in a WebKit View is simple. We have to get the URL, create a request, and ask the view to load it.

```
import UIKit
import WebKit

class ViewController: UIViewController {
   @IBOutlet weak var webView: WKWebView!

   override func viewDidLoad() {
      super.viewDidLoad()

      if let webURL = URL(string: "https://www.google.com") {
         let request = URLRequest(url: webURL)
         webView.load(request)
      }
   }
}
```

Listing 27-7: Loading a website with a WebKit View

The example of Listing 27-7 assumes that we have added a WebKit View to the interface and it is connected to the **ViewController** class with an Outlet called **webView**. To prepare the request, we get the **URL** structure with the address we want to access and initialize the **URLRequest** structure with standard values. Finally, the request is loaded with the **load()** method and the website is shown on the screen.

Do It Yourself: Create a new Single View Application project. Add a WebKit View to the initial view and pin it to the edges of the main view. Connect the WebKit View to the **ViewController** class with an Outlet called **webView**. Complete the **ViewController** class with the code of Listing 27-7. Run the application. You should see Google's website on the screen.

With this process, we can load any website we want, including those specified or selected by the user (we just have to remember to prepare the URL the way we did before for links in Listing 27-2). But users need more control over the content. For instance, if we use the previous example to perform a search in Google, we will notice right away that there is no way to go back to the previous page or start again from the beginning. WebKit views offer several methods to manipulate their content, and also a delegate we can define to respond to changes. To introduce these tools in our application, we are going to work with an interface that includes a Navigation Bar with three buttons to go back, forward, and refresh the page.

Figure 27-3: Custom web browser for our application

Before modifying the content of a WebKit View we need to know what we can do and what we can't. For example, we can only go backwards if the user has already navigated forward. This is when the delegate becomes useful. Implementing the **webView(WKWebView, didFinish:)** method, we can check the status of the content every time a new document is loaded. The following is the **ViewController** class for the initial view of the interface of Figure 27-3.

```
import UIKit
import WebKit

class ViewController: UIViewController, WKNavigationDelegate {
    @IBOutlet weak var backButton: UIBarButtonItem!
    @IBOutlet weak var forwardButton: UIBarButtonItem!
    @IBOutlet weak var refreshButton: UIBarButtonItem!
    @IBOutlet weak var webView: WKWebView!

    override func viewDidLoad() {
        super.viewDidLoad()
        backButton.isEnabled = false
        forwardButton.isEnabled = false
        webView.navigationDelegate = self
        if let webURL = URL(string: "https://www.google.com") {
            let request = URLRequest(url: webURL)
            webView.load(request)
        }
    }
    @IBAction func moveBack(_ sender: UIBarButtonItem) {
        webView.goBack()
    }
    @IBAction func moveForward(_ sender: UIBarButtonItem) {
        webView.goForward()
    }
```

```
@IBAction func refresh(_ sender: UIBarButtonItem) {
    webView.reload()
}
func webView(_ webView: WKWebView, didFinish navigation:
WKNavigation!) {
    backButton.isEnabled = webView.canGoBack
    forwardButton.isEnabled = webView.canGoForward
}
}
```

Listing 27-8: Implementing a custom web browser

The **WKWebView** class includes the **navigationDelegate** property to designate a delegate for the view. In Listing 27-8, we assign the view controller as the delegate and then implement the **webView(WKWebView, didFinish:)** method to modify the interface every time a new page is loaded. When the view is displayed for the first time, the buttons are disabled because only one document was loaded into the view at the moment, but after a new document is loaded, this delegate method is executed, and the state of the buttons is modified from the values of the **canGoBack** and **canGoForward** properties, activating the buttons only when there are documents to go to.

 Do It Yourself: Create a new Single View Application project. Embed the initial view in a Navigation Controller. Add a WebKit View to the initial view and pin it to the sides of the view (below the Navigation Bar). Connect the view with an Outlet called **webView**. Add three Bar Buttons to the Navigation Bar (you can change the appearance of the buttons from the System Item option in the Attributes Inspector panel). Connect the buttons to Outlets called **backButton**, **forwardButton**, and **refreshButton**, and to Actions called **moveBack()**, **moveForward()**, and **refresh()**. Complete the **ViewController** class with the code of Listing 27-8. Run the application and search for a word. Click on a link in the results. The buttons in the Navigation Bar should activate or deactivate according to your location in the navigation history.

 IMPORTANT: The WebKit framework also offers tools to process cookies and JavaScript code, which allow us to interact with the web page's content. The topic is beyond the scope of this book. For more information, visit our website and follow the links for this chapter.

App Transport Security

In the latest examples, we opened secure URLs (URLs that begin with the prefix https://), because these are the URLs allowed by default. iOS implements a system called App Transport Security (ATS) to block insecure URLs, like those starting with the prefix http:// (without the s). If we need to load insecure URLs, such as http://www.formasterminds.com, we can configure our app from the info.plist file to circumvent this security measure for every website or specific domains. The option to configure the App Transport Security system is called "App Transport Security Settings". After we select this option, we will see something similar to Figure 27-4.

Key	Type	Value	
▼ Information Property List	Dictionary	(16 items)	
▶ App Transport Security Settings ⬍	Dictionary	(0 items)	
Localization native development re... ⬍	String	en	⬍
Executable file ⬍	String	$(EXECUTABLE_NAME)	

Figure 27-4: Option to configure App Transport Security

Web

The interface includes a + button on the right side of the item to add values to that item. In this case, the button has two functions: if the arrow on the left is pointing to the item (closed), a new item is added to the main list, but if the arrow is pointing down (expanded), the new item is added to the item as a new value (we can click the arrow to close or expand the item). Values added to an item are shown below the item with a little indentation to reflect the hierarchy. The value we need to add to the App Transport Security Settings item to allow insecure URLs to be opened from our app is called "Allow Arbitrary Loads". Figure 27-5 shows what the list looks like after we add this value.

Key		Type	Value
▼ Information Property List		Dictionary	(16 items)
▼ App Transport Security Settings	↕	Dictionary	(1 item)
Allow Arbitrary Loads	↕	Boolean	YES
Localization native development re...	↕	String	en

Figure 27-5: App Transport Security configured to allow insecure URLs

The Allow Arbitrary Loads key represents a Boolean value specified with the strings YES and NO. Setting this key to YES allows any URL to be opened. If what we want is to allow only specific domains, we have to use the Exception Domains key and add to the key additional items with the domains we want to include. These items in turn require at least three more items with the keys **NSIncludesSubdomains** (Boolean), **NSTemporaryExceptionAllowsInsecureHTTPLoads** (Boolean), and **NSTemporaryExceptionMinimumTLSVersion** (String). For example, the following configuration allows documents from the formasterminds.com domain to be opened.

Key		Type	Value
▼ Information Property List		Dictionary	(16 items)
▼ App Transport Security Settings	↕	Dictionary	(1 item)
▼ Exception Domains	↕	Dictionary	(1 item)
▼ formasterminds.com		Dictionary	(3 items)
NSIncludesSubdomains		Boolean	YES
NSTemporaryExceptionAllowsInsecureHTTPLoads		Boolean	YES
NSTemporaryExceptionMinimumTLSVersion		String	TLSv1.1
Localization native development region	↕	String	en

Figure 27-6: App Transport Security configured to allow URLs from formasterminds.com

27.4 Web Content

The Safari view controller and WebKit Views were designed to show content to the user, but the capacity to integrate that content with our app is limited. Sometimes all we need is to extract a piece of information from the document or process its data instead of showing the entire content as it is. In cases like this, we have to load the document in the background and analyze it to extract only what we need. Foundation includes a group of classes to get content referenced by a URL. The main class is called **URLSession**. This class creates a session that manages an HTTP connection to obtain data, and download, or upload files. The following are the type property and initializers provided by the class to create the session.

shared—This type property returns a standard session with a configuration by default that is suitable to perform basic requests.

URLSession(configuration: URLSessionConfiguration**)**—This initializer creates a new session with the configuration set by its attribute. The **configuration** attribute is an object that specifies the session's behaviour.

URLSession(configuration: URLSessionConfiguration, **delegate:** URLSession-Delegate?, **delegateQueue:** OperationQueue?**)**—This initializer creates a new

Web

session with the configuration set by its attributes. The **configuration** attribute is an object that specifies the session's behaviour, the **delegate** attribute is a reference to the delegate object we want to assign to the session, and the **delegateQueue** attribute is the queue in which the delegate methods and completion handlers are going to be called.

The session sets up the connection, but it does not perform any task. To download or upload data we have to create a `URLSessionTask` object with a specific task and add it to the session. The `URLSession` class includes the following methods to create tasks to download data and download or upload files.

dataTask(with: URL, **completionHandler:** Block)—This method creates a task to download data and adds it to the session. The **with** attribute is the URL with the location of the data, and the **completionHandler** attribute is a closure that is executed when the task is completed. The closure receives three optional attributes, a `Data` structure with the data returned by the request, a `URLResponse` object with the status of the request, and an `Error` value to indicate if an error occurred. There is an additional implementation of this method that takes a `URLRequest` object instead of a `URL` structure.

downloadTask(with: URL, **completionHandler:** Block)—This method creates a task to download a file and adds it to the session. The **with** attribute is a URL with the location of the file, and the **completionHandler** attribute is a closure that is executed when the task is completed. The closure receives three optional attributes, a `URL` structure with the location of a temporary file that represents the file downloaded, a `URLResponse` object with the status of the request, and an `Error` value to indicate if an error occurred. There is an additional implementation of this method that takes a `URLRequest` object instead of a `URL` structure.

uploadTask(with: URLRequest, **from:** Data?, **completionHandler:** Block)—This method creates a task to upload a file and adds it to the session. The **with** attribute is a request with the URL where we want to upload the file, the **from** attribute is a `Data` structure with the data we want to use to create the file, and the **completionHandler** attribute is a closure that is executed when the task is completed. The closure receives three optional attributes, a `Data` structure with the data returned by the server, a `URLResponse` object with the status of the request, and an `Error` value to indicate if an error occurred.

uploadTask(with: URLRequest, **fromFile:** URL, **completionHandler:** Block)— This method creates a task to upload a file and adds it to the session. The **with** attribute is a `URLRequest` object with the URL where we want to upload the file, the **fromFile** attribute is a `URL` structure with the location of the file we want to upload, and the **completionHandler** attribute is a closure that is executed when the task is completed. The closure receives three optional attributes, a `Data` structure with the data returned by the server, a `URLResponse` object with the status of the request, and an `Error` value to indicate if an error occurred.

The objects returned by these methods are subclasses of the `URLSessionTask` class (`URLSessionDataTask`, `URLSessionDownloadTask`, and `URLSessionUploadTask`). All these subclasses include the following methods to control the task.

cancel()—This method cancels the task.

resume()—This method starts or resumes the task.

suspend()—This method suspends the task until it is resumed.

When the task is finished, it sends the results to a closure for processing. For example, if we use the `dataTask()` method to get data from a website, the closure for this task receives a value with the data and an object of type **URLResponse** with the status of the request. When we access a URL using the HTTP protocol, the response is represented by an object of type **HTTPURLResponse** (a subclass of **URLResponse**). This class includes the **statusCode** property to return a code that determines the status of the request. There are several values available to determine things like the success of the request (200) or more drastic situations like when the website has been moved to a different address (301). If all we want is to make sure that the data was downloaded correctly, we have to check if the value of the **statusCode** property is equal to 200 before processing anything. The following example shows how to perform a basic request.

```
import UIKit

class ViewController: UIViewController {
    override func viewDidLoad() {
        super.viewDidLoad()

        let webURL = URL(string: "https://www.yahoo.com")
        let request = URLRequest(url: webURL!)

        let session = URLSession.shared
        let task = session.dataTask(with: request, completionHandler: {
(data, response, error) in
            if error == nil && data != nil {
                if let resp = response as? HTTPURLResponse {
                    let status = resp.statusCode
                    if status == 200 {
                        let content = String(data: data!, encoding:
String.Encoding.ascii)
                        print(content!)
                    } else {
                        print("Error")
                    }
                }
            } else {
                print("Error")
            }
        })
        task.resume()
    }
}
```

Listing 27-9: Loading a remote document

The example of Listing 27-9 loads the content of the website at www.yahoo.com and prints it on the console. Because we are just loading a single web page, the standard session returned by the **shared** property is more than enough. We add to this session a task to download data and then call the **resume()** method at the end to perform the task. When the task is finished, we turn the data into a string with the **String()** initializer and then print the string on the console.

A standard session like the one we used in this example comes with a configuration by default that is suitable for most situations, but a custom session requires its own configuration. To configure a session, the loading system provides a class called **URLSessionConfiguration** with type methods and properties to set a specific configuration. The following is a type property we can use to get an object with values by default that we can adapt later to the requirements of our application.

default—This property returns a **URLSessionConfiguration** object with default settings.

The following are some of the properties offered by the **URLSessionConfiguration** class to modify the configuration.

allowsCellularAccess—This property sets or returns a Boolean value that determines if the connection should be made when the device is connected to a cellular network.

timeoutIntervalForRequest—This property sets or returns a **TimeInterval** value (a typealias of **Double**) that determines the number of seconds the session should wait for a request to be answered. The value by default is 60.

waitsForConnectivity—This property sets or returns a Boolean value that determines if the session should wait to perform the request until the device gets connected to the network. The value by default is **false**.

Working with custom sessions only requires us to change how the session is initialized, but the rest of the code remains the same.

```
import UIKit

class ViewController: UIViewController {
    override func viewDidLoad() {
        super.viewDidLoad()
        let webURL = URL(string: "https://www.yahoo.com")
        let request = URLRequest(url: webURL!)

        let config = URLSessionConfiguration.default
        config.waitsForConnectivity = true

        let session = URLSession(configuration: config)
        let task = session.dataTask(with: request, completionHandler: {
(data, response, error) in
            if error == nil && data != nil {
                if let resp = response as? HTTPURLResponse {
                    let status = resp.statusCode
                    if status == 200 {
                        let content = String(data: data!, encoding:
String.Encoding.ascii)
                        print(content!)
                    } else {
                        print("Error")
                    }
                }
            } else {
                print("Error")
            }
        })
        task.resume()
    }
}
```

Listing 27-10: Instantiating a custom session

 Do It Yourself: Create a new Single View Application project. Update the **ViewController** class with the codes of Listings 27-9 or 27-10. Run the application. You should see the HTML code of Yahoo's website printed on the console.

Custom sessions are useful when we need to respond to particular circumstances like the website being redirected or a request for authentication. These situations are managed by delegates of the session. The loading system defines a total of four protocols with methods specific for every type of task. The **URLSessionDelegate** protocol defines methods to handle session events, the **URLSessionTaskDelegate** protocol defines methods to handle events that are common to every task, the **URLSessionDataDelegate** protocol defines methods to handle data and upload tasks events, and the **URLSessionDownloadDelegate** protocol defines methods to handle download tasks events. Usually, a session requires only a few methods to respond to common situations. For example, the **URLSessionDelegate** protocol includes the following method to provide authentication for a secure connection.

urlSession(URLSession, **didReceive:** URLAuthenticationChallenge, **completionHandler:** Block)—This method is called on the delegate when authentication is requested by the server. Our implementation must call the completion handler received by the method with two attributes that define the settings and credentials.

There is also a useful method defined in the **URLSessionTaskDelegate** protocol to respond to a redirection.

urlSession(URLSession, **task:** URLSessionTask, **willPerformHTTPRedirection:** HTTPURLResponse, **newRequest:** URLRequest, **completionHandler:** Block)— This method is called on the delegate when the server redirected the connection to another URL. Our implementation must call the completion handler received by the method with an attribute that defines the new request (the value of the **newRequest** attribute) or the value **nil** if we do not want to follow the redirection.

Some websites, like www.google.com, send the user to a different address that contains a version of the website customized according to the user's location or preferences. This means that the URL we provide is not the final destination; the server does not return any data but instead redirects the user to another document. We can define a custom session with a delegate and then implement the method of the **URLSessionTaskDelegate** protocol to determine what we want to do when the server is redirecting.

```swift
import UIKit
class ViewController: UIViewController, URLSessionTaskDelegate {
    override func viewDidLoad() {
        super.viewDidLoad()
        let webURL = URL(string: "https://www.google.com")
        let request = URLRequest(url: webURL!)
        let config = URLSessionConfiguration.default
        config.waitsForConnectivity = true

        let session = URLSession(configuration: config, delegate: self,
delegateQueue: nil)
        let task = session.dataTask(with: request, completionHandler: {
(data, response, error) in
            if error == nil && data != nil {
                if let resp = response as? HTTPURLResponse {
                    let status = resp.statusCode
                    if status == 200 {
                        let content = String(data: data!, encoding:
String.Encoding.ascii)
                        print(content!)
                    } else {
                        print("Error")
                    }
                }
            }
```

```
        } else {
            print("Error")
        }
    })
    task.resume()
}
func urlSession(_ session: URLSession, task: URLSessionTask,
willPerformHTTPRedirection response: HTTPURLResponse, newRequest request:
URLRequest, completionHandler: @escaping (URLRequest?) -> Void) {
    completionHandler(request)
}
}
```

Listing 27-11: Following a redirection

In the example of Listing 27-11, we define the **ViewController** class as the delegate of our session and call the closure received by the protocol method with the value of the new request. Every time the server asks for a redirection, the protocol method is called and the request with the new URL is executed. The process repeats until the final destination is reached and then the content of that document is again printed on the console.

JSON

Normal websites return documents written in HTML code. This is the basic language used by every website. It is composed of predefined tags that are in charge of delineating the document's data. For example, the tags <title> and </title> enclose the title of the document, so we can use string methods to find the location of the last character of the <title> tag and the first character of the </title> tag and then cut the text in the middle to extract the title. The problem with this approach is that most tags in HTML have the same name, making it very difficult to identify the information we want to retrieve. Also, websites do not follow a predefined structure and their code may be changed without a warning. If we create an app that extracts information from the HTML code of a web page, it may stop working before we even ship the app to the App Store. This is not only a problem for mobile applications but also for web applications in general. The solution was found a long time ago with the creation of formatting languages that have the exclusive purpose of transmitting data through the web. Some are considered programming languages and others are just format specifications, like JSON.

JSON (Javascript Object Notation) proposes a dictionary-like organization for the data. Every piece of data is stored with a key/value pair and related values are enclosed in braces. The advantage of this format is that the information is easy to find. Every value has its unique key.

Because of its format, JSON files can easily be converted into Swift structure that we can process as any other structure in our code. Foundation includes the **JSONDecoder** class to decode JSON data into Swift structures and the **JSONEncoder** class to encode Swift structures into JSON data. The classes include their respective methods to decode and encode the values.

decode(Type, **from:** Data**)**—This method returns a value of the type specified by the first attribute with the information contained by the **from** attribute. The **from** attribute is a **Data** structure that contains the JSON data we want to decode.

encode(Value**)**—This method returns a JSON representation of the data provided by the attribute.

For the structures to be decodable, they have to conform to the **Codable** protocol. This is a protocol that defines initializers and methods required to encode and decode the values of the properties (see Chapter 21). For example, the following is a JSON file that contains information about a book.

```
{
    "title": "The Shining",
    "author": "Stephen King"
}
```

Listing 27-12: JSON file

To convert this data to a value we can process in Swift, we have to create a structure that conforms to the **Codable** protocol and includes all the properties required to represent the values we want to read.

```
struct Book: Codable {
    let title: String
    let author: String
}
```

Listing 27-13: Swift structure

Because the structure conforms to the **Codable** protocol, it is ready for coding and decoding, so we can use it to read the JSON file of Listing 27-12. The following view controller demonstrates how we have to proceed to turn the JSON data into a **Book** structure and read its values (Notice that the data type is declared with the **self** keyword. This is because we want to reference the data type, not a value of that type).

```
import UIKit

class ViewController: UIViewController {
    override func viewDidLoad() {
        super.viewDidLoad()

        let decoder = JSONDecoder()
        do {
            let info = try decoder.decode(Book.self, from: jsonData)
            print("Title: \(info.title)")
            print("Author: \(info.author)")
        } catch {
            print("Error: \(error)")
        }
    }
}
```

Listing 27-14: Decoding JSON data

This example is not functional because it assumes that we have already loaded the JSON data from a file or the Internet and store it in a property called **jsonData**, but it shows how simple it is to extract information from a JSON file and process it. Of course, JSON data is not always that simple. We will usually find nested values that require us to define structures inside structures to represent them. For example, the following JSON file expands the previous example to include information about the publisher and the publication date.

```
{
    "title": "The Shining",
    "author": "Stephen King",
    "publisher": {
        "name": "Random House",
```

```
        "date": "2008-06-24T13:30:52.123Z"
    }
}
```

Listing 27-15: Nested data

To read these values, we have to define a structure that represents the values of the publisher inside another structure that represents the values of the book.

```
struct Publisher: Codable {
    let name: String
    let date: String
}
struct Book: Codable {
    let title: String
    let author: String
    let publisher: Publisher
}
```

Listing 27-16: Defining nested structures

Every time we have to read a JSON structure with nested values, we first have to define a structure to represent the nested values and then include a property of that type to store the values. In the example of Listing 27-16, we define the `Publisher` structure first to represent the values for the publisher's name and date, and then include the `publisher` property inside the `Book` structure to store the values (all the structures have to conform to the `Codable` protocol).

The process to read the JSON file with nested structures is the same as before, we just have to use dot notation to access all the values. In the following view controller, we process the JSON file of Listing 27-15 with the structures of Listing 27-16 and print the value of the `name` property of the `Publisher` structure on the console.

```
import UIKit

class ViewController: UIViewController {
    override func viewDidLoad() {
        super.viewDidLoad()
        let decoder = JSONDecoder()
        do {
            let info = try decoder.decode(Book.self, from: jsonData!)
            print("Title: \(info.title)")
            print("Author: \(info.author)")
            print("Publisher: \(info.publisher.name)")
        } catch {
            print("Error: \(error)")
        }
    }
}
```

Listing 27-17: Reading values in a nested structure

So far, we have interpreted every value in the JSON structure as a string, but JSON can also include numbers. Furthermore, some of the values, like dates and URLs, are not processed as strings in Swift but as values of a specific data type, such as `Date` and `URL` structures. For numbers and URLs, the process is simple, we just have to declare the properties as `Int`, `Float`, or `URL`, and the decoder takes care of converting the values for us, but for the correct interpretation of dates we have to declare what kind of format the decoder has to use. For this purpose, the `JSONDecoder` class includes the following property.

dateDecodingStrategy—This property defines a strategy the decoder has to follow to decode a date. It is an enumeration of type `DateDecodingStrategy` with the values `millisecondsSince1970`, `secondsSince1970`, `deferredToDate`, and `iso8601`. The enumeration also includes the methods `formatted()` and `custom()` to define custom formats.

As we already mentioned, we have to specify the data types we want to use in the definition of the structures. For instance, if we want to process the date property as a date, we have to declare it of type `Date`. The following code defines the `Publisher` structure we used before with the right data types and an additional property to store the number of the edition.

```
struct Publisher: Codable {
    let name: String
    let date: Date
    let edition: Int
}
struct Book: Codable {
    let title: String
    let author: String
    let publisher: Publisher
}
```

Listing 27-18: Using specific data types

The following is the possible JSON data we may be looking to decode with these structures.

```
{
    "title": "The Shining",
    "author": "Stephen King",
    "publisher": {
        "name": "Random House",
        "date": "2008-06-24T13:30:52Z",
        "edition": 2
    }
}
```

Listing 27-19: JSON data with values of different types

To convert this JSON data into the corresponding structures, we have to tell the decoder the format we want to use for the date. Because in this case the JSON data includes a date in the ISO 8601 format, we just have to assign the value `iso8601` to the `dateDecodingStrategy` property and the decoder will have enough information to decode it.

```
import UIKit

class ViewController: UIViewController {
    override func viewDidLoad() {
        super.viewDidLoad()

        let decoder = JSONDecoder()
        decoder.dateDecodingStrategy = .iso8601
        do {
            let info = try decoder.decode(Book.self, from: jsonData!)
            print("Title: \(info.title)")
            print("Author: \(info.author)")
            print("Publisher: \(info.publisher.date)")
            print("Edition: \(info.publisher.edition)")
```

```
      } catch {
         print("Error: \(error)")
      }
   }
}
```

Listing 27-20: Converting dates

In these examples, we have used a custom JSON file with hard-coded values, but JSON files are usually downloaded from the web. Website share information using JSON to make it easy for other websites or applications to access it. But web pages are not automatically translated into JSON files. Developers decide what information to share and how to share it. For example, Yahoo does not offer a JSON document with the data of its home page, but it does offer a JSON file with information about the weather. These services are specific of each website and are usually included as an additional service with its own website and domain. For example, the API provided by Yahoo to generate JSON documents with information about the weather is available at https://developer.yahoo.com/weather/. From these special websites, we can get the URLs to access the JSON documents and download the data we need for our application. The following is the JSON file returned by Yahoo when we ask for information about the weather in the city of San Diego.

```
{
   "query": {
      "count": 1,
      "created": "2017-11-02T20:18:15Z",
      "lang": "en-US",
      "results": {
         "channel": {
            "item": {
               "condition": {
                  "code": "30",
                  "date": "Thu, 02 Nov 2017 12:00 PM PDT",
                  "temp": "71",
                  "text": "Partly Cloudy"
               }
            }
         }
      }
   }
}
```

Listing 27-21: JSON file provided by Yahoo

To process this information in our app, we have to download the data from the web with a `URLSession` object and then convert it into Swift structures, as we did before. The following is the view controller we have created to process the data in Listing 27-21.

```
import UIKit

class ViewController: UIViewController {
   override func viewDidLoad() {
      super.viewDidLoad()
      let webURL = URL(string:
"https://query.yahooapis.com/v1/public/yql?q=select%20item.condition%20fr
om%20weather.forecast%20where%20woeid%20%3D%202487889&format=json&env=sto
re%3A%2F%2Fdatatables.org%2Falltableswithkeys")
      let request = URLRequest(url: webURL!)
      let session = URLSession.shared
```

```
        let task = session.dataTask(with: request, completionHandler:
{ (data, response, error) in
        if error == nil && data != nil {
            if let resp = response as? HTTPURLResponse {
                let status = resp.statusCode
                if status == 200 {
                    self.getValues(jsonData: data!)
                } else {
                    print("Error")
                }
            }
        } else {
            print("Error")
        }
    })
    task.resume()
    }
}
```

Listing 27-22: Loading a JSON file from Yahoo

The code of Listing 27-22 loads the JSON document and then calls a method called **getValues()** to read the data. The values provided by Yahoo are nested one inside another, so we have to create several structures to represent them. The following is a possible implementation of our **getValues()** method (we have defined the structures inside the method to simplify the example).

```
func getValues(jsonData: Data) {
    struct Condition: Codable {
        let temp: String
        let text: String
        let date: Date
    }
    struct Item: Codable {
        let condition: Condition
    }
    struct Channel: Codable {
        let item: Item
    }
    struct Results: Codable {
        let channel: Channel
    }
    struct Query: Codable {
        let results: Results
    }
    struct JsonResults: Codable {
        let query: Query
    }

    let formatter = DateFormatter()
    formatter.dateFormat = "EEE, dd MMM yyyy h:mm a z"

    let decoder = JSONDecoder()
    decoder.dateDecodingStrategy = .formatted(formatter)
    do {
        let info = try decoder.decode(JsonResults.self, from: jsonData)
        print("Temperature:
\(info.query.results.channel.item.condition.temp)")
        print("Condition:
\(info.query.results.channel.item.condition.text)")
```

```
        print("Date: \(info.query.results.channel.item.condition.date)")
    } catch {
        print("Error: \(error)")
    }
}
```

Listing 27-23: Converting JSON data

Except for the number of the structures we had to define, there is no difference between this process and the one used before to read our custom JSON data. The only change we had to perform is in how the decoder is going to interpret the date. The date provided by Yahoo is in a custom format, so we had to define the same custom format with a **DateFormatter** object (see **DateFormatter** in Chapter 4). After converting the values, the method prints them on the console.

 Do It Yourself: Create a new Single View Application project. Update the **ViewController** class with the code of Listing 27-22. Add the method of Listing 27-23 to the class and run the application. You should see the value of the temperature in San Diego on the console. You can get the link to the JSON document from Yahoo's website. Go to **developer.yahoo.com/weather/**, select the example of San Diego from the list, and select the option JSON from the responses. The web page shows the JSON code generated for the document and the link to the document. You can select other examples and adapt the code to extract the information according to the keys available in each document.

 IMPORTANT: Working with values downloaded from the web is never safe. The values may be corrupted or modified before getting to the user's device. In these examples, we have just printed the decoded values, but when they have to be processed or stored in the device, you should always check that their data types are correct by converting them with the **as?** operator. For more information on how to decode and protect your users, visit our website and follow the links for this chapter.

 The Basics: The keys used in a JSON document are selected by the developer. Every developer decides what keys to use and how to structure the information. To know the keys used to construct the hierarchy, you have to load the JSON document in your browser or find examples on the website.

XML

XML is similar to JSON, but instead of key/value pairs it uses tags, like HTML. The difference between XML and HTML is that the tags use custom names, so every tag is defined by the developer and may represent a specific value. Foundation provides the **XMLParser** class to create an XML parser. The class includes the following initializers.

XMLParser(contentsOf: URL)—This initializer creates an XML parser to parse the XML document at the location specified by the **contentsOf** attribute.

XMLParser(data: Data)—This initializer creates an XML parser to parse the XML document provided by the attribute. The attribute is a **Data** structure with the data returned by a request.

The initializers load the XML document and create the **XMLParser** object, but the parsing is controlled by the object's methods.

parse()—This method starts the parsing of the document.

abortParsing()—This method interrupts the parsing of the document.

The way an XML parser works is different than a JSON parser. The XML document is read line by line and every time a new element or content is found the parser calls delegate methods to process the values. Foundation includes the **XMLParserDelegate** protocol to define these methods.

parserDidStartDocument(XMLParser**)**—This method is called on the delegate when the parser begins parsing the document.

parserDidEndDocument(XMLParser**)**—This method is called on the delegate when the parser ends parsing the document.

parser(XMLParser, **didStartElement:** String, **namespaceURI:** String?, **qualifiedName:** String?, **attributes:** Dictionary**)**—This method is called on the delegate when the parser finds an opening tag (e.g., **<title>**).

parser(XMLParser, **didEndElement:** String, **namespaceURI:** String?, **qualifiedName:** String?**)**—This method is called on the delegate when the parser finds a closing tag (e.g., **</title>**).

parser(XMLParser, **foundCharacters:** String**)**—This method is called on the delegate when the parser starts parsing the characters enclosed by the tags. The parser may take several attempts to parse all the characters. To get the entire value, we have to concatenate the strings received from the **foundCharacters** attribute until the closing tag is found.

Because a parser may be created from a URL, the code to load the XML document is simpler than the one we used to parse JSON documents. We have to create the **XMLParser** object with a URL pointing to an XML document and then call the **parse()** method to start parsing the document.

```
import UIKit

class ViewController: UIViewController, XMLParserDelegate {
    override func viewDidLoad() {
        super.viewDidLoad()
        let webURL = URL(string:
"https://query.yahooapis.com/v1/public/yql?q=select%20item.condition%20fr
om%20weather.forecast%20where%20woeid%20%3D%202487889&format=xml&env=stor
e%3A%2F%2Fdatatables.org%2Falltableswithkeys")
        if let parser = XMLParser(contentsOf: webURL!) {
            parser.delegate = self
            parser.parse()
        }
    }
    func parser(_ parser: XMLParser, didStartElement elementName: String,
namespaceURI: String?, qualifiedName qName: String?, attributes
attributeDict: [String : String] = [:]) {
        if elementName == "yweather:condition" {
            print(attributeDict["temp"]!)
        }
    }
}
```

Listing 27-24: Parsing an XML document

The Yahoo weather API does not store the values between tags but in attributes inside the opening tags (e.g., `<yweather temp="58">`). For this reason, we only need to implement the `parser(XMLParser, didStartElement:, namespaceURI:, qualifiedName:, attributes:)` method that is called when an opening tag is found. This method receives the name of the current element and a dictionary containing the names and values of its attributes. To get the value we want, all we have to do is to check if the current tag is the one containing those values and then read it from the `attributesDict` dictionary. In Listing 27-24, we check if the value of the `elementName` attribute is equal to the element that is storing the weather data (yweather:condition) and then read its temp attribute to get the temperature.

Do It Yourself: Replace the `ViewController` class in the project created for JSON documents by the class in Listing 27-24 and run the application. You should see the value of the temperature printed on the console. You can get the link to the XML document from Yahoo's website. Go to **developer.yahoo.com/weather/**, select the example of San Diego from the list and select the option XML from the responses. The web page shows the XML code generated for the document and the link to the document below. You can select other examples and adapt the code to extract the information according to the keys available in each document.

27.5 Social Networks

Social networks like Facebook and Twitter also provide their own services to share data. Using these services, we can get information from the user's account and also post messages and pictures on behalf of the user. These are very complex services that usually require us to open a developer account, register our application, and even ask permission to implement some features, but Apple has simplified the process by letting applications share information between them. The service is provided through the Activity View Controller.

Activity View Controller

The Activity View Controller is created from the `UIActivityViewController` class. The class presents a view with icons to let the users select the application they want to share the information with (the applications are called *Activities*). The controller cannot only send the information to social networks but also to applications such as Mail, Notes, Camera Roll, and the printer, among others.

The `UIActivityViewController` class is a very powerful but simple class. To create the view controller, we just have to initialize the object and determine the options we want to offer. The following are its initializer and property.

UIActivityViewController(activityItems: [Any], applicationActivities: [UIActivity]?)—This initializer creates an Activity Controller to send the information specified by the **activityItems** attribute. The **activityItems** attribute is an array with the data we want to share, and the **applicationActivities** attribute is an array with values that represent the custom services we want to include in the list (declared as `nil` when we only need to present the activities provided by the system).

excludedActivityTypes—This property sets or returns an array of values that represent the activities we want to exclude from the controller. The values are provided by properties of the ActivityType structure included in the **UIActivity** class. The properties available are `addToReadingList, airDrop, assignToContact, copyToPasteboard, mail, message,` openInIBooks, postToFacebook, postToFlickr, postToTencentWeibo, postToTwitter, postToVimeo, postToWeibo, print, saveToCameraRoll, and markupAsPDF.

The information that is going to be sent to the view controller depends on the destination we consider appropriate for our application. For example, if we want to let the user store a message in the Notes application, we just have to provide the text. Social networks can receive three values: a message, a URL, and an image. In the following example, we decided to use the capacity of Facebook and Twitter to post images and created an interface to let users post pictures taken with the camera.

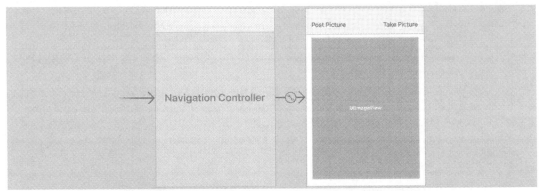

Figure 27-7: *Interface to post pictures on social networks*

The interface of Figure 27-7 includes an Image View to show the picture and two bar buttons, one called Take Picture to open the **UIImagePickerController** controller used to take the picture and another called Post Picture to open the **UIActivityViewController** controller to let the user post the picture in the social network of preference.

The code to configure and open the view controller for the camera is exactly the same we used in Chapter 26. When the user takes a picture, we store it in a property for later use.

```
import UIKit

class ViewController: UIViewController, UINavigationControllerDelegate,
UIImagePickerControllerDelegate {
    @IBOutlet weak var pictureView: UIImageView!
    var picture: UIImage?

    @IBAction func takePicture(_ sender: UIBarButtonItem) {
        let mediaPicker = UIImagePickerController()
        mediaPicker.delegate = self
        let sourceAvailable =
UIImagePickerController.isSourceTypeAvailable(.camera)

        if sourceAvailable {
            mediaPicker.sourceType = .camera
            mediaPicker.mediaTypes = ["public.image"]
            mediaPicker.allowsEditing = false
            mediaPicker.cameraCaptureMode = .photo
            present(mediaPicker, animated: true, completion: nil)
        } else {
            print("The media is not available")
        }
    }
```

```
    func imagePickerController(_ picker: UIImagePickerController,
didFinishPickingMediaWithInfo info: [UIImagePickerController.InfoKey :
Any]) {
        picture = info[.originalImage] as? UIImage
        pictureView.image = picture
        dismiss(animated: true, completion: nil)
    }
    func imagePickerControllerDidCancel(_ picker:UIImagePickerController) {
        dismiss(animated: true, completion: nil)
    }
}
```

Listing 27-25: Taking a picture to send to social networks

There is nothing new in the code of Listing 27-25, we just get the picture, assign it to a property, and show it on the screen. The code responsible for posting the picture is in the Action for the Post Picture button. In this method, we have to use the picture stored in the **picture** property to initialize a new **UIActivityViewController** object and present it on the screen.

```
@IBAction func postPicture(_ sender: UIBarButtonItem) {
    if let image = picture {
        let width = image.size.width / 2
        let height = image.size.height / 2
        let imageSize = CGSize(width: width, height: height)

        let render = UIGraphicsImageRenderer(size: imageSize)
        render.image(actions: { (renderContext) in
            let context = renderContext.cgContext
            UIGraphicsPushContext(context)
            image.draw(in: CGRect(x: 0, y: 0, width: width, height: height))

            let items = [renderContext.currentImage]
            let controller = UIActivityViewController(activityItems: items,
applicationActivities: nil)
            present(controller, animated: true, completion: nil)
        })
    }
}
```

Listing 27-26: Posting the picture

Pictures may be posted in some services with the original orientation. This means that if we take the picture with the device in landscape mode, it could have the wrong orientation in the final destination. To avoid the issue, in the code of Listing 27-26, we create an Image Context and generate a new image that will always have the same orientation. Due to the high resolution of the cameras, we also reduce the size of the picture in half, to create an image that can be managed by the controller and is more suitable for social networks.

The **items** array in our example includes only the picture we want to post, but it could also include a text and a URL (a **URL** structure). The controller takes this information and presents it to the user in an additional view after the social network is selected. This view allows the user to incorporate to the post additional information such as the location or who is going to be able to see it. Figure 27-8 shows the views generated by the Activity Controller.

Figure 27-8: Posting to Facebook with the Activity Controller

By default, the Activity Controller shows every service available, but we can exclude some of those services with the controller's **excludedActivityTypes** property. For instance, if we want to exclude everything except Facebook, we can replace the **postPicture()** Action by the following.

```
@IBAction func postPicture(_ sender: UIBarButtonItem) {
   if let image = picture {
      let width = image.size.width / 2
      let height = image.size.height / 2
      let imageSize = CGSize(width: width, height: height)

      let render = UIGraphicsImageRenderer(size: imageSize)
      render.image(actions: { (renderContext) in
         let context = renderContext.cgContext
         UIGraphicsPushContext(context)
         image.draw(in: CGRect(x: 0, y: 0, width: width, height: height))

         let items = [renderContext.currentImage]
         let controller = UIActivityViewController(activityItems: items,
applicationActivities: nil)
         controller.excludedActivityTypes = [.postToTwitter,
.postToWeibo, .message, .mail, .print, .copyToPasteboard,
.assignToContact, .saveToCameraRoll, .addToReadingList, .postToFlickr,
.postToVimeo, .postToTencentWeibo, .airDrop]
         present(controller, animated: true, completion: nil)
      })
   }
}
```

Listing 27-27: Excluding activities

 Do It Yourself: Create a new Single View Application project. Embed the initial view in a Navigation Controller. Add an Image View and two bar buttons to the initial view called Post Picture and Take Picture (Figure 27-7). Connect the Image View to the **ViewController** class with an Outlet called **pictureView**, the Take Picture button with an Action called **takePicture()**, and the Post Picture button with an Action called **postPicture()**. Complete the class with the codes of Listings 27-15 and 27-16. Run the application. Take a picture, press the Post Picture button, and select the Facebook icon. You should see something similar to Figure 27-8. Remember to include the "Privacy - Camera Usage Description" option in the info.plist file to explain to the user why you need to access the camera.

Chapter 28
Internationalization

28.1 Internationalization

Apple has presence in more than a hundred countries and apps are distributed in dozens of languages and dialects, but we cannot publish multiple copies of our application, we have to create only one version and adapt it to each market. This includes not only translations but also organizing the elements in the interface, formatting numbers, etc. The adaptation process is divided in two parts called *Internationalization* and *Localization*. Internationalization is the process of preparing our application to be able to work in any region and language, while Localization is the process of translating the interface and resources to each language.

Most of the internationalization process is done automatically for us. For example, the constraints defined with Auto Layout organize the interface according to the direction of the language (right-to-left or left-to-right) without us having to do anything about it. But we still have to format values, such as dates and units of measurement, and translate strings to the respective languages.

Formatters

Formatters are objects that prepare data to be displayed to the user. In Chapter 4 we have already introduced some of the formatters available in Foundation, including `DateFormatter`, `NumberFormatter`, and `MeasurementFormatter`. These formatters automatically create a string according to the language and region where the user is located. For example, if we format the value of a `Date` structure with the `DateFormatter` class and set the style for the date as `fullStyle`, the formatter will create the string "Saturday, January 2, 2018" for users located in the US that speak English and the string "sábado, 2 de enero de 2018" for those located in Spain that speak Spanish. This basic behaviour is enough to get the expected results, but some of these classes also provide convenient methods to create localized strings. The following is the type method available for the `DateFormatter` class.

localizedString(from: Date, **dateStyle:** Style, **timeStyle:** Style)—This type method returns a string with the value of the date specified by the **from** attribute and with a format according to the values specified by the second and third attributes. The **dateStyle** and **timeStyle** attributes are enumerations with the values `none`, `short`, `medium`, `long`, and `full`.

The `NumberFormatter` class also includes its own type method to localize numbers.

localizedString(from: NSNumber, **number:** Style)—This type method returns a string with the value of the **from** attribute and with a format according to the value specified by the **number** attribute. The **number** attribute is an enumeration with the values `none`, `decimal`, `currency`, `percent`, `scientific`, and `spellOut`.

Besides these classes, we also have classes for specific units or periods of time, such as `DateComponentsFormatter` and `DateIntervalFormatter`. The `DateComponents-Formatter` class provides the following type method to create a localized string from date components.

localizedString(from: DateComponents, **unitsStyle:** UnitsStyle)—This type method returns a string with the components specified by the **from** attribute and with a format according to the value specified by the **unitsStyle** attribute. The **from** attribute specifies the date components we want to include in the string, and the **unitsStyle** attribute is an enumeration that defines how the components are going to be described. The possible values are **positional**, **abbreviated**, **short**, **full**, **spellOut**, and **brief**.

Values are only localized when we use the appropriate formatters and methods, so we have to implement these classes every time we want the values to be shown with the right format in every region and language. The following example illustrates how to localize values for dates and numbers with the methods we have just introduced.

```
import UIKit

class ViewController: UIViewController {
    @IBOutlet weak var dateLabel: UILabel!
    @IBOutlet weak var daysLabel: UILabel!
    @IBOutlet weak var priceLabel: UILabel!

    override func viewDidLoad() {
        super.viewDidLoad()

        let today = Date()
        let date = DateFormatter.localizedString(from: today, dateStyle:
.medium, timeStyle: .none)
        dateLabel.text = date

        let calendar = Calendar.current
        let components = calendar.dateComponents([.day], from: today)
        let days = DateComponentsFormatter.localizedString(from:
components, unitsStyle: .full)
        daysLabel.text = days

        let price = NumberFormatter.localizedString(from: 120.59, number:
.currency)
        priceLabel.text = price
    }
}
```

Listing 28-1: Localizing values

The code of Listing 28-1 generates the localized strings with random values and assigns them to labels on the interface (the example assumes that we have an interface with three labels to show the values). Figure 28-1, below, illustrates how the values are presented in different regions and languages. The picture on the left is what the user will see when the device is located in the US and configured for the English language, the picture at the center shows the values in Spanish for people in Spain, and the picture on the right will be seen in Egypt by people that speak Arabic (in this case, the labels are automatically moved to the right place on the screen because they were pinned to the sides with Leading and Trailing constraints).

Figure 28-1: Same interface in different regions and languages

Internationalization

Do It Yourself: Create a new Single View Application project. Add three labels on the left side of the initial view with the texts "Date", "Days", and "Price" and pin them to the Safe Area with Leading constraints. Add another three labels on the right with placeholders for the values and pin them to the Safe Area with Trailing constraints. Connect the labels on the right to the **ViewController** class with Outlets called **dateLabel**, **daysLabel**, and **priceLabel**. Complete the **ViewController** class with the code of Listing 28-1. Run the application. You should see the labels on the right with values formatted according to your location and language. Next, we explain how to change these parameters to test the app for different countries and languages.

Languages

Formatting the values to adapt to every language does not make our app ready for international markets. Some of the information, like the currency symbol, is region-dependent, but some, like the name of days and months, is language-dependent. By default, the app is distributed to every market with the Base language (the language used in development), but we can add the rest of the languages we want our app to work with in the project's settings. The project's settings are available in the app's settings panel. We have to open the app settings (Figure 28-2, number 1), click on the button at the top-left corner of the Editor Area to open the menu (Figure 28-2, number 2), and, instead of selecting the Target as we did before to configure the app, we have to select the project (Figure 28-2, number 3).

Figure 28-2: Project's settings

After the project is selected, the Editor Area lists a few sections with the project's settings. The section that allows us to edit the languages available is called *Localizations*, as shown in Figure 28-3.

Figure 28-3: Languages available

The Localizations section shows the languages currently available (number 1). If we did not add a new language before, the only one on the list will be the Base language (the language used in development). To add a new language, we have to press the + button at the bottom of the section (number 2) and select the language from the popup menu. After the language is selected, Xcode displays a window where we have to select the resources the language is going to be associated with (usually all the resources are selected) and press Finish to add the language. Figure 28-3 shows what we see when the process is over (for this example we added the languages Spanish and Arabic).

Internationalization

779 | P a g e

▼ Localizations

Language	Resources
Arabic	2 Files Localized
English — Development Language	2 Files Localized
Spanish	2 Files Localized

+ —

Figure 28-4: New languages available

From this moment, our app is ready to work with all the languages on the list, but if we run it, it will still show the strings according to the region and language set on the simulator or the device. This is because the application automatically detects these settings and formats the strings accordingly. To see what the application will look like when it is executed by our international users, we can simulate a region and a language from the Scheme.

We introduced Schemes in Chapter 5. A Scheme determines where our application is going to be executed and the settings it will use. The advantage of using a Scheme is that we can configure the target with the values we want. The Scheme settings are accessible through a popup menu that opens when we click on the Scheme button in the toolbar (Figure 5-4). The menu offers an option to edit the current Scheme or create a new one, as shown in Figure 28-5.

Figure 28-5: Scheme's menu

When we select the Edit Scheme option, Xcode displays a window where we can select the process for which we want to configure the Scheme. Figure 28-6 shows the options available.

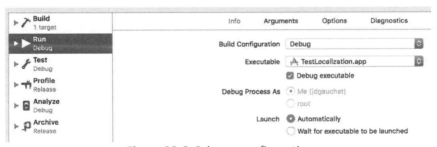

Figure 28-6: Scheme configuration

If what we want is to see how the interface adapts to a different region or language when the app is executed, we have to change the settings for the Run option. When this option is selected, the panel on the right offers four tabs: Info, Arguments, Options, and Diagnostics. The values for the region and language are shown in the Options tab. At the bottom of the list, there are two controls with this information called Application Language and Application Region. Figure 28-7 shows what the controls look like when we change the values to Arabic and Egypt.

Figure 28-7: Scheme's region and language

Internationalization

After the new region and language are selected, we can execute the app and check the strings produced to confirm that the app is ready for that particular market.

 Do It Yourself: Open the app's settings (Figure 28-2, number 1). Click on the button at the top-left corner of the Editor Area and select the project from the menu (Figure 28-2, number 3). Go down to Localizations and press the + button to add more languages. Add the Arabic language (Egypt) and press Finish. Repeat the process for Spanish (Figure 28-4). Press the Scheme button and select the Edit Scheme option. Select the Run option and open the Options tab (Figure 28-6). Set the language and region to the ones you want to test. Run the application. You should see the interface adapted to the new settings.

Translation

The project developed so far formats the values according to the region and language set on the device, and even reorganizes the elements on the interface according to the direction of the language (right-to-left for Arabic), but it does not translate the text we defined in the Storyboard for the labels on the left. The word "Date" is shown always as "Date", no matter the language selected in the app's settings (see Figure 28-1). The texts are not automatically translated; we have to translate them ourselves one by one.

The process of translating every single text in our application could be exhausting and error prone, but fortunately Xcode offers a tool that extracts the texts and puts them inside a single file we can send to a translator. The option is available in the Editor menu. We have to open the app's settings (Figure 28-2, number 1), go to the Editor menu, and select the option Export for Localization, as shown in Figure 28-8 (the option is only available when the app's settings panel is open).

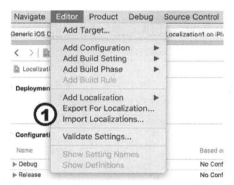

Figure 28-8: *Localization options in the Editor menu*

A window pops up to ask where we want the files to be stored and the system creates a folder in this location containing the translation files, one for each language. For example, if we create the translation files for our previous project, the folder will include a group of folders that include the files ar.xliff for Arabic and es.xliff for Spanish (English is not included because it is the language used in development).

 The Basics: The xliff files contain XML code. As we have seen before, this is a language that uses tags to delimit the values and declare their purpose. The original texts are enclosed in <source> tags, and the translations are enclosed in <target> tags. Translators have special software that allows them to access and modify these values, but you can do it yourself from Xcode. Open the Finder application, find the folder where the files were stored, and open the file you want to edit. Search for the <target> tag, translate the word, and save the file.

Once the files are translated, we have to import them back to our application. The Editor menu offers the Import Localizations option for this purpose (see Figure 28-8, number 1). When this option is selected, Xcode shows a window that exposes the errors found (e.g., texts that the translator forgot to translate or differences between the new file and an old file already in the project) and lets us decide whether to import the file or not. After the files are imported, the translations become available for our application. Figure 28-9 shows what the app looks like after the translations for Arabic and Spanish are imported.

Figure 28-9: Interface translated to Spanish and Arabic

 Do It Yourself: Open the app's settings (Figure 28-2, number 1). Go to the Editor menu and select the option Export for Localization. Select the folder where you want to store the files and press the Save button. Xcode generates files with the xliff extension for each language. Open the files in Xcode and translate the strings between <target> tags. Go to the Editor menu again and select the Import Localizations to import back the translated files. Press the Scheme button and select the Edit Scheme option from the popup menu (Figure 28-5). Select the Run option, open the Options tab, and change the language and region to the one you want to test. Run the application. You should see something similar to Figure 28-9.

Localized Strings

All the strings in the interface are automatically included in the translation files, but the strings defined in code are not. The system does not know which strings in the code are going to be shown to the user and require translation. To turn the strings into localizable strings, Foundation includes a function called **NSLocalizedString()**. The most frequently used version of this function takes a string with the original text and a second string with a comment that provides additional information about the string to help the translator get the most accurate result.

NSLocalizedString(String, **comment:** String**)**—This function returns a localized string. The first attribute is a string with the original text, and the **comment** attribute is a string with a comment that describes the purpose of the text to help the translator.

The strings in our code that we want to include in the translation files must be created with the **NSLocalizedString()** function. The following code creates a localized string for a label.

```
import UIKit

class ViewController: UIViewController {
    @IBOutlet weak var titleLabel: UILabel!
    override func viewDidLoad() {
        super.viewDidLoad()
        let text = NSLocalizedString("Hello User!", comment: "Welcome
message for new users")
        titleLabel.text = text
    }
}
```

Listing 28-2: Creating localized strings

Internationalization

The **NSLocalizedString()** function returns a **String** value with the string specified by the first attribute ("Hello User!"). If a translation is found, the **String** value returned by the method includes the translation instead.

 The Basics: The process of translating the texts is the same as before. When we export the files, Xcode takes the strings from the interface and all the strings in the code that are localized with the **NSLocalizedString()** function and includes them in the translation files for each language.

The **NSLocalizedString()** function can also work with formatted strings, but because the placeholders are usually moved to a different place during the translation, the string requires additional processing. The **String** structure includes the following method for this purpose.

localizedStringWithFormat(String, Values**)**—This type method creates a string from a localized string. The first attribute is the localized string we want to format, and the second attribute is the list of values we want to include in the string separated by comma.

To format a localized string, we have to create the localized string with the placeholders first and then call the **localizedStringWithFormat()** method with the values we want to use to replace the placeholders. The translator will translate the string but keep the original placeholders, so we can assign the corresponding values.

```
import UIKit

class ViewController: UIViewController {
    @IBOutlet weak var titleLabel: UILabel!

    override func viewDidLoad() {
        super.viewDidLoad()

        let localizedText = NSLocalizedString("%d hours and %d minutes",
comment: "For how long the app was running")
        let text = String.localizedStringWithFormat(localizedText, 2, 35)
        titleLabel.text = text
    }
}
```

Listing 28-3: Formatting localized strings

 Do It Yourself: Create a new Single View Application project. Add a label to the initial view and connect it to the **ViewController** class with an Outlet called **titleLabel**. Complete the class with the code of Listings 28-2 or 28-3. If you want to see how the strings are translated, you can follow the same procedure we used before to create and import the translation files.

Resources

Besides text, applications usually contain images, videos, and audio files that need translation. Of course, the way we work with our translator in this case is different; we have to ask the translator to translate the texts and then create different versions of the media for each language. To load the right media, we can use localized texts. For instance, we can localize the names of the files to load one image or another according to the language.

```
import UIKit

class ViewController: UIViewController {
    @IBOutlet weak var logoImage: UIImageView!

    override func viewDidLoad() {
        super.viewDidLoad()
        let logoFile = NSLocalizedString("logoen", comment: "File name.
Replace suffix")
        logoImage.image = UIImage(named: logoFile)
    }
}
```

Listing 28-4: *Localizing files*

The code of Listing 28-4 localized the string "logoen". In the comment, we suggest to the translator to replace the suffix "en" by the one corresponding to the language. This allows us to load the image corresponding to the user's language. For our example, we have prepared three files, one for English (logoen.png), another for Spanish (logoes.png), and one more for Arabic (logoar.png). If we export the translation files and translate the string to "logoes" and "logoar", we will see an image on the screen depending on the device's settings, as shown in Figure 28-10.

Figure 28-10: *Localized images*

 Do It Yourself: Create a new Single View Application project. Add an Image View to the initial view and connect it to the **ViewController** class with an Outlet called **logoImage**. Complete the **ViewController** class with the code of Listing 28-4. Add to the project the languages Spanish and Arabic (see Figure 28-4). Export the translation files (Figure 28-8). Translate the "logoen" string into "logoes" and "logoar" and import the files back into the project. Download the logoen.png, logoes.png, and logoar.png files from our website and add them to the Assets Catalog. Set the language you want to try (Figure 28-7) and run the application. You should see the image corresponding to the selected language (Figure 28-10).

If all we want to do is to change the image when the language of the user is written right-to-left, we can use the Assets Catalog. Each image in the Assets Catalog includes an option called *Direction* that we can set to select when the image is going to be shown. Figure 28-11 shows the values available.

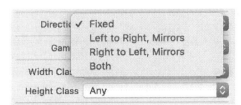

Figure 28-11: *Direction options for images in the Assets Catalog*

Internationalization

Chapter 29
App Store

29.1 Publishing

At the beginning of this book we talked about Apple's strict control over the applications the users have access to. Because of Apple's policies, we cannot sell mobile applications on our own; we have to publish them in the App Store. The process is performed from Xcode, but there are a series of requirements we must satisfy for our app to be published.

- We need an Apple Developer Program membership.
- We need a Distribution Certificate.
- We need a Provisioning Profile for distribution.
- We need an App ID for each application.
- We must register the app in the iTunes Connect website.
- We must create an archive with our app to send to Apple's servers.
- We must upload the archive to iTunes Connect for review.

Apple Developer Program

Developing and testing can be done with a free account, but publishing our app requires a membership to the Apple Developer Program. The option to enroll in this program is available in the **developer.apple.com** website. We have to click on the Discover/Program options at the top of the screen, press the Enroll button, and follow the instructions to register an account for an Individual or an organization. At the time of this writing, the membership costs 99 USD a year.

Certificates, Provisioning Profiles, and Identifiers

Apple wants to make sure that only authorized apps are running on its devices, so it requests developers to add a cryptographic signature to each application. There are three values that are necessary to authorize the app: certificates, provisioning profiles, and identifiers. Basically, a certificate identifies the developer that publishes the application, the provisioning profile identifies the device that is allowed to run the application, and an identifier, called *App ID*, identifies the application. These values are packed along with the app's files and therefore Apple always knows who developed the app, who is authorized to run it, and in which devices.

As we will see next, Xcode automatically generates these values for us, so we do not have to worry about them, but Apple offers a control panel in our developer account in case we need to do it manually. Figure 29-1 shows the menu we see after we go to developer.apple.com, click on Account, and select the option Certificates, IDs & Profiles.

Figure 29-1: Web page to manage certificates, provisioning profiles, and identifiers

In this page, we can create, edit, or remove certificates, provisioning profiles and identifiers. The page contains two panels, the left panel offers a list of options to select the type of values we want to work with and the right panel shows the list of values available and buttons to create new ones.

iTunes Connect

The first step to submit our app is to create a record on Apple's servers. Apple has designated a special website for this purpose. Because iTunes is the system Apple uses to manage user's applications, the website is called iTunes Connect, and it is available at **itunesconnect.apple.com**.

iTunes Connect is integrated with Apple's developing system and therefore it already contains information of our developer account. To login, we have to use the same Apple ID and password we use to access our account at developer.apple.com. Figure 29-2 illustrates the options available.

Figure 29-2: *iTunes Connect menu*

From this panel, we can insert our financial information required to put our apps on the market (Agreements, Tax, and Banking), publish our apps (My Apps), and see how the business is going (Sales and Trends). The first step is to create a record of the app we want to publish from the My Apps option. When we click on this icon, a new window shows the list of our apps and a + button at the top to add new ones.

Figure 29-3: *Menu to add apps to our account*

To add a new app, we have to click the New App button and insert the app's information. The first window asks for the platform (iOS or tvOS), the application's name, the primary language, the bundle ID, and a custom ID (SKU) that can help us identify the app. The name and language are values we already have, and the SKU is a custom string, but the Bundle ID is a value generate by Xcode. Xcode creates a Bundle ID and submit it to iTunes Connect when we enable services from the capabilities panel. If our app does not use any of these services, we will not find its ID on this list. In this case, we have to select the option "Xcode iOS Wildcard App ID - *" and insert the app's Bundle Identifier (available in the app's Settings panel). Figure 29-4 shows the information we have to insert to register an app called Test that was created with the Bundle Identifier com.formasterminds.Test.

App Store

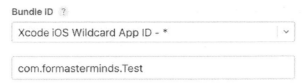

Bundle ID ?

Xcode iOS Wildcard App ID - *

com.formasterminds.Test

Figure 29-4: Bundle ID

After these values are inserted, we have to press the Create button and complete the rest of the information required. This includes the app's description, screenshots, and personal information. We also have to select the option Pricing and Availability on the left to set the price and where the application will be available. Once all the information is provided, we can finally press the Save button and go back to Xcode to prepare the files for uploading.

Submitting the Application

The application and resources must be compiled in a single archive and then submitted to iTunes Connect. The option is available on the Xcode's Product menu. The option is only available when a device is selected on the Schemes, so we have to select the device and then click on the Archive option inside the Product menu (we may use the Generic iOS Device option, or the device currently connected to the computer).

Figure 29-5: Archive option

After we click on this option, Xcode compiles the application and creates the archive. The next window shows the archive and offers buttons to validate and submit the app.

Figure 29-6: List of archives created for our apps

Figure 29-6 shows an archive created for an application called AnotherTest (number 1). The item representing the archive includes the date it was created, the app's version, and the number of the archive (we can send multiple archives to iTunes Connect and later decide which one we want to be reviewed by Apple).

 The Basics: The app's version is determined from the app's settings editor (by default it is set as 1.0). If we want to specify a different version, we have to declare the numbers separated by one or two periods (e.g., 1.0 or 1.2.5). The values represent different revisions of our app, with the order of relevance from left to right. The actual meaning of the value is arbitrary, but we are required to change it every time an update is published to the App Store to reflect how big the update was.

Although it is not required, we should always validate the archive before submitting the app to iTunes Connect. The process allows Xcode to detect errors and suggest a fix or do it for us. To begin the validation process, we have to press the Validate button (Figure 29-6, number 3). The first window presents three options to tell Xcode how to configure the archive and what to include in it.

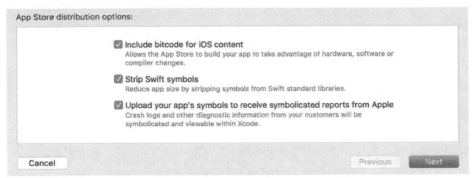

Figure 29-7: Options to configure the archive

All of these options are recommended. The first one tells Xcode to include code that improves the app's performance, the second includes symbols that represent code from the Swift standard library, which reduces the size of the app, and the last option uploads the necessary information for Apple to be able to report errors and perform diagnostics.

The next window lets us select how we want to sign the app. With automatic signing, we let Xcode take care of everything for us (recommended).

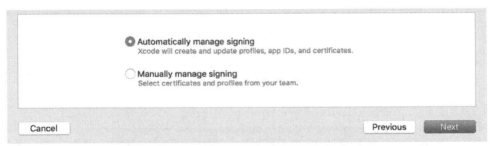

Figure 29-8: Option to select automatic signing

The last window displays a summary and provides a button to initiate the validation process. Once this process is over, if no errors are found, we can finally submit our app to iTunes by pressing the Distribute App button (Figure 29-6, number 2).

As we already mentioned, we may submit multiple archives to iTunes Connect. For this reason, we have to go back to the iTunes Connect website, open the description of our application, and select the archive we just uploaded (it may take a few minutes to be available). Figure 29-9 shows the option with the archive (build) we just uploaded for the AnotherTest application.

Figure 29-9: Selecting the build to send to the App Store

App Store

After the archive is selected, we can press the Save button to save the app's description. If all the required information was provided, we can finally press the Submit for Review link at the top of the page to submit the application. The system asks us a few questions and then the application is sent for review (the message Waiting for Review is shown below the app's title).

The process takes a few days to be completed. If everything is correct, and the app is accepted, Apple sends us an email to let us know that the app has become available in the App Store.

App Store

Index

Made in the USA
Middletown, DE
04 January 2020